HOW
MOVIES
WORK

HOW MOVIES WORK

Bruce F. Kawin

UNIVERSITY OF COLORADO

University of California Press

BERKELEY · LOS ANGELES · LONDON

University of California Press
Berkeley and Los Angeles, California

University of California Press, Ltd.
London, England

Kawin, Bruce F., 1945–
    How movies work / Bruce F. Kawin
        p.   cm.
    Reprint. Originally published: New York : Macmillan, 1987.
    Includes bibliographical references and index.
    ISBN 0-520-07696-6 (pbk.)
    1. Motion pictures. 2. Cinematography. 3. Motion pictures
industry. I. Title.
[PN1994.K34   1992]   91-23049
791.43—dc20   CIP

Printed in the United States of America

08   07   06   05   04   03   02   01   00
9   8   7   6   5

The paper used in this publication meets the minimum requirements of ANSI/NISO Z39.48-1992 (R 1997) (*Permanence of
Paper*). ⊗

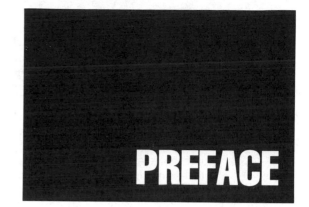

PREFACE

This is a book of film appreciation. Although it is primarily designed to be used as an introductory textbook, it should answer many of the questions anyone might have about the movies. *How Movies Work* is addressed to the filmgoer who wants to know more about the art, to the prospective filmmaker, and to the critic/student, in school or not. The movies are their own school, and most readers will already have learned a great deal there before ever opening this book.

As a subject, "how movies work" covers a lot of ground: how they achieve their aesthetic purposes, how their essential technology functions, how they are produced, and how their parts work together so that from them we generate the impression of a whole. Subject to the limitations of space, all of these matters are examined from a variety of viewpoints, of which the most pervasively applied is systems analysis. Part II, for example, concentrates on the cinema as a signifying system, and Part III looks at filmmaking as a creative system in state-of-the-art detail. *How Movies Work* is dedicated to an understanding of film that is at once technically sophisticated and intellectually intriguing. It is just as important to learn how a camera crew works with a director as to realize how a pattern of reverse-angle cross-cutting can create the impression of a conversation between two characters.

Rather than track down the "best" ways to compose and intercut shots or the "best" reasons to make a movie, we shall take an inventory of those that have been the most widely adopted, whether commonplace or intriguing, conventional or radical, shot by independent film poets or by union crews. While concentrating on the model of the Hollywood narrative 35mm feature (which is what most people mean by "a movie"), we shall pay significant attention to the non-Hollywood product as well as to the nonfiction, animated, and avant-garde film. Whatever generalizations may arise about the cinema will be rooted in the close observation of particular movies, and in most cases, frame enlargements will be offered as evidence and as material for further study.

The illustrations are very much part of the text and, in fact, took the same amount of time to prepare. They have no captions, but their figure numbers are in boldface so that you can readily match the photo with its discussion in context. Nearly all of the illustrations are either frame enlargements or production stills. A frame enlargement is a blow-up of a complete individual frame from the film as released; see **Fig. 2-73** (p. 175) for one from *Citizen Kane*. A production still is taken with a still camera, on the set or at various other stages of the filmmaking process; it relates to the film but is not from it. It can be of anything from a storyboard to a posed version of a scene in the film, like **Fig. 2-72** (p. 174), also from *Kane*.

Classical examples are taken from silent and sound films, virtually from Georges Méliès to George Lucas and from *Mothlight* to *Once Upon a Time in America*. The use of the moving camera, for instance, is explored along with frame enlargements from two of the most resonant shots in the history of the art, one from the moonlit tryst in *Sunrise* and the other from the vertiginous hotel-room kiss scene in *Vertigo*. The differences among the long shot, full shot, medium shot, and so on are illustrated by such shots of the same actor in the same movie (*The 39 Steps*). When scenes from *Citizen Kane*, *King Kong*, and *Hiroshima, mon amour* are analyzed, at least one high-quality frame enlargement is provided for every shot and significant movement, and any dialogue transcriptions are complete and taken from the screen, not from the script. Soundtracks, music, and songs are considered in detail, and in one case (*Cabaret*), musical and theatrical beats as well as poetic stresses are integrated into a discussion of editing and camera rhythm. The related arts of photography, painting, drama, literature, and dance are brought to bear on the cinema, and so are the disciplines of chemistry, physics, history, psychology, semiotics, economics, and sociology.

As an introduction, then, this book adopts a diverse, far-ranging, and open-minded approach to the art. It simply accepts that film study is a phenomenally rich field — one that can give you a great deal more than a degree in Godzilla — and that film appreciation is a comprehensive, developing, and intensely exciting process.

Although this book is occasionally quite technical, it also turns to the central issues of film criticism and theory. As a guide to some of the issues that dominate contemporary writing about film, *How Movies Work* highlights such controversial matters as the auteur theory, narrative structure, audience response, the portrayal of sex roles, the implications of continuity editing, the role of ideology, the uses of genre, and the continuing relevance of classical film theory. At the same time it presents the most comprehensive explanation of professional filmmaking procedures available in any single book, introductory or otherwise, unraveling in the process such tail-credit mysteries as "Best Boy," "ADR," and "Foley."

Film is the art of light — filtered by crystals and dyes, and casting some kind of shadow on a screen (or, for that matter, a photocell). Most of the interest in film study is in what kind of shadow that might be, how it looks and why its elements have been arranged in a certain way. But that study will do well to be grounded in a solid understanding of the medium itself, its physical properties and the circumstances of actual film production, not in a critical vacuum. Otherwise we won't really know what it is we are appreciating.

For many people, the appreciation of literature begins with the love of stories. But the study of literature and a real grasp of its immense resources would not get very far without such terms as "word," "line," "sentence," and "stanza." It is the same with film. *How Movies Work* provides a working vocabulary of film terms. Like "shot" in this introduction, some of these terms are inevitably used before they are defined — otherwise page 1 would be 200 pages long. (All crucial or problematic terms can be found in the Glossary.) As each term is defined or significantly redefined, it is printed in **boldface.** Out of these terms, the structures of film emerge: the frame, the shot, the scene, the sequence.

Acknowledging the fact that we all talk about movies in general and those we admire or despise in particular, whether or not we have ever been on a set, let alone studied any film shot by shot, this book begins with a discussion of the cinema as an art and examines many completed films, both as individual works and as members of such significant groupings as genres. In attempting to show how movies achieve their purposes, Part I concentrates on the relationships between film and the physical world — particularly on how photography, framing, and cutting create signs and images as well as records. It discusses the major categories of the narrative, nonfiction, animated, and avant-garde film; the relations between montage and mise-en-scène; what one might want to know about any movie before discussing it; and some of the more useful critical methodologies for organizing an understanding of film.

Part II examines film as a physical object and as a structured discourse. It starts with the raw materials of filmstock, tape, and equipment, then builds the cinema from the individual frame to the shot. Then it explores scenes and sequences, the primary structures into which shots themselves are assembled. Part II begins with a box camera and works its way up to a close examination of the baptism sequence from *The Godfather*. It is a structural description of the art.

Part III outlines the stages of film production, from the development of an idea to the release of a projectable print. If Part I offers a number of ways of thinking about movies and Part II takes a detailed look at what film is in the first place, Part III explains how movies are made. Where Part I discusses montage, for example, Part II illustrates the various kinds of cuts, and Part III at last pays attention to the editor.

Each part ends with a series of close readings, in which various interlocking ways of thinking about and paying attention to movies are shown in action. Some of these apply the critical methods and perspectives introduced early in Part I; for example, the discussion of sex-role stereotyping and the ways women are often defined, limited, and denigrated in the movies, which plays a small role in the section on feminist criticism and *A Clockwork Orange*, becomes the focus of the relatively lengthy reading of *High Noon* in Part III and concludes with the reading of *Flashdance*, also in Part III, where the female subject is shown to be a "split" construct, both ideologically and cinematically. (*A Clockwork Orange* is taken, in Part I, not as an exemplary film but as a random example of a movie about which many valid but conflicting critical observations might be made.) The majority of the readings are devoted to exploring one or more key elements of the cinema: a scene from *King Kong*, for example, for what it reveals about the dramatic and editorial construction of a scene.

As the readings become more detailed, the *intensity* of film study catches hold, and the value of the close and well-informed look begins to speak for itself. One comes to respect and enjoy — in a word, to appreciate — just how frame-by-frame study can unlock the editing strategies of one scene in *The Birds*, for example, as well as what that scene reveals about the relations between shooting and editing in general, or how Eisenstein made composition serve his purposes, or how framing and camera movement define and clarify what is going on between the characters in one shot in *Citizen Kane*. To perform a deconstructive reading of *Flashdance*, as odd as that might sound, or to compare *Alien* and *Heaven's Gate* in terms of genre strategy, becomes as exciting and satisfying as to find that one understands *exactly* how the most complex special optical effects are achieved, or why depth of field makes a difference.

What this book teaches, then, is a series of ways of looking deeply and carefully at movies, together with a great deal of more-or-less universally applicable information about the key elements of film construction (the frame, the shot, light, sound, etc.) and a scrupulously researched introduction to the intricacies of film production. All of these interlock continuously throughout the book, and they accumulate eventually into a full-fledged model for the appreciation of film. If there is a credo here, it is not that of any particular critical school; rather, it is an attitude of openness, curiosity, and respect. It is in that spirit that such different matters as the job of the sound editor, the focal properties of a biconvex lens, and the implications of camera movement are discussed in equal detail.

Many of the films discussed here are classics; some are just interesting and wonderful. This is not a film history book (and a good one, along with a host of other books, journals, and movies, ought to be consulted as you proceed — see "For Further Reading"), but great films from all periods and avenues of film history are called forth and worked with, so that sooner or later virtually every significant aspect of film study and filmmaking is touched on and, however briefly, made vivid.

There is no rule that a movie must be difficult in order to be worthwhile. In practice, much of the best work appears almost transparently simple — from the classical Hollywood continuity practiced by Howard Hawks to the ineffable clarity of a *Days of Heaven* or the brilliant grace of a Keaton gag. We can learn as much from *The Wizard of Oz* as we can from *Potemkin*. And from Chuck Jones and Alfred Hitchcock, Stan Brakhage and Richard Leacock, Dick Smith and Nestor Almendros, Bernard Herrmann and Douglas Trumbull, Sergio Leone and Alain Resnais, Walter Murch and Greta Garbo.

This book is open to all of them, to others like them, and to all the artists behind them who rarely are heard of. It attempts to be open to the whole of film and to respect each of its elements. As it examines and builds up a working technical and critical vocabulary, it also keeps in touch with the extraordinary pleasure and animating genius of the movies, the touch of the glittery wand on the sequined slippers. Because there will always be a part of us where they *are* made of rubies.

A great many people helped to make this book possible. I have never encountered such a host of generous experts, people who spent hours explaining their jobs, hunting down stills, opening doors, checking over what I had written, and offering professional advice. Many of them found in this book the opportunity to set the record straight: to sort out and present accurately, for the use of a generation of students, the primary creative, technical, economic, and critical aspects of the cinema. Although I have been teaching film history and analysis for many years and have had some dealings with the film industry, more than half of the "elementary" information finally presented here was news to me, and to run my well-meaning ignorance to earth was no solitary project.

Those interviewed specifically for this book include Jack Anderson (cameraman), Jim Berkus (agent), Stan Brakhage (filmmaker), Norman Burza (costume designer), Joy Gorelick (production assistant and editor), Ricky Leacock (filmmaker), Avi Levy (estimator), Tom Luddy (producer), Chester Luton (lab director), Bill McLeod (publicist), Herbert Nusbaum (lawyer), Bonnie Rothbart (researcher), Fred Runner (sound man), Dick Smith (makeup artist), Agnès Varda (director), Betty Walberg (musical coordinator), Rose Ann Weinstein (writer and editor), Marcia Sakamoto Wong (choreographer), and a development executive at a major studio who requested anonymity. These people not only spoke about their work and provided me with invaluable materials but, in most cases, read over and corrected portions of the manuscript. I owe special thanks to William Hines, the author of *Job Descriptions*, who shared information that has never before been available to academic researchers and who corrected the whole of Part III of this book.

While researching other projects or through various happy accidents, I have in the past interviewed other film artists whose indirect contributions to this book are significant. Among them are Robert Breer (filmmaker), Linwood Dunn (special effects artist), Gabriel Figueroa (cinematographer), Horton Foote (writer), Lillian Foote (producer), Lillian Gish (actress), Howard Hawks (director), Chuck Jones (director), Sam Marx (story executive), Brian Moore (writer), Marcel Ophuls (director), Alain Robbe-Grillet (writer), David Seltzer (writer), Peter Watkins (director), Meta Wilde (script supervisor), and Fay Wray (actress).

The actual process of obtaining high-quality prints and shooting frame enlargements was nearly as formidable as that of securing the legal permission to print them in this book. Bob Harris, of Images Film Archive, provided extraordinary prints and unfailingly expert advice, both technical and historical. In the Film Studies office at the University of Colorado at Boulder, where I commandeered the Steenbeck every morning for a year, Virgil Grillo, Marcia Johnston, Jim Palmer, and Don Yannacito were consistently helpful and encouraging. The negatives were printed under the extremely careful supervision of Tito Roberts and Fred Woelfel at Jones Drug and Camera in Boulder. Superior 35mm negatives of *Kane* and *Kong* were struck specifically for this book by George Herndon of Guffanti Labs, and Paramount provided 35mm interpositives of sequences from *The Godfather*. Among those whose practical, technical, and legal assistance proved invaluable are James Boyle (educator), Kevin Brownlow (historian), Ernest Callenbach (*Film Quarterly*), Anna Catalana (editorial assistant and interviewer), Sam Chavez (Dolby Laboratories), Don Civitillo (Cine 60), Mary Corliss (Museum of Modern Art Film/Stills Archive), Nancy Cushing-Jones (MCA), Stacy Endres (Academy Library), Kim Fowler (Foley artist), Dore Freeman (MGM), Daniel Furie (Paramount), Gretchen Gerken (Tyler), James James (LTM), Jim Kincaid (critic), Stan Kinsey (Disney), Diane Lawrence (Columbia), Susan Lewis (Cinema Products), Ivy Orta (Columbia), Bill and Stella Pence (Telluride), Adam Reilly (Denver Center Cinema), Tom Savini (makeup), Harold Schechter (special effects), Don Shay (*Cinefex*), Judith Singer (Warner Bros.), Jerry Sole (New Yorker Films), Robert Stein (Criterion), Terri Tafreshi (Lucasfilm), Earl Weldon (Disney), Drake Woodworth (Technicolor), and Ruth Zitter (RKO).

Editors Paul O'Connell and Sara Black saw the manuscript through its crucial first stages; the book was, in fact, Paul's idea. Julie Levin Alexander, D. Anthony English, and J. Edward Neve, of Macmillan, edited the final versions and realized the finished product. The designer was Andrew Zutis. Among those who critiqued the complete manuscript line by line, I wish particularly to thank Robert Carringer, Bill Costanzo, Dan Greenberg, Beverle Houston, and Gerald Mast.

I also want to thank my first film teachers, Gordon Beck and Hugh Grauel, and the many friends and colleagues whose encouragement and support meant so much as this book was being written.

Boulder, Colorado

Acknowledgments

The author and publisher gratefully acknowledge the following sources and thank them for their permission to reproduce owned and/or copyrighted materials in this book:

Alinari/Art Resource, NY, for Raphael, *Marriage of the Virgin*.

Stan Brakhage for stills from *Mothlight*.

Kevin Brownlow, Rachel Ford, David Gill, Dave Kent, and Pam Paumier for stills from *Unknown Chaplin* (Thames Television Ltd.); see "Kobal," "Roy," and "Thames."

Cine 60, Inc. for Fig. 2-11. Courtesy of Cine 60.

Cinema Products for Figs. 2-25, 2-31, 2-32, and 2-33. Courtesy of Cinema Products Corporation.

Columbia Pictures and Steven Spielberg for the still from *Close Encounters of the Third Kind: The Special Edition*, © 1977, 1980 Columbia Pictures Industries, Inc. Courtesy of Columbia Pictures.

Walt Disney Productions for stills from *Snow White and the Seven Dwarfs*, © 1937 The Walt Disney Company.

Larry Edmunds Cinema Bookshop for Figs. 3-50, 3-73, 3-75, 3-91, 3-136, and 3-137.

Dore Freeman for Fig. 3-65. Photo by George Hurrell. From the collection of Dore Freeman.

Hudson Bay Music Inc. for lyrics from "Tomorrow Belongs To Me" (John Kander, Fred Ebb), © 1966 Alley Music Corporation and Trio Music Company, Inc. All rights administered by Hudson Bay Music Inc. Used by permission. All rights reserved.

Images Video & Film Archive for stills from *Battleship Potemkin*, *Breathless*, *Broken Blossoms*, *The Cabinet of Dr. Caligari*, *The Cameraman's Revenge*, *Entr'acte*, *Flash Gordon Conquers the Universe*, *Hiroshima, mon* amour, *Intolerance, It's A Wonderful Life, Ivan the Terrible Part II, The Last Laugh, Man With a Movie Camera, Ménilmontant, Metropolis, Napoleon* (© Copyright 1981 The Images Film Archive, Inc. All Rights Reserved. Courtesy of Images Film Archive/Zoetrope Films), *Nosferatu, October, Olympia, The Passion of Joan of Arc, Return to Reason, La Roue, Strike, A Study in Choreography for Camera, Symphonie Diagonale, The 39 Steps, The War Game, Wild Strawberries,* and *Young and Innocent.*

The Kobal Collection for Fig. 3-1, © The Kobal Collection.

LTM Corporation of America for Figs. 2-42, 2-43, 2-44, and 2-45. Courtesy of Herbert Breitling and Gilles Galerne-LTM Corporation of America.

Lucasfilm Ltd. for stills from *Star Wars* (© Lucasfilm Ltd. (LFL) 1977. All rights reserved), *The Empire Strikes Back* (© Lucasfilm Ltd. (LFL) 1980. All rights reserved), and *Return of the Jedi* (© Lucasfilm Ltd. (LFL), 1983. All rights reserved). Courtesy of Lucasfilm Ltd.

MCA for stills from *Duck Soup* (© 1933 by Universal Pictures, A Division of Universal City Studios, Inc.), *Earthquake* (© 1974 by Universal Pictures, A Division of Universal City Studios, Inc.), *The Egg and I* (© 1947 by Universal Pictures, A Division of Universal City Studios, Inc.), *The Mummy* (© 1932 by Universal Pictures, A Division of Universal City Studios, Inc.), *The Phantom of the Opera* (© 1925 by Universal Pictures, A Division of Universal City Studios, Inc.), *Taza, Son of Cochise* (© 1954 by Universal Pictures, A Division of Universal City Studios, Inc.), *Vertigo* (© 1958 by Universal Pictures, A Division of Universal City Studios, Inc.), and *The Wolf Man* (© 1941 by Universal Pictures, A Division of Universal City Studios, Inc.). Courtesy of MCA Publishing Rights, A Division of MCA Inc.

MGM Entertainment Co. for stills from *Anchors Aweigh* (© 1945 Loew's Inc. Ren. 1972 Metro-Goldwyn-Mayer Inc.), *Ben-Hur* (© 1959 Loew's Incorporated), *The Boy Friend* (© 1971 Metro-Goldwyn-Mayer Inc.), *Casablanca* (© 1943 Warner Bros. Pictures, Inc. Ren 1970 United Artists Television, Inc.), *Devil Doll* (© 1936 Metro-Goldwyn-Mayer Corporation. Ren 1963 Metro-Goldwyn-Mayer Inc.), *Diane* (© 1955 Metro-Goldwyn-Mayer Distributing Corporation. Ren 1977 Metro-Goldwyn-Mayer Inc.), *Doctor Zhivago* (© 1965 Metro-Goldwyn-Mayer Inc.), *Forbidden Planet* (© 1956 Loew's Incorporated. Ren. 1984 MGM/UA Entertainment Co.), *Gone With the Wind* (© 1939 Selznick International Pictures, Inc. Ren. 1967 Metro-Goldwyn-Mayer Inc.), *Greed* (© 1925 Metro-Goldwyn-Mayer Corporation. Ren. 1952 Loew's Incorporated), *Mad Love* (© 1935 Metro-Goldwyn-Mayer Corporation. Ren. 1962 Metro-Goldwyn-Mayer Inc.), *Poltergeist* (© 1982 Metro-Goldwyn-Mayer Film Co. and SLM Entertainment, Ltd.), *Queen Christina* (© 1934 Metro-Goldwyn-Mayer Corporation. Ren. 1961 Metro-Goldwyn-Mayer Inc.), *Royal Wedding* (© 1951 Loew's Incorporated), *Thirty Seconds Over Tokyo* (© 1944 Loew's Inc. Ren 1971 Metro-Goldwyn-Mayer Inc.), *2001: A Space Odyssey* (© 1968 Metro-Goldwyn-Mayer Inc.), and *The Wizard of Oz* (© 1939 Loew's Incorporated. Ren. 1966 Metro-Goldwyn-Mayer Inc.).

Mike Minor for stills from *Flesh Gordon.*

Moviecam for Figs. 2-6, 2-7, and 2-8. Courtesy of Moviecam.

The Museum of Modern Art for Fig. C-3: Salvador Dali, *The Persistence of Memory*, 1931, Oil on canvas, 9½ × 13″. Collection, The Museum of Modern Art, New York. Given anonymously.

The Museum of Modern Art Film/Stills Archive for stills from *Broken Blossoms, The Conjuror, Drame chez les Fantoches, Dream of a Rarebit Fiend, Entr'acte, Fatty and Mabel Adrift, The Great Train Robbery, Intolerance, The Love of Jeanne Ney, The Man with the Rubber Head, Nosferatu, Olympia, Sunrise,* and *Vampyr.*

NASA for Figs. 1-4, C-1, and C-2.

The National Film Archive/Stills Library, London, for Fig. 3-12.

New Yorker Films for stills from *The 400 Blows* and *2 or 3 Things I Know About Her.* Courtesy of New Yorker Films.

Paramount Pictures for stills from *Friday the 13th — Part I* (© 1980 Paramount Pictures Corporation. All Rights Reserved) and *The Godfather* (© 1972 Paramount Pictures Corporation. All Rights Reserved). Courtesy of Paramount Pictures.

RKO Pictures for stills from *Citizen Kane* (© 1941 RKO Pictures, Inc. All Rights Reserved), *The Hunchback of Notre Dame* (© 1940 RKO Pictures, Inc. All Rights Reserved), *King Kong* (© 1933 RKO Pictures, Inc. All Rights Reserved), and *Son of Kong* (© 1934 RKO Pictures, Inc. All Rights Reserved). Courtesy of RKO Pictures, Inc.

Raymond Rohauer for stills from *Sherlock Jr.* Courtesy of Raymond Rohauer.

Roy Export Company for Figs. 2-22, 2-23, and 2-99, © Roy Export Company Establishment.

Fred Runner for Fig. 3-135. Photo by Fred Runner.

Tom Savini for stills from his collection (*Dawn of the Dead* and *Friday the 13th*).

Dick Smith for stills from his collection (*Little Big Man*).

Swiss Professional Movie Equipment, Ltd. for Fig. 2-10.

Thames Television Limited and David Gill for Fig. 3-139, © David Gill.

Olivia Tiomkin. Volta Music Corporation for "High Noon" lyrics.

Tyler Camera Systems for Figs. 2-29 and 2-30. Courtesy of Tyler Camera Systems.

Warner Bros. Inc. for stills from *A Clockwork Orange* (© 1971 Warner Bros. Inc. and Polaris Productions, Inc. All Rights Reserved), *Blade Runner* (© 1982 The Blade Runner Partnership. All Rights Reserved), *Duck Amuck* (© 1953 The Vitaphone Corporation. All Rights Re-served), *East of Eden* (© 1955 Warner Bros. Pictures Inc. All Rights Reserved), *The Right Stuff* (© 1983 The Ladd Company. All Rights Reserved), and *Them* (© 1955 Warner Bros. Pictures Inc. All Rights Reserved).

Zoetrope Studios for the still from *Apocalypse Now* (Fig. 3-48). Photograph courtesy of Zoetrope Studios. All rights reserved.

Figs. C-93, 2-89, 3-44, 3-45, 3-46, 3-47, 3-128, 3-129, 3-130, 3-131, 3-132, 3-134, and most of the frame enlargements were shot by the author. Owned materials not listed above come from private collections (anonymity requested), are in the public domain, or have been specifically approved for reproduction here under "fair use" conventions.

SHORT CONTENTS

CONTENTS

Film and the Physical World

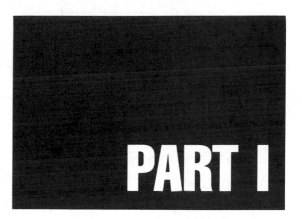

PART I

1. Film Appreciation

Ingmar Bergman was six years old when he saw his first movie. It was *Black Beauty,* and the fire scene scared him so badly that, according to one account, he hid under the seat. Soon he had bought the book and had learned the fire scene by heart. That is the way most of us first come to the movies — as children. The screen and its figures are huge, like the world of adults but even bigger, full of intriguing shadows and bright colors, charged with messages that may be difficult to figure out, capable of opening up vistas of experience and fantasy, mysterious and overwhelming and fun. Like the challenge of life itself, the movies become something to learn about and to grow into. The beginning filmgoer of whatever age has some of this child inside, and that child, with its love of movies and all that they can show, remains a continuing resource, even as critical innocence is supplemented by knowledge and experience. Many adult filmgoers are sustained by the hope of encountering a work that will bring forward again that quality of surprise and freshness that they may have experienced when encountering film for the first time.

Saturday Night at the Movies

People go to the movies for different reasons. After a hard day at work, or in the middle of an unstructured afternoon, it can be relaxing and exciting to be swept into another world. The movies can provide entertainment, a temporary "escape" from the routines of daily living. And they can also provoke enlightenment, can organize the terms of the world into a significant and resonant structure.

Entertainment, Enlightenment, and the Bottom Line. Although the movies certainly have their limitations, they also have special capacities, like the ability to present a fragment of history as it occurred, or to include a landscape rather than a backdrop, or to jump instantly from one unit of time and space to another, virtually at the speed of thought. Although there is no device that *only* the cinema can manipulate, it is still true that the cinema is a unique structure, and to understand that structure is an engaging and rewarding project.

A movie can give us a lot more than we may have bargained for when plunking down our cash for a ticket. Some films are virtually bottomless — endlessly interesting. And even in a garden-variety entertainment there may be resonant images, subtly arresting sounds, intriguing characters, and significant story lines that will stick with us whether we want them to or not. For some people, there is no clearer way to think through the nature of romantic obsession, for instance, than by talking about Alfred Hitchcock's *Vertigo* (1958).*

*Please note that at the first mention of any film in this text, it is identified by director, title, and release date. This is purely a convention and is not meant to imply that the director was the sole author of that movie. Where more than the director(s) are named, however, collaborative authorship *is* implied.

The movies can affect us in subtle ways that have little to do with entertainment or enlightenment. Whether or not being macho is a problem for him, a boy may carry around the images of John Wayne and Montgomery Clift, Mel Gibson and Clark Gable, or Eddie Murphy and Morgan Freeman, and may consult these, even unconsciously, as he sorts out the options for "correct" masculine behavior. A girl may begin by internalizing — and later on, evaluating — a host of sex-role stereotypes, including the good girl, the bad girl, the wife, the mother, the mistress, the careerist, and the adventuress, and go on either to model herself after one of those types or to begin a deliberate and even urgent search for a more personally appropriate role model. Decisions about how to live and what sort of person to become will be made in reference to social pressures and normative expectations, and the movies are an important contributor to such social codes — at times, even a force for social control.

Like any art, film is one of the ways a society talks to itself and exchanges information with other cultures. It is an art, a business, and a medium of international understanding. It is the site where the aspirations of the artists, the calculations of the backers and distributors, and the expectations of the audience come together.

Each of these groups may have a different conception of the "bottom line." For someone primarily concerned with the business angle, the bottom line is whether the picture earns a profit. For the filmmaker, the crucial question may be how well executed the picture is, the degree to which it has approached or surpassed its original artistic goals. For the audience, what may finally matter is how interesting and entertaining the film is, how it stacks up as an experience. For the critics and film students in the audience, the bottom line may be how "good" the movie is — in other words, how it relates to the critic's own set of informed standards and what it may be contributing to the history of the art.

Such standards are relative, of course; notions of "good" and "bad" change as the art, the conditions of its reception, and the critic's own sophistication develop. But most people who care about the movies and spend a lot of time thinking about them and going to them carry some kind of "excellence meter," an expectation of how good any film can be, when they open themselves to a new work. A "poor" film may leave us feeling not only that we have wasted our time, but also that something important has been betrayed — that everyone has missed an opportunity. But when the opportunity has been appreciated and fulfilled, the movie really shines, and what it shows us takes on a special, charged quality, like a privileged communication or a moment of vision.

The Business of Art. No one really knows what this opportunity is or what makes it tick. If there were a formula for making a good movie, the lives of Hollywood executives would be considerably more calm. Even without having to worry about making back advertising costs and selling $40 million worth of tickets, the filmmaker has to confront that blank moment before getting an idea, the glimmer of insight, the gradual changes of structure and texture as the idea takes shape, the suspicion that the idea positively stinks, and the problem of what it might mean to communicate that idea to an audience.

Some filmmakers begin with something to say and a style in which to say it, and from that point they may have to go out and convince someone to invest millions of dollars to realize the project. Others may begin with a marketable proposal, have the good luck to get backing for it, write a screenplay with the available talent and budget in mind, direct and cut the film, and find at the end of it all that some message *has* expressed itself in an effective style.

Some filmmakers have nothing personally urgent to say but are good at their jobs, that is, good at bringing projects to full realization and letting those finished projects make their own points in their own terms. Some filmmakers are crass and stupid, and others, like Charles Chaplin, have been among the authentic geniuses of the century. There are also those who simply need to believe that they are geniuses and have to work out a compromise between their egos and their achievements. But all of them are in the business of filling a movie theater with the best possible material, with something they respect. It is important to remember that virtually no one sets out to make a bad film.

Within the film industry — a term that denotes Hollywood and its subsidiaries and imitators around the world — the normative expectation is that an audience will see a movie once, even though big money flows in only when word of mouth is so good and the experience so worth repeating that audiences go back to see it several times during its first release and even when it is re-released. Some films, like Steven Spielberg and George Lucas's *Raiders of the Lost Ark* (1981), are calculated both to work in the short run and to attract repeat audiences, making their statements and portraying their actions in ways that are clear enough to be absorbed the first time around, yet in a manner so direct, efficient, and complete in itself that it will be a pleasure to see those things again. Others have twists and turns that become entirely comprehensible only with repeated viewings, like Ingmar Bergman's *Persona* (1966). Oddly enough, the videocassette revolution has increased the demand for pictures that have what Hollywood is now calling "repeatability," as there is little point in owning a copy of a film that one intends to see only once. But the classics have always been worth seeing repeatedly.

The key here is the self-sufficiency of the work, the way it forms a universe of style, mood, and action. Its primary references may be to the outside world, but its primary lines of communication are internal. That is, it works in its own terms, in terms that it creates and interrelates, and the connections among those terms are the laws of that movie's world. To recognize those laws and to stick to them are matters of artistic integrity, of following out the rules of a particular movie's game. To codify those laws into a formula that can be imitated is a matter of business acumen, and it does not always lead to an artistic success.

Film and the Industry. To anyone who takes a hard look at the current state of the industry, it is clear that film — at least, narrative film — is a business, and that an individual picture is a deal, a package of talent. That package is assembled not by an expert in film aesthetics but by executives with access to experts in marketing.

It used to be true that the industry depended on films and that films depended on the ticket dollar, but that is no longer the case. At this point many of the major studios are subsidiaries of giant corporations. These corporations are so large that the revenue contributed by their motion picture and TV divisions, even in the year of a major hit, might amount to less than 20 percent of that corporation's annual profits. These corporations do not, then, absolutely depend on studio profits and, to that extent, do not depend on films.

Nor is film revenue as dependent as it used to be on box office receipts, for although blockbusters earn their $100 million primarily in theaters, a picture that performs indifferently in theaters can still make back its costs through sales to TV. In this sense, releasing a movie can be like sending up a trial balloon. If a picture proves to have "legs" — that is, shows signs of being able to attract large audiences — it will be promoted more extensively, perhaps with a new ad campaign and a shift in release pattern. If a picture does poorly in its first week or two — as measured by the number of admissions and the gross revenues reported in the industry's daily tabloids, like *Variety* (called "the trades" because they are trade publications) — that picture might well be pulled from domestic distribution, hustled into video stores, and leased in a package with more desirable films to cable and network TV.

A picture that the studio considers a "bomb" may be released to hundreds of theaters at once, so that it can make its money before word of mouth catches up with it. An anticipated hit, or a very good film that the studio feels will need to build up a reputation before a chance is taken on wide release, usually opens in one theater in each of several major cities. This approach often creates a widespread desire to see the film that "everyone" is talking about, and when that desire is measurable, the film comes to local theaters. Reviews, as useful adjuncts to ad campaigns, are important here only when they are raves. Film criticism is ignored, film history is irrelevant, and film theory is a joke. Audience appeal is measured in terms of how many people will go to see a movie on the basis of its title, cast, and ad campaign, especially during its first week of release.

Although there would be no blockbusters without the industry, it is still true that the cinema, as a medium of human expression, does not entirely depend on the industry. The executive in search of a marketable hit is very different from the artist who has something to say and feels the urgent desire to say it in the language of cinema.

With the passage of time, the cinema has become open to independent filmmakers, and the studios have lost their monopolistic control of the medium. There are independent producers and filmmakers who finance and complete their own pictures and then sell them to studios, which distribute them under the studio logo (this is called "negative pick-up," as the studio buys the finished negative), or make deals with unaffiliated distributors. There are TV companies that produce films directly for broadcast — called "TV movies," even if many of them are shot on motion picture lots — and some of these have turned out to be important works. There are businesses that make movies for internal distribution, and there are amateurs who make low-budget films for their own amusement or as an adjunct to the family album.

Most significantly (from an aesthetic, if not from an economic, point of view), there are those filmmakers who used to be called "independent" — until that term was co-opted by the producers and directors not affiliated with the studios but emphatically part of the narrative film industry — and who now have no name, though it is convenient to label them "avant-garde." These artists, who often work in solitude and have little or no access to theatrical distribution, make films for the sake of making films and advancing the terms of the art. The importance of documentaries and animated films too is inestimable. No overview of the state of film production or the aesthetic opportunities of filmmaking would be complete without taking all of these into account, and it is possible to argue that the real health of cinema, its living and breathing, depends much more on the state of the art in general — as measured by the excellence of particular films, no matter what category they fit into — than on the state of the industry.

Just as there is no recipe for making a successful film, there is no rule for determining what constitutes a great one. There is, however, that matter of respect and the question of self-sufficiency. It is unlikely that anyone will do wonderful work on a picture that he or she doesn't respect. People set out to make "good" films, not just because they are investing years of their lives, their reputations, and their (or their meal ticket's) financial resources in a single project that could make or break them — in an absolutely unpredictable manner — but also because they want to make something worth all that effort and risk and, above all, worth watching.

The serious filmmaker usually tries to make a picture that will be clear and interesting to an audience that will see it only once, yet rewarding to those who will see it again. Shakespeare did much the same thing, writing *Hamlet* so that one could follow it if one were interested only in swordfights and sneaky poisons, or if one had seen it before and knew how it came out, or if one knew it backward and forward and were in a position to study every word. The aspiration to contribute to film history is made of this stuff: to create a work of art that declares its own terms and forms a complete world, that is self-sufficient even if it also forms part of the mortal universe.

Patronage and Response. To achieve what is sentimentally called the immortality of art, a work has to make sense by itself and has to continue to demonstrate its integrity even when the culture that gave rise to it has vanished. It may be hard, looking at a film like Jean Renoir's *Grand Illusion* (1937) or Orson Welles's *Citizen Kane* (1941), to remember that it was made in the context of a film industry, that it had to make back its costs, and that it was subject to flip reviews in the daily papers. It is hard because such films have been accepted as classics, but even Shakespeare's sonnets and many of the paintings we are accustomed to seeing in public galleries and museums were made for hire, commissioned by patrons.

It might be nice if the studios and the deal makers considered themselves the patrons of new and proven talent, but they do not. They are most interested in making or buying a product that they can sell, and they naturally try to get the most capable and reliable people to do the job. Because they control the purse strings, studio executives have the decisive say on which projects the studio will consider developing, which they will "pass" on (reject), and which they will actually produce and release. Just as the history of literature is, for better or worse, the history of what happened to get published and not the totality of human literary expression, the history of film is the history of *produced* films. And it is a familiar line in Hollywood that "No one ever got fired for saying no" — even to Spielberg's *E.T.* (1982).

Even if it is the "money men" who determine which pictures get made — and *somebody* has to pay for every movie — it is not the executives but the filmmakers, the critics, and the informed audiences who have the real voice in determining the ultimate *value* of a picture. They can "vote" with their ticket money, selecting a "good" movie from those that happen to be available; they can gather around an interesting picture as if it were an oasis; they can think about it, be influenced by it, write about it, and pass it along to future generations as an object of special merit.

What people do when they make such a determination is a complex process involving degrees of personal satisfaction, a sense of what matters in film history, and an intuition about the nature of great art. They do not check off a given film against a list of rules for good filmmaking. If anything, they check it against their hearts, their sense of form, and their most enlightened and unbiased critical range. A film that passes this test will be seen repeatedly, and not only when it is re-released by a studio. It may be shown in a class, for instance, and written about in magazines, journals, and books. If it stands up to such a torrent of interest and scrutiny, then the film might ultimately be called a classic: not in the sense of box office performance, but in the context of the history of art, as an achievement of enduring value. Such a distinction almost never means additional revenue for a studio, though it can give prestige to a long-term portfolio. It means a great deal, however, to filmmakers and to those who care passionately about film as an art and as a medium of communication.

What keeps the movies alive is the wonder of vision: the filmmaker's quest for an appropriate and memorable image, sound, or scene and the audience's appreciation of the achievement. "Appreciation" is a term that can sound rather cold and distant, but in its best sense it refers both to enjoyment and to understanding, and both of these responses are most effectively tapped in a mood of intense engagement supported by a long-term critical education. The sense of wonder, the emotional and intellectual excitement generated by a compelling image or a perfectly realized sound effect or a brilliant line of dialogue — that is the essence of film appreciation and the foundation of film study.

Critical Approaches to Film Appreciation

When I was a kid, I thought that movies were made in an hour and a half and that they were shot in sequence. I was vaguely aware that there had to be a camera, but I imagined that it could change setups instantaneously. I figured that films were like Chinese dinners, with the food washed and sliced for hours in advance, then prepared in minutes once everything was ready to go. It took a long time for me to realize that movies are *made*. I had to step back even further to notice that they are made of shots, that each shot is a unit in itself as well as part of the whole, and that it is possible for the way a film is shot to convey its meaning.

Howard Hawks's *Land of the Pharaohs* was released in 1955. These days people watch it because it gave Joan Collins her first starring role, or perhaps because they are interested in Alexander Trauner's art direction or in William Faulkner's contributions to the screenplay. But when it came out, the principal attraction was the way the gigantic pyramid sealed itself through an ingenious use of sand hydraulics, trapping the evil Collins. What most children and innocent filmgoers *get* from a movie, besides a good time in the theater, is the idea or spectacle that makes the movie exciting and unique: in this case, the pyramid. Watching the sand pour into the central chamber and the huge blocks slide into place, we don't count the setups or categorize the shots. We say "Wow!" and let it go at that.

Beyond "Wow!" But one of the first things you learn to notice in film study is how a film is put together out of individual shots, and at first, noticing all the cuts and thinking about how the artist is getting the job done can interfere with the simple pleasures of filmgoing. You begin to look *at* the film, like a painting, rather than *through* it, like a window. You get used to seeing films over again, surrendering the pleasure of not knowing how they will come out and concentrating instead on the *presence* of each shot and the ways it does its job. After a while this new way of looking at a movie begins to pay off, and you can see why certain artistic decisions were made and how they work.

When you come out the other side of the tunnel, when you really understand how movies work, all this noticing becomes second nature. You find yourself watching a new film or an old favorite with all the absorption in premise and spectacle that you felt as an "innocent," and with a rich, almost automatic understanding of the techniques that went into the film's construction. A brief closeup may excite you not only because it presents, say, a quick view of a gun in a crowd, but also because you have come to appreciate how that information was presented, the choice of the proper camera position and lens. At the end of the analytical route — of picking things apart to see how they work — knowing all about how Trauner, Hawks, and Faulkner designed the pyramid and how the climax works as a cinematic unit, you may find that all that sophistication was, in fact, focused on putting across the core idea — the spectacle, the pyramid — in an effective and unobtrusive manner. In other words, all that expertise was put in the service of clearly presenting what, as a 10-year-old, you may have entirely understood. As T. S. Eliot wrote at the end of his poem *Four Quartets*, you get back to where you started from and "know the place for the first time."

There are many filmgoers — and believe it or not, filmmakers — who have never heard of Sergei Eisenstein, who don't know that Chaplin directed the films he starred in, and who wouldn't know an answer print from an answering machine. Once Chaplin and Eisenstein have truly come into your life, however, their works become part of the way you see things — and not just cinematic things. This may be true whether or not you *like* what they do. The way Eisenstein conceived of the shot as a montage element, or the way he composed his images, will stick with you, and you will never see film editing in the same way again, any more than you will forget the ending of Chaplin's *City Lights* (1931). After a while you might come to expect that any filmmaker will have Eisenstein in the back of his or her head while thinking about a current project; you might expect the art to build on its own achievements in full appreciation of those achievements. You might wish that the fellow who thinks he invented camera movement had studied F. W. Murnau's *The Last Laugh* (1924) and Welles's *The Magnificent Ambersons* (1942), or that the raw youth who decides to show what life is really like in the Bronx had heard of Rossellini and *Open City* (1945). At that point the problem is to avoid becoming a film snob.

Whether or not every filmmaker or filmgoer thinks about these matters, the fact is that cinema itself *is* a coherent body of work and manner of expression that does have a history and a tradition and that does build on what has been learned and achieved in previous films. To want to learn more about this is to be interested in film history.

It is also true that an image, whether or not the person who found or imagined it was worrying about this at the time, is a prob-

lematic construct, at once both a real thing (an image) and a fictitious presence (an image of something that isn't really there). This
doubleness is part of the way cinema functions as a language, even
in its most nonverbal moments (because language is a system of
references, not of literal presences). To want to know what film *is*
and to sort out its fundamental structures and paradoxes is to be
interested in film theory.

And there are other things to learn about: how movies are made
(production), how they work as art (aesthetics), how to evaluate
them for an audience (reviewing), how to interpret and analyze
them (criticism), what they reveal about the workings of the mind
(psychology), how they interact with the cultures that produce
them (marketing, sociology, and ideology), and so on.

Where to Start? Film study begins with you and with films. As
you set out on this journey, examine the assumptions you already
hold about the movies. Do you think they are "just entertainment"? Does the "just" keep you from taking them seriously, or
from taking entertainment seriously? Do you take them *only* seriously? Do you agree that at six bucks and carfare, a movie had
better be good? How do you feel about subtitled foreign films?
Given a free block of time, would you rather go to a movie or work
in the garden? Do you make a fuss when the picture is not in
focus? Do you get irritated at people who point out "deep meanings" in movies? Whatever you bring to film study will affect the
encounter, and it may be best to arrive at a neutral critical posture,
open to whatever turns out actually to be in the art.

There are many ways to approach the study of film and to organize an understanding of it, and it is best to have command of
several of them and to be at least on speaking terms with the rest
— and, of course, with new ones as they arise, because film studies
is a rapidly developing field. Some people do become utterly committed to one particular methodology (a systematic way of thinking
about and analyzing a subject) to the exclusion of others. In most
cases, of course, they will have checked out their methodological
alternatives extensively before having settled on the one that best
answers the questions that most interest them. They might focus
on a single aspect of the field — for example, the art of the director
(an emphasis that can promote the impression that film history is
a lonesome train each of whose cars is the work of a great director,
and that's it), or the psychology of audience response, or the ideological aspects of representation, or the encoding and constitution
of the female subject within the film, or the history of film technology, or genre work, or whatever. But all of these matters are
interesting, and there is no reason not to test many of them on a
movie one cares about and is in the mood to analyze deeply. At
first that might feel like opening every door in a long hallway when
all you really want is to find the bathroom. Even so, there is no
telling what you may find when you take a good hard look at a film
from a number of different perspectives. Very often a valid and

surprising critical insight will flash out at you from the unexpected fit between a movie and a method.

Frankenstein Meets the Ivory Tower. It is a familiar complaint of filmmakers that film critics have little or no understanding of how movies are made and that they are always finding meanings where none were intended. And some critics retaliate by arguing that only those filmmakers who think about high art and who labor to put complex and personal material into their pictures are worth discussing, as if those people had struggled out of an oily sea of ignorance and commercialism. This is one battle that really ought to end.

There was a study group that spent months looking at a print of Carl Theodor Dreyer's *Vampyr* (1932), one of the all-time great horror films. They noticed that the image went totally black from time to time, even in what appeared to be the middle of a scene. They worked up a very complex analysis of why Dreyer had "as if randomly" cut these black areas into his film. When they presented their findings, someone who knew a thing or two about how films are copied for distribution pointed out that they had been using a print made by a faulty machine — that the printer's shutter had not stayed open when it was supposed to be open. When the shutter had remained inappropriately closed, the frames on the printing stock had not been exposed; they came out black. The occurrence of the black areas was random because the shutter malfunctioned at random. There was no "secret message" being conveyed by Dreyer, and the study group could have saved itself from embarrassment by checking another print of the film and by learning the ins and outs of contact printing.

We cannot ask the current crop of filmmakers to cancel their shooting schedules and enroll in film courses. We may never get some of them to see that the industry was wrong to give such a hard time to D. W. Griffith, Abel Gance, Erich von Stroheim, or Orson Welles. But we can hope that those who intend to go into film production as a career will take the time to study film aesthetics before they are swept into the industry, and that they will cultivate their aesthetic ideals along with their business acumen. To be a professional is not just to know how to do a job; it is also to have a vision of the range and importance of that job and to feel that it is worth a lifelong commitment.

And in the meantime, we can learn the language of the professionals, study their working methods, learn about their priorities. If the proverbial mountain won't come to us, we can still go to it. We can avoid the disastrous and embarrassing situation of making big statements when we don't really know what we are talking about. We can work out a balance between aesthetics and production — as film itself already has.

Vital Statistics. There are some things we are going to want to know about any film before making up our minds about what it is and what it says. They help to anchor the terms of discussion and put the shadows in context.

As a random example, take Stanley Kubrick's *A Clockwork Orange* (1971). That simple citation tells us the name of the director, the exact title of the picture, and the year it was released to the public. That's a good start.

Director, Title, and Release Date. The director's name is significant for a number of reasons, the most controversial of which is the assumption that the director is the ultimate "author" of the picture. Film is a collaborative enterprise, and it is sometimes hard to see how a group of people could put together a coherent movie. If we assume that one person — the director — was in a position to coordinate all the filmmakers, that would make it simpler to discuss the coherence of the picture, as if it had proceeded full-grown from the mind of that person. But there are many films that were the product of significant top-level collaborations. Out of the hundreds of people who worked on *King Kong* (1933), for example, there were four who were absolutely essential: Merian C. Cooper and Ernest B. Schoedsack, who co-directed and co-produced the film; Ruth Rose, who wrote the final screenplay; and Willis O'Brien, who acted as chief technician and, among other things, animated the model of Kong. And that is not even to mention the lead actors — Fay Wray, Robert Armstrong, and Bruce Cabot — nor the people who designed and executed the optical special effects. In the absence of reliable production information, to identify a film by its director is little more than a critical convenience. In Kubrick's case, as it turns out, there is considerable evidence that he *is* the primary creator of "his" movies.

The title of a picture may seem a simple matter, and in the case of *A Clockwork Orange*, it is. But *Vampyr* is known by many titles: *The Dream of Allan Gray, The Strange Adventure of David Gray, Castle of Doom, Not Against the Flesh,* and, of course, *Vampyr.* Which is the "right" one? (And *what's* the name of the main character?) The most acceptable title is the one that the picture bore in its country of origin when it was first released. In the case of a foreign film and an English-speaking audience, the film may also be known by an English title, although that might not be a literal translation of the original. Some of these new titles can be as far-fetched as *Castle of Doom.* In the case of Vittorio De Sica and Cesare Zavattini's *Ladri di biciclette* (1948), the American release title was *The Bicycle Thief.* Translated literally, however, the title would be *Bicycle Thieves.* Because there is more than one bike-stealer in that picture, the literal translation would be preferable — but most Americans call it *The Bicycle Thief* anyway. When citing a foreign-language title, it is important to observe the capitalization and punctuation conventions of that language. Film titles are conventionally printed in italics (underlined in manuscript).

But the title of a film does more than just sit there and demand to be cited accurately. Often it is a significant key to the work, calling attention to its central figure or point. In the case of *Ladri di biciclette*, the point is that the central character is not simply the victim of a thief but becomes one himself. *A Clockwork Orange* evokes the image of a mechanical fruit, a wind-up toy. The implication is that the garden of this particularly empty and over-controlled world can produce only imitation fruit. This notion extends to the main character, Alex, who is conditioned to behave "well," but at the expense of his free will. As a specific Cockney slang expression, "a clockwork orange" is something useless, especially something uselessly technological; that describes both Alex and his rehabilitation. Although the film reveals no sympathy for the means by which Alex is conditioned (and points out their similarity to narrative film techniques), it does not imply that Alex is any valid heroic alternative. Instead it continually asks us to consider the value of Alex's freedom — not just to be upset at the ways his society controls people — because, when he has freedom, he usually puts it to destructive purposes. The title may also be thought of as a self-descriptive gesture, for the film itself has a mechanical quality: it is a cold movie, elegant and nasty, with an extremely formal and linear structure. In contrast, a film like Alexander Dovzhenko's *Earth* (1930) could be thought of as an "organic" orange, a natural plenitude.

The release date is the exact day (loosely, the year) a picture was first shown publicly to a paying audience. It does not necessarily indicate when that picture was made. It took several years to plan and shoot *A Clockwork Orange*, but rather than write those years inclusively, it is simpler to have a date by which the picture was *known* to have been completed and after which it could have become an influence on other filmmakers. When the release date is several years later than the date of completion, it is best to provide both. Chris Marker's *La Jetée* was finished in 1962 and released in 1964, and so the date citation could be written "(1962, rel. 1964)." The date citation can be helpful in sorting out films that share the same title: *King Kong* (1933) is not at all the same movie as *King Kong* (1976).

Script and Source. Kubrick directed *A Clockwork Orange*, but he didn't exactly make it up. The film was based on a novel of the same title by Anthony Burgess. Right away we know something significant about a film when we learn that it is an adaptation of a pre-existing work. Whatever artistic decisions were made by the filmmakers can be compared with what went on in the source, on the assumption that what was changed was changed for a reason. Some changes will have been mandated by the change of medium: what Burgess could write, Kubrick had to show. Others may have been made because the filmmakers were trying to make their own points or to change the emphases of the story.

On the whole, *A Clockwork Orange* is a "faithful adaptation" of Burgess's novel: it tells the same story, and in much the same way, and it seeks out effective visual equivalents to the novel's crucial narrative devices and ironic tone. Nevertheless, the adaptation is not at all slavish and reflects a distinct interpretation of the material. The song "Singin' in the Rain," for example, does not appear in the novel, but it plays a significant role in the movie and was obviously a thoughtful — and nasty — addition. Novel and film end differently, too. The British edition of the novel ends with a chapter (deleted from the American edition) in which the main character and narrator, Alex, begins to grow up. The film ends, like the American edition, by quoting the last line of what was originally the next-to-last chapter, when growing up is the furthest thing from Alex's mind: "I was cured all right." In the last scene of the film, then — to accompany and illustrate this line — Alex is shown cavorting with an undressed woman while some upper-class types applaud in slow motion; it is an image that is supposed to show that he has been cured of his anti-sex-and-violence-and-Beethoven conditioning. (In fact, a variant of that image does appear in the novel, but it comes a few pages earlier.) In the novel, when Alex notes that he has been *cured*, what he is fantasizing about is not antiseptic decadence and stylized lovemaking but slashing the face of the world with his lovely razor. That change makes quite a bit of difference.

The script of *A Clockwork Orange* happens to have been written by Kubrick. It is the screenplay that provides the underlying structure for the majority of films, and so it is very important to identify the writer. Where the director is also the writer, we can feel slightly more comfortable about crediting that person with the fundamental design of the movie. And there are many cases in which the most significant contribution was made by the writer and not by the director or anyone else. Whether or not it was directed by Bruce Beresford, *Tender Mercies* (1983) is primarily the work of its writer, Horton Foote, and it looks and sounds more like the other films Foote wrote (among them Robert Mulligan's *To Kill a Mockingbird* [1962], Joseph Anthony's *Tomorrow* [1972], and Ken Harrison's *1918* [1984]) than the other films Beresford directed, such as *Breaker Morant* (1979). In *A Clockwork Orange*, one of the most significant decisions that Kubrick made as screenwriter was to preserve the bizarre teen slang that Alex speaks in the novel; even if that slang made the movie more difficult for the audience, it preserved the essential tone of the original and kept in touch with a good deal of its aesthetic energy.

While thinking about the writer, we might well take a look at the picture's narrative structure — that is, the way its storytelling is organized. Narrative structure is in part a question of time: the decision to present certain information in a certain order, and with an almost rhythmically calculated degree of emphasis. As in the mystery, such decisions may amount to a "narrative strategy." But narrative structure takes shape not only as the work *unfolds* in time but also as it *comes together* for the audience; it takes on a kind of conceptual shape in the consciousness of the viewer, as it develops into a vision of the organized whole.

If *A Clockwork Orange* has a shape, that shape has three parts. The first and third major segments of the movie trace essentially the same series of encounters and locations, except that in the first part Alex is the aggressor, and in the third part he is the victim. Acts 1 and 3, then — though they do not have those names in the script — are mirror images of each other, the outer wings of a triptych. Act 2, the shortest of the major segments, relates the story of Alex's imprisonment and conditioning; it is the turning point of the story, and it is structurally appropriate and aesthetically pleasing that it should also form the center, or perhaps the hinge, of the narrative structure. The symmetry of the first and last hours of the movie gives Alex's story, and the film itself, a sense of rigor, a formal elegance, and what might almost be called the quality of a demonstration or a formal proof. It also encourages before-and-after comparisons, as precisely as a well-rehearsed argument, between Alex's natural and conditioned lives.

There are, of course, other ways of conceptualizing structure, not all of which are so logical, and many other kinds of structures than Kubrick's elegant 1-2-1'. The structure of Alain Resnais and Alain Robbe-Grillet's *Last Year at Marienbad* (1961), for instance, can only be described as involuted: not just convoluted, but also turning back inward on itself, like some chambered-nautilus tape loop or Möbius strip. The structure of *Vampyr* is linear, but it has been built to include and to shift among various levels of waking, dreaming, and unnatural reality. *Dead of Night* (1945) is a loop within which there are at least five distinct stories, each of which is told in its own style and with its own particular strategy. A great deal of what we respond to in a film like *Dead of Night is* its structure, and the same might be said of *The Godfather, Part II* or *La Jetée*.

Narrative structure is also a matter of masks and voices. The author (or, in the case of an anonymous or collaborative project, the *authorial level* of intention and decision, which is implied by the majority of texts and which might be thought of as "the impression that this text comes from an author of some kind") often masks his or her voice. That mask might be a "narrative persona," which is neither a specific character nor the actual author, but instead a characterized way of speaking, a tone or a pose that performs the function of a mask, obscuring the author and offering an adopted face. The Woody Allen who narrates *Manhattan* (1979) is an authorial persona, although he is also a character in the story; a purer example might be the characteristic tone and implicit presence of "the master of suspense," who is not the same as Alfred Hitchcock. A classic example from literature is Jonathan Swift's *An Argument against Abolishing Christianity*.

There are also authors who speak in their own voices — especially in documentaries — and there are complex syntheses of medium and maker that cannot be sorted out, as I believe is the case with Abel Gance. It sounds gushy, but is also accurate, to say that *Napoleon* (1927) is narrated by the cinema and Abel Gance.

Voice is itself a complex structural concern. Who is chosen to tell a part or all of the story, or whether it appears to tell itself, are decisions that affect the conceptual shape as well as the ironies of any narrated work; they determine a great deal of what is meant by the *form* of a work, and they are the way its attributed meanings are organized. *Citizen Kane* may be quite adequately described as a sequence of narrative voices (accompanied by the ubiquitous "voice," or personalized narrating presence, of the camera, which in *Kane* is unusually curious, resourceful, and intent). So may Faulkner's *As I Lay Dying*, and the play of presenters is no less complex in *Kane* than it is in that novel.

Both the novel and the movie of *A Clockwork Orange* are narrated in the first person, and by Alex. In the movie, Alex addresses the audience voice-over, so that we hear him talking to us about the events we are watching; he takes us on a guided tour of his past. But it is much more interesting to note that the whole film reflects Alex's personal attitudes toward his situation, and that that is the subtler and more interesting way that the discourse of *A Clockwork Orange* becomes first-person. If Alex finds violence in Beethoven, that is how the film presents Beethoven. If Alex thinks that he feels real pain but that his victims do not, that is how the audience is led to feel about what Alex does and what happens to him. The audience may find itself rooting for this character (because he is shown having a hard time) and utterly ignoring the horrible ways in which Alex has treated his own victims, because that is how Alex sees it. He is the narrator, and this is how he presents the story. Alex is not the same as Kubrick; we do not know from this movie whether Kubrick enjoys violence, nor even whether he is celebrating it. At the same time, of course — and just like Burgess before him — Kubrick *is* presenting the story as he sees it, using Alex as a vehicle for his own ironies, and standing behind him but, one imagines, well off to the side.

Before and Behind the Camera. Alex is also not the same as Malcolm McDowell, the actor who played that role. The narrative cinema is unthinkable without actors (a term that refers to both males and females), and we will want to know who they are when we begin to think about the film they helped to create. Whereas Alex is an abstraction in the novel, a flow of discourse to be fleshed out by the reader, in the film he is inseparable from McDowell. Nor is McDowell the only actor in this picture; some of the supporting players are superb, especially Anthony Sharp in the role of the Minister of the Interior/Inferior.

We would also want to know who *designed* the picture, who gave it its clean, hard, outlandish look. The cinematographer on this film was John Alcott; he balanced the lights, selected the lenses and the filmstock, and supervised the placement and movement of the camera. The production designer was John Barry; he was responsible for coordinating the design of the sets and costumes, the choice of props, and the overall color scheme. The costume designer, the art directors, the set decorators, and the hairdressers all contributed to the visualization of Alex's world, but it was Barry who ensured that their creations would work toward a particular and calculated effect. The design of the picture was the result of a collaboration among Kubrick, Alcott, and Barry, with

Kubrick making the final decisions — not as director, but as producer.

Producer and Studio. The producer is the one who raises the money to make a picture and who decides how it will be spent. As Kubrick was both director and producer, he was in a position to approve his own spending plans, but directors in a less fortunate situation must be prepared to have their more expensive ideas rejected or modified. When a picture "looks expensive," it is said to have high production values; in other words, the film reflects how much the producer was willing to spend on it. Most of Kubrick's films have very high production values, but so did Joseph L. Mankiewicz's *Cleopatra* (1963), and they didn't save the picture. The important issue is not really how much money was available, but how well it was spent. As the person in charge of those decisions, the producer plays a crucial creative role in the film-making process. Even without knowing the name of the director, you can immediately recognize that certain of the great MGM musicals were produced by Arthur Freed, just as you can tell that Victor Fleming's *Gone With the Wind* (1939), King Vidor's *Duel in the Sun* (1946), and William Dieterle's *Portrait of Jennie* (1948) were all produced by David O. Selznick. Your critical sensitivity to the "style" of a particular film artist — whether it be a director, a producer, an actor, a cinematographer, a choreographer, or a production designer — will increase as you see more films and take note of who did what in each of them.

It is also valuable to know the name of the studio that released the picture. There are many studios that have had recognizable styles in specific periods. In the 1930s, for example, MGM was associated with polished, high-quality dramas, whereas Warner Brothers concentrated on graphic urban melodramas and Paramount turned out sophisticated comedies. But this is not just a matter of genre (a particular type of story, like a Western, with recurring figures, like horses). Karl Freund directed one horror film at Universal in 1932 *(The Mummy)* and another at MGM in 1935 *(Mad Love)*. They are both great films; they share genre and director and were made within three years of each other; yet *Mad Love* has the high production values of an MGM picture, a certain classy approach to its subject, and *The Mummy* has the uniquely intense flavor of a Universal horror film. In many cases, to identify a picture by its studio is to provide at least as much reliable information about it as to identify it by director or writer. But not always. There is little point in implying that the author of Abel Gance's *Napoleon* was the Société Générale de Films; all it did was distribute what Gance had created and Charles Pathé had helped to finance.

In the case of *A Clockwork Orange*, the studio was Warner Brothers. But if you look carefully at the credits, you will notice that Warners acted only as releasor/distributor. The film was produced by Kubrick's own company, Hawk Films Ltd., and it was made in England. This was not, then, "a Warner Brothers picture," but it is still significant that Warner Brothers contributed to the financing and agreed to release and distribute this controversial movie.

Running Time. It is valuable to note the running time of a film. Because films are sometimes recut after first release, perhaps to attract a wider audience or to merit a different rating, different versions usually have different running times. Five versions of Sam Peckinpah's *The Wild Bunch* (1969) were shown during the year of first release, running 190, 148, 145, 143, and 135 minutes. It can be assumed that the earliest version (190 minutes) reflected Peckinpah's intentions, in other words, that it is the most authoritative text — but only the 145- and 135-minute versions remain in circulation. *A Clockwork Orange* is a bit more tricky. The original release version ran 137 minutes and was rated X. In order to obtain an R rating, the film was cut by a few seconds. The R version, too, is 137 minutes long.

You will also want to know who edited a film, the person or group who trimmed what was shot on the set and put the pieces in their final order. Even if he or she works in close consultation with the director, it is the editor who gives the picture its ultimate rhythm and draws all of the parts into a whole. One of the most striking differences between Kubrick's *Dr. Strangelove* (1964) and *A Clockwork Orange* is in their editing rhythms, and they were, in fact, cut by different people: *Strangelove* by Anthony Harvey and *Clockwork* by Bill Butler.

Sound and Music. Sound makes an essential contribution to most films today — and has ever since the "talkies" took over the industry in the late 1920s. Although a sound crew includes many hardworking professionals, it is most valuable for the critic to be aware of who recorded the sound and who mixed it. To capture the texture of an environment, as did John Jordan (the sound recordist on *Clockwork*), is a matter of great skill. And to edit and mix a soundtrack can be as demanding and exciting as to edit a picture track (the sound editor on *Clockwork* was Brian Blamey). Of the many pictures that Francis Ford Coppola has directed, notice the differences in their soundtracks. Those supervised by Walter Murch — notably *The Conversation* (1974) and *Apocalypse Now* (1979) — have far more interesting effects than some of those on which Murch did not work, like *One from the Heart* (1982).

As a simple example of how much the soundtrack can contribute to an image, consider a silent shot of a hammer's pounding a nail into a board. That shot will convey the essence of the action; it will show us what happened. But with sound added, we might also discover how hard the hammer hit the nail, how thick the board was, perhaps even what kind of wood it was, and what kind of room or environment the action took place in.

Music is especially important in *A Clockwork Orange*, partly because Alex is a great fan of classical music. The selection of the best possible recordings was made, in this case, by Kubrick, who to that extent acted as his own music editor. An original electronic score was also composed by Walter Carlos, and it filled out the musical landscape.

These are some of the most important roles in the filmmaking collaborative, but there are many others — as you will see in Part III of this book. Depending on which movie you are working with, it might be crucial to know who did the makeup, who designed and executed the special effects, and so on. But you will always want to know the title, the release date, the director, the writer, the source, the producer, the production designer or art director, the lead actors, the cinematographer, the editor, the studio/distributor, and the original running time.

An Educated Look. Now that you know which film you are talking about and the names of some of the people who worked on it, you are ready to make use of the information, to make sense of it. You can draw on a variety of critical tools and see which of them yields the most interesting and accurate view of the movie, that is, which provides the most useful approach.

The first thing to do, of course, is to watch the movie. Ideally, your first viewing should be uninterrupted so that you can have something like the original theatrical experience and can see the film as it was intended to be seen. And you should, if at all possible, be looking at a complete release print of the film in its original format. A film that was released in 35mm (the norm for theatrical exhibition) has far more visual information per frame than a 16mm copy of that same film. In fact, the 16mm is *not* the "same film" but an approximation of it.

Some 16mm and TV prints have been seriously modified during copying. A wide-format image may include significant information throughout the frame, but a TV print can show only part of that image at a time. At any given moment, you will be looking at only a portion of the image, and there will be cases where what was one shot in the original will have been made into two or more shots in the cropped print. Outside the domain of TV, there are 16mm prints that can yield a wide-format image and full-frame 16mm prints of pictures with standard formats. But even there, the visual information is much less dense — there is about one-fifth the area of a 35mm frame, so the loss of detail is noticeable — and it just can't be the *original* picture.

But you take what you can get. Whether or not you are looking at an original print in its theatrical gauge, give yourself a chance to enjoy the movie. See what it does to you. Check out how you feel at the end of the picture and compare that with how you felt before it began. Then write down the ideas that occurred to you during this first viewing.

There is not always an opportunity to see a film over again whenever that happens to be convenient, and so you should train yourself to remember accurately what you see and hear. Try this experiment with a TV. Turn on a movie or a commercial and watch it for a few seconds. Then turn off the set and write down the last shot you saw. Describe it in detail: where the camera was, whether and how it moved, what was in the shot (actors, actions, and backgrounds), what was on the soundtrack (including the exact dialogue), and approximately how many seconds the shot lasted. Then repeat the procedure, building up your skill until you can describe five continuous shots. This experiment works better with a videotape or a laserdisc because you can check your descriptions against what was actually being shown.

The next time you see the film, feel free to take notes. Note taking is quite distracting, and in a first viewing, you ought to restrict yourself to writing down only those insights that you expect to forget or that are really stunning. You may want to get a pen with a built-in flashlight so that you can write in the dark; that is preferable to watching the film in a lighted room because the ambient light washes out the picture. Or you can train yourself to write in your lap while looking at the screen — whatever works best for you. During this second or third viewing, you will get a better grasp of how the movie has been organized and perhaps why it was shot as it was — but keep in touch with your first impressions, too.

Any field of study has its special emphases. When you are looking hard at a painting or trying to talk about it, you notice the brushstrokes, what kind of paint was used, whether the backing was canvas or wood, and so on, and you use such terms as "line," "value," and "composition." You pick up on references to other paintings and note the ways certain conventions have been employed. In film study, there is a great deal of emphasis on the look and organization of the image — light values, for instance, and the arrangement of people and objects within the visual field — and on the ways images work with each other and with the soundtrack. In the narrative film, there is a further emphasis on story values, narrative structure, dialogue, and characterization. Among the many other areas of special interest are factuality, the psychology and politics of audience response, the theatrical experience, and the influence of distribution networks.

What you have to ask yourself is, What difference does it make that this is *a movie* rather than a painting, a novel, or an outdoor swimming meet? In answering that question, you will know what to emphasize in your analysis, what goes to the heart of this particular work. Thus a great deal of the interest in *A Clockwork Orange* is in the cinematography and the production design, the use of music, and the way Alex functions as a cinematic narrator. In a film like Hitchcock's *Psycho* (1960), many of the essential communications are made via the editing, the framing of the images, the music, the tone of the lighting, and the extremely ironic twists of the story. The point to remember is that when you talk *only* about the story of a movie, you might as well be talking about a novel.

As a general rule, then, you will want to keep your eyes and ears open as well as your mind. In Part II of this book, you will learn more about the essential sound and picture elements that make up a film and, in Part III, about the practice of film production. Distributed through both of those discussions is information about aesthetic intentions and priorities, so that you can see, for instance, why a filmmaker might have wanted to use a low-angle shot (where the camera points upward) to create a certain effect, or what an editor might have been trying to accomplish while cutting a picture. But you will have to supplement that information with a deliberate effort to become especially sensitive to light values, composition, sound textures, and significant relationships among films (historical and otherwise), because no one can make you see what you just don't see.

Criticism. Critics are sometimes thought of as parasites on the juicy body of art. Rather than create their own work, they take potshots at the work of others; they don't take the same risks that artists do, and whatever they do publish can be only, at best, "secondary" work. In truth, some critics deserve to be characterized in such a manner, although "parasite" is rather harsh; perhaps "sniper" (a term that would allow the major critic to be a "big gun") would be better. But, as with any other professional commitment, one must come to understand the nature of the work — in this case, criticism itself — before one can make judgments about its worth or the stature of those who do it well.

The point is that criticism is an independent activity, a primary field in its own right, sharing as much with philosophy as it does with the art of writing essays. It is, in most cases, an analytic discipline; one spends a good deal of time taking things apart, to see how they work, and then making sure that they function properly when reassembled. It is an interpretive discipline, too; the goal is to make sense of what one has found interesting, to clarify and perhaps to enlarge upon the questions raised by the work or to sort out what the artist has accomplished. Not all criticism is about works of art, of course; there are social critics, critical theorists, critics who criticize critical works ("metacritics"), and so on. Criticism is often descriptive (like this book) as well as analytic and interpretive. And very often, though not always, criticism is evaluative.

That, however, is where the vague, public notion of the critic usually begins and ends: that the critic is one who makes value judgments about the fruits of the labors of others, the one who gives the work "thumbs up" or "thumbs down." But even the critics who *are* of the evaluative persuasion do not simply "like" or "dislike" a work. That level of personal preference is not particularly worth sharing with a public audience; we don't care whether George liked the movie, we want to know whether *we* are liable to like it (if George writes reviews), or just what made it so enjoyable and interesting, or why it's worth paying attention to in the first place, or where it came from and who made it, or what it reveals about the state of the art in general (if George isn't meeting a journalistic deadline and has the time to write full-length criticism). If the film critic makes an evaluation, that rarely springs from matters of sheer personal preference; instead the critic evaluates the film *as* a film, putting it to a variety of tests. Is this as good a film as it might have been? How has it made use of the cinematic potential of the material? How attentive were the filmmakers to (the critic's favorite) technical and aesthetic problems? What does this film set out to teach its audience, and what means does it use to reach that audience? What wonderful ideas does it give rise to? And so on.

But to ask all possible questions and to take on a film comprehensively, whole-hog, may fling open too many doors at once; the critical discussion might not achieve sufficient focus to yield insights of value. Therefore the critic has access to a variety of critical methodologies, each of which, in its own way, facilitates and clarifies the encounter with the text. The text or work, here, might be thought of as a painted splinter that is being analyzed in a lab; first one looks at it through a microscope (Method A), then one might dunk it in a test tube full of some useful solution and run it around in a centrifuge (Method Q), and so on, until one compares the results and finds out what it is.

Methodologies are tools of analysis as well as areas of critical concern. Those who specialize in feminist critical methodologies, for example, are likely to be concerned with feminist issues. A work may be extremely diverse, but a methodology will ask a certain question of it and will be best equipped to work with the answer it receives to that particular question. In other words, if you ask what kind of a Western Michael Cimino's *Heaven's Gate* (1980) is, and concentrate on that aspect of the work, you may not find out very much about the images of women, or the conceptual space within which the diegesis (see the glossary) takes place, or whatever. The critic who has worked long with a variety of critical tools and approaches learns eventually which set of tests and questions will unlock not simply one aspect of a work but the entire work and the best of its secrets. Say that the work is a screw that needs tightening; the critic might take a hammer out of the toolbox, but the better choice, in this case, would be the screwdriver.

The film student's critical toolbox includes a growing number of methodologies, which are systematic ways of tackling and thinking about a subject. These include auteur criticism, deconstruction, genre analysis, political criticism, production analysis, semiotic analysis, and more. None of these is inherently better than any other, but some are more useful for particular applications and some are especially useful to the beginner. Semiotics, the study of signs, will be taken up in the next major section of this part of the book, "Parts and Wholes"; deconstruction will have to wait until the discussion of *Flashdance* in Part III. Ideological criticism in general takes up a significant portion of "Film and Society" in Part III. But some of the others will be introduced shortly, and all of them are used at various times throughout this book.

Beyond the matter of analyzing works of art or social conditions, and as a direct extension of that activity, the critic is often in the process of exploring (or reflecting a commitment to) a certain view of the world and a system of values. Most people are. But the critic is especially concerned with the ways those matters find expression and focus in the subject at hand, in other words, with applying the system of values and the work (or whatever) to each other.

Critics share the assumption that things are worth talking about. That implies that discourse itself matters.

A significant critical work is not just a parasite on the body of some other work or problem. It is a work on its own, an original contribution to human thought. That is not to say that a review is independent of the film it is reviewing, nor a film history free of its period; it is to suggest that the best critical works are also able to stand on their own merits and that they have their own things to say. Many of the more interesting critical works are those that directly tackle major and even philosophical matters (a school that dates at least from Matthew Arnold), rather than specific works. Others set up a dialogue with the text or problem under discussion, to see where its leads can lead; a movie can prove a jumping-off place for an original argument, a kind of pre-text. Among those whose criticism sets up this level of intense dialogue with the cinema and with movies, André Bazin and Stanley Cavell are eminent examples.

Criticism can be playful or somber in tone and method, but it is almost always both serious and creative. An idle critic does not hold an audience, nor does one who reveals ignorance about the subject. The seriousness of criticism lies in its commitment to sorting out things that need to be sorted out. That can be a matter of separating the true from the false, the great from the ordinary, or the irresponsible from the necessary. If someone wrote a book saying that heroin was good for you, a critic would take seriously the effort to set the author and the public straight — assuming that the critic had carefully researched the issue before forming a judgment. The creativity of criticism is often a matter of bringing things into new combinations, putting this idea next to the other, or testing that movie against both of those methodologies. Creativity itself has often been defined as the ability to achieve fresh juxtapositions. An intellectual structure can have just as much beauty as any other, and it can require just as much artistic skill to bring an argument into a satisfying balance as to write a poem or to design an interior.

Values and Value Judgments. A critic wants to make sense of something, to show what's going on. In most cases, he or she is committed to a model of the truth, and "truth" is a word that means different things to different people, like "reality." It is a cultural fact that value systems vary among different groups and periods; they also change and develop. That relativistic perspective does not tell us anything about what might be going on *outside* the system of human values, nor about whether any particular view of the truth corresponds to The Truth. But however the critic happens to think about his or her values and sense of the truth, the odds are that he or she believes in them as much as in anything else, if not more so.

When the film critic tests a movie against a vision of the possibilities of film, that vision is being tested as much as the film is. If a terrible picture moves a critic to denounce it as a betrayal of cinema, it is the value system of cinema, as that critic sees it, that is being defended. And the critic does not simply defend a vision of the true and the good, but continually re-examines and attempts to improve it. In the best cases, the critic does not *assign* value but *finds* it, opens it up to the light. Critically, the bottom line is rarely a matter of "good film/bad film," but instead a spirit of working with and honoring a film and the questions it gives rise to.

When reading evaluative criticism, it is important to remember that value judgments change and develop, even as value systems and conceptual models do. The Academy Awards provide an example of an implicitly critical, evaluative system. True, the Oscars are not awarded by critics, and sometimes the judgments of the members of the Academy of Motion Picture Arts and Sciences utterly fail to jibe with both critical and box office judgments. But they are awarded as the direct reflection of a clearly understood set of standards (in this case, professional ones), and they have followed a relatively consistent logic over a long history. So it may be of interest to offer Academy Awards as value judgments that reflect their specific origins as well as some of the general attitudes of the times in which they were awarded.

In 1952, the year of John Ford's *The Quiet Man*, the Oscar for Best Picture went to Cecil B. DeMille's *The Greatest Show on Earth*. That is a value judgment that most people today would not support, even within the Academy. The inherent characteristics of the two pictures have not changed in the meantime, but some of the ways in which we think about the cinema have.

In 1947, the Best Picture Oscar went to Elia Kazan's *Gentleman's Agreement*, a "problem picture" about anti-Semitism. But these days, *Gentleman's Agreement* looks stodgy and tame compared to Edward Dmytryk's *Crossfire*, which was also in nomination. And the 1947 films that have the greatest interest today, utterly eclipsing *Gentleman's Agreement* (which is lost somewhere in Outer Late Show), are the films noirs, the dark melodramas, like Henry Hathaway's *Kiss of Death*. All this shouldn't imply that "we now know the truth and those poor fools couldn't see their own period correctly." There has simply been a change of emphasis, a change in the way we see things and in what we find of interest.

In the Best Supporting Actor category, both Richard Widmark and Edmund Gwenn were nominated; Gwenn won. Gwenn had played St. Nicholas in George Seaton's *Miracle on 34th Street* and had done so brilliantly. Widmark had played the sleazy creep who pushed an old woman in a wheelchair down a staircase in *Kiss of Death*. Today Widmark's performance is considered a definitive example of great character acting. He won, from our perspective, the larger contest. At some future time, Gwenn's performance may well come to look better than Widmark's, as it apparently did to the Academy in 1947. What will be interesting is the critical shift that would make such a value judgment defensible. Outside the realm of the Academy, there are countless examples of analogous shifts in critical consensus. In the early 1960s, for instance, Douglas Sirk's melodramas were not given serious attention while Michelangelo Antonioni's masterpieces were being acclaimed and argued about around the world. Today Sirk's *Imitation of Life* (1959) is held in higher regard by many critics, and is certainly more widely discussed, than Antonioni's *La Notte* (1961).

As much as some artists bemoan the reception of their works by critics or complain that critics have no understanding of what it means to be on the front lines, it is also true that the critic is on another kind of front line — that of reception and analysis — and that it is important for the artist to feel that "someone is listening," that a well-informed critic is out there to pay attention to what the artist may have achieved.

Training yourself as a student is much the same as training yourself to be a critic. You learn the subject as deeply as possible, feeling your way through its structures and implications, trying to see it from the inside and the outside. In the process, you learn what matters about the subject and how that might relate to other things that matter. And as you learn to explain the subject to yourself, you also discover the urge to communicate that understanding to others, to explain to them what you have learned. In that sense the critic is always on the edge between student and teacher — and so is the artist.

Critical Options. A methodology is a kind of filter, and it can make the subject easier to see or reduce its "colors" to a single wavelength. The following are some of the more widely applied methodologies.

The Auteur. Auteur criticism posits that a significant film has an author or a guiding creative intelligence. That person, usually the director, becomes the offscreen site or implicit source of coherence. This is one way of accounting for the apparent "intentionality" of what is clearly a collaborative effort.

A film like *A Clockwork Orange* could be analyzed not just as an independent work but as a segment of Kubrick's artistic development. One might work up a "biography" of Kubrick's imagination, arguing, for instance, that Kubrick has always been interested in irony and that he has found different ways to express it.

One of his early melodramas, *The Killing* (1956), was about a robbery, and it ended as the loot spilled out of a suitcase and blew all over the landscape. (That image itself could be compared with the ending of John Huston's *The Treasure of the Sierra Madre* [1948], where the gold dust is blown back to the mountain it came from; in that case, one would be examining how movies build on, influence, and refer to each other, which is one aspect of cinematic "intertextuality.") In *Paths of Glory* (1957) Kubrick exposed the self-serving hypocrisy of the officer class in World War I, but the irony exploded into anger. Not since *Paths of Glory* has a Kubrick protagonist "lost his cool" as the colonel (played by Kirk Douglas) does in that film, spelling out for the audience that the bad guys are bad guys. In *Dr. Strangelove* irony is the dominant tone, and there is no inner "lecture" about what constitutes good and bad behavior; instead, virtually everyone in the film is a little crazy — or a lot — and the tone of "black humor" is unrelieved. In *2001: A Space Odyssey* (1968) the Kubrick world appears to have turned much colder. The editing rhythms have nothing like the urgency and complexity of those in *Dr. Strangelove* (which is, in fact, one of the best-edited films of its decade); instead Kubrick begins to pursue what has been called a "one-point-per-scene" method. *2001* can be interpreted as the point where Kubrick's cinema turned cerebral and where his ironies came under very tight control. *A Clockwork Orange* is so thoroughly and unrelievedly ironic that it is difficult to find in it any positive vision for the human race. Although that tone tended to jibe with Burgess's, it was a bit foreign to Thackeray's *Barry Lyndon*, which Kubrick adapted in 1975, and had nothing whatever to do with Stephen King's *The Shining*, which Kubrick adapted in 1980. His next film was *Full Metal Jacket* in 1987.

But *The Shining*, which builds on the heartless elegance of *A Clockwork Orange* — particularly in its production design and color scheme, all that clean white and red — is a very interesting film in its own right, and where King's story is explicable, Kubrick's is not. Instead it is a cold labyrinth, and the camera tracks through the corridors of the Overlook Hotel just as it does through the hedge maze and through the twists of the story; it is all a labyrinth, a telepathic trap, and at its center is a frozen victim. It is also interesting to note that *A Clockwork Orange* is the first Kubrick film to have a first-person narrator, that *Barry Lyndon* experiments with a more impersonal voice-over narrator, and that *The Shining* tackles the problem of subjective vision even more rigorously than *2001*.

The point of all this would be to show how Kubrick has developed as an artist, to set *A Clockwork Orange* in the context of a coherent body of work. That would not have to be done in terms of authorial irony or narrative sophistication. One could just as easily examine the differences between Kubrick's color and black-and-white movies, or his American and British ones, or those he wrote alone and those that were co-written with Jim Thompson (a novelist of bitter genius, author of *Savage Night* and *The Killer Inside Me*, who worked on *The Killing* and *Paths of Glory*), or his reasons for adapting certain novels. To carry out such discussions, however, it is necessary to have some proof that Kubrick has, in fact, been the guiding artistic intelligence of the pictures he has directed.

Auteurism works well with Kubrick because he has written or co-written most of the scripts he has directed, in addition to acting as his own producer or co-producer. There is a great deal of power associated with approving a production design, telling people where to put the camera and what to do with it, and insisting that actors perform a scene in a certain manner, and so it is often reasonable to think of the director as the "maker" or "author" of a movie. On the other hand, you will not learn much about *The Cabinet of Dr. Caligari* (1919, rel. 1920) by studying the career of its director, Robert Wiene, for Wiene contributed much less to that picture than did its writers, its producer, its designers (whom he did help to select), and the first director assigned to the project (Fritz Lang).

Production History. Another methodology that can prove useful, then, is production analysis. This is a matter of finding out just what happened, both on the set and in the front office, when a particular picture was being planned and made, and then applying that information when examining the finished product. In studying *Caligari,* a look at the production history reveals that the basic story concept — which can be found in the original screenplay — was modified by the producer (Erich Pommer) and by Lang before Wiene ever got his hands on it; the bright idea the three of them shared, which was that the tale should be told by a lunatic, sabotaged what Janowitz and Mayer had written. Wiene cannot take exclusive credit for that interesting disaster, but he is often awarded it. What remains is a very intriguing movie, and one of the more effective ways to sort it out is to examine the different ideas that its various makers held about it as it was being readied for shooting. It can be just as important to know when the filmmakers might have run out of money, whether the film was taken out of the director's hands during the editing process, whether the ending was changed in response to preview reactions, and so on.

Sometimes a creative act turns out to have begun as the solution to a technical or economic problem. In the movies this is practically the rule. During pre-production on *The Shining,* for instance, there were serious attempts to design mechanical special effects that could realize King's shape-shifting animal hedges, but the results were unsatisfactory and very expensive. The hedge maze, with its high, wide corridors, was easier to construct, and it was used as a departure for the design of the hotel. The result was that the hotel corridors became a related maze, and the whole picture was structured as a labyrinth. Even if it was not "true" to King's concept, the maze had a visual and dramatic integrity of its own. The point is that none of this was part of the original plans for the movie — yet it dominates the finished work.

In another sense, production analysis is, quite literally, the analysis of a production. On a general level, a film crew may subscribe to or reflect an attitude (which might even be an industry-wide consensus during a particular phase of film history) in regard to what constitutes good filmmaking practice. The specific manner in which a film is shot may reflect not just industry standards, however, but virtual ideologies of shooting. A cultural code may be embedded in the consistently different framing of men and women in midshot, for example, or in the ways the gauze filter comes and goes in *Gone With the Wind*, depending on which actress is on-screen. The overall manner in which Hollywood films were shot in the 1930s or 1940s (the highpoint of the "classical Hollywood cinema") is of considerable interest in itself, and to recognize it as a relatively consistent structure, however complex, is to have a handle on the movies whose form and manner it determined.

Reading the Mise-en-Scène. Mise-en-scène analysis is the study of the "look" of a film, the selection and organization of the elements of the image. A movie can be full of meanings that are almost entirely visual.

In *Citizen Kane*, for instance, there is a moment when Kane (played by the director, Orson Welles) walks between facing mirrors that extend his image into infinity (see **Fig. 2-125**). While the "story" element here may be simply that Kane walks down the corridor, the implications of the *image* are vast: notably that Kane is himself an unknowable figure, an infinite series of reflections — like the versions of him presented by those who "knew" him — rather than a single object. The key elements in the mise-en-scène here are the mirrors and the angle from which one of them is seen by the camera.

When performing this kind of analysis, pay attention to the layout of the visual field. Ask what the camera is doing while the characters go about their business, and notice how the actors are arranged and where they move. Check out the sets and props, the lighting, the shadows, the color scheme. Look for recurring images or compositions and ask yourself what they may have to do with the overall project of the film. Ask why, for instance, a character steps into the shadows while saying a particular line. In the case of *The Shining*, it is a real key to the picture to notice that the corridors of the hotel and of the hedge maze are similar, and one could go on from there to compare the ways in which the camera moves down the trenches in *Paths of Glory*.

Tales and Telling. Narrative structure can be studied in many kinds of films, not only in those that tell stories. To narrate is to tell, to present something to an audience and often to color that presentation with a particular point of view or way of seeing the subject — whether or not that subject is imaginary. In the case of *A Clockwork Orange*, you will not get very far without asking what Alex contributes as the narrator. Is this his vision of the world, or Burgess's, or Kubrick's, or that of the film as a whole? We have already considered the triptych form of *Clockwork*'s narrative structure, so let us take up a more ambitious example.

In *Citizen Kane*, the complexity of the narrative structure is particularly interesting. On the one hand, it is a series of "inner" narrations (preceded by a newsreel), visualizations of the monologues delivered about Kane by several different characters. Those inner renditions are sometimes highly subjective, and as we look at them, we notice what they reveal about their tellers as well as about Kane, their ostensible subject. On the other hand, the camera itself functions as a kind of narrator, a more objective one, and part of the fun of watching that movie is to sort out the objective from the subjective, to navigate our attention among the various kinds of narration that are going on, often simultaneously.

Genres and Codes. Genre analysis takes for its point of departure what kind of film a film is. Within the domain of the narrative film, there are such major genres as the Western, the mystery, the romantic melodrama, and so on. It would be hard to say much about *2001* without acknowledging that it is a science fiction film and wondering how it relates to other works in the same genre. By the same token, *The Shining* is a horror film, *Barry Lyndon* is a period piece, and *Dr. Strangelove* is a political satire. But *A Clockwork Orange* is a bit more problematic. Set in the future and full of intriguing techology (notably the conditioning equipment), it has claims to being science fiction. But it may be more precise and more useful to think of it as a satire, in the Swiftian mode, and to identify its genre as that of the dystopia, or the vision of a society with which something is terribly wrong. Since the dystopian fiction is often set in the future (from Samuel Butler's *Erewhon* to Aldous Huxley's *Brave New World*), it may well be considered a subgenre of science fiction in any case, but the value of considering *Clockwork* a dystopia is to lay the emphasis on its social satire rather than on its attitude toward the continuing drama of humanity and technology, or on the ways it re-imagines the limits of the possible.

To decide what genre a picture belongs to is to make a decision about its narrative project, what it appears primarily to be attempting to accomplish. A horror film, for example, often sets out to scare the audience, just as a musical often attempts to generate terms of artifice. Some pictures follow generic formulas closely and try to live up to them, but it is just as common for a picture to *play* with generic expectations and even to work against them. And there are many films that cannot be neatly pigeonholed into particular genres or that set out to work in terms of several genres at once.

It often happens that the recurring figures, images, and story situations of a genre are used as a kind of coded reference system, a nonverbal shorthand. In the early Westerns, for instance, black and white hats had relatively consistent meanings: white for good, black for bad. One way to complicate that moral universe might have been to dress the hero in a *black* hat. The audience would begin by recognizing the black hat as a sign of a bad guy — through familiarity with other Westerns and their narrative conventions — and then go on to enjoy the ways in which this film plays with and against the codes of the Western.

In some cases, familiarity with generic conventions can be a key to the problematic aspects of a work. At the end of John Ford's *The Searchers* (1956), Ethan (played by John Wayne) walks off into the landscape even though he has the opportunity to settle down. The hero of George Stevens's *Shane* (1953) does the same thing. In fact, many Westerns end this way, for reasons that genre analysts continue to probe. Wim Wenders and Sam Shepard's *Paris, Texas* (1984) ends as the father heads for the hills just when he has, after great difficulty, reunited his wife and son. If *Paris, Texas* were primarily a romantic melodrama, that ending would make very little sense. But once you realize that Wenders and Shepard were trying to make a modern Western — to examine the survival of that mystique in the West of the 1980s — it becomes clear that the father is simply following out the dictates of the genre, and that recognition opens up the most basic intentions of the movie, that is, why this particular story has been conceived in this manner.

There are also genres within other major cinematic categories. The nonfiction film is a major category, and some of its genres include the industrial documentary, the home movie, the educational film, the newsreel, and cinéma vérité.

Political Criticism. Rather than a specific methodology, political criticism implements a set of concerns and questions. Typically it adopts, of course, the political vantage point of the critic, who may lean to the left or the right. The critic may be concerned with the issue of social realism, for example, hoping that a particular class or group will be represented in a certain manner in mainstream pictures, or praising an obscure picture because it raises what the critic considers to be *the* important questions about the world and the ways it is represented on film.

Political criticism is attentive to the overt and covert political content of specific films as well as to the cinema itself as a political entity (comparable, perhaps, to a highly expressive and influential member of a community). In general, it seeks to clarify and interpret what a particular movie might be arguing about the proper organization of people in society, the political aspects and dynamics of the relationships among the characters, and the role that film, or the medium of cinema itself, can play in creating and/or reinforcing a set of political attitudes.

An interlocking set of attitudes, assumptions, values, and expectations concerning how the world works and ought to work is called an *ideology*. Although an ideology may be personal, in the sense that an individual or even a text may hold or reflect one, the term normally refers to the system of attitudes and values shared by a group, a subculture, or an entire culture. The members of a society tend to accept the dominant ideology and to ignore it, so that the filter it imposes on their perception of unsocialized reality becomes familiar, automatic, and finally invisible. A good deal of political criticism is concerned with identifying and analyzing the ideological content of specific films and even of certain aspects of filmmaking practice.

If an ideology is a way of representing and interpreting the world, it is appropriate to ask how an ideology may be reflected in a particular system of representation, such as an industry-wide consensus as to what constitutes good filmmaking, or in a particular representative system, such as a movie. Many critics today value the subversive project of movies that set out to challenge what they consider "the dominant system of representation," by which they often mean continuity editing, the untroubled perspective of the normal lens, narrative and thematic closure, and characters who are either good, bad, or good/bad. If a movie imposes its way of seeing and organizing the world on an audience (whether its sway is temporary or nagging or, in some cases, overpowering), then the way it has been structured to represent the world is an issue of power, both politically and psychologically. Texts have real power in a culture; they also *express* power and may reinforce power relationships.

A picture may be evaluated, then, in terms of the degree to which it reinforces, undermines, or departs from the dominant ideology, as well as the (related) ways it encodes and represents the "real." In this light, virtually any film is a political film, whether or not it treats an overtly political topic.

A work of art may, however, *choose* to address a political subject or a representative public concern. In this sense, Alan Pakula's *All the President's Men* (1976) is a political film, and so is Costa-Gavras's *Z* (1969). The critic might evaluate such a film for its historical accuracy or the credibility of its falsehoods; how successfully it puts across or dramatizes a political message; the value of that message; and how likely the movie is to be able to persuade an audience to agree with it or take issue with it. One criterion of value might well be the quality of public discussion (about the issue, not about the film) the movie has been calculated to generate or has proved to have generated. Does the movie provide facile solutions to serious problems? Are facts distorted for emotional or rhetorical reasons? Does it shove the audience, or lead it, or stimulate independent reactions?

The political critic has good reason to investigate the production history as well as the social, historical, and ideological contexts that affected and are reflected in the cinematic product. It makes a difference, for example, to know that one movie about urban poverty was made by the actual members of a slum and was distributed through an underground network, whereas another was made by the fat cats in Hollywood and was intended to be shown to people who could pay five or six dollars to see it. The former picture might be radical, and the latter either oppressive or "out of touch," but it would be just as possible that the former would aspire to the conservative narrative structures of the "bourgeois" entertainment film and that the latter would be subversive.

The critic might also examine the politics of audience response: Does this film make people comfortable with existing conditions, even if those are unjust and even if it appears to be demanding some kind of change? The picture may well do that if its story presents the problem as having been resolved by the actions of the characters. There can be a "worked-out-ness" to any dramatically resolved situation, so that the resolution of the *story* appears to settle the problems of the real world. Rambo freed no prisoners, and Mr. Smith did not clean up the real Washington. There are also pictures, like Adrian Lyne's *Flashdance* (1983), that almost deliberately present political and social arguments while they appear to be overwhelmingly concerned only with the "personal" problems of the characters. (Part of a thoroughly political perspective is to see personal problems as political ones in any case, as reflections or specific expressions of more general conditions, but in this case the critic might well point out that a distinct political project is being *masked* by a personal one.) The success of the main character in *Flashdance* implies that "America works," and a political critic might be especially concerned with pointing out that this "innocent" film is a subtle exercise in propaganda.

In the worked-out film, the audience is encouraged to identify with the character who, in most cases, provides the solution to whatever problem the picture is addressing. That character's triumph becomes ours, and we may not notice that the solution has taken place only in the realm of fantasy. Such works are sometimes referred to as "bourgeois art," whether or not they have any political project or touch on political subjects. The point is that they provide an escape but also strengthen the prison.

What the term "bourgeois art" implies is that such works, produced within capitalist cultures, reflect the interest of the dominant class (in capitalist culture, the middle class or bourgeois, a term that dates back to the middle ages, when a trading class emerged in the towns or "burgs," a class that was made up neither of nobles nor of serfs and that exchanged the goods produced by others) or of the government. Assuming that there were some political problem that the official culture (the government and the media) did not want people to worry about and perhaps change, one way to keep the public happy surely would be to encourage them to pay attention to other (resolved) or unreal problems, or to divert their attention into realms of neatened fantasy. The political critic might well wonder about the effects (both on people and on the distribution and exercise of power within the culture) of our spending our evening hours in front of the tube or in a movie theater. Commercial television can easily be interpreted as a continuous indoctrination in a tightly coordinated world of product preferences, role models, and summarized news, in other words, an entertaining lecture on the coherence of capitalist culture. Whether or not all this constitutes a conspiracy between government and media, or a coincidence within a consistent ideology, it is hard to shake off that image of a contented audience (and hard not to ask whose interest this engaged passivity might serve), sitting in the dark and having their values reaffirmed, or rehearsing and assuaging their anxieties, or just enjoying some very good art, while outside the theater the real problems of the real world continue undisturbed.

But a good audience is not cattle. The playwright Bertolt Brecht found that if the audience's desire to identify with the characters and to believe in the illusion were frustrated or systematically discouraged, the audience might adopt a more critical view of what was presented. The figures in the play (or movie) could be held at a distance, *estranged*, rather than embraced and taken as models for fantasy identification. The "estrangement effect" or "alienation effect" stimulates the audience to evaluate the story and to devise its own solutions to the (usually unresolved) problems presented. A number of filmmakers, notably Jean-Luc Godard, have been influenced by Brecht, but there is also a long history of reflexivity in the cinema that has proved capable of being politicized in a diversity of ways, not only Brechtian ones, and there are many films that set out to engage and heighten the audience's critical and creative awareness.

As suggested before, politically-oriented people tend to view virtually all conditions and relationships as inherently political. Everything becomes a political decision, from the choice of a car to the selection of a pronoun. Nothing is innocent. Any individual film is produced under specific historical conditions and, upon release, becomes an element in the discourse, or the exchange of texts, that is society. And the same may be said, on a much larger scale, of the discourse of film itself, the role that the movies in general play in our lives and in the models we construct for ourselves of how *to* live. If society is a language system, or even a cluster of texts, cinema is one of its tongues.

What sort of political act is *A Clockwork Orange?* It has a political subject, perhaps several. Its dystopia is a parody of some aspects of British government and culture as well as a projection of a very oddly socialist future. Its battleground is the familiar one of personal expression and free will versus government control. It appears to argue that this particular government and society (and sociopathic narrator) are the interlocking elements of a nightmare, or in any case that this is no way to run a world. But it makes that world be fun. It appears to endorse Alex's "cure" on the grounds that free will is preferable to government control. Furthermore, it identifies free will with artistic flair and government control with the dreary or horrific. Alex is the one who has *style* in this picture, and the picture has style (and the violence is "only stylized violence," the pain, it was said, not painful), and so to the extent that we appreciate the artistry and clean boldness of the film, the more we have to be on Alex's side. We may enjoy Beethoven, too. But as much as Alex wants us to consider ourselves his "only friends," some of us may persist in not liking him one bit. We may feel or respect some of that pain, in spite of all the irony. Alex may be held at arm's length, not our secret other self but a stranger from whom we are critically alienated. The estrangement effect, to the extent that it is a calculated aspect of *Clockwork*'s narrative strategy, augments the film's satiric project. At such a juncture, political and genre criticism would both be useful.

One could go on to ask what *Clockwork* teaches its audience or encourages them to think about the world. Some have criticized it for offering pure stylishness as an elitist alternative to political chaos; others have seen it as an oddly direct extension of *Dr.*

Strangelove and *2001*, both of which present politicians in an extremely ironic and unfavorable light. If the generals were yelled at in *Paths of Glory*, they were skewered in *Dr. Strangelove*, brought down to size in *2001*, and coldly parodied, in *Clockwork*, as monsters of genteel power and as air-conditioned bureaucrats. But this is still not a movie that is calculated to side the audience entirely with Alex and against the government, nor to sprout a generation of punks. It may even have been perceived as an apolitical project. One way to focus and test this is to look critically at the ways women are portrayed and treated in the film. After watching *A Clockwork Orange*, do you feel like kicking a woman?

Feminist Criticism. It has been argued that the relations between the sexes are inherently political, that "male" and "female" are as much social classes and power levels as are "noble" and "peasant" or "boss" and "worker." And there clearly are movies that imply that men should do some things whereas women should do others (see the discussion of *High Noon* in Part III), and that ground those notions in often sexist constructs of what the natures of men and women "really" are. One concern of feminist criticism is to analyze a film for its "images of women," in other words, for the evidence of these constructs across a spectrum of roles, role models, and stereotypes. But the image of woman on the screen is itself a problematic one, virtually regardless of what a female character might be shown doing (or doing for a living), and that problem is of very active interest to feminist critics today.

Ever since Méliès trotted out a line of showgirls in *A Trip to the Moon* (1902), the image of woman has been used, among other things, as a spectacle. She compels the gaze. It can be argued that the camera has a more intimate relationship with the faces of Greta Garbo or Ingrid Bergman or Grace Kelly than it has with Gary Cooper, Cary Grant, or James Stewart. It can be argued that Jane Russell is there (on the screen) to be looked at in a different way than James Stewart is. Now it can also be argued that the camera has a more intimate relationship with Henry Fonda than with Jane Fonda, and that male and female viewers have different responses to Grace Kelly and Cary Grant, respectively. But it remains well within the realm of possibility, and has given rise to much valuable debate, that the cinema of a patriarchal or male-dominated culture may be determined by a patriarchal structure of discourse (a patriarchal society or, more precisely, the terms in which that society prefers things to be phrased, which determines the terms and the structure of communication and of self-definition within that society, which itself can be seen as a structure of interlocking texts). There may be a "male camera" and an implicit male viewer to whom the spectacle of woman is presented, and the female viewer may be prompted to identify with the implicit power of that gaze. Or the camera may be neutral (making all of this a matter of projection, the viewer's reading-in), or neutral only when a woman is not onscreen, and the female viewer may have any of a variety of responses to the spectacle and to the camera. These questions are wide open.

Feminist criticism has taken many avenues. The examination of woman as a sign, as a spectacle, and as a subject who acts independently has called on and interwoven the disciplines (and the textual strategies) of semiotics, psychoanalysis, Marxism, and poststructuralism, as well as feminist theory itself. Such a cluster allows the feminist critic to analyze, for example, the ways that human subjects (both onscreen and in the audience) are "ideologically positioned" within the text and in relation to the text, focusing in particular on the ways we are led to read films and on the ways women are portrayed and defined.

On a less academically complex level, feminist criticism has explored ties with genre theory, film history, and production analysis. The critic may find that it makes a significant difference whether women were behind the camera as well as in front of it. It could prove of interest, for example, that the role played by Sigourney Weaver in Ridley Scott's *Alien* (1979) was originally written for a male, or that the crudely exploitative *The Slumber Party Massacre* (1982) was made by women (directed by Amy Jones and written by Rita Mae Brown). Along with the growing critical interest in women filmmakers (particularly those of Martha Coolidge's generation), there has been a real opening-up to women within the industry itself. The majority of job descriptions have been revised so that they will not imply that the job is customarily done by a male or a female: "script girl" is now "script supervisor," for example, and "prop man" is "prop handler," although "best boy" and "cameraman" remain.

Feminist criticism is concerned, among other things, with the politics, or politicized nature, of sex in films. Although the manner of portrayal of specifically sexual activity is of interest (at one extreme, as it takes place in pornography; at another, in romantic comedy), the more interesting questions revolve around *the* sex of a character or the power-and-role dynamics of encounters between men and women, mothers and daughters, etc. To examine a movie for what it appears to be saying about — or implicitly in the terms of — sexual politics is one common aspect of feminist criticism, and the field is called that because the feminists were the first to take seriously this set of problems. Nevertheless, males are invited to practice and to learn from feminist criticism, and males are subjects of feminist analysis nearly as often as females are. The "images of men" in cinema are no less limited and programmatic, and effective as conditioning, than the "images of women."

Women have created many crucial forms of artistic expression: arguably the dance, certainly the lyric poem (Sappho) and the novel (Murasaki Shikibu, *The Tale of Genji*). World literature has, however, been dominated by males, just as politics has, with the result that we have an extensive library of largely male perspectives on the world. The first autobiography in English, for example, was written by an illiterate woman, Margery Kempe; but when her male scribe died, the book had to remain incomplete, and it was not even discovered until 1934, some 500 years after the unknown date of her death. In all the films made by men, how has the reality of woman's experience been expressed? Is the story told differently when it is told by women, and is there an emerging gynocentric discourse that may find its own expressive terms and cinematic codes? How would a cinema made by and for women proceed, and what might it accomplish? Film can be a way for women to talk to women, as men have long talked to men; that is of just as much interest as the filmmaking opportunities that have allowed women as well as men to address everybody.

Of some movies, one might ask to what extent they represent contributions to a genuinely feminist discourse. Examining a story, one might ask whether the women are active or are acted upon: whether and how genuinely they are talking to each other; for what reasons they have been placed in the foreground or the background of the image or the action; and whether they are defined primarily in relation to the men around them (that is, as Norma Jean Baker, as Marilyn Monroe, or as Mrs. Arthur Miller). Some genres have embedded formulas that may well be considered sexist, like the emblem of "the monster and the (fainted or screaming) girl." The death of the beautiful woman, which Poe considered ineffably Romantic, is felt everywhere in the cinema from *Camille* to *Rambo*. It may be quite valuable to examine a picture in terms of whether it critiques or throws into question sexist treatments of women in the movies as well as in life.

And there are, of course, those films that unabashedly portray women as sex objects, as dependent bubbleheads, as black widows, as helpless victims, and as deserving victims. Some films, like *A Clockwork Orange* or like Sam Peckinpah's *Straw Dogs* (also 1971), may readily be perceived as "male" films, comfortably ensconced in the dominant patriarchal discourse, and may even be perceived as pernicious and offensive.

Looking at the sexual politics of *A Clockwork Orange*, there is a great deal of upsetting and problematic material. The film opens with a scene in a drugged-milk bar, and the furniture looks like naked women. One might defend this controversial piece of art direction by saying that milk, after all, comes from female mammals — but that would be to ignore the implied message that women are furniture. All of the major characters in this film are males. The women appear to matter only because of the ways they relate to Alex, and they are given a limited repertoire: the ludicrously weepy mother, the half-nude model whose sexiness tests Alex's conditioning, the pickups, the rape victims, and the murder victim.

There is only one woman in the entire film who is presented as being in charge of her own life. She takes care of her body, appreciates art, and lives by herself — with some cats. Alex beats her to death with a phallic sculpture. While that choice of weapon might be taken as an intentional irony, a critique of the "only males and their problems matter" attitude of this picture, the fact is that only males and their problems *do* matter in this picture. The audience is manipulated to root for *Alex* throughout the murder scene, and the victim is made to look ridiculous. (As observed before, this is his version.) To add insult to injury, this woman is identified in the cast list not by her name — which would have acknowledged her existence as a significant character — but simply as "Catlady."

Thus there is a problem with the so-called existential humanism of *A Clockwork Orange*, one that seems not even to have occurred to its makers. Bureaucracy and conditioning are threats to freedom, and the major point about Alex is that his freedom, no matter how he exercises it, is morally valuable. But no one in the story seems to care about what happens to the women. They become sacrifices, the vehicles for Alex's self-expression, furniture on which he can rest his storm-trooper boots. And at no point is the audience encouraged to see past or to correct this perspective. It is not a movie about freedom, but a movie about male freedom.

Close Reading. Critical attention is not necessarily a matter of examining a text in relation to a particular theoretical perspective and by means of a particular analytic methodology. Nor is it necessary to discover who created an effect, or even a whole movie, in order to enjoy, respect, and interpret it. Although any text is related to the culture, time, and people that produced it, it is also an independent and self-contained structure.

Of all the available "methods," the one that is indispensable and that is also the most open (in the sense that it requires an open mind and yields results that are often open-ended) is simply that of watching a movie carefully, surrendering to it and seeing where it goes and how it gets there — in effect, how the movie, as a discourse, proceeds and succeeds; not just what it does right, but what it does; how it *works*.

This is a matter, first, of appreciating the movie *as* a movie, of discovering its major terms and observing how they are established, clarified, interrelated, and, in general, played with. It is a matter of finding the rules of a particular text *in* that text, of observing it closely and drawing out its apparent meanings. In both literary and film criticism, this process is known as "close reading"; it is the equivalent of a long, tight, mental closeup, an intense act of critical attention to every nuance, every camera movement, every line — in fact, every aspect of the text itself, as it declares and deploys its major and minor terms. This is, not surprisingly, the primary analytical and critical method followed in *How Movies Work*, a book that developed out of the close study of films and whose goal is to demonstrate how meanings are expressed and recognized in cinematic works.

In 1958 — to take a simple example of a recognizably cinematic expression — William Wyler's *The Big Country* appeared on American screens. It opens with a series of shots of a stagecoach crossing a vast landscape, over which the opening titles are superimposed. The main title, THE BIG COUNTRY, appears over an extreme long shot of the dry prairie; the coach is approximately in the middle of the frame, but the camera is so far away that the coach appears small. The wide screen is filled with country. What one immediately notices — or, in any case, is inevitably affected by — is the huge scale of the image. The wide screen format reveals the "bigness" of the country, and the choice of an extreme long shot accentuates just how large and rich a field the wide, color image is capable of surveying. This is, in other words, a deliberate use of the wide format to convey a wide impression, and it reflects back not only on the expanse of the West but also on the expanse of the wide screen. The fact that the coach remains more-or-less in the center of the image asserts its dramatic importance *and* implies that both the lead character (who is, unknown to us, in the coach and on the way to his destiny) and the big country are to be the movie's central subjects — in other words, that the figure and the landscape, microcosm and macrocosm, are of equal importance here; that the story concerns both people and their environment; and, by implication, that the character will have to rise to the demands of the landscape just as the country will itself be changed by the morally elevated actions of the central character.

When the main title is superimposed, the music states its principal theme; the music is both exciting and, in its own way, definitive: it points to the central subject and says, in essence, *here* is the title statement and this is how its essential energy feels. The coming of the title itself accomplishes a similar grounding of the text, a sense of having arrived at the subject, even as it marshalls and releases the narrative momentum, the spectacular drive, of the beginning of a long and dynamic presentation. All of this adds up to a spectacle, a wide-screen vista of color, music, and so on — a sense of "big," of "country," and of "cinema." For what one is watching is both a well-calculated long shot and a view of the Old West — the spectacle of the cinema as well as the spectacle of the immense landscape, both of which light up and somehow erase the front wall of that box full of seats, the theater.

It is not absolutely necessary to worry about who devised that juxtaposition of image, music, and title, nor even who took the long shot. One *could*, of course, go to town on the question: read the script to see whether this shot is described there in this manner, interview people who worked on the set, identify the composer and compare his other work with his work here, etc. The odds are, in fact, that this was a second-unit shot, taken by the second-unit cinematographer, and that its placement was determined by the supervising editor who may, in fact, have orchestrated this entire opening sequence. But for a full appreciation of the credits sequence of this movie, one will necessarily return to the shots themselves: to the ways they have been arranged, to the fact of their projected "presence," and to the ways they, in themselves, affect us.

There is a scene in Fritz Lang's *Fury* (1936) that may help to clarify this way of reading movies. The story concerns Joe Wilson (Spencer Tracy), an innocent man who is accused of murder and apparently burned to death in his prison cell by a small-town mob As it turns out, Joe survives the conflagration but pretends to be dead so that his murderers (it is not, as Joe continually points out, *their* doing that he was not actually killed) will be condemned. The ruse demands that Joe's fiancée (Sylvia Sidney) not be told of his survival, because Joe knows that she would not support his revenge by lying on the stand. In the end, in order to regain his self-respect and in the hope of effecting a reconciliation with his beloved, Wilson appears in court as the verdicts are being read.

About halfway through the movie, Wilson shows up as his brothers are discussing his death. Up until now, Tracy's face has been evenly if not brightly lit. Now his face is in shadow, and his makeup is dark. In raincoat and hat, he appears shrouded, a figure of the shadows — and "shroud" and "shade" are terms long associated with the dead. Standing in his brothers' doorway, dressed and made up and *lit* as he is, he appears to be (as his brothers see him) a figure returned from the dead. But the lighting also shows the brothers, and particularly the audience, that Wilson's character and attitudes toward the world have changed. He is now very dark inside, and the lighting implies this by darkening his outside.

A movie is a structured revelation. *Fury* opens by establishing the "terms" of the lovers and of the quality of emotional honesty and moral innocence they share; this relationship becomes a criterion of value, something for the audience to root for and the filmmakers to endorse. As the story develops, the lovers are separated, and we observe how each of them reacts to the devastating turn of events. Wilson's decision whether to reveal himself to the court and save his enemies is, in these terms, a decision whether to continue in his exile and solitude. He chooses relationship and human community, and so the separated threads of man and woman are woven together again at (and *as*) the resolution of the story and of its meanings, as Joe and his fiancée embrace. The fact that this reconciliation occurs in the courtroom asserts that it is also a social gesture, a coming to terms with the larger forces of social order and the law. In this way the coming together of the lovers clarifies the healing of the culture and implies a comprehensive system of values. The lovers incarnate a value that is challenged, redefined, strengthened, and mended by the course of events; their reconciliation shows the resetting of the moral order that was fractured at the lynching.

Two other scenes from *Fury* reveal some of the fundamental pleasures of simply watching a movie for all it's worth. In a barber shop, where some of the townspeople are discussing the Wilson case, the barber lets the customer whom he is shaving — and a nearby deputy — know that he has often felt the impulse to cut throats rather than groom them. The camera holds on the barber and the deputy during the last half of the barber's speech. The barber then returns his attention to the customer, but the customer has, understandably, disappeared. The flight of the customer is not shown. Instead, the camera pans over to the empty barber chair and then to the front door, which is just swinging closed. What the camera is doing here is acting as the vehicle of the barber and deputy's attention, and also of ours; all of us notice, at the same time, that the customer has fled. It would have been possible for the camera to show the man's leaving and the barber's speaking at once, as they purportedly occurred in the "time of the story," but this particular narrative strategy — of showing the discovery of the man's just having left — enhances the comedy of the scene and puts us, for a moment, in the barber's shoes. Out of the many snippets of time and space and action that might have been shown, these snippets were chosen. These are the time/space fragments that constitute the story and its presentation; this is the path that leads us through these woods; this series of shots is the gold vein that runs through this pre-filmic mountain of quartz. The camera, or the particular series of views, charts a path by selecting and following certain actions, certain sections of time and space; this path is the work.

Looking at that scene, we can also observe the play of continuity. A shot of a door's swinging closed need not "mean" anything in particular, but in this context and in this order, this shot implies that the customer (unseen) fled (unseen) for reasons (unseen) that we fill in. We fill in virtually all of this, in fact, supplying the emotions and the comedy ourselves (which makes them more vivid for us, more a matter of our *own* experience) on the basis of a carefully calculated visual hint.

We can learn something similar about camerawork and narrative strategy in general by considering the scene in which Wilson feels pursued by his soon-to-be victims, walks hurriedly home, and decides to turn himself in. As he walks down the street, Wilson turns to look over his shoulder. The next shot is of the pavement as it unrolls behind him. What it actually is is simply a low-level tracking shot. The shot of Wilson's looking behind him and the shot of the receding pavement work together and encourage us to read them in terms of each other, almost as if there were an invisible staple or "suture" between them. We understand that the pavement shot is taken from Wilson's vantage point and that (since he turned around and since the pavement is receding) he is thinking not of where he is going but of what he is trying to walk away from or, in context, being pursued by (the unseen ghosts of his victims; in other words, his conscience).

All we have been doing here is looking at a few shots — *as* shots, as choices, and as clues. We could well go on to examine *Fury* in relation to other pictures directed by Lang, noticing the ways it relates to his 1931 German picture, *M* (which is an equally complex treatment of the nature of justice and which also ends with a lengthy trial) and to the other American films he made that dealt with the problem of revenge, such as *Rancho Notorious* (1952) or *The Big Heat* (1953). We could study *Fury* in relation to other courtroom melodramas, other Tracy performances, other MGM pictures of the 1930s, other "problem pictures," other visions of America directed by recently arrived foreigners, and so on. Wherever you start, the point is to *keep going*.

As our tour through *A Clockwork Orange* has demonstrated, it is possible to say a great many things about a movie, and it is important to have a grasp of critical discourse. As a corrective, by way of *The Big Country* and *Fury*, we have also seen that simple attention to what is onscreen at a given moment can reveal just as much as can the well-informed application of, say, genre criticism. In film appreciation, it is film and not the critical apparatus that is primary; it is the movies that have the secrets and that reveal them to our patient and involved scrutiny. Accordingly, this book concentrates on movies and draws appreciative strategies out of *them*.

Whether a movie is a controversial piece of "high" art like *A Clockwork Orange*, an intensely political and romantic melodrama like *Fury*, an action spectacle like *The Big Country*, or a paradoxical trap like *Dead of Night*, it can prove intriguing once you take a close look at it. But before advancing a rigorous critical argument, it is necessary to have a grasp of the art as a whole. Before analyzing what kind of movie the picture that interests you is, or how it employs the terms of the art, you have to know what a movie is in the first place and what the most important of those terms are.

That means that we will have to start from scratch: with the eye and the ear, the screen and the projector, the filmstock and the frame. As a way of anchoring and organizing all this, the discussion will repeatedly touch base with one critical problem and one major text. The text will be *Citizen Kane*, a phenomenally rich film that so thoroughly explored the possibilities of the cinema that one could explore the cinema by studying that movie. The critical problem will be the "auteur theory," and it will be tested against the complex realities of production. But many other films and problems will come under discussion, and we should finish this inquiry with a relatively full understanding of the art, an understanding on which a deep appreciation can be based.

Terms As Tools. None of this is a matter of learning rules, although one does learn a great many *terms*, like the names for certain kinds of shots and how certain pieces of equipment are used. One learns these because they are the fundamental tools of the craft of filmmaking as well as of film analysis. One doesn't, responsibly, import a slew of terms from literature or psychoanalysis or Marxism and use them to explain what is happening in a film — or at least, if those terms do prove useful and appropriate, one has to set them in relation to the terms of actual film practice. The film student has to learn the filmmaker's language, and beyond that the student or critic has to use that language clearly, not to obscure matters with a cloud of jargon.

What all this leads to is an understanding not of rules but of *conventions* and *options*. There are many ways of making films, none of them graven in stone, and the filmmaker has the option of selecting whatever will work — or of inventing something new.

These options expand with time as more and more films demonstrate new ways of achieving their purposes.

Cinema and the Movies. The first term to learn is **cinema**, the name for the whole shebang. Cinema denotes the system of film, the "language" that all movies "speak"; it is a collective term for motion pictures.

The origin of the word tells a great deal about it. When Edison introduced the Kinetoscope (a nonprojecting viewing device) and the Kinetograph (a camera), he had in mind the Greek word that is also the basis of the word "kinetic": *kinein,* "to move." The Lumière brothers, who were the first to project films for a paying audience (on December 28, 1895), called their integrated camera/printer/projector the Cinématographe, and the French *c* eventually replaced the Greek *k*, leaving the English word "cinema." The German *Kino* and Russian *kinó* reveal the same root. Just as "photography," made up of the Greek for "light" (*phōs*) and "to write" (*graphein*), means something like "writing with light" or "written light," **cinematography** denotes written movement, or the process of recording motion. This sense of the motion picture as a picture of motion is not only descriptive; it also shows that what was first considered important about cinema was its ability to capture and re-create the illusion of movement. Its aesthetics, then, are rooted in kinetics, and that implies that there is something "uncinematic" about a movie that doesn't move. Of course, the opinions of those who coined the word in the late nineteenth century do not have to mandate certain kinds of film practice in the late twentieth century — there have been a lot of good, unmoving images in films — but this is a useful way to understand how "cinema" advances a position about the nature of the art and the process of making movies, while it also functions as a neutral, collective term.

Movie began as a slang term for "motion picture." It too has built into it the implication that movement is the crucial and definitive aspect of a film. It denotes the finished product of the cinematic process, the "speech act" of that "language" (perhaps, to extend the metaphor, a speech act in the "tongue" of a particular genre). It is also a collective term for motion pictures, as in "the movies."

Film, which is loosely considered interchangeable with both "cinema" and "movie," specifically denotes the physical medium — the celluloid strip — on which the images are imprinted, although it also refers to the totality of the finished product, as in "that was a good film," and to the whole of the art, as in "film appreciation." If "movie" spotlights the importance of the picture's moving, "film" emphasizes the importance of the plastic material and its specific qualities of transparency, flexibility, the ability to be **spliced** (taped or cemented together), and so on. In this fairly rigorous context, "cinema" — the medium-specific process of intermittent movement and projection — is what allows "film," the plastic material, to become a "movie," or moving picture.

Within the industry, an idea that is being considered for production is often called a **property**, whereas a film that is in production or that has been released is usually called a **picture**. These terms are revealing and precise: a property is something that can be bought, owned, and sold; a picture is something to look at, to be seen by an audience.

From here, things get a little more complicated. In common usage "cinema," "film," and "movie" are considered denotatively interchangeable, whereas their connotations are very different. "Cinema" can refer to a theater, and "film" and "movie" can refer to what is shown there. If "movie" is a populist term whereas "film" is a highbrow or academic one, "cinema" can sound positively snooty. The underlying notion that a movie is something to eat popcorn with, whereas a film is something to ponder, is well entrenched, though it is unfortunately misleading. Any motion picture, if it is good enough, is there to be appreciated in the fullest sense.

Most countries refer to motion pictures by some variant of "cinema," that is, of "to move" + "to write." The Chinese, however, have an extremely interesting term, *dianying*, which means "electric shadows." In this word the emphasis is not on the content of the image (on whether it is a moving or a still picture) nor on the process of its recording, but on what the spectator sees in the theater: the shadows cast on the screen as the electrically generated light is blocked and filtered by the frame in the projector. The implication here is almost like that in Book VII of Plato's *Republic*, where the world is compared to a cave in which an audience is shown only the shadows of real things, and in which it is argued that one must leave the cave entirely if one is to find out what is ultimately Real. Whether or not a Platonic interpretation of cinema proves useful, *dianying* puts its finger squarely on the problem of the nature of the image and its relation to reality, while also grounding itself in the theatrical experience.

Sherlock Jr. There are two sequences in Buster Keaton's *Sherlock Jr.* (1924) that address all of these problems. Keaton plays a projectionist (call him Buster) who wants to be a detective. At one point, despondent at being rejected by his girlfriend for a theft that he didn't commit, Buster goes to the theater and starts up the movie *Hearts and Pearls*. Then he falls asleep, and his dream self leaves the projection booth and eventually jumps into the screen. What he has to learn is that film (and fantasy) work in a manner different from the world. For one thing, a film can be cut. The landscape begins to shift instantaneously, suddenly yanking Buster from a garden to the middle of a busy city street. At one point he finds himself on a rock in the ocean; he starts to dive into the water, but there is another cut, and he lands in a snowbank. Eventually he is incorporated into the image — so that he is not left in the same screen position while everything around him shifts with every cut — and takes on the idealized fantasy role of "Sherlock Jr." When he wakes up, the audience has to make a similar image–reality shift, thinking of him not as "Sherlock Jr." but as "Buster" again, while remaining aware all along that he is also "Keaton," the actor and director.

The girlfriend is in the projection booth now, having proved herself the better detective and discovered the thief. Their engagement is on again, but Buster is hopelessly shy. He looks through the window of the projection booth, at the end of *Hearts and Pearls,* which is still being shown. He takes his cues about what to do from what is done by the people on the screen — conveniently, a romantic couple. When the screen hero kisses the heroine, Buster kisses his girlfriend; when his role model produces an engagement ring, so does Buster. But what to do next? On the theater screen there is a fade-out on the romantic couple and a fade-in on them as a married couple with children. This transition — which has discreetly skipped over the reproductive process — leaves Buster scratching his head, because he cannot figure out how to accomplish such a shift in the physical world. He doesn't yet know where movies come from.

What Buster has to learn, and what Keaton is showing us, is that the cinema has its own way of working. We may use movies as a vehicle of escape or of fantasy, as Buster does when he imagines himself to be Sherlock Jr., "the world's greatest detective." We may confront them as a metaphysical problem, as Buster does in the landscape montage and at the end in the projection booth. We may enjoy the ways in which they are able to refer to their own processes, the way *Sherlock Jr.* is a reflexive film — that is, a film that calls attention to the fact that it is a film. But no matter what, we have to know what we are looking at before we try to maneuver our imaginations through the world of the movies. We have to know how they are different from the physical world, what are the terms of their art and the tools of their craft, who makes them, why people watch them, and what they are capable of meaning. We have to know what movies are and how they work.

Our experience of the world is a relationship. Between the subjective reality of the self — our thoughts, emotions, and physical condition — and the objective reality of the external environment, we draw connections so rapidly and efficiently that we are often unconsious of the process. Yet even the simple impression of walking down the street is something we construct out of a great many pieces of information.

The feet feel the pressure of pavement, shoe, and sock. The skin feels the temperature of the air. The inner ear adjusts to the pull of gravity and to shifts in position, maintaining the body's balance and equilibrium. Muscles all over the body contract and stretch, sending messages without which coordination would be impossible. The nose samples the environment, reporting a pleasurable sensation from the new-mown grass on the left, an unpleasant one from the car exhaust on the right. The ears and brain decipher sound waves into a robin, a chittering squirrel, the wind, a car that needs engine work, the shoes on the pavement. The eyes discern color, shape, depth, movement, and distance, seeing the street, the grass, the car, the animals, and a good portion of the body. And the conscious mind selects which of these items is to receive particular notice, shifting from the robin to the reason for taking this walk — the memory of an appointment, perhaps, and the plans for what to do upon arrival — in some manner inhabiting the past, the present, and the future at once, while holding a sense of who the person is.

The sense of being oneself and of being in a place and time, which feels like a whole, is an automatic accomplishment, an integration of data from inside and outside the body. Even if the mind, in this example, may be entirely preoccupied with the appointment that will start in five minutes, the brain keeps doing its job, both reporting on and constructing the relationship of subject and object, self and world.

2. Parts and Wholes

Fragmentation and Synthesis

We are always making connections. Consider the eyes and the fact that we have two of them. Each eye receives a two-dimensional image, and that image is inverted as light passes through the lens. The brain does not simply accept the information on the retina; it knows, through experience, to turn that information upside down — that is, "right" side up — so that the visual impression will coincide with the way things are in the outside world. The brain receives two flattened and inverted images, each of them complete. Computing the parallax created by the angles at which each eye sees the objects before it, the brain constructs an impression of a three-dimensional image that neither eye can see, and this hallucination is what we take for granted as visual experience. What the eye cannot see at all — X-rays and so on — we may consider irrelevant or somehow not there.

Or consider language. Each word is an individual symbol, a fragment of a referential system. To express a complete thought, we usually have to string words together in a sentence. And to interpret a sentence, we have to break it down into its components, understanding each word both as an independent symbol and in relationship to the symbols that surround it. A sentence is a whole, and it is made up of parts. The most obvious such parts are the individual words; others include such syntactic structures as phrases and clauses, which may be thought of as subsystems.

There is a difference between a string of words and an understood sentence, and that difference may be a response to the "systemness" or the systemic coherence of the organized parts. A **system,** as a whole, is greater than the sum of its parts, just as a working automobile is something more than a ton of car parts. To learn to read is to discover how words work individually and in significant arrangements, to unlock the secrets of the linguistic system. When speaking or listening, writing or reading, we are always breaking wholes down into fragments and reassembling fragments into wholes, and that activity is not very different from the normal process of integrating sensory data into a model of the world around us.

Frames and Shots. We draw on much the same skills when watching a movie. Although the soundtrack is continuous, the picture track consists of a series of individual still pictures.

Fig. 1-2 is a diagram of a section of 35mm film. The width of a piece of film is called its **gauge**, and most movies are shot and printed onto stock that is 35 millimeters wide. Other commonly used gauges are 8mm, 16mm, and 70mm. Running down the outer edges of the film are regularly spaced perforations called **sprocket holes**; these are engaged by toothed wheels, or gears, called **sprockets**, so that the film can be advanced and stopped in the camera and in the projector. Each individual picture is called a **frame**, and in most 35mm systems, each frame is four sprocket-holes high. The unexposed area between frames is called the **frame line**. The soundtrack runs between the frames and the left sprocket holes. In 16mm there is only one line of sprocket holes (on the left side), each frame is one sprocket-hole high, and the soundtrack runs down the right side, as shown in **Fig. 1-3**. There are 16 frames per foot of 35mm film and 40 frames per foot of 16mm film.

In almost all cases, sound film is projected at 24 frames per second (abbreviated 24 **fps**). This projection rate was standardized with the advent of the "talkies." Silent films usually ran at between 16 and 20 fps; the higher rate of 24 fps yielded better sound fidelity, and in any case sound required a predictable and consistent projection rate. The length of a silent film was measured in feet, meters, or reels; the length of a sound film is measured in minutes. A **reel** is approximately 950 feet of 35mm film, with a maximum length of 1,000 feet, and approximately 380 feet of 16mm film, with a maximum length of 400 feet. At the more-or-less standard

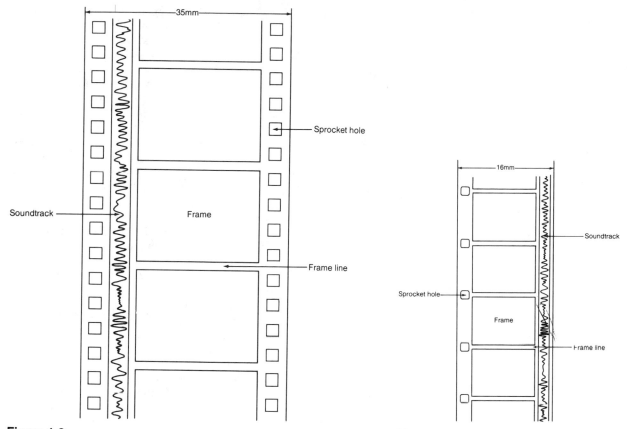

Figure 1-2

Figure 1-3

silent projection rate of 16 fps, a full reel took about 15 minutes to project; at sound speed, a reel lasts about 10 minutes. The standard projection reel today holds up to 2,000 feet of 35mm film, but "one reel" remains a standard, if approximate, unit of measure.

One process that is peculiar to the cinema (in other words, "medium-specific") is that of generating the impression of a *moving* picture. Like a still camera, a movie camera can take only one picture at a time, and the same is true of a projector, which can show only one frame at a time. The strip of film does not move during the split second necessary to expose the negative or to shine a light through the image onto a screen. In both camera and projector, the film moves *intermittently*, driven and stopped by the sprockets, which, in turn, are driven by a crank or a motor. When the film is held still, a rotating plate with one or more wedges cut out of it (the **shutter**) is positioned so that an open wedge is between the film and the light source, allowing the light to expose the frame from the front (in a camera) or to shine through it from the back (in a projector). While the film is moving from one exposure or projection position to another, the shutter is closed — that is, shut. The shutter is open about the same amount of time that it is closed; therefore, for about half the time we are watching a movie, the screen is totally dark.

The flicker from which the "flicks" got another one of their names is caused by the opening and closing of the shutter during projection. Below 12 fps, this flicker is extremely distracting; at 16 fps, it becomes relatively unnoticeable — to the conscious mind, that is. But the brain works very rapidly and is, on some level, aware of each frame as a still picture and of the dark intervals. To render the flicker even less noticeable, it is now common for each frame to be shown and blocked out as many as four or five times, depending on the design of the shutter. There will still be a new frame every twenty-fourth of a second, but the flicker rate might be as high as 120 per second.

The illusion of motion in a movie depends on a physiological quirk and a mental process. As it happens, the retina retains a brief afterimage of each still — a quirk that is enhanced by keeping the theater dark, so that each frame makes a particularly distinct impression. This effect, called the **persistence of vision**, accounts for our not being especially aware of the darkness between frames, because the retina continues to "see" the image even when the screen is dark. When a coin is spun and both sides appear to be superimposed, or when a burning stick is whipped in rapid circles and we see curlicues rather than a moving orange point, those "unreal" sights are the product of persistence of vision.

But that effect is not enough to account for the impression of *movement*. The eyes see one distinct frame after another — successive glimpses, for example, of a hand in the act of waving. The brain applies the real-world laws of cause and effect to this series of stills and deduces that the hand *must have moved* from one photographed position to another — and so we imagine that we have actually seen the object move. This process, called the **phi phenomenon**, is comparable to the hallucination of a noninverted three-dimensional field generated by the brain from what the eyes actually register: two inverted two-dimensional images from predictably different vantage points. On the very simplest level, then, watching a movie involves making connections among fragments (frames) and generating a holistic impression, even if most of this is done without conscious effort.

A more conscious process is involved in making connections between one moving picture and another. It is very unusual for a movie to consist of only one shot.

A **shot** is a continuously exposed piece of film, or the view provided by that continuous series of frames. In camera terms, a shot begins when the camera is turned on and ends when the camera is turned off, although on the set that continuous exposure might be called a **take**, that is, an attempt to get a shot on film (one may shoot many takes before being satisfied with the shot). In the terms of a completed film, or from the perspective of the editor, however, a shot begins and ends with a cut or with some other transitional device, such as a wipe or a dissolve.

A shot may also be thought of as a **printed take**, in other words, a take that is approved by the director and is printed (copied) so that the editor can cut it into the film. The editor may divide a single take into several shots or may use only part of the take as a single shot.

A shot can be as short as a single frame, though most last for a few seconds. When an edited shot lasts longer than a minute, it is sometimes called a **long take**. To **cut** or **edit** a film is to join its shots together physically into the order in which they are intended to be projected.

It is impossible to take a picture of the whole world at once. (Even from outer space, the camera would see only one half of the planet at a time.) Instead, the photographer or filmmaker selects a portion of the visible field and records that in a still or a shot. The movie audience watches each shot and is led — by the film-maker or by an understanding of basic cinematic conventions — to assemble those parts into a conceptual or spatial whole. In Shot A, for example, we may see a man who is leaning against a brick wall and looking to his right while doffing his hat and saying, "Hello." Shot B may show a woman who is leaning against a brick wall and looking to her left. In the absence of further information, we would assume that the man in Shot A is saying "Hello" to the woman in Shot B, that they are looking at each other, and that they are leaning against the same wall. If the woman looks up and points to something at the end of Shot B, and Shot C shows a flying bird, we would assume not only that she is pointing at *that* bird — which might have been photographed five years ago in Tibet, for all we know — but also that the sky in Shot C is above what we can see in Shots A and B, even if it has not been shown in Shot A or B.

The world is a whole, but the filmed world is usually a series of selected fragments. Our experience of the visible world is itself constructed out of a series of glimpses. The eyes do not simply stare and absorb; they move about almost continually. The part of the retina where the optic nerve joins it is blind, and only one portion of the retina (the fovea) is extremely acute. The eyes keep moving — in what are called "saccades" — in order to direct the fovea toward the thing we want to see best at the moment. These saccadic movements are so brief and rapid that we accumulate many distinct perceptions into an impression of a focused visual field.

It is easy to test this process by looking at someone who is watching a train pass by. While the person may have the simple experience of seeing that train, the eyes will flick back and forth, directing the fovea to one car after another. Even when people make eye contact, unless they are having a staring contest, their eyes dart from one part of the face to another: the mouth, the hair, this eye, the other eye. One reason that television induces a kind of mental numbness is that the screen is so small that saccadic movements are minimalized and, with them, the degree of conscious alertness. (Reading, conversely, stimulates mental alertness.) In a movie, where the image is larger, the eye moves about in the visual field much as it does in the physical world, taking in various bits of information and integrating them into a sense of the whole. Much of the art of making an interesting film is in keeping the audience's eyes moving, not just to forestall boredom — which would set in quickly if the viewer were not distracted from the experience of simply sitting in the dark for hours — but also to trick the brain into thinking that it is looking at or moving around within something like the real world.

The Filmed World. There are many ways in which the image on a movie screen is not like the brain's impression of the visible world. Most obviously, it is two-dimensional, like the image seen by one eye. The black perimeter of the image does not correspond to our experience of the limits of peripheral vision. Only a part of the visual field can be shown at a time — something that frustrates amateur or home movie makers, who often attempt to defeat the limits of the frame by panning and tilting all over the landscape, trying to fit it all into one shot. Size relationships are constantly changing, so that a face may be twelve feet high at one moment and two feet high the next. A black-and-white image converts colors to shades of gray, and even a color film has a limited repertoire of dyes and chemicals.

It has been argued that it is the ways in which film is *not* like reality that allow it to be an art. Rudolf Arnheim, for one, made the case that because the frame cannot include the whole visual world and is limited by a black rectangle, the border can be used as a structuring principle, like the frame of a painting. An image can be *composed* in relation to the shape and limits of the frame, and to include or exclude part of the visual field can become a matter of artistic choice. Black-and-white offers a controllable palette, and these days even colors can be precisely selected and modulated. And because the film image is (leaving 3-D out of this) two-dimensional, perspective can be exploited, size relationships varied, and so on.

It has also been argued, by theorists like Siegfried Kracauer and André Bazin, that film is justified by its resemblance to the physical world and that its ideal is realism. A photo can have the authenticity and authority of a fingerprint, as if the physical world had imprinted its image directly on the photosensitive emulsion. Even if realism is not reality but a way of looking at or conceptualizing reality, it remains true that the technology of photography gives film a special claim to being an art of the real. Something that would "have to be seen to be believed" can be shown in a photo or a nonfiction film and can then demand to be believed. A drawing or a verbal description would not have the same virtually automatic claim on belief.

To have a complete grasp of what film is, it is necessary to understand how both of these arguments are, in their own terms, correct. Film gives us a picture that is both like and unlike the world. It works, most often, with the materials of audible and visible reality, and it both transforms those materials and arranges them.

One of the original polarities in film history and one that remains useful in sorting out the cinema is that between the work of the Lumière brothers and that of Georges Méliès. The striking achievement of Auguste and particularly Louis Lumière was that they put an objective view of physical, daily reality on the screen. Although they also dabbled in the narrative film (*The Gardener and the Little Scamp* [1895], remade as *The Sprinkler Sprinkled* [1896], was *the* first narrative film) and in cinematic manipulations of reality (*Demolition of a Wall* [1896] was sometimes cranked backward), they are best remembered for their recorded fragments of human activity. They chose their subjects from the ordinary world, or posed their friends, or encouraged people to show off for the camera. Louis thought the cinema was a toy, but he knew it was a *great* toy. The Lumières, whose name means "light," delighted in capturing the world and projecting its image on a screen; each film was a single shot and had no reason to be any longer. That was the key to its integrity.

Georges Méliès, the magician who made *A Trip to the Moon*, exploited the cinema's ability to transform reality — stopping the camera in mid take, for instance, to allow a man to change into a woman or to turn a moon dweller into a blast of smoke. Méliès knew the cinema was magic.

The Lumière/Méliès dichotomy may be expressed as the tension, in almost any film, between the *actual* and the *fantastic*. These are opportunities, creative decisions, that the photographer and the filmmaker can pursue, faced with the world. (It has sometimes been expressed as "realism versus expressionism," but that formulation takes "realism" — which is problematic — for granted and confuses the desire to transform the real with a particular artistic movement.) The selected and photographed image is linked to the physical world, the actual, by the technology of photography. Yet it can be framed, cut, arranged, and made to function however the filmmaker desires.

Within Frames and Between Them. Shots and cuts make up virtually the entire visual world of film, much as words and their ordering make up the sentence, or a sequence of sentences makes up a book. The general term for what has been arranged within the shot is **mise-en-scène**. The general term for how shots are joined together is **montage**. (These are two of the most important and problematic terms in film study, and they will be defined at greater length in the course of this book, but for now it is useful to introduce them as relatively simple notions.) Just as the viewer interprets the mise-en-scène to establish, for example, what is important within a given shot and how it corresponds or does not to the physical world and the world of the imagination, the viewer interprets the montage to establish what these separate views may have to do with one another.

Let us return to that walk down the street, but this time with a movie camera. One way to shoot this epic might be in a single continuous shot — a long take that would privilege mise-en-scène. We select a lens with a fairly wide angle of view so that we can take in the sidewalk, the lawns to the left, the street to the right — but probably not the moving body, as a lens with that wide an angle would introduce "fish-eye" distortions, bending straight lines into pronounced curves. We decide between a hand-held camera, which will convey the shifting of our body as we walk (but not too much, as our brain compensates for such motion when walking, and we do not experience the visual world as bouncing up and down), and a dolly shot, where the camera moves smoothly on a wheeled platform. We turn on a tape recorder and obtain a continuous soundtrack, complete with bird, squirrel, passing car, and footsteps. As the bird attracts our attention, we swing the camera over to the right, and this movement induces some blurring that does not correspond to our real-world experience, but cameras have their limitations at 24 fps. Then we swing back to a forward view, and so on. After a while the audience may become bored with this unchanging point of view and may feel as if the camera were staring, regardless of whether we have chosen to let it bounce or glide.

For the sequel, *Sidewalk II*, we opt for montage. This time we begin with a wide field of view (a long shot) to establish the setting and the action. We maintain the illusion that the camera is showing what the walking character sees (subjective camera), but this time we can vary the distance between camera and object to indicate the relative importance of the objects in the field, not only in themselves but also to the character who is noticing them. When the squirrel chitters, we cut to a closeup of the squirrel, indicating that it is the principal current object of attention by excluding other objects from view, and suggesting its importance by making it large. (The closer view might indicate that the character has moved closer to the squirrel, but more often it would indicate that the character has *concentrated his or her attention* on the squirrel. In that sense the cinema is capable of imitating or alluding to the activity of the mind, as the early film theorist Hugo Münsterberg observed.) We cut and move the camera back — or change the lens — for a view of the branch and more of the tree (a medium shot) as the squirrel becomes aware of us and leaps away. Then we cut to a long shot of the sidewalk, similar to the establishing shot but taken from several yards further down the street, to indicate that a certain distance has been traveled in the meantime and also that all these actions are to be considered continuous, part of a single extended action.

If we wanted to give an even fuller impression of what is going on here, we might cut to a long shot, taken from the middle of the street or from somewhere further down the sidewalk, showing the character in the act of walking. This would mean abandoning the device of subjective camera in favor of an objective, exterior view, and its principal advantage would be to let the audience know just who is doing the walking. We might give the piece some rhythm by cutting to a closeup of the character's shoes (like the opening of John Badham's *Saturday Night Fever* [1977]), or we could alternate shots of shoes and legs in a regular rhythm (each shot on the screen for the same length of time), making the walking more kinetically immediate. We could then inject some drama by cutting to a medium shot of the car's passing suddenly by, suggesting that the character is surprised by it, and then to a closeup of the robin's flying away, suggesting not only that the bird is startled by the car but also that the character and the bird share a certain perspective, both of them regarding the car as an intruder. In that case, we would have made the camera's limited view work *for* us, arranging the parts in the interest of a particular significance.

Continuity. The car and the robin might have been shot on separate days, but the audience will read the montage as if the events shown in the two shots are related and will attempt to discover or invent a reason for this juxtaposition. The various shots of the sidewalk, the character, and the environment will be connected by the viewer into an impression of **continuity**, the even flow of events from shot to shot.

This applies not only to conceptual continuity — as in "bird plus walker versus car equals a symbolic statement about being in harmony with nature" — but also to spatial and temporal continuity. Continuity demands that the events portrayed in Shot 3, in most cases, follow and conform with those portrayed in Shot 2, and that the *spaces* of Shots 2 and 3 both be locateable on some kind of mental map. Thus, if the character opens his top shirt button in Shot 2 while in the middle of the block, that button had better be open in Shot 3, where he is shown a few steps further down the block. If there is no deliberate time-juggling going on, a cut from an actress with a half-finished cigarette in her hand, as she begins a speech, to that same actress with a three-quarter-length cigarette, as her speech continues, will be interpreted as a **continuity flaw**, a mismatch.

But a continuity flaw is not necessarily an error. Because film works with fragments, it has the ability to assemble parts into any kind of whole. This is one of the essential ways it plays with time, space, and logic. Film allows us to put the future before the past, to make a memory appear to live, to cut from a "real" landscape to an artificial one, and to violate the laws of cause and effect. One of the most brilliantly sustained continuity "flaws" in film history was Luis Buñuel's using two actresses to play the same character in *That Obscure Object of Desire* (1977). Another occurs in the "Odessa Steps" sequence of Eisenstein's *Battleship Potemkin* (1925), where a baby carriage begins to roll down a staircase over and over again; here "real time" is stretched into a highly expressive "cinematic time," an effect that could never have been achieved if Eisenstein had felt compelled to observe normal continuity.

One filmmaker's "flaw" may be another's "creative effect"; it depends on what the filmmaker wants to accomplish. Keeping in mind that presentation and structure are artistic choices and that the cinema allows a story, a record, or a vision to be presented in *any* order, most students and filmmakers begin by studying continuity — which is a matter both of shooting and of editing — because it requires a mastery of normal continuity in order to create (or understand) significant discontinuity.

In the absence of signals to the contrary, the shots in a film are normally assembled — by the editor and by the viewer — into the most likely impression of completeness and continuity, giving the sense that there is a 360° three-dimensional world within which the eye could roam if it chose to do so. One mark of an accomplished filmmaker is that he or she shows the audience something just when (or just before) the audience wants to see it — cutting to the squirrel, for instance, when the viewer may want to know what is making that funny sound — because this gives the impression that the viewer is free to look where he or she wants to, as if in the spatial and temporal whole of the physical world.

Film As a Language

Photography itself, on which the medium of cinema principally depends, directs the viewer in two opposite directions, and to reconcile these directions is a vital aspect of understanding any movie or even any shot. When speaking of the Lumière/Méliès distinction, we naively assumed that all one had to do, in order to have a reality fragment to leave alone or to distort, was to take a picture of it. But a photograph is not a simple thing, and once several photographs are arranged into a structure, that structure reveals a mystery of its own, for it begins to display some of the attributes of a language: a signifying system.

Signs and Referents. On the one hand, photography offers us a picture of a thing or an event that had to exist in the physical world long enough to be photographed. The fact that the event may have been staged by actors — in other words, that it may be part of a fiction — does not take away from the fact that the actors were real and were there to be photographed. In a nonfiction shot — a highly magnified view of feeding microbes, for example — what is most important is that it presents the record of an actual occurrence.

On the other hand, photography is a signifying system, comparable to language in that it does not give us the referents; instead, it refers to them. While a shot is present, its referent is literally absent. And the cinema gives us audible and visible signs — which evoke the mental images of their referents — in a particular order. In that sense, the cinema is an artificial, arranged structure that can be manipulated like any other language, not a torrent of referents but a series of signs.

Semiotics — also known as **semiology** — is the study of signifying systems, including everything from a thermometer to *Moby-*

Dick. The root of the word is *seme*, Greek for "sign" or "symptom." (Diagnosis is the art of interpreting symptoms, which are signs of particular disorders; it was the original semiotics.) The goal of this science is to identify the minimal units of signification and the necessary logic of their arrangements if they *are* to make sense in relation to other units of meaning.

Photography poses special problems for semiotics because so much information — often of differing types — is presented at once: in the foreground and background, for instance, or as a complex action. To sort all this out, the semiotician hunts not only for signs but also for **codes**, subsystems by which information is organized and selectively emphasized. An image may be "encoded" and in need of "decoding." A low-angle shot can encode the subject as a figure of power, just as a white hat can encode a cowboy as a hero and a jump cut can act as a code for discontinuity.

Each word is an individual symbol. The word "tree" stands for a certain kind of vegetation; "tree" is the **sign**, and the leafy wooden thing is the **referent**, the thing being referred to. In *Sidewalk II* the medium shot of the tree is a sign, and the tree itself is the referent. Watching that film, we would never see the referent — only the sign, the picture.

Yet even as a discrete item the sign cannot be understood on its own; it depends on our understanding of its role in a relationship. As a verbal sign, a word is not simply a "name" for a "thing," nor is a photo simply a "picture" of a "thing." The sign is itself a relationship between a **signifier** (a sound or image) and a **signified** (a concept or idea). The picture of a tree evokes not the actual tree but an idea of the tree, a mental construct of it. This is obvious in verbal language, but it is just as true in the cinema.

As a referent, the tree may be signified via the written word "tree," the spoken sound "trē," a drawing, a photograph, or even a gesture such as pointing to a particular tree. When you say "tree," you do not bring the plant itself into the room, or language would be a cluttered business. Nor do you bring back a complete event when you remember it (memory is a sign system). It is more accurate to say that "tree" works as a reference, or sign, because both the speaker and the listener are familiar with the relationship between t-r-e-e or trē (the signifier, whether read or heard) and the general idea or particularized abstraction (the signified) of the leafy wooden thing (the referent). Signifier and signified are interlocking abstractions. As a team they constitute the sign.

If you do not know Japanese and are looking at a page written in that language, you are confronting something that you suspect is intended to signify something, although you don't know what. Although each Japanese character is a sign (a signifier and a signified, working together to evoke an image of the referent in the mind of a native speaker), to you it may appear to be a "pure" signifier — something that is meant to stand for or to evoke *some* mental construct or other. If you had never learned any language but had an image in your head of something that you didn't know was called a tree, you might be having an experience of a "pure" signified. The connection between signifier and signified is made so rapidly, by one who knows language, that it is difficult, without such examples, to consider what a pure signifier or signified might be like, and the fact is that they cannot exist independently of one another.

To understand the sign "tree" is to know that t-r-e-e and the idea of a certain class of objects go together, that signifier and signified are linked. The next step is to know that "tree" is the sign for that referent. Once this set of connections has become second nature, it becomes easy to forget that the signifier t-r-e-e is not the sign "tree," just as the signified (the concept of a tree) is not the referent (the tree itself). The character in Jean-Luc Godard's *Les Carabiniers* (1963) who tries to climb into a bathtub with the heroine of a stag film — and, of course, tears the screen — has lost sight of the distinction between sign and referent.

Nor are words the only kinds of signs. The level of mercury in a thermometer signifies the temperature. (The degree marks on the thermometer are a code — specific to *that* shape and size of thermometer — by which the level of mercury can be interpreted.) A red octagon on an American street tells the driver to come to a full stop before proceeding through the intersection. A picture of an apple refers to an apple, and a photograph of your face refers to your face.

The *kind* of sign, or category, depends on the kind of relationship that exists between the signifier and the signified. An **icon** or **iconic sign** functions by the *resemblance* or *likeness* between its elements: a picture of an apple looks like an apple. (Actually, to perceive this you have to learn how to "read" the sign. Until you see that it is a photograph and know what that implies, the object could look simply like a piece of stiff paper with a random pattern of light and dark on one side.) An **index** or **indexical sign** points to or *indicates* its referent, and this reference depends on some essential and inevitable *link* between signifier and signified, as seamless and predictable as a physical law and often a matter of cause and effect. A weathervane points (like an *index* finger) in the direction of the wind that is blowing at the time, just as an increase in temperature causes the mercury in a thermometer to expand in an inevitable manner. A **symbol** or **symbolic sign** is one in which the relationship between its elements is *arbitrary* or agreed upon. Most words are symbols. The idea of a tree is agreed to be signified by t-r-e-e in English, B-a-u-m in German — an arbitrary system, but one that works because it is consistently applied in those languages.

In the cinema any given sign may take on more than one of these properties. A picture of Paul Newman, for instance, is iconic in the sense that it resembles the real Paul Newman. And it is indexical, because the pattern of light and shade that we recognize as Newman's image is the product of light's having struck the photosensitive filmstock in a specific manner; a photo can be as indexical as a fingerprint. It may also be symbolic if the audience is expected to read Paul Newman "as" Cool Hand Luke (in Stuart

Rosenberg's 1967 film) rather than as Newman himself — and even more intricately symbolic if Luke, stretched out on the prison dining table, is encoded as a reference to the crucified Jesus.

Syntagms and Paradigms. It is one thing to understand a sign, another to draw or perceive the connections among several signs. For verbal language, this problem is most directly raised by the sentence. The rules of grammar and syntax help us to sort out the words and the possible or intended relations between them, and the habit of reading or speaking in sentences suspends our sense of full understanding until the sentence has been completed.

It is possible to analyze a sentence in a way that clarifies how meaning is built up from word to word. Each word to be presented or interpreted occupies a discrete place in the sentence, and for each word that is in that place, there are others that might have been chosen. These two properties of every word — that it is in a certain place and that it, rather than some other word, is there — can be described in terms of the syntagmatic and paradigmatic axes that semioticians find at work in every sentence.

The **syntagmatic axis**, which runs horizontally across the page or forward in time, denotes the sequence of words as they are linked by the relations of syntax. In the sentence "I went to the store," "went" follows "I" on the syntagmatic axis and bears the syntactic relationship to "I" of verb to subject. The adverbial phrase "to the store" falls into place once we understand the previously established relationship between "I" and "went" and have gone on to ask, prompted by the syntax, "Went" where?

The **paradigmatic axis**, which runs vertically, contains all the words that could make sense in the same context at a given point in the sentence. At the point in this sentence where there is to be a verb, a position along the syntagmatic axis currently occupied by "went," there is a whole category, or paradigm, of alternative words: "ran," "stumbled," "drove," and so on. Taking another selection from the paradigm, one could say, "I drove to the store" or "I ran to the store," or one could make other choices from other collections of alternatives and say, "I ran from the store" or "I hid from the monster." Although the paradigms are astronomically extensive, it is possible to simplify and condense the system into something like this:

He	ran	from	a	house
She	drove	around	one	district
Bill	walked	into	that	theater
I	went	to	the	store

In this sentence there is one syntagmatic axis, and there are five paradigmatic axes. Their points of intersection are linguistic decisions in time.

These axes are tidy systems, governed by rules. If a word is in a given position, it obeys the rules of that position. In this sentence, "store" cannot be replaced by a word taken from the paradigm of verbs because no verb would make sense in that context in that position. "I store to the went" may be interesting, but under the constraints of this particular structure, it doesn't signify.

No one has worked out an entirely satisfactory way of analyzing film editing in these terms. Film may, in fact, have no firm syntax, and a shot is not the same as a word in any case. But in the simple case of a shot of two people who are being held at gunpoint, followed by a closeup of a revolver's being fired, the audience will wait for the third shot to find out who, if anyone, gets wounded. That third shot could be of the bullet's striking Person A, or Person B, or a lamp in the back of the room. Any of these would make sense at this point and would complete the action, and all might be thought of as having come from the same paradigm.

Because it is made up of parts and also has a working, functional integrity that appears only when those parts have been assembled, film is a system. What makes film different from other referential systems is that the referents appear to be almost present, so that one appears to be looking at *the* world. What makes film like other signifying systems is that it can present only signs. Whether or not the arrangement of cinematic signs can be analyzed with a methodology that has proved useful for the sentence is another matter. There is still a great deal we do not know about how, exactly, a moving picture and a sound field communicate what we take to be their meanings, that is, how they signify. But it is clear that both picture and sound are selections from the continuum of the physical world and the world of the imagination, and that those parts are organized into an act of communication that depends on a referential system, the language of cinema.

The cinema can be divided into four major categories or avenues of expression: the narrative film, the nonfiction film, the animated film, and the avant-garde film. In practice there are many films that belong in several of these categories — like Walt Disney's *Snow White and the Seven Dwarfs* (1937), which is an animated film and which tells a story. But in theory these classifications can be very useful as guides to the possibilities of cinema. Even when we have a grasp of some of the essential characteristics of cinema as a signifying system and as a stew concocted from the materials of the world, we need to take stock of its most general applications. As an analogy, consider the English language: a coherent system, but one that reveals different resources in a poem, a novel, or an entry in an encyclopedia.

3. Primary Categories

The Narrative Film

Perhaps because of the important role played in film history by the narrative film and those who merchandise it, the first thing most people want to know about a film is whether it tells a story, and then what kind of story that is.

Narrative films tell stories. Usually the term "story" refers to a fictitious series of events, but it is also possible for a narrative film to tell a true story.

Story and Discourse. Within the majority of narrative structures, whether or not what is being related is a fiction, useful distinctions can be drawn among story, plot, and discourse. The **story** is the series of hypothetical events as they "happen" in the time of the fiction or of factual events in history. The **plot** is the order in which selected story-events are arranged; it is the site of narrative strategy. The story of *Citizen Kane* begins when Kane's mother decides that her son should be raised by a banker, but its plot begins with Kane's death.

The **discourse** is the narrative line, the vehicle and manner in which the story is told or presented to the audience; it is the site of style. The discourse of *Kane* begins with the opening titles and presents the story, structured as a plot, in a complex and intriguing style. In a movie the time of discourse is the time of projection: in the case of *Kane*, 119 consecutive minutes.

Although "narrative" is properly an adjective, some people use **narration** to refer to the act of telling and **narrative** to refer to what is told. Within fictions, the recounted story is sometimes known by the ancient Greek term **diegesis**; the laws and events of the recounted world are **diegetic**, and what comes from outside that world or pertains only to the discourse is **extra-diegetic**.

It is conventional to use the past tense when recounting any event that occurred in real or historical time, including the activities of filmmakers. Thus, "Hitchcock directed *Vertigo*." Within the time of the fiction, the convention is to use the present tense, with past and future tenses referenced to the narrative present.

Thus, "When Scottie meets Judy, he remembers how Madeleine looked."

Showing the Story. Whether or not a film sets out to tell a story, every film does set out to show something. In most cases the whole does not need to be shown, and in any case the fragmented nature of the filmed universe — chopped into shots — makes it appropriate to suggest a whole by presenting carefully selected parts of it. There may not be any inherently more significant parts in any whole, but the fact that the filmmaker has selected certain parts rather than others asserts their importance and defines both the story and the discourse.

Suppose that we want to make a film in which a man gets out of a car, walks into a building, goes up a staircase, unlocks a door, and goes into an apartment. To get from the car to the living room, he has to go through all these actions, but to show his doing this, we do not have to shoot every step. We could leave out his ascent of the stairway as well as the walk to the building, cutting from the closing car door to the opening apartment door. Or we could devote most of the screen time to his going up the staircase, perhaps to suggest that his eagerness or reluctance to reach his goal is the most important element in this phase of the story. In the earliest days of filmmaking it was considered essential to show complete actions, just as it was a rule to show the actors from head to foot. D. W. Griffith changed all that by demonstrating that fragments of actions and bodies could be built up into a whole, with each fragment's bearing its own particular significance and emphasis. The working assumption then became that whatever was included in a film was there for a reason; the irrelevant could be (and, presumably, had been) left out.

A narrative film tells a story by showing us parts of it. The choice of which parts to show clarifies the intentions and announces the emphases of that movie. A competent filmmaker selects these parts carefully and shows the audience how to interrelate them. A "part" might be an event, an image, a shot, a track, a portion of a shot such as an action or camera movement, a scene, etc.

Some stories are easier to show than others. Even if there is no kind of story that one could confidently say the movies cannot tell, it has proved true that the dramatic and pictorial strengths of the film medium have made it easier to figure out how to shoot a Western than how to shoot a philosophical tract. However exciting it may be to sit at a desk and stare out the window while writing a love letter, most filmmakers would prefer to dramatize how boy met girl than to show how it feels to write that letter or to get into the drama of the exact choice of phrasing. In virtually any narrative film something has to *happen*, and to happen in such a way that it can be watched with some degree of comprehension. Whether or not they are intellectually complex, the movies work primarily with action and emotion.

The ancients divided literature into such master categories as the epic, the lyric, and the drama. Most narrative films are dramas in that they are meant to be performed. **Dramatization** is the art of making something clear in performance, of constructing a presentation so that what is important about the subject can be shown or acted out.

If dramatization is the narrative film's stock-in-trade, the willing suspension of disbelief is its currency. What the **willing suspension of disbelief** means is that the audience voluntarily agrees to believe in the reality of a fiction — to forget, for example, that there have not been any Star Wars except those created through special effects and to hope that Han Solo will be able to save Luke Skywalker from Darth Vader. The audience of a nonfiction film sometimes has to think in the other direction, to notice that **Fig. 1-4**, for example, is *not* a frame from a science fiction movie but NASA footage of the actual surface of the moon, with the Earth rising in the background. And in avant-garde films one must sometimes undermine the concreteness of the referential system in the interest of noticing the pure interplay of the images.

Figure 1-4

Escapism. With the willing suspension of disbelief comes the problem of escapism. But to "escape" from the world is not always to be free of it, nor is it always an evasion or avoidance of confrontation.

The worlds of life and fiction are often very different from each other. Not everything in the real world has a beginning, a middle, and an end. Not everything works itself out in relation to a paradigm of poetic justice. Nor is every meaningful event a matter of conflict, although drama would have it so. When a narrative cliché is offered as the resolution of what the audience recognizes as a real-world problem, such an artificial gesture may feel like a cop-out. As Roger Ebert once put it, "Car chases may solve the problems of the director, but they have nothing to do with real life."

On the other hand, it can be very satisfying to enter a made-up world that is tightly organized. We do not know what will finally happen in our own lives. We can, however, become interested in fictional characters and find out what happens to them, to some degree allaying anxiety about the unknown ending of our own story. We can share in a life more exciting and colorful than our own, or one that is more depressing, or focused, or significant. A "good story" (which does not, of course, begin to exhaust the possibilities of fiction) has a pattern, a structure, a significant order; it creates expectations and lets them fall into place, as life often does not. "Once upon a time" takes us to a place of order and arrangement, of meaningful actions with meaningful and related consequences. The "escape" it offers is often not to a world of car chases and trivial pastimes, but to one in which vital matters are clarified.

Manuel Puig's novel *Kiss of the Spider Woman* is a wonderful exploration of the paradox of escapism. It concerns two cellmates in a Buenos Aires prison. Molina, a homosexual with no interest in politics, tells the stories and evokes the images of his favorite movies. Valentin, a political activist, listens to these tales with increasing fascination but insists to Molina that they are only fantasies with no relevance to the revolution, and he almost resents the way they allow him to forget about his problems for a while.

The fact that they are imprisoned makes this tale spinning appear a perfect model of escapism — the desire to avoid the reality of one's immediate situation. But as the novel progresses, we come under the spell of Molina's versions of Val Lewton and Jacques Tourneur's *Cat People* (1942), a Nazi romance, and others, and we begin to understand the importance of their beauty. We may even question whether they are politically useless. Movies are the web Molina spins to seduce Valentin, and he has to teach his literalist cellmate how to love them, how to share his passionate attachment to them and recognize their disarming profundity. In this romantic otherworld, where everything has meaning and is perfectly realized, the two characters surprisingly confront the terms of their imprisonment and find hope.

In the course of the action the two men switch roles, with Valentin participating in a homosexual encounter and Molina — released by the prison officials in the hope that he will lead them to Valentin's comrades — getting killed "like the heroine of a movie" in his first and only political gesture. And Puig gracefully allowed the novel to have a happy ending, in which the mechanics of oppression are suspended for a moment, long enough for Valentin to dream a vision of kindness and political integrity in the terms of one of Molina's movies.

Gather Round the Fire. In Peter Bogdanovich's first film, *Targets* (1968), Boris Karloff played an aging star of horror films, Byron Orlok. At one point Orlok tells the following story (slightly reworded from its source, W. Somerset Maugham's 1934 play *Sheppey*):

Once upon a time, many many years ago, a rich merchant in Baghdad sent his servant to the marketplace to buy provisions. And after awhile the servant came back, white-faced and trembling, and said, "Master, when I was in the marketplace, I was jostled by a woman in the crowd and I turned to look, and I saw that it was Death that had jostled me. And she looked at me and made a threatening gesture. Oh Master, please, lend me your horse that I may ride away from this city and escape my fate! I will ride to Samarra, and Death will not find me there." So the merchant loaned him the horse and the servant mounted it and dug his spurs into its flank, and as fast as the horse could gallop, he rode towards Samarra. Then the merchant went to the marketplace, and he saw Death standing in the crowd, and he said to her, "Why did you make a threatening gesture to my servant when you saw him this morning?" And Death said, "I made no threatening gesture; that was only a start of surprise. I was astonished to see him here in Baghdad, for I have an appointment with him tonight — in Samarra."

That is an efficiently told, perfectly constructed, "good" story. It begins by establishing a relatively stable situation — Baghdad, the marketplace, and the normal course of human activity — and two central characters, the merchant and his servant. Then something happens to jar events into motion: the servant meets the antagonist, Death, in the marketplace. (The rules of this story's world are revealed at this point and are honored from here on; they are that Death can appear as a woman in a marketplace and that one's fate is inescapable.) The servant arrives at a course of action and, in a brief but complete scene, convinces the merchant to help him realize it. Then the merchant himself confronts Death, and the situation is given a brilliant twist that puts everything in a different perspective, teaching a lesson about destiny and announcing a resolution — that the servant and Death will meet again in Samarra — that has exactly the right combination of the unanticipated and the inevitable.

Audiences gather around the light source of the movie or the television screen just as they once gathered around a fire to submit to the spell of a storyteller. And although film dramas are primarily intended to be watched, there are moments when the power of telling a story in words — the age-old power of narration itself — proves compelling in the cinema. When the old entertainer tells the Samarra story in *Targets*, Bogdanovich declined to cut, letting the tale unfold in one continuous shot. This is not to suggest that visual and verbal values are opposed in cinema (nor to imply that there is anything uncinematic about a long take), but to indicate how both are useful and how they may sometimes step out of each other's way.

Hollywood Formulas. The makers of narrative films often rely on classical precepts about what constitutes a "good story." These can be summarized as follows: There ought to be one or more major characters. They ought to be in some kind of conflict. That conflict ought to be acted out (dramatized). Some degree of tension ought to accumulate as the events proceed, until that tension peaks and is released at a climax. The climax should be followed by a resolution that wraps up the threads of the story. Both the characters and the meaning of the events ought to be clarified and advanced by this progression from exposition, complication, reversal (or twist), and climax to resolution.

To the extent that it can be codified, the Hollywood formula depends not only on the conservative dramatic principles outlined above, but also on **audience identification** and **rooting interest**. That is, the members of the audience are presented with characters with whom they can identify — usually played by stars — and conflicts in which they can be led to feel that they have a personal stake. The audience identifies with the hero, in the simplest of all formulas, and collectively roots for him or her. We are led to care about the characters and to hope that they will get what's coming to them.

In a film like Sidney Lumet's *The Verdict* (1982), for example, the central character is a seedy, unreliable, and alcoholic lawyer in the full momentum of professional decline — someone with whom one might not expect an audience to want to identify. But that lawyer is played by Paul Newman, who is physically attractive and a star, and this makes it easier for the audience to enjoy playing with the idea of being in his shoes for a couple of hours. This lawyer is defending the interests of a highly sympathetic client, and the opposition is presented as a huge and inhumane organization, practically in league with the Devil. That is where rooting interest comes in: we want the lawyer to discredit the bad guys, to win his client's case, and to clean up his own life. Having created those desires, the film goes on to satisfy them.

"Identification plus rooting interest" is not a new formula. It is at work in *The Odyssey*, *King Lear*, D. W. Griffith's *Intolerance* (1916), and Frank Capra's *Mr. Smith Goes to Washington* (1939). But there are many works — like Bertolt Brecht and Kurt Weill's *The Threepenny Opera*, or Jean-Luc Godard's *Weekend* (1967) — that set out to undermine that formula or turn it against itself, encouraging the audience to adopt a distanced, critical attitude rather than to behave like an emotionally manipulated mob.

One of the most time-tested ways for an artist to get across a point or to convey a value judgment is to identify a character that the audience likes with an idea that the artist likes, and to link a villain with a position that the audience is encouraged to reject. This strategic manipulation of identification and rooting interest is so effective that even a sophisticated audience is liable to find itself rooting for the Ku Klux Klan at the climax of Griffith's *The Birth of a Nation* (1915).

A newer formula, buried in jargon but very powerful today (perhaps because no one is quite sure what it means, but everyone feels answerable to it), is "high concept and a hook." To get past many studio heads in the 1980s, a story must be **high concept**. What this means is that its plot and appeal should be capable of being summarized in a short, clear sentence. This does not mean that the story should be organized around a concept or idea, nor that the idea ought to be elevated or high; it means that the film as a whole should be a marketable and easily identifiable product. It will achieve this status if its "concept" — something between a gimmick and an organizing principle — is both intriguing and easy to understand. "High" means something like "highly visible." This does not make for great movies.

One of the first properties recognized as high concept was Goldie Hawn and Howard Zieff's *Private Benjamin* (1980). Its concept was "Goldie Hawn plays a 'Jewish American Princess' who joins the Army." Such a sentence often serves as the basis for an ad campaign and may end its days as a descriptive blurb in a newspaper's TV listings. High concept is not just a demon of the marketing executives but a full-fledged story criterion as well as an indication of the importance of marketing considerations in the process of story approval. If the story can't be summarized that directly and with that much attractiveness and market visibility, the dominant assumption — valid or not — is that people won't go to see it.

A more genuine structural value is embedded in the mystique of the hook. A **hook** is what hooks or immediately captures the audience's interest in a story. But the term is also used as another word for "structure." In that sense the hook is the spine of the story, what the ribs latch onto, what everything hangs on. It is the central, intriguing idea that motivates the story and dictates its primary elements.

In Colin Higgins's *9 to 5* (1980), whose subject is office politics, the hook (or dramatic premise and approach) is that a group of secretaries become so angry at their boss that they kidnap him. For a screenwriter, to find the hook hiding in his or her material is to know how to tell that story, much as Michelangelo looked for the sculpture that was latent in a block of marble. For an agent, to identify the hook is to know how to sell that story.

There are times when a formula will work against originality or will occupy the place of invention. But there are many cases in which a formula can provide a structure on which the filmmaker can improvise creatively. What Gertrude Stein said about truly original work was that it strikes its first audiences as ugly or somehow disturbing. Once its time is past, it is recognized as a classic, and from then on, all that anyone says about it is how beautiful it is. It is not that a great artist is ahead of his or her time, she argued, but that the audience is behind *its* time. At present, however, the disturbingly stimulating represents too extreme a financial gamble. So the Hollywood ideal, at least in the 1980s, appears to be a product that will depart enough from its predecessors to be recognized as new (like a NEW version of the laundry soap you've been using for five years), but not so drastically original that no one will know what to make of it. This is one reason that so many original works today are genre films, because the generic formula keeps the audience and the executives oriented, while the filmmakers are free to slip in their variations, subversions, and innovations.

Genre. A **genre** is a particular variety of film that deals with a characteristic subject and that is often organized around a specific repertoire of conventions and recurring figures. When people ask what kind of film a film is, what they usually want to know is its genre.

Familiar genres include the Western, the musical, the stag film, the horror film, the science fiction film, the mystery, the gangster film, the satire, the romantic melodrama, the screwball comedy, the biography or "biopic," the problem picture, the martial arts film, and the adventure film. There are also subgenres, like the backstage musical or the adult Western, and genres that remain to be explored, like the letter.

Most genres are distinguished by their use of certain elements. The Western almost necessarily includes the American West in the latter half of the nineteenth century, horses, guns, fledgling towns, cattlemen, sweet young women and tough old women, good guys and bad guys. But a genre can also be characterized by an *attitude*, not just by a cluster of *elements*. Thus the Western typically involves a split attitude toward the call of the wide-open spaces and the importance of a warm hearth and a safe, honest town, and it organizes itself around the moral validity of heroic and often violent action. There are films not set in the American West that behave like Westerns — like *Paris, Texas* or Michael Winner's *Death Wish* (1974) — just as there are films set in the frontier that behave like horror films (Edward Dein's *Curse of the Undead* [1959]).

Although most genres involve the meshing of common subject matter and shared attitude, there are many films whose elements and attitudes appear to be moving in different directions. In such cases, what validates or informs the decision to place a film within a particular genre is the nature of the element or attitude that dominates the system. Fred Zinnemann's *Oklahoma!* (1955) is more a musical than it is a Western. Even though Howard Hawks and Christian Nyby's *The Thing From Another World* (1951) and Robert Wise's *The Day the Earth Stood Still* (1951) share the elements of flying saucers with intelligent alien pilots who challenge both military and scientific personnel, *The Thing* is a horror film, and *The Day* is a science fiction film.

In *The Thing*, the scientist who wants to communicate with the alien is presented as a fool, whereas the soldiers who decide to destroy it are presented as correct. In *The Day*, the scientists who respect the alien and listen to his messages are presented as the hope of the world, whereas the soldiers who attempt to kill him are presented as shortsighted and destructive. It is typical of the science fiction film to celebrate the scientific imagination, to be curious about the unknown, and to open its system — as the human community in *The Day* is opened to the possibility of joining the galactic community. It is typical of the horror film to surrender to curiosity and then reject it as dangerous, to show the follies of the scientist who would play God, and to reclose the system and heal the damage done by the eruption of the monstrous or the repressed — as the community in *The Thing*, having destroyed the monster, is urged to "keep watching the skies" in the event that any other monsters should make their appearance. The difference between these two films is one of attitude, though they share virtually all the same elements. This is a particularly useful example because both films were made in the same country during the same year, and because both were addressing the same contemporary problem, the Cold War — to which *The Thing* took an isolationist and militaristic attitude, whereas *The Day* argued that international cooperation and nuclear disarmament were absolutely necessary.

Genres create expectations as well as ritual formulas. There are thousands of Westerns that follow the formula exactly and offer their audiences the satisfaction of attending a ritual performance, like a ceremony in which everything is in place and shows up at the right time. It can be extremely pleasant for someone who is addicted to horror films to go through the familiar progression of the introduction of the threat, the killing of the "first victim," the emblem of "the monster and the girl," the solution of the problem (the Blob hates cold!), and the restoration of normality. Sometimes these expectations can be fulfilled in a bizarre manner, making little sense in the world of the story but making perfect sense as ritual elements of the genre. Thus in Gene Fowler's *I Was a Teenage Werewolf* (1957), which is set in America in the late 1950s, the sheriff's posse carries torches rather than flashlights.

Some of the best generic payoffs come when a formula is respected but is approached from a slightly unusual angle or is given a twist, like the wonderful use of the "first victim" figure in *Alien*, whose curiosity compels him to touch the vicious egg while the audience is screaming "Don't!" but knows that he will, and who survives only long enough to be victimized a *second* time — or like that moonlit moment at the end of Reginald LeBorg's *The Mummy's Ghost* (1944) when the monster *gets* the girl. Much of the delight in watching Mark Sandrich's *Top Hat* (1935) comes not just from enjoying Fred Astaire's dancing, but also from recognizing that it is time for a certain kind of "number" to begin and appreciating what Astaire does with that opportunity, how he varies and enriches the formula for his own purposes.

Narrative Structure. In a story the beginning, middle, and end succeed each other in chronological order; a plot need not answer to such restrictions, and beyond that a plot can be presented to the audience in a variety of discourses. A **linear structure** is one in which the beginning, middle, and end follow each other in chronological order not only in the story but also in the plot, as if along a straight line. Information, often in the form of scenes, is provided as needed or appropriate. However complex or simple the narration (the telling), the narrative (plotted story) proceeds from first event to last. A linear structure may be organized around a single string of events or narrative line, or it may interweave several narrative lines that share the same time frame.

In the simplest narrative structure, then — the one common to the majority of narrative films — a linear story is presented in a linear discourse. (Discourse includes plotting as well as such other properties of the telling as style and voice; strictly speaking, it is the film — the image and soundtrack.) At the beginning of the film a relatively stable situation is catalyzed into significant action; it unfolds and develops; and near the end of the film, it is resolved. The unfolding middle is usually the longest portion, and it evolves out of the conditions established at the start. In fact, what makes a certain cluster of events *the* beginning is that it does establish the conditions that will evolve into *that* particular confrontation or dramatic situation.

By the same logic, the dramatic situation ought to dictate the conditions of its own most appropriate resolution, and what makes an ending *the* ending is that it does resolve the problems of the central action. This is called a **closed ending**, one that wraps up loose ends or has a strong sense of conclusion, like the last scene of Howard Hawks's *Red River* (1948). An **open ending** prefers to leave matters up in the air or to adjourn while the story can readily be imagined as continuing, like the last scene of *City Lights*. As different as they may be, both endings conclude the film at what feels like the "right" moment.

Acts. Many dramatic film structures are divided into acts. An **act** is a major structural unit, usually consisting of more than one scene, that moves the plot forward while accomplishing a relatively self-contained dramatic action. Acts are a standard screenwriter's convention; a three-act structure is the norm today. We can see how acts work in a linear structure by taking a brief look at Francis Ford Coppola and Mario Puzo's *The Godfather* (1972).

The Godfather has five acts, each of which corresponds to a major plot development. The overall story concerns the transfer of power from Vito Corleone (Marlon Brando) to his son Michael (Al Pacino). The five acts may be identified as follows: (1) King Vito, (2) Sollozzo, (3) Prince Sonny, (4) Prince Michael, and (5) King Michael.

The first act shows Vito in power. The values by which he lives and runs his business are clarified by the ways he handles various requests on his daughter Connie's wedding day, and the wedding itself is a ritual that implies family continuity and valorizes tradition. What hides in this situation, the seed of imbalance and dissolution, is Carlo, the new son-in-law, who lacks judgment and integrity.

In the second act Vito's power is challenged by Sollozzo, who wants Vito to bankroll a narcotics operation. Vito refuses, and Sollozzo has him shot. From there on, the principal conflict is between the Corleones, with their Old World sense of family and business values, and the *relatively* unscrupulous forces of the "new" Mafia: Sollozzo, Barzini, and the rest. Because it is a historical fact that the new Mafia won this battle, the Corleones become the "underdogs" at this point and hook the audience's rooting interest. At the same time, we root for them as a family.

The third act shows how Sonny, the eldest son and heir apparent, takes over while Vito is in the hospital. Sonny uses power badly, showing a murderous lack of self-restraint and political judgment. The third act includes Michael's killing of Sollozzo and the policeman, Barzini's covert manipulations of Connie's marriage, Michael's Sicilian marriage and the murder of his bride, and the death of Sonny, all of which are related to the ways in which Sonny uses power and the family's attempts to cope with Vito's absence. Sonny's death is the plot's *turning point*, upsetting the succession and making it necessary for Michael to play a more active role.

In the fourth act Michael takes control of the family business but continues to take direction from his father. Michael's power is equivocal here, partly because he is not entirely independent (though this makes him a better don than Sonny was) and partly because his character is in transition, but mostly because the Barzini threat is still present. This act ends with Vito's death by natural causes shortly after he has given Michael a last crucial piece of advice (how to identify the man who will try to assassinate him).

In the fifth act Michael comes fully into his power, killing off all his enemies. Because he has got rid of Barzini and the other heads of "the Five Families," Michael has removed the immediate threat first introduced by their agent, Sollozzo; that implies a new stability, which is formalized in the final line of dialogue when Clemenza kisses Michael's ring and calls him "don Corleone." But because Michael has also taken vengeance within the family (by killing Connie's husband), because he has violated the essence of a fundamental ritual (by playing the hypocrite at the baptism of Connie's baby), and because we have just seen him lie to his wife at a crucial moment, the foundations of Michael's new regime are perceived as corrupt. Thus the ending has an unsettling edge, however neat its sense of closure. There is a new Godfather, but he does not know best.

Narrative Complexity. Not every interesting line is a straight one. In more complex situations, a linear story may be told out of chronological order *(Citizen Kane)*, or a story that defies chronology entirely may be told in whatever order will do the job *(Last Year at Marienbad)*.

The Greek epics typically begin *in medias res* — in the middle of the action — and then double back to present the beginning. Martin Scorsese's *Raging Bull* (1980) begins in 1964 as the hero, Jake La Motta (Robert De Niro), rehearses for a one-man show, and it ends when he leaves the dressing room to go onstage. Within this bracketing **frame** or framing story (the dressing-room scene, which establishes a narrative reference point), the story of La Motta's career is presented in a series of flashbacks. We see what happened to him between 1941 and 1957 and come to understand how this trim contender became an overweight loser. In *Betrayal* (1983), directed by David Jones from a play and screenplay by Harold Pinter, the order of the discourse begins with the end of the story and advances, in a complex forward-and-backward progression, to the beginning of the story.

The Godfather has a linear structure, but Coppola's *The Godfather, Part II* (1974) tells the stories of Vito's rise and Michael's fall in parallel, alternating from one to the other in 40-year leaps and letting each story comment on the other. When these two films were edited into a linear discourse for presentation on network TV, beginning with Vito's story, moving through *The Godfather* itself, and ending with the rest of Michael's story, the story was easy to follow, but the discourse was much less interesting than it had been originally. It is not just that the stories of Michael and Vito collide ironically in *Godfather II* to generate a statement that neither story can make on its own, but also that the linear structure of the first film collides with the intricate structure of the second film. Together they show that there is more than one way to tell a story, just as the careers of Vito and Michael, taken together, imply that there is more than one way to run a family business.

A linear structure is organized around one major plot and may involve various subplots, like the subplot of Michael's Sicilian marriage. In more complex structures there may be several major plot lines, and each may have its own pace and logic, its own time frame, and its own degree of verisimilitude. The classic example of multiple plot lines is *Intolerance*, which presents four stories from different historical epochs and intercuts them to demonstrate that they share a common lesson. Rather than present one complete story after another, Griffith cut back and forth among all four, joining them into one narrative drive. In Akira Kurosawa's *Rashomon* (1950), several different versions of a crime are related by those who participated in it and by a woodcutter who saw what "really" happened. Each of the renditions is different because each narrator saw things from his or her own perspective and is trying to justify his or her own actions. The truth that emerges from a comparison of the stories is that none of the narrators behaved as well as possible. The four stories in *Intolerance* are all presented as true, and the audience's job is to find the lesson or theme that emerges from their juxtaposition. The stories in *Rashomon*, on the other hand, undermine each other's apparent veracity; the complexity of Kurosawa's structure complements and advances the complexity of his insights into human behavior.

Another way to achieve complexity is to play against the audience's structural expectations. Nicolas Roeg's *Walkabout* (1971) has two endings, one in which the heroine grows into an impossibly exact image of her urbanized mother and one (framed as a memory) in which she still enjoys the romantic innocence of nature. Rather than end the story, the two scenes—which present the dialectic of her walkabout, between the overcivilized and the wild—conclude the argument. Although the audience may at first believe that the urban scene happens, it comes to realize that both scenes are extrapolations launched from an open ending.

Paradoxical Structures. The **narrative present** is the time in which the primary action is taking place. In *Citizen Kane* the narrative present is that in which the reporter attempts to find out the meaning of "Rosebud"; the story of Kane's life belongs to the **narrative past**. The narrative present in *Raging Bull* is 1964, the time of the frame. But in *Last Year at Marienbad* there is no last year, no Marienbad, and not even a fictitious year and place in which the movie's actions can be thought of as "taking place." There is only the present in which the film is projected, and all of its "realities" are equally suspect.

Marienbad points, then, to another order of complexity. It is not just intricate, not just multiple, but authentically paradoxical. A paradox is an impossible fact, a contradiction that makes sense or feels true. The task of a paradoxical structure is to enmesh us in a pattern that may appear absurd but that eventually becomes compelling as we learn its rules. One of the only ways to talk sensibly about this kind of film is to talk about its narrative structure.

A good example of a paradoxical narrative is *Dead of Night*, which was directed by Alberto Cavalcanti, Charles Crichton, Basil Dearden, and Robert Hamer, and released in England in 1945.

The frame story concerns a man named Walter Craig (Mervyn Johns) who has been troubled by a recurring dream that changes abruptly into a murderous nightmare and that he can never entirely remember upon waking. As the film starts, Craig arrives at a cottage in the English countryside where he has never been before. He meets six people, all of whom he recognizes from his dream. Five of them, prompted by Craig's growing concern that he is now living out his nightmare and that the recurring dream has offered a warning to which he had better pay attention, tell stories about their own encounters with the supernatural, with madness, and with prophetic warnings. Eventually the catastrophe occurs: Craig strangles one of the storytellers, a psychiatrist who has refused to believe in the power of the supernatural. Then the characters from the inner stories pursue Craig, and one of them kills him. Then he wakes up, shakes off the dream, and is invited to spend the weekend at a cottage in the countryside . . . The film ends with exactly the same shots that began it, in exactly the same order.

There are two ways of reading that ending — as first-person or third-person — and both of them make sense. It is clear that the whole film, up to the point of Craig's waking and receiving the invitation, has been a dream — in fact, *the* recurring dream — and that Craig is the dreamer. That interpretation makes him, however unconsciously, the primary narrator or presenter of the film, within which five of his country companions act as secondary narrators of their own supernatural stories. What is not clear is whether the ending is still part of his narration, that is, whether it is the dream's starting up again, or whether this is the actual visit against which the dream has been warning him, narrated in an objective voice. Because the dream is presented as an absolutely accurate foreknowledge, its fulfillment would look the same as the dream does.

If the ending rebegins the dream, *Dead of Night* is a loop, an infinite structure. If the ending is supposed to be "real," the implication is that Craig will behave just as he did in the dream. Either way, he is trapped by a warning that he cannot entirely remember and from which he cannot escape. The paradox is that neither Craig nor the audience can tell whether the ending is a dream or a reality, because it would have to look exactly the same in either case. It *can* be either and is somehow both. And beyond that is the implication that the line between dream and "reality" cannot easily be drawn, in this movie or anywhere else — but *especially* in a narrative film, which looks factual but is also an illusion. When one of the characters says that she is a figment of Craig's imagination, she is right — but what she does not know is that she is also part of the "dream" called *Dead of Night*.

Voice. One way to complicate a structure, or to find a discourse that can communicate the complexity of experience, is to work with more than one narrative voice.

In the majority of narrative films the discourse is presented "directly" by the **cinematic apparatus** — which it is sometimes convenient to call "the camera," but which might just as well be the filmmaking enterprise or the screen — as if by an invisible, single, and objective narrator. Sometimes that narrator or presentational apparatus transfers authority to another voice and steps aside so that we can see things the way a character within the story sees them or can listen to another storyteller. There are numerous ways to keep the audience abreast of these shifts in narrative voice — so that we know an objective from a subjective image, if we are supposed to be able to — and it can be useful to think of many of those ways as codes.

In a sentence it is always easy to indicate who is speaking, that is, who is the source of the utterance. The first-, second-, and third-person pronouns are highly efficient signs. But in film, which has no pronouns, it is necessary to encode an image so that it may be decoded by the audience (or may not, if the paradox is good enough, as in *Dead of Night*). In Victor Fleming's *The Wizard of Oz* (1939), for example, the Kansas scenes are objective — are presented as really happening in just this manner — whereas the dream of Oz is subjective, a private vision that appears to Dorothy after she has been knocked out during a Kansas tornado. To make this clear to the audience, the waking material is in black-and-white, most of the dream material is in color, and the transitions between these sequences are marked by whirling optical effects. At the end of *Walkabout* we realize that both endings are hypothetical because each contains highly improbable material. The wilderness ending includes a living character who has died a few scenes ago, and the urban ending shows the heroine in her mother's clothes and kitchen, now married to a man who behaves like an idealized fantasy of her father. So it is possible to encode an image as hypothetical or subjective by bracketing it within special transition effects and/or by shooting it in an unusual but consistent manner, as in *The Wizard of Oz,* or by including "unreliable" subject matter, as in *Walkabout*.

Dorothy is not aware of sharing her dream with an audience; we eavesdrop on her unconscious. Yet she is the one who presents the dream of Oz, rather as does Walter Craig. Her narration is **unauthorized**. An **authorized** narration is one whose presenter is aware of the act of telling, like the stories told by the characters in the country house in *Dead of Night*, or Alex's deliberate presentation of *A Clockwork Orange*. All of these can be thought of as first-person narrations, "delivered" by characters in their own words and/or images, showing how they "see" things, in contrast to the third-person voice of the cinematic apparatus, which presents what happened to him, her, it, or them in an apparently objective manner.

First-Person Voices. There are several common ways to encode cinematic discourse as first-person: voice-over narration, subjective sound, subjective camera, and mindscreen.

In **voice-over narration** the narrator, who may or may not be a character within the fiction, speaks directly to the audience but is not shown while speaking. We hear his or her voice **over** the continuing soundtrack. Voice-over — abbreviated **V-O** — is free to encode itself with the pronouns of spoken language, and so it is easier to use and much less problematic than voices that must be encoded visually. When voice-over is used by a character, as in *Apocalypse Now* or *A Clockwork Orange,* we can be certain that a first-person narrator is deliberately telling the story as he or she sees it. (Voice-over is also a common convention for interior monologue, where authorized narration and direct address are rare.) When it is used by someone outside the fiction, as when Orson Welles identifies himself voice-over during the final credits of *The Magnificent Ambersons,* it often sounds like the voice of authority, an objective presenter who is very much in charge of the system and is willing to guide us through it.

Subjective sound directly presents what a character hears or imagines hearing. In Hitchcock's *Strangers on a Train* (1951) the villain meets a woman who reminds him of a woman he killed in an amusement park while the merry-go-round was playing "The Band Played On." As he looks at this second woman, he "hears" that song again, and so do we. Although it is clear that no carousel is in the vicinity — so that we can tell right away that its music is heard only by the villain — the music is distorted and given a slight echo, and here these function as codes of subjectivity.

In **subjective camera** the camera adopts the position of the character's physical eye, so that the audience sees more-or-less what the character sees. Another name for subjective camera, and the one used in the film industry, is the **POV shot**; "POV" stands for "point of view," and it is a specific camera instruction. The most common way to encode an image as POV is to have some character look directly at the camera as if meeting its gaze, and to indicate in that or another shot that the character is looking at the narrator (the character whose view is, usually without authorization, being adopted by the camera and shared by the audience). Another way is to begin with a shot of the looker, then cut to a shot of what he or she is looking at (the POV shot itself), and then return to a shot of the looker. This sequence might be called a "POV sandwich." (Some critics call it "suture editing.") Although the subjective camera is normally used only for brief intrusions, some entire films have been shot in this voice, notably Robert Montgomery's *Lady in the Lake* (1946). In Sean Cunningham's *Friday the 13th* (1980) the subjective camera often stood in for — and thus masked the identity of — the killer.

In Hitchcock's *The 39 Steps* (1935) we share the visual experience of the hero (Robert Donat) while he scans a newspaper (for a report on the spies-and-murder conflict in which he has become involved) and peeks above the paper at a man who is studying him with unnerving curiosity. Part of this scene is shown in **Figs. 1-5** through **1-11.** In the first shot (**Figs. 1-5** through **1-7**) the hero borrows the newspaper from a man sitting across from him in a railway compartment and begins to read the story; it is a POV

Figure 1-5

Figure 1-6

Figure 1-7

Figure 1-8

Figure 1-9

Figure 1-10

Figure 1-11

shot. Shot 2 (**Fig. 1-8**) is an objective view of the hero as he begins to look at the curious passenger. This is followed by another POV shot (**Figs. 1-9** and **1-10**). The shift in focus from **Fig. 1-7** to **Fig. 1-9** indicates that the hero is looking at the other passenger rather than reading the newspaper. In **Fig. 1-10**, the view after the paper has been lowered, we can see the meeting of the camera's gaze that is one way of encoding POV, and in **Figs. 1-8** and **1-9**, the start of a "POV sandwich." **Fig. 1-11** is an objective shot of the compartment. If the whole scene had been shot from the camera position of **Fig. 1-11**, the emotional content of the peeking would have been less clear or immediate, and so this change of voice, this momentary personalization, is dramatically effective.

A **mindscreen** presents the landscape of the mind's eye, much as subjective camera presents what is seen by the physical eye. This term is not in wide use. I coined it myself because the term "dream sequence" seemed inadequate. There are many instances in which the contents of a character's mind are displayed on the movie screen (or in which the movie screen behaves *like* a mind), and not all of them are intended to approximate dreams. The mind may wander, or dwell on a memory, or be in the grip of a hallucination, or think through a problem. And beyond that, a character may envision a story while in the act of relating or hearing it. Dorothy's dream of Oz is an unauthorized mindscreen, and the mad narrator's tale in *The Cabinet of Dr. Caligari* is an authorized mindscreen. A mindscreen can show what a character *thinks* — the cinematic equivalent of "stream of consciousness."

There is a scene in Gance's *Napoleon* where Napoleon is asked what tactics he would employ if *he* were to break the siege of Toulon. Gance cut to a closeup of Napoleon's upper face (**Fig. 1-12**) and then to a torrent of overlapping images — hundreds of them in less than a minute — some of which are shown in **Figs. 1-13** through **1-16**. These images of maps, models, flashing lights, soldiers, equations, and explosions are visualizations of Napoleon's battle plans. They are what he "sees" in his mind's eye, and they also bear the stamp of his enthusiasm. **Fig. 1-12** is the exact equivalent of the start of a "POV sandwich," but not all mindscreens — nor all POV shots — require such clear encoding.

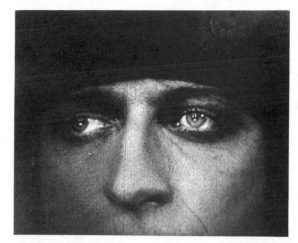

Figure 1-12

Figure 1-13

Figure 1-14

Figure 1-15

Figure 1-16

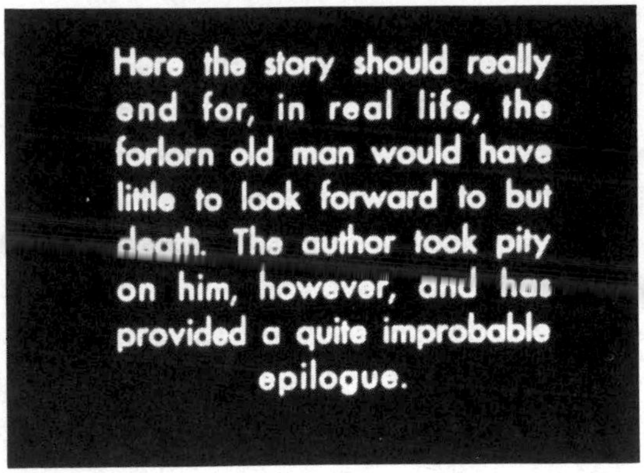

Here the story should really end for, in real life, the forlorn old man would have little to look forward to but death. The author took pity on him, however, and has provided a quite improbable epilogue.

Figure 1-17

Reflexive Voices. Another voice that can come into play is that of the actual filmmaker. At several points in *2 or 3 Things I Know About Her* (1966), Godard whispers on the soundtrack, telling us what he was trying to do in a given sequence, re-editing it to see whether it works out better, and asking himself what "all these signs" are supposed to signify. It bothers him that the real does not stand out clearly from the imaginary, and he presents himself not as the absolute controller of the system but as *one* of the voices involved in and partially directing that system.

There is a particularly effective **authorial intrusion** near the end of F. W. Murnau's *The Last Laugh* (1924), a silent film about a doorman (Emil Jannings) who is demoted to lavatory attendant. This demotion makes him so depressed that he loses all interest in life, and his family and neighbors reject him because he no longer wears the doorman's splendid uniform — their connection to the realm of power in this class-conscious society. When the doorman is at his lowest point, and his only friend is the hotel's night watchman, the author (in this case a persona adopted by Carl Mayer, who wrote the script) intrudes via the movie's only **title card**, which is shown in **Fig. 1-17**. After this **intertitle** the look of the film (which was shot by Karl Freund) changes from the shadowy and depressing to the brilliantly lit. We see how the old man enjoys a huge, sudden, and extremely unlikely legacy, treating the night watchman to a generous lunch in the hotel and then leaving forever the site of his former humiliation.

This intrusion is an example of what Bertolt Brecht called an **alienation effect**, a gesture or strategy that encourages the audience to *suspend* its willing suspension of disbelief, to back out of believing the story and take a critical look at it. In the case of *The Last Laugh*, the audience is told directly that the author is aware of the artificiality of the narrative system, that he is making all this up and can steer it in any direction at his whim. That intrusion makes it almost impossible to continue to believe in the story. The audience realizes that the happy ending is an improbable artifice and has to ask itself how it feels about all this sweetness and light (in fact, dessert and bright lighting). The ending is evaluated rather than swallowed whole. But as the story picks up, there is a strong impulse *to* believe in the ending, and we are left rather like Buster at the end of *Sherlock Jr.*, trying to come to terms with a world of compelling illusion that is somehow both true and false.

Finally, it is possible for a film itself to have a voice. As if leaving the author or filmmaker out of the picture, a movie can appear to be aware of itself *as* a movie and to authorize its own narration. This happens throughout Bergman's *Persona*, which is a film in search of its own laws, the relations between pure light and the imagery that is its mask ("persona"), which is comparable to the relations between Being and personality. The film appears to generate its own discourse without any help from Ingmar Bergman. When the story of *Persona* reaches a point of apparently irreconcilable conflict, the discourse breaks down. The film rips, the projector goes on a kind of holiday, and the image must reconstruct itself from scratch in order for the discourse to continue. In this sense *Persona* presents the mindscreen of its own self-conscious awareness: it has a systemic voice.

This is a rigorous and unusual example of a **reflexive**, or self-mirroring, self-referential, and self-regarding structure. Reflexive films, which often employ alienation effects, call the audience's attention to the fact that it is watching a movie. One way to alert the audience that this sort of narration is going on is to have a character realize that he or she is part of an artificial or narrated situation, as in *Dead of Night*. Another is to fill the film image with images of film, like the projector breakdown in *Persona* or the murderous camera in Michael Powell's *Peeping Tom* (1960). A definitive example of cinematic reflexivity can be found in Dziga Vertov's *The Man with a Movie Camera* (1929). A sequence of city traffic is interrupted in the middle of a shot, and the editor is then shown at her bench. She unrolls several shots — and we see them played — then selects one and cuts it into the sequence, which then resumes. At that point it becomes impossible for the audience to forget that it is watching an edited reality.

Creating Under Pressure. In the best movies, it is hard to imagine that the story could have been told differently. If *Citizen Kane* had begun with the story of Kane's childhood, had killed him off in the middle, and had then followed the reporter on his "Rosebud" quest, it not only would have been dull but also would have sacrificed a whole matrix of interconnections, the emerging logic of Kane's life as it is rendered through the partial perspectives of the various narrators and through the momentum of the reporter's (and the camera's) investigation.

It is just as hard to realize that a great story might itself have been different, since the logic of its narrative development appears so solid and satisfying. But filmmaking does not simply take place in the imagination. The filmmaker must grapple with the real world at virtually every stage, and some of those real-world constraints will affect even the story.

Let us consider briefly some of the pressures and creative solutions that went into the making of Abel Gance's *La Roue (The Wheel)*, shot between 1919 and 1921 and released in 1922. Gance's original intention was to make an epic melodrama about a railroad engineer (Sisif, as in Sisyphus) who saves a baby girl (Norma) from a train wreck and raises her as his own daughter. Sisif's own son (Elie) falls in love with Norma but believes her to be his sister. Sisif, unfortunately, is also in love with Norma. About two hours into what was originally a nine-hour movie, Sisif's boss (Hersan) marries Norma and takes her away from the railroad yard where she has been living, and they enter an empty life of luxury.

The first half of the film was shot in the south of France in a real railroad yard, partly because Gance wanted the mise-en-scène to be as authentic as possible. The immediate consideration, however, was that the woman with whom Gance was in love, Ida Denis, had developed tuberculosis, and her doctor advised that she needed the Mediterranean air. For that reason Gance decided to work in the railroad yards of Nice.

Even in Nice, however, Ida's health declined, and the doctor prescribed another change of air — this time to the mountains. Gance accordingly revised his script. Sisif is partially blinded by steam in an accident, then destroys his own train in a failed suicide attempt. In consideration of his years of good service, Sisif's employers send him to Mont Blanc, where his limited vision will still allow him to conduct a funicular train up and down the slopes. The shooting then continued in the mountains, and Gance devised a clever way to bring Norma and her husband to a nearby resort, further developing and finally resolving the tragic story.

At this point the "black" of the railyards and the "white" of the snowy mountains suggested itself to Gance as a structuring visual principle, and he made his film "a symphony in black and white." If he had already been interested in trains as "a world made for the cinema, a world of machines, rails, and signals," he now found a way to put those signs and engines in an even more purely cinematic context, the black-and-white of filmstock. The result is a brilliant movie that uses, and is about, the full resources of light and dark, framing and composition, entrapment and open space, signs and communication, blindness and insight, and desire and forgiveness. On the day that shooting was completed, Ida died, and the devastated Gance left for America, where he met D. W. Griffith and they compared notes. When Gance returned to France, he edited *La Roue*, and that six-month hiatus had given him time to rethink what he had shot and to devise a final structure that is so tight and powerful that one would never suspect, looking at the finished film, that it had not been conceived from the start in just the way it eventually turned out.

Advice from the Masters. Two of the finer storytellers in the history of American cinema were Howard Hawks and Sam Fuller. Both of them understood the necessity for action, for good scenes, for solidly drawn characters, and for careful structuring of the narrative line. The way Fuller put it, "Youth, romance, a little error, a big error, and then violence — *that's* a picture."

For Hawks, a good picture was one that was entertaining and had "four or five good scenes." A good director was one who "didn't annoy you" and had a recognizable personal style. Hawks chose material that interested *him*, and within the disciplining framework of a narrative structure, he felt free "to jump to whatever I think is interesting." He considered himself lucky that audiences shared his personal tastes, and he felt free to indulge his own intuitions: "If I think a thing's funny, then people laugh at it. If I think a thing's dramatic, the audience does. I'm very lucky that way. I don't stop to analyze it. We just made scenes that were fun to do."

Hawks may have been lucky, but he was also a master at putting across the objects of his enthusiasm, at telling a story so that others could see what he saw in it. "A director's a storyteller," he said, "and if he tells a story that people can't understand, then he shouldn't be a director. I don't care what they do as long as they can tell it well. We haven't run out of stories."

The Nonfiction Film

On the way to the moon, the Apollo 17 spacecraft took a photograph of the Earth. That photo is reproduced in this book as **Fig. C-1** in the color-plate insert. In looking at this picture, a significant part of our response comes from recognizing its factuality. We realize that this *is* how the planet looked during the instant this photo was exposed. Knowing that the view is authentic, we can look at Africa, the South Pole, and the cloud cover and feel that we are seeing how they really looked from outer space. That is the authority of the objective, nonfiction image.

Over 10 years later, NASA released **Fig. C-2**. The photo of the Earth is the one taken by Apollo 17, but the star background was added by an artist. In this picture, the actual and the artificial are made to work together, and although the result is spectacular, it does not have the absolute authority of **Fig. C-1**.

Nonfiction films are primarily concerned with recording real events: audible and visible facts. People appear as themselves, not as made-up characters. In the most programmatically objective films, there is an implicit contract with the audience that what is shown will not have been faked for the camera, that there will be no star background added by an artist. But not every nonfiction film is objective, and many nonfiction filmmakers set out to work *with* the materials of reality and to create a compelling work; they might enjoy the way **Fig. C-2** included the real Earth and then did something with it.

The difference between these two pictures is the difference between the authentic record of the Nazi concentration camps shot by Allied troops in 1944 and Alain Resnais's *Night and Fog* (1955), a documentary that includes both archival black-and-white footage of the camps in operation and color views of Auschwitz as it looked in the mid-1950s. Resnais intercut these two sets of factual material, and the result is a profound movie about the nature and importance of memory — not only our own urgent need to remember and confront this social atrocity, but also the question of how much of their own past the camps carry with them, the extent to which *they* manifest and efface their own history. Both sets of footage have authority, but their juxtaposition is transformative and accomplishes an artistic, political statement.

There are many types of nonfiction film, ranging from the home movie to the newsreel, but three of the most interesting are the documentary, the actualité, and cinéma vérité. As we briefly examine these subcategories, keep in mind how pervasive the image of reality is in virtually any photograph, how the real Earth keeps popping up against even the most painted of star fields.

Documentary. A **documentary** is a movie that has a particular point to make or perspective to advance concerning the factual material that is being presented. Like any nonfiction film, the documentary *documents* an occurrence. Its signs have factual referents and are not fantasy structures, so that a shot can be taken as evidence, or documentation, that a certain event did take place. But the true documentary typically does more than present objective records of factual material; it uses that material to document an argument or to meditate on the real, as if thinking along with the world — just as Resnais used the concentration camp footage in *Night and Fog.*

Although it is sometimes said that "the camera cannot lie," it is clear that the way a filmmaker decides just what the camera will be allowed to record can bias the presentation considerably. In *Triumph of the Will* (1935) Leni Riefenstahl used many low-angle shots of Hitler, pointing her camera up at him to make him seem a powerful and imposing presence, and intercut closeups of his face with long shots of excited crowds to suggest that Hitler was a galvanizing speaker who could excite, control, and lead his people. A British news company might have represented the same event (a Nazi Party convention) in a very different manner, giving the impression that Hitler was dangerous and erratic, a lunatic conqueror at the head of a pliable and frightening mob. Even a documentary on the making of steel may turn out to be centrally concerned with arguing the importance of a well-run factory, the prominence of the steel industry, and the superiority of the free-enterprise system.

In *Nanook of the North* (1922), the movie that established the terms of the modern documentary, Robert Flaherty did not simply record and present the basic elements of Eskimo life but selected and arranged those materials in the light of his own perspective. Some of the scenes were rehearsed, and many were staged for the camera. *Nanook* presents a personalized vision of the relations between man and nature, of life as a quest for food and shelter, of the universality of human values, of the art of craftsmanship, and of the institution of fatherhood. The scenes in which Nanook fashions an ice window for the evening's igloo are representative, as they organize factual materials into a subtle argument in favor of the values that Nanook appears to incarnate in those moments. He is a resourceful craftsman who makes a home out of the materials of nature, a responsible father, the leader and protector of his family, and a tireless worker with a sense of humor. As an ethnographic study *Nanook* is too subjective (if not patriarchal) to be reliable, but as a documentary it is coherent and complete.

Because it allows so much room for personal expression and social commentary, the documentary can be a much less objective form than is commonly supposed. Connie Fields's *The Life and Times of Rosie the Riveter* (1980) uses interviews, newsreel footage, graphics, and government propaganda films to clear up the historical record and to advance an argument about the role of women in the American work force during and shortly after World War II. Even the investigative documentary, whose job is to establish the truth, is charged by the filmmaker's conviction that his or her conclusions *are* true, and some of these, like Marcel Ophuls's *The Sorrow and the Pity* (1969) or John Lowenthal's *The Trials of Alger Hiss* (1980), have remained personal while markedly affecting our sense of what really happened during a controversial historical period.

Carlos Saura's *Blood Wedding* (1981), though not strictly a documentary, does purport to be a record of a rehearsal of a dance based on Lorca's *Blood Wedding*. But as the rehearsal proceeds, the willing suspension of disbelief takes over, and both the dancers and the film's audience surrender to Lorca's story. By the end, much more than a rehearsal appears to have taken place — and more than a story as well. *Blood Wedding* is very much like **Fig. C-2**.

Actualité. There are also films that present factual material without interpreting it. The French called them *actualités:* unbiased recordings of real objects and events. The very first projected film, *Workers Leaving the Lumière Factory* (1895), is a good example: one shot in length, it simply shows workers leaving the factory at the end of a working day. The majority of home movies and medical films are actualités, and factual objectivity is one of the ideals of the news film. As an alternative to the French term, the actualité might be called the **factual film**.

Cinéma Vérité. This nonfiction genre goes by many names: in America, **direct cinema**; in England, **free cinema**; in Russia, **kinópravda** ("film truth"); in France (and America), **cinéma vérité** ("film truth"). Filmmaker Richard Leacock calls it "CV." It is an amalgam of documentary and the actualité that acknowledges the interaction between filmmaker and subject as a way of attaining comprehensive realism.

As James Agee discovered while writing the book-length essay *Let Us Now Praise Famous Men*, it is impossible simply to drop in on people, capture the essence of their way of life, and record it in an objective manner. Agee was a Harvard-educated Romantic, sent — with photographer Walker Evans — to investigate and describe the lives of three sharecropping families in Alabama during the Depression. His employer was *Fortune*, the magazine of big business. Unless he could bring Harvard and *Fortune* and his personal reactions into play, Agee would have been paralyzed by the incongruity of his situation. And following the implications of physicist Werner Heisenberg's "uncertainty principle," which holds that one cannot observe any system without exchanging energy with it, *any* reporter aspiring to complete objectivity would be in Agee's position, that is, forced to include and acknowledge his own subjectivity and his impact on the subjects with whom he necessarily interacts. Because Agee and Evans were living in the sharecroppers' homes while preparing their lengthy article — which *Fortune* declined to publish — their awareness of interaction was especially acute.

Cinéma vérité builds on this awareness by acknowledging the presence of the camera and the filmmaking crew. It brings into the foreground what a film like *Nanook* seeks to hide. For Alan King's *A Married Couple* (1969), a film crew spent ten weeks with Billy and Antoinette Edwards, recording their intimate lives in the privacy of their home. Of course, daily life does not proceed in a normal fashion when a film crew is present and every facial tic is exposed to a lens, if not to posterity. The situation to be recorded includes the crew. Once that presence is acknowledged, it is possible for the subjects and the audience to come to *forget* about the camera, and CV lives for those moments when an unstaged and unself-conscious gesture or speech can open up the essence of a real person or situation. This roundabout manner of capturing reality often has more integrity — and can lead to a greater sense of realism — than the actualité's shortcut of pretending that the camera is not present. It is one of the most reflexive genres in all of cinema.

In cinéma vérité the key figure is not the director, and certainly not the writer (most such films have no scripts), but the cameraman — the link between subject and film. Next in line comes the person who records the sound — and, in fact, the two of them might constitute the entire crew. Voice-over narration and dubbing (dialogue replacement) are ruled out: it is essential that the soundtrack be authentic, live, and recorded on the spot.

Contemporary cinéma vérité would be almost unthinkable without the **zoom lens,** which has a variable focal length and thus can take in a wide, normal, or narrow field of view, depending on how it is adjusted. The zoom lens allows the cameraman to turn his or her attention from a group to a face to a hand gesture to another face without distracting the people who are being photographed; there is no need to stop the camera and move it or to change a lens. This makes it all the more likely that if enough film is exposed, the fleeting word or expression or action that reveals the essence of the subject will be caught on film.

The sounds are recorded live, as the images are being shot, and one can often hear the whirr of the camera's motor in the background. Camera noise, lens flare, and especially the constant shifting of the frame as the zoom lens probes the environment for significant actions and moves in and out of focus — all these are not technical flaws but acknowledgments of the immediacy of the situation and the presence of the camera.

The Look of the Real. Like everything else in the dynamic and living world of movies, these categories can overlap, and their techniques can be put to each other's purposes. Peter Watkins's *The War Game* (1965), for example, is emphatically a documentary, even though the "events" it records — glimpses of a nuclear attack on Britain — are hypothetical. It uses many of the methods

Figure 1-18

of cinéma vérité as well as of TV journalism. By using a hand-held camera, a zoom lens, and grainy black-and-white filmstock, and by covering each scene with a single camera, Watkins created the impression that these staged events were unstaged. They appear to have been captured by newsmen who both recorded them on the fly and interacted with some of the participants — as when a police officer refuses to let the crew record an execution, or when a rioter makes an obscene gesture at the camera (**Fig. 1-18**).

Watkins clearly held an opinion about his subject, and he made this opinion obvious by having the voice-over narrator dwell on the failures of the civil defense system or the actual characteristics of a firestorm, or by cutting from a rapid and horrific scene in which a family scrambles for shelter in their living room to an authentic quotation from a churchman to the effect that one can learn to accept the Bomb "if it is clean and comes from a good family." The authorial irony of that cut is blatant, and it implies that such remarks could be made only by those who have no grasp of the reality of nuclear war. The project of *The War Game*, then, was to show how a nuclear attack might *actually look*, so that such ignorance could be dispelled and discredited.

The challenge of nonfiction film in general is to capture something real and to present it in a way that will allow it to look real. Depending on one's attitude toward the nature of reality and the problem of objectivity, one will arrive at different ways of letting the real declare itself. It is important to remember that a record of the real may not always seem real, and also that absolute objectivity is a nearly unattainable goal in any medium or discipline.

The capacity to record real events, persons, and objects is not unique to film, but it is one of film's most distinctive elements. Nonfiction film can have the authority of evidence and the excitement of privileged witness. Although there are other ways to tell a story than on film, there is not quite any other way to record an event with such a capacity for accuracy.

The Animated Film

Animation is the process of creating in an unmoving object the impression of movement, of making the inanimate appear to live. Its root is the Latin *animāre*, "to fill with breath," from *anima*, which means "breath" or "soul." There are several different ways to achieve animation, but in almost all cases the movie is shot frame by frame and then projected at a normal rate.

Varieties of Animation. Strictly speaking, "animation" refers only to the process of photographing a series of two-dimensional graphics, drawings, or paintings — but it also refers loosely to the master category (frame-by-frame shooting). A short animated film is called a **cartoon** or an **animated short subject**; one that is longer than an hour is usually called an **animated feature**.

Each frame of virtually every cartoon is a photograph of a painting or drawing. Although a drawing can be done on paper, most paintings are executed on transparent sheets of celluloid called **cels**; the general term for this process is **cel animation**. To save labor and to ensure consistency from frame to frame, the background is painted on one cel, and the "moving" elements are painted on other cels that are mounted on top of it and usually changed for each frame. Major stages of action are first mapped out on **storyboards**, which resemble comic strips, and later the individual paintings that will "move" the figures from one major position to another are executed by **animators**. The **multiplane camera**, a device that allows cels to be separated from each other in order to create an impression of depth, was used to great effect in *Snow White and the Seven Dwarfs* as well as in several 3-D cartoons.

Pixillation is the art of animating a person or an object that is capable of moving under its own power. If a man walked up a hill and only a few frames were shot every few seconds, on film the man would appear to flit erratically up the hill, as if he were possessed by the pixies (mischievous fairies). A similar effect could be obtained by posing the man, taking a frame or two, and then posing him further up the hill.

In **stop-motion animation** a single frame is shot of a model, a puppet, or a cutout; then the object is moved slightly, and the next frame is shot. This technique, which reached its aesthetic zenith in Willis O'Brien's work on *King Kong*, was discovered during the infancy of the cinema. Well before 1910 a number of "trick" films had been produced in which furniture moved around a room as if under its own power.

There are also films in which the camera is stopped in the middle of a *live* action and then restarted after a significant change in the action area; this technique is called **stop-motion photography**. Georges Méliès is said to have discovered this trick accidentally while taking an actualité of Paris traffic. His camera jammed in mid-take, and when he developed the footage, he found that a bus had changed into a hearse. In *The Conjuror* (1899) Méliès used stop-motion photography to change a woman into a man (**Fig. 1-19**). The intermittent or frame-by-frame shooting of live, continuing action — without such spectacularly staged flourishes — is a more common use of stop-motion photography.

What defines stop-motion *animation* is that a three-dimensional object is photographed in a series of still positions. Thus the Muppet films, photographed in real time, are not animated even though they use puppets. But George Pal's "Puppetoons" and the **Claymation®** (animated clay) effects used in Will Vinton and Bob Gardiner's *Closed Mondays* (1974) — and further developed by Vinton for Walter Murch's *Return to Oz* (1985) — do fit the bill.

Enter the Computer. The animated film has made good use of the computer revolution. **Computer animation** uses a computer to generate graphics that can then be photographed (or, since the mid-1980s, scanned onto film). Pioneered by John Whitney, Sr., and his brother James Whitney, this technique was first used for avant-garde and scientific purposes. In John Whitney's *Permutations* (1967) and James Whitney's *Lapis* (1963 1966), where all the imagery is computer-generated, the systematic transmutation of abstract forms attains the fascinating rigor of music.

John Whitney, Sr., was also a pioneer in **motion-control photography**, which is a sophisticated technique for photographing models either frame by frame or at any desired rate of exposure. Let us say that the filmmaker wants a model of a spaceship to approach the camera and then suddenly veer to screen right. (**Screen right** is the right side of the screen as seen by the audience; the other side is called **screen left**, and between them is the **center**, or **center screen**.) Rather than keep the camera stable and move the model an eighth of an inch between every single-frame exposure, it is possible to keep the model steady and to move the camera up to it (creating the sense of approach) and then off to the left (creating the turn to screen right).

The computer keeps a record of exactly where the camera was in relation to the model at the time each frame was exposed. This allows the camera's movement to be duplicated exactly in subsequent takes. In an outer-space battle sequence there may be one such camera movement, controlled and recorded by a computer, for each rocket ship, space torpedo, planetoid, and background field. The movement of these objects — in relation to each other and to the camera — will appear to occur in real time and within the same visual field, even though each object was shot separately, perhaps even at a different rate of exposure. An exploding ship, for example, may well be shot in slow motion. In other words, a model may be equipped with a small charge and exploded in real time while a camera records the event at perhaps 240 fps, giving

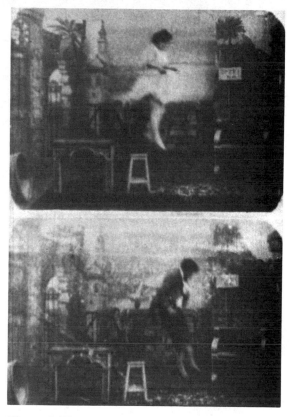

Figure 1-19

the fragments a greater impression of mass when the shot is projected at 24 fps. All of these shots or elements will have to match exactly if they are to be combined into a single image, and the computer helps to make that possible.

Motion-control photography, which today is used almost exclusively for special effects, relies on models (see **Fig. 3-111**). Thanks to recent developments in the field of computer animation — notably those created for Nick Castle's *The Last Starfighter* (1984) by Digital Productions, a company founded by John Whitney, Jr., and Gary Demos — it is possible to create an apparently three-dimensional computer image, complete with minuscule "moving" parts, that can be positioned, colored, lit, and manipulated electronically. The result is virtually identical to a photograph of a model, and so there may be no need to build one. Instead the "object" can be displayed in various major positions, as if on a storyboard, and the computer can calculate all the intervening positions and display them. Once they have been photographed and projected, these successive displays or images create the impression of movement.

Computer animation creates an individual image by defining and combining vast numbers of pixels into rasters. A **pixel**, or picture element, is the smallest bit of information on a TV or computer screen, a dot with a particular color and brightness. A **raster** is a single image field made up of these dots. In *The Last Starfighter* each raster or frame consists of 24 million pixels. For each of the three primary colors, the computer is capable of discriminating among 4,096 intensity levels. To generate an individual frame by this method, a supercomputer like the Cray XMP must perform between 7 and 22 billion calculations; nowadays that takes about 2½ minutes per frame, at approximately 160 million calculations per second.

Computer animation is not just a way to avoid using models, however. It is a fast, precise, and relatively economical way to generate successive images of any kind, to see how they will look in motion, to turn them around — and light them — within an imagined spatial field, and to combine them in new relationships. As one of the creators of Steven Lisberger's *Tron* (1982) remarked, that film contained nothing that could not have been done with conventional animation "given $45 million and 100 years." Like film itself, the computer is a meeting place between art and technology, and whether computer animation is used to streamline the painstaking process of generating successive representational images or to explore and systematically vary abstract forms, its hour has definitely arrived.

Direct Animation. There are also films in which the effect of animation is created without the aid of a camera, a process called **direct animation** or **constructed film**. In the simplest case, the images are painted directly onto clear filmstock, or they may be scratched onto the surface of black or colored filmstock.

If you take a yardstick and position it so that its top is at the

Figure 1-20

right edge of the filmstrip and its bottom is at the left edge, then run a pin along it and scratch off the emulsion, you will have a transparent diagonal line. When you run that strip through a projector, less than an inch of that line will be visible at any time. The line will appear very nearly vertical because its angle (moving an inch or so to one side over a distance of three feet) is so slight. The line will appear to move from one side of the screen to the other, and this motion will have been created almost entirely by the projector, whose access to the scratched line happens one frame, or projection position, at a time.

One of the most remarkable examples of direct animation is Stan Brakhage's *Mothlight* (1963). Brakhage made this film by shaking out the contents of his ceiling light fixtures and arranging moth wings, leaves, and other natural materials on the sticky side of a length of 16mm splicing tape. (**Splicing tape** is transparent, has the same dimensions as filmstock, and is perforated with sprocket holes.) He then painstakingly laid another length of splicing tape over that, sticky side down and with the sprocket holes lined up. Then he ran the whole thing through a printer, and when the print was projected, the result was a frantically changing pattern, a series of images with which Brakhage intended to convey a sense of the moth's life.

Figure 1-21

Each frame of this film was meticulously composed, with the sprocket holes used as reference points. **Fig. 1-20** shows a strip from *Mothlight*, and **Figs. 1-21** and **1-22** are frames of leaves and wings respectively. It is almost a pity that these beautiful images go by so rapidly, but it is their animation that evokes the sense of life, as if the moths were flitting around the light of the projector in a radically compressed and energized time, or as if the world of the moth had been essentialized to the terms of light and motion.

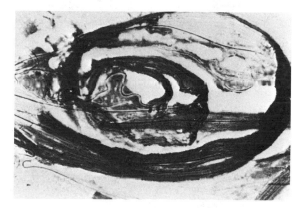

Figure 1-22

Brakhage has not lost his interest in animation. As this book goes to press, he is painting *existence is song* on Imax footage, advancing at seconds per month. Some of the huge, densely layered frames look like dried tide pools or exploding oil slicks.

Animation and the Cinema. Although animation can be uniquely free of the normal cinematic practice of photographing the physical world — free even of the camera itself — it is very much a cinematic art. The movies are, by nature, single frames in series, and it does not make an *essential* difference whether 24 frames are shot in a second or a week: it's still a movie.

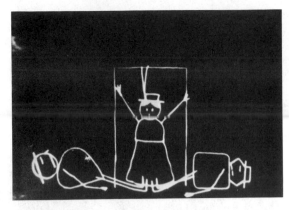

Figure 1-23

Figure 1-24

Figure 1-25

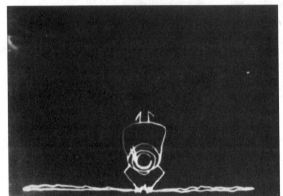

Figure 1-26

Figure 1-27

Although it makes sense to think of cinema as an extension of photography — first there was the still, then the sequence of stills with their impression of movement — the fact is that the earliest cinematic experiments were devoted to making *drawings* move, and it was in such toys as the Zoetrope that the principle of the shutter was first investigated.

The **Zoetrope** was a black drum — a low cylinder looking something like a hatbox — that was painted matte black and had slits cut at regular intervals along its upper half. A strip of drawings fit inside the drum, occupying its lower half. The drum was mounted on a rod and could be spun by hand. Looking through a slit and downward across the interior of the drum, one could see an individual drawing. When the Zoetrope was spun, the whole drum acted as a shutter, blocking one's view for a few degrees of spin and then allowing one to see, through the next slit, the next drawing. The drawn action would repeat with each complete revolution of the drum — forward or backward, at whatever rate one chose — and the loop of drawings was the earliest "film strip." What this implies is that the animation of individual stills, whether they are drawn or are taken from nature, is the essence and genesis of the cinematic. The **motion picture** can be thought of as any image that has been given the illusory property of movement.

Without question, animation has given the cinema some of its finest works and even some of its major stars. The only screen figure who is as well-known, worldwide, as Chaplin's tramp is Mickey Mouse. Without Mickey, Bugs Bunny, Daffy Duck, Jiminy Cricket, and Betty Boop, this world would be a different place.

Freed from physical limitations, the animated film is capable of indulging in an original plastic logic, a holiday of the impossible. The transformation of figures, first explored by Méliès, became utterly fluid in the hands of Emile Cohl, who turned one image into another in celebration of the animator's creative freedom, as in this sequence from his 1908 cartoon *Un Drame chez les fantoches* (*A Love Affair in Toyland;* **Figs. 1-23** through **1-27**). And in *Symphonie diagonale* (*Diagonal Symphony,* 1924) Viking Eggeling extended that experiment into the realm of pure form (**Figs. 1-28** through **1-31**). This play with form is one of animation's greatest continuing resources.

The Avant-garde Film

Avant-garde films are made outside the industry, usually by individual artists or small groups, and are often designed and executed in order to explore some aspect of film or to advance a specific aesthetic. If the mainstream narrative film can be compared with popular fiction, the avant-garde film can be compared with poetry: a form of compressed and heightened discourse, often personal, and addressed to an audience of other poets as well as to the appreciative general reader. Because they are made on relatively small budgets, avant-garde films do not need to reach huge audiences, but many of them have proved to be far more influential than their limited circulation might suggest.

Figure 1-28

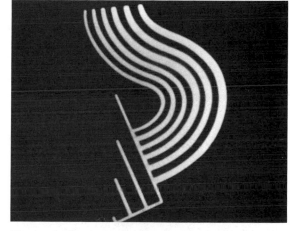

Figure 1-29

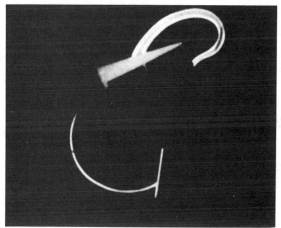

Figure 1-30

Figure 1-31

An Open Name. The term "avant-garde" ("in the front ranks") implies that such films are both outside and in advance of the mainstream of film practice. Most of them are embattled with conventional notions of realism and "good style," not because their makers belong to cliques that share certain aesthetic attitudes, but because, for most of these artists, to arrive at a viable way of making a worthwhile film is to resolve a lifelong quest. There is nothing so personal as a worldview, and nothing so difficult as to share an inner vision in a way that will both do it honor and make it clear. To find the terms of an aesthetic after years of trial is as personal and urgent as to come to terms with one's own life, and may well involve the same issues.

This category has gone by many names, some of which are still in use: **experimental film**, **underground film**, **personal film**, **poetic film**, **abstract film**, **absolute film**, **visionary film**, **structural film**, **art film**, and **independent film**. "Independent film" was among the better of these terms because it was free of value judgments and aesthetically unspecific, leaving the door open for any kind of film made by an artist who worked on his or her own. That term was, however, successfully appropriated by mainstream narrative filmmakers whose independence is from the studios, not from normative structural expectations. No matter how much you may appreciate an independently-produced picture like George Romero's *Night of the Living Dead* (1968), that is clearly not the same *kind* of movie as Maya Deren and Alexander Hammid's *Meshes of the Afternoon* (1943) or David Lynch's *Eraserhead* (1978).

"Experimental film" implies that the artist is always trying out things that may not work (sometimes taken as a license to be sloppy), and furthermore that mainstream filmmakers never take artistic risks. "Underground film" sounds like a convention of moles, and "art film" has also been used to refer to pornography. "Abstract film" perfectly describes a subcategory, but many avant-garde films include representational photography. Although in its most negative sense "avant-garde" conjures up an image of a self-righteous and hyperaesthetic artist, sitting in the corner and nursing a private project whose goals only an "in" group can understand, or waving a can of film above the battlements, the advantage of the term is that most people have accepted it. As Robert Breer put it, avant-garde is "a deteriorated term, but it's OK with me."

This terminological walkabout yields a valuable insight into the richness and complexity of the films in this category, which refuse to conform to or even to suggest an adequate label. What do you know about something once you have named it? Does that mean that you have successfully identified and honored its integrity, or that you no longer have to think about it or fully confront it? Sometimes, to reflect the living quality of a subject, the description of that subject must be made new. As Gertrude Stein and Ezra Pound demonstrated during the Modernist period, not just a word or a phrase but the entire language can atrophy if it is not continually prodded and renewed. Avant-garde film has kept itself new while its old names have expired. No other area of filmmaking has provoked so many attempts at definition, and that is one proof that it is a living art. We shall adopt "avant-garde" here, but that does not close the discussion. The name is open, and it will doubtless give rise to others.

Representationality and Abstraction. A representational painting is a picture *of* something. An **abstract film** is comparable to a *non*representational painting; working with pure forms and colors, and sometimes with music or a constructed soundtrack, it aspires to a condition of absolute self-sufficiency. The majority of abstract films set out to be purely visual events, sustained by and often commenting on their own formal principles. They may be thought of as abstract paintings endowed with the gift of time, or as music that can work with color and space. But to the extent that they rely on photography, even many abstract films are forced to present pictures of things.

Some filmmakers avoid representationality by avoiding photography entirely, painting or scratching directly on raw filmstock. Some use photography but restrict their subjects to pure shapes, lines, and colors — with or without sound — or resort to animation, as Viking Eggeling did in *Symphonie diagonale*, which is one of the definitive examples of abstract film. Nonrepresentational film might be thought of as a choreography of light — a light that is not descriptive, not a representation of anything but itself.

The majority of avant-garde films use representational, photographic imagery but systematically defeat the normal signals by which such imagery becomes conventionally comprehensible. The filmmaker may throw the lens out of focus, frame only part of an object without ever revealing what it is, cut so rapidly and erratically that no consistent setting can be established, refuse to tell stories and undermine whatever threatens to establish a coherent narrative, or deliberately insert continuity flaws. Fernand Léger's *Ballet mécanique* (1924) is such a film. All this is very much like what Gertrude Stein did with language, using terms that were inevitably representational (any word is) but repeating and rearranging them in a syntax of her own invention so that the reader was encouraged to see each word as a new and exciting construct. Like much of Stein's work, many of these films are embattled with representation rather than utterly free of it.

Dada and Surrealism. A number of avant-garde films were outgrowths of specific radical movements in the arts. Among the most influential of those movements were Surrealism and Expressionism.

Lautréamont encapsulated the pleasures of Surrealism in his famous image of "the chance encounter of an umbrella and a sewing machine on a dissecting table." **Dada**, the movement out of which Surrealism evolved in the mid-1920s, applied both wit and sarcasm to the project of undermining the traditional bases of social

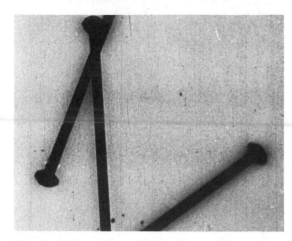

Figure 1-32

Figure 1-33

and aesthetic order. Among the few films that the Dadaists produced, Man Ray's *Return to Reason* (1923) is representative. Working overnight, Ray scattered nails (**Fig. 1-32**), salt and pepper, and other debris (**Fig. 1-33**) over raw filmstock, turning on the light to expose the footage; he also cut in images taken with a camera. At its premiere this 3-minute film literally caused a riot.

The Surrealists, under the guidance of André Breton, endorsed this dismantling of established values but felt that it was necessary to explore the interstices of the network that the Dadaists had exploded. **Surrealism** set out to discover the logic of the unconscious mind. In the hope of discovering new and significant relations beneath the mundane surfaces of the all-too-well-organized world, the Surrealists threw images together in a spontaneous and often unplanned manner, trusting to the promptings of the unconscious that might yield juxtapositions of obscure yet startling validity.

In this respect their films resemble dreams, working in the language of condensation and displacement explored by Sigmund Freud in *The Interpretation of Dreams*. This is not to say that the Surrealists were Freudians — most of them were not — but to single out their interest in the relations between dreaming and language. (One of Freud's major insights was that dreams can be a key to the language or the signifying system of the unconscious.) The Surrealists were interested in the coherence of the apparently incoherent, the revelatory value of puns and secret messages and weird juxtapositions. They sought to liberate the unconscious, to explore or create situations in which the odd transitions and resonant images of dreams erupted into daylight, and to critique the complacency of those who felt that the world made a rather dull but entirely reliable kind of sense.

Like the Dadaists, the Surrealists often deliberately assaulted contemporary expectations of proper behavior and narrative continuity. Luis Buñuel and Salvador Dalí's *Un Chien andalou* (1929) opens with a brutal assault on the audience, as what looks like a human eyeball is slit open by a straight razor. This scene is introduced by a title that reads "Once upon a time," and the tones of the scene and this title clash ironically. Within the scene, two similar visual elements predominate: a thin, dark cloud passing over the round moon, and the line of the razor across the eyeball. If this juxtaposition has a logic, it is the logic of dreams.

When a Surrealist "explains" an image, what often emerges is an obscure psychological association. Dalí once told an audience at Columbia University what he meant by the melting watches in his 1931 painting *The Persistence of Memory* (**Fig. C-3**). He said, "Christ is Camembert cheese." Under a certain amount of baffled prodding he grinned, stroked his extravagant mustache, and outlined the association. The watches have the runny yet pliable shape of warm Camembert, Camembert has the consistency of flesh, Christ vanquished time, and/but Christ was mortal and of the flesh. Dalí's concern was not that the viewer should understand his painting in those exact terms, but that the obscurity and precision of its imagery should open a conduit to the viewer's unconscious.

Expressionism. Expressionism relies more on the emotions than on the unconscious, though it too is concerned with uncovering hidden — and sometimes repressed — material. In its most general sense, **Expressionism** is the art of rendering inner states as aspects of the outer world. In its loosest sense, it means creatively motivated distortion. As a specific movement in the arts that reached its peak between 1880 and 1920, primarily in Germany and Northern Europe, Expressionism was an outgrowth of nineteenth-century **Romanticism**, whose special concern was the points of contact and correspondence between the natural world and the world of the imagination. But even in the work of Vincent Van Gogh, who straddled both traditions, it is clear that Expressionism had a far more tragic and frustrated outlook on both of those worlds than Romanticism ever did. As an image of the Romantic, think of William Wordsworth out for an elevating walk in the country; as an image of the Expressionist, think of Franz Kafka's supplicant, dying outside the gates of the Law.

In Edvard Munch's 1895 lithograph *The Cry* (**Fig. 1-34**) a curved figure with a skull-like head is shown on a bridge. His hands cup the sides of his head; his mouth is open in a shriek. The entire landscape is made up of thick, harsh, wavy lines, as if *it* were screaming. Down at the other end of the bridge are two dull, conventional figures who appear not to notice any of this — the bourgeois, sworn enemies of the radical artist.

What the landscape is doing, here and in the majority of Expressionist art, theater, and film, is *expressing* or pushing outward the emotions that would otherwise remain locked up inside the subject. In *The Cry* the landscape is manifesting the essence of the cry. Near the end of *The Cabinet of Dr. Caligari*, a definitively Expressionist film, a figure clearly modeled on Munch's screamer is shown on the verge of death (**Fig. 1-35**). Here, too, landscape and figure are part of a coherent and interreferential system, expressing each other's essential condition in similar visual terms — equally transfigured by the burden of irrepressible emotion.

Expressionism is the world of the tortured Romantic, but it is also the world of the visionary who sees the secret meanings of things and finds a way to make them directly observable. (Think of Van Gogh's *Starry Night*, which has the emotion of a visionary breakthrough.) It fosters and depends on a heightened imaginative intensity — an intensity of insight that can be personally overwhelming whether it is attuned to horror, mysticism, and death, or to more positive intimations of transcendence. Its focus can be on repressed inner states that are somehow to be revealed, or on powerfully controlling exterior forces that have somehow to be resisted.

Masks and madness are among its recurring concerns. The mask is a resonant means of hiding a physical face while revealing either

Figure 1-34

Figure 1-35

a true spiritual face or an even more calculatedly false face. Part of the Expressionist's task was to recognize when a face or a surface was hiding something, and either to tear off the false mask, to leave it on but exaggerate its falsehood, or to substitute a new mask that revealed the deepest possible inner workings of that person or condition.

If the Surrealists saw the logic of the unconscious as a rich alternative to rationality, the Expressionists feared that the only alternative to reason — in fact, its shadow — was madness. Masks, madness, and shadows come together in the Expressionist horror film, where the threatening figure is often uncontrollably destructive, sexually aggressive, masked or in heavy makeup, and acting out some culturally repressed impulse. A figure of the shadows in more ways than one, such a monster conventionally must be destroyed, but its eruption is the centerpiece of the horror film as well as the key to its message. In most such films, the monster is a figure of truth as well as a kind of victim, like Karloff's Frankenstein monster.

The Expressionist tendency has infiltrated mainstream narrative filmmaking more decisively than has any other avant-garde perspective. It is evident in the visionary style of Werner Herzog, who has said that he searches the world for "landscapes that do not exist on this planet" and who hypnotized the actors in *Heart of Glass* (1976) in order to exteriorize their inner states of mind and being. It infuses the images of madness and the monstrous that have long sustained the horror film, from Murnau's *Nosferatu* (1922) to Tobe Hooper's *The Texas Chain Saw Massacre* (1974) and Wes Craven's *A Nightmare on Elm Street* (1984). It can be found in such cinematic nightmares as *Dead of Night* and *Peeping Tom*, as well as in such studies of the extremes of violence, spiritual pain, and the unnatural exercise of control as *Alien* or James Whale's *Bride of Frankenstein* (1935). It gave birth to the threatening atmosphere of **film noir**, a genre that flourished in America in the 1940s and 1950s, charged with sudden violence and spiritual corruption and expressing the true condition of the world as a trap full of oppressive shadows. Its interest in saturated colors, bold lines, and sharp graphics have had an equally powerful influence on the musical.

Washing the Windows. The central ambition of the avant-garde film is to create an opportunity for the renewal of perception. If the eyes are the windows of the mind, avant-garde films set out to wash the windows. Some use Windex, and some install warped, cracked, distortive new panes, but all are concerned with getting at the heart of what is on the other side of the glass, what is revealed — if only for a fraction of a second — within the limits of the frame.

It is their heightened awareness of the possibilities of vision that has prompted these filmmakers to create new visual structures. Although some consider their films assaults on complacent or inadequate understandings of reality, others leave the bourgeois —

and Hollywood — to their own devices and simply explore the fun they can have in, say, turning the ocean upside down, or playing the image forward while the sound runs backward, or having a dancer leap up in a gallery and land on a cliffside, or exploring how light travels through a glass ashtray. By refusing to follow the rules, avant-garde films can reveal new kinds of rigor. By refusing to look pretty in an easy manner, they can show the gracefulness and assurance of integrity.

A Beautiful Friendship

Narration, nonfiction, animation, and the avant-garde are all very large cinematic categories. Even so, they do not cover every possible kind of film. What they do indicate are four of the primary possibilities and implicit characteristics of filmmaking: the ability to tell a story, to make a record of the world, to give stills the impression of movement, and to incarnate a vision. All of the aspects of cinema that have been considered here have some relevance to virtually any movie, though in different proportions and for different purposes. What defines these categories is the ascendance of a particular aspect of film form, but all of those aspects are capable of working together. Almost all of them come into play when we analyze or respond fully to any shot or scene in any film, narrative or otherwise.

For example, when Rick and Ilsa say goodbye to each other at the end of Michael Curtiz's *Casablanca* (1942), we may be caught up — via the willing suspension of disbelief — in the story of their love for each other and the reasons for their parting. Nevertheless, we are just as attentive to the play of light and shadow on their faces; the ways the mise-en-scène creates a mood that is both ro-

Figure 1-36

Figure 1-37

mantic and patriotic; and the cross-cutting of closeups that separates Rick and Ilsa into different frames (**Figs. 1-36** and **1-37**), expressing their separation, but that also makes their faces the most important things shown and, by treating them equally and in alternation, asserts their similarity, their connection, their romance. And we are also grateful to the recording medium that has given these stills the illusion of life and placed two great, deceased actors, Humphrey Bogart and Ingrid Bergman, before us again, capturing not only their performances — the real events being recorded — but also the ghosts of their presence.

The Soviet director V. I. Pudovkin observed that the difference between an event as it occurs in the world and the way that event is presented in a movie is the essence of the art of cinema. Film-making transforms the **pre-filmic** reality (what is available to be photographed and recorded) into a cinematic construct, a *filmed world* that is also a *film world*.

There are several drastic differences between the filmed and the pre-filmic worlds. The framing of an image selects a block of data from the flux of the world and asserts that what is presented has significance. A cut accomplishes an instantaneous transition in space and time, and it has virtually no equivalent in the physical world. The only things that come close to it are purely *mental* shifts of attention (which suggests that cinematic structures are more analogous to those of consciousness than they are to those of the objective world) and the quantum leap, which is subatomic and paradoxical. But cuts are quite normal in movies.

As an example of both these transformative structures, consider the moment in Dmitri Kirsanov's *Ménilmontant* (1925) when a girl (Nadia Sibirskaïa) discovers that her parents have been killed by an ax murderer. In the pre-filmic continuum, she stands in one spot while her face expresses shock and horror. The way Kirsanov filmed it was to shoot five closeups of her face, each one **tighter** (closer to the subject) than the last. The framing isolates her face as the most significant element in the visual field, and the cutting expresses her sense of shock. Later in the film, as a grown woman, she sees her lover in the embrace of her sister, and there is a similar series of closeups. The repetition of this cinematic **trope** (a figure of discourse) lets the audience know that this second shock is as great as the first and feels much the same to her. The framing and cutting patterns are not at all random; they efficiently and appropriately communicate what Kirsanov wanted to reveal about his subject. That, in a nutshell, is how movies work.

Organizing the Filmed World

There is more to telling a story on film than simply having it acted out in front of a camera. Much of the story is told *with* film, ex-ploiting cinematic devices to create meanings and clarify relation-ships.

The shot is the fundamental unit in the cinematic system. Within the shot, elements are set in significant arrangements (mise-en-scène). When shots are juxtaposed in series, that series itself becomes a significant arrangement (montage). One works in space, the other in time.

Mise-en-Scène. Originally a theatrical term meaning "staging" or "production," **mise-en-scène** translates roughly as "put in place" or "made into a scene." "Mise" comes from the French verb *mettre*, "to put." In a theatrical sense, the most significant aspects of the mise-en-scène are lighting, production design and set dec-

4. Montage and Mise-en-Scène in the Narrative Film

oration (**art direction**), and the choice (**casting**) and placement on the stage (**blocking**) of actors.

In the theater a director is given a text and has to bring it to life in performance. The text must be realized, dramatized, *played*. The director must establish how lines are to be read, the characters clarified, and the scenes staged. In cinema these responsibilities are similar, but they are complicated and enriched by the resources of the camera. The first thing one looks for in cinematic mise-en-scène is how the text has been made into scenes, as if those scenes were being played on a stage. How are the actors situated? Do the sets, props, and makeup contribute to the intended dramatic purposes of the scene? Is the realized whole an effective dramatic unit? A film director must have these basic theatrical skills, just as a cinematographer must be able to light a scene in a theatrical space that will translate well to cinematic space.

In cinema, mise-en-scène is a function of the relations between the scene as a dramatic unit played out in theatrical space (the set or landscape) and the camera that reshapes that space into a two-dimensional rectangle of light and shadow. The cinematic scene is typically divided into several shots, whereas the theatrical scene is played out in the seamless time and space of the stage. Thus each shot also has a mise-en-scène of its own, created primarily by the way a given fragment of action is composed and framed by the camera, selected out of the pre-filmic whole and given a particular shape and texture. It matters how the actors move in relation to the setting and to each other, as on the stage, but it also matters how they move in relation to the camera and how the camera moves in relation to them. Their ultimate stage is the frame.

Although the fundamental elements of mise-en-scène in both theater and cinema are those of lighting, blocking, and production design (costumes, props, and sets), cinematic mise-en-scène also includes such elements as the choice of filmstock (black-and-white or color, fine-grain or grainy), of aspect ratio (the proportions of the screen), of framing (how much of the set or cast will be shown at a time), of camera placement and movement, and of sound environment. All of these elements are selected and put in place — or set in motion.

Montage. As soon as a film is made of more than one shot, editing comes into play. When one shot does not simply follow another, and their juxtaposition has a dynamic significance, one speaks not of editing but of montage. The French term for simple continuity editing is **découpage**; it denotes "ordinary" sequential cutting, where one shot follows another in a linear, easy-to-follow manner. Montage — from the French verb *monter*, "to ascend, mount, or assemble" — denotes the way one shot is *mounted* next to another, but it has the connotation of an ascending or heightened effect. **Montage**, then, is the art of assembling individual shots into a dynamic system.

There are four commonly used varieties of montage. The first, and the most familiar, is **rapid cutting**: a great many shots follow one another in a short period of time. This can create a shock rhythm and can feel like an avalanche of images. Its primary function is rhythmic, and it is often used to heighten the audience's sense of dramatic urgency or to realize the energy of a climax. One of the most startling and violent examples of rapid cutting occurs at the very start of *Ménilmontant*. In less than 40 seconds more than 50 shots present the ax murders with horrifying suddenness. The shower murder in *Psycho* provides an analogous example from the sound period.

Figure 1-38

The second variety of montage is **linkage editing**, a structure primarily associated with the work of Pudovkin, both in his theoretical writings and in his film *Mother* (1926). As the term suggests, individual shots are joined together to present a whole; they are linked into a system. (This is also called **constructive editing**, as if shots were bricks.) Linkage editing is far more fragmented and dynamic than normal continuity cutting, because the individual shots are true fragments and, to some degree, retain their integrity as autonomous units, whereas those in continuity editing tend to flow together. Although **continuity editing** is the single most common type of editing, it is often excluded from the cate-

Figure 1-39

Figure 1-40

Figure 1-41

Figure 1-42

gory of montage because it is at pains to "hide" cuts so that the audience will not become aware of them. In true montage, shot juxtapositions are deliberately called to the audience's attention. By the same token, not every shot can be said to have a mise-en-scène; a simple intertitle, for instance, rarely asserts a significant arrangement.

The third is **dialectical montage** (sometimes called **intellectual montage**), a trope primarily associated with Eisenstein but still practiced by Nicolas Roeg, Alain Resnais, and others. Rather than *linking* with each other like the pieces of a jigsaw puzzle, the shots in a dialectical montage *collide*. They do not fit easily together but appear to be in conflict, and the audience must reason out what these shots have to do with each other. Griffith used dialectical montage as a structuring principle in *Intolerance* (though he had no special name for it), telling four separate stories among which the audience had to discover a common theme. In *Strike* (1925), Eisenstein offered a shot of a slaughtered animal and then a shot of massacred strikers (**Fig. 1-38**). The animal had nothing to do with the plot of *Strike*, but the two shots, taken together, implied that the workers had been not simply attacked but *slaughtered* like cattle.

The fourth is **Hollywood montage**, where the images overlap as they succeed each other. In the three previous types, the images are separated by **straight cuts**: without any special bridging device, one shot ends, then the next begins. Hollywood montage "softens" the abrupt transitions of classical (Gance, etc.) montage, providing a series of double (or more) exposures, usually accompanied by music rather than dialogue, and generally used to give a whirlwind impression of an event or an overview of a transition between scenes. In *Citizen Kane* the essence of Susan's operatic career is shown in such a montage (**Figs 1-39** through 1 12).

Montage and mise-en-scène overlap in the tropes of multiple exposure and split-screen. The term Abel Gance coined to describe both of these was **polyvision** (any image made up of several images), and both polyvision and rapid cutting are as permanently associated with his name as dialectical montage is with Eisenstein's. In **split-screen** two or more distinct images are mounted next to each other within the limits of the frame. Early in *Napoleon* Gance showed a pillow fight in a boy's dormitory (**Fig. 1-43**). As the scene progressed, he divided the shot into four distinct image fields (**Fig. 1-44**) and then into nine (**Fig. 1-45**). In **multiple exposure** two or more images are superimposed. Gance overlapped as many as 16 separate exposures in order to convey the excitement of another stage of the pillow fight (**Fig. 1-46**). Polyvision reached its peak in the triptych sequences (originally there were three) of *Napoleon,* when Gance spread his images across three screens. What makes polyvision different from other varieties of montage is that its juxtapositions are simultaneous rather than successive or sequential; still, it may be thought of as *montage within the frame* or montage *as* mise-en-scène.

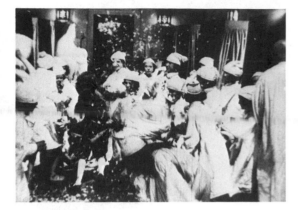

Figure 1-43

Figure 1-44

Figure 1-45

Figure 1-46

To sum up, let us return to the semiotic playground of paradigmatic and syntagmatic axes. Looking at any given shot, we realize that there were many ways that that shot could have been lit and composed, many ways that the frame could have been occupied — but that *this is what was chosen,* what was selected and arranged. Thus mise-en-scène reflects a selection from the paradigmatic axis of the pre-filmic world. Within a shot, or from one shot to another, certain items are called to the audience's attention, and that sequence of significant percepts runs along the syntagmatic axis, the flow of the film in time.

Citizen Kane

One of the reasons *Citizen Kane* is so highly praised is that it exploited the full resources of both montage and mise-en-scène. Some of its shots were filmed entirely in long takes, with the camera moving from one object of interest — and composition — to another. These camera movements made some conventional uses of cutting unnecessary and enhanced the impression of a coherent and seamless visual field. By the use of deep focus photography, cinematographer Gregg Toland kept foreground, middleground, and background objects in focus, further integrating the visual world into a richly composed mise-en-scène.

On the other hand, the film as a whole consists of several distinct segments: a view of Kane's death; a newsreel that reports his death and gives much information about Kane's life; a story about the reporter (Thompson) who compiled that material and is sent out to discover the meaning of "Rosebud"; the story of Kane's childhood and business career as recounted in the memoirs of Kane's banker (Thatcher); four separate interviews with Kane's friends (Bernstein and Leland), his second wife (Susan), and his butler (Raymond); and a concluding scene at Kane's mansion. Each of these segments has something different to say and to reveal about the central character, and they all have to be put together if the audience is to understand Kane and his story. That is a montage process, projecting an integration by presenting fragments, and it is just as important in this film as the mise-en-scène (composition in depth and the long take) that projects its own sense of shifting relations within a coherent field.

Two brief excerpts from Citizen Kane should indicate the complexity of that film's narrative devices and some of the ways in which montage and mise-en-scène can be useful in telling stories.

"Rosebud." The first excerpt comes from early in the film. The camera has gone past a "No Trespassing" sign, surveyed the grounds of Charles Foster Kane's Florida mansion, Xanadu, and finally gone inside Kane's bedroom. Whirling snowflakes are superimposed on a shot of Kane's window. Then there is a cut to an extreme closeup of a model house with snow falling around it. This turns out to be the inside of a glass paperweight filled with water and synthetic snow (when the globe is shaken, the snow appears to be falling). We recognize this globe as the source of the "snow" that was superimposed on the previous image and that continues to appear over several shots in this brief scene. Without cutting, the camera pulls rapidly back to reveal the globe in a man's open hand (**Fig. 1-47**). Then there is a cut to an extreme closeup of a man's mouth; the lips say a single word, "Rosebud" (**Fig. 1-48**). No one appears to be in the room to hear "Rosebud," but the butler later says he was there. This is followed by a cut to a closeup of the globe's dropping from the man's relaxed hand (**Fig. 1-49**). The soundtrack is now only music, and when the globe falls and breaks in this and the following shot, no glass is heard.

Putting this together, we gather that the hand and the mouth belong to the same person. We also wonder, but have as yet no way to know, why that man is shown in fragments rather than all at once. Later on we may realize that the montage structure of this film presents Kane in parts all along—partial views, subjective interpretations, conflicting evidence—and that our task is to assemble all this information into a whole figure that the film will not or cannot present outright in the narrative present.

Because the wrist comes from screen right in **Fig. 1-47** and from screen left in **Fig. 1-49**, and because the globe falls away from the bed in **Fig. 1-49**, we note that the camera has reversed its direction between those two shots. Because the mouth is shown in **Fig. 1-48**, we gather that it and the previous shot offer an outsider's view of the man on the bed and that **Fig. 1-49** shows the falling globe as seen *from* the bed — in other words, that **Fig. 1-49** is a POV shot. This offers one answer to the question why an image of falling snow is superimposed over the shot of the falling globe in **Fig. 1-49**; that we are seeing the inside of the globe (the synthetic snowfall) as Kane sees it, as well as the Colorado snowfall of which it has reminded him. His dying consciousness is still taking in or thinking about the snowy vision (mindscreen) even while his eyes register the fall of the globe (subjective camera). We do not hear

Figure 1-47

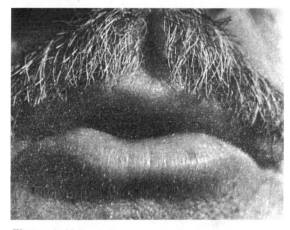

Figure 1-48

Figure 1-49

the crash because the dying man does not (subjective sound). All this is part of the standard process of reading a film's narrative continuity. We see the hand and the globe this way, then the lips, and then the hand and the globe the other way. Therefore we understand that the camera has "trespassed," has found what it was looking for, and has then turned back, perhaps in search of the rest of the story. In the process, it has partially shared with Kane the moment of his death (**Fig. 1-49**).

But there is more to be gathered from these three shots, which are a good working example of dialectical montage. Eisenstein's point was that, given two distinct and perhaps apparently unrelated shots, the audience will generate for themselves a way of reading the two images together or in terms of each other. He considered this process **dialectical** in that the conflict between the two shots — comparable to the conflict between *thesis* and *antithesis* in Hegelian and Marxist philosophy — gives rise to a *synthesis* that is different from either of the initial terms but that somehow reconciles and goes past them. In cinema, the *synthesis* is the concept or the linking idea that arises from the juxtaposition of two or more shots and that could not itself be photographed. (It is hard to take a picture of an idea.)

In historical terms, we may think of the French monarchy as the **thesis**, or first term; of the French Revolution as the **antithesis**, or opposing term, that arose in opposition to the monarchy and worked on entirely different principles; and of the figure of Napoleon Bonaparte — a believer in the revolution who went on to become the emperor of a new political system — as the **synthesis** that arose spontaneously from this conflict and that itself went on to become the thesis, or first term, in a new historical cycle. Hegel argued that this process would end only when history did, with the achievement of an ultimate synthesis. In these three shots from *Citizen Kane,* if the thesis is the shot of the globe and the antithesis or counterterm is the lips saying "Rosebud," what is the synthesis?

The rest of the movie gives us enough information to realize what is being implied in this brief series of shots. Kane's mother had run a boarding house in Colorado, and one winter a guest had paid for his room with a deed to a mine that turned out to be extremely valuable. Mrs. Kane had arranged for Thatcher, a banker, to invest her funds and to raise her son in affluence. One day Thatcher comes to sign the papers and collect the boy. Unhappy about leaving, Kane hits Thatcher with a sled. Much later, as an adult, Kane is on the way to a warehouse where he intends to look over his late mother's possessions, but he meets Susan — who later becomes his second wife — and enjoys the way they both seem to understand "how mothers are." Susan has a glass globe on her dressing table — the same one that will later drop from Kane's hand in death. When Susan leaves him, years later, Kane wrecks her room. In the course of this rampage he sees the globe, picks it up and shakes it, and says "Rosebud." At the very end of the film, the camera "trespasses" into one of the vast rooms of Xanadu, where apparently worthless items from Kane's estate are being burned. One of these items is the sled with which Kane hit Thatcher. The camera goes into the furnace and shows the word "Rosebud" in closeup.

Although this is not the full story of Kane, it is a key to an important aspect of him. By remembering the sled on his deathbed and also at the breakup of his marriage, Kane is expressing a nostalgic longing for the world of his boyhood, for his mother, and for the unity of love and acceptance that eluded him when he became rich. Rosebud is Colorado, and his mother, and also a prized personal possession that he did not want to lose — perhaps one root of the compulsive collecting of art objects in which Kane indulged as an adult. Kane may well be realizing on his deathbed that he should have hit Thatcher harder, that Rosebud was his last hold on an authentic life.

Looking back, we can see that the synthesis in this sequence is the identity and the significance of Rosebud, the sled from snowy Colorado. The landscape inside the glass paperweight evokes the Colorado home of Mary Kane (and the boy's last winter there), just as the globe itself is an image of a self-contained world, and what the montage teaches us is to search for a link between all that the paperweight symbolizes and the word spoken in the following shot. The third shot, repeating the paperweight, further emphasizes the potential relations between "Rosebud" and the globe.

What all this finally shows is not just that Rosebud is the Colorado sled, and that Kane misses not the sled but the home and world of which it was a part, but also that to understand "Rosebud" is to understand the self-contained wholeness of the mystery of Kane's life, a wholeness that shatters at his death. The ending of the film lets us know what "Rosebud" literally meant, but by implication it also takes us back to the image of the globe: an isolated and innocent universe. The globe is a symbol of Kane's desire to hold the world in his hand and make it do his bidding, as well as the symbol of his longing for a simple life, and beyond that, an image of how he feels that those contradictory desires can be reconciled. It is like the paradox — or collision — of the film's title, which shows Kane's desire to be an ordinary *citizen* but also identifies him with *Cain*, the social outcast, and Kubla *Khan*, the emperor who built the mythical Xanadu.

To reduce this "Rosebud sandwich" to its simplest terms: Snowy globe-world plus "Rosebud" equals Colorado, mother, ideals, possessions, innocence, love, loss, control, and sled. But "plus" does not quite do the job, because the collision among the elements in a dialectical montage is less a matter of addition than one of dynamic interaction. Rather than the *sum* of its elements, the synthesis is their *product*.

The point is not that we should have understood the meaning of Kane's dying word when we first saw these three shots, but that this sequence is used to set up the final revelation. The film maintains a continuous coherence; its meanings are not contained entirely in the closing punch line but are displayed all along.

"A Desert Island." **Figs. 1-50** through **1-55** are from one continuous shot near the middle of the film. Kane (Orson Welles), who has just lost the race for governor because of a scandal involving the "love nest" he has shared with Susan (Dorothy Comingore), has gone back to his newspaper office. There he encounters Jed Leland (Joseph Cotten), a lifelong friend who had taken the idealism of Kane's campaign seriously and who has gotten drunk.

The mise-en-scène in **Fig. 1-50** is full of props that pertain to the campaign, notably "KANE for Governor" signs and piles of spent confetti. The clutter of confetti suggests the failure of the campaign, a mess of jubilant expectation that now, in the absence of celebrants, is just a mess. The camera is at a low angle, and this angle makes two things possible: a view of the skylight, which may be taken to symbolize the idealism of the campaign and an openness to the outside world (the subjects of Leland's dialogue in this scene), and an exaggerated sense of perspective that allows the figure nearer the camera to appear unnaturally large and the distant figure unnaturally small. Welles and Toland used this perspective "flaw" to vary the apparent sizes of Kane and Leland throughout the shot, and this turns out to comment upon and clarify what the characters say to each other. This scene is a clear example of how the camera can define and explore relationships between characters. It also illustrates what Rudolf Arnheim meant when he argued that it is the ways film distorts or cannot match physical reality that allow it to be an art. The arrangement of the actors within the visual field, the framing of the image, and the compositions created by that framing are all significant aspects of the mise-en-scène, and here they work together with the set design and decoration to enrich the presentation of this phase of the story.

There is no music in this shot, only dialogue and simple sound effects. In the previous shot, which is part of this three-shot scene, Leland has announced his drunkenness, and Kane has asked him not to deliver a lecture about Susan, then has understood that Leland is more upset about Kane's letting his personal life get in the way of "the sacred cause of reform." Kane has gone on to say, "All right, if that's the way they want it, the people have made their choice. It's obvious the people prefer Jim Gettys to me."

Now the shot begins, at **Fig. 1-50**. Leland says, "You talk about the people as though you owned them. As though they belong to you. Goodness! As long as I can remember, you've talked about giving the people their rights, as if you could make them a present of liberty, as a reward for services rendered." Kane replies, "Jed." At this point the mise-en-scène presents a tiny man talking to a huge man, and his subject is politics. This makes Leland appear to be a representative and spokesman for "the people" and, in that respect, functions as a parody of the attitude toward "the little guy" that Leland argues Kane actually has.

Now the tiny man has a chance to bring the big man down to his own size, to show that they are equals. The way Welles accomplished this was to have Kane walk away from the camera and toward Leland. This makes not only a political point but also a personal one, because Kane and Leland are at a critical point in their friendship, and to show them near each other and on the same scale would be a visual way to call attention to that friendship and to suggest a way for it to survive. The viewer who cares about this relationship will be rooting for something like **Fig. 1-53** and will perceive other compositions and perspective relations as advances toward or retreats from this balanced stability. The friendship and the political issues are both engaged in this shot and are shown to be closely related — in fact, to depend on the same terms.

At the words "as a reward for services rendered" Leland steps forward, growing in screen size as if his words had granted him some extra stature (**Fig. 1-51**). Kane's "Jed" is a rapid interjection, and on the same beat Leland says, "Remember the working man?" Now the political theme is uppermost, and Kane tries to dodge it. "I'll get drunk too, Jedediah, if it'll do any good," he says, and Leland replies, "It won't do any good. Besides, you never get drunk." Now Kane takes a few steps toward Leland, probably because Leland's joke has offered the prospect of some warmth between them. But Leland continues, "You used to write an awful lot about the working man — " and Kane breaks in, "Aw, go on home."

Now that the two men are nearly the same size, Leland launches his major attack. "He's turning into something called organized labor," he says (**Fig. 1-52**), and it is as if the little working man has turned into the confrontational force of the labor movement, capable of taking on Kane and the major capitalist forces he represents. "You're not going to like that one little bit," he goes on, "when you find out it means your working man expects something as his right and not your gift. Charlie, when your precious under

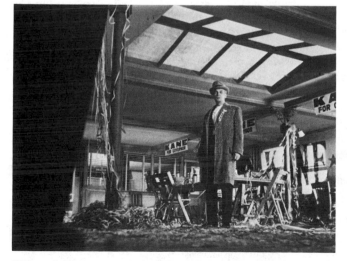

Figure 1-50

Figure 1-51

Figure 1-52

Figure 1-53

privileged really get together — oh, boy. That's going to add up to something bigger than your privilege, and then I don't know what you'll do. Sail away to a desert island, probably, and lord it over the monkeys." The desert island reference echoes the theme of the controlled world of the paperweight, while Leland's general message is that the day of the benevolent aristocrat has passed.

Now Kane makes what, in the terms of this composition, is a solid gesture of friendship — again perhaps responding to the joking tone on which Leland has closed — by turning to face him from the closest distance they ever achieve (**Fig. 1-53**). Kane's dialogue, appropriately, concerns friendship, but it also suggests, in both the visual and the dramatic contexts of this shot, that good politics is carried out between equals who respect each other. "I wouldn't worry about it too much, Jed," he says. "There'll probably be a few of them there to let me know when I do something wrong." Dodging the fact that Kane has nearly called him a monkey, but also displaying some petulance, Leland replies, "You may not always be so lucky." "You're not very drunk," says Kane, and Leland snaps, "Drunk — what do you care? You don't care about anything except you." Because Leland's words and attitude amount to a rebuff of Kane's hopes for their continuing friendship and a criticism of Kane's lack of insight and compassion — in fact, his failure to pay attention to the desires and thoughts of those around him — Kane turns from Leland and walks away, toward the office bar, and the camera pivots to follow him.

"You don't care about anything except you," Leland has said. And at this point (**Fig. 1-54**) we do see Kane moving off into an isolated space, alone with himself. Walking at an angle that brings him gradually closer to the camera, Kane increases in apparent size. What this means, visually, is that Kane has withdrawn from the interaction with his critical friend. It means that he is unwilling to continue functioning as his friend's equal, that he will not take the risk of descending to the level of the working man, that he is retreating to a position of privilege and power (because he is beginning to loom over the audience), that the alternative he perceives to engagement is isolation, that he is beginning his retreat into Xanadu, that he cannot take criticism, and that Leland's analysis of Kane's problems is correct. Of course, it is important to note that this section of the film is narrated by Leland, who is talking with the reporter in the narrative present; naturally, then, the visual presentation reinforces Leland's attitudes toward Kane at this phase of the story.

Now that Kane is entirely alone in the frame, Leland finishes his harangue: "You just want to persuade people that you love them so much that they ought to love you back." Kane reacts (**Fig. 1-55**) as if Leland has struck a sore spot (an economical and dramatic way for Welles to show how Kane is feeling), and Leland's offscreen voice concludes, "Only you want love on your own terms." The fact that Kane is alone in the shot epitomizes the tragic flaw in Kane's vision of intimate relationships, the futility of attempting to dictate the conditions of love. It is an emotional strategy that will leave Kane on his own, no matter how much he wants to be loved.

We notice at this point that the skylight has disappeared, so that the ceiling appears to press down on the character whose inadequate understanding of relationships — and politics — so limits him. In the next shot, Kane proposes a toast "to love on my terms," making a bitter joke out of his choice of isolation but also making an effective point, which is that one's own terms *are* the only terms that one really knows. Although Kane declines to learn enough about the terms of others, in order to understand Kane we must try to understand how *he* saw the terms of his own life and

Figure 1-54

Figure 1-55

how his isolation is both a key to his paradoxical greatness and an expression of the tragedy of his character.

The design of the ceiling, and the ways in which its lines are framed, works with the design of the room and the blocking of the actors to complicate the mise-en-scène even further. One conventional reading of the direction of lines is to see *horizontals* as stable and calm, *verticals* as less stable but strong, and *diagonals* as dynamic. Kane and Leland are standing on a diagonal line that runs from one corner of the set to another, and this in itself contributes to the highly charged atmosphere of their confrontation.

If we look at the line created by the spine of the skylight, we notice that it is most nearly horizontal in **Fig. 1-53**, which is the moment when the friendship theme is visually reinforced by the natural size relationships of Kane and Leland. **Fig. 1-53** also shows Kane next to the strong vertical of a pillar that is also prominent in **Fig. 1-52**, where Kane is approaching his friend and conscience. But when Kane turns to walk away, the stable skylight and the strong pillar are removed from the image, and what we see instead is an *X* (**Fig. 1-54**), as if Kane were walking into the business end of a pair of scissors (**Fig. 1-55**). One of the ceiling diagonals extends the line of the skylight, and the other interrupts or cuts it; at the axis is Kane's head (**Fig. 1-54**). The point here is that the stability of the friendship and the personal power that Kane might have found there have been cut off, and that it is Kane's movement or reaction that has created this shift; Leland is left behind with the skylight.

In **Fig. 1-55** the diagonal ceiling lines are at their dynamic, upsetting maximum, and this *X*, although onscreen for a very short time, is sufficient to give the audience the impression that this looming figure is both powerful and isolated, yet trapped — boxed in by the line of the bar, the edge of the frame, and the two lines on the ceiling. The pillar is far to screen right and no longer reaches the top of the frame, and so has lost its connotation of strength, as Kane has lost real strength by retreating into this position of apparent power.

The scene continues for another lengthy shot, but the interaction and its largest meanings have already been communicated here, not only by the dialogue but also by the drama of shifting size relationships, of closeness and isolation, of horizontals and diagonals, of who is under the skylight and how much confetti is shown — in short, of the mise-en-scène.

Close Encounters

King Kong pushes with all his strength against the barred gate that has separated his world from that of the villagers (**Fig. 1-56**). The villagers and sailors, from their side of the ancient barrier, push back (**Fig. 1-57**). Then the bar gives, and Kong storms into the village (**Fig. 1-58**). What the montage has separated, the mise-en-scène unifies.

It is almost as if the civilized humans have been trying to keep the primitive Kong in a separate shot. The dramatic energy peaks, in this case, when the fragmentations of montage are overcome, when the two worlds become one.

In the scene of Kong at the gates, montage and mise-en-scène work together to define and enhance the drama of assault, resistance, and synthesis. We may arrive at a summary understanding of what has been introduced so far by looking at a sequence from Steven Spielberg's *Close Encounters of the Third Kind: The Special Edition* (1980; first edition, 1977) in which the separation and juxtaposition of signs is a crucial aspect of the drama and a key to the meaning of the story.

"Stay Out of the Area!" *Close Encounters* is a science fiction film about the first thoroughly documented contact between Earthlings and extraterrestrials. Several of the characters have seen alien spacecraft and have suffered "implanted visions" of a moundlike shape that they feel must somehow be significant, though they do not know why, and some have heard a five-note musical sequence. Army and U.S. government intelligence forces, working with a team of scientists, have recognized that an at first baffling radio signal (a sequence of six numbers) refers to the latitude and longitude of Devil's Tower National Monument in Wyoming, which they have correctly interpreted as the site of a forthcoming alien landing. To clear the area so that the government can monopolize this event (because this is, among other things, an anti-Establishment film informed by the populist idealism of the 1960s), a phony nerve-gas spill in the Devil's Tower area has been announced to the media, and an evacuation has been scheduled.

Roy Neary (Richard Dreyfuss) has been sculpting an image of the mound in search of what it means, first in his shaving cream, then in his mashed potatoes, then in clay, and finally — on a larger scale and using much of his garden — in the basement. His wife and children think he has gone crazy and eventually leave him. A woman Roy met at one sighting, Jillian Guiler (Melinda Dillon), has previously been seen drawing a similar mound while her son has been playing the five notes on his toy xylophone. It is approximately halfway through the movie that the following sequence starts.

Roy is holding a plant and wondering where on the model to put it. The camera pulls back from a closeup of Roy and the plant to a view of the mound. Roy walks almost completely around the model, and as the camera follows him, a TV set can be seen at screen right. Near the end of the shot, Roy is at screen left, still with the plant in his hand; then he lowers it as if temporarily defeated. The soundtrack has been dominated by the TV program, a soap opera. Because the audience has not seen the TV until late in the shot, there has been some question whether it is Roy's doorbell that has been ringing and whether he is alone in the room, and the TV's appearance both settles this question and draws the audience's attention to the set.

Figure 1-56

Figure 1-57

Figure 1-58

There is a straight cut to a closeup of a window as Roy pulls the curtain aside and looks out. Another straight cut, reversing the camera angle, shows his neighbors, busy at their gardening and other routine tasks. During these two shots the soap opera's theme statement is heard — "Like the sands through the hourglass, so are the Days of Our Lives" — and this comments ironically on the shot of the neighborhood while expressing what Roy may be thinking to himself about the futility of routine daily experience and the apparent futility of his project. The camera pulls back a few feet (it has been inside all along, shooting through the window) as Roy closes the curtain and turns to look at the offscreen monument, exhausted and almost disgusted.

By now the soundtrack has gone to a Budweiser commercial. Because Roy himself drinks Bud (there is a can on top of the set), the playing of the commercial may represent little more than an extreme promotional consideration worked out between the brewery and the studio, Columbia Pictures, but Spielberg put the words of the commercial to ironic use. "The king is coming, let's hear the call," sings the chorus, as if parodying what Roy is trying to do. The brewery, of course, is referring to what it considers "the king of beers," but the phrase inevitably echoes the Christian expectation of the return of Jesus, whose "call" mortals ought to attend to. In this context, where Roy is attempting to decipher the "call" he has received from the aliens and whose coming he anticipates, the ironic implication is that transcendental summonses are not easy to interpret. The symbolic connotation is that the aliens are a benevolent extraterrestrial agency whose coming may lead to a new and better era. But Roy himself is immanent, is about to discover his own mission, and we can understand this additional connotation by remembering that in Old French, "Roy" means "king."

Next there is a cut from a close shot to a relatively long shot, showing Roy as he continues to look at the baffling sign of the model (he has a signifier on his hands, but no signified to go with it) and to listen to the commercial: "When you say Bud, you've said it all." This is a totally ironic deferring, or putting off, of clear meaning. "All" is not being declared or said here. Instead, Roy is set between two signs or signifying systems: the model, whose meaning he cannot understand, and the commercial, whose meaning is so evident that it cannot be useful.

The next cut is a little confusing. The shot begins with a closeup of the TV set as the commercial concludes and an ABC news bulletin comes on. The camera then pulls back to show that Roy is on the phone, having an argument with his wife; she wants a separation and will not discuss the matter with him in person. The TV's picture and sound tracks have been continuous, but the phone call is presented as having gone on for at least a few minutes. This continuity flaw creates an odd time sense, disorienting the audience and prompting it to share the limbo of Roy's obsession, so that what *has* continuity is the search for the elusive meaning of the mound shape, whereas the events of "the days of our lives"

Figure 1-59

sink to futility or simply go on in a less-than-significant order. This is a good working example of the cinema's ability to manipulate time.

As this shot continues, Roy paces around the room, still talking on the phone, while the TV's images remain in full view of the audience. The bulletin reports the nerve gas spill and civilian evacuation while teasing the movie audience with glimpses of Devil's Tower, which resembles the model of the mound. In this case what the mise-en-scène is showing us, via the similar shapes of mound and monument, is that the model is *of the monument.* Roy does not know this yet, and we feel frustrated because Roy, engaged in a losing argument with his wife, is looking away from the set at the instant (**Fig. 1-59**) that this information might become available to him — the instant when the solution comes "into the area," more or less as Kong bursts into the village. What Roy would learn, if he looked, is that he has been telepathically invited by the aliens to be present at the landing, and where it will take place. If the words of the bulletin are false, its images are true.

His wife hangs up, and Roy finally looks at the TV. Just before the shot ends, music starts up — a repeated two-chord sequence sung by a chorus, almost an "ah-haaaa" or a gathering of breathlike energy. This music continues till the end of the sequence and expresses the dawning revelation, now Roy's but soon to be Roy's and Jillian's, of the meaning of the shape. Not only the music and the mise-en-scène but also the montage now work together to advance the sequence and to clarify its narrative project.

There is a straight cut to a closeup of Jillian as she looks at something offscreen — with the music, of course, continuing. Another straight cut, to a long shot of Jillian's motel room, shows us that she, too, is looking at the TV bulletin. She gets up quickly and goes over to the set, and as she arrives, the camera pulls in for a closeup of her touching the screen. At the instant she begins to trace the image of the monument, there is a straight cut to Roy as *he* crouches to look at the monument. At this point Roy and Jillian are linked and paralleled by the similarity of the two shots and by the fact that these shots immediately follow one another.

Technically this sequence is one of **parallel montage** or **cross-cutting**, which works by cutting back and forth between actions that are then seen as developing in parallel. Roy's and Jillian's revelations are unfolding in separate locations and at the same time. But this is also an instance of dialectical montage, although a fairly simple one, and the concept that arises from the juxtaposition of these two shots is that Roy and Jillian are both recognizing the source of their "implanted visions" through the same means; we see that their quests are parallel, and that their insights and visions have brought them together. Several scenes later, this theme is fully articulated when Roy and Jillian look at the actual monument together, in Wyoming and in the same shot, as if the fragmentations of montage — which can separate terms as well as interrelate them — have been overcome.

The rhythm of the first long takes in this sequence has been slow, but now the lengths of the shots shorten and the cross-cutting establishes its own more excited rhythm. The next shot picks up Jillian just where her last shot had left her. Pulling her hand back from the set, she turns, smiling. The camera reverses its angle of direction over the cut (this is called a **reverse-angle shot**) to show the opposite wall of the room, the one at which she was looking in the previous shot. We see her go to the wall, on which her sketches are hanging. She looks back at the TV and then at the sketches — clarifying the connection between her own attempts to understand the mound image through art and the broadcast image of the monument — and then begins to take one sketch down. The camera moves to the left and in close, to end the shot with a close view of another of Jillian's drawings. Then there is a straight cut to the monument on Roy's TV set. This restates, quite forcefully, the relatedness of the three central signs: Jillian's pastel sketch, Roy's clay model, and the televised image of Devil's Tower.

The project of this sequence has been the interpretation of a sign, a sign that appears in three fourths of the shots in this sequence. (It cannot be called a scene because it takes place at more than one location.) The audience has been allowed to interpret the sign only a minute or so before Roy has. Now Roy looks away from the set to his model and stands up for a full view of it. The TV, no longer a primary source of information, is allowed to leave the frame, and that transfers our attention from the TV set to the model as Roy's attention is redirected. The sequence ends with a reverse-angle shot of Roy's face as he looks at the model and listens to the TV, which is now repeating an instruction to "Stay out of the area!" As the music peaks, Roy marshalls his distrust of the government and the media and realizes that the news story is a blind and that people are being kept out of the area on false pretenses. So we are not surprised when the next sequence begins (with a straight cut and a different, more ugent music track) with a shot of Roy in his truck, reading a map and already in Wyoming.

This final shot of Roy's looking at the offscreen model and listening to the offscreen TV serves to focus and summarize two major themes: the identity of the mound shape and the problem of interpretation. The latter includes not just the difficulty of deciphering a sign but also the reliability of certain sources of information. The most important element of the soundtrack here is the command, "Stay out of the area!", and the visual element that coordinates with these words is Roy's smiling, brightening face. This coordination is, of course, an opposition, as what Roy's expression communicates is his realization that he ought to get *into* the area as soon as possible. The government-controlled media have given him valid information while attempting to mislead him, and the key to understanding such a communication is distrust of the source: the realization that the Establishment is of course lying. This returns us to a further consideration of the Budweiser commercial.

The "king" that is coming is neither a deity nor a beer; the "call" that is so difficult to interpret is not scriptural nor commercial; you have not "said it all — la-la-la" when you say "Bud," even if the aliens will turn out to be our buddies. There is more to say, to understand, and to do in life than simply to fall in with some commercial procession or to live as if in a soap opera. Although all the ironics noted earlier in relation to this commercial remain appropriate, it is important to add the observation that the commercial *trivializes* Roy's quest, reducing it to terms of merchandising and product preference, the programmed solution to an artificial problem (which beer to buy).

Most of us distrust commercials automatically, but most of us also tend to believe what we hear on network newscasts — or at least we begin with a posture of tentative acceptance. But the Devil's Tower news bulletin is a lie, and Roy knows enough to dismiss it. What the newscast has communicated honestly — its only truthful element — is what Devil's Tower looks like. In this sense the sign of the monument (the dominant element in the mise-en-scène here, whether drawn, sculpted, or broadcast) has itself the authority of truth, the ability to cut through any corruptions or perversions of the process of communication. It is a powerfully authentic sign, and this authoritative presence is forceful — however enigmatic — wherever it appears.

Roy and Jillian are both able to seize on this authentic sign despite the corrupted information context. When they crouch before their sets, they are not kneeling before the altar of television but are expressing awe and gratitude in the presence of the solution to their quests, the picture of the monument itself. It is a truthful image, a fragment of the world given meaning.

The phony aspects of the newscast are as opposed to the communication of truth as the commercial is indifferent to the resolution of authentic quests. It is clear, then, that this sequence is concerned not only with the problem of interpreting an enigmatic sign but also with the importance of sorting out truthful from false information within a corrupted signifying structure (a lying newscast in the service of a "me-first" government). It is, after all, a central problem with communication systems that they can be used to distort information as well as to convey it, and any sophisticated audience knows the importance of being able to discriminate between what is true and what is presented as being true.

In this context, it is worth noting another montage effect confined to the broadcast itself: the end of the commercial is immediately followed by the beginning of the newscast. This implies that the newscast is another kind of commercial — in fact, a commercial for the government. This **sound cut** is a subtle demonstration of governmental manipulation and perversion of the communications media, and in the context of a movie about the discovery of authentic communication, both the media (whether or not the newscasters are aware of reporting a hoax) and the government are guilty of the worst sin against human progress. Language is an urgent business, and this movie knows it.

This sequence encapsulates the whole project of *Close Encounters*. Its political perspective, its realistic approach to science fiction (as opposed to the "space opera" approach of George Lucas's *Star Wars*, also 1977), and its idealism all contribute to, and can be expressed in terms of, one central theme. That theme is the discovery of the possibility of communication — not just contact — between species, the search for a common language, a meeting ground. The story line in this sequence takes Roy from a posture of frustration and confusion to the moment when he at last understands what the image of the mound means — and one shot further, to the moment when he understands the full meaning of the newscast. Though it shows her less often, it brings Jillian along the same route. They have discovered the referent of the sign, after having been teased by the conviction that the mound image must be not simply a shape but a signifier, that — as Roy says — "this must mean something."

Roy's and Jillian's quests for the meaning of this sign have been paralleled throughout the film with the attempts of a scientific team to link up their own experiments in a language of gesture with the musical code (the five tones) received from the aliens. This attempt leads to two climaxes: one in which tones and colors are integrated in a language exchange with the aliens, and another in which the chief scientist (played by French director François Truffaut, a maker of invaluable pictures) communicates with one of the aliens by using five hand gestures that correspond to the five tones. The latter, in fact, is the climax of the entire movie, an instance of person-to-"person" communication having little to do with words as we understand them and nothing at all to do with computers, high tech, or commercial television. The meaning of these tones and gestures is never spelled out for the audience by being translated into words, but that matters little in comparison with the evidence of communication itself.

The terms of this new language are color, sound, gesture, and — if we include the monument — shape. Those are also major terms of the language of cinema, its means of and vehicles for signification. So the opening of a new era of communication between species is also, in this context, a reflexive praise of cinema and of the vehicle it offers for the expansion and enrichment of human communication. Finding the referent of the sign by making the connection between one image (televised) and another (sculpted), Roy prepares himself to join the new community. He draws this connection by comparing two signs, and the film itself performs the same task through its own clarifying and integrating devices, montage and mise-en-scène. What Roy, Jillian, the scientists, and the audience all discover is something akin to cinema itself: a language that transcends the verbal, and a means of realizing the connections that exist among the discrete fragments of experience.

From Shot to Sequence

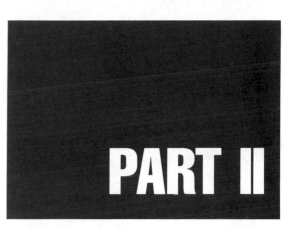

PART II

1. Raw Materials

As an integrated, finished product, the motion picture is familiar to us as something capable of being projected: a series of images and sound information, synchronized on a ribbon of celluloid. From the perspective of the audience, the images are reflected from a screen as the sounds are emitted by one or more speakers. The theater becomes an environment of programmed light and moving air. But behind this nearly immaterial experience are a great many pieces of equipment and a host of practical considerations.

In this part of the book we will be starting from the raw materials of filmmaking — the basic physical materials and the most representative equipment — and then we will go on to consider a chain of aesthetic units and structures, from the frame to the shot and soundtrack, all the way to the scene and the sequence. Having achieved an overview of the most basic theoretical, analytic, and critical considerations in Part I, we are now ready to consider "the thing itself": film and the fundamental elements of cinematic structure. Once these have been understood, we will go on in Part III to take a look at all of the specific jobs involved in making a movie and at the people whose work is, like the cinema itself, a functional integration of the material and the aesthetic.

The Camera and the Eye

The eye is designed to receive images in the form of light, and so is the camera. Even if one is an organ controlled by the brain and the other is a machine controlled by a photographer, both can be thought of as photosensitive instruments.

The Still Camera. Fig. 2-2 is a simplified diagram of a box camera. Its basic elements are a lens, an iris diaphragm, a shutter, a light-tight (perfectly dark) box containing a sheet of film, and a viewfinder.

Light is reflected off an object (the photographic subject) in all directions, and some of that light enters the **lens**, a curved piece of glass. The lens used in most cameras is curved outward on both sides (**biconvex**), and it took its name from the lentil seed of which it reminded the ancients. It is also a **converging** lens, which means that it bends the light rays as they pass through it and causes them to converge at a point behind it. Because of its shape, it **refracts** the light (bends it as it passes *through* the glass) rather than **reflects** it (bounces it back). The **viewfinder** allows the photographer to see which part of the visual field is being photographed. The viewfinder may be lined up with the lens, more or less like a rifle sight; a through-the-lens, or **reflex**, viewfinder — used in most professional movie cameras — shows the photographer *exactly* what the lens sees, thanks to a system of internal mirrors.

Behind the lens, an **iris diaphragm** allows only the desired amount of light to continue on its way into the body of the camera. The iris is a system of thin metal plates (**Fig. 2-3**), and the hole at its center can be made larger or smaller. That hole, or opening, is

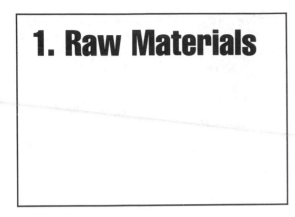

Dark interior
Shutter
Iris diaphragm
Film
Light path
Lens

Figure 2-2

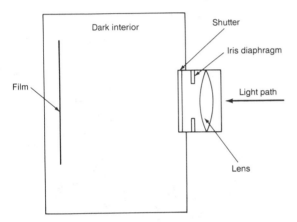

Figure 2-3

called the **lens aperture**. The wider the aperture, the more light passes through it. There are many kinds of film, and each has a limited range within which it can produce acceptable results. If too much light hits the film, the picture will be **overexposed** and the negative will be very *dense*; too little, and it will be **underexposed** and *thin*.

Next the light encounters a metal barrier that can be opened or closed completely: the **shutter**. It is opened only during the instant of exposure, and it can be set to remain open for varying lengths of time. The longer it is open, the more light passes through it. The interior of the camera is dark so that only the light that has passed through the lens, the iris, and the shutter reaches the film. The film itself is coated with a photosensitive surface called the **emulsion**, a gelantinous medium filled with silver halide crystals that turn black when they are exposed to light.

The Eye. The camera was designed on the model of the human eye (**Fig. 2-4**). The eye has a lens, an iris, a dark chamber, and a light-sensitive retina. The pupil is its aperture, the eyelid its shutter. The crucial difference is that the retina does not have to be changed for each new image — nor does it keep a permanent record of an image.

As light enters the eye, it is refracted by the cornea and passes through a thick transparent liquid called the aqueous humor. The iris, a pigmented membrane, involuntarily expands and contracts to compensate for the dimness or brightness of the visual field, thus varying the size of the hole in its center, the pupil. The pupil appears black because the interior of the eye is dark, filled with another thick liquid called the vitreous humor.

After passing through the pupil, the light is refracted by the lens of the eye. This lens can be made fatter or thinner thanks to the action of the ciliary muscles, which squeeze and pull it. The width of this lens determines which objects in the visual field will be in focus, that is, which light rays will converge on the retina. In a camera, focus is manipulated by moving the lens closer to or farther from the film.

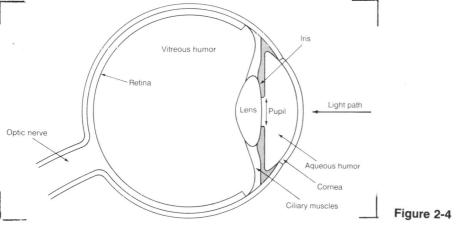

Figure 2-4

When the light strikes the retina, its cells react and send signals to the brain along the optic nerve. Whereas the retina can process an image and be done with it, the photographer must set a fresh piece of film into position to record each new image. And that is where the movie camera comes into play.

The Movie Camera. **Fig. 2-5** is a schematic diagram of a movie camera, and it shows the path that the film takes from the feed reel, through its exposure position, and to the take-up reel. To flesh out this diagram, **Figs. 2-6** through **2-8** show a 35mm camera manufactured by Moviecam.

Although there are many movie cameras whose feed and take-up reels are located within the body of the camera, that severely limits the amount of film that can be exposed without reloading. Virtually all professional movie cameras can be fitted with light-tight boxes called **magazines**. The Moviecam magazine is shown in its closed and open positions in **Fig. 2-7**. The magazine is usually attached to the top or rear of the camera body, much as the lens is attached to the front of the body (**Fig. 2-6**). The magazine houses a spool of unexposed film (the **feed reel**) and another spool onto which the film is wound after it has been exposed (the **take-up reel**). The film is threaded from the magazine, into the camera body, and then back into the magazine (**Fig. 2-8**).

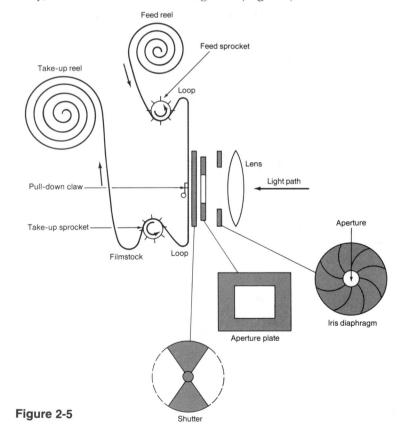

Figure 2-5

Figure 2-6

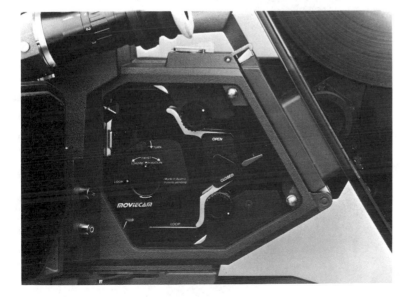

Figure 2-7

Figure 2-8

Figure 2-9

Figure 2-10

The place where the film is exposed to light is called the **film gate**. Film gates vary in design, but most of them are fitted with a **pressure plate** that keeps the film flat during the instant of exposure and with an **aperture plate** that determines the proportions of the frame.

Throughout most of the history of the cinema, the shape of the rectangle through which the light passed, and thus the shape of the frame, was four units wide by three units high. Now called the "Academy ratio," this shape is usually expressed not as 4 : 3 but as an aspect ratio of 1.33 : 1. The most common aspect ratio in use today, however, is 1.85 : 1. Fortunately, a supplementary aperture plate can be changed as easily as a lens.

The sprocket holes along the sides of the film allow it to be engaged and advanced by sprocket wheels (**Fig. 2-9**). In the film gate there is an even more precise mechanism for advancing the film *and stopping it* during exposure; it is called the **pulldown claw**. Inspired by the mechanism that drives the needle of a sewing machine, it converts the rotation of the shaft from the motor into an up-and-down, forward-and-backward movement. The claw moves forward into the film path and engages the sprocket holes, then pulls them and the film down, and then retracts. Then it moves up again and forward to engage the next set of sprocket holes.

All of this rapid jerking would tear the film if there were no **loops** above and below the film gate. The loops provide some slack, but not so much that the emulsion will be scratched by the interior walls of the camera.

The motor of the camera may be spring-loaded, like that of the 16mm Bolex camera shown in **Fig. 2-10**; the crank, shown in its disengaged position, is the handle at the side of the camera. More often the motor is electrical, and it is driven either by a portable generator or by a battery. A Cine 60 battery belt is shown in **Fig. 2-11**. Although the motor usually runs at 24 fps, it can be adjusted to run slower or faster than that. The Bolex, as you may be able to see from the dial on its side, can be set at any rate between 8 and 64 fps. **Slow motion** is achieved by shooting at *more* than 24 fps; **fast motion**, by shooting at *less* than 24 fps. When an action shot at 48 fps is projected at 24 fps, it will take twice as long to show, yielding the effect of movement at half-normal speed.

Figure 2-11

The motor drives both the pull-down mechanism and the shutter, whose actions must be coordinated exactly. The shutter of a movie camera usually has one or two **blades**, and it turns in a circle. The one shown in **Fig. 2-5** is a two-bladed shutter; a one-bladed shutter resembles a pie with a huge wedge cut out of it, and the size of that wedge, in degrees, identifies the shutter. Thus a 180° shutter is a hemisphere; most are between 120° and 175°. At 24 fps, a 180° shutter will let in light for one forty-eighth of a second. The cinematographer does not have as much freedom as the still photographer when it comes to setting the shutter speed, as the normal upper limit is well under one twenty-fourth of a second (under one twenty-fourth because it takes some time for the film to advance while the shutter is closed). The normal exposure time is one fiftieth of a second. For that reason, most movie frames are slightly blurred, though this blurring becomes unnoticeable in projection. Many movie cameras are equipped with a **variable shutter** whose degree of openness can be adjusted, yielding greater control over exposure.

At the instant of exposure, the shutter's open area is between the film and the lens, allowing the light to pass through. While the film is being advanced, a blade blocks the light. During that instant, a mirror on the blade reflects the scene into a reflex viewfinder.

The line along which the film is moved through the gate is called the **film plane**. The cinematographer focuses the lens by varying the distance between the film plane — the place where the film is — and the optical center of the lens.

After leaving the film gate, the film makes its way over a take-up sprocket wheel and past a series of rollers back into the magazine, where it is rolled up on the take-up reel.

The Movie Projector. The essential difference between a movie camera and a movie projector is that the light comes from inside the projector and from outside the camera. But there are other differences as well.

The majority of projectors in use today can run only at 24 fps, though many have a switch that allows them to run at 16 or 18 fps to approximate silent speed. Projectors have no need for exposure controls and thus no iris diaphragm, though they do have interchangeable aperture plates. The shutter may have up to five or six blades in order to show each frame several times and render the flicker less noticeable. The lens is designed to **throw** an image and to make it converge on a screen.

The film path in a projector is slightly more intricate than in a camera. The film is wound off a feed reel, is advanced by a feed sprocket, and is formed into loops above and below the film gate. After reaching the take-up sprocket, however, its movement is smoothed out by several rollers in order for the soundtrack to be read continuously by a magnetic head or by a photoelectric cell. We shall take up the soundtrack in a later section, but for now it is enough to note that the soundtrack that is meant to accompany

Figure 2-12

the frame in the gate must be read when the film is moving evenly rather than jerking up and down, and so it is usually located 21 frames ahead of the picture on the same strip of celluloid. "Ahead" means nearer to the take-up reel; the start of a length of film is called the **head**, and the end is called the **tail**. After passing by the sound reader, the film is wound onto the take-up reel.

The reels on a projector can accommodate only a certain amount of film, depending on the design of the projector. In the silent period, the upper limit was 1,000 feet of 35mm film, and that length was — and still is — called a **reel**. Throughout the sound period, the majority of theatrical projectors have been loaded with **double reels**, that is, single but larger metal reels that can hold up to 2,000 feet of 35mm film. Feature films are longer than 20 minutes, and so it has always been common to use two projectors and to **change over** from one projector to another as one reel ends and another begins, a shift that is called a **changeover** and that is flagged with **changeover marks**. The marks themselves are tiny white dots or circles that appear briefly in the upper right corner of the frame, just before the end of each reel. A changeover mark from *Napoleon* can be seen in **Fig. 2-12**. (When the film is projected through an anamorphic lens, the marks widen to ovals. Thus if you see elliptical changeover marks in a theater, you know you're watching scope; if you see them in a flat or TV print, you know you're watching pan-and-scan.) The marks appear briefly, twice; in order for the projectionist to see them, each circle appears for 4 consecutive frames.

At the head of each reel is a strip of film with numbers that count down, usually to 3, called the **head leader**. From the start of the countdown to the first frame of picture is a distance of 12 feet (in 35mm). The last few feet of the head leader are opaque. By the time the reel being shown (call it Reel A) is nearly over, Reel B has been loaded into the other projector, perhaps with the head leader's "7" or "9" in the gate (that is, in projection position). Upon seeing the first changeover mark, the projectionist turns on the *motor* of Projector B. The two marks are separated by a distance of 11 feet, and in that interval, Projector B has time to get up to speed. (Knowing the projector intimately, the projectionist has learned which number to start from.) Upon seeing the second changeover mark, which ends 20 frames from the last frame of Reel A (after which comes the **tail leader**), the projectionist has just under a second to switch on the *lamp* in Projector B and to switch *off* the lamp in Projector A (or, leaving both lamps on, to block one beam and unblock the other). If a changeover is performed properly, the audience will never notice it; if it is performed perfectly, the first frame of Reel B will be gleaming in the gate at the instant that the last frame of Reel A calls it a night.

In order to avoid changeovers, it is now possible to splice the reels of an entire feature together and to wind all that film onto a horizontal metal platter. The film runs over rollers into the projector and then back onto another horizontal platter. These platters, which might be thought of as open-faced magazines, are incredibly heavy when fully loaded, and even they cannot hold much more than two hours of film; thus for those longer movies that rarely are booked into cineplexes (rarely, for just this reason), an intermission must be scheduled in order to allow time to reload the single projector.

There are several different light sources that can be used in projectors, from high-intensity lamps to carbon arcs. In a standard 35mm projector, two rods of carbon are brought into proximity (**Fig. 2-13**), and an electric current jumps, or *arcs*, between them (**Fig. 2-14**). (These frames, like **Figs. 2-3** and **2-9**, come from Vertov's *The Man With a Movie Camera*.) An **arc-light** projector produces the best possible light, a pure white with an even brightness. But the rods are consumed in less than an hour (another reason for changeovers), and their burning produces carbon monoxide. Trading quality for convenience, other projectors use lamps that last many hours and produce no gases. The majority of 16mm projectors use a **tungsten-halogen lamp** or a **quartz arc lamp**. The best alternative to the standard carbon arc is the **xenon lamp**; only a trained eye can tell the difference between the light from a xenon lamp and that from a carbon arc, and the lamp lasts longer. The xenon lamp is found in the majority of new 35mm projectors.

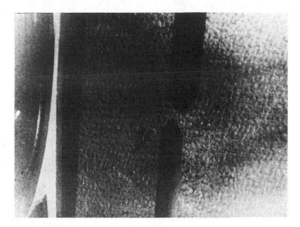

Figure 2-13

Figure 2-14

Film

Unexposed film is referred to as **filmstock** or **raw stock**. Once it has been exposed, it is usually called, simply, film; a specific length of exposed film is called **footage**.

Filmstock consists of two materials: a transparent, flexible support called the **base** and a light-sensitive coating called the **emulsion**. The only essential difference between filmstock and film, in these terms, is that the emulsion — the image-bearing area — on processed film is no longer photosensitive. **Leader**, which is primarily found at the heads and tails of reels and has many uses in film editing, is clear or colored film base.

Base. From the 1880s through the 1940s, most base was made of *cellulose nitrate*. **Nitrate film**, as it was called, produced an extremely sharp and richly detailed image. Unfortunately, it was highly inflammable — even explosive. Flaherty once lit a cigarette while working on early footage for *Nanook*, and not only the entire negative but also the editing shack were blown to cinders. Nitrate base had a tendency to shrink with time and could not tolerate moisture, so that after 10 or 20 years, unless they had been stored under ideal conditions, nitrate prints could not be projected.

Since 1951 a relatively noninflammable support made of *cellulose tri-acetate* (an improvement over cellulose acetate) and called **safety base** has been used exclusively. Although its image-bearing qualities are inferior to those of nitrate base, safety base will not blow up in your hands and will not shrink or deform as readily as nitrate did. A good proportion of the budgets of many film archives is devoted to transferring nitrate prints to safety-base stock.

A new polyester base called **Estar** is especially flexible and scratch-resistant; it is used only for high-wear prints.

Emulsion. Most photographic emulsions consist of photosensitive silver halides — usually silver bromo-iodide — suspended in gelatin. This gelatin includes several organic compounds, one of the most bizarre and highly prized of which is prepared from the ears and cheeks of calves that have grazed on certain ranges. The gelatin dissolves in warm water, so that it is easy to apply to the base, then chills to a solid gel whose flexibility improves the life of the stock and keeps it from becoming brittle. The gel allows processing solutions to reach the suspended crystals easily, yet keeps the crystals from clumping together. Its organic compounds improve the light sensitivity of the silver halides.

Once they have been developed, the silver halides turn to metallic silver, each crystal of which is a unit of film **grain**. This grain becomes noticeable when a very small negative is blown up on a large screen, when the emulsion has been developed at a very high temperature, and under certain other conditions. An extremely **grainy** film resembles a field of madly jiggling salt and pepper. In general, **fine-grain** emulsions produce a perfectly detailed, clean image and are *slower* — that is, they require more light for proper exposure. (See **Fig. 2-53** for an example of a grainy image.)

Film emulsion comes in two major varieties: negative and reversal. **Negative** stock, the kind used by most professionals, yields an image whose black and white values are reversed. This happens because silver halide crystals turn black when exposed to light. When the negative is printed onto a second strip of negative stock, these values are reversed again, and the result is a **positive** copy whose black and white values match those of the original subject. In color negatives the situation is similar: the color values are reversed, and the negative bears the complementary color, that is, a blue sky will appear orange, and a blue-green shirt will appear red. When a print is made from a color negative, these values are reversed to normal.

Reversal emulsion, designed for reversal processing, produces a direct positive image. The same film that is run through the camera can be projected, because it has been processed to yield normal color or black and white values. As a camera stock, reversal is the most common choice for amateur use, where it is expected that no prints will be made from the original, and for newswork, where a projectable copy may be needed almost immediately. Projection scratches film and exposes it to dust, and it is virtually unheard of for a professional filmmaker to project a camera original. Instead the original is stored in a dark, dust-free environment from which it is removed only to be cut into final form or to be used to make intermediate prints. Reversal is quite useful as a laboratory stock — for example, when striking a printing negative directly from the camera negative.

A print is a copy of a film. Because a print has a useful life of less than 400 runs through a *clean* projector before it is unacceptably scratched or torn, it is important to have a source of new prints. The **camera original** — the negative or reversal stock that was run through the camera and then edited — is copied onto special **printing stock**, and this **intermediate print** is used for making **release prints**, which are the only professional prints intended to be projected. Printing stocks are typically more fine-grained than camera stocks.

Another kind of stock, **magnetic film** or **mag stock**, is not intended to be run through a camera. It is coated with magnetic oxide, just as is magnetic tape, and it carries the soundtrack. It has the same base and comes in the same sizes as filmstock, and it is perforated so that it can be kept in synchronization with the picture track during the editing process and sometimes during projection.

Small quantities of dyes are mixed into the emulsion just before it is dried onto the base. Without these dyes, filmstock would be sensitive only to blue and ultraviolet light. Most silent films were shot on **orthochromatic** stock, which is sensitive to blue and green. **Panchromatic film** is sensitive to the entire visible spectrum, from blue to red; since 1926 it has been the most widely used black-and-white stock. Most color filmstock has three layers of emulsion separated by binding and color-filtration layers, allowing each layer to respond to a primary color or its complement. Color stock will be discussed at length in a later section.

Gauge. Filmstock comes in several standard **gauges**, or widths, of which the most common are 8mm, 16mm, 35mm, 65mm, and 70mm. 8mm (as Super8) is used almost exclusively by amateurs. 16mm offers the least expensive results that can be considered professionally acceptable. 35mm is the standard professional gauge. 65mm is a camera stock, and 70mm is exclusively a printing stock. The wider the stock, the heavier and more expensive the film — and, in most cases, the better the picture quality.

Fig. 2-15 shows three lengths of film, each of them six frames (¼ second) long. They have been reproduced life-size. In order to facilitate comparison, they all show the same image: part of the head leader on a reel, just before the countdown starts. The one on the left is 70mm, 35mm is in the middle, and 16mm is on the right.

They have been turned upside down and flipped left to right, so that "PICTURE START" will be easily legible. Remember that any biconvex lens, whether in the camera or in the eye, inverts the image. In order for the image to look correct on the screen, the action of the projector lens must be taken into account; thus when film is loaded into a projector, its head faces *downward*. In this figure, the head is near the top of the page, the tail near the

Figure 2-15

bottom. The diamond will be projected one sixth of a second *after* "PICTURE START." In projection position, then, with the head down and as seen by the operator (facing the screen and looking through the film), the 35mm soundtrack is to the right. In viewing position, however — as projected on the screen or printed in this book (see **Figure 2-16**), the 35mm soundtrack is to the left of the upright, frontal image.

When you look at this figure, it should be clear why a wider gauge can yield a better image. Each silver crystal is an information storage unit, and only so many of them can be crammed into a square inch. What appears as a comb in the background of a 35mm image may well appear as a fat line in the background of an 8mm image. The larger frame is capable of including finer detail; it can also, assuming that screen size and screen/projector distance are constant for purposes of comparison, yield a less grainy image. The standard 35mm frame area is more than four times larger than the standard 16mm frame area, and all things being equal, a 35mm print of *Casablanca* will have almost five times more visual information than a 16mm print of *Casablanca*.

16mm film has one sprocket hole per frame, directly adjacent to the frame line. In projection position, the sprocket holes are on the right, and the optical or magnetic soundtrack is on the left. The sample in **Fig. 2-15** has no soundtrack, but the area where one would go has been blacked out, so that the frame area (in this case, "PICTURE START") appears to be set off to one side.

35mm film has eight sprocket holes per frame, four on each side (assuming that the camera has a four-perforation pulldown). In projection position, the optical track runs between the frame area and the right sprocket holes. Some 35mm stereo formats use four magnetic soundtracks: one along each outer edge of the film, and one between each line of sprocket holes and the frame area. 35mm has a much wider frame line than 16mm and is easier to splice.

70mm film is used to make prints of films shot on **65mm** camera stock (the extra width provides room for the soundtracks) or blown up from 35mm anamorphic (more on that later). It has ten sprocket holes per frame, five on each side. At the frame line, on the right side, it also has a small hole between two of the sprockets. During projection, a registration pin engages this hole and keeps the film absolutely steady. 70mm prints usually have six magnetic soundtracks: one along each outer edge of the film, and two between each line of sprocket holes and the frame area.

Two new formats have recently been developed. **Imax** uses 65mm stock in the camera and 70mm stock in projection, but it runs the film horizontally rather than vertically. This yields a frame area just over 70mm wide and 52mm high, capable of storing approximately three times as much detail as a standard 70mm frame (which is approximately 52mm wide and 23mm high). It runs at 24 fps and produces a large, very sharp and detailed image. When projected onto a curved screen or an overhead dome, it is called **Omnimax**. **Showscan**, developed by Douglas Trumbull in the late 1970s and first marketed in 1983, runs 70mm prints at 60 fps. Because so many more phases of movement are captured, even an individual raindrop — which appears as a streak in most films shot at 24 fps — can be seen distinctly, and the spokes of a turning wheel, which appear to move backward at 24 fps, will be seen as turning in the proper direction. Audiences whose pulse rates and galvanic skin responses were monitored while watching films made to be projected at different speeds showed the highest responses when the image ran at 60–72 fps, perhaps because of the denser flow of information.

Both Imax and Showscan — and some conventional formats — have picture and sound on separate, synchronized lengths of stock. The sound, on mag stock, is read by a machine whose motor is mechanically linked, or **interlocked**, with that of the projector. This is called **double system sound**. When picture and sound are on the same strip of film, that is called **single system sound**. Most movies are edited in double system and projected in single system.

Lenses, Exposure, and Focus

A lens consists of one or more pieces of glass, called **elements**. Each element has a particular *refractive index*, a characteristic way of bending the light that passes through it. To design a lens to do a specific job, lensmakers assemble various elements based on their individual characteristics and on the ways in which they work together.

Lenses are identified in terms of a number of characteristics, of which the most important are speed, focal length, and squeeze. The quality of a lens is a matter of its sharpness and resolution. **Sharpness** refers to the lens's ability to produce an image with clear, well-defined *edges*. **Resolution** refers to the resolving power of a lens, its ability to produce fine detail *within* the image.

Speed. The **speed** of a lens is its widest possible *f*-stop setting. An *f*-**stop** is an expression of the aperture of a lens at a particular iris diaphragm setting, and it is derived by dividing the diameter of the diaphragm opening into the focal length of the lens. As the apertures get smaller, the *f*-numbers get larger. This happens because the smaller the diameter of the iris becomes, the more it can be divided into the focal length. Each standard iris aperture lets in twice (or half) as much light as the next standard setting. The standard *f*-numbers — in the order of widest to narrowest aperture — are *f*1, *f*1.4, *f*2, *f*2.8, *f*4, *f*5.6, *f*8, *f*11, *f*16, and *f*22. A lens set at *f*8 will let in twice as much light per second as one set at *f*11, but only half as much light as one set at *f*5.6. The larger the maximum *f*-stop, the **faster** the speed of that particular lens — that is, the more rapidly it can gather light.

Even at the same aperture settings, different lenses vary in the efficiency with which their elements transmit light. Many professional lenses are calibrated not in *f*-stops but in **T-stops**, which allow for these differences. In a lens with 100% efficiency, the T-stops and *f*-stops would be the same. By regulating exposure via T-stops, one can be sure that the desired amount of light will actually reach the film. If the lens is relatively inefficient, and *f*8 worth of light is necessary for proper exposure, T8 for that lens will be slightly wider than *f*8 would be on a perfectly efficient lens.

Focal Length. A **focal point** is a point at which light rays converge (an instance of **real focus**) or from which they appear to diverge (an instance of **virtual focus**).

Principal focus is computed in terms of the behavior of parallel rays as they pass through a lens system. Any lens has two principal foci. In the case of a biconvex refracting lens (see **Fig. 2-17**), there are *anterior* and *posterior* points of principal focus. (For a reflecting lens, both points may be anterior.) The posterior is the side nearer the film. Light rays appear to *diverge* from the **anterior focal point** — that is, from the object on which the lens is focused — and do *converge* at the **posterior focal point**, the film plane.

When the lens is focused at **infinity** (for a sharp image of a far-away object), the rays from that object are *parallel* as they enter the lens, and they converge on the film (that is, at the film plane). The **focal length** of a lens is the distance from the film plane to the optical center of the lens when it is focused at infinity. (The optical center of a lens is not always halfway through the glass, but that is a convenient way to think of it.) A 50mm lens will produce a sharp image of a faraway object when its optical center is 50mm from the film plane; the lens may be adjusted to focus on nearer objects, but it will still be a 50mm lens.

A lens with a fixed focal length is called a **prime** or **primary lens**. One with a variable focal length is called a **zoom lens**. Prime lenses come in three categories: short, normal, and long.

A short or **wide-angle lens** takes in a broader field of view than a normal lens. A long lens — the longest are called **telephoto** lenses — takes in a narrower field of view, which means that it has a higher factor of *magnification*, filling the frame with a relatively small or faraway object. The most commonly used prime lens is the **normal lens**, so called because it reproduces *perspective* much as seen by the human eye, and it has a field of view midway between wide-angle and telephoto. It is important to remember that focal length affects perspective just as much as it does the broadness or tightness of the field of view (magnification).

A normal lens is "normal" for a particular film gauge. The same magnification and perspective effects will be obtained if a 50mm lens is used with 35mm film and if a 25mm lens is used with 16mm film. For this discussion, focal lengths are given as if the film gauge were 35mm. In current Hollywood practice, which is referenced to the widescreen format, 25–32mm is considered normal. 14–20mm are commonly used wide-angle lenses. 50–75mm are "tight" lenses and are often used to provide a closer view of the subject from the normal camera position. 100–150mm are the ones usually referred to as "long," and from 200–1200mm they are called "telephoto." Broadly speaking, however, a **short lens** is one with a focal length of less than 25mm, and a **long lens** is one with a focal length greater than 50mm.

Perspective. A short lens tends to *exaggerate* depth relationships. The nearer an object is to a wide-angle lens, the deeper, fatter, and more spherical it will appear. A long lens tends to *flatten* depth relationships. Perspective relations depend on the *real distances* between objects and the lens (or observer). The farther from the observer, the closer together equidistant planes appear to be.

Long lenses are most often used to give a view of an object that is far from the camera, but they do not actually *bring* that object closer; instead they gather light from a small area of the visual field. The perspective relations are the same in that magnified area as they are in the complete visual field. In an extreme telephoto shot, then, the planes of perspective appear to be separated by less space than is actually between them, and the field appears to have been flattened. A telephoto lens can make a traffic jam look worse than it is.

Near the end of Mike Nichols's *The Graduate* (1967), Dustin Hoffman is shown running down a sidewalk, in a hurry to stop his girlfriend from marrying someone else. A telephoto lens flattened the field and gave the impression that the character was covering little distance although he was running as fast as he could, and this let the audience share his anxiety that he might not arrive in time. If a wide-angle lens had been used, the character would have appeared to be nearing the camera much more rapidly.

Zooming. The modern zoom lens came into general use only in the 1950s. Before then (leaving aside experimental and limited zoom technology dating from the late 1920s), if the cameraman wanted to shift from a wide to a narrow field of view, the lens would have to be changed or the camera would have to be moved. It is important not to think of a forward or backward camera *movement* as a zoom, and in fact they look very different from one another on film.

The most common term for a forward, backward, or lateral movement of the camera is a **track** or a **tracking movement** (also called **trucking**). When a camera moves closer to an object, it **tracks forward** or **in**; when it retreats, it **tracks back** or **out**. When a zoom lens is adjusted from a short to a long focal length, that is a **forward zoom** or a **zoom in**; the reverse is a **back zoom** or a **zoom out**.

One of the basic ways we perceive depth is by noticing the relationships between background and foreground planes (or objects situated at those planes, that is, those distances from the point of observation). When the camera tracks forward or backward, these relationships change — not only spatially, but also in time. In a zoom, the spatial relations between foreground and background objects do *not* change with the passage of time, even though the field of view does. Because the field appears deep when viewed through a wide-angle lens and shallow when viewed through a telephoto lens, a forward zoom can mash its subject flat.

Zoom lenses are identified by their range of focal lengths: a 20–200mm zoom lens can be set at any focal length between 20mm and 200mm. In a good zoom lens, the same objects remain in focus while the focal length is changed. The act of changing focal length while the camera is running is called **zooming**. The great advantage of a zoom lens is *not*, however, that it makes zooming possible, but that it is an integrated, perfectly matched lens system with consistent light-transmitting characteristics.

When one is using several prime lenses, care must be taken to ensure that all of them have the same sharpness, resolving power, and efficiency. Because the zoom is, effectively, one lens, its elements will handle light in the same way regardless of whether it is set at 45mm or at 145mm, and in that sense it offers the cameraman the equivalent of a matched set of, say, 100 lenses. The zoom lens is extremely convenient when one is framing an image; the only drawback is a slight loss of sharpness and resolving power, relative to what can be obtained with a top-quality prime lens.

Cameramen (male and female) disagree about the merits of zooming during, rather than while setting up, a shot. On the one hand, the zoom is an aesthetic device like any other, capable of being put to a variety of creative uses, including but not limited to the rapid forward zoom's sudden concentration on a detail within a field. On the other hand, some filmmakers use the zoom only as a cheap substitute for a track shot. It is, after all, easier than moving the camera platform. The trouble is that a zoom can always be recognized *as* a zoom because of its effect on perspective; what it shows, above all, is that the camera has *not* moved. That can of course be a desirable effect. In *The War Game* Watkins zoomed in on an execution in order to emphasize that the cameraman had not been allowed to approach any closer.

In *Vertigo*, Hitchcock exploited the perspective differences between the zoom and the tracking movement to great effect. The hero, Scottie (James Stewart) is afraid of heights. At several points during the movie, he looks down the side of a building or down a stairwell (see color **Figs. C-4** and **C-5**). As he looks, the stairwell appears to become much deeper. Hitchcock accomplished this effect by simultaneously tracking in and zooming out. (He used a model stairwell set on its side; all movements were horizontal rather than vertical.) The backward zoom increased the impression of depth within the image. The forward track compensated for the zoom, keeping the same parts of the model in view. The shallow perspective produced by the telephoto setting can be seen in **Fig. C-4**; the deep perspective produced by the wide-angle setting can be seen in **Fig. C-5**. The fact that more of the side window can be seen in **Fig. C-5** is a giveaway that the camera tracked forward.

Squeeze. Lenses vary according to how they treat horizontal and vertical relationships. **Spherical** or **flat** lenses, which are by far the more commonly used, preserve the normal horizontal and vertical relationships found in the subject. **Anamorphic** or **scope** lenses are lenses that **squeeze** (compress) or **unsqueeze** (expand) the horizontal dimension without affecting the vertical dimension. In many wide-screen processes (to be taken up in a later section), the anamorphic camera lens squeezes a wide field of view horizontally, yielding an image that is half as wide as normal but just as high, so that the wide field can fit on the normal-sized film. **Fig. 2-16**, from a 35mm print of David Lean's *Doctor Zhivago* (1965), shows two sequential squeezed shots; you can just see the splice on the frame line. During projection, another anamorphic lens exactly reverses this distortion, spreading the image out and restoring the original height-to-width relationships. In *Jules and Jim* (1961), Truffaut let the scope lens spread out flat, nonanamorphic newsreel battle footage for an unforgettable effect.

A spherical lens is not actually flat. The term arose in the 1950s when CinemaScope® (the first major 35mm anamorphic process,

Figure 2-16

from which "scope" was derived as a general term) and other wide formats introduced a deeply curved screen. "Flat" films can be shown on flat or slightly curved screens. When a CinemaScope film is projected onto a flat screen in a large theater and the center of the field is in focus, the outer edges are too far from the lens and appear out of focus; the curved screen keeps its left, center, and right areas equidistant from the lens, ensuring fieldwide focus.

Focus. As mentioned before, the cameraman focuses the lens by turning a ring that moves its optical center closer to or farther from the film plane. What this adjustment actually does is to select a point of virtual focus so that the rays diverging from the desired object are *those* that will converge on the film as a point of real focus.

In practice, however, a *point* in the visual field appears as a *circle* at the point of posterior focus; even if to all intents and purposes it looks like a point, what it actually is is the smallest possible circle. That circle — the image of a focused point — is called the **circle of least confusion**. Any point closer to or farther from the lens than this one will appear as a slightly broader circle, called simply a **circle of confusion**.

Fig. 2-17 should make some of this less confusing. Here we see a biconvex lens; the film plane is indicated by a vertical line near the left edge of the diagram, posterior to the optical center of the lens. In the anterior field — the world in front of the camera, at the right side of the diagram — there are three objects on which the cameraman might want to focus: A, B, and C. Light diverges from A, B, and C; is refracted by the lens; and converges at the posterior points A, B, and C. In this diagram, the point where the rays from B converge happens to be exactly where the film is. On

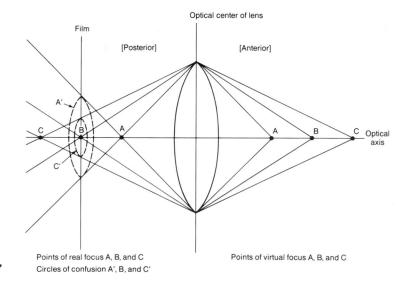

Figure 2-17

Points of real focus A, B, and C
Circles of confusion A', B, and C'

the posterior side, then, B will appear as the circle of least confusion; in other words, B will be in perfect focus.

The rays emerging from point A, however, do not converge at the film plane. They converge at posterior point A. By the time they reach the film plane, they will have broadened, and *on the film* they will appear as circle of confusion A′. The rays from point-of-virtual-focus C will appear as circle-of-confusion C′ on their way to their point of real focus, posterior C. In summary, then, with this lens in this position, point B will be **in focus** — will appear as the smallest possible circle on the film — whereas points A and C will appear as relatively broad circles. If point A were not a point but an object, its outlines might be fuzzy or blurred. If that same object were where B is, its outlines would be sharp. On the other hand, if this lens were adjusted so that the posterior-point-of-focus A were where the film is, then A would appear as the circle of least confusion and B and C would be thrown **out of focus**.

Because the eye naturally gravitates toward objects that are in focus, the control of focus is a crucial aesthetic device. Consider the following frames from *Napoleon*. The setting is a rainy battlefield at night. Frustrated at how the senior officers are handling things, Napoleon walks forward through the rain and denounces the others as "Speech-makers!" At the beginning of the shot (**Fig. 2-18**), Napoleon is out of focus. As he continues to advance, he walks into focus (**Fig. 2-19**). A similar effect could have been obtained by having the actor remain stationary while the lens was refocused, but the way Gance set up the shot is more interesting. What he implied is that Napoleon is here responsible for his own coming into clarity and forcefulness.

The shifting of focus in order to keep a moving figure in focus is called **follow focus**, and it is usually smooth and unobtrusive. A shift of focus from one object of attention to another — often rather abrupt — is called **rack focus** or **focus pull**.

Depth of Field. For a particular lens at a particular setting, the **depth of field** is the range within which objects remain in focus. It is expressed in terms of feet or meters — real distance between focal planes — and can be characterized as broad, normal, or shallow.

Let us say that the distance between points A and E in **Fig. 2-20** is 30 feet and that point A is 12 feet from the camera. Points B and D are each 5 feet from point C. In the top example — a broad depth of field — objects A through E are all in focus. Put another way, any object between 12 and 42 feet from the camera is in focus. Put correctly, this lens at this setting has a depth of field of 30 (or 12–42) feet, or of 15 feet before and behind the plane of focus. In the bottom example — a shallow depth of field — only objects B through D would be in focus, and the lens would have a depth of field of 10 feet (that is, 5 feet before and behind the plane of focus).

Depth of field is primarily controlled via lens aperture. In general, the narrower the iris opening, the broader the depth of field.

Figure 2-18

Figure 2-19

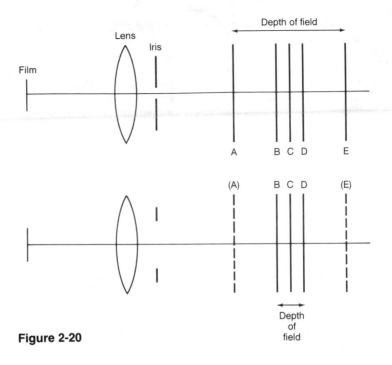

Figure 2-20

It is also affected by focal length: wide-angle lenses have greater depth of field. A long lens at its widest aperture has a *very* shallow depth of field.

The advantage of a shallow depth of field is that it allows the filmmaker to keep only a few objects in focus and thus to make sure that the audience will look *there*. The effect that Gance achieved in **Figs. 2-18** and **2-19** would have been impossible with a broad depth of field, and so would most rack-focus shots. The advantage of a broad depth of field is that it allows many planes and objects to remain in focus. Significant information can be included in the foreground, the middleground, and the background.

Although the technique had been used before, cinematographer Gregg Toland made exceptionally fine use of deep focus in his work on *Citizen Kane* (**Fig. 2-21**). **Deep focus** creates a field that is sharp from foreground to background (a very broad depth of field) and in which the foreground and the background appear to be widely separated (thanks to a short lens). In order to achieve these effects, Toland used a wide-angle lens, set it at a narrow aperture, and had to increase the amount of light on the set in order to compensate for that aperture; his work was facilitated by the introduction of new, high-powered arc lights and more sensitive filmstock.

Exposure. There are several basic and interrelated ways to control exposure. The filmstock itself has a discrete range of sensitivity or **exposure latitude** within which it functions properly. A medium-gray object, correctly photographed, will yield a medium-

Figure 2-21

gray image. Overexposed, that same object will look too white (too black on the negative). On color reversal stock, a yellow object will come out too red when overexposed, too blue when underexposed. So one way to control exposure is to select a more sensitive (or **faster**) emulsion for low-light conditions, and a **slower** emulsion for very bright conditions. Emulsions have speeds much as lenses do: a high-speed emulsion is the more photosensitive. Slow emulsions are usually more fine-grained than fast ones, and if grain is the paramount consideration, the amount of light that is to reach the film must itself be controlled, with the film's sensitivity — and 24 fps — a given.

Exposure can be regulated within the camera body by adjusting the opening of the variable shutter, if the camera has one. Exposure can be regulated in the lens by changing the f- or T-stop. But a change in aperture will also affect the depth of field.

A way to cut down the amount of light without changing the aperture is to put a filter in front of the lens. Most **filters** cut out discrete portions of the spectrum. A **neutral density filter** is unique in that it only reduces the amount of light (usually by two stops) without altering its colors.

Given all of these optical considerations, the preferred method for exposure control is to control the amount of light that is being reflected off the subject. That approach allows grain and depth of field to be selected for aesthetic reasons, rather than varying emulsion and aperture simply to make sure that the picture comes out. The best way to ensure complete control of light is to shoot in a studio on a windowless **sound stage**. Lighting will be taken up a bit later, but it is important to note here that a **light meter** is used to measure the amount of light in the visual field; it lets the cameraman know, for example, that to expose this particular gray as gray, given this much light and an exposure rate of one fiftieth of a second, the lens will have to be set at $f4$.

Camera Equipment

The word "camera" originally meant "chamber" or "room," and the earliest form of the camera *was* a room. The **camera obscura** ("dark room"), developed during the late Middle Ages and the early Renaissance, was a small room, one of whose walls had a small opening in it; in later experiments, this hole was fitted with a lens. On the opposite wall, a flipped and inverted image would be thrown of whatever was on the other side of the punctured wall. As recently as the nineteenth century, a portable version of the camera obscura was still being used as an aid to accurate drawing. The lens threw an image onto a sheet of paper mounted inside the rear of the box, and the artist opened the top and traced the outlines of the image onto the paper. In this context, photography began as a labor-saving device, introducing treated papers or pieces of metal that would retain images through chemical action rather than the work of the sketch artist.

However elegantly and efficiently designed, the camera today is still a dark box. Interchangeable lenses and magazines are attached to the box, along with other accessories, and the camera itself usually rests on some kind of support.

Basic Equipment. Fig. 2-22 shows Chaplin directing an unknown actress. Behind him is a simple 35mm camera, clearly a box. The lens, which cannot be seen in this photograph, is mounted at the front, and the magazine is mounted on top. The

Figure 2-22

Figure 2-23

cylinder attached to the left side of the camera is a simple view-finder. The camera rests on a three-legged support called a **tripod**. On top of the tripod is a gear-driven **tripod head**, to which the bottom of the camera has been screwed or bolted. The camera-man's left hand is on one of the cranks of the head. One crank allowed the camera to **pan** — to pivot from side to side — and the other allowed it to **tilt** — to pivot upward and downward.

In **Fig. 2-23**, which shows Chaplin (at the left) directing a scene from *The Gold Rush*, we have a view of a slightly more sophisti-cated setup. Here we can see the belt that drives the magazine, and the crank in the cameraman's right hand. The camera itself is a Mitchell, for years the workhorse of the industry. This camera is equipped with a **lens turret**, a plate on which several lenses — in this case three — are mounted. The turret rotates so that the cam-eraman can quickly change lenses, moving whichever one is wanted into the taking position.

In front of the lenses there is a **matte box**, which could have been used to hold a **matte card** that would block out part of the image, but that in this case appears simply to be acting as a sun-shade. Matte cards were used to *mask* the image — for example, to make it look as if the subject were being viewed through a key-hole or binoculars — and to block out part of the frame area for special-effects work. Using a matte card to block out the right side, the camerman could shoot an actor in the left of the frame; then the film could be wound back, a complementary card or **counter-matte** could be placed in the matte box to block out the left side, and the same actor could be shot in the right frame area. The result would be that the actor could play a scene with his or her other self, and each part of each frame would have been exposed only once. Matte boxes are also used to hold filters and, in some cases, aperture plates. Today aperture plates and filters are often inserted behind the lens in a filter slot.

Behind the camera is a large, square **reflector**, which is bouncing some of the sunlight into the scene. Where direct light may prove too harsh, a reflector is used to take some of the edge off and to bounce a more *diffused* and muted light onto the subject.

Motors and Tripods. In terms of basic camera mechanics, not that much has changed since Chaplin's day, but there have been many improvements in design and operation. **Fig. 2-24** shows cinematographer Caleb Deschanel on the set of Philip Kaufman's *The Right Stuff* (1983). The camera is a 35mm Arriflex. The magazine has a "2" on it so that the camera crew can keep track of which magazines have been used and in what order. A gauge on the side of the magazine indicates how much of its load has been shot. The hanging cord powers the camera's motor, whose speed can be precisely controlled. The motor itself is that nearly vertical cylinder. The reflex viewfinder can be seen sticking out to the rear from the far side of the camera; looking past the cord, you can see its rubber eyepiece. At the front of the camera a zoom lens is mounted, and attached to the front of that is a matte box.

Between the camera and the Panavision tripod is an O'Connor **fluid head**, which allows for panning, tilting, and locking the camera at virtually any angle but without the use of cranks or gears. That light-colored lever is a friction lock, and when it is released, the camera can be set at or moved smoothly through a variety of

Figure 2-24

positions. The long handle coming from the back of the head is used to move the head and, with it, the camera.

To set a camera on a tripod, and to set that tripod on firm ground, virtually guarantees a stable image. Whether the cameraman uses a fluid head or a gear-type head like Cinema Products' Mini-Worrall (**Fig. 2-25**), he or she can be sure that the camera will pivot smoothly or will remain locked in position.

Virtually all professional cameras today are driven by motors rather than cranked by hand. The motor provides a reliable 24 fps exposure rate, and it can also be adjusted for slow or fast motion. It is powered by a portable generator or by a battery pack, to which it is connected by cables. In many shooting situations it is convenient for the camera operator to wear the battery pack as a belt (**Fig. 2-11**).

Dollies, Tracks, and Cranes. A camera platform is a wheeled mount that supports the camera, the tripod, and the camera operator(s). It is used for moving the camera smoothly across the floor or the ground — in other words, for tracking movements. The track shot got its name from the steel **tracks** — much like those used in railroads — on which the camera platform's metal wheels rode smoothly forward and backward.

A camera platform that is equipped with large rubber wheels and can be pushed silently across the floor without any tracks is called a **dolly**. The **crab dolly** got its name from its ability to move sideways — laterally, like a crab — at a turn of the wheels. Track shots and dolly shots (the terms are now used almost interchangeably) are taken from the ground, but the ground is not always as smooth as one might wish. In **Fig. 2-26**, a production still from

Figure 2-25

Figure 2-26

Figure 2-27

Edward Dmytryk's *Raintree County* (1957), the 65mm camera rests on a dolly, but the dolly is moving on two boards; the boards compensate for the uneven ground and perform, essentially, the function of tracks.

To lift the camera off the ground and move it fluidly through the air, a **crane** or **boom** is used. **Fig. 2-27** shows director Vincente Minnelli (topmost) setting up a crane shot for *Yolanda and the Thief* (1945). The crane arm's platform is here supporting both the director and two camera operators.

More of the crane can be seen in **Fig. 2-28**, a production still from the making of *Gone With the Wind*. Here the arm (or boom) supports three men, a three-strip Technicolor® 35mm camera, and a light (to the left). Just over Vivien Leigh's head, a **boom microphone** is being held by a crew member. The advantage of a boom over a fixed microphone is that it can be moved silently, following the actors and yet remaining out of camera range. Just as the boom allows the microphone to be dangled from a pole, a true boom or

Figure 2-28

crane allows the camera crew to hang out in space and to execute movements of exceptional smoothness.

In the mid-1980s, a lightweight, remote-controlled camera support called the **Louma crane** came into wide use.

Sea and Sky. Even the boom shot depends on the ground for support. For shooting at sea or from an airplane, other sophisticated support mechanisms have been developed.

Fig. 2-29 shows a 35mm Panavision® camera mounted on a Tyler Gyro Platform®. The Gyro Platform is an electro-hydraulically stabilizing unit that is used to keep the camera level even when one is shooting in a rough sea. Between the camera and the platform is an O'Connor fluid head. The camera itself is a Panaflex®, equipped with a crystal-controlled motor, a variable shutter, and a reflex viewfinder. The magazine is mounted to the rear, and the lens is a Panavision zoom lens.

In **Fig. 2-30** we can see a 35mm Arriflex attached to a helicopter by a Tyler 206 Nose Mount®. Just below the camera is a Cine 60 battery, to power the motor. The lens turret has been fitted with a prime wide-angle lens. The camera can be tilted — even straight

Figure 2-29

Figure 2-30

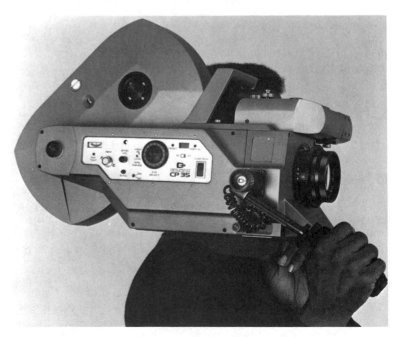

Figure 2-31

down or upside-down and backward — from inside the aircraft. A setup like this was used to shoot the opening of *The Shining*.

Hand-Held Shooting. In many situations it is desirable or necessary to hold the camera oneself and perhaps to walk around with it. Cinema Products' CP-35 (**Fig. 2-31**) is a 35mm camera designed for **hand-held** operation. As shown, with a fully loaded 500-foot magazine, a self-contained battery, and a lens, it weighs only 25 pounds. But even when working with a lightweight 16mm camera like Cinema Products' GSMO (**Fig. 2-32**), shown here with a reflex viewfinder and an Angenieux zoom lens, it may be difficult to keep the image as stable as one might wish.

In situations where smooth, rapid, hand-held camera movements are desired, the **Steadicam®** has proved ideal. It was invented by Garrett Brown and was developed by Cinema Products, and its makers won a technical Oscar in 1977. The Steadicam Universal Model III, as shown in **Fig. 2-33**, is worn by the cameraman. As the cameraman moves, the Steadicam system automatically compensates for any body motions. Steadicam works thanks to a patented spring-loaded arm and a perfectly engineered balance and counterbalance system. With the Steadicam one can obtain a stable, fluid shot even while running over a rockpile and can squeeze gracefully into places where a dolly cannot fit. In this photo the unit is shown with an Ikegami EC-35 Electronic Cinematography camera, and the box at which the operator is looking is the viewfinder, a high-intensity video monitor.

Blimps and Barneys. Because the noise made by the camera can be picked up by the microphone, the camera requires some

Figure 2-32

Figure 2-33

Figure 2-34

kind of soundproofing. **A blimp** is a rigid soundproof cover that can be fitted over the camera. **A barney** is a padded bag that performs the same function. Many cameras today are **blimped**, which means that they have excellent *internal* sound insulation.

In this production still from the making of Douglas Sirk's *Taza, Son of Cochise* (1953), a boom microphone can be seen at the left (**Fig. 2-34**). On the right are two studio-sized lights, which are often used in outdoor shooting. A portable generator, complete with cables, provides electricity for the camera, the sound, and the lights. The puffy bag in the center of the photo is a barney, and inside it is a 3-D Technicolor 35mm camera.

Lights

Light itself is one of the most essential of film's raw materials. It provides the image that is recorded on film, and it carries that image from the film to the screen. A projected image is actually a shadow — the shadow of the frame. Whether the frame is in black-and-white or in color, its shades and hues are subtracted from the pure white light provided by the projector.

One of the first things that one notices about a film set is how many lights there are, both overhead and at eye level, and what intense heat they emit. The lights are selected and arranged in order to model the subjects, to cast or eliminate shadows, and to give the image its most significant textures. In addition to the aesthetic resources of controlled and modulated light, the constraints

Figure 2-35

of exposure time and lens properties make it vital that the subject be adequately — not just artistically — lit.

Light Meters. To measure the light level and ensure proper exposure, a light meter is used. The type being used in **Fig. 2-35** — which shows Elizabeth Taylor's lipstick being tested for *Raintree County* — is an incident meter. An **incident light meter** measures the amount of light that is actually *falling on* the subject, and the measurement is taken from the position of the subject, facing the camera. A **reflected light meter** measures the light being *reflected from* a subject, and the measurement is taken from the position of the camera. Another way to put this is to say that an incident meter measures the actual, consistent brightness of the source, and a reflected meter measures how much of that light is reaching the camera's position. (Through-the-lens meters, which are rarely used in the film industry, are reflected light meters.)

A reflected light meter with a very small angle of view is called a **spot meter**, and it allows one to measure the light reflected from a small or distant area in the visual field. To measure and balance the color temperatures of various light sources, one uses a **color temperature meter**. As we shall see in a moment, color temperature has a crucial effect on the exposure of color filmstock.

Key and Fill Lighting. The principal light illuminating the subject is called the **key light**. In the film industry, **key** means "principal"; the key grip supervises the other grips, and the key light establishes the basic look, form, and texture of the subject. It is

Figure 2-36

usually placed to one side of the camera and at an angle (cross-frontally). It tends to produce a "hard" light with distinct shadows. (Parallel or focused light rays create hard effects; diffused or scattered light creates soft effects.) When one is shooting in daylight, the sun is the key light.

To soften the hard-edged quality of these shadows, to balance the total lighting effect, and to reveal detail in otherwise shadowed areas, a relatively "soft" light called the **fill light** is used. Key and fill may each be single lamps or systems of lamps. The fill light usually comes more-or-less from the camera's direction, and it "fills in" the shadows cast by the key light. In this frame from *Citizen Kane* (**Fig. 2-36**), the key light, directed from the upper right corner of the frame, is much brighter than the fill light, and the shadows on Leland's face are hard and distinct.

Contrast Ratios. A lighting mood can be described in terms of the degree of contrast between the bright and dark or hard and soft areas within the visual field. This **contrast ratio** is determined by the relationship between key and fill lighting, and it is expressed as the ratio of *key plus fill light* to *fill light*.

The key light is set first, then the fill. The higher (brighter) the fill light, the less difference there is between key and fill, and the softer the shadows are in relation to the more brightly lit areas. If the key light were switched off, the contrast ratio would be 1 : 1 (in other words, zero key plus *X* fill to *X* fill). If key and fill were equally bright, the ratio would be 2 : 1, and if the key were twice as bright as the fill, the ratio would be 3 : 1. Two of the most common contrast ratios are known as low-key and high-key lighting.

Figure 2-37

Figure 2-38

In **low-key lighting** the contrast ratio is high, and the set is dimly lit, with rich shadows and occasional highlights. **Fig. 2-37** shows an example of low-key lighting from *Mad Love,* and **Fig. 2-38** offers another from Rouben Mamoulian's *Queen Christina* (1933). These stills illustrate two of the regular uses to which low-key lighting is put: to provide a dark and brooding atmosphere *(Mad Love)* or to provide a rich and subtly expressive palette of highlights and shadows *(Queen Christina).*

In **high-key lighting** the set is brightly lit and has a relatively low level of contrast. High-key lighting is illustrated in **Fig. 2-39**, from George Sidney's *Anchors Aweigh* (1945), and in **Fig. 2-40**, from *2001.* The high-key mood accounts for much of the rich, colorful look of the great MGM musicals. Working against normal audience expectations, however, some filmmakers have used high-key lighting to suggest low-key situations, in other words, to imply that dark things are going on even if we cannot see dark shadows. Kubrick and Alcott did that in *The Shining.* As will be evident from this choice of examples, the terms "high-key" and "low-key" apply in both color and black-and-white cinematography.

Figure 2-39

Figure 2-40

Figure 2-41

Supplementary Lights. There are many other lights beyond the primary ones of key and fill, and they are known by the functions they perform. A **back light**, which illuminates the subject from behind, can be used to separate the subject from the background. A very bright back light can turn the subject into a silhouette, as in this frame from *Citizen Kane* (**Fig. 2-41**). An **effects light** is used to produce specific highlight areas — the effect of candlelight on a face, for example, when the candle itself provides inadequate illumination. In **Fig. 2-38**, Greta Garbo (Christina) is separated from the background with a back light, and effects lights create the impression of reflected firelight.

The **kicker** is a back light coming from behind and to the side. The **base light** provides diffuse (soft) illumination for the entire set. A hard light used to reveal texture and form is called an **accent light**. Other types include the rim light, the cross light or counter key, the edge light, the eye light, the hair light, the clothes light, and the top light.

Color Temperature. Any light source has specific color characteristics, and some of these are related to temperature. If a cold bar of iron is placed in a furnace, it will change color as it heats up. Eventually it will become orange, and at its hottest it will turn blue-white — hence the expression "white hot." **Color temperature** refers to the specific energy distribution of a black body that has been heated to a specific temperature. A **black body** is a perfectly efficient radiator — and an abstraction, as no such object exists. It absorbs all the radiant energy falling on it, and when it is heated, it radiates with no distortion or loss of energy.

Color temperature is measured in degrees Kelvin, where 0°K is absolute zero — the point at which molecular motion ceases, expressed as −273° on the centigrade scale. The color temperature of a light source is expressed as the temperature to which a black body would have to be heated in order to produce light of that color. Lamps are identified by their color temperature. A 3,200°K lamp would not burn at 3,200°K (because, like any real object, it is not a perfect radiator) but would produce the same kind of light as a black body burning at 3,200°K. When using color film, it is important to provide light of the proper color temperature for the emulsion being used, because color film is balanced for specific types and intensities of illumination. Some emulsions are balanced for daylight, others for particular kinds of artificial light. If the color temperature of the light source is wrong, the colors will be distorted.

Lamps, Housings, and Lighting Equipment. A light consists primarily of a **lamp** (the light source or **luminant**) and a **housing**, in which the lamp is mounted. Previously we have identified lights by their functions; now we shall look at specific types of lighting instruments.

In the simple **scoop** light, a bulb or floodlight is held in a matte-finish aluminum bowl (the scoop) that reflects the light forward and outward in a broad, diffuse field. A **broad** or **broadside light** has a trough-shaped reflector and uses a tubular quartz lamp; a small broad is called a **nook light** (from "nookie"), and a large one, a **large broad**. The general name for a lighting instrument is a **luminaire**. In the cases of the scoop and many broads, the lamp socket and the reflector that houses it make up the entire instrument. In order to focus the light, some luminaires are fitted with lenses, of which the most commonly used is the **fresnel** or "stepped" lens.

Fig. 2-42 shows one of LTM's Pepper 100 spotlights with its lid opened. Behind the lamp is a highly polished reflector, and at the front of the housing is a fresnel lens. Notice the protruding handle attached to the lamp/reflector assembly, which allows it to move in relation to the lens. When the assembly is placed at the posterior focal point of the lens, the light rays emerge as a parallel beam, which produces the hardest possible illumination. (So does the sun, whose rays are parallel because the source is so distant.) When the assembly is moved nearer to the lens, the light beam *spreads,* converting this instrument into a small **floodlight.** When the assembly is moved farther from the lens, the light beam *narrows* to produce a **spotlight.** A small spotlight is sometimes called a **baby spot. Fig. 2-43**, again of the Pepper 100, gives an idea of how small a baby can be.

Some of the biggest lights derive their illumination from carbon arcs, like those in many projectors; they are called **arc lights.** A very large carbon arc light is called a **brute.** In **Fig. 2-34** the brutes to the right of the frame are being used to balance the intensity of the sunlight. **Fig. 2-44** shows the Luxarc 12,000, the largest and brightest light currently made for the film industry,

Figure 2-42

Figure 2-43

together with the 12-KW (Kilowatt) transformer that provides its AC power.

To control the shape and texture of the light once it has passed through the lens, there are two commonly used accessories, the barn door and the diffuser. A **barn door** consists of up to four hinged flaps, usually made of metal and painted flat black. Barn doors allow the crew to light specific areas of the set while leaving others alone (to light an actor, for instance, but not a nearby wall or couch) or to keep the light from adjacent sources from overlapping, to create shafts of "sunlight," and so on. A **diffuser**, which can be anything from a net to a graded filter, modifies, scatters, and softens the light uniformly and is mounted in front of the lens. On the set or on location, light can also be bounced and diffused by a reflector, which is usually hand-held. **Fig. 2-45** shows three LTM spotlights on their stands and, in the foreground, three boxed lamps, three barn doors, and four diffusion filters, together with the case into which all this equipment fits. Filters made of glass or gelatin (**gels**) can also be used to color the light; they resemble the diffusion filters shown here.

Other ways of structuring the light beam include the use of **cookies**, which look like cutout stencils and produce patterns and shadows of particular shapes, like that of a rose window; **scrims** or

Figure 2-44

Figure 2-45

nets (the large-mesh ones are called **butterflies**), which soften and reduce the light in local areas; and **gobos**, large black panels that can hide a light from the camera or restrict a light beam to a certain area. Small gobos, mounted several inches or feet in front of a light and used to produce hard or soft shadows of any shape, are called **flags**. A black, horizontal gobo, hung from above and used to give the impression that an opposite window or doorway is admitting only a certain rectangle of light that does not reach the ceiling, is called a **black**.

As you will have noticed, some of these names are a bit bizarre. When cameraman Jack Anderson showed up for his first day of work, he wondered what universe he was in when he heard someone call, "Hang the black, throw a net over the broad, and kill the baby!"

An individual frame of film presents a single picture. The term **frame** can be used to refer both to this individual picture area and to its perimeter or boundaries. To frame a shot is to decide where the boundaries of the image will be located, in other words, to decide what will be in the frame, or what will be framed by its limits. We shall begin by looking at the frame as a cinematic unit with particular physical characteristics, then go on to examine some of the ways in which the contents of the frame may be arranged.

2. The Frame

The Perimeter

In Chuck Jones's great cartoon *Duck Amuck* (1951), Daffy Duck is doing his best to act in a film that he does not realize is being drawn by an unusually playful Bugs Bunny. At one point the limits of the frame turn into a heavy black gook that Daffy tries to keep out of the picture area (**Fig. 2-46**), a clever way for Jones to dramatize the paradoxical physicality of the frame and the ways that subjects work within and are partially defined by its boundaries.

At another point the "projector" slips a bit, and Daffy is shown in two adjacent frames (**Fig. 2-47**). This gag (also found in H. C. Potter's *Hellzapoppin'*, 1941) calls attention to the fact that the cinematic subject is repeated from frame to frame, which itself poses the problem of whether each image is equally *the* subject. Jones brought this out by having the two Daffys argue about which of them is himself, and the joke is topped by having the second Daffy—the one who popped up in the lower frame—carry on the action for the rest of the movie. By raising the issue of the frame, Jones and his cohorts addressed the cinema itself.

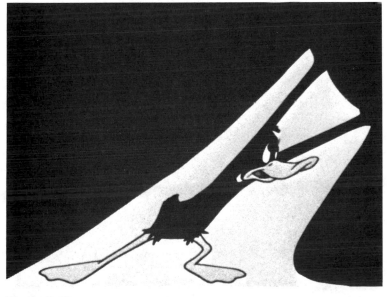

Figure 2-46

Figure 2-47

The Inner Frame. If the world is framed in any shot, one of the more reflexive ways of calling attention to this structuring process is to set a frame within the frame of the image. This might be compared with the "play within a play" device in *Hamlet*. At the end of *Sherlock Jr.* the real lovers are framed within the window of the projection booth, while the screen lovers are framed within the theater screen. This reminds the audience that each of these couples is a category of cinematic illusion, the real lovers "more real" than the others only because the latter are "really supposed to be in a film," whereas the truth is that both are in *Sherlock Jr.* Much the same idea is conveyed by this production still (**Fig. 2-48**), which corresponds to a scene near the middle of the film, in which Buster looks at the theater audience(s) before entering the inner frame of the projected image.

Less philosophically heady uses of the inner frame can be found in many movies. Shown through a window or a doorway, or within a box, a character may look confined, isolated, or even "at home." Inner framing calls attention to what it frames. When the young Kane is shown through the window of his mother's boarding house near the beginning of *Citizen Kane* (**Fig. 2-49**), the point is clearly made that he is the subject of the controlling discussions going on inside. He is isolated as the subject of discourse within another discourse (the shot), as his future is determined.

Throughout *Rear Window* (1954) Hitchcock used the device of the window frame to limit the characters in space and to give them discrete, line-of-sight access to each other's privacy. The story concerns a photographer (James Stewart) who takes what he considers an innocent, voyeuristic pleasure in spying on his neighbors

Figure 2-48

Figure 2-49

through the telephoto lens on his camera. The problem arises when he discovers evidence of a murder and when the murderer looks back at *him*. The window frame ironically reminds the audience of the screen's rectangle, through which *we* are spying on the world of the film. Although the murderer will not climb through the screen and show up in our private space, we are still led to think about the nature of voyeurism, its relation to filmgoing, and the threat or challenge of authentic participation. Quite often, and not just in *Rear Window*, the inner frame is used to call attention to the problem of vision and discourse, of seeing and being seen within an artificially limited structure.

Geography and Gravity. In many cases the frame is "read" in a consistent manner. If we project a kind of map onto the frame, screen left is identified with west, and screen right is east. In the majority of Westerns, a pioneer wagon advances from screen right to screen left. Of course, the simplest reverse-angle shot will flip these directions, but most films are made so that all of the spaces within frames can be coherently mapped in continuous (that is, synthesized) space.

One of the ways this synthesis is encoded and decoded is in terms of **screen direction**: the orientation of screen action to three-dimensional space, expressed as the direction or trajectory of a movement within the frame. If a ball is thrown to screen left in one shot and enters from screen right in the next shot, the screen direction of the ball is consistent. Filmmakers keep track of these directions by drawing an imaginary line straight through the set, more-or-less perpendicular to the direction in which the camera is

Figure 2-50

first facing. The camera can be put *anywhere* on its side of that **line** (the **axis of action**) and will yield consistent screen direction from shot to shot. But if the camera **crosses the line**, the screen directions in that shot will be reversed, so that a conversation might take place between two figures who are both facing the same edge of the screen. When the line or axis is crossed, the results will not "cut together" (in continuity).

The top of the frame is the north or skyward direction, and the bottom heads south or to the ground. This convention gives the bottom edge of the frame a sense of gravity.

Of course, all of these expectations can be played with or deliberately reversed. The Japanese director Yasujiro Ozu crossed the line with impunity. In these frames from Stanley Donen's *Royal*

Wedding (1951), Fred Astaire exploits the expectation that the bottom edge has the most gravity and dances on the walls and the ceiling, courtesy of a turning set (**Fig. 2-50**). He is playing with the nature of the frame as much as with the room.

Inclusion and Exclusion. The frame is defined by what it includes and excludes. What is in the frame is what the camera has been directed to include, and therefore what the audience is supposed to notice at a particular time. What is framed out may be irrelevant — or crucial, like an unseen killer sneaking up on a victim, or Leland as he lectures Kane about "love on your own terms."

Consider these two frames from Erich von Stroheim's *Greed* (1924). *Greed* was adapted from Frank Norris's novel *McTeague*, and in this scene McTeague (Gibson Gowland) shows up with the intention of taking a large sum of money — the $5,000 she has won in a lottery — from his estranged wife Trina (Zasu Pitts). Trina has found work as a scrubwoman in a school. The schoolroom is decorated for the Christmas season, but it is late at night, and the hour motivates some very rich low-key lighting. As it turns out, McTeague has to kill Trina in order to steal the money.

Fig. 2-51 shows McTeague's entrance and Trina's first reaction. Their estrangement is signified by their being at opposite edges of the frame, which is as far apart as they can be and remain in the same shot. The lines of light on the floor dramatically interrelate them, as if McTeague or his plans point directly to Trina. Baby spotlights isolate their faces, giving them further dramatic weight, and also the bucket, the key prop defining Trina's occupation. The lights draw our attention, like Trina's, from the bucket she has been thinking about to the threatening figure she must now deal with, and back from McTeague to Trina like the vector of his intentions. All of this information is included in the frame, a temporary but self-sufficient world.

But it is also possible to have significant offscreen information. In **Fig. 2-52**, McTeague exits the frame to screen left, and in this offscreen space he will murder his wife. Although we know what is going on, it can be more effective for us to imagine the bloody scene than to watch it. At this point in the novel, Norris wrote the simple and powerful sentence, "Then it became abominable."

In the sound film, offscreen sounds are often used to suggest what is going on outside the limits of the frame — what we could see, if the camera would only move.

To decide what to put in the frame can be a playful act, an exercise in style and irony. There is a scene in Hawks's *Scarface* (1932) in which a criminal played by Boris Karloff is shot down in a bowling alley just as he is bowling a strike. Rather than lingering on the victim, the camera pans to the left, following the ball down the alley. All but one of the pins fall; the last one spins and tilts. A second burst of gunfire is heard offscreen, and the pin keels over. We gather that it took the second volley to finish off the victim: the final pin has fallen as Karloff's surrogate. What might have

Figure 2-51

Figure 2-52

been simply a violent scene has been transformed, by the choice of camera position, into a wry joke.

Aspect Ratio and the Shape of the Frame

Masking. The inherent shape of the frame is a horizontal rectangle. By masking the borders of the frame, it is possible to change this shape in order to give an individual shot a particular impact.

An **iris** card masks the frame into a circle (see **Fig. 2-158**). At several points in *Broken Blossoms* (1919), Griffith and his cameraman G. W. Bitzer added top and bottom masks in order to make the frame extremely wide (**Fig. 2-53**). (This frame enlargment, made from a 16mm color print, is also an example of excessive film grain.) In **Fig. 2-54**, from *La Roue*, the vertical frame emphasizes the direction, speed, and linearity of the railroad track, so that at this moment the most important element is simply a line.

Aspect Ratio. In most cases, however, the frame has one shape and maintains it throughout the film. This shape is expressed as an **aspect ratio**, the ratio of the width of the image (written first) to its height. Aspect ratio can be controlled in the camera, by a change of aperture plates; in the matte box or filter slot, by a mask; in an optical printer, by a reframing of the image while it is being copied; or by the choice of a particular lens.

Like the lenses that photograph and project them, movies are either flat or anamorphic. Until the 1950s, the normal aspect ratio for a flat film was 1.33 : 1. Regardless of whether they achieve their effects through anamorphic lenses, films with an aspect ratio

Figure 2-53

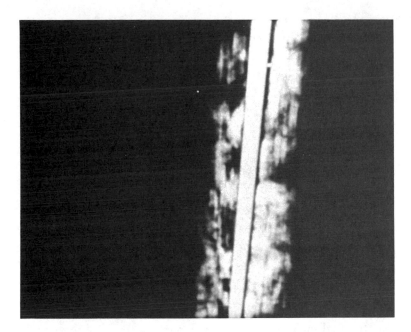

Figure 2-54

greater than 1.33 : 1 are considered **wide screen** or **wide format**; that is, they are **wide-screen** films. As a separate term, **widescreen** (though it is often used loosely to refer to wide screen) denotes a *flat* film with an aspect ratio of 1.85 : 1 (1.66 : 1 in Europe), and that is the most common flat format in use today. A wide, anamorphic format would be wide screen but not widescreen. Before we get into this, a short table should prove useful:

Common Aspect Ratios

1.33 : 1	Academy (35mm flat)
1.66 : 1	European widescreen (35mm flat)
1.85 : 1	American widescreen (35mm flat)
2.2 : 1	Super-Panavision and Todd-AO (70mm flat)
2.35 : 1	Panavision and CinemaScope (35mm anamorphic)
2.75 : 1	Ultra-Panavision (70mm anamorphic)

In the silent period, the frame occupied virtually the entire area between the lines of sprocket holes, and its aspect ratio was 1.33 : 1. An aperture plate in the camera ensured that the frame's borders would be hard and straight but did not crop the image. When single-system sound became the norm, the frame had to be reduced in size in order to allow room for the soundtrack — but its proportions remained 1.33 : 1. In order to take full advantage of the frame area on the negative (the larger the negative, the better the picture can be), it became common to use a full-screen aperture plate (0.98 in. × 0.735 in.) in the camera and a smaller one in the printer and the projector. That smaller opening was standardized as the **Academy aperture** (0.864 in. × 0.63 in.). The **Academy ratio** remained 1.33 : 1.

Pan and Scan. The Academy ratio is also standard for most TV screens, so it is possible to view older films on TV with a minimal loss of image area. Actually the TV image is reframed just inside the borders of the original motion picture image, and so cinematographers who expect that their work will be shown on TV inscribe a slightly smaller frame inside that of the viewfinder. They keep significant actions within this inner frame, whose limits are called the **TV safe area**. But when the frame is extremely wide, it is necessary to pan and scan the image with an optical printer, moving the 1.33 : 1 viewing area around to coincide with the site of the most interesting action or information. The pan-and-scan process, which is done in a laboratory, is used both for TV prints and for some flat theatrical prints. A **flat print** is a nonanamorphic copy of any film, whether or not the original was flat; the term also applies to a two-dimensional print of a 3-D movie.

Flat and Anamorphic Systems. The most common flat formats are 1.33 : 1 (Academy), 1.66 : 1 (European widescreen), and 1.85 : 1 (American widescreen); they have the same aspect ratios in 16mm and 35mm. To widen a flat frame, the usual method is to mask off the top and the bottom of the full-frame area; in projection the resulting image is magnified more than normal so that full screen height will be reached. The major exception, **VistaVision®**, runs 35mm film *horizontally* through the camera, recording the image on as much stock as would normally be consumed by two adjacent frames. VistaVision flourished in the 1950s (*Vertigo* was shot in it), but today it is used primarily for special effects work because of its large negative; the VistaVision aspect ratio varied in practice from 1.33 : 1 to 1.96 : 1, but 1.66 : 1 and 1.85 : 1 were the most common.

The 65mm frame is already a wide screen format, and more often than not it is flat. A flat film shot on 65mm stock has an aspect ratio of 2.2 : 1. (Release prints will be on 70mm stock.) Flat 65mm systems include **Todd-AO®**, introduced in 1955, and **Super-Pan-avision®**, the format in which *2001* was released (**Fig. 2-55**).

But 65mm can also be shot anamorphically. In **Ultra-Panavision®** the squeeze ratio is 1.25 : 1 (most anamorphic lenses have a

Figure 2-55

Figure 2-56

squeeze ratio of 2 : 1). The squeezed image fills the wide frame area and is unsqueezed during projection to an aspect ratio of 2.75 : 1. *Raintree County* was the first film shot in Ultra-Panavision. Most people saw it in 35mm Panavision, however, because the 70mm houses were all showing Mike Todd's *Around the World in 80 Days* — in Todd-AO.

In the 1950s the most common anamorphic process was **CinemaScope®**, which made its debut in Henry Koster's *The Robe* (1953). At first, CinemaScope had an aspect ratio of 2.55 : 1, but this was soon reduced to 2.35 : 1 in order to make room for the soundtrack. By the end of the decade, CinemaScope had given way to **Panavision®**, which remains the dominant 35mm anamorphic process in use today and whose aspect ratio is also 2.35 : 1. Both of these systems use standard 35mm film, onto which the image is laterally compressed (**Fig. 2-16**). The majority of 70mm films today are flat prints derived from 35mm anamorphic negatives (it vastly increases costs to shoot in 65mm).

In passing, it is worth noting the dialectical aspects of the history of aspect ratio. The Academy ratio, as "thesis," was most decisively challenged by the "antithesis" of CinemaScope; the flat widescreen format emerged as "synthesis." Although it is hard to imagine anyone's having worked this out deliberately, it happens that 1.85 : 1 is almost exactly midway between 1.33 : 1 and 2.35 : 1.

Multiple Screens. There is another way to produce an extremely wide image, and that is to project several flat images side by side. The first person to do this was Abel Gance. At three points in *Napoleon*, though only the last of these sections appears to have survived, three projectors operated simultaneously, producing a **triptych** image with an aspect ratio of 4 : 1. The three images could line up in a single panorama, as in **Fig. 2-56**. Often each image was of an entirely different subject, allowing Gance to construct a genuine triptych or triple image whose parts would enhance or comment on each other. Sometimes the two outer images would be identical, except that one of them would be reversed left-to-right; symmetrically they flanked the central image.

In 1952 the triptych process was theatrically revived as **Cinerama**. The three images in Cinerama were almost invariably used to produce wide panoramas rather than three-part structures. The Cinerama image, whose combined aspect ratio was approximately 2.6 : 1, was taller than normal and extremely sharp. The projected image area was nearly as wide as that of human peripheral vision, and this effect was enhanced by a large and deeply curved screen.

3-D

Since the silent period, there have been many experiments in taking and projecting a **stereoscopic** or three-dimensional image (abbreviated as **3-D**). One reel of *Napoleon* was shot in 3-D, though Gance decided not to release it. Like wide screen, 3-D was one of the formats Hollywood exploited in the 1950s in its battle with television (so was the shift to making most features in color), and it enjoyed a brief revival in the 1980s — perhaps in a battle with cable.

Stereoscopy. Humans perceive a three-dimensional visual field because each eye sees the world from a slightly different angle. Those angles are consistent for each individual because the eyes are a fixed distance apart, and the brain computes the point from which the different rays of light must have diverged, compensating for the parallax of each view.

In 3-D photography, there are two frames for each image, often on separate, synchronized prints. One presents the subject as seen by the camera on the left (the view from the left "eye"), and the other as seen by the camera on the right. The lenses of these cameras are usually kept as far apart as the left and right eyes: 2½ inches. In 3-D projection the view from the left camera is filtered so that its information reaches only the left eye of the audience, and the converse is done with the image from the right. Thus the audience sees the left-eye image with the left eye, and the right with the right, and the brain is then able to process these into a 3-D integrated image.

Separating the Views. There are several ways of filtering the images to achieve this result. In black-and-white 3-D, one image is projected through a red filter and then is refracted through a red lens (which also blocks or filters out the blue-green image) on a pair of 3-D glasses; the other image passes through a blue-green filter and is seen only by the eye behind the blue-green lens on the glasses. This process is called **anaglyphic 3-D**. Rather than true black-and-white, it produces a shimmering, muddy color — part of its charm.

In order to obtain an image with natural color, polarizing filters are used. One full-color image is polarized as it leaves the projector so that it is a pattern of vertical lines, and a matching lens on one side of the 3-D glasses allows only these vertical lines to reach the eye; the other full–color image is polarized horizontally and reaches the other eye. This process is called **polarized 3-D**.

A third system, still under development and called **lenticular 3-D**, requires no glasses. An intricately designed screen reflects the light from the left-eye projector more-or-less directly to the left eye of the audience, and the right-eye image to the right eye. To make this system work, the projectors are set at precisely computed angles to the screen, whereas most 3-D projection is perpendicular to the screen.

Holography, which also requires no glasses, uses laser beams to generate a truly three-dimensional image — so that if you were to tilt your head or take a little walk, you could see *around* a foreground object. The basic limitation of holography in cinema is that no magnification of the image is yet possible, and the frames must be the same size as the screen.

Using the Stereo Window. 3-D is often used simply as a novelty, a way of invading the audience's private space with landslides, burning arrows, and even credits. Its effect on composition can be a mixed blessing, as 3-D has a tendency to become *planographic*; in other words, one often sees a number of nearly flat images separated from each other in depth. With their wide fields and curved screens, some CinemaScope films actually conveyed more realistic impressions of depth and roundness than did 1950s 3-D — without causing headaches.

When used carefully and with restraint, however, 3-D can be a definite asset. Although *Dial M for Murder* (1954) was released "flat" — that is, in a two-dimensional version — Hitchcock shot it in 3-D, and the 3-D version was revived in the early 1980s. Much of *Dial M* takes place in one living room (it was adapted from a play), and the 3-D gives this room the feel of a rich and complex set, a defined space within which the actors move and which they turn to their own purposes. At only two points in that film did Hitchcock make an image protrude drastically through the **stereo window** (the apparent proscenium): when Grace Kelly, as the intended murder victim, reaches behind her to grab a lethal pair of scissors, and when the detective extends in his open palm the latchkey that implicates the real murderer. Those were the two crucial twists in the plot, and Hitchcock's restrained use of the protruding image gave them extra dramatic weight.

Composition

As one aspect of mise-en-scène, **composition** refers to the arrangement of the elements of the image in relation to the boundaries of the frame and to each other — the organization of two-dimensional space. The frame itself provides the reference points and defines the field; it makes composition possible. People, objects, and light itself become elements of a composition, aspects of an arrangement. They become lines and fields, vacuums and volumes.

To frame an image is to decide not only what will be included or excluded but also what the visual relationships among image elements will be. In a carefully composed image, the placement of elements within the frame clarifies their relative importance and can define or comment on their interactions (as seen in **Fig. 2-51**).

Balance and Symmetry. Each element has its own visual "weight," which may be a matter of volume, color, line, or placement. A **balanced composition** is evenly weighted, though it need not be bilaterally symmetrical. A symmetrical image with a vertical rectangle to the left of center and another rectangle of the same size to the right of center would be *very* balanced. If there were

Figure 2-57

only a rectangle on the right and a blank space on the left, that composition would be unbalanced to the right — as if the center of the frame were a kind of fulcrum. In the proper position, a small volume can balance a large one.

A completely balanced composition may seem less than dynamic, and it may be the slight departure from symmetry that makes such a composition interesting. In Raphael's 1504 painting, *The Marriage of the Virgin* (**Fig. 2-57** — signed and dated above the door), the overall composition is bilaterally symmetrical (the left side mirrors the right). Its perspective lines would converge somewhere behind the door of the building, at infinity.

A closer look reveals that Raphael subtly unbalanced this symmetry to increase visual interest. There are more figures in the right background than in the left, and the rabbi's head is inclined toward the right of the frame. The bending heads of Mary and Joseph mirror each other, but a look at the perspective lines behind them reveals that they are each slightly off-center. What is actually at the center of the frame is the ring held in Joseph's hand, and its centrality declares its importance as well as making it the fulcrum and the balance point of the scene. The ring is exactly lined up with the middle of the middle row of steps and tiles (the central perspective line). The rabbi's beard has been combed into two parallel strands, and the shadow line between them leads the eye directly to the ring. This artful composition asserts the stability of the marriage, which is a matter of the ring even more than of the couple; it draws attention to the major action, which is the putting of the ring on the bride's extended hand; and it provides enough variety and visual relief to keep the whole from seeming *too* arranged.

Geometrical Composition. Some compositions can be described as circular, triangular, or rectangular if their elements fall

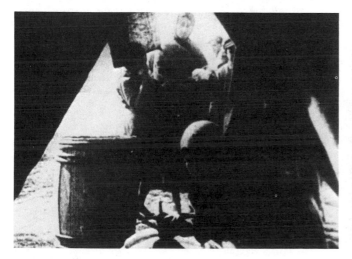

Figure 2-58

Figure 2-59

Figure 2-60

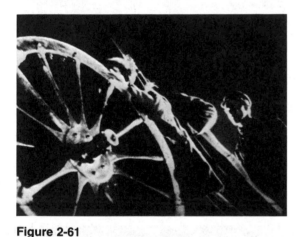

Figure 2-61

into standard geometrical relationships. Both **Fig. 2-58** and **Fig. 2-59** are triangular compositions. The triangle in **Fig. 2-58**, from Eisenstein's *Battleship Potemkin* (1925), is created by the tent flaps as if by a mask; that in **Fig. 2-59**, from Eisenstein's *Ivan the Terrible, Part Two* (1946), is created by blocking and camera placement.

When the base of the triangle is at the bottom of the frame, the image usually has an impression of extreme stability, and the apex of the triangle is the site of greatest power. This is one reason that a low-angle shot is often used to depict a powerful figure, because the figure's trunk or base is broadened by perspective, while its head or top is narrowed, and a triangle set on its base is incapable of toppling. An inverted triangle gives the opposite effect, wobbling on its apex in the most unstable of all geometrical structures.

In **Fig. 2-59** Czar Ivan plays a deadly game of pretending to place his young, simple-minded rival on the throne. Ivan's line of dialogue, "I am not rooting out oaks to clear a place for aspens," is meant to mislead the court into thinking that he considers the would-be prince a strong, oaklike figure, but his true intentions are ironic. The composition declares that Ivan is the oak and that the figure seated on the throne is little more than an aspen. The throne itself has a triangular peak, and its occupant might, given another framing, have appeared impressive. But it is Ivan who dominates the triangular composition in this framing; thus we can *see* that he is still the true czar. In **Fig. 2-58** the triangle is used to connote not power but rest and stability (the scene is a wake for a sailor whose corpse is at the bottom of the frame). The roof of the tent creates a mood of intimacy and enclosure, and the broad base gives the image a sense of groundedness and solid presence.

The Line. As elements within a composition, most photographic subjects can be reduced to the terms of line and volume. A volume is an occupied area, whether the occupant is a person, an object, or a patch of light, color, or shadow. Where volumes have visual

Figure 2-62

Figure 2-63

weight, lines have direction. Together with vacuum (space) and medium, they create plastic form.

Sometimes the line has a purely formal value. The line of the jetty in the Odessa harbor, also taken from *Potemkin* (**Fig. 2-60**), is simply a sinuous curve, and it works with the boundaries of the frame to create a composition.

Film composition is drastically affected by camera placement, not just in terms of camera-to-subject distance but also in terms of angle. A horizontal line, seen from a certain angle, can become a diagonal or even a vertical. In **Fig. 2-61**, from Eisenstein's *October* (1928), cinematographer Eduard Tisse and assistant Vladimir Nilsen used a low, oblique camera angle in order to obtain what they called "the proper dynamic distortion" of the figures. The figures are part of a military procession, opposing the counterrevolutionary campaign of General Kornilov. They appear to be leaning into a powerful wind and straining as if uphill, but they move horizontally from screen right to left. When this scene was shot, the procession was actually moving uphill, and the low camera angle gave the figures some dynamism. The full effect was realized when Tisse tilted the camera to one side, lining up the bottom of the frame with the line of the hill (the sloping platform).

According to many filmmakers and art historians, the point of greatest interest within a frame is located along a diagonal line that runs from the bottom of screen left to the top of screen right. Eisenstein exploited this principle throughout his work, most clearly in this frame from *October* (**Fig. 2-62**) where the flag in Lenin's hand runs along that very line, visually reinforcing the dynamic energy of the Bolshevik movement.

Although rules were made to be broken, or at least to be redefined in practice, the general rule is that horizontal lines imply stability, verticals are powerful but relatively unstable, and diagonals are the most dynamic. In the Odessa Steps sequence of *Potemkin*, Eisenstein varied his compositions so that their dominant lines would comment on the action and increase its dramatic impact. The situation is that a ruthless line of soldiers is descending a wide, outdoor staircase in the town of Odessa and firing on a group of citizens who have turned out to show their support for the mutineers who have taken over the battleship *Potemkin*; the time is 1905.

In **Figs. 2-63** and **2-64** the diagonal compositions make the soldiers and their rifles especially powerful, whereas **Fig. 2-65**, with its virtual grid of horizontal lines, mocks the apparent safety of the Odessa Steps via an ironically stable, yet top-heavy, composition. The cuts among these and similar views give the entire sequence a marvelous dynamism, a sense of continually shifting frames of reference that communicates the upheaval of revolutionary conflict and the chaos of surprise. In an earlier shot (**Fig. 2-66**), Eisenstein set lines in conflict within the frame. One line of mutineers runs diagonally from right to left while another line runs from left to right. Attempting to follow both movements, the eye is excited into sharing the contradictory rush of the moment.

Figure 2-64

Figure 2-65

Figure 2-66

Figure 2-67

Coping with Scope. Because the perimeter provides the points of reference that allow a composition to be structured, the aspect ratio plays a significant role. The Academy ratio has long been valued for its ability to define and enhance the greatest variety of interesting spatial arrangements. The more elongated rectangle of the wide screen enhances horizontal compositions but limits what can be done with the vertical.

The problem is to use the entire frame area in an interesting manner, not necessarily to fill it. One mark of a good wide image is that it *cannot* successfully be panned and scanned. **Fig. 2-67** is a production still from Elia Kazan's *East of Eden* (1955), but it has been cropped to CinemaScope proportions. The whole frame has integrity as a unit, and there is no 1.33 : 1 rectangle that can include all of its significant elements at once, let alone express the James Dean character's isolation from the others. Note how the line of the trough integrates the composition — or imagine the frame without it and evaluate the difference.

Figs. 2-68 through **2-70**, from Fred Wilcox's *Forbidden Planet* (1956), illustrate the compositional challenge of the wide frame. In **Fig. 2-68** the composition is balanced, with significant information at the left and right sides of the screen, but it feels as if the middle were being avoided (the table helps to alleviate the problem). In **Fig. 2-69**, a conventional two-shot that would have worked well in the Academy ratio, all the information is in the center, and the sides are left hanging. But in **Fig. 2-70** significant information is distributed throughout the frame, and the diagonal composition in depth further enhances visual interest.

Composition in Depth. Compositions can be organized in relation not only to the boundaries of the frame but also to the line that runs from the camera to infinity. Both foreground and back-

Figure 2-68

Figure 2-69

Figure 2-70

ground, although differently weighted, are equally significant image fields, and their relationships can be structured so that the frame takes on a sense of depth — or loses it, depending on the filmmaker's intentions. In this frame from *Citizen Kane* (**Fig. 2-71**) the planes of the image are interrelated by having Kane, in the background, throw his coat to Leland, in the foreground. Following the moving coat, the eye travels through the depth of the image.

Composition in depth is the art of placing significant information in widely separated image planes, often along or in relation to the camera-to-subject axis.

Although it might be assumed that the most straightforward way

Figure 2-71

to indicate the importance of a figure would be to put him, her, or it in the foreground, front and center, composition in depth can give just this kind of importance to a figure in the background. In this production still from *Citizen Kane* (**Fig. 2-72**) — which is quite similar to this shot in the film — Kane dominates the composition

Figure 2-72

Figure 2-73

even though his volume is small. He does this partly because he is isolated in the center of the frame, but primarily because his figure is at the point of convergence of the deep *V* whose foreground points are Bernstein and Thatcher. This composition is triangular, but in depth.

Fig. 2-73, a frame enlargement from *Kane*, shows how a composition can be organized both laterally and in depth. It also shows how lines of sight can alert the audience to a composition, can direct the eye along selected imaginary lines. The composition is in a *V*; down from Leland and past Bernstein (Everett Sloane) to Kane, then up to Thatcher (George Coulouris) on the right. But it is also a *V* in depth: forward from Leland in the background, to Kane in the middle ground, and to Thatcher in the foreground. The center of interest, the point at which the lines of the *V* converge, is Kane.

The fact that the characters are looking down these lines makes the lines even more prominent and clarifies the reason for the composition. In this scene Thatcher is confronting Kane, a powerful but upstart editor. Lined up behind Kane, Bernstein and Leland appear to be extensions of his personal power; even if we are interested in them, our eyes follow the line they make down to Kane, like the line in the beard of Raphael's rabbi. That line also gives visual importance to the telegram that Bernstein is reading, the temporary center of dramatic interest. But the line of Thatcher's sight points directly to Kane, and that line tells us that Thatcher is more interested in Kane than in the telegram.

Vacuum and Volume. The "empty" spaces of a composition are just as significant as its occupied areas. Vacuum and volume inev-

Figure 2-74

Figure 2-75

Figure 2-76

itably work together: it is the relatively empty background area that allows Kane to dominate **Fig. 2-72**, just as the line in **Fig. 2-60** is created equally by the ocean vacuum and the jetty volume.

A composition can clarify not only what is in the frame but also what is missing from it or is about to happen in it. If a figure is alone in the frame — near screen right, for example, and facing the right edge of the frame — we normally expect that someone will sneak up on that person from the left. A large, empty field may call out to be occupied; a composition can demand to be balanced by an absent figure.

In *Intolerance,* when Griffith wanted to indicate the moral isolation of a boss named Jenkins, he framed him in long shot so that Jenkins is surrounded by fields of barren room (see **Fig. 2-162**). A wonderful use of space that calls out to be occupied occurs near the beginning of *Top Hat.* Fred Astaire is shown walking, and the camera pans to follow him — but it moves more than it would have had to if all that had been intended was to keep him in view. The camera soon takes in an open area of parquet floor, and the attentive viewer knows that Astaire will soon complete the composition by dancing in the space of that floor. The camera, slightly anticipating Astaire's movements, works with him here like a dance partner. Because it does more than simply to keep Astaire in view, the new visual arrangement sets us up for what is to come. This expectation arises when we read the composition.

Composition and Meaning. Early in *Queen Christina* the Swedish king is killed in battle, and his young daughter Christina is promoted to the throne. She is so small that the crown must be held above her head by two courtiers. In **Fig. 2-74** Christina is slightly off-center, with the courtiers to either side and her adviser at screen right. That composition clarifies the power structure at this point and implies that Christina needs — or in any case will receive — the adviser's help; the group of four is centered. The queen has just been asked how she intends to continue her father's military campaign, and she is delivering a prepared speech when she forgets a phrase. "We promise — " she says, and falters.

Then there is a **cutaway** (a cut away from a setup to which the camera may soon return in a **cutback**) to a closeup of the adviser (**Fig. 2-75**). He prompts her, whispering, "To wage it with courage." The closeup gives him an impression of power, and as a cutaway it facilitates the change of camera position seen in **Fig. 2-76**.

In this final frame — the cutback — Christina is central. The frame has been redefined to exclude the adviser, who, of course, has not moved. What she says here is "We promise to *win* it!" This charming line is significant because it is in the girl's own language; it indicates that she understands the issues and will handle them herself and in her own way. The composition asserts the same thing, showing her in a position of centrality and autonomy. She has balanced the frame herself: Mamoulian's way of showing that she has resolved the political crisis of the succession.

Another fine bit of authorial commentary, and one that helps to clarify the emotions of the main character, comes near the end of the film. Christina has abdicated the throne in order to live a more fully human and spontaneous life, and in a profoundly moving scene she has removed the crown from her head with her own hands. But as she addresses the court, the camera has been positioned so that a carved figure of the crown in the background appears directly over her head. That composition asserts that she is still essentially a queen, both for the audience and for the director; it also shows how the aura of the throne remains a part of Christina's being, how this transition feels to her. For further examples of how composition affects meaning, review the "desert island" scene between Kane and Leland, discussed in Section 4 of Part I.

Movement and Succession. What makes cinematic composition fundamentally different from composition in painting and still photography is the element of motion — the challenge of composing movement, not just stable geometry. Regardless of whether it is the camera or the subject that changes position within the shot, it is important that they move from one significant composition to another and that those compositions work together. As organized movement, cinematic composition can well be thought of as choreography.

Whereas the composition in a painting or a still can be analyzed at leisure, a cinematic composition must declare itself quickly, must make its impression before it is displaced by another shot. Along with this constraint comes the opportunity to devise compositions that will succeed each other in an interesting and significant manner.

Many of the shots in *Citizen Kane* were set up so that continual reframing and reblocking create several distinct compositions, one after the other. A more conventional practice is to cut between compositions, as Eisenstein did. In a nonfiction film, where the subject is usually autonomous, the cameraman's challenge is to frame the figure in an interesting manner. From Fred Wiseman's *High School* (1968) to Jeff Margolis's *Richard Pryor — Live in Concert* (1979), there is a subtle drama as the camera follows the subject, achieves focus, and seeks out a composition.

It should be kept in mind that many filmmakers are more-or-less indifferent to composition and simply make sure that the subject of interest is visible, in focus, adequately lit, and — as often as not — in the central foreground and within the TV safe area. But that does not tell against those filmmakers who respect composition and know how to make it work for them.

3. Black-and-White and Color

The frame may be in color or in black-and-white. This aspect of the frame is so important and provides the filmmaker with so many artistic resources that it requires a separate discussion.

The earliest photographs and movies were all shot in black-and-white. Many early films, however, were presented to their audiences in color. In some cases the individual frames were hand-painted. More often the entire image was bathed in a single color; this was done on the print after the film had been shot in black-and-white.

In the 1920s some films began to be shot in color. In the 1930s and 1940s the dominant color system was Technicolor, a process that in most cases used three strips of film to transfer dyes onto a single print. The 1950s saw the advent of Eastmancolor, a single strip of film capable of recording the entire visible spectrum instantaneously.

One way or another, then, filmmakers have long had the choice whether to present their films in black-and-white or in color, even if *shooting* in color was a relatively late development. Since the 1950s it has been common practice to shoot features in color — at first, because the competition, TV, could not broadcast color, and now because color TV is a major market for films — but the resources of black-and-white remain available, and so does the opportunity to mix the two within a single image.

Black-and-White

According to one school of thought, the mark of an excellent black-and-white photograph or movie frame is that it includes the com-

Figure 2-77

Figure 2-78

plete range of tones from black to white, with fully realized and distinct intermediate grays.

These production stills from *Broken Blossoms* (**Fig. 2-77**) and *Casablanca* (**Fig. 2-78**) live up to those demands. In the *Broken Blossoms* still there is a clear separation between black and white, and the subdued grays under the stairs and the brighter grays in the display case are equally clear and well-defined. The range in the *Casablanca* still is more limited, with most of the grays in a complex middle range, but the emulsion has still done justice to the pianist's dark coat, the high-lit champagne bottle, and the bright sheet of music, which is, of course, "As Time Goes By."

Although black-and-white may be thought of as the "absence" of color, it is actually a complete palette or repertoire of shades. It is a system with its own terms, comparable to the two-dimensionality of the frame: its limits make its art possible. Nor is it devoid of "psychological" color, because many people read color values into the grays and may find color film overstated — in fact, psychologically limiting because it provides so *much* definite information. Because many of the resources and techniques associated with black-and-white have been covered in previous discussions of filmstock and lighting, we shall concentrate here on a few examples of what can be done with black-and-white *itself*.

Two Vampires. Mention black-and-white, and the first thing many people will think of is the opportunity to work with shadows. In color, shadows are in danger of being washed out or of appearing as patches of muted color. But a shadow in black-and-white can be rich, deep, and satisfyingly dark. Black-and-white lends itself

readily to the age-old symbolic opposition between light and shadow, good and evil, freedom and enclosure, lightheartedness and sorrow. As closely tied as it can be to such symbolic structures and emotional moods, it is also a self-sufficient system that can be experimented with and organized in numberless original ways.

Both Murnau's *Nosferatu* (**Fig. 2-79**) and Dreyer's *Vampyr* (**Fig. 2-80**) tell stories about vampires. Murnau often let his vampire appear as a distillation of darkness, a hard-edged and angularly distorted shadow. Dreyer, on the other hand, rarely presented his vampire (the old woman with the cane) as a shadow. For **Fig. 2-80** cinematographer Rudolf Maté directed a light into the lens in or-

Figure 2-80

der to achieve a highly diffused image. Here the range of grays is limited but extremely effective, and the foggy texture of the scene is palpably frightening.

Where **Fig. 2-79** works with the extremes of the gray scale, **Fig. 2-80** works with the midrange, and where the lighting in one is hard, that in the other is soft. Yet both are intensely atmospheric, and each defines the categories of spirituality and nightmare in which it is interested. *Nosferatu* is concerned with an incarnation of absolute evil, whereas *Vampyr* examines the interfusion of evil and God's grace. Both images are just as concerned with the opportunity to use black-and-white as they are with the nature of the vampire and the imagery of night.

Texture. The texture of an image is not only a matter of grain, nor of hardness and diffusion, although all of these do have pronounced effects. A careful use of proximate grays (tones that are near or next to each other on the gray scale) can give the image an almost tangible texture.

In these two frames from the night battle in *Napoleon* a soldier has been pushed beneath the surface of a pool of mud; his hand gropes around for solid ground. In **Fig. 2-81** the shadow makes it easy to see the hand. **Fig. 2-82**, without the shadow, is less arresting at first but more interesting in the long run, because here the hand and the mud share much the same texture. Hand and mud are all one field, and the threat of their merging — which would kill the soldier — becomes oddly beautiful. Like the frame from *Vampyr,* these images can be appreciated for the subtle textures of their surfaces and their masterly control of shading and tone.

Separation and Depth. When a dark figure is against a dark background, it is easy for that figure to get lost. It is relatively simple to isolate centers of interest and to keep them from bleeding together when working with color, but to separate one gray from another may require careful blocking and lighting.

In **Fig. 2-83** a back light has been used to separate Raymond, Kane's butler (Paul Stewart), from the stucco wall behind him and to accentuate the texture of that wall. The match flame separates his hands from his face and motivates a rich shadow. A **motivated** lighting effect is one that has its apparent origin in a light source that is part of the set: a ceiling fixture, a table lamp, a window, a flashlight, a match — and in the case of exteriors, the sun, moon, clouds, and sky.

Light can also contribute to the impression of depth within the frame. This goes well beyond considerations of depth of field (focus) or perspective. Even when they are in focus, one may need to separate disparate planes further through lighting effects, perhaps by giving each area of the set its own texture, by interposing light and dark areas, or by introducing clearly readable perspective lines. In **Fig. 2-84**, also from *Kane*, it is the lighting that is most responsible for the apparent depth of the image. If the set had been fully illuminated, it would have appeared more shallow

Figure 2-81

Figure 2-82

Figure 2-83

Figure 2-84

even if the depth of field remained unchanged. **Fig. 2-84** may also serve as a summary example of a rich and fine-grained black-and-white field whose motivated low-key lighting creates a full range of grays.

Black-and-White Versus Color

Both color and black-and-white have their own distinct merits. Given the choice, filmmakers decide on one system or the other because of what it can contribute to the project at hand. As a simple indication of how drastically this decision can affect the finished product, imagine how much would be lost if Disney's *Fantasia* (1940) had been in black-and-white, or if *Psycho* had been in color.

Or imagine if *It's A Wonderful Life* had been in color. When *Video Review* (June 1986) asked James Stewart his opinion of **colorization** (imparting colors to black-and-white movies), he said:

I think it's terrible. It's a shame that they're doing it. Frank Capra and I talked them out of colorizing *It's A Wonderful Life* last year, but the picture's in public domain now, and nobody can really stop this colorization thing for long. I think it's an insult to the people who did the movies in black-and-white. . . . In black-and-white, you had to mold not only the people's faces but also the background and everything, to give it depth and to make it interesting to look at. . . . When they put that color on a girl's face, a face that had these beautiful lights at a correct angle, then all those shadows are taken off and she just has sort of a light-orange face. And the background — one thing's red, the other thing's green. There's no composition to the thing.

George Romero's decision to shoot *Night of the Living Dead* in black-and-white was deliberate. That is one film anyone can agree is better for being in black-and-white, for it is a dark, relentless nightmare of the Vietnam-and-civil-rights-movement period (it was released in 1968), and its deep shadows and sharp contrasts heighten the tension and emphasize the quality of massive, cheap, uncanny nightmare. It proved just as appropriate that Romero's *Dawn of the Dead* (1979) be shot in color, for it is (in the uncut version) an extremely funny parody of the more professedly "open" and narcissistic 1970s, of "mall consciousness" and elevator music, yet with a keen eye to contemporary urban conflicts and the failures of the media. Color, daylight, and comedy worked together in *Dawn*, as black-and-white, night, and terror had in *Night*. Neither film lacked in horror or in gore.

To show the world in natural color, color film is necessary — but beyond that, color can function as a coded system, with certain moods and meanings assigned to certain colors. (At the start of *Dial M for Murder*, for example, her red dress encodes Grace Kelly as a "scarlet woman.") The palette, or range of colors used, can be limited to certain hues and degrees of saturation. The kinetic and psychological effects of particular colors can be exploited: a restful blue, for instance, followed by a bright orange.

The overwhelming limitation of black-and-white — that it can show only a range of grays — is also its greatest advantage. By reducing the world to a consistent and single spectrum, black-and-white has a scale of values that can be precisely controlled and interrelated.

Using Both. A number of movies have included both color and black-and-white, sometimes within the same image. A *little* color can be extremely powerful.

In Byron Haskin's *War of the Worlds* (1953), colored flames were superimposed around the edges of black-and-white footage of running crowds and falling buildings. The newsreels shown in theaters at the time were invariably in black-and-white, and so black-and-white gave these scenes the aura of authenticity: one could have assumed that one was looking at genuine news footage. The colored flames link those images with the world of the rest of the film, which is in color, and provide an effect that is visually exciting in itself.

In Coppola's *Rumble Fish* (1983), the fish of the title are in color, and the rest of the film is in black-and-white. The fact that the heroes see the fish as colored tells a great deal about their romanticism and their isolation, and it trades on a conventional reading of black-and-white as "colorless." It is also a simple way to call special attention to the fish, to lend them symbolic weight, to make them more vivid than the world, and to create some utterly beautiful images.

Black-and-white and color have also been used in alternation, most notably in *Night and Fog* and *The Wizard of Oz,* whose Kansas is inconceivable except in monochrome.

Color

Basic Terminology. Any color can be defined in terms of its hue, its saturation, and its brightness.

The **hue**, which can most simply be thought of as the name of the color, defines the relation of a particular color — say, burnt orange — to a primary reference color, like pure red. The range of hues can be thought of as linear (like the line of the spectrum that runs from red to violet) or as an endless circle that runs from red to yellow to green to blue to violet to red (the arrangement of the **color wheel**). If you think of orange as occupying a position on the color wheel comparable to that of 2 o'clock on the face of a watch, then a particular burnt orange may be located on the wheel at 1:57; that position is its hue. Some colors, like black, white, and gray, have no hues and are called **achromatic colors**. Those that have hues are called **chromatic colors**.

Saturation indicates how much a given chromatic color differs from the nearest achromatic color — how different it is from gray. A pure white or black would have zero saturation, as would gray. Dull or pale colors have low saturation, and intense, vivid colors have high saturation.

Brightness refers to how light or dark a color is, in other words how much light it is emitting or reflecting. The sun is brighter than the moon, and a rose in full sunlight is brighter than a rose seen by moonlight.

Brightness can be divided into the factors of luminosity and lightness. **Luminosity** is the amount of light that appears to be coming from a specific color patch or colored area; that is, how much light comes from the portion of the visual field occupied by the rose. **Lightness** is the proportion of the total available light that is being reflected by the color patch; that is, how much of the light in the complete visual field is being reflected by the rose.

Directly across the color wheel from any hue is a hue with opposite properties. Pairs of opposite hues are called **complementary colors**. Blue and yellow are complementary colors. A color that cannot be produced by the mixture of other colors is called a **primary color**. Any other hue can be produced by the mixture of primary colors in specific proportions; thus orange, which is not a primary color, can be made by the combination of red and yellow, but no combination of orange and violet will yield the primary red. On a color wheel, the primaries are equidistant.

Additive and Subtractive Systems. There are two sets of primary colors, depending on whether the color system is additive or subtractive. In an **additive** color system, whose primaries are red, green, and blue, the various *lights add* to each other so that the final color is the sum of their information. When all three primaries — or any two complementary colors — are projected onto a screen at the same levels of brightness and saturation, they add to white. In a **subtractive** color system, whose primaries are yellow, cyan, and magenta, the various *dyes and filters absorb* color information — subtract it from white — so that the resultant color is what they leave to be seen. When the subtractive primaries — or any two complements — are mixed equally, the result is black.

The subtractive primaries are the complements of the additive primaries: cyan is the complement of red, magenta of green, and yellow of blue. For convenience, the primaries are abbreviated to **RGB** and **YCM** (or **CMY**). In the case of colored bodies or paints (not lights), the subtractive primaries are red, yellow, and blue.

Color film is a subtractive system. Colors are produced by the selective removal of hues from the spectrum of white light. If you look at life through rose-colored glasses, all the wavelengths except pink are being subtracted from the spectrum. The color emulsion (and black-and-white emulsion exposed through a colored filter) keeps a record of the wavelengths it has absorbed. Dyed, that record is a color image.

Three Emulsions. The most satisfactory way to record a complete color image is to work in terms of the primaries: to make discrete records of the cyan, magenta, and yellow information. (YCM is for negatives, RGB for positives.) This can be achieved with three separate strips of film or with a single strip of base coated with three emulsions; the latter is called an **integral tripack** or **monopack** system, and as Eastmancolor it was introduced in 1951. We shall take up three-strip Technicolor® and some of the older color processes shortly.

If a cyan filter is placed in front of an emulsion, the complement (red) is removed from the spectrum, and the emulsion will be exposed only to the cyan information in the visual field; for this reason a cyan filter is often called **minus-red**. A magenta filter is **minus-green**, and yellow is **minus-blue**. In monopack, each of the three sandwiched emulsions responds to approximately one third of the spectrum. As the light passes through each layer, some of its color information is absorbed by that layer and is not allowed to pass further.

Monopack color depends on both filters and couplers. Between the blue-sensitive emulsion and the blue-and-green-sensitive emulsion, for example, the light encounters a yellow filter. Each emulsion layer includes **dye couplers**, fine globules that react during development to release their dyes. These dyes form colored images that remain suspended in the gelatin in a pattern dictated by the exposure of the silver halide crystals with which they are associated, or "coupled."

During processing, the exposed silver halides are developed into metallic silver, and the couplers react to form colored dye images. Then the silver image is removed by bleaching and fixing, leaving the colored image. That single image is, of course, three perfectly superimposed microthin images, each of which subtracts its information from the white light of the projector.

Technicolor. **Imbibition printing**, also called the **dye transfer process**, was perfected by the Technicolor company. From 1926 to

1932, complementary color records were exposed onto two strips of black-and-white film; beginning in 1932, the RGB records were exposed onto three strips of black-and-white film; and in the 1960s and early 1970s the camera was loaded with monopack stock. Much as in the process of silk-screen printing, the YCM dyes are applied directly onto the printing stock by means of individual matrices.

The three-strip Technicolor camera — which went out of use with the introduction of monopack Technicolor, but whose operation is easier to explain — exposed three frames at a time, each on a separate strip of film. The camera had two magazines; the first ran a single roll of stock, but the second magazine was loaded in bi-pack, which means that it ran *two* rolls of film at once. Without getting into the intricacies of bi-pack camera loads (which we will take up along with special effects cinematography in Part III), let us just say that the camera simultaneously exposed frames on three perfectly synchronized rolls of stock and that those frames were kept in tight horizontal registration during the instant of exposure. Each frame was exposed through a primary-color filter (or the equivalent), so each recorded its third of the spectrum in black-and-white. These three negatives were then used to produce three positive matrices.

The **matrix** is a celluloid strip bearing various thicknesses of hardened gelatin, and it both absorbs dyes and sheds them. It absorbs more dye where the negative is denser, that is, where there would be more of a particular color. The information from the red record is converted to a matrix that soaks up cyan dye. Then each matrix is laid on top of the print stock, and the dye is transferred onto the print. After one pass from each matrix, the Technicolor print is complete.

The dyes used in the integral tripack represent a working compromise between the color effects desired and the fact that these dyes have to go through many chemical processes that must be compensated for in advance. Imbibition dyes simply have to be absorbed by the matrix and deposited on the film, and so they can be relatively pure. In the color stills pages **Fig. C-6** has been reproduced directly from an original Technicolor frame, and it may help to suggest how an instant of John Huston's *The African Queen* looked when the film was first released in 1951. (To convey the full effect, that frame would have to have been printed by the publishers in dye transfer.) The last American film made in Technicolor was *The Godfather, Part II*, in 1974. It used monopack camera stock and matrix printing.

Hand-Painting, Tinting, and Toning. During the silent period there were three principal ways of adding color to a black-and-white image. The earliest, used rarely because it was so expensive and time-consuming, was to **hand-paint** every single frame. **Fig. C-7** is a hand-painted frame from Edwin S. Porter's *The Great Train Robbery* (1903).

The more widely used silent color processes were tinting and toning. Both were achieved during the printing stage rather than in the camera. For **tinting**, the black-and-white negative is printed onto specially colored filmstock (or else the print is run through a vat of dye), and the image is evenly monochromatic. A blue-colored tint might be used for night scenes, sepia for interiors, or red for battles. **Fig. C-8** illustrates the red tint used for a night battle in *Napoleon*. **Fig. C-9** shows the sepia tint, here used for a *Napoleon* daylight exterior, and **Fig. C-10** shows the blue. The image in **Fig. C-10** is rushing water (cut by Napoleon's boat as he fled Corsica, much earlier in the film): one wing of *Napoleon's* concluding triptych, which at this point has blue water at one side, white (untinted) water in the middle, and red water at the other side: the colors of the French flag. This is one example of a stylish gesture that can lift color into the realm of symbolism and authorial commentary.

For **toning**, the black-and-white image is chemically converted to a colored image, and the color appears only where there are silver crystals. Where the print is transparent, or free of silver, the dye does not adhere to the filmstock. Thus the darker the image, the deeper the color. Note the whites of the soldier's eyes in this toned frame from *Napoleon* (**Fig. C-11**), and compare them with Napoleon's eyes in the accompanying tinted frame (**Fig. C-12**).

Tinting and toning afforded the artist a great degree of emotional and aesthetic control over the image, well at odds with conventional realism. Some of the colors in *Broken Blossoms* are unusually beautiful and appeared in no other films, like the rich purple of the harbor in **Fig. C-13**, or the delicate pinks in **Fig. C-14.**

Monochromatic color effects did not, however, disappear with the silent film. In **Fig. C-15**, from *2001*, the full-screen red not only characterizes the otherness of the computer area but also acts as a sign for the danger of the astronaut's situation. Tobe Hooper's *Poltergeist* (1982), from which **Fig. C-16** is taken, often uses a single color to characterize a scene. When the child sits in front of the TV, early in the film, the image is an eerie gray-blue, as if the light from the TV were about to engulf the living room. When the mother attempts to rescue her children from their chaotic bedroom, the image is red. In **Fig. C-16**, where the heroes are about to enter the spiritual territory of the ghosts, the wash of blue light is both calming and mysterious; if the light had been red, the connotations of violence and danger would have been emphasized. This frame also indicates the cinematic power of colored *light*, which can be as specific to cinema as colored pigments are to painting. Furthermore, as an effect that can be found in Spielberg films from *Close Encounters* to *E.T.* (Spielberg produced *Poltergeist*) but that has no precedent in Hooper's work, this flood of immaterial blue may prove important in sorting out which of the two brainstorming collaborators was most responsible for creating particular sections of this movie. In other words, an attitude toward the use of color can be part of a filmmaker's personal style.

Color and Realism.

A system of carefully chosen and integrated colors is called a **color scheme**. A color scheme can be extensive, like those in *Gone With the Wind* or *The Wizard of Oz* (both of which were shot in Technicolor), or it can be deliberately limited for particular effects. **Figs. C-17** and **C-18** are production stills from Ken Russell's *The Boy Friend* (1971). **Fig. C-17** has a subdued color scheme, mostly in grays and blues with little saturation, whereas in **Fig. C-18** the palette is saturated and bright, almost to the point of loudness.

Although there is a noticeable difference between natural and artificial colors, some filmmakers are determined to get the actual colors of the world into their movies; that is, they use an intensely realistic color scheme. Brakhage accomplished this in *Mothlight* (**Fig. C-19**) by taking his images as directly as possible from nature. Apart from the *Mothlight* solution, which involved no camera, realistic color is a matter of choosing the proper filmstock, lighting the subject at the correct color temperature, and developing and printing according to precise, normal specifications. One can obtain unrealistic color — to create a mood, express a state of mind, or redefine the world — by changing the natural color of the subject (painting a tree blue), using filters, unbalancing the light, developing at an unauthorized temperature, or whatever else works.

Most filmmakers achieve their color schemes by realistically photographing a visual field whose colors have been *preselected*, like a room full of silver furniture. Sets, costumes, props, and even flesh tones may be chosen with an eye to what they will contribute to the complete color effect, which is an important aspect of mise-en-scène. What most filmgoers do not realize is how carefully the colors for a "realistic" scene are chosen and how much they contribute to the design and even the meaning of the film.

In an expressionistic film like Masaki Kobayashi's *Kwaidan* (1964), where pure blue dyes fall through clear water or a wild red painting can stand in for the sky, it is easy to appreciate that color is being used as an emotional vehicle or even as an exercise in sheer artistic flair. On the other hand, consider the green light that illuminates Judy's transformation back into Madeleine ("both" played by Kim Novak) near the end of *Vertigo*. This light, which has a great deal of symbolic value in context, is motivated by a neon sign outside Judy's hotel room. We could look at the light and say, well, it comes from the sign — or we could appreciate the way it acts as a magical, glamorous force, a transformative and romantic agency. This is a classic example of the expressive potential of "realistic" color and lighting.

Color Composition.

Just as a black-and-white image may aspire to the full range of grays, some color schemes attempt to include the majority of the visible spectrum. In this production still from *Gone With the Wind* (**Fig. C-20**) high-key lighting brings out the brightness and saturation of a wide range of hues: the variety of reds, yellows, greens, browns, blues, and even the pure blacks and whites. There is a similar range of colors in **Fig. C-21**, from *The Wizard of Oz*, but here the color areas have been separated within the frame. To screen right, Dorothy and the scarecrow and the yellow brick road occupy an area of brightness and enthusiasm; to screen left, the gray tree and the witch's black cape promote darkness and doom. These two areas, which themselves *are* the dramatic content of the scene, are integrated by a clever use of green: the grassy bank that borders the yellow brick road leads our eye to the green face of the witch. Finally, the bright apples unify the scheme, distributing spots of red across the top of the field and bringing the two areas together. Both of these are good examples of what is meant by **color composition**.

As one aspect of composition, color can be used to highlight the center of interest. In the production still from *Gone With the Wind* shown in **Fig. C-22**, the eye is immediately drawn to the spot of red that is Scarlett's dress.

Heightened and Expressionist Color. Some filmmakers completely depart from realism in the interests of personal style, authorial commentary, or even outright Expressionism. Eisenstein experimented with color in a sequence near the end of *Ivan the Terrible, Part II*. In **Fig. C-23** he divided the image into bands of red, black, and green, apparently out of sheer delight at being able to compose in color. At another point, figures in black robes and carrying candles are seen against a vivid red background: a stylish gesture with classically Expressionist intentions.

In **Figs. C-24** and **C-25** Eisenstein changed the lights falling on the subject to render the core of the dramatic situation as an aspect of the visible world. In **Fig. C-24** a loyal subject asks Ivan, "Does not the blood we shed tie us closer to you?" What he is really asking is why Ivan might consider elevating a numbskull to the throne, rather than choosing a successor from among those who have proved loyal to him. Although the lighting at this point is more-or-less realistic, with the questioner in a red-brown shadow that may have been motivated by the reddish light of the room, the light changes instantly when Ivan answers, "You are not my kin" (**Fig. C-25**). Now both figures are washed by a blood-red floodlight; the questioner falls into an even deeper shadow, signifying his disappointment and his fears. Ivan is truly terrible in this moment — formidable and in charge. The light on his face is as bloody as his true thoughts (he has no intention of keeping his kin on the throne but will have the pretender murdered within a few minutes). This unmotivated shift in color — no "realistic" red light source has entered the room — is entirely artificial, genuinely expressionistic, and dramatically to the point.

Color can also be manipulated to characterize a world. The green face of the witch in *The Wizard of Oz* (**Fig. C-26**) defines her character and is inseparable from the fun of that movie. Colors were played with throughout *Oz* in order to separate the phases of the landscape (the Emerald City and the yellow brick road), to heighten the emotional tone of a scene (the red hourglass), or for the sheer pleasure of changing colors (the horse of a different color — colored not with lights but with dry Jell-O).

Color and Animation. The animator has complete freedom to choose colors and to apply them with all the control of a painter.

In the transformation scene from *Snow White and the Seven Dwarfs* (**Fig. C-27**), the wicked queen is enveloped in great, free strokes of green, yellow, and red — in effect, a whirlpool of pure color. In **Fig. C-28**, which shows the dwarfs backlit by the sunset as they walk across a tree bridge, the animator's choice of colors has been restricted by the intention to make this look like a natural scene. Even within those limits, however, this frame shows a great deal of creative expression. The yellows, browns, and reds of the sunset are coordinated with the darker brown of the tree, and all these earth tones give the scene a quality of easy, grounded naturalness.

In more abstract animations, like Oskar Fischinger's *Composition in Blue* (1935) or *Motion Painting #1* (1949), colors may be selected because of the pure ways in which they interact. Both for Fischinger and for John Whitney — who has explained some of his ideas in a book called *Digital Harmony* — the systematic play of colors is comparable to that of musical tones.

Lighting for Mood. In the hands of a great cinematographer it is possible for color to achieve many of the effects regularly associated with great black-and-white, and we can close this section with a look at two masterful examples of color lighting. **Figs. C-29** and **C-30** offer two frames from *The Godfather*, which was shot by Gordon Willis. Both show the same set, but the lighting in each is quite different.

Fig. C-29 comes from the beginning of the movie, where don Vito Corleone (Marlon Brando) dispenses his own brand of justice from the sanctuary of his office. The light is at once rich and subdued; the yellows and browns give the office a sense of intimacy, comfort, and security. What the colors establish here is the position from which the Corleones will fall when don Vito is replaced as the head of the family business. There is an Old World quality to Vito's values, a sense of propriety, good manners, and warmth that is reflected not only in the feel of his private office but also in the way he is dressed here: a black tuxedo and a white shirt, tastefully highlighted by a red rosebud.

Fig. C-30 comes from a later scene, in which Tom (Robert Duvall) has to give Vito the news of the death of Sonny. The tone of the image here is considerably darker. Rather than being seen in a white light at the rear of the frame, upright in his desk chair, Vito is seen in a yellow-brown light that expresses his sadness, while other subdued lights call attention to the desk chair, now empty, in the rear at screen right. The fall has clearly begun.

The soundtrack is the final component of the contemporary shot. In this section we shall examine a few of the basic principles of sound recording, the nature and placement of the soundtrack, the issue of synchronization, and several representative and creative uses of sound in the cinema.

4. The Soundtrack

The Ear and the Microphone

When something vibrates, it causes the medium around it — air, water, or whatever — to move. Should an object move rapidly forward and backward, it generates waves of pressure (with the forward movement) and rarefaction (with the backward movement). The same happens when an object vibrates slowly, but the frequency may be too low to hear. The range of human hearing is approximately 20–20,000 Hz (cycles per second). A **cycle** may be thought of as an individual sound wave; the number of cycles per second is the **frequency** of the sound, the rate of vibration.

The Ear. The ear is divided into three sections: the outer, middle, and inner ear. The outer ear gathers sound waves and channels them into the middle ear. At the entrance to the middle ear is the tympanic membrane, or eardrum. It vibrates in response to the advances and retreats of the sound wave, at the same frequency; in other words, it is pushed and pulled by the air. These vibrations are then transported via three small bones, which convert the waves so that they can be interpreted in a fluid rather than a gaseous medium. The inner ear, a shell-like structure called the cochlea, is filled with liquid.

There are two channels in the inner ear, and the upper channel is lined with extremely fine hairs. As the fluid vibrates, the hairs respond to individual frequencies. Should a gong produce a C#, the hairs whose position in the narrowing channel allow them to respond to C# bend and send nerve impulses — one per bend, or cycle — to the brain. The lowest frequencies (the longest waves) are picked up by those hairs at the narrowest, deepest end of the channel. What enters the ear as a movement of air is thus made readable as a complex of distinct frequencies.

Volume, as opposed to frequency, is conveyed by the intensity of the pressure of the sound wave, not by its rate of vibration. The harder a gong is struck, the louder it sounds. Volume is measured in decibels (**dB**). The **decibel** denotes a ratio between two amounts of power, whether electrical or acoustic. Because decibels are logarithmic, every 10-dB increase involves multiplication by a factor of 10. Thus the sound waves from a gong at 10 dB would have 10 times more acoustical energy than the gong at 1 dB, and a gong at 20 dB would have 100 times more energy than the gong at 1 dB. Power, however, does not translate directly into perceived changes in volume. Volume doubles with every increase of 3 dB.

The Microphone. Just as the ear converts sound waves into nerve impulses that can be interpreted as sounds, a **microphone** converts sound waves into electrical energy. Microphones vary substantially in design, but in most cases the sound waves encounter a diaphragm that vibrates rather as the eardrum does. As the air pressure changes, the diaphragm moves, and these changes in pressure are converted into changes in electrical voltage.

Recording. The microphone's electrical signal is fed into an instrument capable of recording it. Assuming that the sound is not fed into a computer and digitalized, the electrical waveform remains *analogous* to the acoustical waveform: as one goes up, so does the other, and the electrical waveform is as continuous as the acoustical waveform. As opposed to **analog** communication, which is continuous and signifies differences by having more or less of something, **digital** communication works in a binary fashion, as when a current is either on or off, and information is highly discrete. Virtually all theatrical film soundtracks are analog.

Today, most film sound is recorded on magnetic tape. The ¼-inch tape recorder of choice is the Nagra; in a recording studio or mixing room the sound might be recorded directly onto 35mm magnetic stock.

Like film, tape has a backing — usually plastic — and a coating. The ferromagnetic coating, which contains the particles to be magnetized, is like the emulsion that contains the photosensitive chemicals. Magnetic patterns are inscribed and later retrieved by the recording and playback heads. A **head** is a transducer (something that changes one form of energy into another), and it converts electrical into magnetic energy for recording, or magnetic into electrical energy for playback. Eventually the speaker, as a transducer, converts electrical energy into sound waves.

After the sound has been recorded, edited (on mag stock), and mixed down (integrated into one monaural or several stereo tracks, also on mag stock), it is copied. That final soundtrack may be optical or magnetic, and it may be run on a separate machine (double system) or "married" to the picture track (single system).

Sound Please!

Fig. 2-85 shows Daffy during an unnaturally quiet moment in *Duck Amuck*. The soundtrack is the system of black and white lines just outside the frame. The rascally rabbit has turned off the sound just when Daffy is ready to play a solo. When the sound is restored, the guitar sounds like a machine gun. Thus this frame lays out two important considerations: the physical nature and placement of the soundtrack and the problem of creative synchronization.

Optical and Magnetic Tracks. A magnetic **soundtrack**, or **mag track**, is a strip of magnetized iron oxide particles; in single sys-

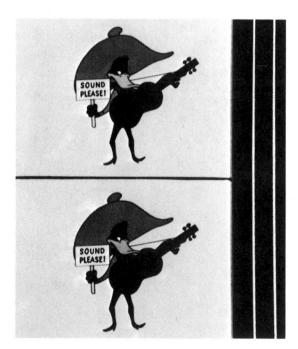

Figure 2-85

tem, it is bonded to the print. (That is, the **magnetic stripe** that is bonded to the print has the sound recorded onto it, in real time.) In double system, it is on mag stock. It has been used in the film industry only since 1949. It provides high-quality sound, and its only real drawback is that it can be erased if brought too near a strong magnetic field. As explained previously, the single-system stereo magnetic soundtrack is transferred onto several magnetic stripes that fit between the image and the sprocket holes.

An **optical soundtrack**, which usually is in black-and-white even if the film is in color, is designed to let various amounts of light pass through it to a photocell. The **photocell**, or **photoelectric cell**, converts this light to an electrical impulse whose characteristics vary with those of the light.

There are three common types of optical soundtrack: variable area, variable density, and Dolby Stereo®. The first two are monaural; all three are the same overall width and fit between the frame and one set of sprocket holes.

The **variable area** track, like that used in *Duck Amuck*, has a constant density but varies in width (amplitude modulation). In **Fig. 2-85** the full-width track blocks most of the light and produces the effect of near silence — "near" because a slight rippling at its edges provides **room tone** or **ambient air**, the sound made by an empty room. True silence is strikingly noticeable, and room tone is often used for an effect of inhabited silence, or to smooth out transitions or cover up little problems. When the frame falls on Daffy's head, the soundtrack looks very different (**Fig. 2-86**). Some variable area soundtracks use one band, as in these examples; others use two identical bands.

A **variable density** track is of constant width but becomes darker (denser) or lighter in response to variations in the sound. A variable density track can be seen alongside the frame from *The African Queen* (**Fig. C-6**). Both kinds of soundtrack can be read by the same photocell, as both get their results by varying the total amount of light that will reach the cell.

Dolby Stereo uses two variable area tracks that must be read by a special photocell and decoded with Dolby equipment. The two tracks carry separate information, phased for four separate channels (left, center, right, and surround). In 70mm, Dolby uses six *magnetic* tracks, adding "baby boom" channels just to the left and right of center.

Fig. 2-87 shows two strips of 35mm Dolby optical stereo, from the restored version of *Napoleon*, and one variable area track (with two bands) from Bergman's *Wild Strawberries* (1957). Note the extreme differences between the tracks in the center strip.

Noise Reduction. Whenever a signal is recorded on magnetic tape, some **noise** (random information) or tape hiss is introduced. As various tracks are re-recorded and mixed, the noise level builds up considerably.

Dolby noise reduction (or **Dolby NR**®) — named for its inventor, Dr. Ray Dolby — is a system for reducing tape and other

Figure 2-86

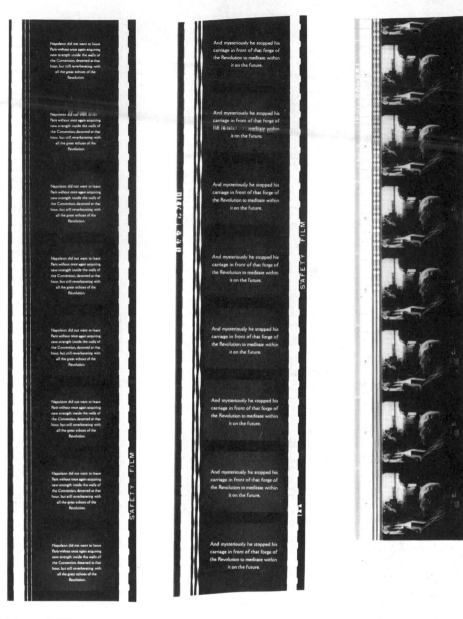

Figure 2-87

noise. Before it reaches the recording head, the signal is *compressed;* this compression allows the signal to be recorded at a higher than normal **level** (volume). After it leaves the playback head, the signal is *expanded*, and this has the effect of depressing or pushing the noise floor down about 10–15 dB. The entire process is known as **companding**.

Fig. 2-88 is a schematic diagram of the Dolby NR process; "O VU" means "zero volume units" as displayed on a **VU meter** in dBs. In an unprocessed signal, the difference in volume between the quietest parts of the signal and the tape hiss may be very slight; companding increases that difference, rendering system noise virtually inaudible.

For best results, Dolby noise reduction processes a signal at every stage from the initial recording, through multiple re-recording, to projection. **Dolby A**, the type of noise reduction used in the film industry, treats low, middle, and high frequencies differently, because each frequency group has different compression requirements.

Advance to the Rear. As previously explained, the soundtrack that is meant to be heard while a given frame is projected cannot be right next to that frame on the print. In most cases the sound is **advanced** 1 or 2 feet up the print, toward the head. The sound

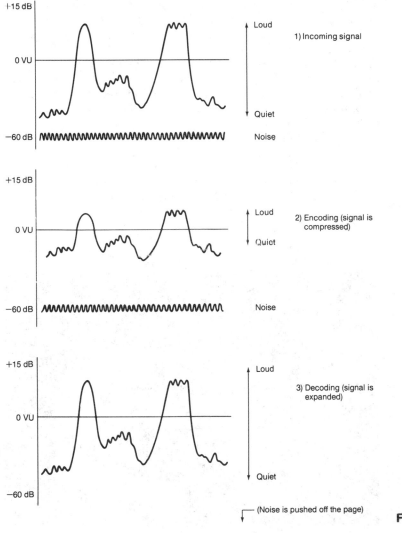

Figure 2-88

you see in **Fig. 2-86** will not be heard until just over a second later; it is in advance of its proper frame on the print.

In 35mm optical sound, the sound is 20 frames ahead of the picture; in 16mm optical sound, it is 26 frames ahead of the picture. In 35mm magnetic sound, the sound is 28 frames *behind* the picture, and in 16mm magnetic sound, it is 28 frames ahead of the picture. In 70mm magnetic sound, it is 24 frames behind the picture.

If the loop is too large during projection, the film can be thrown out of synchronization (sync), so that the right sounds are heard at the wrong time.

Synchronization

Ideally, any completed film will be in sync. This means that certain pictures and sounds will have been coordinated so that they will be heard and seen at the same time. Because mag stock is perforated, any given frame can be matched and aligned with a given "frame" of sound. For editing purposes, sound and picture tracks are kept in mutual registration by a machine called a **synchronizer** (**Fig. 2-89**), a system of interlocked, sprocketed wheels. Optical soundtracks (obsolete in editing) are also on perforated 35mm base.

At the head or tail of each take, there is a notated point where sound and picture are known to be in perfect sync. This sync point can be marked by fogging (drastically overexposing) a frame in the camera and simultaneously sending a sound pulse to the tape recorder, but the more common practice is to use a clapstick and slate.

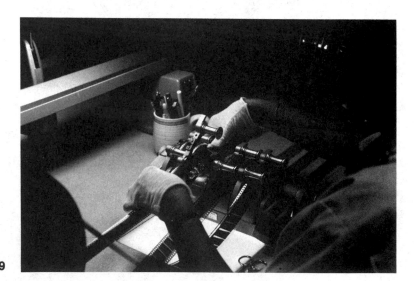

Figure 2-89

The **slate** is a small chalkboard on which is written such information as the title of the film, the names of the director and the cinematographer, and the numbers of the scene and the take (see **Fig. 2-35**). The **clapstick** is a thin, hinged board, and it makes a sharp, distinct sound when it is brought down to hit the top of the slate. Making a loud short clap by whatever means available is called **hitting the sticks**.

By matching the picture frame in which the stick hits the slate with the sound frame in which the clap is heard, the editor can line up the two tracks so that they are in sync from head to tail. The tracks are edited in parallel (**editorial sync**) and advanced or retarded only on single-system prints (**projection sync**).

Lip Sync. In many cases, synchronization can be one or two frames off without the audience's noticing. When one is watching a car tear down the highway or listening to an actor whose back is turned to the camera, tight sync is not necessary. But when an actor speaks while facing the camera, the movements of his or her lips must precisely match the dialogue track. That is **lip sync**, and any discrepancy greater than half a frame can ruin the show.

Lip sync is the acid test of synchronization, and to make sure that it is perfectly maintained during recording, many cameras (or independent units) send a regular pulse to the tape recorder. This pulse keeps track of the exact speed of the camera, or in some cases regulates both camera and recorder. It can be monitored during playback — when the sounds are transferred from ¼-inch tape onto mag film — to regulate the speed of the recorder so that it matches that of the camera. Sometimes called a **pilot tone**, this **sync pulse** is recorded and played back by a special head and has its own track on the tape. A recording made without camera synchronization is called a **wild recording**, and it can be mixed into the soundtrack wherever lip sync is not required.

Dubbing. Most soundtracks are made up of sync and wild tracks. **Post-synchronization** is the art of matching the picture with a recording made after the picture has been shot; it allows essentially wild tracks to stand in for unusable or missing sync tracks. **Dialogue replacement,** the recording and post-synchronizing of a replacement dialogue track — properly called **looping** or, depending on the technology involved, **ADR** — is more commonly known as **dubbing**, though the latter term refers primarily to the act of re-recording a track, as when transferring or mixing, and to the recording of a foreign-language dialogue track; for all these terms, see the glossary.

The problem with using location sound — and in some cases, live sound in general — is that outside the controlled environment of the soundproofed sound stage, the world goes about its business with little regard for the problems of filmmakers. It can really throw off a historical romance when a jet streaks by overhead or somebody starts up a lawnmover.

The solution is to re-record the sound under studio conditions, using the original, synchronized track (and the picture) as reference. The effects and music tracks are created separately, and they, too, can be brought into sync with the dialogue track and the picture.

Dubbing (in the sense of the systematic replacement of dialogue) is also used to present a foreign-language film in the audience's native tongue. Many film industries, notably the Italian, post-synchronize virtually all dialogue as a matter of course. But most people prefer their sound **live**, (that is, recorded during shooting) and acceptable sound-stage dialogue tracks are not normally replaced, at least in Hollywood.

Creative Synchronization. When a sound film aspires to realism, or to making its illusions convincing, synchronization is a high priority. The audience will want to hear how the object on screen actually sounds — will want to hear Garbo's real voice, or the muffled click of a toggle switch.

Or they will want to hear how it *should* sound. There is a scene in *The Right Stuff* when John Glenn (Ed Harris) reaches out of camera range and appears to be flipping switches. Actually there were no switches, but the actor went through the correct movements. When the sound editor synchronized these movements with the sounds of switches, the effect was realistic: the post-synchronized sounds made the switches present.

According to some filmmakers, notably Eisenstein and Vertov, this kind of thinking makes sound and picture mutual slaves and produces effects that are ultimately boring and predictable: *that* object with *that* same old sound. In *L'Age d'or* (1930), on the other hand, Buñuel accompanied an image of gushing lava with the sound of a flushing toilet.

As one creative alternative to realism, **contrapuntal sound** is the art of deliberately mismatching picture and sound, allowing the two tracks to play off each other and to present the audience with fresh and surprising juxtapositions. This is what happens when Daffy's guitar sounds like a machine gun. In the great Laurel and Hardy film *Way Out West* (1937, directed by James W. Horne), there is a scene where Stan Laurel sings "The Blue Ridge Mountains of Virginia" in a bar. First, we hear his own voice, then a deep bass voice, and finally a woman's voice. All three tracks are in tight sync, which plants this outrageous gag in the context of realism.

Sound and the Camera

Realistic sound can generate the impression of a complete and continuous world beyond that portion of it shown in the frame. When we hear a sound **off–camera** — that is, coming from a hypothetical location that is not in camera range — we tend to imagine a complete field of action.

In Val Lewton and Jacques Tourneur's *The Leopard Man* (1943), one devastatingly well-controlled sequence implies, but does not entirely show, how a young woman is pursued and killed by a wild animal. Her mother has sent her out for a sack of corn meal, though it is very late. On her way home, the camera is mostly on her. First, we hear the sound of dripping water, then a loud passing train — jerking us from the creepy to the startling — and then a very effective silence. She sees the leopard, it growls, and she runs. We hear the sounds of her running feet on the dirt road and the fall of the bag of corn meal when she stumbles. Then the camera cuts to the inside of her home, where the mother has decided to teach her a lesson about dawdling: she has locked the front door. Outside the door, we hear the woman pleading with her mother, then screaming. The screams and animal snarls reach maximum intensity while the mother and her young son try to open the door. Then the screaming stops, and blood leaks under the door; when it hits the perpendicular crack formed by a floorboard, it almost seems to flow into a cross. Just as the pool of blood is more powerful than a view of the actual mauling would have been, this use of off-camera sound stimulates the viewer to imagine the unseen in all its vividness.

Sound can also *lead* the camera, just as it leads the audience's attention. There are countless movies in which a door slams or a vase is dropped off-camera, the actor turns to look, and the camera pivots or cuts for a view of what made the sound. At the climax of Hitchcock's *The Man Who Knew Too Much* (1956), a woman (Doris Day) is singing downstairs while her kidnapped son is being held upstairs. The camera follows the gradually diminishing sound of the mother's voice out of the room in which she is singing, over to the staircase, and then up several flights until it finds the boy — in other words, until her voice reaches him. The decreasing volume and increasing echo of her voice point to another important device, **perspective sound**, which is the art of making a sound appear to originate at a certain distance from the camera.

Creating in Sound

Some of the sounds in films are made up. According to sound designer Alan Splet, who worked with director David Lynch on *Eraserhead, The Elephant Man* (1980), *Dune* (1984), and *Blue Velvet* (1986), about 80 percent of the effects for *Dune* were "made." Many of the weapon sounds, for example, began with a 50-foot oil tank that was being kicked and beaten with bars, hammers, and chains. The voices of a horse, a baboon, a puma, and a pig were mixed to produce the roaring of the sandworms. Once the natural sound has been recorded, as Splet put it, "you just go get it — distort it until it's right."

Sound distortion can serve a variety of purposes. In many American films made during World War II, the Nazis' rifles sounded

Figure 2-90

Figure 2-91

brutal, whereas the Americans' sounded clean-cut, neat, and efficient.

Sound Montage. Soundtracks employ audible montage relationships. A straight cut from one sound to another is called a **sound cut**; a sound dissolve, where one fades in as the other fades out, is called a **segue**. It is extremely common for the soundtrack to be multilayered and to have been **built** (assembled) out of many separate tracks. Walter Murch mixed more than 140 tracks for the helicopter assault on the beach in *Apocalypse Now*. As a general term, **sound montage** refers to the way one sound collides or overlaps with another, whether or not their boundary is a visual cut, and also to the mixing together of a great many tracks. For more on contemporary sound montage, see the discussion of sound editing in Part III.

One instance of countrapuntal sound montage, which has been imitated so often that it might now seem a cliché, can serve for its brilliance as a summary example. It comes from *The 39 Steps*. In one shot (**Fig. 2-90**) a cleaning woman discovers a body and turns to scream. Then there is a straight cut to a shot (**Fig. 2-91**) of a train, blowing its whistle as it comes out of a tunnel. We do not hear the woman's voice; the shriek of the steam, instead, *becomes* the scream.

A good soundtrack can enhance realism, fill out the visual world, and bias audience response. It can also comment on the world, characterize it, or transfigure it. It can include silence as the silent film cannot, and it has led to an art that is very different from that of the silent film — not its replacement, but its complement.

After the frame, the shot is the next major unit in the structural hierarchy of the cinematic system. In order to provide a catalog of the most commonly used shots, a few terms introduced earlier will be defined here again, but this time with examples taken from released films. Then we will go on to examine the structures into which shots can be organized: scenes and sequences.

5. The Shot

Takes and Shots

For shooting purposes, a **scene** is a unit of action staged for or captured by the camera. In these terms, a scene can be photographed in a single continuous exposure. In dramatic terms, however, a **scene** is a dramatic event or interaction taking place in a single location, and it may end up being composed of many shots. When a slate reads "Scene 24, Take 3," that denotes the third attempt to photograph this unit of action from this camera position or setup.

The term **setup** is used to indicate the position, in real space, of the camera and the lights at the start of any take. Should the camera be moved for the next take — or remain in the same position but be fitted with a different lens — that would be another setup.

A **take** is the footage exposed between the time the camera is started and the time it is stopped. Usually it includes slating frames and unwanted bits of action, and so takes are **trimmed** by the editor; in other words, their heads and tails — and sometimes parts in between — are removed. The portion of a take that appears in a completed movie as an integral unit of sequentially photographed frames is called a **shot.** Where a shot has not been trimmed from a take — in cel animation, for example — it is defined as the interval between two transitional devices such as cuts or fades; such a shot gives the *impression* of having been continuously exposed, which is the point.

More generally, a **take** is defined as a single attempt to get a shot on film, and a **shot** is defined as *any* continuously-exposed series of frames, whether it begins with a cut, with a fade, or with the starting of a camera motor.

Shot Duration. **Shot duration**, the amount of time a shot remains onscreen, can be measured in units of time or length. The most precise way is length: 2 feet and 4 frames. The alternative is time: 1½ seconds. That last calculation assumed 35mm stock, which has 16 frames per foot, so that "2 ft., 4 fr." equals 36 frames; divided by 24 fps, the yield is a duration of 1½ seconds. But 16mm stock has 40 frames per foot. In 16mm this same shot would be less than a foot long. One way to ensure that a length duration will be applicable, no matter what gauge a shot is printed on, is to dispense with feet and count only in frames. Time notations can use some awkward fractions, but where rounding off is acceptable, they are convenient and simple to work with.

The minimum length of a shot is one frame. A shot two frames long can be just barely comprehended. Most shots run between 1 and 10 seconds. A shot that lasts for a minute or more is called a **long take**. When a complete scene is covered in a single long take (often with intricate camera movement), that is called a **sequence shot**.

It is generally true that a shot will remain onscreen only long enough to get its point across, assuming a viewer of average intelligence and attention span. When a shot goes on longer than we at first think it needs to, we look around in the visual field to find out what the real point of the shot may be — something we may have missed at first glance. To cut away from a certain image field may bring the audience a sense of relief, and some filmmakers will have reasons *not* to release concentration — or boredom — in that manner. When Godard shot a traffic jam in one 6-minute sequence shot in *Weekend* (1967), the experience of watching it was almost as frustrating as being *in* such a jam.

Aside from its effect on the perception of image content, shot duration is a vital element of cinematic rhythm. Just as a dance may be made up of brief and slow movements, or a paragraph of long and short sentences, variations in shot duration can establish a **visual rhythm**. Just as important is the variation of movement within the shot; the two rhythms work together. When a number of successive shots last for exactly the same time — an effect Eisenstein called **metrical montage** — the rhythm is immediately noticeable. Subtler effects can be achieved by juxtaposing brief and lengthy shots in patterns that are often arrived at intuitively.

One way to sensitize yourself to these rhythms is to think of a cut — or a distinct movement or a pause within a shot — as introducing a **beat**, like the downbeat in a bar of music. If you are alone in the theater, you may even want to stamp your foot or tap your thigh to keep track of the beats. After a while you will "hear" these rhythms as an intricate visual pulse. They are simpler to notice in silent films; sound introduces a rhythm of its own, and to appreciate how it works with and against the visual rhythm, it is best to begin with an appreciation of the latter.

Shot Description

In the majority of screenplays, a shot is identified simply as taking place during the day or at night, and in an interior or exterior setting. These are capitalized and abbreviated as: DAY, NIGHT, INT., and EXT. Most directors do not like to be told by the scriptwriter where to place the camera.

The full notation or description of a completed shot includes its duration, a record of the action, the distance from the camera to the subject, the angle from which the camera views the subject, whether the camera is moved and in what direction, and sometimes the shot's specific function. Thus we could speak of a certain shot as a hand-held medium shot, another as a track from long shot to closeup, and still another as a low-angle close shot — or we could go for broke and describe a shot fully: a daylight exterior high-angle long establishing shot of a crowded freeway (3½ seconds).

Camera-to-Subject Distance. There are three broad categories of camera-to-subject distance: the long shot, the medium shot, and the closeup. **A long shot** gives a wide view of the visual field, and a human subject usually takes up less than half the height of the frame. **A medium shot** presents a view somewhere between those of the long shot and the closeup, and a human subject may take up the full height of the frame or may fill it with half of his or her body. **A closeup** offers a very narrow view of the field, and a human subject may fill the entire frame with his or her face or hand. Actually these distinctions depend not on the real physical distance between camera and subject, but on how far away the camera *appears* to be. A closeup taken with a telephoto lens from a distance of 100 yards would still be a closeup. It is also not crucial to refer to the relative screen height of a human subject. The area needed to present a long shot of a mouse or a toy may well be the same as that for a medium shot of a person. To call something a long, medium, or close shot, then, is to reference the field of view to the person or object that is identified as the primary subject.

Within these three categories there is a spectrum of subdivisions. The spectrum runs from extreme long shot (**ELS**) to long shot (**LS**), medium long shot (**MLS**), full shot (**FS**), medium shot (**MS**), medium close shot (**MCS**), close shot (**CS**), closeup (**CU**), and extreme closeup (**ECU**). This is how they look:

Fig. 2-92 is an **extreme long shot** from Leni Riefenstahl's *Olympia* (1938). **Fig. 2-93** is an extreme long shot referenced to the human figure and taken from *The 39 Steps*.

Figure 2-92

Figure 2-93

Figure 2-94

Figure 2-95

Fig. 2-94 shows the same figure from *The 39 Steps*, this time in long shot. He is seen from an even closer view in **Fig. 2-95**. This frame is still within the range of the long shot, but to indicate the relatively shorter camera-to-subject distance, this one would be called a **medium long shot**. **Fig. 2-96**, from René Clair's *Entr'acte* (1924), is a tighter medium long shot. The closer the camera is to the subject, the **tighter** the field of view.

The **full shot** presents the human subject from head to foot, together with a reasonably complete view of the set. It is a variant of the medium long shot. **Fig. 2-97** is a full shot from *Broken Blossoms*. Pursuing our figure from *The 39 Steps*, we find him in a tight full shot in **Fig. 2-98**.

The **medium shot**, which is the most widely used field of view, usually presents less than a full view of the human subject, from approximately one quarter to three quarters of the body. It is also called a **midshot**. You can see most of Chaplin's body in the medium shot from the unreleased *How to Make Movies*, shot in 1917

Figure 2-96

Figure 2-97

Figure 2-98

Figure 2-99

(**Fig. 2-99**). **Figs. 2-100** and **2-101** are both medium shots taken from *The 39 Steps*, but **Fig. 2-101** would more precisely be identified as a **medium close shot**. **Fig. 2-102** is a medium shot from *Nosferatu*.

A **close shot** brings the camera nearer than medium close, but not so near as a closeup. In terms of the human subject, it usually provides a view from the top of the head to the upper part of the chest. **Fig. 2-103** is a close shot from *Citizen Kane*.

A **closeup** fills the frame with a tight view of the subject. For a person, this means that a foot, a face, or part of a face will take up virtually the entire field. A closeup is often used to show a portion

Figure 2-100

Figure 2-101

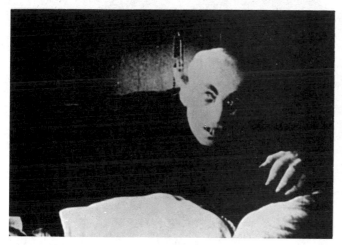

Figure 2-102

Figure 2-103

Figure 2-104

Figure 2-105

of a larger subject or a full view of a very small subject. It is commonly used to reveal details or for emphasis, as in the practice of cutting to a closeup when a character is about to utter a particularly important line. A closeup means, "Pay attention to *this*." **Fig. 2-104** is a closeup from *Ménilmontant*. **Fig. 2-105**, from *October,* shows a hand reaching for a sword handle in closeup.

A **tight** or **extreme closeup** shows even less of the subject than a closeup does. **Fig. 2-106** is a *tight* closeup from Hitchcock's *Young and Innocent* (1937). **Fig. 2-107**, from *Citizen Kane,* shows just how tight the field of view of an *extreme* closeup can get. In this scene, Kane is typing the word "weak." The ECU and the correspondingly intensified sound of the keys on the paper (perspective sound) make this "weak" effect very strong.

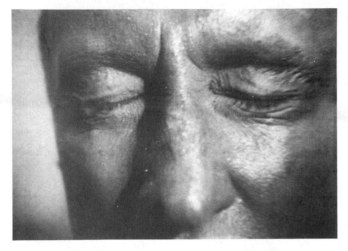

Figure 2-106

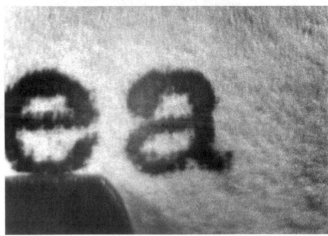

Figure 2-107

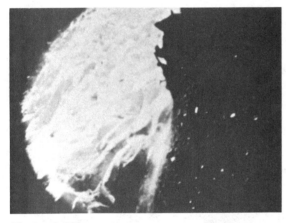

Figure 2-108

Camera-to-subject distance markedly affects the direction of the viewer's attention. The camera moves close to something because we need to see it now, and up close, or it pulls back so that we can see more about that object's position in space and its relation to other objects. The control of vantage point also affects the *tone* of a presentation. There is a scene in Blake Edwards's *Victor Victoria* (1982) where a cockroach gets loose in a restaurant. Instead of indulging in a free-for-all of close, comical views, Edwards cut to an exterior long shot. Through the windows of the restaurant we see a tiny riot of people and chairs, which contrasts elegantly with the cool, detached stability of the camera — making the riot, in fact, more funny.

Figs. 2-108 through **2-110** are three frames from *La Roue*, showing a young man hanging from a cliff. Taken together, they illus-

Figure 2-109

Figure 2-110

trate the effectiveness of concentrating the field of view on various parts of the whole. The extreme long shot (**Fig. 2-108**) shows the man with his knee bent, a good portion of the mountain, and a dog at the top of the cliff. Although the details are hard to make out, the broad scope of the situation is clear. **Fig. 2-109** takes us to a close shot for a better look at the man. From this distance we can see, and momentarily share, the extremity of his pain and anxiety. In **Fig. 2-110** a closeup of his hand lets us see an even finer detail: the way his thumb flicks the root to which he is clinging in a spasm of impatience. Each view conveys and emphasizes one detail of the scene. By using several of them in a calculated editing pattern, Gance was able to throw the emphasis where and when he wished.

Camera-to-Subject Angle. The camera does not always meet its subject head-on, with a level gaze. The tilt or inclination from which the camera views the subject is called the **camera angle**.

The spectrum of camera angles runs from the bird's-eye view (looking straight down) through the high-angle shot, the eye-level shot, and the low-angle shot, to the worm's-eye view (looking straight up). Where the camera's line of sight markedly diverges from the horizontal and vertical axes of the scene, that is called an **oblique angle** shot. When the camera simply tilts to the side, without other angles coming into play, that is called an **off-angle** or **Dutch tilt shot**. Fig 2-111 is an oblique low-angle shot from *October*.

A **bird's-eye view** is taken from directly above the subject. **Fig. 2-112** is a bird's-eye shot from *Vertigo*. The point of view is Scottie's as he hangs from a rain gutter and watches the policeman who has tried to save him fall to his death. The same action, viewed from below or from the side, would not have been the same: this angle emphasizes verticality, the length of the fall, and it also shows how all of this fools to Scottie, who will be driven by this unhappy conjunction of acrophobia and guilt for the rest of the movie.

There is a marvelous bird's-eye shot at the end of Karel Reisz's *Morgan!* (1966), which concerns a hyperromantic Marxist who is eventually committed to an asylum. The doctors are pleased that he is calmly trimming the hedge. An overhead shot lets us see that he has cut the hedge into the shape of a hammer and sickle.

In a **high-angle shot**, the camera looks downward toward the subject at an angle less than the vertical. In the high-angle shot from *King Kong* shown in **Fig. 2-113**, the downward angle of sight is approximately 45°. The high-angle shot can be used simply to provide a view of a low object, like a letter slipped under a door; in other words, it can correspond to the act of looking down to see something. It also has an effect on perspective. A rectangular object seen from a high angle tends to narrow at its base and widen at its top, and this effect can promote the impression of instability. Thus to look down on a subject may be to encode it as relatively powerless or as being on the verge of toppling over.

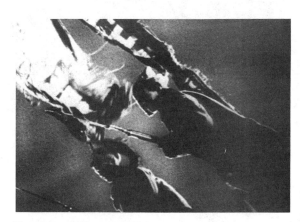

Figure 2-111

Figure 2-112

Figure 2-113

Figure 2-114

Figure 2-115

Fig. 2-114 is an **eye-level shot** from *King Kong*. As you can see from this frame, the term "eye-level" has little to do with whether the camera is planted firmly on the ground. What it means is that the camera is placed at the eye level of the principal subject — that if the subject were to look at the camera, he or she would meet its gaze without having to look up or down.

"Eye level" can have another meaning, however: that the field is seen as it would be perceived by a standing adult — in fact, by a standing Western male adult. This convention may well have begun as a convenience because for a long time most Western filmmakers *were* standing male adults, and the camera was set at a comfortable position for them. The French director Chantal Akerman, who happens to be rather short, has deliberately violated this convention by shooting many of her films from her *own* eye level, putting a "female" stamp on the gaze of the camera. For the Japanese director Ozu, the normal, eye-level view of an interior scene was only a few feet off the ground, the way someone would see it if he or she were sitting on the floor. Eye level, then, is a culturally relative matter, and it can also affect the sexual politics of a film.

There is good use of the low eye-level shot at the start of *E.T.* The jangling key ring on the waist of a running man is seen straight on, which suggests that the perceiver is the height of a child. This angle not only prepares the way for the friendly relationship between the boy and the short alien, but also places the audience within the worldview of a child, enhancing the processes of identification and empathy with the figures whom the choice of angle has declared to be the central characters.

In a **low-angle shot**, the camera looks up at the subject. In the low-angle shot from *King Kong* shown in **Fig. 2-115**, the upward

Figure 2-116

Figure 2-117

angle of sight is about 70°, and it increases our impression of the height of the building. It also corresponds to the normal activity of looking up to see a high object.

The low-angle shot affects perspective in a manner directly opposite to that of the high-angle shot. Seen from below, a rectangular object appears to widen at the bottom, so that it resembles the most stable of all geometrical forms, the triangle set on its base. Thus low-angle shots are often used to encode a subject as powerful or intimidating. In the frame from *Nosferatu* shown in **Fig. 2-116**, the triangularity of the vampire and the rigging is particularly noticeable. **Fig. 2-117** shows the preparations for a low-angle shot — part of the scene in which Kane trashes Susan's bedroom. Even though the angle of view is not especially steep, the crew still had to tear out part of the floor of the set.

For a **worm's-eye view** the camera is pointed directly upward. **Fig. 2-118** offers a worm's-eye view of a dancer, taken from *Entr'acte*.

Figure 2-118

Pivoting and Moving the Camera

Once mounted or held, the camera can be moved forward or backward or to the side; it can pivot from right to left, or from a low to a high angle; it can sweep through the air; or it can stay where it is.

Pivoting and Zooming. When the base that supports the camera remains in the same spot throughout the take, movement can be introduced in two ways: by pivoting the camera along a hori-

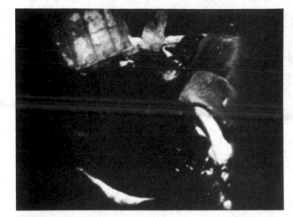

Figure 2-119

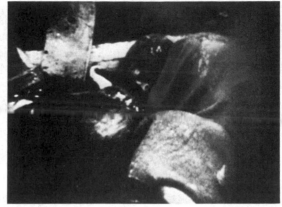

Figure 2-120

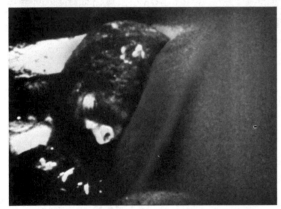

Figure 2-121

zontal or vertical axis, or by using a zoom lens. As previously explained, forward and backward zooms introduce only *apparent* camera movements. **Figs. 2-119** through **2-121** show a forward zoom from *The War Game.*

In a **pan** or **panoramic shot** the camera pivots on a vertical axis; that is, it turns in a horizontal plane. It can swivel from side to side or rotate in a complete circle (a **360° pan**). A rapid pan that renders the image as streaks is called a **swish pan**. The pan can survey a wide, horizontal field of view, or it can swing from one subject to another within a more limited field. One straightforward use of the pan is to follow a subject that is moving horizontally, as when the camera follows a wave until it breaks over the lovers in Fred Zinnemann's *From Here to Eternity* (1953).

Figs. 2-122 through **2-125** illustrate how a pan can be used to

Figure 2-122

Figure 2-123

Figure 2-124

Figure 2-125

introduce new information within the changing field of the shot. Kane has just wrecked Susan's room and pocketed the snowy globe. As if unaware of the watching servants, he walks by a pillar and in front of a large mirror. The camera arrives at the mirror before Kane does; what we are seeing in **Fig. 2-124** is his reflection; Kane himself is in the foreground in **Fig. 2-125**. To set up this shot, another mirror was made to face the one in the frame. In this shot, the physical or integrated Kane turns before our eyes into an infinite series of reflections; this pan is symbolic, then, of the entire narrative project of *Citizen Kane*.

In a **tilt** or **tilting shot** the camera pivots on a horizontal axis,

Figure 2-126

Figure 2-127

that is, moves in a vertical plane. **Figs. 2-126** and **2-127** show a tilt shot from *Kane.* The camera begins at the young Kane's eye level, then tilts upward until it provides a low-angle view of Thatcher as he rather commandingly wishes the boy a "Merry Christmas."

Figure 2-128

Figure 2-129

Figure 2-130

Figure 2-131

Figure 2-132

Figure 2-133

Moving Camera Shots. In the course of many shots the operator or camera platform will move from one location to another. The most common of these **moving camera shots** are hand-held, track, dolly, and crane shots. A pan or tilt is also considered a camera movement, but of a different kind.

Since the introduction of the Steadicam, a **hand-held shot** can be perfectly smooth. Nevertheless, the instability of the normal hand-held shot can introduce a desirable jerkiness, a feeling of informality, or the impression of impromptu shooting under realistic conditions. In the shot from *The War Game* shown in **Figs. 2-128** through **2-133**, the hand-held camera is used to convey, in purely visual terms, the chaos of a food riot; the shot is as unstable as the event. The jerking movements indicate that the cameraman is being jostled about, not only increasing our kinetic participation in the scene but also giving the impression that this is a real riot photographed by a news team. It has a refreshing and realistic sense of not having been shot in a studio by comfortable professionals.

In a classical **track** or **trucking shot** the camera platform moves along rails that are very like a pair of railroad tracks. **Track shot** is also used as a generic term for any forward, backward, lateral, or curving camera movement executed on the ground, regardless of whether the platform has rubber wheels (a **dolly**) or moves on steel rails; the term can even refer to the use of a moving car or a wheelchair. **Figs. 2-134** and **2-135** show a backward track from *The 39 Steps.*

Because the dolly can be pushed or pulled wherever the floor is clear, the **dolly shot** can involve more intricate movements than the average track shot. In *The Conformist* (1970) Bernardo Bertolucci staged a dance scene in which the camera crosses the dance floor and almost seems to dance itself. These complex turns and diagonal movements *could* have been executed on tracks, but the

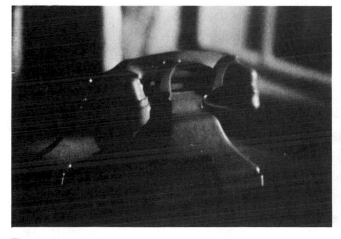

Figure 2-134

Figure 2-135

5. THE SHOT **215**

dolly was clearly a more flexible alternative, and in any case, any full view of the dance floor would have shown the system of rails.

In a **boom** or **crane shot** (the terms are interchangeable), the

Figure 2-136

Figure 2-137

Figure 2-138

Figure 2-139

Figure 2-140

Figure 2-141

Figure 2-142

Figure 2-143

Figure 2-144

Figure 2-145

Figure 2-146

camera is mounted on a large, cantilevered **boom** or arm that is itself attached to a vehicle called a **crane.** The whole system is balanced for grace and smoothness; on the finest booms, rather than feeling hauled up into the air, one may have the impression of remaining stable while the ground goes down. When the camera support actually leaves the ground — when it is a helicopter, for instance —the result is called an **aerial shot.**

An intricate crane shot from the climax of *Young and Innocent* is shown in **Figs. 2-136** through **2-150.** The shot begins by showing the lobby of a hotel (**Fig. 2-136**), then pans to the right and tilts downward (**Fig. 2-139**) for a view of the hotel restaurant (**Fig. 2-140**). The camera pans rapidly over the tables and dancers until it catches a view of the band (**Fig. 2-143**). It then begins to move forward for a closer view of the band (**Fig. 2-144**). The song they are performing concerns "the drummer man." By **Fig. 2-145** we can see that the camera is particularly interested in the drummer, but we might take this interest as a reflection of the content of the song. By **Fig. 2-146** we can see clearly that the drummer is in blackface. Once the camera gets as close as it is in **Fig. 2-148**, we

Figure 2-147

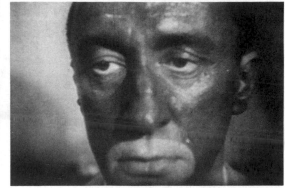

Figure 2-148

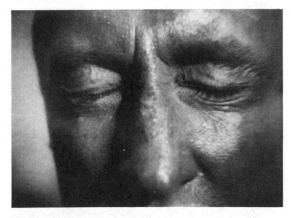

Figure 2-149

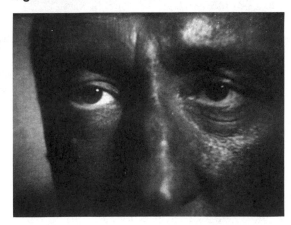

Figure 2-150

can recognize this man as the villain whom the heroes have been seeking. They are looking for a white man with a nervous habit of rapidly twitching both eyes. When the drummer blinks this way in **Fig. 2-149**, his identity is confirmed, and after the twitches have stopped, his face subsides briefly into the cold, lost gaze seen in **Fig. 2-150**. If all this had been presented in 5 or 10 separate shots, the elegant flow of the crane movement would have been lost and, with it, the sense of the camera's infallible pursuit and identification of the villain, who at first appears to be just another figure in a populous landscape. This shot is a working lesson in the value of taking a closer look, and it is a perfect and characteristic Hitchcock irony that it ends by meeting the gaze of the villain.

Specialized Functions and Characteristics

Some shots are identified not by the position, angle, and movement of the camera but by the specialized functions they play in a film, or by other unique characteristics. These include the establishing shot, the master shot, the POV shot, the cutaway, the insert, the two-shot, the follow shot, the reaction shot, the matte shot, the composite, and the superimposition or "double exposure." Beyond these, any shot can be notated as having slow, fast, or normal motion.

The **establishing shot** introduces or establishes the location where the action will take place. It is typically a long shot. **Fig. 2-151** is the first shot in *King Kong*, and it shows the Hoboken Docks. It establishes that the opening actions will occur in the vicinity of New York, but its immediate focus of interest is the large ship in the central middle ground, and the first scenes are, in fact, set near and on that ship. When the location changes or a new sequence begins, another establishing shot may introduce the new setting.

The **master shot** provides an overview of a scene that is capable of taking in all of its major action. It is almost always a full or long shot. Closer or more particularized views are cut into the master

Figure 2-151

shot, to flesh out the scene. The master shot will be discussed more fully in the context of the scene, in the next section.

For a review of the POV shot, see the discussion of the railway carriage scene in *The 39 Steps* (**Figs. 1-5** through **1-11**). For the cutaway shot, review Christina's coronation (**Figs. 2-74** through **2-76**).

An **insert** is a shot of an object, usually unmoving, that is cut into a scene or a sequence. Although the typewriter is working, the shot of w-e-a-k (**Fig. 2-107**) is an insert shot, and so is this map from *The 39 Steps* (**Fig. 2-152**).

The **two-shot** is a view of two people. Not surprisingly, a view

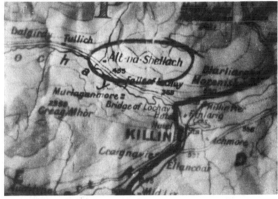

Figure 2-152

Figure 2-153

Figure 2-154

of three people is called a **three-shot**, and a view of one person is a **one-shot**. **Fig. 2-153** is a two-shot from *Napoleon*. **Fig. 2-154** is a **tight two-shot**, or "tight two," from *The Last Laugh*.

In a **follow** or **following shot** the camera pivots or moves in order to keep a moving subject in view. The pan in **Figs. 2-122** through **2-125** is a follow shot, but in the majority of cases the camera keeps perfect pace with the subject. **Follow-focus** is the art of keeping the moving subject in focus.

Near the opening of *The 39 Steps* there is a lengthy following shot involving a police officer and the start of a fight. At the end of that shot we see the agitated crowd (**Fig. 2-155**). Then there is a cutaway from the principal action to a close shot of a firing handgun (**Fig. 2-156**). **Fig. 2-157** is not only a cutback to the crowd but also a **reaction shot**: it shows their reaction to the gunshot.

Figure 2-155

Figure 2-156

Figure 2-157

A **reverse** or **reverse-angle shot** is one that reverses the field of view, usually by an angle between 120° and 160°, though a 180° reverse or a complete turnaround is what the term strictly means. The regular alternation of such reversed views is called a **shot/reverse-shot** pattern, and it is often used for conversations between people who are facing each other (See **Fig. 2-1,** from *It's A Wonderful Life.*) A view over one person's shoulder to the face of another is called an **over-the-shoulder shot.**

Matte Shots and Composites. The mask or **matte card** produces an image of a certain desired shape. **Fig. 2-158** shows an **iris** or circular mask from *Intolerance,* and **Fig. 2-159** shows a **keyhole** mask from Ladislas Starewicz's *The Cameraman's Revenge* (1912). A **matte shot** is one in which part of the frame has been blocked out; the term also denotes a single image created through the sequential use of a matte and a counter-matte; shots whose mattes are complementary can be combined into a single image without overlap. As we shall see in the discussion of optical special effects, a matte can also be an opaque pattern that changes shape with every frame; this is called a **traveling matte**, and one was used to add the figure of the falling policeman to the bird's-eye shot in *Vertigo* (**Fig. 2-112**).

Whether or not a fixed or traveling matte is used, a shot that has been composed from the material in several different shots — or pre-print materials — is called a **composite.** (A **composite print** is one that has both picture and sound.) The alignment of its visual elements must be absolutely precise; otherwise one will see a **matte line** between them. When a composite is perfect, as in this frame from *King Kong* (**Fig. 2-160**), the various images cohere

Figure 2-158

Figure 2-159

Figure 2-160

Figure 2-161

without a seam. At screen left is a waterfall photographed in the High Sierras. The background mountains have been painted on glass. In the foreground is a miniature model tree, and in the bottom right corner, there is live action.

A **superimposition** or **multiple exposure** is a shot that includes two or more images photographed at different times. No mattes are employed, and so one or more of the images may appear transparent. **Fig. 2-161** is a multiple exposure from *The 39 Steps*. This shot could also be described as a mindscreen: it shows how the hero remembers the recently deceased woman's warning about the dangerous figures whom he can see outside his window at the phone booth.

Shot Transitions

The usual way to get from one shot to another is via a **straight cut**, in which the end of one shot is spliced directly to the beginning of another. **Fig. 2-162** shows a straight cut from *Intolerance*. In context, this cut implicates the corporate boss, Jenkins, in the death of the old man who is shown with his grieving son in the previous shot (the upper of the two frames). But the straight cut can be used for virtually any purpose and is the simplest transitional device.

A **fade** presents the image as evenly emerging out of or retreating into complete darkness. When the image emerges out of darkness, that is a **fade-in**; the reverse is a **fade-out**. A fade can also be to a white or colored field; hence **fade to black**, **fade to white**, or **fade to red** (used to great effect in Bergman's *Cries and Whispers* [1972]). Examples of fades can be found in the scene from *Hiroshima, mon amour*, discussed in the next section (see **Figs. 2-235, 2-236, 2-268,** and **2-269**).

For an **iris-in**, the circular mask is opened so that the image

Figure 2-162

Figure 2-163

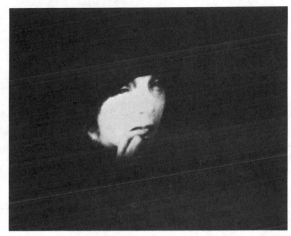

Figure 2-164

appears as a growing circle; an **iris-out** is the reverse. **Figs. 2-163** and **2-164** show an iris-out from *Greed*. Trina is biting her finger and wondering where her husband got liquor money. *Greed* concerns not only miserliness but also its psychopathology, and there are several scenes in which Mac bites Trina's fingers in order to force her to give him money. The reason the finger is so important here — and is emphasized by its placement within the contracting iris — is that Trina, in a miserly mood, is biting it herself.

A **dissolve**, in which one image melts into another that comes to replace it, is produced by superimposing a fade-out over a fade-in. At the midpoint of the dissolve, both images are equally half-present. **Figs. 2-165** through **2-167** come from a 48-frame (2-second) dissolve from *Citizen Kane*. In this case, a series of dissolves is used to convey the passage of time — a period Susan fills up by doing jigsaw puzzles. Elsewhere in *Kane* short dissolves are used

Figure 2-165

Figure 2-166

Figure 2-167

Figure 2-168

to smooth transitions between shots, basically as an alternative to the straight cut. A dissolve can also create the impression that something has disappeared. In this frame from *Nosferatu* (**Fig. 2-168**) the vampire dissolves into thin air when he is trapped by the sunrise. The shot of the count (Max Schreck) was faded out while the shot of the room continued without a fade. It is likely that this particular effect was achieved in the camera, but most dissolves and optical effects are created in the laboratory.

When one image displaces another without any fading or overlap, so that parts of both are onscreen at the same time, the transition is called a **wipe**. In the most common form, one image appears to be pushed offscreen by the arrival of another, with a **wipe line** (their point of conjunction) sweeping across the screen. When the line moves from screen right to left, or the reverse, that is a **horizontal wipe**, and many of them were used effectively in the

Figure 2-169

Figure 2-170

Figure 2-171

Star Wars films. **Figs. 2-169** through **2-171** show a **vertical wipe** from *The 39 Steps*. Here the downward vertical movement of the wipe line complements the action — the characters are taking the elevator upstairs — as if the lower floor were being pushed down by the view of the upper floor. The most extravagant wipes, named after the spirals, irises, and other geometrical forms they manipulated, were found in the serials of the 1930s and 1940s. **Figs. 2-172** through **2-174** show a fancy wipe from Chapter 10 ("The Death Mist") of *Flash Gordon Conquers the Universe* (1940).

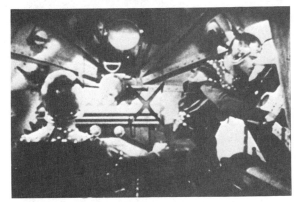

Figure 2-172

Shot Relations

The study of shot relations is more than the study of editing: it goes beyond that to concentrate on how shots are constructed so that they *can* be cut together. The careful design and placement of shots prompt us to imagine the arrangement and even the meaning of the whole.

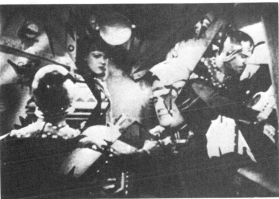

Figure 2-173

Making Connections. **Fig. 2-175** shows two consecutive frames from *Intolerance*. The woman (Mae Marsh) is attending her husband's trial for a murder he did not commit. Rather than present

Figure 2-174

Figure 2-175

her in a single shot, Griffith isolated her face and hands into different shots, giving special emphasis to each. The face shows one aspect of her anxiety, the hands another. Taken together, these parts suggest the whole.

More to the point, these shots were photographed so that they demand to be interrelated. The camera is eye-level on Marsh's face, then slightly high-angle on her hands — as if it had looked down to see the hands. The costume and lighting are consistent in both shots, as is the tone of anxious concern. In another two frames from *Intolerance* (**Fig. 2-176**), the screen direction is consistent, and we are prompted to imagine that the soldiers in the first shot are firing on the workers in the next shot. But in **Fig. 2-177** there is a continuity flaw. Jenkins holds a dime in his left hand in the first shot, but in his right hand in the inserted closeup. These shots cannot be cut together in continuity, whereas the others can.

In the color insert, **Figs. C-31** and **C-32** are frames from two consecutive shots in *The Godfather* — the scene in which Vito's friend Luca Brasi is murdered. (These are full-frame enlargements, by the way: they show the entire 1.33 : 1 image photographed at the time of production. The left edge has been dark-

Figure 2-176   **Figure 2-177**

ened; that is where the soundtrack would eventually go. When printed for projection, the whole image would be reduced, and its top and bottom would be masked to 1.85 : 1.) **Fig. C-31** is a close shot, and its tightness determines that the subject matter to notice at this moment is Luca himself: his pain and surprise, the furious and desperate look in his eyes, and the way he is surrounded by his enemies.

Fig. C-32 is a full shot of the next phase of the same action, but the change of setup radically alters the content of the image. Here Luca is a figure in the distance, and if we feel for him, it is with a different kind of intensity: he is already lost. The brownish red color scheme injects an impression of blood, or bloody business, and it contrasts markedly with the blue-gray scheme of the later scene in which Vito is shot down in the street, as if the key to this scene were its reddish violence and the key to the latter its downbeat, cold winter blue. Still later, the Corleones will be informed that "Luca Brasi sleeps with the fishes" — in other words, that he is dead. This line is set up in **Fig. C-32**. The fish are seen here to be an important part of the bar's decor, and they stamp Luca's fate. Taken together, these frames show very clearly how significant aspects can be isolated out of a field of action and given selective emphasis through camera placement and control of color. Each shot has distinct content, and the shots are linked by the continuity of action and setting.

Creative Geography and the Mozhukhin Experiment. It is important to realize that most films are shot **out of sequence**; that is, the shots are not taken in the order that they will follow once the picture has been edited. This is a matter of simple economy: it makes sense to shoot everything that will take place on a particular set at the same time. In a shot/reverse-shot conversation, there is no reason to change setups after every speech; the whole scene can be run through with the camera looking over the first actor's shoulder, then again looking over the second actor's shoulder. Whether continuity or discontinuity is the filmmaker's goal, each must be carefully anticipated during shooting. In either case, the audience will do its best to read sequential shots in terms of each other, making sense of the ways they clash or cohere.

When the Russian director Lev Kuleshov was first trying to establish how movies worked, sometime in the early 1920s, he conducted an important experiment. He found some old footage of a pre-Revolutionary actor named Ivan Mozhukhin, a single long take (probably a makeup test) in which the face showed an unvarying, neutral expression. Kuleshov then cut three different shots into this take: one of a child playing with a toy, one of a bowl of soup, and one of an old woman in a coffin. The sequence went as follows: face, child, face, soup, face, woman, face. When he showed this short film to an audience (although this may be a bit of cinematic folklore), they remarked what a great actor Mozhukhin was. They enjoyed the subtle way he expressed affectionate delight at the child's playing, hunger for the soup, and grief at the death of the woman, whom they assumed was his mother. The Mozhukhin experiment, as it has since been called, had a permanent impact on the theory of screen acting. It showed that audiences will read shots in terms of each other and therefore that a film actor — who ought ideally to underact — could allow the montage to suggest some of his or her emotions and thoughts. The point for our immediate purposes, however, is simply that the impression of continuity is often generated by the audience.

In a related experiment, Kuleshov cut together views of a walking man, a waiting woman, a gate, a staircase, and a mansion. All of the shots had been taken in different locations, and the mansion was in fact the White House, but when the shots were assembled, the audience read them as having both spatial and temporal continuity. They imagined (or decided) that they saw a man meet a woman in front of a gate, beyond which were stairs leading to a mansion. Kuleshov called what he had discovered "the artificial landscape" or "creative geography." The filmmaker has the opportunity, then, not only to shoot out of sequence but also to join together shots that come from utterly unrelated sources.

One familiar use of creative geography is to intercut studio interiors with location exteriors. Another is to lift shots from previous films: when Hawks made *The Road to Glory* (1936), he took much of the battle footage from a French film by Raymond Bernard called *Wooden Crosses* (1932). In terms of sound, an analogous practice is to intercut lip-sync shots with shots that were photographed silent. There is usually no reason to record live sound in a scene that does not include dialogue. When a film is "salted" with lip-sync shots, distributed every so often, the audience will bring its expectation of continuity to bear and will think that the whole movie is in perfect sync.

Intercutting and Cross-cutting. The regular alternation between any two ongoing actions is called **cross-cutting**; because it implies that the actions are somehow parallel, or proceeding in the same dramatic direction — usually in the same time frame — it is also called **parallel montage**. The process of inserting shots into another series of shots is called **intercutting**; it does not necessarily involve a regular pattern of alternation. An insert shot, for example, is **cut into** an ongoing scene.

As a representative example of cross-cutting, consider this scene from G. W. Pabst's great romantic thriller, *The Love of Jeanne Ney* (1927). Jeanne (Edith Jehanne) and her lover Andreas (Uno Henning) are spending the night together at a hotel. They open the window and look across the street at a wedding reception, and the sight upsets them. They feel that being unmarried makes them a less-than-legitimate couple. Then Andreas takes a closer look (**Fig. 2-178**) and sees that the bride is looking tearfully at *them* (**Fig. 2-179**). To their surprise they find that she envies their romantic freedom and how good they look together. We can tell that they are looking at each other because the shots are separated by an angle of less than 180° — the line has not been crossed. Shortly

Figure 2-178

Figure 2-179

Figure 2-180

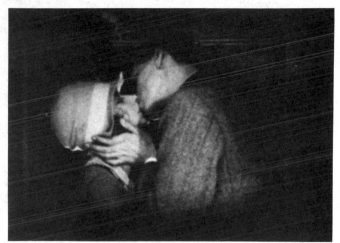

Figure 2-181

afterward we see why she is crying, for the boyishly unattractive and weepy figure who embraces her in **Fig. 2-180** is her new husband.

At first, Andreas and Jeanne had judged themselves for being unmarried; now they realize what a good couple they are in their own terms, and they kiss, in a shot taken from inside their hotel room (**Fig. 2-181**). The pattern of alternation — the cross-cutting — has had two effects. First, it has let us understand who was looking at whom, while the characters' actions suggested what they felt about what they saw. Second, it has encouraged *us* to make the same kind of comparisons and eventually to endorse Andreas and Jeanne's conclusions. The final shift to a camera position inside their room signifies that the comparison has served its purpose and that the characters can now go on to explore their intimacy.

Match and Jump Cuts. Some filmmakers do their best to hide cuts from the audience's attention in cases where they may prove distracting. In *The Love of Jeanne Ney* Pabst often *cut on movement*. A character might move his hand in a medium long shot, and after a straight cut, that hand might still be shown moving in a medium close shot. He also *cut on eye movement:* an action in one shot might lead the audience's attention to the upper right corner of the frame, and the next shot might begin with something moving in that same screen position or along the same trajectory. In order to conceal the "madeness" of its illusions (a pervasive concern amounting almost to an ideological project), Hollywood has made a science out of these practices.

Within the scheme of continuity cutting, the most rigorously

Figure 2-182

Figure 2-183

Figure 2-184

Figure 2-185

similar or analogous shots are said to be bridged by match cuts. Over a **match cut** there is a change of setup while an action appears to continue seamlessly.

Figs. 2-182 through 2-185 show a rigorous match cut from *The 39 Steps*. The woman has just told the man that he can identify a certain character by his missing pinky-joint; the man frees his hand and gets up from the kitchen table. The first shot (Figs. 2-182 and 2-183) ends as he begins to rise. Between Figs. 2-183 and 2-184, which are consecutive frames, a match cut intervenes, and the second shot shows the completion of his action from a more distant setup. A slight change of camera angle usually makes a match cut less noticeable.

Whereas the two elements of a match cut "match" each other, the elements of a **jump cut** do not match each other seamlessly, if at all. A jump cut leaps over time or creates an odd transition, and it often creates the impression that something has been left out. If you have a 1-minute take of a woman putting on eye shadow, and you delete the middle 40 seconds, the result will be a jump cut from her beginning to apply the makeup to her examining the completed job.

Figs. 2-186 through 2-191 show a series of jump cuts from Godard's first feature, *Breathless* (1959, rel. 1960). The hero (Jean-Paul Belmondo) is driving down a country road, and he is impatient to pass any vehicles that happen to get in his way. In the first shot (Figs. 2-186 and 2-187) he passes a white car; the view is through his windshield. Then there is a jump cut to the second shot (Figs. 2-188 and 2-189), which shows his passing a gasoline truck. By the position of the trees, it is clear that the driving time between the two passes has been deleted. This cut conveys the driver's impatience and speeds up the presentation of the complete action, as if both time and distance were being leapt over. The action "jumps" forward. Another jump cut takes us to the third shot (Figs. 2-190 and 2-191), where a black car is passed.

A jump cut can also be defined as a *mismatch* between shots that are not ordinarily put together — what some would call a "bad cut." Time is not necessarily a factor in this kind of cut, nor is the leaving out of some aspect of a process. An example of a "bad" cut would be from one medium shot of an unmoving figure to a similar medium shot of that same figure. Such a figure will appear to "jump" from one position to another. Even when the figure is moving, if the second shot picks up the action in a position earlier than that at which the first ended (producing a brief jump backward in time) or just slightly ahead of that point (producing an odd leap forward), the flow of events may be jarred.

We can summarize by saying that the shots in a jump cut do not "go together," whereas those in a match cut go together perfectly. Between these alternatives are what may be called ordinary cuts, those that are neither seamless nor radically odd. It is an important aspect of the development of film style that some filmmakers experiment with new approaches to continuity, some of which — like Godard's jump cuts — are eventually accepted as valid, revising

Figure 2-186

Figure 2-187

Figure 2-188

Figure 2-189

Figure 2-190

Figure 2-191

audience expectations and enlarging the syntactic possibilities of the medium.

Symbolic Interrelationships. In semiotic terms, a symbol is a sign in which the relation between signifier and signified is arbitrary, or agreed upon. In more conventional — but clearly related — terms, a **symbol** is a figure that stands for more than itself; Joseph Conrad's "heart of darkness," for example, is more than a condition of the light, and James Joyce's Leopold Bloom (in *Ulysses*) is both Odysseus and an Irish-Jewish salesman who wanders through a Dublin that is charged with symbolic overtones of the ancient Mediterranean world. Symbolic content is often enriched in films by encouraging the audience to draw comparisons among particularly resonant shots and images.

At the end of Part I of Michael Cimino's *Heaven's Gate* (1980), a pessimistic alcoholic (John Hurt) sits on his horse and, realizing the full extent of mortal failure, says, "What are we?" and takes a long drink from a silver flask. At that moment a huge dust cloud blows into the frame and hides him from view, and when the dust has passed, the man is gone. Clearly this dust is more than just dust. As a symbol, it stands in for the forces of nature and history, before which man is an insignificant and passing figure. When dust clouds come to dominate much of the mise-en-scène in Part II, they continue to bear this symbolic content.

Fig. 2-192, a frame from Murnau's *Sunrise* (1927), shows a simple loaf of bread. The situation is that a man (George O'Brien) has long been happily married, but he has recently begun an affair with a "woman from the city" (Margaret Livingston). The setting is the countryside, and the loaf has just been set out by the wife (Janet Gaynor). She has cut the loaf in half, cut one half into slices, and set it all on a plate on the dinner table. In this, the only close shot of the bread, it is seen from an angle that makes it look round and whole. This is the loaf as the husband sees it as he leaves to meet his lover while his wife is in the kitchen getting a bowl of hot soup.

What this choice of angle means is that married life is itself a whole and that the husband feels guilty about the wholeness he is betraying. The loaf is also a symbol for life in the country, where bread is kneaded and baked at home — not something presliced and sold in a bag. It has the integrity of well-understood and time-honored values. We eventually realize that it has this specific meaning because we are encouraged to compare it with another symbolic loaf in a later scene, shown in **Figs. 2-193** through **2-196**.

In the interim between these scenes the man has invited his wife on a trip to the city, and along the way he has tried to drown her. Although at the last minute he changed his mind, the wife has — understandably — not yet forgiven him. In an attempt at reconciliation he takes her to a restaurant and orders bread. The bread comes on a plate and has been cut into neat little cubes (**Fig. 2-193**). These cubes are as different as possible from the round country loaf, and they imply not only how things are organized and distanced from nature in the city, but also what a mess the man's actions have made of their once-whole marriage.

As he offers the bread, he is also offering life — because bread is food. This gesture is the opposite of attempted murder, but of course, it reminds her of how nearly she missed never eating again. She understands the gesture, as we can see from her expression in **Fig. 2-194**. She is almost afraid of the bread and all it implies. She tastes it, then bursts into tears (**Fig. 2-195**). In the next

Figure 2-192

Figure 2-193

Figure 2-194

Figure 2-195

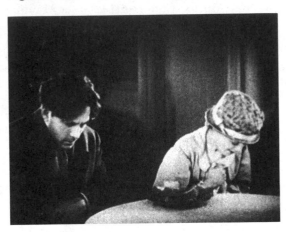

Figure 2-196

shot we can see what has happened to the couple. In **Fig. 2-193** he leaned toward her while she leaned at once toward and away from him. The next shot concentrated on her experience. In **Fig. 2-196** they have both been sucked down into private despair: he to his guilt and she to her grief, with the cut bread between them.

The Moving Camera

Complex interrelationships can be developed within the shot, not just among shots. In this section we shall examine two brilliant uses of the moving camera, one from *Sunrise* and the other from *Vertigo*. In both cases camera movement was used to introduce a variety of information within a continuous field and also to encode that field both subjectively and morally.

Sunrise. Figs. **2-197** through **2-215** are frames from a continuous track shot that lasts 1 minute and 28 seconds; it shows the meeting

Figure 2-197

Figure 2-198

Figure 2-199

Figure 2-200

Figure 2-201

Figure 2-202

Figure 2-203

Figure 2-204

Figure 2-205

Figure 2-206

Figure 2-207

Figure 2-208

Figure 2-209

Figure 2-210

Figure 2-211

Figure 2-212

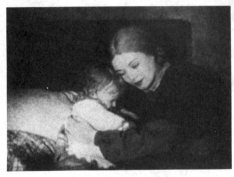

Figure 2-213

Figure 2-214

Figure 2-215

Figure 2-216

between the faithless husband and the woman from the city. This shot is bracketed fore and aft by unmoving two-shots of the wife and her child at home; their stability contrasts with the fluid rambling of this long take. When the wife and the child are cut back to (**Fig. 2-216**), their sad hug declares an authorial value judgment on the embrace of the lovers.

As the man walks through the branches and underbrush on the way to meet the woman, the camera follows him in an intricate and beautiful pattern. The shot begins with a diffused view of the moon at screen left and the man walking away from the camera

(**Fig. 2-197**). The camera follows him at a distance, moving forward and slightly to the right (**Fig. 2-198**). When he turns and walks to the right (**Fig. 2-199**), the camera makes the same turn and pans right while continuing to track forward (**Fig. 2-200**). When he ducks under a tree (**Fig. 2-201**), the camera stops advancing on him and instead begins to move to the left (**Fig. 2-202**), catching a view of him as he walks toward the left in the distance (**Fig. 2-203**). As he approaches a fence (**Fig. 2-204**), the camera is still tracking to the left. He climbs over the fence (**Fig. 2-205**) and begins to walk toward the camera (**Fig. 2-206**).

Now the camera stops moving until he has nearly walked past it (**Fig. 2-207**). It begins to track to the left again, as if in search of the woman from the city. It knows where to find her, for in **Fig. 2-208** she is obscured by a clump of trees, yet the camera pushes through them (**Fig. 2-209**) until the woman is shown in full moonlight, impatiently twirling a flower (**Fig. 2-210**). At this point the shot has gone on for 50 seconds, and from here till the end, the camera no longer moves.

After a while she hears him coming and throws away the flower (**Fig. 2-211**). Then she quickly powders her face (**Fig. 2-212**) and waits. When he does appear, it is from the left side of the frame (**Fig. 2-213**). We might have expected him to appear from screen right, and this surprise is the heart of the shot. Not only is it disorienting, but it also indicates that the man and the camera have taken different routes to the woman. It is as if the camera knew just where it was going, whereas the man took a less direct route, perhaps as a way of stalling and perhaps because he is not sure of his own intentions. He walks forward and backward, to left and right, and even in this last unshown circle. The woman, on the other hand, stays put. She knows what she wants and what she is doing, and she has settled on this picturesque, moonlit spot because it will display her to the best romantic advantage. Because of the unexpected way the man shows up in **Fig. 2-213**, we are almost as surprised to see him here as he must be himself, even if we have been following his progress and expecting the meeting to take place. Now he stands still, and the woman advances to meet him (**Fig. 2-214**). They embrace (**Fig. 2-215**), and then there is a straight cut to **Fig. 2-216**.

In its own right, this shot is a masterpiece, and it was one of the reasons that Charles Rosher and Karl Struss won the first Oscar for cinematography for their work on *Sunrise*. Through the intricacy of its movements, the camera communicates the man's psychological uneasiness about the way his life is changing, his role in that change, and his suspicion that the change may be for the worse. He wanders, yet he continues to advance toward his goal. The moral value of his affair is both presented and judged by these same movements, both of the man and of the relatively more intentional camera. The woman's psychology is conveyed just as efficiently by the camera's *not* moving, and that stability is followed by the disorientation of the man's entrance from the "wrong" side of the frame. When she moves to meet him, the camera stays where it is. The camera, then, does not respond to her movements as it does to the man's, and it is his psychology — and moral quandary — that dominates the shot.

Vertigo. In order to clarify what is going on in the famous circular track shot from *Vertigo* (see the color insert for **Figs. C-33** through **C-42**), it is necessary to reprise a bit of that film's complex plot.

Scottie (Stewart) has been retired from the San Francisco police force after nearly falling from a building and watching the police officer who tried to help him fall to his death. As he explains to his former fiancée Midge, Scottie has discovered that he has acrophobia (fear of heights), which gives him vertigo, which makes him dizzy. Vertigo (from the Latin *vertere*, "to turn") is the sensation that the world is spinning around one, or simply a dizzily circling movement.

An old friend, Gavin Elster, hires Scottie to tail his wife Madeleine, who he says is obsessed with the figure of Carlotta Valdes, her suicidal ancestor. Scottie follows Madeleine (Novak) and eventually falls in love with her. She leads him to the mission at San Juan Baptista, and at one point they go into the livery stable, where Madeleine tells Scottie a "memory" that appears to belong to Carlotta and includes the figure of a gray horse. Scottie goes to a wooden horse in the stable and identifies it as the one in the memory — a memory that he explains may have been part of her own experience as Madeleine. "You see," he says, "there's an answer for everything." But Madeleine leaves him and runs into the church. Scottie pursues her up the stairs of the mission tower, but an attack of acrophobia and vertigo incapacitates him. He sees Madeleine's body fall to a low red-tiled roof, as if she had finally reenacted Carlotta's suicide.

Scottie goes into a major depression. One day he spots a woman named Judy (Novak) who reminds him of Madeleine. He compels her to dress up as Madeleine. By this time Hitchcock has informed us that Judy and the "Madeleine" Scottie met are in fact the same woman. She had been Elster's mistress, and Elster had manipulated both her and Scottie as part of his plan to murder his wife, the real Madeleine. Knowing that Scottie would not be able to make it up the mission stairs in time, Elster had been waiting in the bell tower with Madeleine's dead body, which he had thrown down to the roof when Judy disappeared from Scottie's view. Then he had broken up with Judy.

The problem is that Judy has fallen in love with Scottie, and she submits to his demands that she pretend to be Madeleine, knowing that she is risking prison, but unable to refuse. She takes this risk in the hope that Scottie will fall in love with *her*, with the real Judy. But he only has eyes for Madeleine. When she returns to her room in the Empire Hotel after a trip to the beauty parlor, her clothes and makeup are right, but she has declined to put up her hair. She wants part of this fantasy woman to remain like Judy, but he insists otherwise. Frightened and exasperated, Judy goes into the bathroom to put up her hair. When she reappears, transformed into Madeleine as if, in Hitchcock's word, she were her "ghost," they kiss. We shall return to that scene in a moment.

After an interlude during which they apparently make love, Judy makes the "mistake" of putting on Carlotta's necklace, a souvenir from her affair with Elster, and Scottie realizes what has been going on. He insists that they drive down to the mission. At this point he is as much a detective as he is a vengeful lover, a man who resents having been played for a fool. He forces her to go up the stairs with him, and this time he makes it to the top. While they are in the bell tower, a nun appears out of the shadows, and Judy is so frightened — as if of the ghost of Madeleine — that she falls to her death on the same red roof. Scottie looks down at her body, apparently cured of his vertigo. This ambiguous, dark, and essentially perverse ending makes several points: (1) that Judy has been justly punished for playing with death; (2) that Scottie has lost Madeleine in the instant of finding her again; and (3) that Scottie has murdered Judy, that his project of turning her into the image of the dead Madeleine has ironically succeeded.

The made-up problem was that Madeleine might compulsively repeat Carlotta's suicide. The ironic development is that Judy repeats the circumstances of Madeleine's "suicide." The unsuspected irony, and the central subject of the picture, is that it is Scottie who is driven to repeat the event that ruined him emotionally. This related series of repetitions, some illusory and some real, turns *Vertigo* into an authentic tragedy. Like a good detective, Scottie has found that there is "an answer for everything," even if it is not the answer he wanted to find. Like Oedipus, Scottie is forced to confront his own role in the problem he hoped to solve. And like many tragic heroes, Judy has gambled on her ability to dodge Fate, has persevered in a self-destructive course of action that she considers necessary and correct, and has been destroyed.

During the scene in which Scottie had convinced Judy to go to the beauty parlor, she had been backlit by the green light of the neon sign outside her hotel room. In silhouette, she had looked all the more like Madeleine. Green has been associated with Madeleine throughout the film — she often dresses in green, and drives a green car — and green is also a color favored by Hitchcock to express the complexities of sexual desire. When she returns with the wrong hair-do, she looks in the mirror. About half of the mirror's depths reflect the green light. This implies that Madeleine is Judy's reflection, her other self. That same light bathes her like a ghostly vision when she steps out of the bathroom. As she steps forward, out of the cloud of light, she becomes physical. When seen directly — looking right at the sign — the light actually appears slightly more blue-green than green, and so we interpret the extra greening of the light in the mirror and on the bathroom door as a reflection of Scottie's desire and as the sign of Judy's transformation into the object of that desire. She *is* Madeleine now, back from the dead, and he moves to embrace her (**Fig. C-33**).

As soon as he touches her face, the room begins to spin in a slow, languorous, vertiginous movement. Between **Figs. C-34** and **C-35**, we can see by the position of the picture on the wall that the room is moving in a clockwise direction, from screen left to screen right. The lovers are also turning as they kiss, also clockwise. They move in the same direction but at different rates (the room moves faster), and both room and lovers make approximately one complete turn. It becomes slightly dizzying for us to follow this shot, which lasts 1 minute and 15 seconds. There is never a point when we can say with assurance just what the relations are, in real space, between the camera and its subjects, nor even whether Scottie and Judy are supposed to be thought of as turning or standing still. It is likely, however, that the lovers are not turning: during the kiss they feel that the room is spinning around them and that they themselves have lost their bearings, their reference points in space.

Here is the way this shot was actually created. Hitchcock began with a circular set, most of which was like Judy's hotel room but part of which showed the livery stable. Cinematographer Robert Burks then photographed this room with a circular movement of the camera — probably a 360° pan, though he may have used a circular track. Then Hitchcock stood the actors on a small turntable, set the camera in front of them, and turned them slowly around. Behind them, the shot of the room was rear-projected onto a screen and rephotographed while the lovers turned in the foreground. The camera moved slightly forward and backward during this take but did not otherwise move. The ultimate movement on screen, then, was created by forward and backward tracks, turning actors, and the circular movement in the background (process) shot.

Beginning with **Fig. C-36**, the background begins to change. The room disappears, and an obscure view of the livery stable glides into view (**Fig. C-37**). In **Fig. C-38**, Scottie looks up for a few seconds, and his face shows his confusion. It is as if kissing Judy has been so much like kissing Madeleine that he has been transported to his memory of the last day he saw her and to the moment when he felt that everything could be explained. He feels that he is back in the stable with Madeleine, not in Judy's room. The shift in background expresses his disorientation, but it is also the seed of the solution he will eventually find. At this point he is 180° away from the position in which he began the kiss. He is opposite, then, to the mood of surrender with which the kiss began and will end. On the other hand, he is also opposite from the position in which he was aware of his real surroundings. What this shows is that he has been thoroughly drawn into the fantasy and that part of him remains skeptical. He both believes and wants to believe in the transformation, glad that Judy is so like Madeleine but suspicious that she is so like Madeleine.

Then Scottie returns to the full embrace (**Fig. C-39**), and soon the stable disappears. As the room comes back into view, the camera moves forward while the circling continues (**Fig. C-40**). By **Fig. C-41**, the neon sign has returned to the frame. At screen right, backlit by an expanse of blue-green light, Scottie bends for a deeper embrace (**Fig. C-42**), and the shot fades out as Bernard Herrmann's music, which has been playing the "Madeleine" theme throughout this shot, peaks and fades. Like a circle, this shot ends much as it began, with the emphasis on romantic transformation and dizzying surrender. In its course, the circle has included a moment of skepticism, confusion, and transformation.

As a circular movement — let alone as an intricate double circle — the camerawork here is part of an elaborate symbolic pattern. Scottie's acrophobia has been an important part of the plot — the key to Elster's plans. The stretching stairwell has vividly rendered his giddy, vertiginous reaction to heights. But this is also a story about guilt — not Elster's, but Judy's and particularly Scottie's. As mentioned earlier, the association between height and guilt is first made in the scene of the policeman's death, for which Scottie is partly responsible. The circular kiss, for all its dizzy romanticism, begins another kind of guilt and a more elaborate moral trap. While Elster manipulates his acrophobia-vertigo, Scottie's love for Madeleine involves him in romantic vertigo. In the whirl of emotions, he cannot be sure who this double woman is, cannot get his bearings; he is caught between his own authentic emotions, however perverse they may be, and the sense that he is caught up in some indecipherable manipulation. The mystery, the murder, and the romance — the three central elements of *Vertigo* — are linked in this one shot, and inseparable from all three is the problem of guilt: the link between love and death, between desire and murder.

Up to this point in the film, Scottie has been seen mostly as a victim. When he takes Judy to the mission, we are a bit distanced from him as the center of sympathy because we know more than he does about Judy's true feelings. (When one sees the film again, Kim Novak's performance is revealed in its true complexity, and our sympathy for her becomes even stronger. Throughout the film she plays either Judy or Judy-as-Madeleine. She is utterly Madeleine only in the circular kiss, which itself is one of the most brilliant gestures in the picture.) Once they return to the mission, we see Scottie as — to whatever extent — her executioner. His surrender to his romantic obsession and his professional code is murderous, as if Hitchcock were remembering Oscar Wilde's observation that "each man kills the thing he loves." It is also an act of self-healing, of shaking off the burden of guilt and finding that he was not responsible for Madeleine's death; it is that realization that cures him, at the end, of his vertigo. But he is left looking down at the body of the only Madeleine who ever mattered.

The dynamics of guilt and disorientation, the key to Scottie's vertigo as it is fully realized in the kiss scene, are conveyed by the circular movement of the camera. It is the circle of obsession and of the loss of control. It is also the romantic high point of the movie, and the truest and falsest moment in their tragic relationship. It is in the kiss that the execution of Judy begins, the seed of an extraordinarily intricate guilt, and Judy surrenders to it just as Scottie does. It is this vertigo, and not acrophobia, that gives the film its title. (The original novel, by Pierre Boileau and Thomas Narcejac, was called *Among the Dead.*) And it is this long take that gives vertigo, and the title, their full meaning.

The scene is an occasion for significant behavior and dramatic interaction. As a theatrical unit taking place in continuous time and space, it has a long history of definition.

In conventional English dramaturgy, scenes are divided according to changes in time and location: the living room at noon (one scene) and at midnight (another scene), the front yard at midnight (still another). The French theater divides scenes according to their participants: two people talk in a living room (one scene), and then another person enters, setting the stage for a three-way interaction (another scene). Regardless of how scenes are conventionally divided, however, both playwrights and directors understand the scene as a distinct dramatic entity with its own beginning, middle, and end, and often with its own momentum toward climax and resolution — in fact, a miniature play.

As explained at the start of the previous section, "scene" is used in two related ways in motion pictures. Within the screenplay and as a production term, a **scene** is a complete unit of action *capable* of being covered in a single shot, although in the completed movie it may be presented in more than one shot. But **scene** is also used in its conventional dramatic sense, which we can simplify as a significant event taking place in a single location, often involving only one character but usually a heightened interaction between characters. In this section we shall concentrate on the scene as a dramatic unit, not as a production term.

Dramatic Unity and the Task of the Scene

In theatrical terms, a scene is a portion of an act. Each act carries the story through a major phase of the action. In Samuel Beckett's *Waiting for Godot,* for example, the action divides logically into two parts, and each is given its own act. The five-act structure of *The Godfather* was discussed in Part I of this book. The term "act" is not universally employed in motion pictures, however; a group of logically and dramatically related scenes is often called a "sequence," even though "sequence" can also denote any series of related *shots*.

What sets a scene apart from the simple flow of action is the way it brings dramatic elements into focus. Let us imagine a story in which a man walks agitatedly down the streets of a major city. He has just discovered that his wife is a spy, although she has led him to believe that she simply works for an answering service. After pacing in front of the office building where his wife works (Scene 1), he walks into the lobby and asks to see the manager (Scene 2). When he enters the manager's office, he confronts the boss with the truth, and they engage in a major argument (Scene 3). That last scene will stand out in the viewer's memory as a *scene,* a moment of heightened drama, whereas the two previous scenes may be absorbed, in memory, into the general flow of events.

Confrontation and Resolution. Whether or not it resolves the action of a whole story, a scene does not usually end until it has

6. The Scene

dealt with the issues and the dramatic opportunities that generated it. Each scene has a job to do. It brings the characters from one state of affairs to another, from dramatic point A to B. It may be a question of an understanding, so that by the end of the scene the characters know more about each other, or perhaps of confrontation, as in a showdown. It is vital, then, to consider what the characters *bring* to a scene and what the writer, actors, and director want that scene to accomplish — what it contributes to the forward momentum of the story.

Capra's *It's A Wonderful Life* is the story of George Bailey (James Stewart), a man who has markedly enriched the lives of many of his neighbors in the small town of Bedford Falls, particularly by opposing the financial manipulations of a heartless capitalist named Potter. When everything goes wrong for George at once, he contemplates suicide but is saved by Clarence, his guardian angel. Responding to George's wish that he had never been born, Clarence shows him how Bedford Falls — now named Potterville — would look if George had never lived. This is a powerful and terrifying sequence. George recognizes everyone, but they have no idea who he is, and the town itself has turned into a nightmare of nightclubs, low-key lighting, and hardened, combative people.

Within this sequence there is a scene in which George goes to the boarding house run by his mother (Beulah Bondi), and they talk at the front door. What George brings to this scene is the desperate need for his mother to recognize him, to acknowledge his existence and to prove that he is not going mad or the victim of some hypnotic prank. What the mother — who, of course, does *not* recognize him — brings to this scene is the whole of her alternate life, the one she would have led had George never been born. In this version of her life, her son Harry (saved by George during a youthful winter accident) died in childhood, and the family business fell victim to Potter's manipulations. She has become lonely and bitter.

These two sets of attitudes and expectations — George's and the alternative mother's — collide, which both makes the scene and drives it to its conclusion: the mother does not know who George is and tells him to go away (the scene's climax), which leaves him even more upset (its resolution). This scene does not resolve the entire story by any means, but it does set George and his mother on a collision course, play out their interaction, and through that interaction effect a change in their lives.

The George who staggers away from his mother's door is not quite the same man who arrived there. What he brought to the scene was his need to be recognized; what he takes away is a heightened despair. When a character takes away the same things that he or she brought to a scene, there may be something wrong with the scene. One way to begin to analyze a scene, then, is to ask what the characters bring to a scene, to compare that with what they take away from it, and then to discover how the scene has effected that change. It is important to ask what difference the scene has made to them — what it has taught the characters about themselves and each other, and what it has taught us about them.

Distinct from what the characters bring to this scene is the task that Capra and his co-writers wanted it to accomplish: another step in George's terrifying but steady enlightenment. Each time he meets another character, he comes closer to understanding Clarence's point, which is that every life touches other lives and that George's has been "wonderful" because he has helped so many people. In the scene with his mother and in the confrontation that follows with his wife (now an "old maid" librarian), George's nightmare education climaxes, and when the world is finally returned to normal, the audience's relief is almost as great as his own. Capra did not let go of these scenes, or cut them off, until they had fulfilled their dramatic and structural purposes. Each scene is a crucible, transforming the elements that are "heated" within it.

Business. Some scenes include elements that might at first appear extraneous or superfluous. The most common of these are distractions called **business**. They can be used to provide extra visual interest in a scene whose primary element is dialogue — having someone fiddle with a prop, for example — or they can give a secondary character something to bring to the scene.

In Ford's *The Quiet Man* there is a scene in which a woman (Maureen O'Hara) goes to talk with her priest (Ward Bond) about problems she is having with her husband (John Wayne). She brings to the scene her embarrassment and her need to confide. If the priest had been in church, he would have brought only his role as listener. Instead, Ford's priest is on the verge of landing the big fish he has been trying to catch for years. This gives him something extra to bring to the scene, and the result injects comedy into their serious confrontation.

The priest is torn between his duty to listen to the wife and his desire to catch the fish. The fish is way ahead. This bit of business enriches the scene but does not detract from its essential purpose, which is the wife's confiding in the priest and his giving her some impatient advice. Only when the important lines have been said between them — in other words, when the basic "story-advancing purpose" of the scene has been accomplished — does the trout bite. But the business is more than a capricious distraction in this case; in itself it coheres with and advances the comical tone of the film, and it is also one of many examples of the conflict between the demands of a conventional social role and the quirks and attitudes that make each person unique, which is a central theme in this story of an ex-prizefighter who refuses to act in a conventionally "masculine" manner.

Character and Action. Part of what *we* bring to a scene is the expectation that a character will act in character. Character has a logic of its own, and there are some things that some people simply will not do, or that they will consistently do. Much of the drama of watching a scene depends on our not knowing exactly what a character will do, but when the action does occur, it should fall into place with an intuitive sense of "rightness."

It's A Wonderful Life goes to great pains to ensure that George's thoughts of suicide will make sense, will be in character, will appear to have developed logically out of the situation and his personality. Because a film character is often played by a recognized actor and is, in performance, virtually inseparable from that actor (an identification that is momentary in the theater, as one role can be played by different actors in the course of its history, and irrelevant in prose fiction, where the character is not enacted), the logic of *character* can yield to the logic of *persona*. In this sense, "George" is a mask being worn by Stewart, and we would have different expectations of George if he were played by Gary Cooper or Woody Allen.

We should not forget, however, that certain films deliberately set out to violate our expectations of character and story logic. The eye-slitting scene in *Un Chien andalou* has a Surrealist illogic that teases our notions of what makes sense and of what sense is. There is an independently produced feature called *Out* (1982) by Eli Hollander in which the characters change identity every few minutes. Like the novel by Ron Sukenick on which it is based, *Out* has a purposeful *alogic* of character. Because these shifts are as "logical" as everything else in the film, *Out* manages to remain dramatically consistent in a very unconventional manner: its rules are odd, but they are observed as rules. In other words, any movie sets up certain terms, selecting them out of an infinite number of possibilities. These choices determine other choices; they become parameters. Once a character has been defined, certain actions and attitudes will follow. Once an action has been set in motion, it will develop on its own terms. This is what many writers mean when they say, "The character made that decision, I didn't," or "It had to turn out that way."

It is sometimes said that "action is character." The scene is the site where that is most true, where what someone *does* lets us see who that character really is. In the Thanksgiving dinner scene from *The Gold Rush*, the ways in which the tramp (Chaplin) and Big Jim (Mack Swain) eat the shoe — one in disgust, the other converting it into an elegant feast — tell us plainly who they are. Near the end of that film, when the narcissistic dance-hall girl (Georgia Hale) offers to pay the tramp's passage, thinking that he is a stowaway, that action lets us know exactly how she has changed since we and the tramp last saw her.

In a fiction film, the challenge is to construct characters whose actions will appear to be autonomous and appropriate so that the audience will forget that they have been made up. In a nonfiction film, the problem is to find and record an action that will reveal the nature of the truly autonomous characters who have not been made up. In either case, every well-considered scene moves the story or presentation in a desired direction, like an individual step in a staircase. To *plot* either a story or an argument is to structure the staircase — to decide which steps need to be present and in what order.

To examine some of these workings more specifically, let us consider two complete scenes — one classical and one relatively recent — that have markedly different visual styles and that function as essential steps in the staircases of their stories. The first, from *King Kong,* reveals the workings of conventional master-shot construction. The second is the "finger-twitch" scene from Resnais's *Hiroshima, mon amour* (1959), which has an intrusive mindscreen and a subtle yet definite visual unity. Both of these might well be contrasted with the long-take style in *Kane* (review the "desert island" shot, which is one of three in its scene but is itself capable of having been constructed out of many more conventional, limited shots).

King Kong: The Scream Test

Adventurer and filmmaker Carl Denham (Robert Armstrong) has cast Ann Darrow (Fay Wray) to play the female lead in a picture he plans to make about the legendary Kong. She has no acting experience, and while they are en route to Skull Island, he gives her a screen test. **Figs. 2-217** through **2-234** are frame enlargements from the 14 shots that make up the entirety of this scene.

Construction. The scene fades in as Carl finishes setting up his camera and Ann comes up the stairs (**Fig. 2-217**). "Oh, you've put on the Beauty and the Beast costume, eh?" he says, and she replies, "Mn-hmn. It's the prettiest." "All right," he says, "just stand over there." What the dialogue implies here is that Ann naturally inhabits her role in Carl's proposed movie. She has selected, on her own, the costume that epitomizes his vision of the project. This continues a theme that has been running through *King Kong*: that illusion and reality often overlap. (The film's first line is "Say, is this the moving picture ship?") It is in this scene that Ann begins to play the role of Beauty to Kong's Beast, not in the planned film but in the action of *King Kong* itself. She has been cast better than Carl Denham could have known. Eventually he will lose control of Kong and the rest of the show, but for now he is very much in control, and Ann's choice of costume has made it easier for him to treat her as the object of his creative fantasies.

There is a match-cut to shot 2 (**Fig. 2-218**), a medium shot of Ann. She tells Carl that she is nervous she may not photograph well, but he reassures her and she smiles. "What'll I do?" she asks. In the next shot (**Fig. 2-219**) a reverse-angle cut shows Carl beside the camera in medium shot. "Well," he says, "we'll start with a profile. When I start cranking, why, hold it a minute and then turn slowly toward me. You see me —"

Then there is a cut to the fourth shot (**Fig. 2-220**). He continues to speak, so that the cut is bridged both by matching action and by the continuity of the soundtrack: " — You smile a little, then

Figure 2-217

Figure 2-218

Figure 2-219

Figure 2-220

Figure 2-221

Figure 2-222

Figure 2-223

Figure 2-224

you listen, and then you laugh." His voice is fainter now, an instance of perspective sound. The camera (that is, the one controlled by the real makers of *Kong*) has moved away from Carl, and his voice is as it would be heard from this more distant camera position. "All right?" he asks, and then he gives himself the instruction, "Camera," and starts to crank.

This fourth shot is the master shot in this scene. A **master shot** includes or is capable of taking within its purview most of the significant action of a scene. It is almost invariably a full or long shot. When the master shot is the first to appear in a scene, it is called an "establishing shot," but there is no reason that it cannot pop up in the middle of a scene, as it does here, or intermittently, as it does in the helicopter/beach attack in *Apocalypse Now*. In general, the conditions established in the master shot must be repeated in the scene's other shots in order to ensure continuity of action. To digress for a moment in a way that will make this point clearly, that beach attack in Coppola's film (and master shot) had to be reenacted for the background of almost every other shot. According to one of the costume designers who worked on *Apocalypse Now*, it was like living in hell for the two weeks it took to shoot that scene.

Coverage — one of the very first things a director learns — is the art of covering, or being sure that there is a usable shot of, every important action in a scene. The simplest and most widely practiced means of ensuring proper coverage is first to shoot the entire scene in a master shot. Then closer or more distant views are taken from various angles and positions, and each of these shots can be cut into the scene, each replacing a portion of the master shot. The soundtrack, in sync with the master shot, continues unaffected. Should any of the closeups or medium shots prove unacceptable, that portion of the scene can still be covered by the master shot. Of course, if the scene is "covered" by several cameras, the tighter views can be taken at the same time as the master shot.

In this master shot, we can see the deck of the ship, Carl with his camera, Ann in her acting position, and two men looking down on the action. In **Fig. 2-220** these men are just coming into view, and in **Fig. 2-221** they have arrived. They are Captain Engelhorn (Frank Reicher, at the right) and Jack Driscoll (Bruce Cabot). Jack is the romantic lead in *Kong* — unless you see that as Kong's role. Later on (**Fig. 2-228**), a two-shot of Jack and the captain will be cut into the action, a simple example of the editing pattern just mentioned. The only thing not covered in this master shot is the view provided in **Fig. 2-224** of the three sailors who are also looking over the scene. The shot also does not give a good view of Ann's face. The master shot, then, is not a substitute for an edited scene but a way to ensure coverage and to clarify, if necessary, the spatial relationships among the other fields of view.

At the end of Shot 4, Ann turns as Carl has instructed her (**Fig. 2-221**). There is a match cut to Shot 5 (**Fig. 2-222**), in which she continues to act silently until she faces the camera directly (**Fig. 2-223**). Then there is a cut to Shot 6 (**Fig. 2-224**), in which the sailors comment on the action and the woman. "Looks kinda silly, don't it?" says the man in the middle. The topmost sailor says, "Pretty dame, huh?" At the bottom, the Chinese cook asks, "You think maybe he like to take my picture, huh?" The top fellow answers, "Those cameras cost money. Shouldn't think he'd risk it." This joke about the cook's breaking the lens with his looks gives the scene a lighter tone, a bit of comic relief that will make the serious conclusion of this scene all the more effective. This shot is a cutaway.

Figure 2-225

Figure 2-226

Figure 2-227

Figure 2-228

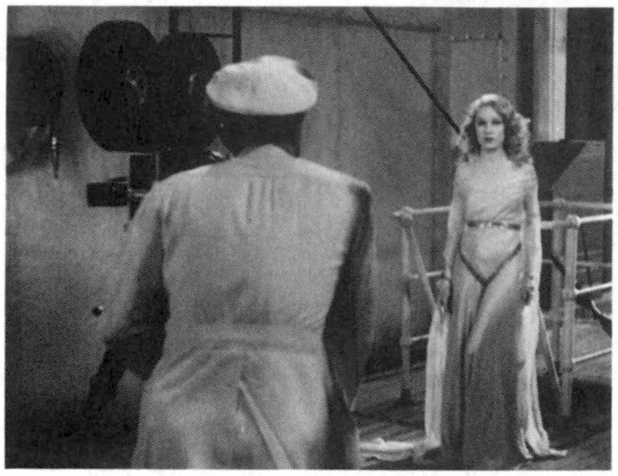

Figure 2-229

Figure 2-230

Now there is a cut back to the same setup used in Shot 3 (**Fig. 2-219**). It is clear that Shots 3 and 7 (**Fig. 2-225**) were originally part of the same take. (As an exercise, scan the photographs and count the number of setups used in this scene.) In this shot, Carl finishes his cranking and then says, "Now that's fine, Ann. Now we'll try one with a filter, eh?" There is a 180° reverse-angle cut to Shot 8 (**Fig. 2-226**). Carl and Ann are facing each other directly, making eye contact. Why was a shallower reverse angle not used? The answer is that Cooper and Schoedsack here wanted to play a bit with the audience's concept of the camera.

Unless you have the frame enlargements in front of you and can study the relative positions of the actors and the direction of Carl's camera, especially in **Fig. 2-225**, it is not at all easy to tell whether the view of Ann when she faces the audience (**Fig. 2-226**) is how she is seen by Carl, or how she is seen by Carl's camera. In fact, **Fig. 2-226** is an instance of subjective camera, Carl's POV. But it is easy to miss this and to assume that we are watching the film Carl is shooting. It is the difference between seeing Ann as a figure in the world photographed by *Kong's* camera and seeing her as a figure within a shot photographed by Carl's camera. It becomes difficult to separate the categories of world and filmed world. In other words, this slightly ambiguous camera position itself advances one of the major themes of the picture, making us unsure of just what we are looking at while reminding us that, one way or the other, this is a movie photographed with a camera just like the one Carl is using. The further implication is that Carl and his camera are almost interchangeable. During this eighth shot Ann asks Carl, "Do you always take the pictures yourself?"

In the ninth shot (**Fig. 2-227**) Carl answers her while removing the filter holder from the matte box, inserting a filter, and then putting the holder back in front of the lens. "Ever since a trip I made to Africa," he says. "I'd'a got a swell picture of a charging rhino, but the cameraman got scared. The darn fool — I was right there with a rifle. Seems he didn't trust me to get the rhino before it got him. I haven't fooled with cameramen since — I do it myself." Another of the illusion/reality jokes in this scene, this story actually happened to one of *Kong's* directors while he was shooting an earlier movie.

Carl and Jack were based largely on Cooper and Schoedsack, and most of the script was written by Ruth Rose (Mrs. Schoedsack), who had met her husband while they were on an expedition. Ann shares much with Rose, who was responsible for the "moving picture ship" joke that opens the movie and who had a lot of fun cramming *Kong* with private references not only to the makers' personal lives but also to the making of *Kong*. Not all of these references were meant to exclude the viewer. The 1933 audience, for instance, knew Cooper and Schoedsack as the makers of expeditionary documentaries and might have known that their most recent pictures had done poorly at the box office because they did not contain "romantic interest." At the start of *Kong*, Carl is furious about having to put a woman in his picture as a concession to public taste. *King Kong* itself is an expedition film with a strong romantic interest. Thus the original audience could have realized that *Kong* is filled with references to the process of its own making. These references are personal (Jack as Schoedsack, etc.), economic (the need for romantic interest), and — particularly in this scene — technical.

In Shot 10 (**Fig. 2-228**) Jack turns to the captain and asks, "Think he's crazy, Skipper?" The captain replies, "Just enthusiastic." In contrast to the comic relief provided by Shot 6 (**Fig. 2-224**), Jack's remarks to the captain are a serious commentary on the action. They shift our interest away from Carl and Ann, clarifying Jack's growing concern for Ann and giving another perspective on Carl's obsessive fixation on the picture he wants to make. In fact, Jack is not simply a bystander but the third principal figure in the scene. What he brings to it is his curiosity; what he takes away is suspicion and protective concern.

Now the scene's crucial action begins, with a cut to Shot 11 (**Fig. 2-229**). "Now, Ann," says Carl, "in this one you're looking down. When I start to crank, you look up slowly." He continues to speak in Shot 12 (**Fig. 2-230**): "You're quite calm; you don't expect to see a thing. Then you just — follow my directions. All right? Camera." As he starts to crank, there is another reverse-angle cut to Shot 13 (**Figs. 2-231** through **2-233**). As Ann carries out Carl's directions,

Figure 2-231

Figure 2-232

Figure 2-233

Figure 2-234

which continue throughout this shot, the sound of the cranking is very distinctly heard. Shot 13 has the same setup as Shot 2, to distinguish it from the setup in Shots 5 and 8. One setup indicates eye contact; this one *may* indicate the view from Denham's camera. As we shall see in a moment, this shot is being taken in much the same manner as were many of *Kong's* special-effects shots, and the reflexive link is there for us to make if we choose to think about it.

Ann begins Shot 13 as instructed, looking down (**Fig. 2-231**). We hear Carl's directions off-camera; that is, we do not see him while we hear his words. "Look up slowly, Ann," he begins, " — that's it. You don't see anything. Now look higher. Still higher. Now you see it! You're amazed! You can't believe it! Your eyes open wider. It's *horrible*, Ann, but you can't look away. There's no chance for you, Ann, no escape. You're helpless, Ann, helpless! There's just one chance — if you can scream. But your throat's paralyzed. [**Fig. 2-232**] *Try* to scream, Ann. Try! Perhaps if you didn't see it, you could scream. Throw your arms across your eyes and scream, Ann, scream for your life!" And Ann does scream, fully and believably (**Fig. 2-233**). The fact that it sounds like a genuine, heart-felt scream follows naturally from the illusion/reality tropes discussed earlier.

There is an immediate cut to the final shot of the scene (**Fig. 2-234**). Jack grabs the captain's arm and says, "What's he think she's *really* going to see?" The captain nods, and the shot ends with a fade-out. The entire scene has lasted 2 minutes and 27 seconds.

Role in the Film. This scene advances several important themes and story points. It is significant that we never see Carl Denham's reaction to Ann's scream. Instead we see Jack's concern, and the dialogue tells us that his concern is for Ann and not for himself and the rest of the crew (otherwise he would have said "we," not "she"). As part of the romantic plot, then, this scene brings Ann and Jack closer together; until now he has treated her as an inconvenience, a "*girl.*"

In terms of the filmmaking plot, the relations between Carl and Ann are also advanced. If nothing else, Carl learns that Ann can take direction, that she can do what he wants. By showing Carl with his camera and Ann alone, the seed of their separation (when Kong takes Ann away into the jungle) is planted. It will be Jack who goes after Ann while Carl returns to his gas bombs and makes new plans. Carl's film project will leave Ann on her own, as she is in these shots, and he will never think fully about anything but his camera or the stage show that comes to replace it.

Carl's vision of the film, the central image of "Beauty and the Beast," is brought up at the start of the scene, and some of its ramifications have already been discussed. This theme is repeated excessively throughout the film, but it *is* a key to the story. The Beast in the fairy tale was, of course, a romantic figure, and all that separates him from Kong is the fact that the giant ape does not turn into a human prince. But he is in love with Beauty (Ann), and that love is one of the things that brings about his destruction. If this theme were not insisted upon, the audience might too readily ask itself why Kong does not simply take Ann away and kill her — the apparent fate of Kong's previous "brides." It is the Beauty-and-the-Beast theme that underscores Kong's tragedy and makes him seem romantic.

As has already been suggested, this scene has many reflexive elements. Without ever completely dispelling the illusion that we are watching a version of reality, this scene nevertheless undermines the willing suspension of disbelief and reminds us that we are watching a movie. The strongest statement of this theme comes in Shot 13, where Ann is instructed to scream at something that is not present. There is a complex observation about acting in Carl's suggestion that Ann cover her eyes so that she cannot see what is not there to be seen in any case. But the key to this shot — and beyond it, to the scene — is that the instructions Carl is giving Ann are exactly those given to Fay Wray by Cooper and Schoedsack. Most of the live action in *King Kong* was shot first. The special-effects shots took much longer to complete. And although Kong's head, foot, and hand were constructed full-scale for some of the shots, Kong was most often a model less than 2 feet high. So in a shot where Ann is supposed to see Kong or a dinosaur and scream, Fay Wray would, in fact, be looking in the direction where the effects team would later insert a monster. She would be screaming at something that was not there. Thus what this shot encapsulates is the actual shooting method of the film in which it appears — simplified, of course, but still on the same track. This is, in fact, the most sophisticated juncture of illusion and reality in the entire movie, as well as a foreshadowing of danger and romance.

Hiroshima, mon amour: The Twitching Hands

Alain Resnais's first feature, *Hiroshima, mon amour* was written by the French avant-garde novelist Marguerite Duras, photographed by Sacha Vierny and Takahashi Michio, edited by Henri

Colpi, and scored by Georges Delerue and Giovanni Fusco. It stars Emmanuelle Riva in the role of a French actress and Eiji Okada as the Japanese architect with whom she has a brief affair in Hiroshima in August 1957. Released just after Truffaut's *The 400 Blows* (1959) and before Godard's *Breathless, Hiroshima, mon amour* was one of the crucial films at the crest of the New Wave.

This film works with several levels of reality. There is the story of the love affair, set in the realistic context of a rebuilt Hiroshima and answerable to the everyday concerns of business schedules, marital responsibilities, passionate infatuation, and simple tourism. There is the pressure or presence of the past as well: the city's memory of its holocaust, the actress's memory of her love affair with a German soldier during the Occupation of France, and the architect's memories of fighting in the war (although the architect is more interested in the present; he is a rebuilder). There was also what Duras called the "operatic" level, realized most fully in the film's opening act, when the lovers are presented as anonymous bodies shimmering with a radioactive dust that is also the sweat of their embrace, speaking in almost disembodied voices about the nature of Hiroshima. Finally and most directly, there was the nonfiction level, represented by authentic footage of bombing victims, the Hiroshima museum, and a modern hospital.

The "finger-twitch" scene, illustrated in **Figs. 2-235** through **2-269**, lasts 1 minute and 52 seconds and contains 13 shots. It takes place in the actress's hotel room on the morning after their first sexual encounter. That encounter has been treated politically and operatically in the film's opening sequence. *Hiroshima* has a five-act structure, like many of Resnais's films, and this scene begins the second act. With a sophisticated rhythm, this scene presents both objective and subjective images and sounds. It will serve as an example of subjective intrusion and visual unity, as well as of an intricately responsive soundtrack.

Construction. **Exposition** is the art of providing the audience with the facts or background information necessary to the understanding of a story. In *The Godfather, Part II*, for example, an opening title informs us about the Mafia conflict that led to the killing of Vito's father, and in the first Nevada sequence, dialogue lets us know what has happened to Michael since the end of *The Godfather*. The opening act of *Hiroshima* introduced us to the lovers as political and romantic abstractions while filling us in on the 1945 bombing and its aftermath. It is in this scene that we begin to meet the lovers as individuals — a different, more personal level of exposition.

The vital information we learn here is that the actress is haunted by a terrible memory, one that this affair has brought back to life. She is as linked to this memory of the war in Europe as Hiroshima is linked to the day of its destruction. Yet, like the modern, rebuilt Hiroshima, she attempts to ignore the past and live in the present. What Resnais and Duras devised was a powerful and realistic metaphor, both political and romantic, that explores the difficulty of living in time: the problems of needing to remember and having to forget, of not forgiving oneself for surviving and forgetting, of not being able to survive *without* forgetting, and of the emptiness of a life lived without reference to the past. The actress cannot forgive herself for not having died of love when her German lover was shot. To fall in love again with a man who reminds her of the war seems to be a betrayal of herself and of the past that she has locked away in a carefully guarded memory. As her emotions drag her into a heightened sense of being, she finds that she has to come to terms with death, loss, betrayal, and the painful fact that life continues. Although much of this is not verbally explained until the end of the film, it is in this early scene that these emotional conflicts are most forcefully presented.

The first shot, which lasts 24 seconds, begins with a fade-in (**Figs. 2-235** and **2-236**). In long shot, we see a group of bicyclists. The camera pans (**Fig. 2-237**) to a medium shot of the actress on her hotel balcony, holding a cup of coffee (**Fig. 2-238**). As she raises her cup, music starts. This music, which has a Japanese flavor, is in a relatively high register and is dominated by woodwinds. It feels carefree and pleasant, and so does she. Then the actress turns to go inside (**Fig. 2-239**), gracefully swinging herself over the balcony rail (**Fig. 2-240**).

Figure 2-235

Figure 2-236

Figure 2-237

Figure 2-238

Figure 2-239

Figure 2-240

Figure 2-241

Figure 2-242

Figure 2-243

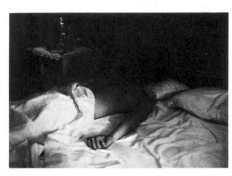

Figure 2-244

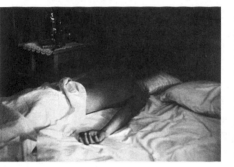

Figure 2-245

Figure 2-246

Figure 2-247

Figure 2-248

Figure 2-249

Figure 2-250

Figure 2-251

Shot 2, shown in **Figs. 2-241** through **2-243**, begins with a perfect match cut, reversing the angle of view as she completes her swing (**Fig. 2-241**). It lasts 8 seconds. The camera tracks back as she advances to the doorway (**Fig. 2-242**) and leans against the frame for a look at her sleeping lover (**Fig. 2-243**). At the very end of this shot, the light music is joined by an ominous, low tone, which grows in intensity through the next shot.

Shot 3 (**Figs. 2-244** and **2-245**) lasts 7 seconds, and it is a motivated POV shot — **motivated**, or accounted for, by her look in the previous shot. It is bracketed by shots of the actress, and the camera's angle in Shot 3 can be traced back along the line of her gaze. As she watches, the architect's hand twitches slightly in his sleep. In the course of this shot, the light Japanese music is completely displaced by the low, building tone. We feel that something bad is about to happen, and we realize that the music is leading us into the actress's feelings. The music reflects the movement of her subjectivity. She does not hear it, of course, but it expresses her emotions — in this case, the shift from carefree happiness to apprehension and resistance.

Shot 4 (**Figs. 2-246** and **2-247**) is a close shot of her face in the doorway. It lasts only 3 seconds. In **Fig. 2-246** her gaze is still directed at the sleeping architect, completing the bracketing of the POV shot (the "POV sandwich"). Then she looks slightly downward, and we can see that she is actually looking into herself (**Fig. 2-247**). As the second shot had prepared us for subjective camera, this fourth shot prepares us for an inner vision, for a sight of what she is thinking about. The ominous tone continues to intensify.

Shot 5 (**Figs. 2-248** through **2-250**) lasts 4 seconds and is a mindscreen. It is "unauthorized" in the sense that she is not deliberately narrating it or presenting it to an audience; it is her memory of the death of her German lover. It begins with a closeup of the German's hand as it twitches in death (**Fig. 2-248**). Clearly what has happened is that the architect's twitch in sleep has involuntarily reminded her of this other hand movement, and the past has intruded involuntarily into the present. There is a very rapid pan up the soldier's body. Midway, at **Fig. 2-249**, the music abruptly stops and is replaced by silence. The camera rests for a second on a tight two-shot of the lovers (**Fig. 2-250**), and we see the actress, 13 years younger, kissing his bloody face. The fact that we see her body indicates that this memory is not presented in subjective camera; instead, we see her as she looked at the time. If this were a completely objective presentation of a past moment, this shot would be called a **flashback**, a leap from the narrative present to a direct view of some past action. (Its complement is the **flash forward**.) Shot 4, however, has made it clear that this vision comes from her, is her memory of the event. It is the view from her mind's eye, and therefore not a flashback (objective) but a mindscreen (subjective). It is motivated by **Fig. 2-247**.

Shot 6 (**Fig. 2-251**) is a closer view of the sleeping architect. It lasts 3 seconds. The only sound is room tone. Then a train whistle is heard in the distance. The soundtrack indicates that the woman has returned to the reality of the present, as does her ability to see the Japanese lover. There is no need for an immediate bracketing shot, a return to her face, to sandwich the mindscreen; the transition is perfectly clear. By keeping this shot approximately as long as Shot 5, Resnais and Colpi emphasized the similarity of the two men, who are linked not only by their twitching but also by her seeing each of them for only a few seconds. Butted against each other, Shots 5 and 6 are an instance of dialectical montage. We must put the two lovers together in order to understand the association that the actress is making. The fact that the view is closer than that in Shot 3 indicates not a physical movement but a change in her attention, a subjective closing-in on the architect.

Shot 7 (**Fig. 2-252**) lasts 2 seconds. The only sound is room tone. The actress's expression is troubled, but she is not quite so lost in thought as she appeared in **Fig. 2-247**. She is somehow between the two times, 1944 and 1957, an emotion communicated to the audience by the juxtaposition of Shots 5 and 6 within these bracketing shots of her face (Shots 4 and 7).

Shot 8 (**Figs. 2-253** and **2-254**) lasts 8 seconds. The camera has moved slightly back from the setup in Shot 6, yet it is nearer than that in Shot 3. At this point there is a return to a normal pattern of cross-cutting. Most of the cuts have been between reverse-angle shots: #2 on her, #3 on him, #4 on her, #6 on him, #7 on her, #8 on him — and that pattern will continue to the end of the scene. Part of what makes Shot 5 an intrusion — besides its coming from a different time period and being entirely subjective — is the way it both disrupts this cross-cutting and fits into it. The editing had prepared us to expect Shot 5 to be of the architect; instead it was of the soldier. But Shot 5 *did* show us what the actress was "looking at" or "facing," and so it did belong where it was.

The duration of Shot 8 is also significant. In this scene, the longer the shot, the more closely it is tied into the narrative present and the context of everyday reality. Shots 4 through 7 are very short, and their durations organize them into a separate unit, a sequence of rapid cross-cuts. Within the scene, they present a single action: her looking at one twitch and remembering another. Along with the return to a more leisurely cutting rhythm, the soundtrack facilitates this return to the present. Over the room tone, the train whistle is heard again. As the architect wakes up, his arm moves over the sheet (**Fig. 2-254**) and makes a sound. The whistle may be taken as what woke him, but it is also a kind of alarm to the actress, a call to get hold of herself. The important thing is simply that she hears it.

Shot 9 (**Figs. 2-255** and **2-256**) lasts only 3 seconds. She snaps herself fully back into the present, deliberately erasing her troubled look. We sense that she has often made such transitions since the end of the war, shoving away her painful memories and presenting a mask to the world and to herself. The problem with this affair is that it will not allow her to put away the past; instead, she will be forced to confront all that it means and all that her life has

Figure 2-252

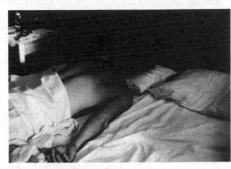

Figure 2-253

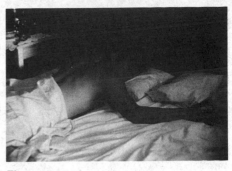

Figure 2-254

Figure 2-255

Figure 2-256

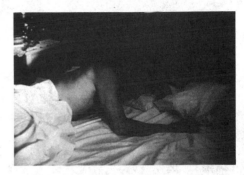

Figure 2-257

Figure 2-258

Figure 2-259

Figure 2-260

meant. But for now the mask is on. His arm can be heard on the sheet.

Shot 10 (**Figs. 2-257** and **2-258**) lasts 4 seconds. By the position of the camera, you can see that Shots 8 and 10 were originally part of the same take. The whistle sounds again, and we still hear the arm as it continues to move over the sheet (**Fig. 2-257**). The architect rouses himself and looks in the actress's direction (**Fig. 2-258**).

Shot 11 (**Figs. 2-259** and **2-260**) lasts 7 seconds. She begins to walk toward him (**Fig. 2-259**) and asks, "Do you want some coffee?" (**Fig. 2-260**). The camera tracks slightly back as she moves, tilting to keep her face in view. As a medium shot, it declares the end of her private, close-shot moment.

Figure 2-261

Figure 2-262

Figure 2-263

Figure 2-264

Figure 2-265

Figure 2-266

Figure 2-267

Figure 2-268

Figure 2-269

In Shot 12 (**Figs. 2-261** through **2-263**), which lasts 18 seconds, the scene takes on a more conventional level of interaction. Having just woken up, the architect does not bring a great deal to the exchange, beyond the generalities of his character and his memory of the previous evening. She, however, brings all the emotions that have been jarred together by her memory of her lover's death and, with them, the whole problem of how to live with or to escape the past. Unwilling to confide in the architect but needing to get some of the experience off her chest, she asks him an indirect question: "What were you dreaming about?"

In **Fig. 2-261** the architect replies, "Uh-huh" to the offer of coffee. The actress enters the frame from the right and gives him her own cup. While he drinks (**Fig. 2-262**), she asks her question. At the end of the shot (**Fig. 2-263**), he says, "I don't know — why?"

Then there is a reverse-angle cut to Shot 13 (**Figs. 2-264** through **2-269**). This shot lasts 21 seconds, almost as long as Shot 1, and gives the editing rhythm a symmetrical balance. That rhythm begins slowly, then accelerates, then becomes very rapid, then slows down, and here it comes to rest. The reverse cut here is purely conventional — a way of following their conversation — and that expresses how far she and the scene have come from the more unconventionally intrusive, subjectively motivated cross-cuts. In other words, she is now thoroughly back in present reality. This editing structure shows plainly how an unconventional cinematic practice can signify an unconventional event or state of mind, and how cinematic norms can be used as analogs to "normal" situations. There is nothing particularly *natural* about cinematic structure, but its norms can be compared with the norms of other structures, the world included.

The actress looks at the architect for a second (**Fig. 2-264**), then looks at his hands and says, "I watched your hands. They move when you sleep." He opens and closes his free hand (**Fig. 2-266**), and they laugh. It is this *action,* this movement of the hand — the one that did not twitch — that gives the scene its ultimate unity.

This is a scene about hands. However different the German and Japanese lovers — one dead and in the past, the other alive and present — the twitching of their hands has rendered them similar, both for the woman and for the audience. Now the preconscious reality of his dream twitch and of her involuntary memory is linked up with the conscious reality of their discussion and his deliberate hand movements. The dialogue concerns hands, too, and running underneath it is the actress's desire to find out what made him twitch in his dream. It is primarily the images of hands that give this scene its *visual* unity, which works with the subjective events and the subject of the conversation to create a *dramatic* unity. The scene is also unified by its symmetrical editing rhythm, its symmetrical fades, and its relatively consistent use of cross-cutting. The scene is disrupted, as is the woman, by the intrusion of the memory, and in order to *contain* this intrusion, the scene must be tightly constructed. Its form must be able to cohere, no matter how disruptive any of its elements may be.

After they have laughed at his hand play, the architect thinks and says, "Maybe it's when you dream without knowing it." This fairly obscure line is translated in subtitled prints as "Sometimes a person dreams without knowing it," but the original line is better. Its vagueness makes sense as the utterance of someone who is not completely awake, but beyond that it compresses the realms of time and dreaming into a hypothetical landscape. She muses, then — a quiet, smiling "hmm" — and rests her head on her crossed forearms (**Fig. 2-267**). Then the shot fades to black (**Figs. 2-268** and **2-269**).

Role in the Film. At the end of the first act the architect had asked the actress, "Why did you want to see everything at Hiroshima?" She answered, "Because it interested me. I have my own ideas about it. For instance, I think looking closely at things is something that has to be learned." This scene at the beginning of the second act continues her education in the art of seeing. It is not enough to look at the present, to visit the Hiroshima museum or tour the hospital, nor even to scrutinize the ultramodern neon city with its apparent compulsion to forget its own past. To see Hiroshima completely, to know it, she must see how she shares the city's problem. She shares it not only because all of us have to come to terms with the realities of the nuclear age, to remember Hiroshima and Nagasaki if we are to avoid their repetition. She shares it because she, too, is afraid of the past, something she has put behind her but has not gotten beyond. Her pleasant, capable, intense face is like the modern city built over an obliterated landscape.

Her relationship with the architect is a confrontation of cities and decades. By the end of the film, he has become simply "Hiroshima" (the source of the film's title, *Hiroshima, My Love*) and she has become "Nevers, in France." It was in Nevers that she fell in love with the German, had her hair shorn as a collaborator, and lived in a cellar until the end of the war. The day she left the cellar, her hair grown to a respectable length, was the day of the Hiroshima bombing. In the Japanese lover, she finds a parallel to the German (both had fought on the Axis side during the war) as well as to herself, for he is a man who survived the war and who has dedicated himself to the erection of a modern, pastless present. To think only of the present is characteristic of impulsive adulterers (both are married). As their emotions deepen into love, the unnamed actress and architect are drawn to learn each other's personal histories and to make sense of the past. But the future remains barred to them, and the film ends when they have come to terms with their pasts — when they have become their cities — but realize that they are destined to separate.

In this scene, the intrusion of the memory is a challenge to the actress's ability to see clearly. It is a glimpse into the secret structure of her life and into the history of her epoch, both for her and for the audience. Its disjuncture provokes thought and demands an attempt at reconciliation. One aspect of this disjuncture that becomes clearer as the film goes on is that the 1944-1945 French scenes, including Shot 5, were photographed by a different camera team and on different filmstock than those set in Japan, and the two crews were not allowed to see each other's work. There were two directors of photography, one French and one Japanese, and two composers, again one French and one Japanese. This made it appear as if the two phases of the actress's life belonged to different films, different lives. In the same way, the nonfiction footage of 1945 Hiroshima and the shots of the rebuilt city seem to be of completely different places. These different landscapes, then, are also different times. Their interrelationship is very similar to that between the past (black-and-white) and present (color) shots of the death camps in Resnais's earlier *Night and Fog*. In a nutshell, then, this scene contains within it all of the major conflicts — personal, political, and even metaphysical — that structure the entire film. And like the rest of the film, it is momentous and mundane at once.

Although it is true that any self-contained action in a single or continuous location can be referred to as a "scene," the scene comes into its full power and significance as a coherent dramatic unit — usually a moment of interaction with clearly defined stakes, although there are many fine scenes that involve only one character. It can be as short as a single shot or considerably longer, but its central characteristic is dramatic unity.

The scene from *King Kong* is a solid example of master-shot construction and continuity editing, whereas that from *Hiroshima, mon amour* has no master shot and includes discontinuity. The *Kong* scene was shot so that it could be correctly assembled by an editor, with adequate coverage of all the events and a unifying soundtrack. The editor of *Hiroshima* was almost as free as *Kong's* and had absolute control over the rhythm of the scene, which is one of its richest and most expressive elements. Both scenes effect changes in their participants in significant and subtle ways, and both encapsulate the major themes of their pictures. The climax of the *Kong* scene — both dramatically and thematically — is Ann's scream, and that in *Hiroshima* is the subjective intrusion. The resolution in *Kong* is Jack's prescient question, and that in *Hiroshima* is the conversation over the coffee cup — a near return to the terms that started the scene, though no complete return to innocence remains possible.

7. The Sequence

A **sequence** is a succession, or consecutive series, of coordinated elements. In cinema studies, the term may refer to a consecutive series of *shots* or to a consecutive series of *scenes*.

Any series of shots or scenes isolated for discussion may be called a sequence. In this loose and general application, all that is necessary is that the shots or scenes in question follow one another consecutively. Thus, one could speak of the "finger-twitch sequence" in *Hiroshima, mon amour* (Shots 3-6), which occurs within a scene. Or one could speak of the "burning of Atlanta" sequence in *Gone With the Wind,* which is a series *of* scenes. A series of brief, dynamically edited shots may be called a "montage sequence," just as a series of song-and-dance scenes may be called a "musical sequence." Although a complete film, too, is a consecutive series of shots and/or scenes, you would not call a film a "sequence"; a sequence is an intermediate level of organization. As a level of *dramatic* organization, the sequence is midway between the scene and the act; as a level of more purely *cinematic* organization, the sequence is midway between the shot and the movie.

The wedding sequence that opens *The Godfather* includes a number of distinct scenes (Vito talks with the undertaker, Luca rehearses his speech, Michael tells Kay about some of the guests, Vito talks with Johnny Fontaine, and so on). It also includes many individual or clustered shots that are not part of scenes but do contribute to the dramatization of the afternoon's events. All of these shots and scenes form an identifiable unit within *The Godfather,* more than a scene and less than an act. The first act of *The Godfather* includes not only the wedding sequence but also the Woltz sequence, most of which consists of scenes between Tom Hagen and the Hollywood producer, and it ends with the discovery of the bloody horse's head. (Act I, you will recall, concerns "King Vito" and is a demonstration of the various ways he uses power.)

A scene is restricted to a single location, and it is not only a theatrical unit and term but also a reflection of the theatrical condition, which is grounded in the physical reality and literal presence of the stage. The cinema, however, is free to leap from one fully realized location to another, to jigsaw the world into a puzzle of its own design and to set down the pieces in whatever order and at whatever pace it sees fit. The sequence is *not* restricted to a single location, and to that extent it reflects the cinematic condition, which is grounded not in any fixed setting but in the showing of *any* setting. What the cinema is grounded in is the look — not simply the look of the attentive eavesdropper, for the theatergoer shares that, but the look, or the series of glimpses, as an analytic and synthetic act of consciousness. As the mind — or creative attention — leaps from one thought to another, or takes things apart, or puts things together, so the sequence cuts from shot to shot.

In its most exclusively cinematic (and more dynamic) sense, then, the sequence is not a string of closely related scenes but a tightly coordinated entity made up of shots. The "Odessa Steps" sequence in *Potemkin,* for example, comprises some 200 brilliantly arranged, consecutive shots and ends the "Odessa Steps" act (Reel 4). It happens to include a number of short scenes (most of which are interwoven with other scenes so that very few of them are presented *as* distinct and uninterrupted scenes), and the majority of the events happen to take place at and around a single location, but the dynamics of that sequence have nothing to do with location. Each shot, in other words, "reports" directly to the sequence and only secondarily to the scene of which it may happen to be a part.

One common use of the sequence is to present and interrelate actions and scenes that are occurring in separate locations. In *The Birth of a Nation*, the "Ride of the Klans" sequence covers a great deal of ground, including scenes in and around a remote, besieged cabin as well as in the center of town, across the hills, and so on. Near the end of *The Godfather*, as we shall see, one scene (in church) is primary while other scenes and autonomous shots are cut into it.

Although in most sequences the separate actions are supposed to be occurring simultaneously, there are also sequences that present two or more events that are taking place at different times, or that present one time as intruding into another. In Nicolas Roeg's *Don't Look Now* (1973), for example, there is an extremely erotic lovemaking sequence in which shots of the husband and wife getting dressed *afterwards* are interwoven with shots of the happy couple in bed. As a structural unit, the sequence alone is adequate to the cinema's freedom in time, its ability to construct time as well as to rearrange it, to characterize and energize it as well as to present it. The sequence may, like the cinema, be all over the map *and* the calendar, and still have a definite beginning, middle, climax, and ending.

To explore the nature of the sequence, we shall take a close look at two great examples. As in the scene discussion, one of these is classic and the other is relatively recent. The first is in black-and-white and comes from a silent film: Eisenstein's *October*. The second is in color and comes from a sound film: Coppola's *The Godfather*. Each of these is, unfortunately, too long to be illustrated and discussed in its entirety; the sequence from *October* alone would require over 300 frame enlargements. Accordingly I have decided to "abridge" that sequence in a way that indicates the major terms and events that are being presented and interrelated in the course of the sequence. For the *Godfather* baptism, I have chosen to present every shot from the second half of the sequence, which is relatively self-contained and is of a manageable length.

October: The Raising of the Bridges ⎯⎯⎯⎯⎯⎯⎯

October was co-written and co-directed by Sergei Eisenstein and Grigori Alexandrov. It was photographed by Eduard Tisse, who was assisted by Vladimir Nilsen and Vladimir Popov. It was shot in 1927, premiered at the end of that year, and was then recut and released to the public in 1928. It was edited primarily by Eisenstein, and he was also the more creatively decisive of the directors. It is important not to confuse *October* (which runs about 2½ hours at silent speed) with *Ten Days that Shook the World,* a shortened and drastically simplified version prepared for overseas release.

The Russian Revolutions. A bit of historical background is necessary if you are to understand this sequence. There were three Russian revolutions. The first occurred in 1905, and it was the setting of such films as Pudovkin's *Mother* and Eisenstein's *Potemkin.* This revolution, which grew out of the civil and economic pressures of the Russo-Japanese War, failed to overthrow the czar but did result in the granting of limited civil rights and the establishment of a parliament called the Duma.

The second revolution occurred in March 1917. In the old Russian calendar, this was actually the month of February, and so it is referred to as the February Revolution. Czar Nicholas II had adopted a repressive, conservative policy, and World War I was causing many economic hardships. There was a workers' strike in Petrograd (Saint Petersburg, now Leningrad). The Duma refused to obey Nicholas's order that it dissolve; instead, it set up a "Provisional Government," and the czar soon abdicated.

Within the Provisional Government, volatile disagreements surfaced quickly. Two parties developed: the radical Bolsheviks (the Reds), under the leadership of Lenin, and the Mensheviks (the Whites), who were perceived as the party of the bourgeoisie (the middle class) and who supported the moderate socialist cabinet organized by Alexander Kerensky in July 1917. This cabinet came to power in reaction against a workers' uprising staged by Lenin in Petrograd that July, and it is that uprising that is dramatized in the "Raising of the Bridges" sequence, which is itself a segment of the "July Days" act in *October.*

The Provisional Government honored the deals that the czar had made with the Allies and committed Russia to continuing to fight in the war. This action aroused extreme opposition, and in any case, the Bolsheviks felt that a bourgeois version of socialism was not a sufficiently radical departure from the autocracy of the czar. The third and final revolution occurred in November 1917 and is referred to as the October Revolution (hence Eisenstein's title) because of its date in the old calendar. It was then that Lenin seized power in Petrograd, and the Bolsheviks quickly passed new laws regarding the ownership of property, civil rights, and the distribution of power. Lenin died in 1924, and by 1927 Stalin had taken control.

The early revolutionary period (especially the years 1923–1927) was a great time for the arts in Russia. The new political structure stimulated and actually called for a new artistic spirit, a more radical and dynamic concept of aesthetic structure. Eisenstein, Pudovkin, Vertov, and others developed an expressive realism that was uniquely powerful and rigorous. When Stalin took over, his conservative tastes and repressive politics led him to oppose such works as "formalist." He preferred an obvious realism and denounced those artists who appeared to put the "form" of the work ahead of simple narrative content and propaganda. One of the first things Stalin did in this context was to mandate the recutting of *October* so that Trotsky's contributions to the revolution would be excised. By the early sound period, the revolutionary cinema was virtually dead in Russia. As you study *October,* then, keep in mind the political context that stimulated its aesthetic strategies and was soon to doom them.

Construction. The "Raising of the Bridges" sequence lasts just over 12 minutes at 16 fps and includes approximately 280 shots and 24 intertitles (it is conventional not to count titles as shots). Although the average shot duration is under 3 seconds, many of the shots last less than 1 second, and some are less than 4 frames long. At least 20 percent of the cuts in this sequence are jump cuts.

The setting is a large demonstration in Petrograd; the date is July 1917. Just before the sequence starts, Lenin is shown stirring up a crowd with a powerful speech. Just after the sequence ends, the First Machine Gun Corps is shown marching slowly and without enthusiasm; they have been "disarmed for solidarity." What this sequence does, then, is to show how the revolt inspired by Lenin led to repressive measures by the Provisional Government.

Representative highlights of this sequence are shown in **Figs. 2-270** through **2-314.** In brief, the narrative content of the sequence is as follows. Vast crowds of workers carry Bolshevik banners through the streets of Petrograd. Although they are strongly opposed to the "capitalist ministers" of the Provisional Government, they agree that the demonstration should be nonviolent. Nevertheless, they are massacred: government militia open fire on the crowd and also order that the drawbridges that separate the workers' district from the rest of the city be raised. One youth does his best to save some banners, but he is murdered by a group of bourgeois, and the banners are thrown into the river. Attempting to cross the bridges before they are raised, many demonstraters are gunned down; one woman falls so that her long hair extends over the midpoint of one bridge, and as the bridge rises, it lifts her hair. On another bridge, a horse drawing a coach filled with banners is shot, and eventually it hangs over the edge of the rising drawbridge. Near the end of the sequence, the horse falls into the water at the same time as the youth's banners.

This sequence consists, then, of a number of closely related actions taking place in several locations. Crowds surge over the bridges, assemble in the streets, are fired upon, and rush in all directions. The woman and the horse are lifted by the bridges. The youth with the banners is killed at the riverside. All of these actions are dramatically related into one large action as the scenes are intercut; the individual shots become part of a dynamic and coherent system, a limited framework within which such terms as the horse and the banners are tightly interrelated.

The best way to appreciate this sequence, aside from watching the movie, is to look at the frame enlargements as a group and to examine how their actions are defined and interwoven.

Figure 2-270

Figure 2-271

Figure 2-272

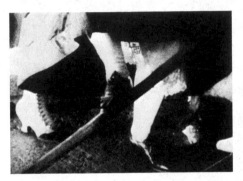

Figure 2-273

Figure 2-274

Figure 2-275

Figure 2-276

Figure 2-277

Figure 2-278

Figure 2-279

Figure 2-280

Figure 2-281

Figure 2-282

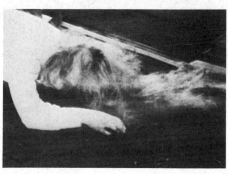

Figure 2-283

Figure 2-284

Figure 2-285

Figure 2-286

Figure 2-287

Figure 2-288

Figure 2-289

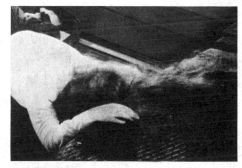

Figure 2-290

Figure 2-291

Figure 2-292

Figure 2-293

Figure 2-294

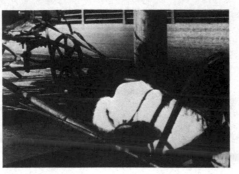

Figure 2-295

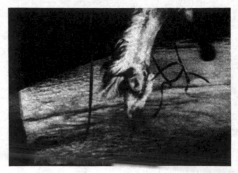

Figure 2-296

Figure 2-297

Figure 2-298

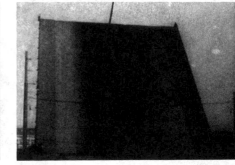

Figure 2-299

Figure 2-300

Figure 2-302

Figure 2-303

Figure 2-304

Figure 2-305

Figure 2-306

Figure 2-307

Figure 2-308

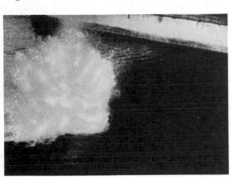

Figure 2-309

Figure 2-310

Figure 2-311

Figure 2-312

Figure 2-313

Figure 2-314

Several of the juxtapositions within this sequence deserve special mention. The action of the machine gun is created by the rapid
cross-cutting of shots of the gun (**Figs. 2-274** and **2-275**) or of gun
and gunner. Each of these shots is only 2 or 3 frames long, and
they occur in bursts — approximately 14 at a time. This stuttering
montage has the binary quality of a machine gun (noise and silence
in rapid alternation), and it visually expresses the kinetic violence
of the firing.

As the horse falls, a bourgeois woman succeeds in breaking the
pole of a captured banner (**Figs. 2-279** and **2-280**). This is a fairly

complex symbolic juxtaposition. On the one hand, it asserts that the attack on the youth and his banners is analogous to the machine-gunning of the demonstrators — that both are part of the same general counterrevolutionary assault. The banners themselves are symbolic of the Bolshevik program, not only because they are carried by the workers but also because they are covered with Bolshevik slogans. And the horse, like the youth, has been attempting to take banners to safety. On the other hand, the white horse itself becomes a kind of banner, a symbol of massacred innocence. All this is asserted when the pole breaks as the horse collapses (the backbone of the demonstration has been broken), and the connection is enriched and complicated until it climaxes with another symbolic juxtaposition (**Figs. 2-307** and **2-308**) as the horse and banners fall simultaneously into the river.

In **Fig. 2-281** the youth is stabbed to death by parasols, and then he, the horse, and the woman are juxtaposed as analogous victims. The horse and the woman are visually linked in an especially forceful manner, as both lie in similar positions across the midpoints of their respective bridges (**Figs. 2-282** and **2-283**). The woman's body is like the coach; her hair is like the horse: vulnerable, natural, and hanging over the edge (**Figs. 2-294** and **2-295**).

As the bridge begins to rise, the woman's hair and hand are lifted away from the rest of her body (**Figs. 2-290** through **2-292**). This stunning image is rebegun and partially repeated for several seconds. If it had been shown only once, the audience might barely have noticed it. As it is, the image absolutely compels our attention, and the way it is stretched out in time gives it special poignancy and power. Like the baby carriage that begins to roll down the Odessa Steps several times in *Potemkin*, this is an example of the expressive control of time.

Now Eisenstein shifted to a larger object that can be seen hanging over the lip of the bridge from a distance: the horse. As you can see in **Fig. 2-297**, the expressive potential of the woman's hair is exhausted once the bridge has been raised only a few feet. Because the hair and the horse have already been rendered symbolically equivalent, this transfer of attention continues the visual argument while shifting between analogous terms.

As the horse continues to rise, there are many shots of the undersides of bridges (**Figs. 2-293** and **2-300**). They loom as symbols of repressive power, but Eisenstein inserted a joke at their expense. In **Fig. 2-299** the coach with its banners is level (because the camera, or point of view, is on the rising bridge), and the horizon is tilted; in other words, it is the *world* that will change whereas the revolution will retain its own dynamic stability as the reference point for a new order.

In **Figs. 2-302** and **2-303** the imposing face of a nearly vertical bridge is compared — in a straightforward instance of dialectical montage — with a statue of an Egyptian pharaoh. The low angle of **Fig. 2-303** reminds us that the pharaoh, like any monarch, was a figure of power, and in this context that power is presented as

Figure C-1   page 79

Figure C-2   page 79

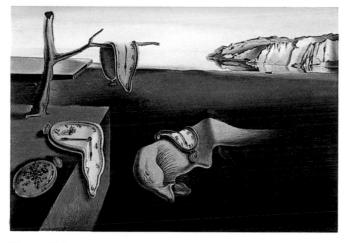

Figure C-3   page 92

Figure C-4   page 135

Figure C-5   page 135

Figure C-6   page 186

Figure C-7   page 186

Figure C-8   page 187

Figure C-9   page 187

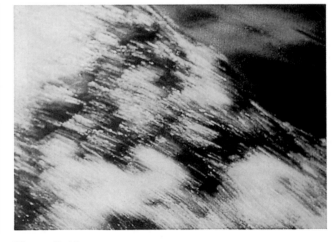

Figure C-10   page 187

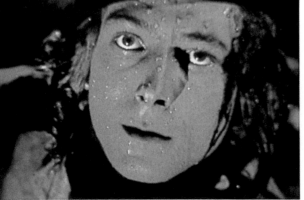

Figure C-11   page 187

Figure C-12   page 187

Figure C-13   page 187

Figure C-14   page 187

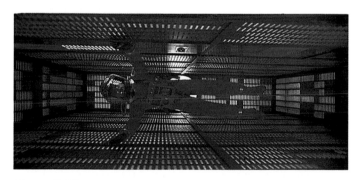

Figure C-15   page 187

Figure C-16   page 187

Figure C-17   page 188

Figure C-18   page 188

Figure C-19   page 188

Figure C-20   page 188

Figure C-21   page 189

Figure C-22   page 189

Figure C-23   page 189

Figure C-24   page 189

C-4

Figure C-25   page 189

Figure C-26   page 189

Figure C-27   page 190

Figure C-28   page 190

Figure C-29   page 190

Figure C-30   page 190

C-5

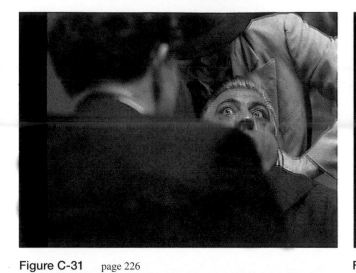

Figure C-31   page 226

Figure C-32   page 226

Figure C-33   page 238

Figure C-34   page 240

Figure C-35   page 240

Figure C-36   page 240

Figure C-37   page 240

Figure C-38   page 240

Figure C-39   page 241

Figure C-40   page 241

Figure C-41   page 241

Figure C-42   page 241

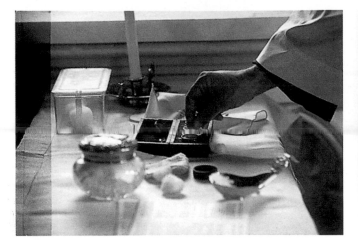

Figure C-43   page 277

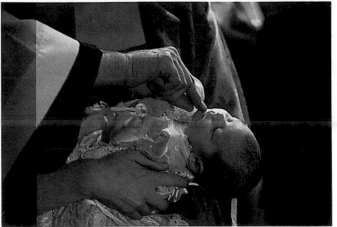

Figure C-44   page 277

Figure C-45   page 277

Figure C-46   page 277

Figure C-47   page 277

Figure C-48   page 281

Figure C-49   page 281

Figure C-50   page 281

Figure C-51   page 281

Figure C-52   page 281

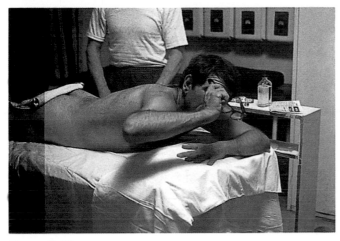

Figure C-53   page 281

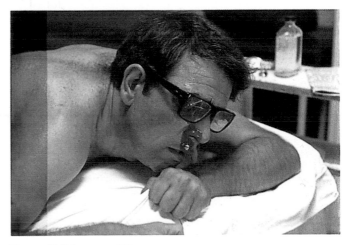

Figure C-54   page 281

Figure C-55   page 281

Figure C-56   page 281

Figure C-57   page 281

Figure C-58   page 281

Figure C-59   page 282

Figure C-60   page 282

Figure C-61 page 282

Figure C-62 page 282

Figure C-63 page 282

Figure C-64 page 282

Figure C-65 page 282

Figure C-66 page 282

Figure C-67   page 282

Figure C-68   page 282

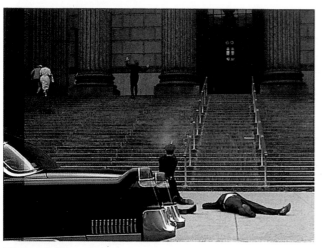

Figure C-69   page 282

Figure C-70   page 282

Figure C-71   page 282

Figure C-72   page 282

C-12

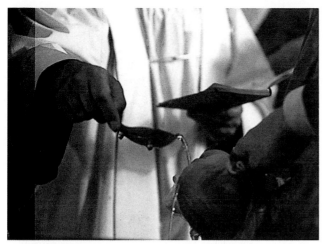

Figure C-73   page 283

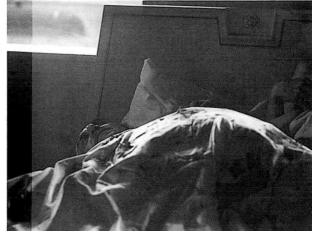

Figure C-74   page 283

Figure C-75   page 283

Figure C-76   page 283

Figure C-77   page 283

Figure C-78   page 350

Figure C-79
page 389

Figure C-80   page 415

Figure C-81   page 416

Figure C-82   page 416

Figure C-83   page 417

Figure C-84   page 419

Figure C-85   page 419

Figure C-86   page 431

Figure C-87   page 432

Figure C-88   page 432

Figure C-89   page 432

Figure C-90   page 432

Figure C-91   page 432

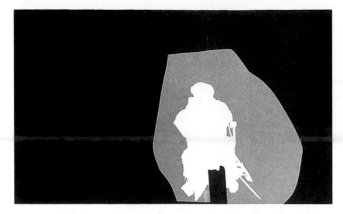

Figure C-92   page 432

Figure C-93
page 477

Figure C-94
page 487

Figure C-95   page 488

Figure C-96   page 488

C-16

oppressive. The bridges themselves are imposing and are often seen from below. The straight cut from **Fig. 2-302** to **Fig. 2-303** makes it impossible to ignore the parallel that Eisenstein was asserting between the autocratic power of the pharaohs and the murderous power of the Mensheviks. The pharaoh would inevitably remind a Soviet audience of the czar, but the crucial point here is that the Mensheviks are themselves being equated with czarism. It was the czar who commissioned this sculpture (*October* was shot entirely in authentic locations, and many of the actors had taken part in the original events), but the Mensheviks are portrayed throughout this movie as endorsing the czar's tastes and carrying out policies that the Bolsheviks opposed as much as they had those of the czar. In other words, Menshevik power (the raising of the bridges) is being presented in czarist terms. The rising bridge in **Fig. 2-304** is a symbol of counterrevolutionary oppression, and the horse dangles from it as a representative symbolic victim, like a flag hoisted up the enemy's flagpole.

Near the end of the sequence, most of the attention shifts back to the aftermath of the youth's murder. Copies of the revolutionary leaflet *Pravda* ("truth") are thrown into the water (**Fig. 2-306**) along with one of the banners (**Fig. 2-307**). At that moment the horse falls, too, and their symbolic equivalence is restated (**Figs. 2-307** through **2-310**). A shot of the dead youth, also in the water (**Fig. 2-311**), ties up the major terms of the sequence.

Without abandoning the image of the bridges, Eisenstein now turned to the river itself; this shift has been prepared by many shots of the undersides of the bridges as they reflect the light from the water. The bridges are an image of oppression, but the river itself has no politics. It has been there since before the czar and will be there, one imagines, long after even Stalin has been forgotten. For now, the water is a medium in which the truth, or the Bolshevik platform, can be symbolically drowned. As horse, leaflets, and banners all fall into the river, they are quite obviously shown to be symbols of the same order. The link between leaflets and banners is summed up in **Fig. 2-312**, where a number of leaflets cling to a flamboyantly floating banner. As a bourgeois gentleman applauds (**Fig. 2-313**), the "truth" sinks below the surface of the river — but the word can still be read (**Fig. 2-314**).

Role in the Film. *October* was made to celebrate the tenth anniversary of the October Revolution. Within that context, the major function of this sequence was to remind the Soviet audience how far they had come since the "July Days." Its extreme violence was meant to justify the October Revolution, to present the Bolsheviks as heroic victims and to re-create the demonstration and the massacre in terms that were at once intensely realistic and symbolic. The Provisional Government is presented as a lackey of the bourgeoisie and as comparable in most important respects to the ousted government of the czar. This asserts that the February Revolution was incomplete and that another revolution was necessary. In other words, this sequence draws extremely clear distinctions between those the Bolsheviks perceived as the good guys and the bad guys.

By building sympathy for the victims, the sequence builds sympathy for their cause. This is a very old trick in the narrative arts, to encourage us to identify with one set of characters against another even when both sets are rather similar. If you step back from *The Godfather*, you will notice that the Corleone good guys and the Barzini bad guys are both bad guys. The Corleones have one attitude toward business, and their antagonists have another, but they *are* in the same business. When Sonny has Bruno Tattaglia murdered, the event does not seem worth showing — but when Sonny himself is killed, we are treated to a long and painful scene of his being massacred by machine guns while en route to help his sister. Although *October* is an outright propaganda film and *The Godfather* is a "**bourgeois**" narrative film (that is, a movie that encourages the audience to be sucked into a fantasy and to forget the political world outside the theater, making the film itself a tool that keeps the ruling class in an unchallenged position of power), both of them manipulate audience identification in the interest of making what their makers considered an ethical argument.

This sequence does more than record an unhappy episode between revolutions. Through its dynamic compositions and extraordinarily kinetic editing rhythm, it celebrates the energy of the coming October Revolution. It projects and realizes the dynamic enthusiasm that Eisenstein felt the revolution brought to the world of politics and of art. By celebrating the revolution in a radically creative way, it *demonstrated* the energetic originality of the new Soviet culture. As we have seen, Stalin did not share Eisenstein's view of the symbiosis between political and aesthetic development — or perhaps he realized that creative artistic attitudes might stimulate further, and for him unwelcome, political developments. Whatever happened behind the scenes, it is in *October* that these two revolutionary energies support each other most completely and in which their causes are asserted to be the same.

Formally, *October* is an experiment in montage, and at its heart is a particular attitude toward the nature of metaphor. Essentially, what a metaphor does is to juxtapose two or more terms that do not immediately appear to have anything to do with one another. The form of the **metaphor** itself compresses these terms into one figure, as in Marcel Proust's resonant image of "the blue flame of a violet." For Eisenstein, the terms could be juxtaposed within a single shot, like that of the tilting horizon and the "level" coach, or in consecutive shots, like those of the slaughtered animal and the massacred workers near the end of *Strike*. He left the audience to draw the terms together and to decode the metaphor.

The dialectically generated synthesis between the terms of a metaphor is utterly conceptual. The proper site for an idea is in the consciousness of a human being, and so Eisenstein provided the audience with images and encouraged them to "connect the dots" on their own. Although this enthusiastic "encouragement" left him in the position of closely manipulating the audience to arrive at certain conclusions, it also made the audience nearly equal participants in generating the final, conceptual work. The audience was led, then, but not spoon-fed.

As a phenomenological whole, virtually any work of art is the product of an interaction between the text and its audience, but not every artist has adopted this as a working principle. Eisenstein's attempt to include the audience in the extended whole of the film experience followed logically and naturally from the Bolshevik agenda, which sought to include the people in those power structures that had previously been controlled by autocrats. The specific way in which the "Raising of the Bridges" sequence contributed to this effort was to present a number of major images in alternation and to teach the audience where to look for points of contact. Putting them together, the audience could discover how all of these were not only characters and props but also interrelated symbols, and how the separate actions joined into the flow of a larger action. The ultimate metaphor to which all of these elements contributed was that of the revolution itself. The juxtaposition and asserted complementarity of political and aesthetic radicalism was the essence of the *October* Revolution, which took place in 1927.

The Godfather: The Baptism

The Godfather was directed by Francis Ford Coppola; was written by Coppola and the author of the original novel, Mario Puzo; was photographed by Gordon Willis; and was edited by William Reynolds and Peter Zinner. The sound — by Christopher Newman, Bud Grenzbach, and Richard Portman — was mixed under the supervision of Walter Murch. The production designer was Dean Tavoularis, the composer was Nino Rota, the costumes were by Anna Hill Johnstone, and the makeup was by Dick Smith and Philip Rhodes. All of these people made substantial contributions to the baptism sequence as well as to the whole. *The Godfather* won the Academy Award for Best Picture of 1972, and its sequel won the same award in 1974.

Two Puns. The story of *The Godfather* begins late in 1945, with don Vito Corleone in power, and it ends approximately 10 years later, with his youngest son Michael in power. The title refers primarily to Vito, but in the baptism sequence the term is extended to include Michael.

For Vito, the role of Godfather is a natural outgrowth of the social, political, and economic structures of his native Sicily. He sees himself as the head of his family, the protector of his friends, and the leader of the family business. That business is, of course, criminal, but it is tied into a social network that is presented as having real validity. At the foundation of this structure are the Old World values of family unity, religious devotion, and personal honor. From his point of view, the godfather rules from a position of moral authority, informed by shrewd business judgment, insight into people, and an efficiency that can be tactful or ruthless, depending on the circumstances.

Michael is a far more ambivalent figure. A war hero with strong family ties, he has been groomed by his father for a role in legitimate politics. By avenging the attempt on Vito's life, fleeing to Sicily, and there marrying Apollonia, he becomes more like his brothers. After his wife is murdered in an explosion meant to kill him, Michael returns to America a changed, hardened man. He marries a Protestant, Kay Adams, and they have children. Counseled by his father, Michael takes over the reins of the business. After Vito dies of a heart attack, Michael finds the opportunity to kill all of his enemies at once. He arranges for his soldiers to murder Barzini, Tattaglia, and several others while he is acting as godfather to his nephew, Michael Rizzi, at the infant's baptism. By the time this sequence is over, Michael is a lost soul. His perversion of the ritual of baptism cuts him off from the moral authority of the role of godfather.

Baptism is a ritual of exorcism, purification, and acceptance into a spiritual community. Its central symbol is water, which washes the infant clean and is a sign of inner spiritual purity. It is also a ritual of anointment, and a mixture of oil and balsam called "chrism" is used to honor the new Christian. The infant, who of course knows no prayers, has no religious convictions, and cannot speak, requires a godfather. The godfather must be a devout, practicing Catholic who will answer for the child when the priest asks him whether he believes in God and the Catholic Church.

As he fulfills this role, Michael Corleone has his mind on murder. Within the context of the ceremony, he is a hypocrite; if nothing else, he is a poor spiritual father to his nephew.

In terms of the story, this series of killings will consolidate Michael's power. Thus he is coming into the role of Mafia godfather even as he "stands godfather" to his sister's baby. Michael is being baptised into a new phase of his life, but the baptism is in blood, not in water. He converts the service into a ritual not of purification but of spiritual pollution. For Vito this would have been a shocking contradiction in terms. For Michael it is a practical solution, and it marks the start of his reign as a "New World" godfather. As the story develops in *Part II*, Michael drifts even further from Vito's values, ultimately turning against his own family in a misguided, paranoid attempt to save it. At the end of *Part II* he is utterly alone, and the family business has no more integrity nor honor than he does.

In this sequence, then, both "baptism" and "godfather" are puns. Coppola presented two baptisms — one in water, one in blood — and showed Michael's standing godfather to Michael Rizzi while coming into his power as Mafia godfather.

These terms are brought together, both as a sequence and as a metaphor, by a pattern of cutting back and forth between the scene in the New York church and the preparation and execution of more than five murders taking place at the same time, most of them in New York but one in Las Vegas. The dominant soundtrack is that from the church service, and its continuity links all these scenes into one coherent action. The ritual device of Michael's answering the questions put to the baby makes it even more clear that this sequence is of *his* baptism, and that becomes the focus of these events of ritual purification and ritual violence. Although some audiences were offended by this sequence — feeling that it respected no discrepancy between baptism and murder, as if both were equal partners in Mafia culture — a close look makes it clear that Coppola was, in fact, emphasizing that discrepancy, exploring its ironies, and using it to dramatize and judge this new stage of Michael's career.

To prepare the pun, Coppola and the editors cross-cut early in the sequence between two shots of anointing (see the color insert for all these full-frame enlargements). In one shot the priest wets his finger from a vial (**Fig. C-43**), and the camera pans to the right as his hand moves to touch the child's chin and mouth (**Fig. C-44**). In the next shot a barber takes shaving cream from a dispenser (**Fig. C-45**), and the camera pans to the right as his hand moves to apply the cream to the chin of his customer, Willi Cicci (**Fig. C-46**), who is getting a shave — in context, a ritual purification — before going upstairs to kill one of Michael's enemies. The parallel montage indicates the events are simultaneous. The exact complementarity of these two shots asserts the equivalence of their content — or makes us look for what is similar in them — while their contents assert their differences. Both are purifications, but only one is innocent. This intensely charged metaphor offers a perfect visual equivalent to Michael's ambivalence and the moral contradictions of his "godfather" project. These two shots are the key to the cutting pattern of the sequence and also to its message.

Construction. The baptism sequence lasts 5 minutes and 1 second; it consists of 67 shots, all of which are bridged by straight cuts. The first 36 shots last 3 minutes and 41 seconds, with an average shot duration of just over 6 seconds. From Shot 37 to the end of the sequence — the part illustrated in **Figs. C-47** through **C-77** — the elapsed time is 1 minute and 20 seconds, with an average shot duration of just over 2½ seconds. In contrast to the sequence from *October,* the *Godfather* baptism includes a great many match cuts and is a good example of continuity editing at its most complex.

Shot 1 is a full shot of the interior of the church. Low organ music is heard, and the baby is crying — but not very loudly. In Shot 2, Michael and Kay bring the baby to the altar. Connie and Carlo, the baby's parents, are in attendance but are not singled out by the camera. The organ continues, the crying stops, and the priest begins to pray in Latin. These become the basic terms of the unifying church soundtrack: the organ, the Latin prayers, and the intermittently crying baby. As the prayer continues, there is a match cut to Shot 3, a medium shot of the priest as he exhales three times in the baby's face. Then comes a close shot of Michael, and the Latin at that point translates, "Let us pray . . ."

In Shot 5, a close shot, Michael and Kay's hands loosen the ribbons and remove the bonnet from the baby's head so that he can be anointed. Then come three shots of one of Michael's soldiers (Rocco) assembling a machine gun in a dingy room. The soundtrack, however, is only that from the church; we hear none of the sounds that Rocco is making in his room, but the organ and the prayers continue uninterrupted. The same is true in Shot 9, a long shot of Clemenza, one of Michael's most trusted lieutenants, leaving his home with a large cardboard carton under one arm and polishing the fender of his car before he gets into it. Shot 10 returns us to the church for a close shot of Michael as the priest's hand makes a cross.

The continuity of the soundtrack accomplishes several things here: (1) it indicates that the actions of Rocco and Clemenza are going on during the service; (2) it makes those actions *part* of the service; and (3) it makes them slightly less vivid or autonomous as scenes. As the sequence progresses, we will come to hear what goes on in these distant scenes while we continue to listen to the service, so that they will all convey their own impression of reality while the service remains dominant and gathers them into its context.

Shot 11 is the anointing of the infant (**Figs. C-43** and **C-44**), and Shot 12 gets the shaving cream onto Cicci's face (**Figs. C-45** and **C-46**). Cicci is in a barber shop in the basement of a hotel. Shot 13 is a full shot of the barber shop, joined to Shot 12 by a match cut. The organ is still going on, rather softly now and with a pronounced echo.

In Shot 14 (also a full shot), Al Neri takes the uniform he used to wear as a police officer out of a suitcase. He is in a dingy room, dressing for the role he will play in the murder of Barzini. The organ is heard, Al is not. Shot 15 is similar to Shot 11, again with a pan as the priest anoints the child a second time, making the sign of the cross on his forehead. Then there is a cut back to Al, and this time we hear him. In Shot 16, a close shot, he takes a police revolver out of a crumpled paper bag, along with his old badge. We hear the paper, the gun, and the clink of the badge distinctly, while the organ and the praying continue; the organ, however, has taken on a lower tone. The deepening of the music is ominous, and the presence of the direct sound makes Al's actions seem more immediate; together they announce that something is about to happen.

In Shot 17 Al wipes the sweat off his face with a cloth. Shot 18 shows Clemenza walking up a hotel staircase, still carrying the carton, and wiping the sweat off *his* face. These parallel actions make it plain that Al and Clemenza are carrying out similar roles. The parallelism helps to knit the sequence together, much as the central figures in the *October* sequence are interrelated. The editing problem here is that the church scene must stand as one of two major terms in the sequence, the other being the series of murders. Because the murders take place in five locations, they could have occupied five sixths of the audience's attention, which would be too much. The editors and Coppola evidently arrived at the strategy of making those five extra-ecclesiastical actions cohere as one, and to do that, they emphasized the parallels among them, creating continuity within fragmentation. The sound works in a similar way: just as we heard Al's actions in Shots 16 and 17, in Shot 18 we hear Clemenza's footsteps on the marble stairs, along with the prayer and the organ.

Shot 19, from the same setup as Shot 2, shows the priest's making a crossing motion in the air. In Shot 20 he touches the baby's mouth. Shot 21 is a close shot of Michael, looking impatient or in conflict. As he looks from the floor to the priest, the organ gets slightly louder. In the next two shots the priest touches the baby's head.

Shot 24 is a closeup of Michael. The closer camera position indicates that this is a critical moment. It is at this point that the editing rhythm begins to accelerate as the sequence narrows in on the killings and on the core of the ritual. This is the moment when Michael must declare his faith and actively play the role of godfather; it lays all of the moral issues on the line. The priest asks him, "Michael, do you believe in God, the Father Almighty, creator of Heaven and Earth?" Michael looks up and says, "I do." The organ continues, rising a little in volume.

Shot 25 is a long shot of Barzini in the lobby of an office building, perhaps a courthouse. He walks to the foreground, and after he leaves the building, he will be killed. The organ is somewhat louder. The priest continues, "Do you believe in Jesus Christ, his only Son, our Lord?" We hear Michael's answer, "I do." "Do you believe in the Holy Ghost, the Holy Catholic Church?" By now Barzini is almost out of the frame. There is a cut to a medium shot (Shot 26) of Al outside that same building. Dressed as a police officer, he knocks on the fender of Barzini's car and motions the chauffeur to drive away; he does this twice, but the driver ignores him. We hear the knocking on the fender, and below that the organ and Michael's answer, "I do." The priest continues to pray in Latin.

The order of the baptism is wrong at this point. In this part of the service the normal order is first an exorcism, then a confession of faith, and then the baptism itself. It is over these shots of Barzini and Al that we hear Michael's confession of faith. The exorcism ("Do you renounce Satan," etc.) will be heard over the actual murders. This rearrangement, which most of the audience could not be expected to notice, is in the interest of more forceful and relevant juxtapositions.

Shot 27 shows Clemenza going up the stairs, turning at the landing, and then starting up another flight. We hear his footsteps, his heavy breathing, the Latin, and the organ. The camera pans to follow him when he crosses the landing. In most of the shots in this sequence the camera does not move. The few movements that do occur, therefore, have more weight.

In Shot 28 Rocco walks to the door of his room with the two machine guns he has assembled and gives one to his partner. The camera pans left to follow him, reversing the movement it has just made to follow Clemenza. The parallel here is that both Rocco and Clemenza are on the way to do murder with the guns they are carrying. We hear the sounds Rocco makes while the church sounds continue.

Shot 29 shows Cicci leaving the barber shop and dragging on a cigarette. We hear the muffled shutting of the glass door — and the prayers and the organ. Shot 30 is a close shot of the priest's red stole, extended toward the baby. This is the part of the service when the infant is to open to the sweetness of God and when the devil is commanded to depart, "For the judgment of God is come."

Shot 31 is very similar to Shot 1, and it effectively rebegins the sequence. We see the interior of the church in full shot. The organ becomes more ominous, and the baby starts to cry again. Now the judgment of God has come. The double message here is extremely ironic. On the one hand, Michael is closing himself to the Lord and making himself liable to Judgment; on the other hand, this is the moment of Michael's judgment against his enemies, the climax of his plans. Either way, we realize that the murders are about to begin.

Shot 32 is a medium long shot of Barzini as he walks down the outside steps. We hear his steps, the organ, the prayer, and the gradually louder crying. His bodyguard walks beside him, and Barzini gestures in the direction of the police officer (Al), who is giving a ticket to the chauffeur: obviously this cop doesn't know the rules. There is a match cut to Shot 33, in which the bodyguard goes down ahead of Barzini and approaches the police officer; the soundtrack is the same as in Shot 32. When the bodyguard reaches the lower center of the frame, there is a match cut to Cicci in the same screen position (a cut on eye movement) in Shot 34, a high-angle full shot of the basement stairs. Cicci walks more than halfway to the top, then stops for a puff on his cigarette. We hear his steps, the organ, the prayer, and the crying. It is as if the baby were crying for all the pain that is about to come.

In Shot 35, Clemenza finally reaches the fifth-floor landing and pushes the elevator button. He wants the elevator to open at that floor. We hear the sounds he makes and the sounds of the baptismal service, just as in the previous shots. Shot 36 is a medium shot of Moe Greene on a masseur's table. He is in the massage room of his own hotel in Las Vegas. The masseur puts oil on his back — another anointing — and Moe twists his neck as if it were stiff, then rests it on his arm, looking preoccupied. We hear all that as well as the continuing service.

At this point all of the murders have been visually prepared for. Al is waiting for Barzini, Clemenza is ready outside the elevator, Cicci is about to trap his victim in the upstairs lobby, Rocco is on the way to Tattaglia's hotel room, and Moe is naked and off guard. The stage is set, then, for the major action.

And the exorcism goes into its climax. In Shot 37 (**Fig. C-47**) the priest touches the baby's mouth and asks, "Michael Francis Rizzi —" At the start of the shot the organ goes into a loud, rapid arpeggio; halfway through "Francis" it becomes silent for the first time in this sequence, as if on a precipice. In shot 38 (**Fig. C-48**) the line is completed: "— do you renounce Satan?" Except for the priest's question, this shot is absolutely silent. Michael just looks. We receive his answer in the following shots.

At the beginning of Shot 39 (**Fig. C-49**) the organ repeats the loud arpeggio as the elevator door opens. The elevator contains two passengers and an operator. At the end of the shot, one of the men catches sight of Clemenza. In Shot 40 (**Fig. C-50**) Clemenza kicks the man back into the elevator, discards the carton, and fires his shotgun twice. We hear the sounds of this scene and the organ.

In Shot 41 (**Fig. C-51**) Michael answers the priest, "I do renounce him." His face reveals that he is looking inside himself, or perhaps thinking about the murders. The juxtaposition of the elevator shootings and his renunciation of Satan is utterly ironic, a montage whose terms, when put together, advance the metaphor of the new godfather and declare Michael's personal damnation. In simpler terms, we can see that he has not renounced anything, except perhaps his peace of mind. Beneath the sound of his voice, the soundtrack of Shot 40 dies rapidly away, leaving the shot in silence.

In Shot 42 (**Fig. C-52**) the organ sounds another loud arpeggio as one of Michael's men walks into the massage room. Now the organ is not part of the church service, but an accompaniment to the murders. This sound trope makes it even more clear that the baptisms are advancing together. It is almost as if the two actions were cross-linked. Up to now the organ has gone naturally with the service, but the play with sound has let it spill over into the murder preparations. In Shot 41, an instant of the murder soundtrack has been heard in the church scene. Now, thanks to Michael, the organ and the service have been made part of the killings themselves; the service has been redefined.

As the thug comes into the room, Moe reaches for his glasses to see who it is. We do not hear his movements, only the organ. There is a match cut to Shot 43 (**Fig. C-53**), in which Moe puts on the glasses. Then there is another match cut to the even tighter Shot 44 (**Fig. C-54**), in which Moe is shot in the eye and his head slumps down. We hear the gunshot and the organ, whose level is fairly loud.

Shot 45 (**Fig. C-55**) returns us to Michael, who looks tired — or as if he would rather be somewhere else. The organ is playing in the background, but now it appears to come from the sites of the killings. The priest asks, "And all his works?"

Shot 46 (**Fig. C-56**) picks up Cicci where we left him on the stairs. The only sound is the organ. Cicci drops his cigarette and heads upstairs. In Shot 47 (**Fig. C-57**) he locks the revolving door in the hotel lobby and draws his gun. Another head of one of the Five Families is trapped. In Shot 48 (**Fig. C-58**) the victim turns around to see what has gone wrong and catches sight of Cicci's gun as it is leveled on him. In both these shots we hear the sounds of the scene (the door lock in particular) as well as the organ. In addition, we note that the baby's crying has begun again.

In Shot 49 (**Fig. C-59**) Cicci finishes leveling his gun; now only the organ is heard. This is a subjective camera shot from the victim's point of view. In the next shot (**Fig. C-60**) the victim yells, and Cicci shoots him twice. In Shot 51 (**Fig. C-61**) Cicci fires two more times, and the glass shatters with each impact until Cicci is nearly obscured, looking totally mad. In both these shots we hear the live sounds and the organ.

Shot 52 (**Fig. C-62**) returns to Michael, who answers, "I do renounce them." The sound of the organ dies out rapidly, like a ricochet. By now it is clear that the organ is not playing in the church.

Now it is time to kill Philip Tattaglia, who is in bed with his mistress. In Shot 53 (**Fig. C-63**) Rocco and his colleague burst through the door, knocking it off its hinges, and open fire. There is a reverse-angle cut to Shot 54 (**Fig. C-64**), showing Tattaglia and especially the woman as they are struck by the bullets. In Shot 53 we hear the organ — now very loud — the crash of the door, the guns, and the woman's "Oh God!" In Shot 54 we hear the organ, the guns, and a second "Oh God!" The religious content of her exclamation is obviously an authorial irony. In Shot 55 (**Fig. C-65**) the camera provides a closer view of the woman as she screams, "Oh —"

At the end of the shot (the frame shown in **Fig. C-65**) she is in the same screen position as Michael will be in the next shot. This is not just a cut on eye movement, but a way of marking Michael as her assassin. She becomes a kind of moral afterimage when we see his face in Shot 56 (**Fig. C-66**, which is the opening frame of that shot). "And all his pomps?" asks the priest. In a resigned, almost exhausted, reserved, and sincere tone he answers, "I do renounce them." The organ, at about medium volume, is heard behind him and continues over the climactic murder of Barzini.

In Shot 57 (**Fig. C-67**) Al shoots Barzini's bodyguard once and the chauffeur twice. Shot 58 (**Fig. C-68**) shows him going into a crouching position and taking careful aim offscreen. Then there is a reverse-angle match cut. In Shot 59 (**Fig. C-69**) he shoots Barzini twice in the back, and we hear the shots. There is another match cut to a medium shot of Barzini (**Fig. C-70**) as he turns and begins to fall. The organ is now very loud. The intensity of the music and the cut to a close view of the principal villain emphasize Michael's triumph and let the audience know that this is the big event. Following another match cut, Shot 61 (**Fig. C-71**) shows Barzini as he falls down the steps. Al runs to the getaway car and escapes. The organ has become a bit softer, and we can clearly hear the sounds of Al's feet, the car door, and the squealing tires.

Shot 62 (**Fig. C-72**) is again of Michael, but this time the camera is closer, urging us to take a closer look at him now that his enemies are dead and the climax of the ritual is upon him. As the actual shootings, building to the major targets of Barzini and Tattaglia, are the climax of their half of the sequence, the actual moment of baptism is the climax of the service. In this shot the priest asks, "Michael Francis Rizzi" — and Michael Corleone looks up — "wilt thou be baptized?" Softly Michael answers, "I will." The organ becomes very soft now, again a part of the service.

In Shot 63 (**Fig. C-73**) the priest pours water onto the baby's head — the moment of baptism. He will do this three times, once at each mention of a member of the Holy Trinity. In this, the most perversely powerful moment in the sequence, the child is baptized in water as Michael is in blood, and the Trinity becomes a trinity of his victims. In Shot 63 we hear the low organ, the sound of the water, and the priest's voice: "In nomine Patris —" ("In the name of the Father").

Shot 64 (**Fig. C-74**) shows the bloody body of Tattaglia in the bed. "Et Filii —" ("and the Son"), says the priest, and at this mention of the "Son" the organ becomes prominent, perhaps a reference to the way Michael is failing to become his own father's ideal son. At the end of this shot we hear the second flow of water. That sound is completed at the start of Shot 65 (**Fig. C-75**), which shows the dead man in the revolving door, and in which the priest completes his line: "et Spiritus Sancti" ("and the Holy Spirit").

Over the start of Shot 66 (**Fig. C-76**), which shows the dead Barzini, we hear the third pouring of the water. The low organ has continued through this morbid trinity, and the water has purified the infant even as it has come to sound, in context, like the pouring of blood. "Michael Rizzi —" says the priest, and in the final shot of the sequence (**Fig. C-77**) he completes his line, "go in peace, and may the Lord be with you. Amen." As the sound of the organ dies out, the camera tracks slowly forward on Michael's face. For the first time we see him with a candle, a spiritual light. As in the rest of this sequence, Michael expresses little or no emotion. Al Pacino's acting here may have taken a hint from Kuleshov's Mozhukhin experiment, because it is the shots around him that suggest what he is thinking and feeling. In any case it is a brilliantly understated performance. As he looks at the light, he appears to be taking stock of all that has happened, all of the changes in his life — but he may well be contemplating the state of his soul. That candle is in itself a summary of the spiritual content of the sequence, and his look is its foregone partner.

Then there is a cut to the outside of the church, punctuated by the tolling of a churchbell.

Role in the Film. In Puzo's novel these climactic events are handled and arranged differently. Although Tattaglia and Barzini are killed much as they are in the movie (but with Tattaglia's mistress being spared), Moe Greene has been killed — by Al — at least a month earlier. To include Moe in this crowd in the movie was a simple measure of narrative efficiency. More significantly, at this point in the novel Michael has Fabrizio killed in an upstate pizza parlor. It was Fabrizio who planted the bomb that killed Apollonia, Michael's first wife. By leaving out this act of *personal* vengeance, the filmmakers were able to emphasize the fact that Michael sees all these killings as *business*.

The service itself is different in the novel and comes at a different time. Instead of a baptism, it is the confirmation of Connie and Carlo's oldest child, and its description takes only a paragraph. It performs the same *general* function as it does in the story of the film; that is, it shows Michael's insincerity — because he is about to murder Carlo — and gives his enemies the impression that he has his mind on family matters and is not preparing a major assault. But it does not have the same symbolic function that it has in the film because it is not a baptism. And because in the novel the killings follow the service rather than accompany it, the religious and business facets of Michael's character are not forced to collide and to generate all this irony.

By studying these changes, we can see what the film was structured to accomplish. At the end of the novel Puzo indicates that Michael's soul needs praying for, but he appears generally pleased with the success of Michael and Vito's plan. At the end of the movie, according to Coppola in an interview, Michael is "a monster." One reason that *Part II* is so much more tragically intense and rigorously formal is that Coppola felt the audience of *The Godfather* had embraced Michael too readily as a hero.

In fact, however, Coppola took great pains, even within *The Godfather*, to underscore Michael's moral failure, and we can appreciate this by examining the scenes that precede and follow the baptism in the movie.

Just before the baptism sequence comes the scene of Vito's funeral. This is a moment for the family to come together and to reaffirm its values and emotional ties. But it is also the scene in which Tessio, one of Michael's lieutenants, approaches him with the news that Barzini wants to set up a meeting. Vito had warned Michael that he would be assassinated at such a meeting and that the man who approached him would be a traitor. At the end of this scene, Michael tells Tom that he has decided to be godfather to Connie's baby — "and then I'll meet with don Barzini, and Tattaglia, all the heads of the Five Families." It is clear that he has finally decided on his plan, and it is both appropriate and ironic that he should have thought of it at the funeral of his father.

Just after the baptism Michael draws Carlo aside and says that he will need him to stay in town for a while (rather than moving with his family to Las Vegas) so that they can talk. Carlo had been responsible for setting up the murder of Sonny, and he had beaten and manipulated Connie simply in order to lure Sonny into a vulnerable position. Once Michael has forced Carlo to admit his guilt — and to identify Barzini as the man behind him — Michael has Carlo garroted by Clemenza.

The movie begins with the wedding of Connie and Carlo (attended, incidentally, by don Barzini). At that point the family and its business are stable and respected. Business problems begin when Vito refuses to support the heroin operation organized by Sollozzo, but the personal problems really begin when Carlo joins the family. As we follow the attempt on Vito's life, the assaults on Connie, and the murder of Sonny, we are indirectly following the progress of Carlo's treachery. Clearly he needs to be dealt with, but the entire culture to which the Corleones belong would reject the solution that Michael finds. Carlo could be banished, he could be shunned, he could be kicked out of the business, but he could not be murdered. At the end of the film, Connie reproaches her brother for violating family ties. Right after that, Kay asks Michael whether he did, in fact, kill Carlo and all those people, and he lies about it, thus violating even the elective ties of marriage.

The film begins, then, with Connie's marriage and ends just after she has been widowed. That provides its overall structure: the plot and her marriage share the same limits. At the start, Michael is a returning war hero in love with a Protestant woman and not expecting to join the family business. At the end, he is married to Kay but does not love her, and he has become the new don Corleone. At the start, the family is intact; at the end, it has begun to pull itself back together, but the cracks are showing.

These generalized transitions are focused in the baptism sequence. That sequence effects the transition from the family funeral, a last moment of unity, to the murder of Carlo, which is a drastic sign of how Michael has lost touch with the Old World values. What happens in between, as we have seen, is that Michael has become the wrong kind of godfather, turning a sacred ritual to profane purposes. In this respect the baptism sequence is an emblem of the whole film, an image that sums up all of its unities, developments, and contradictions. As an insight into Michael's character, it is damning. As an insight into the clash between European values and the ruthless world of corporate America, it is definitive.

The Film Artist and the Movie Business

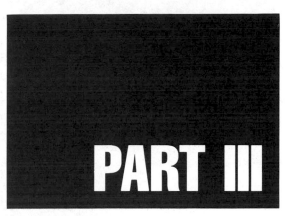

PART III

1. Who Makes a Movie?

The Stages of Production

It is 1978, and we are on the set of *Prophecy* (1979), a generously budgeted horror film about the environmental effects of mercury poisoning. It is 11 A.M. The crew has been setting up a shot since early morning. The floor of the sound stage is covered with cables and is marked with pieces of tape. A cabin has been constructed in the center of the sound stage; it has three walls and a roof. Where the fourth wall ought to be, there is an array of cameras and personnel. Director John Frankenheimer is talking with the cinematographer about the framing of the shot. He has already discussed the shot with the performers, Robert Foxworth and Talia Shire, who are off in their dressing rooms for final makeup. Up on the cabin's roof, two crew members are rigging a stick of dynamite. Now Frankenheimer goes over to a tall youth in a basketball uniform and explains what he wants him to do. The youth smiles affably and climbs into a huge bear suit. Shire appears, attended by a makeup artist who is spraying water into her hair to make her look as if she has just struggled out of a lake. The lake, which is supposed to be just outside the cabin, is actually in the Northwest, and this studio shot must be made to match the details of the previously-shot location material. Foxworth looks all business, and even Shire looks like a businesslike drowned rat.

The soundtrack in this scene will consist entirely of effects: the sounds of feet, a door, and a smashed roof. The production mixer (head of the sound crew) sits behind a blocky console; on a pad, he notes that this shot will be MOS, that is, silent. **MOS** stands for "mit-out sound" and is a continuing industry joke on the German directors who came to Hollywood in the late 1920s and early 1930s and preferred to add sound to their shots in post-production. The production mixer leans over to a colleague and whispers, "I hope his next film is a talkie."

Although there will be no dialogue, this scene is described and numbered in the shooting script, written by David Seltzer. The script supervisor opens the screenplay to the correct page and prepares to take notes. It is her job to keep track of the setups, of exactly how the scene is played before the cameras, and of any dialogue changes that are made at the last moment, so that continuity flaws can be avoided and so that the editor will have an accurate record of each take. The lights have been hung, the actors are ready, and as a guide to the blocking worked out in rehearsal, the floor is marked with the actors' desired positions. The distances from these marks to the film plane in the camera have been precisely measured, and the camera assistant, working with the focus marks etched on the barrel of the lens, will use those measurements as a guide when changing focus during the take. The camera operator, who does not shift focus or focal length, is looking through the viewfinder; the cinematographer, who has verified that the lighting and the framing are correct, tells the director that his crew is ready to shoot. Off in the corner, people set down their styrofoam coffee cups and finish placing their bets in the football pool. An alarm rings, and outside the sound stage a red light goes on to warn passers-by not to enter the building because shooting is in progress.

Frankenheimer nervously plucks at his shirt and says, "Camera." The camera begins to roll, and the assistant watches the motor's gauge; when it registers 24 fps, he says, "Speed." Then Frankenheimer says what only a director can say: "Action."

Foxworth and Shire rush through a door, look rapidly around, and duck down beside a staircase. Then the roof explodes with a terrifically loud noise. (Everyone on the set has been given earplugs.) Through a hole in the roof, the head and paw of a monstrously deformed bear can be seen. The impression is that he has busted through the roof with one blow of his arm. "Cut," says Frankenheimer, and the bear waves happily down at the crew. The take has lasted about 15 seconds.

The next shot will be taken from inside the cabin, and the missing wall will have to be shown. A crew of carpenters and grips pick up flats: sections of wood and plasterboard that look like cabin interior on one side and are unfinished on the other. With startling speed — at least, compared with how long it takes to construct a real cabin — they nail up the six or seven flats while the camera and lights are being repositioned. The actors are wetted down again and sprinkled with ceiling dust. By 1 P.M. this second take of the day has been shot, and it is time to break for lunch.

It usually takes more than 100 people more than a year to make a single feature. At the end of *The Right Stuff* the tail credits list more than 250 names and organizations, yet *The Right Stuff* is labeled "A Philip Kaufman Film." Clearly Kaufman needed many people to work with him: to put up the money, to act, to shoot, to edit, to record and mix the sound, to make and distribute the prints, and to design a marketing campaign. In attempting to sort out who makes a movie, we will not simply be evaluating whether Kaufman or any director deserves such an exclusive creative credit, but will also be exploring the intricacies of authorship: design, development, and execution. This will necessitate our taking another look at the auteur theory (review the discussion of Kubrick in Part I) on the way to a detailed examination of how features are actually made.

Studio Practice. As a model for this inquiry, we will use the full-fledged studio project, the narrative feature film shot in 35mm and intended to be shown to a paying audience. The descriptions of the jobs performed by each member of the production team are based on recent interviews with film professionals — from assistant sound editors to studio executives — and on William Hines's invaluable union manual, *Job Descriptions*, which has only recently become available to the public. These union regulations are extremely specific. Once you have grasped the complexities of a union production, however, you will understand what is involved in virtually any simpler production.

The term "Hollywood" will arise often during this discussion, and in most cases it refers quite directly to the Los Angeles-based vestiges of the world's dominant film industry, with its studio-financed, union productions. A great deal of important production activity takes place elsewhere in America, from the corporate offices and independent companies in New York to the location shoots in Waxahachie. Many projects are brought to the studios' attention only when they are virtually ready to go — or, in some cases, after they have been shot. Yet when a studio is involved at any level, its presence is most definitely felt, and it feels just as seat-of-the-pants authoritative as it did in the 1930s. Around the world there are many different industries, each with its own set of terms and working arrangements. Yet it remains true that there is a generalized "film industry" in the world today and that the old Hollywood has served as its model and occasional standard-bearer. Because the unions and studios are still active, because their procedures are of long standing, and because the majority of filmmaking systems are either adoptions or simplifications of "the Hollywood model" (Japan excepted), there are good reasons to become familiar with the standard working methods of the film business. Hollywood may be an abstraction, or a loose synonym for "the film industry," but it is also a village where things are still being done as they are described here.

It is common practice in Hollywood to divide camera responsibilities among several individuals: the cinematographer, who selects the lighting pattern, the filmstock, the lens, and the filters and supervises the camera crew; the camera operator, who looks through the viewfinder and runs the camera; and two camera assistants, who build and load the camera and take care of focusing and zooming the lens. Similarly, if there is a table on the set, complete with silverware, an ashtray, and a table lamp, on a strict union production the lamp must be unplugged and removed by a lighting technician, the silverware and ashtray must be removed by an assistant prop handler, and the table must be hauled away by grips. In a looser production, on the other hand, one propman or grip could clear and remove the table, or one overworked cameraman could design the lighting as well as set up and operate the camera. But these people would be performing all of the tasks that might otherwise be distributed among several individuals: the overall job still has to be completed. Around the world, various industries go about their business in different ways, but any film anywhere has to be planned, shot, edited, and printed, that is, has to go through essentially the same stages as a Hollywood production, even if they are simplified and condensed.

From Development to Distribution. Any completed film, whether it be narrative or avant-garde, produced in a studio or animated in an attic, goes through five distinct stages.

The first is **development**, in which a draft or an idea is converted into a produceable property, a workable project. The second is **pre-production**, which involves all of the work that must be done before shooting can begin. Next comes **production**, the period of actually staging and photographing the picture. Finally, there is **post-production**, in which the shots are edited, special effects are added, the sound is mixed, and trial prints are made. At the end of post-production a film is ready to be duplicated, released to exhibitors, and shown to the public; once it has been released, the film is in **distribution.**

Each of these stages takes time and a great deal of effort. In an attempt to sort out the nature and the importance of the contributions made by every member of the filmmaking team, and to appreciate the structure of the filmmaking enterprise, we shall take up these stages one at a time. Before doing that, however, let us examine the general problem of authorship in a collaborative enterprise.

Authorship, Design, and Execution

Applauding the Conductor. Imagine that you are at a concert performance of Mozart's Fortieth Symphony. The last movement has just ended, and the audience is applauding the conductor. Not only did the conductor not write the music, he or she has not even played an instrument. Yet it is the conductor whose interpretation of the material is being praised. Next the conductor shakes hands with the concertmaster, and another round of applause ensues. Although the concertmaster's violin was not featured in an extensive solo, this violinist is a representative of the entire orchestra, and now the audience is rewarding them for having played well.

There are at least three artistic entities involved here: the composer, the conductor, and the orchestra. In film terms the composer is often the writer, the conductor is often the director, and the orchestra is a vast array of professionals, from actors to lab technicians. The parallel to the concert hall is the sound stage or location where the movie is shot and the theater where it is exhibited. Behind both operations is a sophisticated financial network that must remain solvent if further concerts or films are to be presented. As a link between the producers and the paying audience, advertisers have let the public know when and where the performance will take place, and they have emphasized those artists whose creative accomplishments are well known and whose personal styles are likely to attract an enthusiastic crowd.

Mozart's Fortieth Symphony existed as a complete textual entity when Mozart finished composing it. Any performance of that composition is itself an artistic event with its own unity and integrity, yet it is still *a* performance of an autonomous text. In a film the situation is markedly different, because the performance *is* the text.

Dashiell Hammett wrote *The Maltese Falcon*, and the novel is still available in its original form for anyone who chooses to read it. It became the basis of three films: Roy Del Ruth's *The Maltese Falcon* (1931), William Dieterle's *Satan Met a Lady* (1936), and John Huston's *The Maltese Falcon* (1941). All four of these are autonomous texts, distinct works of art. In the Huston version, Sam Spade is inseparable from the way Humphrey Bogart incarnated and enacted him, even if we can sort out the differences between Spade and Bogart when we step back from the film. Huston wrote the screenplay and directed the movie, so that the final product became his as much as Hammett's. Yet Huston did not "play an instrument."

The resolution to this quandary is to realize that the instrument that a conductor plays is, in fact, the orchestra. The orchestra members depend on the conductor to keep time and to let them know when and with what emphasis to play. The conductor organizes the performance, and it is therefore up to her or him how the composition will be realized. As the designer of an independent work, the director may have claims to authorship — but such claims are not at all automatic, and film authorship is rarely sole.

The Auteur Theory. Sole authorship is a matter of conceiving, designing, executing, and owning a work. Hammett planned *The Maltese Falcon*, wrote it, and had the sole right to sell it to a publisher. In the majority of films, design, realization, and ownership are necessarily split among many people and companies, and "authorship" becomes problematic.

Recall the moment when Queen Christina removes her crown. The physical movement was executed by Greta Garbo. The position of the camera, with its background view of a crown that cannot be removed, was chosen by the director, Rouben Mamoulian, and by the cinematographer, William Daniels. The action was designed in the first place by a team of screenwriters, based loosely on a historical event. The editor juxtaposed that shot with others that would enhance its impact. And the director, of course, coached Garbo on how to act the scene. But could Mamoulian have *told* Garbo every nuance of that gesture? Who took off that crown? Who should get credit for the brilliant, slow tenderness of Garbo's motions and the exquisite complexity of her face, in that light, at that moment? Who is the author of the total effect, of this scene, of this movie?

In this example there is no sole author. But there may have been a conductor — an artist with ultimate responsibility for approving the work of others — and it may well have been Mamoulian. The director is usually involved — or at least has a say — in all the major creative decisions from development through post-production, notably script approval, casting, production and costume design, the details of performance, and editing. That puts him or her in a position to unify the project and coach the team. But in the absence of reliable information about who did what while a picture was being made, there is little or no justification for assuming that the director has, in fact, performed this unifying function, let alone originated the themes, tropes, and gestures that have proved most distinctive and valuable in the finished work. It is difficult to make sense of the whole body of cinema, or even of any individual movie, until some critical method, informed by a careful understanding of real filmmaking practices, makes it possible to give credit where credit is due. Critical interpretations, especially of creative intentions and decisions, can be more reliable and sophisticated when one knows who the author is; otherwise, intentions are ascribed to a generalized vacuum.

First proposed by François Truffaut in the 1950s and further developed by Andrew Sarris in the 1960s, the **auteur theory** set out to provide just such a critical tool. It begins by acknowledging (or perhaps simply gives lip service to the idea) that film is a collaborative art, then goes on to argue that when a film reveals a thematic and stylistic coherence, that coherence can usually be attributed to the guiding vision of a single artist who was expressing his or her personal convictions and tastes. In order to have such power, the artist must almost invariably have been the director, though it is even better if the director has also written the screenplay. To distinguish this artist from a sole author, he or she is referred to as an "auteur" (French for "author," but used in English to connote this more ambiguous position of control).

The problem with the auteur theory is that it *may* allow the critic to ignore creative collaboration and leap straight to the director. The special merit of the auteur theory is that it is *capable* of acknowledging the collaborative structure of the cinematic enterprise *and* the evidence of patterns of coherence that have the integrity of authorship. These may be stylistic patterns, characteristic approaches to recurring subject matter, or attitudes and strategies that have developed in the course of a career. Hitchcock's work, for example, is characterized by recurring content — notably the problematic relations between guilt and innocence — and a visual style that no one has been able to imitate with authority. This observation does not imply that an artist always says the same thing in the same way; rather, it allows for development and maturation within a structure whose consistency is that of the artist.

In the role of director, then, which touches nearly every aspect of the filmmaking process and may let an artist dominate a work without actually taking center stage, the auteurists found a site for these patterns of coherence. It is quite plain to them that Renoir films are Renoir films, that von Sternberg films could not have been made by Lumet, and that Welles was the auteur of *Citizen Kane*. This makes it simple to talk about a movie as a direct expression of one person's creative intentions. But auteurism has often been applied carelessly. It is by no means true that every film has an auteur. There are auteurs who are not directors, and directors who are not auteurs. Many auteurists have not taken the trouble to check these matters out, nor have they even begun to applaud the concertmaster.

Auteurism has had critical implications that are far-reaching and sometimes off-target. It appears, for one thing, to have been the only academic debate ever to affect the film industry. In its later critical manifestations it has become a cult of personal style, so that a director is considered interesting — or an author at all — only when he or she has exhibited a consistent style and a matrix of recurring interests. Directors in whose work such patterns cannot be discerned have often been dismissed by critics as "hacks." The industry itself has become "director-conscious," while many non-directors have become anti-auteurists. Under the influence of auteurism, many fledgling film artists have gathered that directing is the only important job and that they have to make *their* mark. But there is more to good directing than self-expression, and there are distinctly creative aspects to other film jobs. The public view now appears to be simply that films are made and signed by directors.

Critically, the conventional test of an auteur is that a pattern emerges when all of his or her pictures are viewed together or are considered in relation to each other. But the real value of auteurism — once it is extended beyond directors and as it may be critically applied to a single picture — is that it offers a reasonable explanation for a fact about cinema: that an often personal coherence *can* emerge from a collaborative project.

Even when a film does have an auteur — a Bergman or a Hitchcock, for example — the critical methodology is sometimes applied irresponsibly. Many auteurists want to find a single author and let it go at that. Although they may understand that actress Bibi Andersson and cinematographer Sven Nykvist are independent beings, they prefer to analyze every image and instant of *Persona* as if it proceeded directly from Ingmar Bergman's consciousness. Bergman himself has always been generous in acknowledging the contributions of the group he has worked with and would never endorse such a critical position.

Collaborative Decision-Making. Not every film has a single director, let alone a single guiding consciousness. Both Stanley Donen and Gene Kelly directed *Singin' in the Rain*, and Arthur Freed produced it. Director Vittorio de Sica and writer Cesare Zavattini were lifelong collaborators, from *Shoeshine* (1946) and *The Bicycle Thief* through *A Brief Vacation* (1973). Resnais directed *Marienbad*, Alain Robbe-Grillet wrote it, and the two men disagreed about what happens in the story. The finished film reflects this authorial ambivalence and presents the lovers as having met before (Resnais's interpretation) and as never having met before (Robbe-Grillet's interpretation). This doubleness is responsible for much of *Marienbad's* characteristic tone and style, and it would not be adequate to identify it simply as Resnais's movie. It has as many significant connections with Robbe-Grillet's novels as it has with Resnais's other movies.

Although one can identify most of Spielberg's movies as his, the Indiana Jones films are clearly the result of his collaboration with Lucas. As their producer, Lucas is the auteur of the *Star Wars* series, and his control of those pictures was so personal and exacting that *The Empire Strikes Back* (1980) and *Return of the Jedi* (1983), which he did not direct, are nearly indistinguishable from *Star Wars*, which he did direct. Yet the Indiana Jones films are not the same as the *Star Wars* films, and *Raiders* in particular shares many important characteristics with both Spielberg's *Jaws* (1975) and Lucas's *American Graffiti* (1973). Once you know the pictures, all of these distinctions are obvious, yet a conventional auteurist would approach *Raiders* as a Spielberg film and might dismiss *Jedi* from serious consideration if it did not bear the stamp of Richard Marquand's directorial personality. It is only recently that writers, producers, and actors have begun to be considered possible auteurs, even though it should long have been obvious that there is such a thing as a Horton Foote film, a Walt Disney film, and a Marx Brothers film. But even to settle on such sites of coherence can be to sidestep the realities of development and production.

Let us take up some examples of creative collaboration, both fruitful and unfortunate. In 1943 director Henry Hathaway was developing a story idea about the Unknown Soldier. He kept evaluating suggestions from his colleagues and rejecting them. Finally one writer said, in simple exasperation, "You'll never be satisfied until the Unknown Soldier is Jesus Christ!" Hathaway replied, "Hey, that's a good idea!" This was the key juxtaposition for which Hathaway had unknowingly been searching, and his colleague's quip precipitated the insight. Hathaway and writer William Bacher then drew up a new story idea, and William Faulkner was assigned to develop it into a treatment (an extended story outline from which a screenplay can be further developed). Faulkner warmed up to the idea and turned in a 51-page treatment, but the picture (to have been entitled *Who?*) was never made. Faulkner went on to expand the idea into a novel called *A Fable* (1954), and he gave credit to Hathaway and Bacher on the dedication page.

Eugène Lourié worked as the art director on Jean Renoir's *Grand Illusion* (1937). When he and Renoir were scouting locations for that film, they decided to use the mountain castle of Haut-Koenigsburg, which had been built by Kaiser Wilhelm. Lourié, according to his own account in *American Film* (Jan./Feb. 1985), "noticed a small pot of geraniums on the windowsill of the janitor's lodging. I was impressed by this little speck of color amid the gray stone surroundings. I asked Jean if he would not object to my placing a geranium in Stroheim's room. 'By all means, put it there,' he said, 'I could use it.' This little flower became a highly poetic symbol. Stroheim's cutting this flower became the emotional final touch during the scene showing the death of the Fresnay character." It is clear from this example that the art director did not get the entire idea, did not anticipate how Renoir would ultimately use the geranium in *Grand Illusion,* but it is also clear that there would have been no geranium in the film had Lourié not noticed one on location and intuited that it somehow belonged in the design of the picture. Although Renoir justifiably took credit as the principal author of *Grand Illusion,* he also referred to Lourié as his "accomplice."

Sometimes, however, too many cooks can in fact spoil the broth. Hitchcock's *Suspicion* (1941) was based on a brilliant mystery novel by Francis Iles, *Before the Fact*. The novel is about a woman who discovers that she has married a murderer. When she realizes that he intends to kill her, too, she lets him do it. The scene in which the husband, Johnny, brings his wife a glass of poisoned milk and realizes that she knows what he is doing, yet acquiesces to her demand — "Give it me, Johnny" — is deeply affecting. In what seemed to be perfect casting decisions, Cary Grant and Joan Fontaine were signed to play the leads. But then the RKO studio heads decided that no star of Grant's importance could be cast in the role of a murderer. It became necessary to devise an incredible ending in which the wife is revealed as having misunderstood her husband's good intentions. This happily-ever-after resolution is a classic example of "the Hollywood treatment," and the equivocal terms in which it more-or-less succeeds have nothing to do with the novel.

To see how input from various sources can affect a finished product, even one of classic status, consider the production history of *The Cabinet of Dr. Caligari* (a story vividly recounted by Siegfried Kracauer in his study *From Caligari to Hitler*). The writers, Carl Mayer and Hans Janowitz, developed a story about an insane doctor (Caligari) who forces a somnambulist (Cesare) to commit a series of murders. When the doctor is eventually exposed by the vigilant hero and committed to his own asylum, what Janowitz and Mayer hoped to show was that insane authority can be challenged and even overthrown, that its insanity can be revealed. They saw Caligari — whom each of them drew from a particularly threatening figure in his own past — as a symbol of the criminally deranged, militaristic, authoritarian system and Cesare as a youth turned into a killing machine, like a conscripted soldier.

Producer Erich Pommer bought the script and determined to make, if not an avant-garde feature, then at least an arty movie capable of attracting international attention. He hired Fritz Lang to direct.

Lang suggested that framing sequences be added: one, at the start of the film, to establish that the story (that is, Janowitz and Mayer's script) is being narrated by the central character (Franz or Francis), and one, at the end of the film, to reveal that Francis is insane. In the script and in the body of the movie, Francis is a friend of one of Cesare's victims and is the one who tracks Caligari to his lair, but in the closing scenes he is shown to be an inmate of the asylum run by the benevolent and insightful doctor whom, in his delusion, he calls Caligari. Perhaps Lang conceived this purely as a dramatic twist, and perhaps Pommer appreciated its show business value, but the fact is that their adding the closing frame drastically altered the meaning of the story and sent the writers into a rage. What the revised version preached was submission and self-doubt. Doctor Caligari knows what is good for you.

Lang did not, however, direct the picture; he was reassigned to *Spiders* (1919). Pommer hired Robert Wiene, who did direct it. Wiene agreed with Lang about the value of the framing sequences and the reversal of the story's original intentions. So now it was set: rather than a film of rebellion, *Caligari* was to be a film of repression, of the fear and the denial (and, in fact, the *rescripting*) of rebellion.

It was either Pommer or Janowitz who first conceived of *Caligari* as a film with stylized, painted sets. Janowitz suggested that the designer be Alfred Kubin, but the actual choice of designer was made by Wiene, and he chose Hermann Warm. It was Warm who wrote that "Films must be drawings brought to life," and he and Walter Röhrig and Walter Reimann, all of whom were Expressionist artists, created the sets and the costumes. Without Pommer's approval, however, there is no way that *Caligari* would have become an Expressionist film, and it makes relatively little difference whether Janowitz or Wiene suggested it to him. Under Pommer's guidance, or as a result of the emerging logic of the revisions, the Expressionist style became problematic in the same terms as the framing sequences, and *Caligari* became neither a film of rebellion nor a film of repression but a paradox and a "dream play." As it stands, it might well be compared to a dream whose terms and whose repressed, eruptive meanings have been changed and distorted.

Expressionist distortion was not inconsistent with the meaning and dramatic project of the original script, and Janowitz clearly had no objection to it. In the context of the script alone, the Expressionist distortions would have portrayed and critiqued the state of the culture, or of the German "soul" if you will, shortly after World War I. They would have enhanced the dramatization of the madness of the world that must answer to insane tyranny.

But with the framing sequences added, of course, all these distortions signify is that Francis is crazy. That implies that the world is fine. The action of the closing frame implies that it is not the authority figure but the insightful postromantic rebel who is psychologically disturbed. So far, then, the official message of *Caligari* is almost exactly the opposite of what the writers intended it to be, as the result of suggestions made by Lang and Wiene and approved by Pommer. Creative distortion has become delusion.

Then Wiene made a mistake — or perhaps, in this context, a Freudian slip. He failed to instruct the designers to restore *normal* sets, makeup, and costumes for the closing frame. (The opening frame is relatively neutral.) If the world when it is not being narrated by Francis looks much the same as when it *is*, then all of the Expressionist distortions cannot simply be written off as expressions of the narrator's madness. The Expressionism of the final scenes leaks over from the main story, erupts out of it, and is ultimately both subversive and paradoxical. A hint of what might be called the writer's perspective survives, then, and not only the closing frame but also the entire film appears divided against itself. Thanks to all of these internal contradictions (the impossible closing landscape; the different interpretations of the story held by the writers, Lang and Wiene, and Pommer; the praise of conformity and submission and the impulse to revolt, etc.), *Caligari* actually *does* portray the ambivalence of Germany between the wars, torn between the desire to discover and submit to an authoritarian father figure and the impulse to revolt; it says both things at once. *Caligari* also plays out perfectly the often contradictory message systems of dreaming, and that is one of the reasons, among many, that it became the paradigm of the horror film rather than a unique political melodrama.

None of its makers foresaw how *Caligari* would turn out, and at the very least, it had several authors. The true, or ur-*Caligari* was conceived by Janowitz and Mayer. Wiene directed the film (often very poorly), selected Warm and approved the terms of the design, and is usually credited as the film's auteur. But if anyone had overall creative approval at every stage of production, it was Pommer, the producer. And the addition of the framing sequences, which was as important a development as the decision to use Expressionist sets, was Lang's idea. We are not even speaking here of the definitive, brilliant contributions made by the actors who played Caligari (Werner Krauss) and Cesare (Conrad Veidt), who were cast, as it happens, by Pommer.

Although it may seem rather tangled, the production history of *Caligari* is just as representative as the story of the geranium in *Grand Illusion*. Well after the writer surrenders the script, people are always getting bright ideas, and sometimes the ideas actually enhance what the writer has envisioned. Even a Renoir needs help, and even a script as coherent as that for *Caligari* may be worked over by many people who "improve" it to the point of incoherence. As complex as it is to establish how a collaborative venture may be guided, and to what ends, it is a worthwhile critical effort. And to be comprehensive, that effort must take into account the business context within which feature films are made.

Most of the arts, at some point, touch the world of commerce. If you want to write a novel for your own amusement and satisfaction, that is up to you. But if you want someone to publish it, you will have to deal with business people and listen to many suggestions for improving the work or making it more marketable. In the case of a feature film, where you will have to convince someone to put up at least a million dollars before you can even begin to shoot the picture, the business component is extremely significant.

This is a matter of aesthetics as well as of sheer power. In the first place, the ideas contributed by agents, story editors, producers, and marketing specialists can turn out to be valuable. In the second place, the filmmaker is answerable to an unpleasant reality: filmmaking is one of the only arts that an accomplished artist can be kicked out of. Without the trust of the studios and banks, the artist may simply not be allowed to work. That is what happened to Griffith, Stroheim, and Welles: they were denied the expensive tools they needed to realize their designs. Even a solo filmmaker like Brakhage must scrape together the money to make his films. To ignore this practical context is to introduce the danger of reading a movie in *completely* aesthetic terms and losing sight of the complexities of design and execution — of reading *Suspicion*, for example, as if Hitchcock had had his own reasons for changing the story, or *Caligari* as Wiene's masterpiece.

Collaboration As a System. Many people make creative decisions in the course of a filmmaking project, and several people — at various levels of authority — approve or reject them. The student and the critic must, then, resolve two apparently contradictory facts: (1) that filmmaking is a collaboration, and (2) that some films do reveal the workings of a particular stylistic imagination, one that tends to recur in other films made by the same artist(s).

The auteurists have resolved these contradictions by arguing that the director imposes his or her vision on the entire crew, bucks the system, and heroically conveys a personal statement through the oppressive mechanism of a dense industry. That might be thought of as the model of the conductor and the orchestra, except that the conductor is also being given credit for the equivalent of writing and playing the music. There is something plainly wrong about giving a director credit for the insights and the structural imagination of a writer, especially if the director has worked from a completed script. And even if one views the essence of cinema as lying in the treatment and the mounting of the material — the discourse rather than the story — all that is done by still other professionals who have their own special interests and skills.

Nevertheless, it is simply true that there are styles associated with certain individual filmmakers. There is a "Hitchcock camera" whether or not the cinematographer was Robert Burks. There is a "Toland camera" whether the director was Ford, Wyler, or Welles. There are worlds that can accurately be described as Chaplin's or Keaton's or Lloyd's.

A partial explanation is that a director (and by the same token, a producer) is often given his or her choice of projects. Out of the many available scripts in development at a studio, or sent to the director by agents, the one that the director picks — probably because he or she finds it interesting — is often the one that gets produced. A recognized director also selects his or her major collaborators, knowing their previous work. Part of the "Huston" flavor of a John Huston film can be explained by Huston's having selected only those properties that struck him as "his kind of material," whereas the ones he rejected might wait around to be picked up by other filmmakers who were interested in other things. By the same logic, the look of the image can be read as the one that he hired that particular cinematographer to achieve. In these terms, one can discover Huston's personal tastes — and business acumen — by studying and comparing the properties he agreed or fought to direct. All that is easier if you also know which ones he did *not* want or agree to direct, but it is still possible to find evidence of the connecting thread of Huston through "his" films.

But are they his films? Let me propose that they are "Huston" films. The name is in quotes to suggest that they do have a recognizable and developing style, that that style is reliably associated with all of the films directed by Huston, and that all of them were produced as collaborations. Like Mamoulian in the "crown" example, Huston could not have dictated every significant aspect of all these films. If my argument is correct, the solution to this paradox rests in the intuitive dynamics of collaboration.

Cinematographer Robby Müller has said that he and director Wim Wenders rarely discussed how a scene should be shot but often seemed to share the same ideas. One explanation is that Wenders chose Müller as his cameraman because he liked the way Müller had worked on other projects. But that would not explain the nature of the understanding between them, nor the differences in Müller's work for other directors.

Over and over, in the course of researching this book, I encountered cinematographers who said that although they had their own sense of style and craft, they studied the director and any of his or her previous films in order to discover the director's characteristic approach and to "give the director what he wants." I heard the same thing from film editors, sound mixers, research librarians, assistant directors, and actors. The director is acknowledged as the person who is in a position to have a finger in every pie, at least up to the first edited version of the picture. But it is the position, not really the person, that is at so crucial a place in the film-making system. The director has the opportunity to live up to that position.

It is not that the director issues instructions to everybody in sight and they then carry them out; rather, every creative member of the filmmaking team comes to *share* a vision of how the film ought to be, a vision that they may well identify with the desires of the director. They each do their part, and the parts are coherent because they were each fashioned in relation to an ideal of the whole. The rays come to a point of focus, and whether that point is a shared construct of "what the director wants" or the director as a person, it is most crucially the ideal toward which the film-makers are working and, with luck, the shape of the finished product.

What the group of artists does, in other words, is to agree to work together in a certain style and toward a particular goal. When they are working with Huston, that goal is a "Huston" film. They associate this style with "giving the director what he wants," but that does not mean that the director has or even could have told them all how to do that. What it does mean is that style in a collaborative enterprise is not just the *result* but often the *evidence* of a group effort. The more coherent the style, the better must have been the working understanding among the members of the team.

There are still cases where stylistic coherence reflects the comprehensive and specific instructions of a single person. There are others in which the group ideal has been stimulated not by the director but by the inherent logic of the script, the story to be told — or by the studio, which wants to put out a certain kind of product. But in general, and in the majority of cases, the rich coherence of a movie can be ascribed to the shared vision of its makers.

If that redefined auteur method leaves us examining the politics of Capra, the conflict of guilt and desire in Hitchcock, or the social vision of Ford, there will be no problem — as long as we do not forget that none of those individuals can be given absolute credit for and title to the films they guided to completion. Directors, too, are parts of the system, and if they generate an abstraction that proves to inspire and unify the activities of their many collaborators, that is an intriguing explanation of how the parts of the cinematic system — people, arts, and shots — might be drawn together into a coherent whole.

2. Development

Development begins with the person who gets the original idea for a picture. In most cases that person is a writer, but it often happens that a "concept" originates with a producer or a director. Development ends when the property is approved for production, is entirely abandoned, or is put in **turnaround** (offered to another studio or producer).

The Writer and the Screenplay

Conception. Let us say that a studio executive evalutes the market and decides that in about a year, audiences are likely to be eager for a movie about a scoutmaster who teaches the blind how to river-raft. Perhaps the industry is in the midst of a cycle of pictures about inspiring adults who make contact with isolated adolescents, and perhaps the market has responded consistently to uplifting stories about people who overcome their handicaps. The executive decides that the scoutmaster could be played by Roy Scheider, the rebellious-but-eventually-won-over youth by Matt Dillon, and the girlfriend-who-insists-on-coming-along by Brooke Shields. On the basis of *Rocky* (1976) and *The Karate Kid* (1984), he selects John G. Avildsen as director. He might sign up these four people without so much as a script, and the picture would be well into development.

Many pictures are generated by studios and independent producers in just this manner. What begins as a "concept" is linked with a "package" of **elements**, names with clout and good "track records." A well-known director, a star, a best-selling author, or a highly successful producer can be considered an element, and if one or more of them expresses serious interest in a story concept, it has a good chance of being produced. The more attractive the package, the easier it is to finance and eventually to market. But before such a package can be thoroughly developed, there will have to be a script or at least a treatment, and someone will have to write it. At this point the executive or the producer will hire a writer to work up the idea, and that hiring, strictly speaking, marks the official start of development.

The writer would, in this case, draft a treatment or script and submit it to the executive or producer, who might approve it for expansion, reject it outright, or suggest modifications. Another writer may be hired to revise the script completely, to "punch up" the dialogue, or to polish certain scenes. This process continues until the script has won final approval or has been abandoned.

It is also common for a picture to be based on a published work of fiction or a produced play. In such cases the original work or "literary property" is the seed to be developed, and the producer either buys the movie rights to the work outright or takes out an **option** on them. While the option lasts, the producer commissions scripts and attempts to put together a package deal; when it expires, he or she has the choice of renewing the option or letting it lapse. At any point while the option is in effect, the producer may purchase the rights, but no one else can; once an option has been dropped, the property is back on the open market. Sometimes the producer hires the original writer to adapt the work for the screen; just as often he or she signs up a veteran screenwriter.

Having noted all this, let us concentrate on the tasks of the writer who has thought of an original idea for a movie without any ties to or encouragement from a studio or a producer. This independently conceived story has to be marketed, most often with the help of an agent; it has to be shown to many producers, usually devoid of elements, before it will even be read; and it may turn out to have nothing to do with current studio priorities.

To make the situation almost ideally simple, let us assume that the writer has had a *terrific* idea, is highly accomplished in structuring a narrative, has a good ear for dialogue, and has thought up some profoundly interesting characters. It is a story that will lend itself naturally to visualization, full of significant action and set in an affordable but interesting landscape.

The writer may begin by putting together a **story outline**, a short, relatively informal telling of the core of the proposed picture. It will identify the principal characters and provide a running narrative of the plot.

Practical Considerations. In order for the writer to construct this story outline, he or she will have to grapple with a host of aesthetic considerations in a pragmatic context. Many of these are of the sort that any storyteller needs to master: efficient characterization, pace, and narrative structure. The special constraint imposed on a screenwriter is that all of these must be conceived for presentation in a movie, not on the page.

Sooner or later, a character must reveal the nature of his or her personality through gestures, decisions, and actions that can be *watched*. The screenwriter has to visualize the story and discover how to tell it with pictures and sounds as well as words. If the writer is accustomed to setting the mood of a scene through extensive prose descriptions and subtle verbal twists, he or she has to realize that the camera will present the setting to the audience, often almost instantaneously. Despite all of the visualizing that is absolutely crucial to the construction of a good screenplay, the writer will have to surrender mise-en-scène to the director and the production designer, montage to the editor. Of course the writer can offer impressions of how a scene ought to play, how a character ought to dress, and where there ought to be significant cuts, but most often these will be treated only as suggestions. Of all writers, the screenwriter has the least say about how his or her work will be presented to the public, the least authorial independence (recall Janowitz and Mayer).

What all of the other filmmakers depend on the writer to provide is the spine of the story, its dramatic structure, its characters, its point, and its dialogue. All of these decisions have to be made carefully, by someone who knows how to make them. It is a fairly reliable generalization that producers are interested in a marketable package, directors are interested in the visual and dramatic style of a picture, and writers are interested in narrative logic, believable characterization, the use of words, and the development of a coherent structure. It is far more common for a writer to think in terms of scenes rather than of shots and sequences, of characters rather than of actors, and of story integrity rather than of marketing packages. Yet the story must eventually be designed so that the producer, the director, the actors, the camera crew, the editors, and eventually the distributor can work with it.

If you write a script that begins with 517 green horses leaping from Yankee Stadium into outer space, you will have to consider how that will look to the people who might have to rent and color 517 horses, get a permit to shoot in Yankee Stadium, and pay a special effects team to create the leap. If you think up a story that covers 250 years of history in terms of 43 major characters — which would not be outlandish in a long novel — you will have to reduce it so that the core of the story can be presented in the norm of two hours or less (the "bladder barrier").

As a guide to these matters, there are two books that the aspiring screenwriter would be well advised to consult. William Goldman's *Adventures in the Screen Trade* provides a witty and up-to-date overview of the ways the priorities of the writer and the industry collide and a behind-the-scenes guide to story and script generation. When it comes time to write the screenplay, the recognized manual for the correct way to type and present it is *The Complete Guide to Standard Script Formats, Part I: The Screenplay*, by Hillis Cole, Jr., and Judith Haag.

Script Generations. We left our writer at the point of devising a story outline. The next step, which is sometimes omitted, is to write a treatment. Some writers prefer to leap immediately into a screenplay, but the treatment can be a useful way to break the story outline down into big dramatic chunks. A **treatment** presents the major characters and actions of a story in the order in which they will appear in the proposed film; it translates the story into a plot. Although it has no set format, it often reads like a short story written in the present tense, moving from one scene outline to another, and it usually contains a few sample exchanges of dialogue. It is more precisely descriptive than a story outline, but not as filled-in as a screenplay. Many writers begin with a treatment rather than with a story outline.

The next step is to write the full-length screenplay. At this point the writer may work under contract or "on spec" (speculation). Regardless of how many drafts the writer actually writes, the final product, or the **author's final**, is known as the **first draft** or **temporary screenplay**, because it is the first or earliest version to be submitted and the first with which the producers work.

The author's final may be turned over to another writer, or back to the first writer (this time, under contract), for minor or drastic revision. There may be a **second temporary screenplay**, a **third temporary**, and so on, until the studio or producer is satisfied. The end product of all these revisions is called the **final screenplay**.

(The author's final may also be called "final draft screenplay" or "final draft" — but not "final screenplay.")

The final screenplay, too, may be tinkered with before shooting begins. There may be a **first revised final screenplay**, a **second revised final**, etc. The last revised final — referred to for convenience simply as *the* **revised final** — is the version used on the set. Minor rewriting continues even during shooting, and pages of revised dialogue, on color-coded paper, are added to the revised final as they are approved; these are the **"Changes"** pages, and they are marked with the dates they were composed (or copied by the studio secretaries) and are interleaved in continuity.

A screenplay may be written in a variety of formats. At the author's level, it is rarely necessary to work in the highly technical format of the shooting script. Many writers arrive at their own nonstandard formats, ones that are comfortable to work in. William Goldman, for example, prefers to describe each scene or action in a run-on sentence, punctuated with "CUT TO:" directions. The play format, too, is convenient and adaptable. All the nonstandard screenplay format really needs to do is to pull scenes out of the writer and leave it clear that they are scenes. Stage directions, personal directions, and even camera movements can be called for in parentheses and then shifted to their proper places in the author's final.

The majority of author's finals are written in master-scene format. A **master-scene script** (the simplest of the standard screenplay formats) is broken into scenes rather than into camera setups. Dialogue runs in a central column. Character cues (names) are capitalized and centered above dialogue, and brief personal directions ("angrily," "drinks," "stands," etc.) appear in parentheses, also centered, within the block of dialogue. Stage directions (descriptions of setting, sound cues, camera movements, directions for characters who are not speaking at the moment, entrances and exits, and so on) begin at the left margin and may run several lines. **Fig. 3-2** is a page from the final draft screenplay for *Cannery Row* (1982), written and directed by David S. Ward and based on the novel by John Steinbeck. It is in a formal, author's-presentation, screenplay format. Near the top of the page, "SUZY" is the character cue, "(right in his face)" is personal direction, "'Cause I paid" is dialogue, "Jake stares at her" is stage direction, "46" is the page number, and "57" is a scene number. Scenes 57 and 59 are, in theatrical terms, part of the "same scene," which takes place in Suzy's room at night. Scene 58, however, is an exterior shot (even if it would, in this case, have been shot on a sound stage; *Cannery Row* had an exceptionally large indoor set) and constitutes, in screenplay terms, a separate scene. The capitalized words in the scene headings ("INT. SUZY'S ROOM — NIGHT") establish whether the scene is interior or exterior, where it is set, and the time of day.

Some master-scene scripts are more loosely formatted than Ward's, and the ones that are called "story scripts" may even resemble expanded treatments. Whatever the format, however, by

57   CONTINUED: (2)   57

                                    JAKE
                          What the hell for?

                                    SUZY
                              (right in his
                              face)
                          'Cause I paid $12.99 for this
                          goddamn dress, that's what for.
                          13 bucks so I'd look nice for
                          guys like you. And I ain't
                          gonna take it off till you
                          tell me how you like it.

          Jake stares at her a second. He realizes she's serious,

                                    JAKE
                          It's all right, I like it all
                          right.

                                    SUZY
                          Thanks. You want the light on
                          or off?

                                    JAKE
                          On. Leave it on for a while.

          Jake takes off his underwear and gets into bed. Suzy
          turns toward the window, not wanting to undress facing
          him. She finishes unbuttoning her dress, when the sight
          of something across the street makes her hesitate.

                                                              CUT TO:

58   EXT. WESTERN BIOLOGICAL - DOC - NIGHT   58

          is sitting out on his front porch, drinking the beer
          and eating the macaroons she brought over to him. He's
          looking out at the vacant lot, completely absorbed in
          his own thoughts.

                                                              CUT TO:

59 ˙ INT. SUZY'S ROOM - NIGHT   59

          Suzy moves closer to the window, drawn by Doc's pres-
          ence, strangely glad to see him despite their fight.

          Looking down at Doc, drinking on his porch in the wee
          hours, she senses something shared between them, a
          mutual loneliness, a mutual need. Secure in the
          knowledge that he doesn't see her, she lets her dress
          slip from her hands.

                                                        (CONTINUED)

Figure 3-2

the time of the author's final the movie will have been fully visualized and rendered as a series of playable scenes, with fairly specific camera and sound instructions if the writer's fantasy involvement has been complete. Sooner or later, after producer's and
director's versions of the script have been generated, the screen-

play will be converted into a "set version," which means that it will be put into *the* standard screenplay format, that of the **shooting script**.

In a shooting script, breakdown has proceeded to the level of the setup. What was Scene 57 in the previous draft might now be Scenes 98–102. Every significant change of camera position becomes a new "scene." There will, in most cases, be many more shots in the edited film than there are scene numbers in the shooting script, because of course the editor may trim and rearrange the takes in a variety of ways. The point is to let the people on the set know what *they* have to do, to provide clear instructions for each numbered unit of action, each significant change of view. It is common, by the way, for the shooting script to be prepared in the production office rather than by the writer, but it is likely that the professional screenwriter will have constructed the final screenplay so that this last formal translation will *be* purely formal and will involve no significant rewriting.

The shooting script is an eminently practical format, and the more of them you read, the more natural the conventions become. The margins of a shooting script have been contrived so that one page of script corresponds to approximately one minute of screen time. If dialogue ran from one edge of the page to another, it might take several minutes to deliver. The average shooting script is between 90 and 120 pages. The capitalized scene heading establishes the location, the time of day, the camera angle, and the principal subject, usually in that order. Camera directions and sound effects are capitalized, flagging instructions to the specific crews that will implement them. Once the script has been broken down — analyzed, budgeted, and then arranged in shooting order — it is no longer an odd-looking play but something from which a movie can be *shot*.

The Screenplay and the Cutting Continuity. It is common to save all drafts of a script until production has been completed, and at least one copy of each is usually put into a permanent file in the studio archives. The last "script" or legal version of the screenplay is a **cutting continuity**, and it is always saved. Working from the script supervisor's notes and the final cut of the film, the editor — or sometimes the stenographic staff — makes a thorough record of each shot and its contents, including the exact dialogue. If the screenplay is a guide continually referred to during the production of a film, and subject to continual changes, the cutting continuity is intended to be a precise transcription of the film as released ("intended" because many of them do contain errors).

Some screenplays have such autonomous literary value, or are considered such important contributions to classic films, that they are published. Script publication raises a number of legal and critical questions. Although a completed film is copyrighted, so that title to the work (ownership) is protected for several decades until it enters "public domain" and is considered the collective property of the world, the materials that went into production usually are not copyrighted. These materials, such as the screenplay, the production design sketches, and the budgets, are simply owned outright by the person or the organization that paid to have them generated. They are part of the file on the project and are not intended for public distribution. Many screenwriters, in fact, enjoy the knowledge that their work will *not* be published, but that is another story. For a script to be published, it must be copyrighted as a separate item, not by the writer but by its owner. It is a relatively new practice to copyright the film and the screenplay individually in the year of release.

The question remains: Of all the drafts that have been saved, which is the most important to publish? Many readers will want an accurate record of the dialogue of a favorite movie, keyed to the cuts in the original release print, and they will prefer to have the cutting continuity in book form. But others may be interested in seeing what the filmmakers worked *from*, and they will be most interested in having a copy of the shooting script (the revised final). If they are particularly interested in the writer's career, they will most want to see the original story outline and the final draft. The person who really wants to study the generation of the picture will want to see the story outline, the treatment(s), every draft of the screenplay, all of the "Changes," and the cutting continuity, as well as the most important contracts, sketches, interoffice memos, and transcripts of story conferences. And in many cases, all of that is available in the studio vaults, together with the dates of composition or copying.

Unfortunately, the majority of screenplay publishers do not indicate which draft of the script they are printing and are careless about attributing authorship. The fact that a writer's name appears on the cover of a particular draft does not necessarily mean that he or she wrote *that* draft, and one might have to get into the studio's payroll files to find out the dates on which that writer was actually working on that property and then correlate those dates with the dates on the cover and on the "Changes" pages. Finally, many publishers insist on rearranging the screenplay into the more readable format of a play. Clearly it is better for the reader to have access to a facsimile of an original document and to be offered a well-informed choice between a screenplay and a cutting continuity.

Description and Dialogue. Description is kept to a minimum in a screenplay. Atmospheric details are included as guides to the director, the cinematographer, the production designer, and the costume designer, and details of performance are outlined for the actor, but none of this is written to enrich the experience of the reader. The screenplay has no "gentle reader"; it is not meant to be read by the fireside but is a working blueprint for a specific production.

Screen dialogue typically cannot be as long-winded as it sometimes is in published fiction. This is not to say that it must be simpleminded, but there is a distinct industry and audience preference for the short sentence. Unlike a play, in which language is usually the primary vehicle of communication, a movie is more visually oriented, and a line of dialogue may come into its fullest meaning because of its visual context (like Michael Corleone's "I do renounce them"). But that does not mean that dialogue makes only a minor contribution to a theatrical motion picture.

On the contrary, some of our fondest memories of the movies are memories of dialogue. "They got me!" is pure movie dialogue. When Marlowe (Bogart) is about to shoot Canino (Bob Steele) in Hawks's *The Big Sleep* (1946), he stands up from behind a car and says — with absolute menace — the simple words, "Over here, Canino." Nobody forgets that.

Dialogue is sometimes attacked as "literary" when it does not play well on the screen, though it might read perfectly well on the page. As a pejorative term, "literary" means that something "sounds like literature," as many of Ingmar Bergman's screenplays do. Nevertheless there is an important difference between the "literary" and the "literate."

A literate screenplay is carefully written and intelligently structured. Behind it one senses an artist who respects words and knows how to use them effectively. Such literacy has nothing to do with the level of education of the characters. There are hordes of perfectly stupid scripts about the rich and well educated, just as there are brilliantly written scripts about the illiterate and underprivileged. Literacy reflects back on the writer, not on the subject.

Preston Sturges's screenplays presuppose an intelligent audience, as in that wonderful moment in *Sullivan's Travels* (1941) when a genteel ruffian, driving a studio van, explains to his passengers the meaning of "paraphrase." To indicate just how scared some Hollywood people can be of words like "paraphrase," consider the American release title of John Mackenzie's *Beyond the Limit* (1983), which was adapted from Graham Greene's novel *The Honorary Consul.* Paramount conducted a survey and found that most Americans (whom did they ask?) did not know the meaning of "consul," and so they came up with that energetic but basically irrelevant title. The same kind of market research can prompt memos that encourage writers to keep their dialogue direct and their vocabulary simple. There is, of course, nothing wrong with the simple and direct, and no reason that simple words cannot communicate complex matters. In *Queen Christina*, when the adviser urges Christina to marry so that she will not "die an old maid," she replies, "I shall die — a bachelor!"

At the other extreme is the outright illiterate script. This may be written by a capable author who hates the project to which he or she has been assigned, but it is more often true that the writer is simply incompetent. In the first "all-talking picture," Bryan Foy's *Lights of New York* (1928), there is a scene in which a scorned woman tells her wandering lover, "You think you can take any chicken you want and throw me back in the deck!" One of the all-time awful scripts was written by Ed Wood, Jr., for his legendarily bad film, *Plan 9 from Outer Space* (1959). (Jeff: "I saw a flying saucer." Paula: "Saucer? You mean the kind from up there?" Jeff: "Yeah — or its counterpart.") Wood was the unhappy king of the "they'll never notice" school of filmmaking, but the problem, of course, is that people do notice.

Script Doctoring. It often happens that a writer leaves his or her stamp on a work, whether or not he or she emerges as a full-fledged auteur. (Auteurists may note here that Ed Wood fits the definition of auteur just as much as do Godard, Sirk, Kurosawa, Lucas, Allen, and Antonioni. There is no necessary correlation between the personal controlling of a work and its ultimate quality.) This presence may be felt even when the writer has worked on only a few pages of the script. Near the end of *The Godfather* there is a scene between Vito and Michael in which Vito explains his long-term strategy of wanting to rear a "Senator Corleone, Governor Corleone . . ." That scene was written by Robert Towne, who also wrote Roman Polanski's *Chinatown* (1974). Even though he is not listed in *The Godfather*'s credits, Towne's personal style is evident in the tone and gentle control of that scene, and its contribution to the finished product is significant.

Towne's contribution to *The Godfather* is an example of "script doctoring." A **script doctor** is a writer called in to revise part or all of a script written by others. His or her job is to tinker with the patient in the hope of effecting a cure. A script may pass through the hands of many writers before it is ready to be produced, and even the revised final is likely to be modified by the director and the actors while the picture is being shot. The editor, too, may affect the "script" by deleting a line or a speech that turned out not to play well, and the decisions that follow previews may entirely change the outcome of a story. Screen credits do not generally reflect all these complexities; they attribute authorship to the *principal* screenwriter and his or her immediate sources (for example, "Screenplay by Joanna Smith, based on an original story by Harriet Smith" or "based on the novel by Remington Smith").

The Writer's Credit. The surest way for a writer to protect his or her property is to work through an agent. Studios are extremely wary of "direct submissions" — ideas or scripts brought to the studio for consideration without the help of an agent — because of the danger that the work may not be original with its proposer or may closely resemble a concept on which the studio is already working. When making a direct submission, the writer must sign a release form; this legal document protects the studio from a lawsuit in case it should happen to release a picture that happens to resemble this property. The writer who signs such a form must trust the people with whom he or she is dealing, or must *want* to trust them. As further protection, the writer may register the script with the Writers Guild of America West (WGAw), which keeps a work sealed and on file until it can be opened in a courtroom.

Whether or not the work is registered in this manner, a member of the Writers Guild can ask the guild to arbitrate in cases of disputed authorship. The guild will examine all of the preliminary and final drafts of a screenplay and will determine whose documented contributions were the most significant, the majority of which author's dialogue ended up on screen, and therefore who is to receive screen credit. **Screen credit** means a head or tail credit, part of the released film, that officially and publicly recognizes that a certain person did a certain job.

Part of the fun of researching film history is tracking down **uncredited** contributions, like Towne's to *The Godfather*. It can be just as interesting to discover that a credited artist did not, in fact, do the work for which he or she received screen credit or did work that did not end up on the screen. Raymond Chandler was credited as the principal screenwriter for *Strangers on a Train*, but almost none of his actual writing was used, and very few of his ideas.

There are also cases in which a writer asks that his or her name not be credited because the finished product has somehow failed to measure up. Towne asked that his contributions to Hugh Hudson's *Greystoke* (1984) be credited to his dog, P. H. Vazak. Towne had written and developed *Greystoke*, had planned to direct it, and had then lost it — as an attached asset — during financial hassles over the completion of *Personal Best* (1982), which he had written and directed. The rewritten script of *Greystoke* did not please him, and the film was not directed as he would have directed it, and so he preferred not to take the credit in his own name. At the other extreme are the many victims of the Blacklist (1947–1960) who could sneak their work into production only under pseudonyms. Dalton Trumbo won an Academy Award for the screenplay of Irving Rapper's *The Brave One* (1956) under the name of Robert Rich, and the Academy is still divided over whether the voting members made a daring political gesture or simply did not realize for whom they were voting.

What has been said about writers' credits here applies to most screen credits. The conclusion to draw from all of this is that screen credits cannot always be trusted, although they are certainly useful up to a point. Whether you love or hate some aspect of a film, it is wise not to be too quick to praise or blame the credited artist.

The screenwriter knows — or will rapidly learn — that he or she does not have substantial control over what will happen to the script after it has been sold. Nevertheless the key to the screenwriter's job is to do the best work of which she or he is capable, knowing that it may not be used. Whether or not the released picture has integrity, the writer and the original screenplay must.

Agents and Story Editors

Let us assume that the writer has completed an original screenplay and wants it to be made into a movie. The script will have to be sold to a studio or to an independent producer, and that means that it will have to be read. In the high-pressure world of the industry, it is hard to find time to read anything besides memos and the trade publications, let alone to sit down with a pile of screenplays and to give each the careful reading that it might inherently merit. Many producers prefer to be told a story out loud, or to pay someone to read the script and draw up a synopsis and an evaluation. If a property looks appealing to the producer's reader and sounds good when presented orally (**pitched**, with the producer in the role of batter), the producer may read the actual script.

Preliminary Evaluations. The principal job of an **agent** is to convince a producer, executive, or other potential buyer (for purposes of discussion, simply "the producer") that a property is worth an investment of time and money. The agent, although an interested party (because the agent takes a commission from the sale), is presumed to be a reliable judge of talent and quality in general and to be familiar with the interests and priorities of the producer and the current marketplace. The producer recognizes that the agent would not waste time on a hopeless property. The agent selects a script — or a writer, an actor, a cinematographer, or a director — out of a vast number of alternates and determines that it, he, or she is worth "pushing." If the screenwriter's agent manages to interest the producer sufficiently, the producer will then refer the script to a story editor or a private consultant — or will perhaps option or buy it.

A studio has a **story department**, whose job is to evaluate official submissions and to search the bookstores and newspapers for material that can be developed into pictures. The head of the story department may alert a producer to a submitted property — or to a potential property worth seeking out someone to develop — or else the producer may ask the story department to help evaluate a property of which he or she is already aware. Typically the head of the story department will assign the project to a **story editor**, who will, in turn, assign it to a **reader**. The story editor evaluates the reader's report and turns the whole file back to the department head, who passes it along to the producer and keeps a copy for the studio files.

Whereas the reader must write a precise, nonjudgmental synopsis and a short, well-reasoned summary evaluation of a property — to help the producer see "what kind of a picture could be made out of this" — producers and agents tend to make up their minds judiciously and then to indulge in sheer hyperbole ("hype"). An agent trying to sell a property will let the prospective buyer know, in no uncertain terms, that this is the next *Gone With the Wind* even if it is a corker about a hypochondriacal meteorologist. The producer, trying to raise money from a bank or to obtain backing from a studio, will do the same or worse. Whether or not it is sincerely felt, absolute enthusiasm is the driving force that gets a picture into production and release. There is nothing more important, nothing that is more likely to turn out so well for all concerned, than *Revenge of the Weatherman.*

Getting an Agent. But we have leapt over an important and frustrating step. How does the writer get an agent? If the quest is unsuccessful, the writer may have to submit the script to a story editor without the cloak of hype, sign a release form, and sit by the phone for months. Trying to get the attention of a major studio when you have no previous important sales can be like trying to shake hands with a hummingbird. But it can be even *more* difficult to get the attention of an agent.

Agents typically take on only as many clients as they can promote in the limited amount of time available in the business week. There are small agencies that maintain a short list of clients to whom they can devote careful attention, and large agencies that have many clients. The larger, less "personal" agency is, however, the one most likely to be consulted and immediately trusted by the producer, and this is a trade-off that the client must consider when selecting a representative. And the more powerful the agency, the more fortified is its switchboard against unsolicited calls from prospective clients.

The telephone is the first line of defense against crackpots, starry-eyed self-promoters, and people the agent has never heard of before. Hollywood runs on what I have decided to call "the law of phones": important people place calls, and lucky people get them. The person who places a call, presumably a powerful figure who is going to make some kind of offer, never waits; instead, secretaries place their calls and put the recipient on hold. One of the best understood rules for survival in Hollywood is simply to be there when the phone rings. To attempt to return such a call, should it be missed, may be to start from scratch. When the caller is not well known, many agents and executives either refuse to take the call or have their secretaries pretend that it will be returned.

Many writers complete scores of scripts before ever getting an agent. It often takes an agent to make a sale, and one usually needs a previous sale in order to interest an agent. Although it might take years for a property to attract any attention, once things start to move, they move *fast.* One may have given up on a script and become resigned to a career as a short-order cook, only to find that one has two hours to catch a flight to Hollywood.

But to return to our ideally simplified scenario: should the agent like the property, a contract will be drawn up between the artist and the agency. The agent needs to feel that the artist is capable of doing more work of at least the quality of the property under immediate submission. The agent then becomes a lobbyist for the client, mixing with the right people at parties, embarking on a strategic telephone campaign, and eventually submitting the property to a studio or other potential buyer. If the work sells, the agent takes a commission and helps in the drafting of the deal, much as a real estate agent would.

The Deal. A writer without an established reputation or an agent usually receives only the minimum payment on the WGAw scale (as of 1984–1985, $21,510 for a screenplay, including the treatment, plus $3,075 if the story is original with the writer). A well-represented screenwriter with solid professional credits (a successful "track record") may be paid a great deal more — perhaps as much as half a million dollars, plus a share in the profits of the picture. A more standard payment is 5 percent of the picture's proposed budget.

A deal has a "front end" and a "back end." At the front end — that is, when the deal is signed — one is paid a certain amount of money; the front end fee is "a bird in the hand." Some people contract for less money up front in exchange for profit participation, a percentage of the picture's eventual revenues — in other words, the "birds in the bush." The less one takes from the front end, the more one may be entitled to at the back end. Such gambles are undertaken by independent producers as well as by writers, directors, major stars, and other "elements." By deferring salary, one becomes, in effect, a sponsor of the picture and a patron of its budget. The producer who provides a studio or a releasing company with a nearly completed picture takes more of the risk and accordingly reserves a greater share from the back end of the deal.

An author may also be contracted to write — or, should it be written by someone else, to share in the profits of — a novel whose publication may coincide with the picture's release. Such books are **tie-ins**: products that are merchandised along with the movie. Other tie-ins include toys, sweatshirts, games, and soundtrack albums. To identify the tie-in as an officially related product, it is crucial that the manufacturer secure rights to the artwork associated with the picture. Printed in a certain familiar manner, *Raiders of the Lost Ark* is a trademark. If you decided to write an original novel about the *Star Trek* characters, you would have to secure Paramount's permission; for that novel to sell, it would be essential to have a picture of the Enterprise on the cover and to set the title as viewers are accustomed to seeing it on TV or in the ads for the *Star Trek* movies.

Such deals are also drawn up when no screenplay yet exists. When a novel is sold to a publisher, such subsidiary rights as motion picture and TV adaptations are often reserved to the writer or are left open for future negotiations. A novel may be shown to agents and producers while still in manuscript, and should it be deemed "movie material," the rights may be optioned or even purchased outright before the book is published. Editions of the book may then be coordinated with the release date of the picture (hardcover a year before release; paperback just after release). A package deal may be drawn up, binding a producer, an actor or director, and the literary property. Then a writer may be called in to draft a screenplay. or the original writer may be given first crack at an adaptation. Although many movies begin their histories as literary properties, there are also books that begin as screenplays.

This is obviously true of tie-ins, which are rarely worth reading, but it is more relevant to note that John Steinbeck wrote *The Pearl* as a script for Emilio Fernandez's 1946 movie before expanding it into a short novel.

A property may be sold at this juncture or may simply be optioned. As previously explained, an option gives the prospective buyer the exclusive right to decide to make a movie from that original work. A typical option period lasts six months or a year. During that period, the buyer can **exercise the option** by buying the movie rights; this usually happens only when development is well advanced and the property is likely to be put into production. An option may also be renewed — rarely more than once — and some writers are actually able to support themselves on option money alone.

Once the property has been optioned or sold, the script continues to be tinkered with in **story conferences**, where the writer(s), director, producer, and others kick around some of the problems involved in the script and suggest alternatives. As ideas emerge from these story conferences, writers are assigned to draft a scene or even an entirely new script that incorporates those ideas. These conferences usually work out for the best when they are simply between the director and the writer (and the director can receive a writing credit for this collaboration). When evaluating the results of such development, it is well to remember the old joke that a camel is a horse designed by a committee — and also that a camel can survive under many conditions that would kill a horse.

The Producer, the Studio, and the Money

A movie budget form is divided by a very significant **line**. It separates costs related to the administrative and "creative" personnel (**above-the-line**) from those related to the "technical" personnel and to the logistics, materials, and maintenance required for the production (**below-the-line**). In our orchestral example the conductor and his health insurance would be above-the-line, and the rental of the hall would be below-the-line. The deals just discussed involve above-the-line personnel. With the exception of studio overhead and a catchall category called "other charges," above- and below-the-line expenses constitute the entire cost of making a film. Negotiating a budget is an extremely important facet of film production, and each element, category, and expense is scrutinized in its turn.

At first, above-the-line costs are subject to negotiation while those below-the-line are computed on a relatively fixed basis: it just costs a certain amount to buy and process filmstock, to rent costumes and equipment, and to shoot with a full crew for a certain number of days. On the other hand, once a deal has been signed, those above-the-line figures become fixed commitments, and below-the-line costs begin to look relatively flexible. When above-the-line costs are fixed and below-the-line costs go over budget, both the producer and the production are in serious trouble.

The Producer. Whereas the writer and director are most concerned with the specific design of a picture, the essential job of the producer is to see that the film actually gets *made* — in other words, that the product is produced. Whether he or she uses personal funds, administers studio monies, or takes out a loan, the producer is the one who provides the money to the director and other filmmakers.

A picture can be decisively affected by the amount of money available, and to whom. If millions of dollars can be committed to above-the-line costs, it may be possible to secure the services of a major director, to buy an expensive literary property, and to sign up a bankable star and a well-known supporting cast. (Something is considered **bankable** if a lender feels comfortable banking on it — that is, underwriting a project that includes that element — on the basis of previous performance.) If a great deal of money can be spent below-the-line, the picture is liable to have high **production values**: fancy costumes and sets, for example, or elaborate special effects.

The producer has to juggle such decisions as this one: it might cost as much to sign Stallone (above-the-line) as to design and shoot the actual picture (below-the-line). But Stallone's presence may make the picture easier to finance and ultimately more successful at the box office; therefore it might be a sound financial decision to allocate half the picture's budget to a single actor. It is when thinking about the marketplace and the previous performance of the major elements of a deal that the producer makes practical decisions that can rigorously determine the look and import of the finished product.

Once determined, a budget must be adhered to, and the most important consideration in meeting a budget is how closely the production keeps to the schedule. On a large-budget picture, an *hour* of shooting can easily cost $10,000. (*The Shining* cost $24 to write — the cost of paper, ribbons, and postage — and $19 million to film.) The budget imposes limits that can themselves prompt creativity. Terry Gilliam and Terry Jones's *Monty Python and the Holy Grail* (1974), for example, was completed for less than $500,000. "We never had the money to do things properly," Gilliam told a college audience, "so we had to be clever." The coconut shells clopped by the squires for the skipping knights — a charming and silly device that for many people encapsulates the virtues of that movie — were thought up simply because the production could not afford any horses.

Executive and Line Producers. In general, the role of producer involves both creative input and financial management. The producer hires the filmmakers, provides them with what they need, and obviously has a say in how the money will be spent and to what end. In most cases the producer's responsibilities are divided among several people, each of whom has a different title. To complicate matters, these titles are not consistently applied. "Line producer" is a specific job, but the line producer on a film may end up being credited as "executive producer," and either of them may be credited as "associate producer." For purposes of discussion, we are going to use "line" and "executive" producer as if the terms were consistently applied.

The **producer** is the person who holds the reins from development through release and who retains or can sell title to the picture. On a studio picture, the producer is hired as a temporary employee (and the studio, as production company, owns the picture). The independent producer may never enter a studio's gates or else may sell a property to a studio once it has been developed or even completed (in which case the studio releases the picture under its own logo: **negative pick-up**). In either case, the producer is usually flanked by an executive producer and a line producer.

The **executive producer**, who is not a studio executive, may well be the person who put together the original deal or who put up most of the money. The executive producer may secure the rights to a property, option the services of a star or director, and then make a deal with a studio or with another producer who will actually see that the picture goes further into development. Although "executive producer" is often an honorary title, reflecting a task that has been completed during the first stages of development, there are many executive producers (like George Lucas) who closely oversee the progress of a picture and may even supervise the line producer.

The **line producer** is directly responsible for keeping track of costs, approving expenditures, and making sure that the picture stays on schedule. (In the simplest of situations, the producer acts as line producer.) The **unit production manager** (also called the **unit manager** or the **production manager** — see the glossary), who acts as below-the-line producer, reports directly to the line producer (unless both are the same person), handles the payroll, and usually does the dirty work of collecting receipts and signing purchase orders. The production manager — often a former assistant director, whereas the executive producer may be a former agent — must know a great deal about the practical realities of moviemaking. The director usually retains creative control, but only within the fiscal framework determined by the producer and administered by the line producer. The director, the line producer, and — on the firing line — the production manager have to sweat out below-the-line costs as production proceeds and new, expensive ideas or problems arise.

Script Breakdown. The first major job of the line producer is to "break down" the script and draw up a budget. **Script breakdown** takes place in two major stages. The first is the **budget breakdown**, which happens during development, and the second is the **shot breakdown**, which takes place during pre-production.

To do a budget breakdown, the line producer — working with

an experienced accountant or **estimator** — reads through the script to identify its major production elements: the cast, the extras, the exterior locations, the interiors, the action props, and the wardrobe. Having identified these items, they carefully estimate how much they will cost. A script may call, for example, for authentic exteriors to be shot on location in Rome. That might well involve shipping the whole crew off to Italy, putting them up in hotels, allowing per diem expenses, renting equipment, and paying fees for the use of specific locations, not to mention transoceanic phone calls. If all that looks too expensive, it is the line producer's responsibility to alert the producer to the problem, and perhaps they will agree that a backlot exterior could be made to look adequately Roman.

The shot breakdown, which is usually done by the production manager and first assistant director, entails dividing the script into numbered units and deciding in what order they will be shot. On **breakdown sheets** they note those elements that will have to be scheduled and paid for in order to shoot that scene: cast, extras, stunt doubles, set and action props, makeup, wardrobe, process photography, and so on. For each scene the key information from the scene header ("EXT. BEACH–DAWN"), together with that from the breakdown sheet, is then transferred to a strip of heavy paper. These color-coded strips are then arranged in their proposed shooting order in a shallow wooden box called a **production board.** The production board is the shooting plan of the picture, and there is no way to overestimate its importance to a well-run production. As an exercise, look back at the *Godfather* baptism and identify its production requirements.

Production Executives. A studio usually has a "business affairs" or "production group" unit, consisting primarily of executives and their staffs. It is these executives who make the crucial decisions about which properties will be developed, which of those will actually go into production, and when and in what form a completed picture will (or will not) be released. These people are in business. They *need* to know more about marketing and story considerations than about film aesthetics; it is a matter of survival for them to pay more attention to receipts than to reviews.

When a script has been completed, the production executives have a meeting. They evaluate the script and either reject it or temporarily approve it. Final approval may be conditional on the results of the budget breakdown, or on augmenting the "package." Signing a top director or star, in industry parlance, "puts it over the top and makes it a 'go' picture."

At this point the person who originated the concept or brought the property to the studio's attention may be hired by the studio as executive producer. Because this person may never have been on a set, the studio protects its investment by hiring a line producer. (Conversely, executive supervision of a line producer may be in order.) The typical executive producer may have more than one project in development or production at any given time, whereas the line producer concentrates on a single project.

As the picture is made, its progress is supervised by the line producer and by the studio executives. Strictly speaking, everyone on a studio project is employed by the studio. Although the director often demands the right to have the film released as edited under his or her supervision — called the right of **final cut** — in almost all cases the right of final cut rests with the studio. The director usually has 6 to 10 weeks after the completion of principal photography in which to edit the movie, and this **first cut** is then shown to the executives. They offer their comments and may send the director back to supervise a second cut. Eventually the **director's cut** is previewed on the lot or in a regular theater, and the comments of the audiences are carefully studied. In many cases the studio then insists on another cut, and if they approve the results, that is the version that will be released, whether the director likes it or not.

A studio typically is run by two or three top executives who are answerable to a board of directors. In some countries, studios are subject, further, to governmental supervision (from subvention to censorship); in America, many of them are owned by huge conglomerates. As in most major corporations, there is considerable competition for the services of successful studio executives, who typically move from one top position to another.

In addition to studios and independent producers, there are many independent production companies, and these are usually owned by private individuals. A company may be formed for the production of a single picture, or it may be in for the long haul. Zoetrope Studios, one of the most prestigious of such relatively small companies, is owned by Coppola and has its offices in San Francisco. (It no longer has Hollywood studio facilities.) Zoetrope produces Coppola's films (like *One from the Heart* [1982]) or licenses his services to other producing entities (*The Cotton Club* [1984] was produced by Robert Evans and others for Paramount). Zoetrope also makes negative pick-up deals with independent producers, as they did for Godfrey Reggio's *Koyaanisqatsi* (1983). Sometimes it picks up a film that is ready for release, but just as often it has to advance the money to complete a project. This money can be raised on the promise that the film *will* be completed; in other words, it is possible to borrow against the value of the film before it is even made. Zoetrope can sell foreign distribution rights in advance, and it can also borrow from a lender against other anticipated distribution revenues.

More About Money. What Zoetrope has to go through is representative of what nearly any producer, or even a major studio, must confront early in the development of a picture. One way or another, the money must be raised. A group of independent investors or a financial institution — for purposes of discussion, call it a bank — must be convinced that a property is likely to prove a sound investment. The bankers carefully study the screenplay, the credentials of the proposed above-the-line personnel, the revenues of similar pictures, and especially the budget before recommending for or against the deal.

The bank will insist that its investment be secured, just as a home mortgage loan is secured by the title to the house. Because there is no picture at this stage, security becomes a matter of paper promises. Say that the producer has presold the domestic and foreign distribution rights and has also arranged for the picture to be broadcast on cable and then network TV. All this money will come in only when the picture has been released. The producer asks for a loan on the strength of all these contracts. In the simplest case the bank will advance about 90 percent of the face value of the contracts, using the discounted notes as security. When the picture is completed and the distributors have honored their agreements, the bank will be reimbursed at the notes' full value, which is how the bank earns its interest. The obvious problem is that the picture may never be finished. A star may die in the middle of production, the director may exhaust the budget during the first weeks of shooting, or the underlying literary rights may suddenly prove not to have belonged to the person who sold them to the producer in the first place. The way the bank protects its investment plays an important role in film production.

The bank will insist that the producer take out "errors and omissions" insurance, which will cover any mistakes in the package deal — like an unforeseen conflict over literary rights. The bank will also insist that someone be responsible for cost overruns — a "standby investor" — and may further demand that the producer sign a contract with a penalty structure (so that if a picture goes $100,000 over budget, $200,000 will be deducted from the producer's share of the revenues before the "profit level" or break-even line is determined to have been reached).

Most significantly, the bank will insist on a **completion guarantee** (also called a **completion bond**) from an independent company whose job is to guarantee that the picture *will* be finished. The guarantor's fee is usually 6 percent of the proposed budget. Should it prove absolutely impossible to complete production, the completion guarantor will reimburse the bank's investment. Because that would be financially disastrous for the guarantor, in most cases he or she actually plays a role in the production of the film, keeping tabs on the director and the production manager and making sure that the picture does stay on schedule. The screenplay, at this point, is a legal document, and its terms (what is to be shot) are binding.

Should the picture go over budget in spite of all this planning — and it often does — the standby investor or the completion guarantor is called upon to come up with more money. In that case, one or the other of them may well exercise "takeover rights" — in other words, take over the picture and finish it. In such an event, the vital consideration is not to change the story or to experiment with a new creative approach but to make sure that there is a releasable property of some sort.

Bankers rarely share in the profits of a picture. Their concern is to recoup their original investment at an agreed-upon rate of interest. A group of independent investors, however, is often entitled to profit participation.

The Producer's Job. With the deal completed and funds available, the producer adopts the characteristic role of middleman between the bank account and the creative personnel. If a studio is involved, the producer acts as the link with the studio. During development, the producer is primarily responsible for working with the writers, signing up talent, and, of course, raising money. From that point on, the producer is entitled to supervise every single aspect of production, from giving the director advice to refusing to pay for a costume decorated with real emeralds when fake emeralds would look just as convincing. The producer can hire and fire anybody at any stage — subject to certain guild and union agreements — and often does exercise that right. Every member of the production team reports to the producer or to his or her designated representative (normally the production manager), from the director to the draper. For this reason, directors like Chaplin and Hawks have often preferred to act as their own producers.

The producer must have a way with people, the personal skills to be able to get the artists to do what he or she wants them to do, yet also leave them free to do their best creative work. Often this leads to a friendly working antagonism. Just as a producer can rein in a director who needs hard limits, a director can lead a producer to see the wisdom of spending more money than anticipated on a particular scene.

In summary, the producer's job is to be alert for properties that may merit development, to see the project through to its completion, to arrange for the picture's distribution (usually through a studio or an independent distribution company), and to make lots of money. As the one who brings together the people who will pay for a film and those who will actually make it, the producer has the opportunity to leave his or her "personal" stamp on a work: by selecting the property to be produced, determining the limits of the budget, giving advice, and hiring the writers, director, actors, director of photography, crews, and editors who will realize the project on film.

The Legal Department

Any producer needs access to the services of a lawyer. There can be as many contracts signed during the planning and making of a movie as during the bulldozing of a downtown area to erect a shopping mall. The producer may have a personal lawyer skilled in entertainment law (a branch of corporate, not criminal, law), but for purposes of discussion it is simpler to examine the functions of a studio's legal department.

The legal department is effectively a law firm with one client (the studio). Although the legal department may be involved with a film for many years after release (licensing videocassettes, for example, or the use of stills in film textbooks), its job begins during development just as does that of the producer.

The stages of production and distribution have very specific legal meanings. Where the lawyers and the accountants are concerned, each stage must be clearly delimited so that the studio can keep track of how many projects it has at each stage, and so that costs can be charged to the proper accounts. The following are the official divisions among all these stages:

I. Production
   A. Development. Starts with the hiring of a writer.
   B. Pre-production. Starts when a developed property is approved for production and a "start date" is set for the picture.
   C. Production. Starts with the commencement of principal photography.
   D. Post-production. Starts with the conclusion of principal photography.
II. Distribution. Starts with the delivery of the **answer print** (the first acceptable copy of the picture in its final form).

The finished picture, for legal and accounting purposes, is often referred to as the **negative**. All of the money spent to create the film, from development through post-production (not the cost of making and distributing prints, which is charged to distribution), is the film's **negative cost**. Distribution also has an unofficial second phase, in which the picture has been withdrawn from active circulation but is still available for re-release. A movie that is entirely "out of distribution" may become a collector's item.

Development and Pre-production. Where development officially begins, then, is in the legal department and with the writer's contract. Once the producers have selected a writer and have negotiated a contract according to its terms, the lawyers evaluate and sometimes renegotiate that contract according to its legal implications. (When a prepublished work is involved, for example, they may have to negotiate how many words can be quoted from the original source in any publicity.) Either when the writer is hired or shortly afterward, contracts are also drawn up for the hiring of a producer — and sometimes a director — to supervise the writing. All of these contracts include options. The writer will be paid in stages, as various drafts are delivered and approved, and may not advance to a further draft unless these earlier submissions measure up. The studio is not committed to making the picture at this point, only to covering the preliminary costs of development. Should the project go into turnaround, another studio will be given an opportunity to reimburse those costs and make the picture.

Once a satisfactory script has been approved for production, the director (if not previously signed) and the major actors are hired, and all options are picked up. The director's contract may address the issue of who will have final cut. At this point there will be fully negotiated contracts for the executive and line producers, the director, and the principal players. The legal department does not usually handle "day-player agreements" (contracts for those who will act for a week or less), which are done on preprinted or form contracts and are handled by the production staff.

Research. Then the legal department sends the approved script out for research. This is not the sort handled by the studio's research department (to be discussed in the next section) but involves purely legal and technical matters. A research consultant or firm reads through the script for potential legal problems. They check the names in the script against the names of real people, corporations, and locales. They check whether the filmmakers have used a quotation from something for which permission will be required, whether a given piece of music requires clearance, and even whether the script is accurate or anachronistic. They send their report back to the legal department, where a red star or a similar sign is put beside each truly problematic notation. The report is then forwarded to the producer.

The producer and his or her staff are expected to do something about each of these problems, but red-starred items absolutely have to be resolved, usually by a change in the script. Here are some typical problems. The song "Happy Birthday to You" is not in the public domain, believe it or not, and you have to get a license to use it in a movie. Researching a film about a fictional character named Robert Merriwell who controls the mob in Detroit, a researcher may find that there is a real Robert Merriwell living in Detroit. When there is someone with the exact name of a proposed character, living in the exact city in which the action is to take place, that name is legally "not clear." The lawyers then have to convince the producer to change the name or the city. If a photograph is to be reproduced in the film, it will have to be cleared both with the photographer and with the person whose picture was taken. And if a medical script has been written by someone who is more familiar with car repair than with open-heart surgery, many of the medical terms and procedures may have to be corrected.

Production and Post-production. During production, the legal department handles location agreements and other shooting permits. It also acts as the buffer between the filmmakers and their various guilds and unions. The director cannot begin work on a picture until the legal department has sent a memo to the Directors Guild, advising them of his employment and salary. The legal department is responsible for knowing all the regulations of the

Directors, Writers, and Screen Actors Guilds (the DGA, WGA, and SAG, respectively) and for making sure that the producers observe them. These rules also apply during distribution; for example, there are very specific directions concerning the relative sizes and positioning of the title of the film and the names of the director, the writer, and the principal actors in printed advertisements and on billboards.

When the music and other items requiring legal permission have been selected and cleared, a contract is drawn up so that a composer can be hired; this usually happens early in post-production. Other post-production duties may include helping to resolve a dispute over final cut, particularly with reference to the director's contract.

Titles and Credits. Much post-production legal work is related to the title of the film and its credits. The title of (not to) the film has to be cleared. Titles are not protected by copyright. Most American production companies subscribe to the Title Registration Bureau of the Motion Picture Producers Association (MPPA). The bureau will award "permanent protection" — the exclusive right to use a given title — should the studio copyright an adaptation under the same title as the copyrighted original work (for example, *Gone With the Wind*). Beyond that, a company is allowed permanent protection on up to 250 original titles of its own choosing. (United Artists has nine registration companies and can therefore protect up to 2,250 original titles.) The first company to register a title has "priority" to that title; others who may want to use it will join a prioritized waiting list. Similar titles may be subject to binding arbitration. The title of any released film is protected for four years (renewable once); after that period the company has to decide whether that title will become one of its 250 permanently protected original titles.

The matter of credits can be even more complicated. At the completion of principal photography, the legal department sends the WGA a list of the proposed writing credits on the picture; these might be disputed and require arbitration. The other credits are usually submitted to the legal department by the producer and are evaluated "in-house." Each credit has to correspond with that person's contract. This can mean that a composer was hired as a composer, not as a music editor, and must be credited as a composer; or that a star must be listed above the title of the film because that was a condition in the original contract; or that someone is entitled to a shared or exclusive screen credit even if someone else completed the actual job. If an art director wants to be credited as production designer (a more prestigious title involving a major creative role in the designing of a picture), the lawyers will have to clear that with the Art Directors Guild.

The head screen credits — usually with each on a separate title-card — occur in a specified order, enforced by the guilds. After the releasing company, the prestige credits ("a film by . . ."), and the title of the picture come the names of the principal players not fortunate enough to have been listed above the title. The actors are ranked in clumps of descending prestige: (1) "starring,"; (2) "costarring"; (3) "featuring"; and (4) "with." After "with" may come the name of a famous star who is not the lead; this name is usually preceded by "and" and accompanied by "as" the name of the character. The head credits end with six principal production credits, which currently occur in this order: (1) editor; (2) art director or production designer; (3) director of photography; (4) writer; (5) producer; and (6) director. Occasionally there will be other production credits between the actors and these six — credits for music, for example, or casting — and these are usually included in the head titles as a special gesture, recognizing the importance of that person's contribution to the picture. Tail credits then account for all the important personnel not acknowledged at the start, usually including a reprise of the entire cast. When all of the credits except title and distributor are put at the end of a film, the director's name must appear first, and the producing credit cannot intervene between the directing and writing credits.

Keeping all of this in mind, the producer and the legal department agree on a final list of credits. This list is sent to the art department, which makes up the actual list to be photographed. When the list leaves the legal department, it contains no typos. That is not always the case when it leaves the art department, or when an intertitle, as part of the script, does not receive legal scrutiny. The opening narrative titles of Peter Hyams's *Outland* (1981), to give a glaring example, misspelled "principal" in letters two feet wide.

Distribution. Libel and slander problems, red-starred during the research phase, usually do not crop up this late in the game, but plagiarism suits may well arise once the picture is released, should a starving screenwriter notice the resemblance between that film and a script that he or she may have sent to that same studio. In such a case, the legal files on the underlying literary rights, any release forms, and all of the drafts of the script are readily available to the legal department.

Although true plagiarism is a rarity, piracy is not. As soon as the picture is released — or even as soon as the answer print is made — the studio must be on guard against its being illegally copied. In the first stages of distribution, the problem is not so much that of unauthorized 35mm prints as that of unauthorized videocassettes. MGM found that *The Pope of Greenwich Village* (1984, dir. Stuart Rosenberg) was in cassette before that picture was even released. And it has long been common for pirates and collectors to strike 16mm and 35mm copies of films for their own use or to buy used prints, particularly after the film has secured a critical reputation. Although it can readily and legitimately be argued that many important films would have been lost if collectors had not saved illegal prints of them, it is manifestly true that the pirating of a film that is currently in release is reprehensible, denying the filmmakers the money that they need to pay back their loans and the profits that they have legitimately earned.

In addition to all this, the legal department handles the contracts for all negative pick-up deals as well as a host of internal studio matters.

The "Go"

A studio may put 100 pictures into development in a given year. Out of those, perhaps ten will be given the go-ahead. Those ten or so lucky properties advance into pre-production, which begins with the setting of a production schedule. The other 90 scripts go into turnaround or sit on shelves, all dressed up with no place to go. Out of the ten that go into pre-production — most of which will be completed, barring wildly unforeseen circumstances — perhaps three will make back their negative and advertising costs, and one of those might become a big hit. A studio with three major hits in a single year would be doing extremely well. The big and intermediate hits pay for the losses incurred by the misses and allow the studio to stay in business. Once a property goes out of development, then, it is thought of as a potential hit, all of whose *anticipated* problems have been ironed out in advance.

Once it has been decided that a developed property will actually be filmed, the picture goes into pre-production. **Pre-production** involves all the tasks that must be completed before the actual shooting can begin. The most important of these are (1) casting; (2) location scouting; (3) preparing a final budget and shooting schedule; (4) research; (5) production design; (6) set construction; and (7) costume design.

Casting

To **cast** a picture is to select and hire its actors, from the principal players through the bit players, day players, and stunt doubles. Not all of this is done during pre-production. Principals may have been signed during development, and the casting of extras (background or "atmosphere people," usually with no lines) often happens during production. To get a rough idea of how many extras a big picture can involve, take a look at **Fig. 3-3**, which shows part of the "cast of thousands" as they reported for work on William Wyler's *Ben-Hur* (1959) at the Cinecittà Studios in Rome.

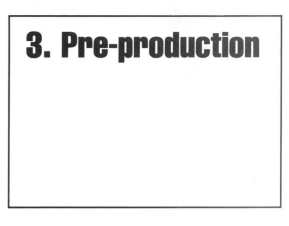

3. Pre-production

Figure 3-3

Major actors are often cast in the following manner. A script is brought to the attention of the actor's agent. The actor evaluates the role for which he or she is being considered and, if the judgment is positive, instructs the agent to negotiate a deal. Some stars will call for changes in the role at this point, and the producer, director, and writers will see to it that the role is revised to take advantage of the actor's particular talents and screen persona.

It can also happen that an actor will hear about a project and ask to be considered for a role. In some cases, the actor will be asked to take a **screen test**, in which a short film is made of the actor reading a scene in character. Looking over the screen tests for *Gone With the Wind*, it is fascinating to see how Hattie McDaniel and Butterfly McQueen had their roles already in hand. They appeared in the tests just as they did in the movie, and their performances stand out from those of their competitors with the authority of the genuine characters.

Casting is such a big job that it is often turned over to a specialist — either a **casting director** or an agency. The casting personnel take a good look at the script and then decide which actors may be best for each of the roles. Casting agencies continually update their files, keeping track of which actors are available for work, which ones are "hot," and which are the most promising newcomers. It is the casting director's job to act as liaison between the abstractions created by the writer and the working actors who may be able to flesh out those roles. As an example of how greatly casting decisions can affect the finished product, consider how different *The African Queen* would have been if the leads had been played — as originally planned — not by Humphrey Bogart and Katharine Hepburn but by John Mills and Helen Hayes.

Location Scouting

A picture that is not shot on a sound stage or in a similarly controlled, artificial environment is said to be shot on **location**. This is not necessarily the location specified in the script, where the events are "really" supposed to be happening, though, of course, it can be. A location is simply an off-studio shooting site. **Location scouting** is the process of looking for a good place to shoot the film. Many pictures are shot both on and off location.

The practical side of location scouting is more difficult than it sounds. With the whole world to choose from, finding the best possible location can be as difficult as reaching into a sack of clear rhinestones and pulling out the one real diamond. A location might turn out not to look right, although in every other respect it will *be* right; one might head out to a genuine factory town, for instance, and then find that it is too clean for the look demanded by the script. Or a location might be perfect in every respect but subject to formidable local controls.

When Werner Herzog was getting ready to shoot his *Nosferatu* (1978), he settled on the city of Delft. One major sequence called for thousands of rats to run through the city streets and, in particular, across a town square. The city had only that year completed a formidable cleanup of the sewer system, getting *rid* of thousands of rats, and it proved very difficult for Herzog to convince them to go along with his plans. But the look Herzog demanded could be realized only in a city that had the specific look of Delft, and to confine the rats to special effects shots would have been unconvincing. Herzog eventually worked out a compromise with the town council, setting the rats loose but taking extraordinary precautions that they would not find their way into the sewer system.

It hardly needs to be pointed out how much the proper location can add to the look and the apparent authenticity of a picture. The makers of *Close Encounters* were probably as excited as Roy and Jillian to have found Devil's Tower in Wyoming. Renoir's *Grand Illusion* and *Rules of the Game* (1939) profited from careful location scouting, as the landscape itself is often a significant element in their mise-en-scène.

Like Renoir and Herzog, some filmmakers allow their ideas about the film to develop out of an interaction with the landscape. The location is chosen because it sets the scene, suits the characters, and augments the action — but it might also be chosen because of the quality of the light at a certain time of day or because it encourages a particular type of composition, letting the filmmakers work *with* the world.

Some films, like *Caligari,* call for a mise-en-scène that can be achieved only artificially. Others, like Michael Wadleigh's *Woodstock* (1970), demand to be shot on location. Just as the Italian neorealist films and many of the early works of the French New Wave adopted a deliberately nonstudio style and shot on location in the interest of greater verisimilitude and less artificiality, the makers of *Citizen Kane* made the deliberate stylistic decision to shoot *in* a studio in order to have complete control over the mise-en-scène.

Sometimes location scouting can itself be an amusing business. Both *1918* and *Places in the Heart* (1984) were shot in Waxahachie, Texas. When Robert Benton tried to lease a local house for the principal location in *Places in the Heart,* he found that it had just been leased by Horton and Lillian Foote for *1918*. And it was the perfect house for both their purposes, even if it was right in the middle of what Hollywood might consider nowhere. Benton, in any case, found another house.

The Final Budget and the Shooting Schedule

The Production Budget. The budget drawn up during development is continually refined during pre-production and adjusted, according to circumstances, during production. When thinking out the production budget, the line producer pays most attention to trimming below-the-line costs, because those above-the-line have already been locked up by contract or are unpredictable, like the number of people the director and the executive producer will want on their personal staffs.

The **production budget** itself is a form — the one with the line — and it is filled out by an estimator or by the line producer. It has entries for the picture's starting date, finishing date, and days in production; for its production number and working title; and for the names of its producer and director. Then come the above-the-line entries: story rights, scenario, producer, director, cast, and fringe benefits. Then comes the line and, below it, entries for extras, staff, art costs, set costs, set strike, light platforms, operating labor and materials, miniatures, cameras, production sound, electrical, special effects, set dressing, drapery, animals and action devices, wardrobe, makeup and hairdressing, process shooting, props, filmstock and processing, stills, transportation, tests, and location expense. All these are subtotaled as the costs of the total production period. Then come the post-production entries: music, post-production sound, special photographic effects, titles, filmstock and processing, projection, and editorial. "Other" covers rental charges, fees, unit publicity expenses, and "miscellaneous." Added to the previous subtotal, these give the total below-the-line expenses.

Onto these is added "overhead," which might be the 20 percent of a picture's budget that a studio typically charges for the use of its facilities. Above- and below-the-line subtotals are now added for a grand total: the budget, the anticipated cost. The form is updated to keep track of actual costs, and it must be signed by everyone from the estimator to the chairman of the board.

More on the Production Board. The approved budget passes into the hands of the production manager and the first assistant director (first A.D.). The latter prepares a "tear sheet," or breakdown sheet, for each numbered scene in the script, as described under "Script Breakdown." The sheet includes all of the cast members, special makeup and hairdressing, costumes, equipment, props, animals, production special effects, and production sound effects that will be required for the shooting of that scene. It also indicates how many script pages (and therefore approximately how many minutes of screen time) the scene lasts, relevant information about the location or sound stage where the scene will be shot, day or night or day-for-night, and a one-line synopsis of the action.

The information from each tear sheet is transferred to a colored cardboard **scene strip**. The strips are mounted in a wooden production board (or **breakdown board**), which is usually at least 5 feet long in order to accommodate the entire shooting schedule. Smaller folding versions of the production board, with space for perhaps a week's worth of scene strips, are designed to be porta-ble, and the first A.D. usually has one on hand at all times.

At the left edge of the board is a column with the names of the cast members, each of whom has been assigned a number. The color-coded strips are in the sequence in which they will be shot and are grouped into shooting days. It is at this stage that the crucial decisions are made about when to shoot what. An actor might be available only at night for a crucial three weeks, for in-stance, or completely unavailable until a month after the picture's start date, and the shooting schedule will have to be arranged ac-cordingly. Scenes taking place in the same location and with the same actors will normally be shot at the same time. The advantage of the scene strips and of the design of the production board itself is that the shooting order can easily be rearranged should prob-lems or opportunities crop up.

The production board is then submitted to, and usually modi-fied by, the production manager, the line producer, and the direc-tor. When completed to their satisfaction, the production board indicates how many scenes can be shot in each working day, which ones they will be, and how many days the picture will be in pro-duction. The approved board is then submitted to the studio ex-ecutives or to the financier/distributor. Should the money people decide that too many shooting days have been proposed, the board will have to be redone and resubmitted.

The Shooting Schedule. Once the board is approved, the actual **shooting schedule** is drawn up — usually by the first A.D. It spells out which scenes (that is, numbered units of action capable of being covered in a single take) will be shot on which specific days and reprises relevant information from the breakdown sheets, to-gether with the exact location where the scene will be shot. All of this information is later transferred to daily "call sheets," used only during production; they let each member of the cast and crew know when and where they have to show up for the next day's work, and they also include extremely detailed production infor-mation (see **Fig. 3-102**). As production itself proceeds, the direc-tor, the first A.D., the production manager, and the line producer continually revise the shooting schedule in order to keep ahead of such unanticipated developments as horrible weather or actors who suddenly decide that they can't work together.

Once all of this work has been done, it is fairly safe to begin spending money on production design, set construction, and costumes.

Research

In order to design the sets and costumes appropriately, it is nec-essary at this stage for the filmmakers to do some extra research. The function of a pre-production researcher, or of a studio research department, is to make sure that the details of the production are accurate and authentic.

Above her desk in the MGM/UA Research Department Bonnie Rothbart hung the sign, "Every question deserves an answer." Questions come into departments like hers from writers, costume designers, propmakers, art directors, and many others. A film might call for an 1872 French country picnic, for example, and it would be up to the research department to find out what kind of utensils and niceties would have been used on such an occasion, how the appropriate costumes would have looked, and which foods might have been brought along.

The makers of Barry Levinson's *The Natural* (1984) wanted to include a night game, and it became necessary to find out when night baseball was first played. They wanted to have the hero's picture on a Wheaties box and thus had to know whether Wheaties were being eaten during the mid-1930s and whether it was then the practice to print sports figures' pictures on the boxes. A call to the General Mills Archives netted pictures of Wheaties boxes from the 1930s and verification that that cereal was associated with sporting figures and health even at that time. The net result was that *The Natural* included a sports-related mention of Wheaties, but no picture of a box with the hero's picture on it. To design the emerald found in Robert Zemeckis's *Romancing the Stone* (1983), it was necessary to gather photographs of many emeralds and to be sure what shape an emerald crystal would take if it were as large as the filmmakers desired; all this research kept the prop from looking like a hunk of green glass.

It is part of the researcher's job to locate odd bits of information, such as the date when Lucky Strike cigarettes switched from a green pack to a white pack (1942). To answer such questions, a research department has access to thousands of books, catalogs, periodicals, and photos in its own collection as well as in other libraries and historical societies. MGM began putting together its research files in the 1920s, and they have been continually updated and enlarged. One old location file from the 1930s, for instance, contained a shot of a baseball stadium in 1935 that proved extremely useful to the makers of *The Natural*. Period films rely on extensive files of costumes and uniforms — how they were worn, by whom, and on which occasions.

When designing the look of *Pennies from Heaven* (1981), director Herbert Ross and production designer Ken Adam (who also designed *Dr. Strangelove, Barry Lyndon,* and most of the James Bond films) spent three or four months looking through films of the 1930s, books on art and architecture, and period photographs. Their careful work was sometimes foregrounded in that film — as when they gave a scene in a diner at night the exact look of Edward Hopper's painting *Nighthawk* — but in most cases the research found more subtle expressions.

Researchers also work with writers during the development of a preliminary screenplay. As opposed to the **pictorial research** described above, this is **background research**. A writer doing a script about a rock singer in the 1950s and 1960s could ask the researcher to provide a list of all the historical events of the period likely to have affected that character, together with a list of all the songs that were most popular during each year that the story would cover. Or a writer who has been assigned a project about a Wonder Woman figure might request pictures from and synopses of every previous treatment of a comic-strip heroine, not only in films but in the comic books themselves.

It is common for research to begin early in pre-production, but it sometimes takes place even during production. When Peter Weir's *Witness* (1985) was being shot in Pennsylvania, a local surgeon, G. Gary Kirchner, was called in as an adviser. The script called for the hero to get shot in the abdomen, not to realize right away that he has been wounded, and then to drive himself and two other characters a distance of 65 miles. The surgeon had to figure out what kind of belly wound would make all that possible and still leave it credible that the hero would survive under primitive medical care. Kirchner advised the makeup people on how the wound would look, how much it would bleed over the course of time, and how much the character would sweat. The actor, Harrison Ford, asked to be coached on how a man with such a wound would walk, sit, and drive. Eventually Kirchner convinced the filmmakers that the bullet would have to go through the character's side but *not* enter the abdominal cavity, and thus an outlandish plot development was realized as a relatively credible series of events.

Production Design

The **art director** is responsible for designing the sets and decor of a picture. The set decorator, the costume designer, the scenic artist, and the illustrator all report to the art director. A **production designer** is an art director who designs the "look" of an entire picture, making sure that the sets, props, and costumes work together to declare the nature of that film's world in purely visual terms. The production designer works closely with the director and the cinematographer and may ultimately prove as important as either of the other two, making creative decisions that will crucially affect the mise-en-scène. The difference between an art director and a production designer, then, is not so much a matter of their job descriptions as one of relative degrees of creative control. Most production designers are art directors, but not every art director is entrusted with the comprehensive task of designing the entire production.

The Art of Art Direction. In the cinema, art direction really began with the work of Georges Méliès. The Lumière brothers were content to take their landscapes as they found them in the natural world, but Méliès took his camera inside a specially designed stu-

Figure 3-4

dio. He designed his sets so that they would best advance the particular visual effects he had in mind. As the first filmmaker to produce movies containing more than a single scene, he also designed sets that would be clearly distinct from each other; as the set changed, the audience understood, so did the scene.

In **Fig. 3-4**, a frame enlargement from *The Man With the Rubber Head* (1901), it is clear that Méliès designed the large central area and its backdrop of black felt so that it would provide a proper space within which to show the head's expanding to amusing proportions. This set, in other words, was designed with that particular special effect in mind and took into account the need for a double exposure. (Méliès himself appears twice in this frame.)

Looking closely at this still, you will notice that most of the props are simply painted on the back wall. Many of the earliest efforts at art direction were confined to the painting of backdrops; that was both an outgrowth of stage practice and a reflection of the assumption that because film is a two-dimensional format, two-dimensional sets should look all right once they had been photographed. Very rapidly it was discovered that three-dimensional sets and props photographed better and looked far more convincing than two-dimensional ones, and the characteristically flat/deep look of the cinematic image was established.

Even if Méliès was his own art director, such a job description did not yet officially exist. The "prop man" was the one who decorated the flats, sometimes with the help of a scene painter, who might have been recruited from a nearby theater. There was no official art director on *Intolerance*, whose impressive sets were built by a master craftsman named Frank Wortman. With *Intolerance*, however, art direction began to be recognized as a vital component of film art. **Fig. 3-5** shows the Babylonian set for *Intolerance* under construction, and **Fig. 3-6** shows it as it appeared in the film. Obviously Wortman had come a long way from the painted backgrounds of Méliès, and his full-scale sets both stimu-

Figure 3-5

Figure 3-6

lated and made possible some of Griffith's most innovative camera movements. **Fig. 3-6**, for example, is taken from an extremely ambitious tracking shot — actually an ancestor of the crane shot — in which the camera moved forward several hundred yards while at the same time slowly descending an improvised elevator shaft. To close in like that on a painted backdrop would have been pointless, but the actual interplay of the camera and the space of the set, as realized in this shot, defined much of the future of cinematic space. **Fig. 3-7** offers a closer view of the staircase visible near the lower right corner of **Fig. 3-6**, and it indicates just how detailed and how carefully thought-out this set was.

A comprehensive production design integrates sets, costumes, and props into a coherent visual structure. As the art progressed, so did the growing sophistication regarding the use of lighting. The fully realized mise-en-scène depends on the integration of art direction and cinematography, and it is part of the director's job to keep the lines of communication open between the art director and the director of photography. In the production still from *The Mummy* shown in **Fig. 3-8**, you can see how the lighting and the more physical design elements work together to enrich the visual space and to communicate the proper mood.

Murnau's *Nosferatu* presents a vampire who has little of the polish and sophistication of Bram Stoker's original Dracula. He is a thing of the night, more like a rat than an aristocrat — a bearer of pestilence. In the production still shown in **Fig. 3-9**, you can see how the sets and costumes, both of which were designed by Albin Grau, helped to incarnate the vision of director Murnau and writer Henrik Galeen. The boards of the trapdoor look suitably old and worn, and the deck of the ship is cluttered with tangled ropes (indicating right away that something is wrong: sailors are notorious for keeping their lines in order). The rat on the vampire's shoulder is a perfect emblem of his character and nature, and the makeup on actor Max Schreck is inspired. Both of them are set off well by the drab, worn, yet somehow formal coat.

An entirely different mood is created in **Fig. 3-10**, which shows

Figure 3-7

Figure 3-8

Figure 3-9

Figure 3-10

Scarlett O'Hara (Vivien Leigh) on the grand staircase of her and Rhett's Atlanta mansion in *Gone With the Wind*. Both this still and **Fig. 3-9** show single figures in characteristic settings, and the difference between them is basically one of art direction. You may want to argue that Scarlett is no vampire and that the Count is no romantic heroine, but the point is that we realize what sort of characters they are and are guided in how we ought to feel about them largely because of their immediate visual environments (especially if we are confined to looking only at these two stills). The production designer on *Gone With the Wind* was William Cameron Menzies; he later designed and directed *Invaders from Mars* (1953).

One of the interesting qualities of this staircase is that it is symmetrical. It is part of the order that Scarlett has established as well as a reflection of her husband's desire to give her the best of everything. Yet as photographed from this three-quarter angle, as it often is in the movie (this is only a production still, not a frame enlargement), the staircase is a dynamic diagonal. This angular orientation adds to the physical weight, sweep, and presence of the staircase, but it also implies that Scarlett's plans for her new life with Rhett (Clark Gable) have been thrown off center. Like this phase of the story, the staircase is opulent, dynamic, imposing, and disturbing. All of these moods and hints are brought fully into play when the staircase becomes the site of Rhett's ravishing of his wife as well as the cause of her miscarriage. What most people remember about that moment when Rhett carries Scarlett up the stairs to the bedroom is that he carries her *up those stairs*.

An art director can be just as important to the look of a picture shot on location as to one shot in a studio. **Fig. 3-11** is a frame enlargement from the night battle sequence in *Napoleon*. This location was not simply waiting around to be photographed. This particular section of ground was selected because its mounds and flat areas could best show off the effect of the rainstorm. The hill in the background would later prove useful, as part of a triangular composition, in the scene where Napoleon finally goes to sleep and is covered with flags as "the victor of Toulon." The trees were selected for their height and bareness, because one of them was

Figure 3-11

to be hit by lightning; you can see that the tree on the left is just now losing its top. That lightning helped to motivate the rich lighting of the whole shot, which descends in a triangle to illuminate the rain, the mounds, and the figure of Napoleon. Napoleon is lit not only from behind, which would ordinarily make his figure a silhouette, but also from the front so that we can see his features; a lantern is placed before him to motivate this effect. And though it is hard to tell from this still, the uniforms and cannons make a vital contribution to the realism of the mise-en-scène. The art director's job here was to help Gance select the location, to modify it however necessary, to design the uniforms and the props, and to see that all of these elements worked together properly. The careful lighting was the responsibility of the cinematographer.

Production Sketches and Storyboards. An art director usually tests out ideas on paper before sets or models are actually built. The person who draws these sketches is the **illustrator**, though he or she may also be called the "artist" or the "draftsman." The **draftsman** is specifically concerned with drawing plans for the construction of sets, scenery, furniture, and models. **Fig. 3-12** shows one of the draftsman's drawings for the mechanical dragon in Fritz Lang's *Siegfried* (1924).

The **artist** typically adopts a freer drawing style and attempts to visualize the look of a particular scene or shot. In some cases the sketches are prepared by the art director and are then detailed, colored, and otherwise augmented by the artist; in other cases the artist creates the entire sketch under the supervision of the art director. In **Fig. 3-13**, a preliminary sketch for the giant spider

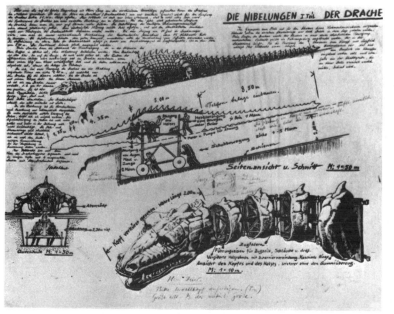

Figure 3-12

Figure 3-13

that was to have inhabited the bottom of a gorge in *King Kong* (the one into which Kong shakes the sailors from the tree bridge), you can see that the artist was more interested in imagining the look of the shot than in providing specific guidelines for the spider's construction.

To sketch something out beforehand can be just as important to a filmmaker as it is to a painter. One advantage of the new Electronic Cinema technology with which Coppola and Zoetrope have been experimenting (notably in *One from the Heart*) is that it allows the filmmaker to sketch a scene on video. A production drawing can be used as a working background for the shot, courtesy of a video mixing board, and the art director can evaluate, among other things, just how much of the set will be in the frame and will therefore actually have to be constructed. But in the absence of that technology, the normal practice is to draw pictures and then to arrange them in sequence like a kind of comic strip.

A **storyboard** consists of a series of sketches, each one corresponding to a particular shot or phase of a shot and arranged in the order that those shots are likely to have in the finished film. Although a storyboard is almost always used in making an animated film — with the secondary animators creating the drawings that will bridge those on the storyboard — it is rarely used in nonfiction or avant-garde filmmaking. It is used on more narrative films than one might at first suspect.

Whether or not they are intended to be part of storyboards, production sketches are crucial to the process of designing a set. Fig. 3-14 shows a member of the MGM Art Department as he

Figure 3-14

Figure 3-15

Figure 3-16

consults an art book while sketching the exterior of a church to be used in Robert Z. Leonard's *The Firefly* (1937). For a good working example of how close a production sketch can be to what actually ends up on the screen, compare **Fig. 3-15**, a full-color sketch for the chariot race in *Ben-Hur* (1959), with **Fig. 3-16**, a frame enlargement of the scene as it was finally realized.

Gone With the Wind: **A Miniportfolio.** As mentioned previously, William Cameron Menzies was the production designer on *Gone With the Wind*. In this MGM publicity still (**Fig. 3-17**) he is shown at work on a large watercolor production sketch. The art director who worked under Menzies's direction, Lyle Wheeler, is shown kneeling beside a storyboard in **Fig. 3-18**. The open drawer contains sketches that have not yet been mounted.

Figure 3-17

Figure 3-18

The two men are shown together in **Fig. 3-19**. In the bottom right corner of that photo, you can see a sketch from the Can-Can sequence. **Fig. 3-20**, a production still, indicates how that sequence looked on the set. **Fig. 3-21** shows Wheeler with the storyboard for the burning of Atlanta. Compare the sketch in the lower

Figure 3-19

Figure 3-20

right corner of the left board with **Fig. 3-22**, which shows Rhett leading the horse and wagon through the burning depot at the height of that sequence.

Models can be just as important as sketches in pre-production. Built to scale, a three-dimensional model can be an invaluable

Figure 3-21

Figure 3-22

Figure 3-23

Figure 3-24

Figure 3-25

Figure 3-26

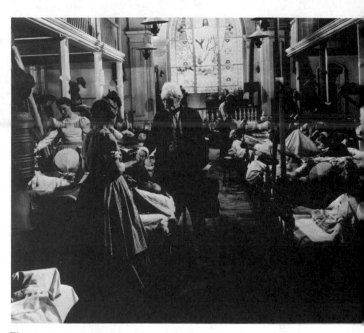

Figure 3-27

supplement to a blueprint while the set is being constructed. And by letting a model stand in for the set, filmmakers can experiment with camera angles and lighting arrangements. Should problems develop at this stage, the unbuilt set can be redesigned. It is not from *Gone With the Wind*, but **Fig. 3-23** offers a very good view of the model for the farm in Chester Erskine's *The Egg and I* (1947), which was used extensively in planning that film's setups. The person shown lifting the roof off the model house is the art director, Bernard Herzbrun. The model was built on a scale of ⅛ inch to 1 foot, and it proved equally useful to the director, the cinematographer, and the studio's construction department.

Fig. 3-24 shows Lyle Wheeler with a miniature of the city of Atlanta. In the foreground is the railroad depot. **Fig. 3-25** is a production still taken of the inside of the constructed depot as it appeared in *Gone With the Wind*. **Fig. 3-26** shows a detail of the miniature of Atlanta — the church — and **Fig. 3-27** shows the interior of the church set.

Set Construction. Once the sets have been designed, they of course will have to be built. The head of the set construction team is the **key set builder**. The key set builder reports to the art director — or, if there is no art director on a picture, to the production manager. The key set builder supervises the work of the carpenters, painters, drapers, upholsterers, paper hangers, tilers, ornamental plasterers, model builders, propmakers, and other essential construction personnel. In most film job classifications, **key** indicates the head of a particular job **category** or subcategory.

Figure 3-28

Figure 3-29

Thus the key set builder is the head of the **set construction category** (as it is officially named), and the key painter supervises the other painters.

Fig. 3-28 shows several sets from *Casablanca*. The top one is a panoramic view of Rick's Cafe, with a studio janitor visible at the far right. The bottom two are views from and of Rick's office. **Fig. 3-29** offers a more detailed view of the Paris railway station where Rick will wait for Ilsa in the rain. To show how the set will look during the rainstorm, the floor has been hosed down. Clearly a great deal of research went into the designing of this set. All of the details are correct, from the wording and layout of the signs to the inscription on the face of the clock. The luggage has been roughed up so that it will not appear to have been just now bought in a Hollywood department store, and the lights have been placed to bring out the set's visual textures and to give the whole a sense of greater depth. As you can tell from the dates on the slates, used to identify each set as part of the production record of the picture, all of these sets were ready to go in early June of 1942, and that date evidently marked the end of the pre-production period on *Casablanca* — at least as far as the sets were concerned.

Set Decoration. The **set decorator** reports to the art director and supervises the property personnel. A **prop**, or **property**, is a physical object used by an actor or displayed as part of a set; the term specifically excludes costumes and those items that are actually part *of* the set — in other words, nailed down. It is the set decorator's job to select furniture, props, and other set dressings and to decide where they will be placed. In making these decisions, the set decorator works closely with the art director, consulting all relevant sketches and models, and with the production manager, who must approve any rentals or purchases. The actual care, storage, and placement of the props is the responsibility of the **property master**, who often relies on the help of an assistant prop handler, or **set dresser**. Although the set dresser takes care of many of the props, any foliage that may appear on a set is the responsibility of the **greens handler**, and any food that may be served or consumed as part of the action of a scene is ordered, prepared, and arranged by the **home economist**. Props break, plants wilt, and food turns dry and ghastly under hot studio lights, so all of the property master's assistants are kept busy. Any props that have to be constructed are the responsibility of the **propmaker**, who reports to the key set builder. Those that can be bought or rented are selected by the set decorator and are then entrusted to the property master.

The choice of props is a vital aspect of production design. This is true even if a prop might make its presence known far more subtly than does *Kane*'s glass paperweight. A copy of Vladimir Nabokov's novel *Pale Fire* sits on the bookshelf of the living room set in Joseph Losey's *The Servant* (1963). *Pale Fire* is about a critic who considers himself more important than the poem he is annotating and than the poet who wrote it, and *The Servant* is about a

Figure 3-30

servant who becomes the master of his boss. The boss is the one who bought *Pale Fire*, has presumably read it, and remains blind to the servant's plans for upending the hierarchy. Of course, only a viewer who knew the novel and had the spare time to scan the bookshelves would catch this reference, but some set decorator did see to it that the book was placed where its title could be read.

Set decoration can define the tone and the mood of a scene almost as conclusively as can the design of the set itself. The landscape of the *Inquirer* office just after Kane has lost the election (**Fig. 3-30**) is less a matter of the ceiling and the pillars — at least in this frame — than it is one of posters, confetti, and a prominent spitoon. All of these join together as signs of waste and loss. The campaign is over, and the set dressing makes it clear not only that this is the case, but also how the characters feel about it.

Set decoration can also play an important role in characterization. The first time you visit someone's home, you might find yourself checking out the landscape in which that person has chosen to live and seeing what you can learn about him or her from the paintings on the walls, the books on the shelves, the relative neatness of the place, the choice of linens, and so on. It is much the same when you meet a character on the screen: you check out the set decoration just as carefully as the costumes and the actor's mannerisms. In his capacity as assistant set decorator on *Intolerance*, Stroheim chose the props for the gangster's private office (**Fig. 3-31**). We immediately notice a liquor bottle next to a pornographic novel (*The Love of Lucile*). This side of the office is dominated by a highly suggestive sculpture of a naked woman embracing a tree of some kind, and the tip of that (in this case, phallic) object is pointed directly at the pelvis of the nude in the painting above it. It is immediately clear that this character has some bad habits.

Figure 3-31

Figure 3-32

Notice how much information about Susan Alexander is conveyed by this frame enlargement from the scene in which she first
takes Kane up to her room (**Fig. 3-32**). All of the framed pictures
are of women. Those at the lower right and left appear to be of
herself when she was younger, and that at the upper right may be
of her mother or another relative. There are at least two bottles of
perfume. Susan herself is framed in the mirror as if this image
were another kind of portrait. And of course there is the snowy
globe on the dressing table, just in front of one of the girlhood
photographs. Aside from what its presence may imply about Susan
(perhaps that she likes pretty things, or that she associates the
globe with her *own* innocence), the fact that that globe is introduced here establishes the crucial link between Kane's old feelings
about his mother and his new feelings about Susan.

Now look back to the color section for **Fig. C-78**. This frame
enlargement from *The Godfather* gives a view of Clemenza's garage workshop. In this scene Clemenza is coaching Michael on
how to use a noisy revolver when avenging Vito's attempted assas-
sination. We notice an open paint can with three brushes sticking
out of it, which is a normal thing to find in a garage, even though
it also implies that Clemenza is careless with some of his tools. In
the upper right of the frame, behind Clemenza's head, a pane of
glass bears the mark of a bullet hole, indicating that this room is
actively used for testing firearms. Next to another two cans of paint
is a bottle of Rheingold beer, which provides a clue to Clemenza's
appetites. Behind and to the right of two tied stacks of books is an
engraving of a priest, perhaps a saint. The fact that he would hang
that picture in a garage indicates not so much a lack of respect as
Clemenza's sense that there is no contradiction between his relig-

ion and his profession. In the upper left of the frame, making odd company for the priest, there are five girlie pictures.

Costumes

Costumes provide important information about characters and also contribute markedly to the look of a picture. Although the production designer will want the costumes to be integrated into the overall design of the film, the actual job of designing or selecting the outfits remains the responsibility of the **costume designer**. The costume designer is most active during pre-production because the clothes have to be ready before shooting begins. During production, the wardrobe unit is headed by the **key wardrobe** person, who is responsible for the care, maintenance, and storage of the costumes. The key wardrobe reports to the art director (or, when no art director is used, to the production manager). He or she is also responsible to the director of photography for the "photographic acceptability" of the costumes and accessories — in other words, for making sure that their colors and patterns will look right on film. The key wardrobe supervises the assistant wardrobe person, or **costumer**, who helps with most of the wardrobe duties to be described, and the **dresser** or **fitter**, who is most often hired for those productions involving a great number of costumes that must be altered and kept in prime condition. In some cases the costume designer and the key wardrobe will be the same person.

Pre-production Tasks. After the script has been budgeted, it is forwarded to the costume designer (or the key wardrobe, if there is no designer). The designer studies the script and makes notes on its historical period, location, weather, and overall tone. A picture might be intentionally upbeat, brightly lit, and set on a contemporary beach, or it might be a dismal period piece set during a three-day rainstorm. The designer has to keep all this in mind when recommending which costumes to use.

At this stage a **wardrobe plot** is drawn up. A wardrobe plot is a costume schedule, and it lists the clothes, the accessories, and the duplicates that will be necessary for each numbered scene as well as the cast members (also numbered) who will wear them.

The next step is research, often carried out with the help of a research department. For a period picture, it is especially important to know how people dressed for specific occasions, or what a 1930 butler — as opposed to an 1830 or 1980 butler — would wear. Having gotten the general feel of the script and the period, the designer then attempts to visualize how each of the characters would look. The designer must come to know each character as a person in order to imagine how he or she would dress in real life.

Once the designer has these preliminary visualizations in mind, perhaps after having talked with the director and the producer about the characters, he or she consults with the production designer or art director. The production designer tells the costume designer which colors will be most important in the picture, what quality of light will be used for which scenes, and how the set will be laid out. Then they compare notes, work out any compromises that may be necessary, and make sure that they are on the same track.

Next the designer meets with the actors who will be playing the roles in question. The actor is measured by the dresser/fitter, and the designer attempts to learn how the actor "sees" the character. When the negotiations are complete and the intuitions fall into place, the designer begins to create the actual outfits. Sometimes an appropriate costume is retrieved from the studio's wardrobe archive, but it is more common for used outfits to be rented from costume houses. Contemporary outfits are usually bought in stores, and in that case the designer decides what ought to be "shopped."

The number of costumes worn by an individual character varies with the film, of course, but there are a few reliable guidelines. In the Middle Ages, for instance, or the Old West, it was common for people to wear the same outfit until it could stand up by itself. Thus someone who plays a page or a ranch hand may require only one outfit. But someone who plays an aristocrat, or — historical accuracy aside — the lead character in a period picture, might change clothes rather often. Each costume makes a statement about the character who wears it, and one way to complicate this "statement," or signifying practice, is to use a carefully chosen variety of outfits, which in this context are signs. For the MGM costume epic *Diane* (1956, directed by David Miller), Walter Plunkett designed an extensive wardrobe for the lead actress (Lana Turner), and **Fig. 3-33** shows Turner posing with all of the costumes she wore, together with some of Plunkett's sketches.

Figure 3-33

From Design to Fitting. A costume design begins with a sketch. **Fig. 3-34** shows a preliminary sketch for an outfit to be worn by Aunt Pittypat in *Gone With the Wind*. The costume designer on that picture was again Walter Plunkett, and all of the sketches reproduced in this section were made by him personally. (Plunkett also worked on *King Kong* and *Singin' in the Rain*.) To the left of the frame, you can see that a routing list has been stamped onto the sketch. That list gives a rough idea of the levels of approval a design has to go through. After lines for the name and number of the movie, there is a line for the "change number"; this can be either the number assigned to the outfit or an abbreviated indication of which scene(s) the costume will be used in. Then there are lines for the "OK" of Mr. Selznick (the producer), the director, the cameraman, and the (Technicolor) color consultant. Finally there are lines for the set number, the date on which the costume is wanted, the days the costume is "in work" (or whether it is yet being made), and a checkoff place for the first through the fourth fittings.

The preliminary sketch is followed by a more detailed drawing. **Fig. 3-35** is a watercolor sketch for one of Mrs. Meade's outfits, again from *Gone With the Wind*. (For an indication of the original size of such a drawing, look back to **Fig. 3-33**.) This drawing is a good example of something more general, however, which is how much careful work goes into the design of a movie but is never seen by the outside world. It takes art to make art. Attention to detail is crucial at every stage of film production, and even the details have details.

Fig. 3-36 is a sketch from *Diane*. The sketch bears two notes: that the covering ought "to match [the] velvet" of the rest of the outfit, and that the cap should be "brown (see script)." **Fig. 3-37** shows Roger Moore in that outfit in the completed film.

Some costumes are directly tied into the story lines of movies or are designed to be permanently associated with certain characters. An example of the latter would be Chaplin's tramp costume, though the same point may be made with the subtler example of Clint Eastwood's Dirty Harry, whose suits have a "bought-off-the-rack" look that James Bond would never tolerate. The one outfit that most people immediately call to mind when they think of *Gone With the Wind* is the green velvet dress, belt, and cap that Scarlett makes out of the old drapes at Tara. Its narrative function is to indicate Scarlett's resourcefulness, as well as her plans to get money from Rhett by looking like a butterfly even while leading the life of a moth. That crucial costume is shown as a sketch in **Fig. 3-38**, and as it appeared in the film in **Fig. 3-39**.

Once the drawing has been approved, the costume must be sewn and fitted. **Fig. 3-40** is the sketch for the "scarlet woman" dress that Rhett forces Scarlett to wear as a negative reflection on what he perceives as her true character. **Fig. 3-41** shows Vivien Leigh being fitted for that dress. This is a preliminary fitting; the dress has not yet been entirely constructed. The final result is shown in **Fig. 3-42**.

Figure 3-34

Figure 3-35

Figure 3-36

Figure 3-37

Figure 3-38

Figure 3-39

Figure 3-40

Figure 3-41

Figure 3-42

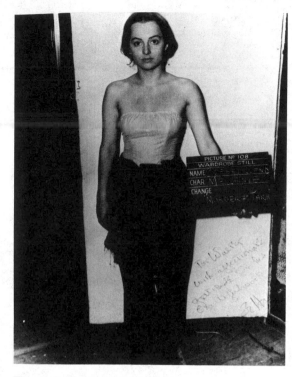

Figure 3-43

When an outfit has gone through its final fittings, a **wardrobe still** is photographed. It shows the actor wearing the outfit and is referenced — via information on a slate very much like that used in the set records of *Casablanca* — to the name of the actor, the name of the character, and the change number. The wardrobe still shown in **Fig. 3-43** is of Olivia de Havilland (Melanie). It was inscribed by de Havilland to Walter Plunkett, "with affectionate gratitude for his beautiful work." Her choice of this, out of all the available wardrobe stills, indicates her sense of humor — but reading beyond her joke, we can realize that even the most mundane or grungy costume contributes to the excellence of a well-designed picture.

Two of the dresses Robert Mackie designed for *Pennies from Heaven* (1981) are shown in **Figs. 3-44** through **3-47**. The one shown in **Fig. 3-44** is a copy of a dress once worn by Ginger Rogers. As an example of just how intricate some of the work on these costumes can be, take a close look at **Fig. 3-45**, and keep in mind that each of those gold bugle beads — like the thousands of silver sequins in **Fig. 3-47** — had to be sewn on individually.

Production Tasks, Stunts, and Effects. Although the costume designer may still be consulted, the majority of the production duties are handled by the key wardrobe person, assisted by costumers and dressers or fitters. These include having the costumes ready to go for each day's shooting. Any cleaning that may be necessary is done overnight by professional cleaners. The costumers have to arrive well before the rest of the crew and, using the actor/change numbers that have been indelibly marked inside the garments and tagged onto the accessories, sort them out and hang them on racks or in lockers marked with the actors' numbers. One of the little joys of this job is dealing with actors who show up at 6 A.M. having forgotten their numbers. Another is to educate movie actors regarding the proper care of a costume, something that stage-trained actors tend already to understand.

The key wardrobe person and the costumers are responsible for seeing not only that each actor's costume is clean, labeled, and ready for that day's shoot (using information from the wardrobe plot) but also that there are enough duplicates of each outfit to satisfy specific production requirements.

Say that an actor is to appear in costume for a scene in which he falls down a flight of stairs and then gets up to say a clever line. Should the actor be injured in the fall, production may be set back or even abandoned. To ensure the principal actor's safety, the fall itself would be executed in a separate shot by a stunt person (most often a **photo double**, someone who looks like the principal when photographed in costume). If you look closely at the outdoor boxing match in *From Here to Eternity*, you will notice that Montgomery Clift and his antagonist are shown in the closeups, but that photo doubles are slugging it out in the long shots. The double needs a costume identical to that of the principal actor. Should the stunt performer tear the costume while falling down the stairs and

Figure 3-44

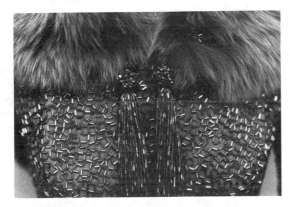

Figure 3-45

Figure 3-46

Figure 3-47

should a retake be necessary, another identical costume has to be ready to go. A conscientious key wardrobe person usually has at least six duplicates on hand. Those numbers add up very rapidly on a picture that calls for a hundred extras to stage a bloody battle.

Squibbing is the process of rigging an actor, a setting, or a costume with an explosive charge, often to simulate a bullet wound or hit. Let us approach, from the point of view of the costumer, the difficulties involved in preparing a costume for a cowboy who is to be shot off his horse. The **squib**, a gelatin capsule with a gunpowder charge, is put inside a **blood bag**, a small balloon filled with imitation blood. The squibbed bag is backed by a concave piece of metal or wood about the size of a silver dollar; when the charge is exploded, this piece of metal or wood directs the force of the explosion — and, of course, the blood — away from the actor's body. The costumer sews that solid backing into the costume and sands or otherwise thins the leather or fabric so that it will be easier for the explosion to open it up. Then the squibbed bag is sewn or taped inside the garment, and wires are run in an inconspicuous manner. The wires, which in this example might run down the cowboy's pants leg and then in a direction where they will not be seen by the camera, are connected to a battery board. On cue, a special effects technician sets off the charge.

Let us say that the squib goes off as planned but that the cowboy overacts when "shot" or falls in such a way that the wires become visible. The costume is covered with movie blood and cannot be used for the retake. The duplicate outfit must be immediately at hand, squibbed in advance. But as we are dealing with a cowboy here, that duplicate — just like the original — has to look as if it has been worn for a long time on the open range. Even if it has just been constructed out of store-bought materials, the costume has to look dirty, sweaty, beat up, *used*. It is part of the costumer's job to **distress** clothing to give it the appropriately used look. A wool coat can be aged by sanding, a leather vest with a wire wheel, or a cotton shirt by being rubbed with fuller's earth. Distressing and aging are usually done in advance, then fine-tuned on location. The "dirt" rubbed into the cowboy's vest, for instance, had better match the coloration of the location's actual soil (red pigment for Monument Valley, but white pigment for an alkali plain in Death Valley).

Much of the costumer's art involves anticipating the desires of the director, trying to figure out how to give the picture what the director will want it to have. There is a scene in John Ford's *Two Rode Together* (1961) in which James Stewart and Richard Widmark walk into a saloon. Stewart is neat, Widmark grungy. When they walk up to the bar, Widmark takes off his gloves and slaps them down, and clouds of dust puff into the air. The costumer, who thought about Widmark, the nature of his character, the shape his clothes would logically be in, and how to bring out the hidden comic elements of the scene, suggested the dust effect to Ford, who approved the gag.

Realism and Continuity. In putting all that dust on Widmark's gloves, the costumer realized, or made real, certain aspects of the character that were latent in the script. But not all films, Hollywood or otherwise, are exclusively concerned with conveying a credible impression of everyday reality. For a costume designer, as for many other film artists who must grapple with the narrative film's paradoxical mix of reality and illusion, to make something "real" is to flesh it out in its own terms, not necessarily to match it with the terms of the normal world. The task is to make sure that the costume appears to belong in — or correspond to the terms of — the world posited by the script, the production design, and the direction.

By making each costume *real for its world*, the designer and the costumer give that world internal credibility and consistency. This contributes to the audience's willing suspension of disbelief, even in the most unrealistic project, just as it can help to make a realistic film all the more convincing. The costumes in *Star Wars* are accepted in the same terms as the rest of the picture: fantastic but true-for-now. The realistic period costumes in *The Godfather* draw us into its world and make it easier to believe that what we are seeing could have happened just this way.

Whether or not a picture sets out to be realistic, it advances certain principles about how its narrated world works. Continuity is more regularly associated with realistic projects, but even the careful use of discontinuity must be managed with reference to continuity. Just as continuity editing can lead the audience to forget about the narrative apparatus and to imagine that one shot flows seamlessly into another, as if what were being presented were a real and internally continuous landscape, **production continuity** is a way of making sure that the conditions presented at the end of Shot A will be matched at the start of Shot B, as if both shots were of the identical subject in consistent conditions. If a character has the two top shirt-buttons unbuttoned in Shot A, which shows him walking up to a street vendor, the costumer and the script supervisor will make sure that those same two buttons are unbuttoned for Shot B, which shows him talking with the street vendor. If the intentions of the project are anti-realistic, however, the costumer may make sure that the buttons are all *buttoned* for Shot B — but to do that, some record would still have to be kept of how the buttons looked in Shot A.

Sometimes wardrobe continuity can involve a lot more than counting buttons. The helicopter beach attack in *Apocalypse Now* was a vast logistical project, shot on location in the Philippines. Because the government disliked the political implications of the story, the U.S. Defense Department refused to cooperate with the filmmakers in any way. The production required a fleet of helicopters that would closely resemble those used by the U.S. Army in Vietnam. It turned out that the United States had provided many such aircraft to the Philippine armed forces, and so the producers worked out a deal with the local militia. On a given shooting day,

Figure 3-48

the call sheet might note that 14 helicopters were to be flown in by Filipino pilots. Because there was a rebellion going on on one of the southern islands, there was actually no way to anticipate how many aircraft might be available on a given day — a straight-forward example of why production schedules often have to be scrapped at the last minute.

Although some of the shots in that sequence were exteriors showing the copters in flight (**Fig. 3-48**), there were also interiors. Many of those were taken from over the shoulders of the pilots and co-pilots, making their helmets prominent foreground elements. On the ground, a small army of local medical students, ex-servicemen, and miscellaneous extras had to be dressed in the style of the U.S. forces in Vietnam, from their boots to their helmets. The helicopters, however, were flown in each day by current members of the Philippine armed forces. Those pilots' flight coveralls and fatigues were acceptably similar to the costumes worn by the extras and the principals, but their own helmets not only looked wrong but also had different kinds of microphones and earphones from those used in Vietnam. The costumers had to provide the pilots with helmets that would have the proper Vietnam look *and* that would function properly when plugged into the Philippine copters' avionics.

The problem was that the Filipino pilots liked the new and quite functional helmets better than their own and very often stole them at the end of the day's shooting. The odds against a given pilot's showing up again were considerable, because pilots were often transferred from the film unit to the ongoing conflict on the southern island.

It was the practice in Vietnam for U.S. servicemen to decorate their helmets with graffiti. Each helmet bore the name of the soldier who wore it, and in addition to normal wear and tear, there were the scrapes and dents made by bullets and shrapnel. After securing hundreds of relatively unmarked helmets from war surplus stores, the costumer had to distress all the helmets so that they would look as if they had been through a war and would reflect the personalities of the characters. Such distressed and decorated helmets would be issued to the Filipino pilot and co-pilot of each copter, and their dents, chipped paint, and markings would be visible in certain shots. Should a helmet be stolen, the costumer had to distress a new helmet overnight, and that task was much more difficult when the original was not there to be used as a model. This exacting and frustrating job made a significant contribution to the apparent continuity of the sequence, and it is just one more example of how much behind-the-scenes work never comes to the specific attention of the audience — unless, of course, the job is done poorly.

Testing

In order to evaluate how it will look on film, **test shots** or **tests** are made of all that has been planned, designed, and constructed so far. Recall Elizabeth Taylor's makeup test for *Raintree County* (**Fig. 2-35**). Testing is how the photographic acceptability of costumes, actors, set color and design, makeup and hairstyling, lighting design, special mechanical effects, and process photography is verified. Makeup and hair styling are discussed in the next section, but their preparation, too, begins during pre-production. Other production personnel hired and at work at this stage include the director of photography, the script supervisor, and the key special effects technician.

With the script broken down, the actors hired, the locations secured, the sets constructed, research completed, the contracts in order, the costumes ready to go, and the tests satisfactorily completed, pre-production is at an end, and the work of actually shooting the picture can begin.

4. Production

One scene in Nunnally Johnson's *The Angel Wore Red* (1960) called for Dirk Bogarde and Ava Gardner to take a walk in the Italian countryside, just the two of them. It was an intimate moment, typical of the events in the lives of characters on which movie audiences are accustomed to eavesdropping. **Fig. 3-49** shows how intimate and isolated that moment was. Gardner and Bogarde are the people near the left of the frame. The arc light illuminating them and the camera taking their picture are mounted on a jeep serving as an improvised dolly. So that the engine will not putter into the soundtrack and choke the actors with exhaust fumes, the jeep is being pushed down the road by four grips. Three other crew members keep the power lines to the light and camera from becoming tangled. The woman in the long coat is the script supervisor. To her left is the location sound assistant, holding a boom mike. To her right is the unit's still photographer, responsible for taking production stills such as this one. An Italian military observer is present, as are about 20 other bystanders and filmmaking personnel. The next time you see any shot in a movie, try to visualize all the people behind the camera. Being aware of their presence is the first step in coming to respect their contributions.

Figure 3-49

Production can be generally defined as the process of putting images on film and sounds on tape, but it has a more specific meaning: the period of principal photography, during which the bulk of the movie is shot. **Principal photography** means the shooting (and the live sound recording) of the principal performers and the essential actions.

The discussions in this section will mostly concern the **first unit**, the group that works under the director and with the principal actors. The **second unit**, whose structure is similar, concentrates on shooting action sequences, special location shots, aerial sequences, "scenics," backgrounds, stunt work, process plates, and inserts — although the latter two may be shot by an **insert unit**. The **second unit director** is not an assistant but a full-fledged director. Although it is typical for the first unit director — usually called simply the director — to be more famous or professionally well established than the second unit director, there are exceptions. On John Wayne's *The Alamo* (1960), for example, the director of the second unit was John Ford.

The Director

With the help of the cinematographer, the **director** selects and stages what will actually be photographed in a given take. As the captain of the production team, the director has numerous other responsibilities — including emergency personal counseling — but the core of the job, the responsibility that makes it possible to identify some directors as the ultimate organizers of their films, is to arrange and direct the action, to indicate where the camera ought to be, and to decide which takes ought to be used in preference to others.

The Director's Job. The director is constantly being bombarded by people with questions and problems that require immediate and effective attention. The director must take care of all these practical matters, balance creative impulses against production realities and business pressures, and still do the intuitive work of envisioning how a scene ought to look in the finished picture. The director needs the short-term memory of a good waiter and the concentration of a master chef. Even if the script has been carefully constructed during development and extensively visualized during pre-production, all of that is on the line when the actual performances and setups are to be effected.

The director who selects or writes the script, is consulted during the hiring of the actors, works closely with the cinematographer and the production designer, and wins the right of final cut is in a good position to steer the picture where he or she wants it to go. Within the contemporary film industry, all this is how the "strong director" may take creative control of a project. As a simpler model of the authorial director — perhaps a model more appropriate to the independent production — auteur Agnès Varda has defined the auteur as "one who writes, directs, and edits a picture." Even the director who does nothing but direct the first unit during principal photography, however, is still entrusted with the opportunity to make significant creative choices that may well determine the movie's ultimate style; one can be a good director without claiming to be an auteur. It is worth remembering that the director who imposed *no* style on the production would still be fulfilling the responsibilities of a director.

Truffaut once said, "Cinema is a question of using time." He was not referring so much to the way in which cinema structures time and space as to the fact that a director must learn how to use time. The most rigorous and well-organized shooting day on the average theatrical feature typically yields only a minute or two of usable footage, and not all of that may end up in the finished film. Although the production manager and the first and second assistant directors keep the set running efficiently, the ultimate responsibility for the efficiency *and* the morale of the production team rests with the director.

The producer delegates to the director full authority over the conduct of the production. Some production members report directly to the producer (for example, the production manager), and others report to the director (for example, the director of photography). These can be thought of as lines of *authority*. But there are also lines of *communication*, and these link the director even with those who answer to the authority of the producer.

How a director communicates his or her desires varies, of course. Some are tyrants on the set; some comment only when something has been done incorrectly. In an article in *American Film* (May 1985), Marcel Ophuls described Truffaut as follows: "Always reluctant to judge, yet persistently assertive, his thought patterns imposed themselves on others in the course of ordinary conversation almost melodically, through sheer strength of spirit." Ophuls was referring to Truffaut's conversational skills, but it is clear that those must have been very useful to him on the set.

Most crucially, the director is responsible for the "cinematurgical" use of production elements. A director's skill is often measured in terms of what he or she can realize — both visually and dramatically — from all that has been planned, designed, and provided. The orchestration of the actors' performances — the most theatrical of the director's major responsibilities — is likewise a matter of making the best possible use of the available resources.

Within certain limits, depending on the creative range of the actor, the director tells the actor how to play the scene. Even the most experienced actor can profit from directorial feedback, for example, from being told which of several approaches to the scene appears to have worked best. The director tells the actor where to stand and when and where to move (**blocking** the scene). Blocking is worked out relative to the set and the camera.

The director needs to let the actor know what he or she wants the scene to achieve and must listen carefully to the actor's concept of the role and the scene; together they can arrive at the best per-

Figure 3-50

formance. As when working with any other creative colleague, the director must know what the actor is capable of doing and must be able to pull that performance out. On a lighter note, **Fig. 3-50** shows Inoshiro Honda explaining what he wants from Godzilla.

The director takes the script bit by bit and realizes each part as a more-or-less theatrical event. Because he or she *stages* the script fragment, one of the French terms for "director" is *metteur-en-scène*, the one who puts things in place and directs how they will play. (Another French term for director is *réalisateur*, the one who

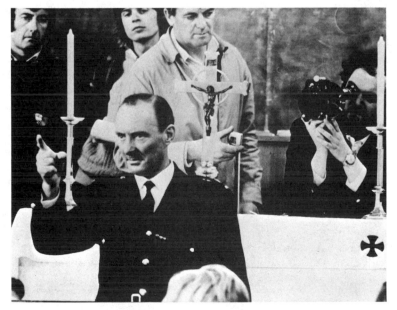

Figure 3-51

realizes the project and fulfills what has been planned.) That theatrical event, planned with the camera in mind, becomes a cinematic event according to the director's instructions, which vary in range and specificity. Although most directors will at some point want to look through the camera — or even to "sketch" on film the way Kubrick (at the right) is shown doing on the set of *A Clockwork Orange* (**Fig. 3-51**) — composing the shot is the normal responsibility of the cinematographer. Getting the right performance is the key responsibility of the director, and that job is theatrical: to stage a dramatic event in such a way that the cinematographer can make the best use of it.

The Director's Crew. There are five crew members, or positions, that are considered the director's immediate team. They are the first assistant director, the second assistant director, the script supervisor, the dialogue director, and the cuer.

The **first assistant director**, or **first A.D.**, is the "on-the-set expediter." The first A.D. works closely with the production manager (the "behind-the-scenes expediter") and helps the director perform any of his or her functions that the director chooses to delegate. The first A.D. is responsible for keeping the production running smoothly and on schedule. Other responsibilities include (1) breaking down the script and identifying the production requirements for each shooting day; (2) roughing out the blocking of the actors and the camera during rehearsals, and occasionally conducting complete rehearsals; (3) arranging background and atmospheric action; (4) managing crowds of extras; (5) overseeing the mechanical special effects crew and occasionally directing their effects; (6) handling release forms; (7) signing employees' time cards; (8) notifying the production manager of the next day's shooting schedule; (9) authorizing overtime; (10) keeping unauthorized personnel off the set; (11) keeping even authorized personnel out of the director's hair; (12) making sure that everything and everybody is on hand, in place, and in the appropriate condition; (13) giving cues to the cast and crew; and (14) supervising the second assistant director(s).

Some of those functions may be delegated to a **second assistant director**. In the majority of cases the second A.D. is not only a general assistant to the first A.D. — as the first A.D. is to the director — but also the person most responsible for handling crowds, whether or not those crowds have been hired to work on the film. It is the second A.D. who keeps bystanders from running up for autographs while a star is acting on location, baby-sits visitors to the set, handles a host of routine contracts, and acts as liaison between the production crew and the immediate outside world.

The **script supervisor**, formerly called the "script girl," keeps track of what is actually shot and reconciles that with what was originally planned to be shot. The script supervisor also *times the script*, estimating how long each scene will run and the ultimate length of the movie. The notes made on the set by the script supervisor are invaluable to the film and sound editors. These notes — made for every single take — include all changes in dialogue and action that are introduced during shooting; the condition and location of props, set dressings, and costumes; the position and any movements of the camera; the lens and lens opening used; the rate of exposure, if it varies from 24 fps; and any comments made by the director, such as working notes on what is most important about a given scene or how it should be edited. The script supervisor gives the scene number to those who will write up the slate, keeps track of which takes the director approves for printing, checks with the sound and camera assistants to make sure *those* takes are printed, cues the actors during rehearsal and times the rehearsals with a stopwatch, makes sure that the director is aware when an actor or camera "crosses the line," lets the director know what he or she either forgot or didn't have time to shoot that day, and takes Polaroid shots of the condition and layout of the set and actors at the beginning and/or the end of a take. All of these notes and cares are essential for maintaining continuity. Done well, the script supervisor's is recognized as the toughest job on the set.

Not every production has a dialogue director and a cuer, but this is what they do. The **dialogue director** lets·the script supervisor know about any dialogue changes that have been approved during off-camera rehearsals. During rehearsals and just before takes, the dialogue director goes over the script with the actors, making sure that they know their lines and occasionally coaching their delivery. After each take, he or she alerts the script supervisor and the director to any departures from the script. Dialogue directors regularly coach the delivery of accents, dialects, and foreign languages.

If cue cards are to be used, the **cuer** takes the dialogue from the script supervisor and sees that it is legibly printed on cue cards, sheets, or rolls. If electronic cueing apparatus — a **teleprompter** — is used, the cuer operates it by remote control, keeping the line display paced to the actor's delivery.

The director's crew may also include a **stunt coordinator** — who designs the stunts for verisimilitude and safety and supervises the stunt performers as well as the necessary equipment — and a **DGA trainee**, an apprentice A.D. from the Directors Guild training program.

The Actor

The actor is the most visible member of the production team. As James Cagney put it, "They need you. Without you, they have an empty screen."

The actor's job is to realize a role. The essence of that job is to arrive at a synthesis between two poles: the actor's personal self, which is real, and the essence or being of the character, which is hypothetical. No actor ever completely vanishes into a role, nor — while acting — is simply himself or herself. Acting is a dialectical art, and a performance is a charged, organic, working relationship between the imagined and the real.

The actor (male or female) is most regularly associated with the narrative or the avant-garde film. Bugs Bunny is a character, not an actor. In most nonfiction films, there are neither characters (invented roles) nor **actors** (people who pretend to be other people), but simply persons.

The issue of realism, which may at first appear to apply only to a certain type of narrative film, is in fact the same for most actors as it is for most costumers. The performance need not correspond to the terms of the everyday or heightened real world, but it must cohere with the terms of the world of the film. The audience must believe that the character would behave as he or she does, given the conditions of the story and the tone of the picture. The actor playing Flash Gordon must be the best of all possible Flash Gordons, even if it would be disorienting to meet such a person on the street. Scarlett O'Hara must carry out her self-contradictory romantic project with dogged consistency, and the audience must feel through the role along with her, even if the viewer who met a real Scarlett might be inclined simply to shake her to her senses.

Getting into the Role. Whatever the reality of the role, the actor must find a way to realize its terms. The actor must know the character, no matter how realistic or fantastic, well enough to incarnate him or her, whether by temporarily becoming that character or by devising a way to imitate the behavior of that character. Those alternatives correspond roughly to the distinction between method and technique acting. To varying degrees, most actors draw for various purposes on both method and technique skills.

Both method and technique acting depend on the actor's crucial skills: careful observation of people and the ability to perform on demand. A **technique** actor like Laurence Olivier or Orson Welles studies how a person looks and behaves under particular circumstances and is then able to imitate and project that behavior. Technique acting is a matter of selecting the proper gestures from a repertory of viable alternatives. A **method** actor like Marlon Brando or Robert De Niro attempts to contact his own inner feelings as a guide to how the character may approach a situation; during performance, he does his best to become that character. Thus the behavior of a method actor comes more from within — that is, the behavior is prompted by how the actor feels through the role — whereas the behavior of a technique actor comes from a more calculated tactic. The method actor knows how it *feels* to feel or do something, whereas the technique actor is skilled at conveying how it *looks* to feel or do something. When Dustin Hoffman (a method actor) got himself into his role for John Schlesinger's *Marathon Man* (1976) by staying up for days on end, breaking himself down so that he could fully realize the behavior of the tortured, bedraggled hero, Olivier is said to have come up to him and asked, "But Dustin — wouldn't it be easier to *act?*"

Method acting — another term for the **Stanislavski method** —

began at the Moscow Art Theater in 1909, when Constantin Stanislavski first presented his actors with a way of achieving realism on the stage. He had observed that those actors who appeared most natural in performance were physically relaxed, that they used props as if they were part of the character's true and familiar environment, and that they "prodded" rather than "forced" their responses. As Stanislavski went on to develop the system, and as it was modified by Americans like Harold Clurman and Lee Strasberg, the method came to emphasize inner techniques such as introspective analysis over external techniques. In Stanislavski's original system, both were equally important.

Many people are unable to cry at will, but an actor can expect to have to cry on cue. Whatever synthesis of inner and outer techniques makes it easier to perform well on demand is the one the actor will adopt. A technique actor may be able to call up the tears — the look of a crying person — at will. A method actor may think of something that was gravely and personally upsetting, tap that emotion, and cry from the heart.

Facing the Camera. The camera is a transformative agency. The actor on film is no longer the actor on the set, but the remnant of a physical presence with the force of a sign. The performance, too, is transformed from a theatrical to a cinematic entity, and the actor surrenders to the camera and the editing some of the responsibility for realizing and interpreting the role. While cinematic realism tends to favor many of the natural-performance goals of method acting, the selectivity of the camera and the manipulations of montage tend to reward underacting (recall the Mozhukhin experiment), as actors from Buster Keaton to Robert Redford have demonstrated. The film actor plays to (or with respect to) the camera, which is not a theatrical audience. Where editing most affects performance is in the question of sequence. Unlike the stage actor, who plays a role from start to finish, the film actor must be able to leap into character at whatever stage of the story is ready to be shot. Within each shot, the actor works with the camera, which may interpret the performance even as it records it and which is also an audience.

The last shot of *Queen Christina* (**Figs. 3-52** through **3-55**) is a particularly fine example of great underacting and of working intimately with the camera. Christina has abdicated her throne in order to run off with her Spanish lover Antonio (John Gilbert) and has arranged to meet him on a ship. When she arrives, she finds that he has been mortally wounded in a duel, and he dies in her arms. The sailors want to know whether she still intends to leave Sweden. "The wind," they tell her, "is with us." "The wind is with us," she repeats, then walks toward the prow of the boat as the sails begin to fill. Her intention, we realize, is to go where she and Antonio had planned to go. When she reaches the front of the ship, the camera begins to move forward (**Fig. 3-52**). This extraordinary crane shot — slow, majestic, and utterly tender — continues until her face fills the frame (**Fig. 3-55**) and holds on that close-

Figure 3-52

Figure 3-53

Figure 3-54

Figure 3-55

up for a long time before the final fade-out. The viewer probes her face in search of what Christina is feeling. Her face appears to express a mix of loss, solitude, perseverance, fidelity, honor, love, and courage. All of those emotions have been generated or set up by the dramatic situation, and all of them would be felt by Christina at this moment. But when asked what *she* was thinking about during that take, Garbo replied, "Nothing."

Actors work out their own ways of dealing with the camera. Because it takes nerve to appear at the focus of all those lenses, lights, and people, many actors avoid a paralyzing self-consciousness by concentrating instead on what the *character* has to accomplish in the scene. The character does not know that the camera is there; the actor, in what has been called a strategy of "controlled schizophrenia," must be well aware of the camera. Once the scene has been blocked out and **marks** (often pieces of tape) have been placed on the floor as a guide to their movements, the majority of actors follow this simple rule: stay on your marks, know where the camera is, and don't look at it.

When the actor looks at the camera, it is as if the character were aware of being observed. Sometimes this will feel as if the character is being observed by the *camera*, and that has the effect of reminding the viewer that all this is a film. Sometimes, however, it will feel as if the character is being observed by the *audience*, making direct eye contact via the intermediary gaze of the camera. This can surprise or intimidate the voyeur in the viewer, the one who would be comfortable watching others as long as they did not look back. The most important reason for the industry prohibition against looking at the camera is to keep the audience comfortable in their voyeurism and to sustain the illusion of the story. The straight-on look is a code of authenticity and directness (which is why it is essential in TV news and is used selectively within fictions). In a POV shot, it indicates eye contact.

Fig. 3-56 is a production still from *Poltergeist*. The mother (JoBeth Williams) is holding her daughter (Heather O'Rourke).

These actors present markedly different inner landscapes, and what makes the difference is the fact that O'Rourke is looking at the camera while Williams is not. Williams appears to be looking inside herself; her gaze is downward and slightly unfocused, as if she were thinking. She comes across as a private being with an interior life, and we can look at her without feeling observed — and perhaps for that reason, read more into her expression. O'Rourke, on the other hand, is looking outward, making direct eye contact with the camera. She is someone who confronts us, and whom we must therefore confront.

In addition to acting in relation to the camera, the actor works in relation to the layout of the set and its lighting. Although most such effects are manipulated by the director, some actors — like Orson Welles — are better than others at incorporating an awareness of lighting into their performances. About half an hour before the end of *The Love of Jeanne Ney*, the seedy villain Khalibiev (Fritz Rasp) murders detective Raymond Ney and then leads the victim's blind daughter until she discovers the body. He leads the daughter (Brigitte Helm) by having her hold onto the empty sleeve of a raincoat and pulling that coat forward. When they are near the body, he drops the coat and backs away from her (**Fig. 3-57**). As he does so, lines of slanted light slice across his face (**Fig. 3-58**). The subtle shift in Rasp's expression in the second frame enlargement indicates that he was deliberately working *with* this lighting effect and making the most of it.

Figure 3-56

Tools of the Trade. The actor's irreducible tool is his or her physical being: the body, the voice, and the face.

Body language was crucial in silent film, but the need for it did not suddenly evaporate with the coming of sound. *The Last Laugh*, you will recall, is the story of a hotel doorman (Emil Jannings) who takes inordinate pride in his pseudomilitary uniform and who becomes hopelessly depressed when he is demoted to lavatory attendant. Although his performance was significantly en-

Figure 3-57

Figure 3-58

Figure 3-59

Figure 3-60

Figure 3-61

hanced by makeup and lighting, Jannings communicated these emotions largely with his *body*, especially through his posture and the easy or labored quality of his movements. **Fig. 3-59** shows him in the full pride of his uniform, near the start of the picture. **Fig. 3-60** shows him after his relatives have uncovered his disgrace and rejected him. His stooped posture in that second frame tells us all that we need to know about his emotions at the moment, and it certainly increases our sympathy for him.

The importance of acting with the body was not lost on Robert De Niro when he portrayed Jake LaMotta in *Raging Bull*. For the early boxing scenes, he had to be trim and in excellent condition. For the later scenes, he had to be fat and out of condition. And for much of the time he would be wearing only boxing trunks. Rather than put on "fat" makeup, De Niro actually gained over 40 pounds.

The actor has to know how to *move*, and part of the secret is to be comfortable in the body. A lot of people are just awkward and look uncomfortable when they move — but the actor must have the *choice* of moving that way or not. The actor who can move well and in character has a head start on getting the audience to accept the character.

Sometimes the best way for an actor to "get" a character is to create the right voice. Peter Sellers always began with the voice and then went on to devise the rest of the character. If you carefully examine the three roles he played in *Dr. Strangelove*, you will notice that his three voices are at least as effective as the costumes, hair styles, and makeup in keeping each of the characters distinct.

A well-chosen gesture communicates a great deal. A flick of the eyes that would go unnoticed in a theater balcony can be momentous in a closeup. At the climax of *La Roue*, after Elie has fallen from the cliff, Norma (Ivy Close) pulls at her hair in an absent, lost way (**Fig. 3-61**), and this understated movement is overwhelming.

The actor's face is quite as important as the body, the voice, and a sense of gesture. Perhaps the single most extraordinary performance in film history is Renée Falconetti's Joan in Dreyer's *The Passion of Joan of Arc* (1928). Unlike most films, this one was shot in sequence so that the actors could have the sense of living their roles through in order. The experience was so draining for Falconetti that she never again acted in a movie; this is her only film role. Her training was on the stage and in comedy, and both of those are far removed from the world of this film. The collaboration between her and Dreyer was luminous. She could not have done the role without his guidance, but there is no way that he could have instructed her exactly how to adopt those expressions, how to call up the fire of her inner being and provide an authentic impression of transcendental power.

At some points she adopts a walleyed look as if she saw to the end of the universe (**Fig. 3-62**). She wears no makeup, and the only significant hairdressing is when her head is cropped bare. When she is bled, they go for an artery; the scene is clearly not faked. She appears to have made an absolute commitment to the role. Rudolf Maté's camera makes the most of her skill at transforming her facial expressions, as you can see in **Figs. 3-63** and **3-64**. In **Fig. 3-62** she is lit from above, and the angle of her head washes her face with clear light. In **Fig. 3-63** the light comes from above and to her left, and her face is given a more forceful, earthly, modeled quality. In **Fig. 3-64** the light is below her and from her left, and together with her closed eyes and the long-suffering, painful set of her lips, this frame softens her and communicates more pain and beauty than one might have thought possible.

Stars and Others. Whereas production realities divide actors into those with and without speaking roles, social and economic realities divide the majority of them into stars, working actors, character actors, and unknowns.

In the script and on the set, the **principals** ("principal players") are those who play the most significant speaking roles, of which two or three might be **lead** ("leading") roles; in the majority of respectably budgeted pictures, the lead roles are played by stars. Some of the principals have stunt doubles who may work with the second unit. A **stunt performer** may or may not be a photo double. A **bit** player has a small speaking role — or, at the least, plays a character who has a name. Bit players are considered minor principals and work with the first unit. An **extra**, hired on a daily or a weekly basis, plays an unnamed character — perhaps someone in a crowd, a pedestrian in the background, and so on — who in most cases has no lines.

A lead role does not guarantee star status. A **star** is an actor who has achieved widespread public visibility and endorsement, in social terms, and in economic terms, one whose announced presence can attract audiences to a film in which they might otherwise have no interest. A star is a public hero. Some actors have parlayed their public visibility into the basis for political careers — notably Ronald Reagan, who became President of the United States. When Reagan first announced his plans to run for governor of California, producer Jack Warner commented, "No — Jimmy Stewart for governor, Reagan for best friend."

The "glamour portrait," or posed and retouched publicity photo, is an important aspect of the star's image, and many of these pictures go out of their way to make the actor look more like a unique being from a higher plane than like a performer who has worked hard to develop his or her talents and has had a string of good breaks. The task, as seen in this glamour portrait of Joan Crawford (**Fig. 3-65**) taken by George Hurrell, is to separate the star from the realm of ordinary mortals while still somehow giving the impression that the star is human and approachable.

The **character actor** is one who is capable of playing a variety of roles but who rarely gets the chance to play the lead. In this sense a character is a "character," a distinctive type or oddball. Some actors who were leads in their 20s are now, in their 60s, playing grandparents and curmudgeons. This is not to suggest that "character" roles are insignificant. Ralph Bellamy and Elisha Cook gave

Figure 3-62

Figure 3-63

Figure 3-64

Figure 3-65

brilliant character performances in Polanski's *Rosemary's Baby* (1968), and Ruth Gordon won an Oscar for hers. Margaret Hamilton's character acting was as vital in *The Wizard of Oz* (the Wicked Witch of the West) as it was in Robert Altman's *Brewster McCloud* (1970).

Acting and Authorship. Without doing the research, there is no automatic way to know whether a certain brilliant gesture was thought up by the writer, called for by the director, caught by the cameraman, or discovered by the actor — even when the gesture proves definitive in establishing the character. In *Apocalypse Now*'s helicopter attack sequence, Colonel Kilgore (Robert Duvall) is most memorably defined by a simple action. When a shell explodes nearby and the people to whom he is talking duck for cover,

Duvall does not even flinch. Whoever thought of it, that was a superior piece of visual characterization.

In *Broken Blossoms*, the battered child Lucy (Lillian Gish) has a repeated and highly significant gesture. Her father demands that she smile, that she appear to be happy, no matter how miserable she is and how badly he treats her. As if her mouth did not know how to smile, Lucy pushes up its sides with two fingers. The effect is terrifying. While the bottom half of her face projects the mask of happiness, her eyes show horror and fear. As Gish tells the story:

That came in a rehearsal. I didn't think of it — I just *did* it. I was just recovering from Spanish influenza, and when I'd come near Griffith I had to put a mask on. He was afraid of germs. But when he saw that, he jumped up and ran up to me and he said, "Where'd you get that gesture? I never saw that gesture before! We'll use it all through!" And I said, "I don't know, it just — came." And he forgot all about the germs and used it all through the film.

Animals and Animated Objects. In Cecil Hepworth's important early British film, *Rescued by Rover* (1904, remade 1905), the best performance is turned in by the dog. Everyone else is over-acting — at least by today's standards — but the dog appears both natural and in character. With unforced realism, Rover appears to inhabit Hepworth's film far more comfortably than do the stage-trained actors.

Perhaps that says something about the photographic nature of the medium. Subjects that are as natural as the landscape itself often appear to belong to the film's world. An animal without either stage presence or stage fright can more easily become a natural photographic subject than can an actor who is self-consciously doing a job. From Rover to Toto, animals have made significant contributions to films and have shown, by implication, something important about film acting.

We can learn as much from inanimate and animated objects as we can from animals, because they, too, present not acting but *behavior*. In Albert Lamorisse's short narrative film *The Red Balloon* (1956), the movement of the balloon is so carefully and consistently controlled that the balloon comes to be seen as a character in the minds of the audience. The balloon appears to be loyal, beautiful, and playful. It waits outside the boy's balcony after a girl has let it go, but it becomes hard for the boy to grab the next morning. It eludes his grasp, follows him, and reverses direction when he turns. All this behavior appears to generate the impression of *willed* behavior, of intentionality, and finally of personality. In a movie, any object that can be endowed with consistent behavior can prompt the audience to imagine it as a character. This happens with the red balloon just as surely as it happens with King Kong.

Acting is a paradoxical business, a game of imitation that has its own reality, of temporary being with access to immortality. Whereas the personal self goes through its own cycle from birth to death, with moments both public and private, the shadow on the screen takes on a life of its own, preserving a record of the actor's being even as it projects a succession of characters whose true life is in the minds of generations.

The Cinematographer

The **cinematographer**, also known in America as the **director of photography** or **D.P.** and sometimes simply as the **cameraman**, determines how the set will be lit and is responsible for maintaining what is called the "optimum photographic quality of the production." One who has been elected to the American Society of Cinematographers is permitted to have **ASC** after his or her name. The cinematographer selects the cameras, the accessories, the lenses, the filters, and the filmstock to be used and determines the exposure (usually in T-stops). He or she works with the director on the general lining up of the shot: the positions, angles, and movements of the camera.

Just who composes the shot will vary. In the most common situation, the director may indicate that she or he wants X and Y to be in the frame, with Z in the lower right corner; wants the camera to pan with character X while she moves from the chair to the door; or simply wants a full shot. Given such instructions, the cinematographer will check out the dynamic composition through the camera viewfinder and then tell the operator how the shot is to be framed. In the British system the lighting is handled by the **lighting cameraman**, and the camera and action blocking are worked out between the director and the **operative cameraman**, a system sometimes followed in American picture-making.

Overall, the cinematographer's principal job is to help the director to translate the screenplay into the best possible visual images. When the **rushes** or **dailies** — hurriedly-processed prints of each day's shooting — are screened, the cinematographer checks them for quality. During post-production, he or she supervises the **timing** or printing exposure of the workprint, used by the editor, and of the answer print.

Stylistic and Practical Considerations. A cinematographer can reveal a personal style and a set of visual standards even when, like a chameleon, adopting the stylistic approaches of the director. Nestor Almendros used a Rohmer style when working with Eric Rohmer and a Truffaut style when working with Truffaut. But the excellence of his eye, his rich sense of color, his preference for motivated light sources, and his avoidance of hard shadows are evident not only in his Rohmer and Truffaut films but also in others: *The Valley Obscured by Clouds* (1972), shot in New Guinea for Barbet Schroeder; the great *Days of Heaven* (1978), shot in Canada for Terrence Malick; and *Sophie's Choice* (1982), shot with full production facilities for Alan J. Pakula. Gregg Toland arrived at a characteristic approach to lighting and composition in depth while working with various directors, notably Hawks, Wyler, and Ford, before guiding the inexperienced Welles on *Citizen Kane*. Some directors and cinematographers work together throughout their careers, and *together* they have a style: Eisenstein and Tissé, Chaplin and Rollie Totheroh, Griffith and Bitzer. Sometimes a new cinematographer provokes a change in a director's style: the Bergman films shot by Gunnar Fischer (*Wild Strawberries*) have a different look from those shot by Sven Nykvist (*Persona*).

On the whole, film historians have paid too little attention to the chain of mentorship and particularly to the crucial ways that cinematographers execute and maintain stylistic traditions. It can easily be argued, for example, that Karl Freund — who shot *The Last Laugh* as well as many Expressionist pictures — brought the German traditions of lighting and camerawork with him when he moved to Hollywood in the late 1920s, made good use of them in the Hollywood films he shot — like Tod Browning's *Dracula* (1931) — and directed (notably *The Mummy* and *Mad Love*), and passed along many of his skills and attitudes to his American colleagues, among whom was Toland, who worked on *Mad Love* and was primarily responsible for the expressionistic lighting in *Kane*. Toland trained Gabriel Figueroa, who extended and personally modified this rich visual style in Fernandez's *The Pearl*, Ford's *The Fugitive* (1947), and Huston's *Under the Volcano* (1984).

The cinematographer has to know what can be put on film and how to put it there. With a trained eye and a good deal of experience, he or she becomes accomplished at knowing how something will look on film as opposed to how it looks before the camera. It is, in many ways, a job for an alchemist. The subject can be transformed by a filter, encoded by a lighting pattern, flattened or deepened by a lens. The composition must be designed in terms of the theatrical aspect ratio, but the TV safe area may also have to be considered.

Figure 3-66

Figure 3-67

Figure 3-68

Figure 3-69

A face can be transformed by light and shadow. **Figs. 3-66** and **3-67** are closeups of Nadia Sibirskaïa in *Ménilmontant*. The soft shadows in **Fig. 3-66** have an entirely different effect from the hard shadows in **Fig. 3-67**. Whereas the former enhance the shape and texture of her face in a meditative moment, the latter dramatize her shock at seeing her lover and her sister in a romantic embrace. By the same token, a landscape or a sky can be dramatically altered by a filter. **Figs. 3-68** and **3-69** are from the diving sequence near the end of *Olympia*. **Fig. 3-68** was shot with no filter, and the sky is a light, neutral gray. For **Fig. 3-69** an entirely different look was needed, as Riefenstahl wanted to enhance the clouds and show the diver in silhouette. A **red filter** brought out the clouds, and the sky, as a backlight, created the silhouette. When deciding how to create a **day-for-night** effect — shooting in the daytime but making the shot look as if it has been taken at night — the cinematographer has to weigh the merits of reducing the lens aperture by two stops — which will affect depth of field, diffraction, and sharpness — or using a colorless **neutral density filter** that will reduce the light by two stops while the aperture and the image properties that it controls remain unaffected.

The set must be lit not only as a stable field but also as a mutable one, and the way William Daniels lit Queen Christina's bedroom (**Fig. 3-70**) is instructive. There are three motivated light sources: a candle near the bedside, a window near the center of the frame, and another window at screen left. The action called for Christina's attendant to cross the room and open each of the windows, and the set had to be lit so that the frame would have continual visual interest at each stage. It had to work with just the candle, with the candle and the central window, and with the candle and both windows. Overall, the lighting design had to create the mood of the scene and to give the set an impression of solidity, depth, and intimacy. Although they are not as sharp as this production still, the frame enlargements in **Figs. 3-71** and **3-72** show how this lighting design actually worked in the film, both as the central window was just being opened (**Fig. 3-71**) and when the set was fully lit (**Fig. 3-72**).

In his recent book, *Man With a Camera*, Almendros pointed out one of the key aspects of the cinematographer's job:

Achieving good composition within a cinematographic frame is, after all, a matter of organizing the different visual elements so that the whole is intelligible, useful within the narrative, and therefore pleasing to look at. In the art of cinema, the director of photography's skill is measured by his capacity to keep an image clear, to "clean it," as Truffaut says, by separating each shape, be it a person or an object, in relation to a background or a set; in other words, by his ability to organize a scene visually in front of the lens and avoid confusion by emphasizing the various elements that are of interest.

Keeping the picture elements distinct can involve lighting design; manipulating the framing, focus, angle, choice of background, and perspective; integrating the lighting and the filmstock with the

Figure 3-70

Figure 3-71

Figure 3-72

production design and the color scheme; thinking hard about the position and movement of the camera; and even recommending to the director that a scene be reblocked.

Balance and Consistency. Laszlo Kovacs once said that the two things a cinematographer has to know about and control are balance and consistency. **Balance** refers to the lighting design within the shot; **consistency** is the continuity of balance from shot to shot.

Within the shot, the lighting has to be balanced so that it will give the effect of a full tonal range from black to white. The light values must be kept within the sensitivity range of the particular filmstock; then those available tones must be brought into balance with each other, creating a visual landscape that is both pleasing and realistic (or consistent with the values of the "world" being filmed).

Once the light has been balanced, continuity comes into play. If two shots are to be cut together and are supposed to be of the same set or landscape at the same time of day, their balances have to be consistent with each other. If one is markedly darker than the other, they may not appear to belong to the same scene. Consistency is the art of making sure that such shots will look right when cut together. What Eisenstein particularly valued — graphic conflicts from shot to shot, including deliberate variations in the lighting — is precisely what most industry professionals go to all lengths to avoid.

The Camera Crew. The typical union camera crew is headed by the director of photography, also known as the "first cameraman."

The "second cameraman" is the camera operator. The "first assistant cameraman," also called the "first camera assistant," is the focus puller. The "second assistant camerman," also called the "second camera assistant," is the clapper and loader. The camera crew also includes a still photographer, who may have an assistant. Gaffers and grips, attached to the camera crew, will be discussed under "The Production Team." Other cinematographers, usually with their own crews, handle second unit work, process projection, and aerial and underwater photography.

The **camera operator** runs the camera as well as pans or tilts it, turning the motor on and off and monitoring the take through the viewfinder. By looking through the viewfinder during rehearsals, the operator is able to tell the sound crew where it is safe to position a boom microphone. If the mike or its shadow comes into the field of view during a take — or an actor misses a mark — the operator is allowed to call the take to a halt.

Retakes can be time-consuming and expensive, but it is always better — and much less expensive — to try another take when the set has been prepared and the actors are in costume and character than to set everything up again at a later date. Although anywhere from half an hour to several days may be needed to set up the lighting for a take (the norm is about an hour), the average retake is a matter of ten minutes. The director can always call for a retake, and so can an actor. Other production personnel must have a good reason — and the authority — to suggest a retake. The most important of those are the camera operator and the production mixer, each of whom is in a position to monitor what is actually being shot and recorded, respectively. It takes time to do good work, and 7 to 10 retakes would not be unusual on a feature; for TV, 3 retakes would normally be considered extravagant.

The **first assistant cameraman** is primarily responsible for **follow-focus**, in other words, for setting and readjusting the focus of the taking lens during rehearsals and takes in order to keep the actor, the action, or the subject area in the best focus. This has to be done without the benefit of looking through the viewfinder during the take, and so the first assistant relies on the focal distance markings on the barrel of the lens and also takes precise measurements from the film plane to the marks, objects, and stand-ins (people who stand where the actors will) on the set. The first or second assistant places the marks on the set and, if the floor will be visible during the take, removes or hides them prior to shooting. **T-marks** indicate the angle relative to set and camera at which the actor should stand: facing the top bar of the T, with its spine between the feet.

In the "invisible" style of classical narrative cinema, it is an accepted rule that the audience should not be made or become aware of the camera — or any aspect of the cinematic apparatus — unless encouraging that awareness makes a dramatic or artistic point. The accomplished first assistant will find ways to "feather" or gently execute a shift in focus so that the change is not noticeable, and the same applies to a shift in focal length (a zoom) — perhaps while the camera is following a moving figure, perhaps while panning across a neutral background.

Whether the lens is prime or zoom, the first assistant must know each individual lens as well as a favorite book — must know exactly how it handles the light, how accurately its T-stops have been calibrated, how sharp it is, and how tight is its range of focus at various stops. Every morning the first assistant "builds" (assembles) and sets up the camera. He or she takes it out of its box, mounts it on a camera support, cleans it, makes sure it is working properly, warms it up, lubricates it, loads it, and puts on the lens that, from long experience, he or she expects the cinematographer to want to use first. The first assistant sets the T-stop as instructed by the cinematographer; makes sure that all lenses, filters, and matte boxes are clean and properly mounted; and keeps a camera report, logging all takes and expended footage and taking whatever notes the cinematographer may dictate.

The **second assistant cameraman**, sometimes called the **loader**, is primarily responsible for the filmstock and for slating each take (**Fig. 3-73**). The second assistant is the one who receives the raw stock from the producer's representative, maintains an up-to-date inventory of all raw and exposed stock, and loads and unloads the film magazines. The job also includes labeling magazines and film cans and preparing exposed film for shipment to the lab, together with any special directions for processing.

In the interest of maintaining continuity, the various production departments take their own Polaroid stills of each scene: records of the condition and placement of sets, props, lights, costumes, hairstyles, blocking, camera position, and anything else that may

Figure 3-73

have to be matched exactly from one take to another. The **still photographer** does not take these Polaroids; instead, his or her job is to take 35mm stills, usually for publicity purposes. These **production stills** are almost invariably sharper and have better resolution than frame enlargements, but they do not have the textual authority of frame enlargements because they do not come from the actual movie. Nevertheless some provide useful records of the look of the set just before or after the shooting of a take.

Process Photography. There are three general types of special effects. The most complex ones, particularly those that involve making composites and using an optical printer, are done during post-production. Mechanical special effects, such as explosions and wire gags, are done during production and will be discussed later on. In relation to the camera crew, the most relevant production effects are those involving process shooting and projection.

You have doubtless seen hundreds of scenes in which the principals are having a conversation in a car while the landscape unrolls behind them. Although it has recently become common practice to shoot such scenes in a real car and on real streets, it is simpler to control the lighting and to record a clean soundtrack when shooting on a set, with the background created through rear projection.

The actors are placed in a mock-up or even a real vehicle, and the microphone is kept out of camera range. Behind the car, and absolutely perpendicular to the line of sight from the camera, there is a screen. Behind that screen, and exactly along the camera's line of sight, there is a projector. That projector is loaded with footage shot by the **process photographer**. In this example, that footage will be of the landscape that is supposed to be unrolling as the car — which may be gently rocked by grips but is otherwise not moving — appears to advance. This footage must be precisely matched by the actions of the "driver," who apparently turns the wheel to the left just before the rear landscape indicates that the car has veered to the left. (Actually a grip, watching the screen, turns the steering mechanism.) Because the process footage is projected from behind the screen, this is called **rear projection**. It is the job of the **process projectionist** to set up and align all this equipment. What is crucial is that the projector display a frame and that the camera rephotograph it — with the new foreground material — at exactly the same instant. To keep their shutters synchronized, their motors are interlocked. **Fig. 3-74** is an example of rear projection from Mervyn LeRoy's *Thirty Seconds Over Tokyo* (1944). In the immediate background of the kneeling players, thanks to an unfortunate floorboard design, you can plainly see the bottom of the rear projection screen.

The major advantage of rear projection is that it allows the stage or set to appear to be on location. The background material, which might involve miniatures or complex and expensive action se-

Figure 3-74

quences, can be shown over and over while the principals perfect their lines and actions in the process takes. Today rear projection is rarely used for car shots but is reserved for cockpits, space travel, and other costly, unlikely, or extremely difficult locations. But it is worth recalling that process work can, as in the turning, mutable "room" in the kiss scene in *Vertigo*, create spaces and locations of its own.

Front projection, a more recent development, entails projecting a slide or film from in front of the process screen rather than from behind it. The actors and the foreground props cast shadows on the screen behind them, but they also block those shadows from the camera's view. The projected information, which under normal lighting conditions would be splashed all over the actors and the props, is washed out by bright foreground lighting.

In the silent and the early sound periods it was normal for the cinematographer to do a number of process shots during production. Multiple exposures were done by backing the film up and running it through the camera again. Matte shots were regularly done in the camera. **Glass shots**, in which part of the set would be painted on glass, were particularly common. For the scenes of the Convention in *Napoleon*, for example, Gance had his people build the bottom of the set and the galleries in which the actors would stand, but for the walls, the ceiling, the windows, and even the beams of "light" coming through the windows, he used a painting on glass and positioned it between the camera and the set. Many of these production processes evolved into sophisticated optical techniques, and they will be discussed in the section on "Special Effects Cinematography."

Makeup

The makeup artist (**Fig. 3-75**) helps the actor to realize a characterization. Although some films achieve realism by having the actors not use makeup — notably *The Passion of Joan of Arc* — in most cases makeup contributes to any theatrical or cinematic project, whether or not the project's goals are realistic. The job is to change the look of the actor into that of the character, and to do it in such a way that the results will look right on film.

It often happens that first impressions of a person or a character are made on the basis of costume, makeup, and hairstyle. Some people know how to manage these in order to create a particular social impression or to declare who they are today, while others look somewhere between messy and personally unconscious. The job of the makeup and hair stylists is to help the actor to look like a character who has made or ignored such decisions, or the course

Figure 3-75

of whose life has left subtler traces on them, such as worry lines, smile creases, aging, or premature baldness.

The Makeup Category. Although some actresses may insist on doing part or all of their beauty makeup, most performers are not allowed to do their own makeup. Under the supervision of the **key makeup artist**, an **assistant makeup artist** may perform the actual application, touching up, and removal. In some cases, makeup between the collarbones and feet is done by a **body makeup artist** of the same sex as the performer.

There are three major types of production makeup: (1) straight or "street" makeup; (2) character makeup; and (3) special effects makeup. (Body makeup — which might be used to give a pale actor a tan for a beach picture — is a relatively minor category.) All of these are designed by the key makeup artist, who must be present on the set during shooting. He or she is responsible to the director and often compares notes with the art director and the cinematographer, as the makeups will have to cohere with the production design and look right on film. The key makeup artist supervises the other hair and makeup artists; for special effects makeup, he or she may work in cooperation with a propmaker or a key special effects technician.

Hair. The **key hairdresser**, who may have an assistant, works both with the actor's own hair and with wigs, toupees, switches, and falls. The hairdresser shampoos, cuts, and styles the actor's hair; touches it up just before a take, perhaps wetting it for a rain scene; and dries it afterward, if for example the actor has been thrown into a pool. As an extreme example of hairdressing, Fig. 3-76 shows all of Peter Lorre's hair being cut off for his role as the obsessed doctor in *Mad Love* (**Fig. 3-77**).

Straight Makeup. Cosmetic makeup that is applied to the actor's face, ears, neck, arms, and hands is called **straight makeup**. It is what most people think of *as* makeup, the cosmetics one might wear in the normal world — hence the alternate term, **"street" makeup**. Except for false eyelashes, it is two-dimensional: eyeliner, lipstick, blush, pigmented ointments, and similar products that can be painted on. Straight makeup that enhances beauty with highlights and shadows is usually called **corrective makeup**. Straight makeup tends to enhance some aspect of the actor's own personality and appearance as well as to define the character in the moment.

Character Makeup. Character makeup, which can be two- and three-dimensional, covers everything from Spock's ears to the Elephant Man; it is used to transform the actor into a radically different personage. A young actor might be given a beard, wrinkles, a longer nose, and hollowed cheeks — or he might be turned into a werewolf. One of the most useful devices in three-dimensional makeup is the **prosthesis**, commonly called an "appliance," which

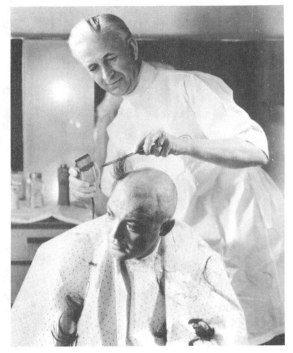

Figure 3-76

Figure 3-77

Figure 3-78

is usually a piece of latex that is applied directly to the actor's face or body and whose edges blend imperceptibly into the foundation level of the cosmetic makeup. Other materials of this specialty include the full range of cosmetic makeup as well as whatever materials can be made to do the job: skullcaps, scleral contact lenses that cover the whole front of the eye, wire, foil, cloth, plastic, and so forth.

The acknowledged master of character makeup was the actor Lon Chaney. For his role as Erik in Rupert Julian's *The Phantom of the Opera* (1923, rel. 1925), Chaney designed and executed a makeup some of whose details are still unknown (**Fig. 3-78**). To lengthen his face, he put on a built-up headpiece, complete with false hair, and taped back his ears. Using cosmetic makeup, he blackened his eye sockets and then painted his lower eyelids white; this gave him a sunken look, highlighted the eyes, and contributed to the prominent look of the cheekbones, which were probably built up with putty. The nostrils were stretched from inside by short cylindrical plugs.

His son, Lon Chaney, Jr., did not design his own makeup but often worked with the next great master of the art, Universal's Jack Pierce — creator of Frankenstein, the Mummy, and — as shown in **Fig. 3-79** — the Wolf Man. Pierce's creepily authentic work always left room for the actor to be expressive, to show the emotional being under the fully-realized mask. The stature of Jack Pierce among makeup artists is comparable to that of Bernard Herrmann among film composers or Willis O'Brien among stop-motion animators. It is appropriate that his undead creations, which continue to walk the screen's night, have been recognized as eternal in value.

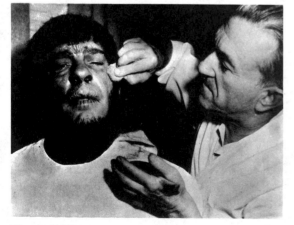

Figure 3-79

Among contemporary American makeup artists, one of the most creative, accomplished, and generous is Dick Smith. Although Smith has done highly influential work in special effects makeup, from the turned-around head in William Friedkin's *The Exorcist* (1973) to the pulsing veins in David Cronenberg's *Scanners* (1981), some of his finest achievements have been in the area of character makeup.

Arthur Penn's *Little Big Man* (1970) called for Dustin Hoffman, who was 32 at the time, to appear as a 121-year-old Indian. The makeup that Smith designed involved ten separate facial appliances, plus two for the backs of Hoffman's hands, and a hump. An **appliance** — something applied to the actor — may be anything from a set of false fingernails to a latex prosthetic. **Figs. 3-80** through **3-88** illustrate the major stages of this particular tour de force of latex prosthesis.

Smith began by making a **life mask** of Hoffman, a plaster model of his head and face. To make a life mask, a flexible moulage — like the powder used by dentists to take impressions — is brushed onto the actor's face, leaving only the nostrils open. Strips of plaster-impregnated cloth are laid over the moulage. All this hardens rapidly into a **negative mold** — one that goes in where the face goes out — which is carefully peeled off the actor's face. The mold is then filled with plaster, which hardens into a **positive cast**. There might be one negative mold for the front of the head and another for the back; when they are removed, the result is a life-sized plaster cast, and any prosthetics are made on this model rather than on the actor. Work this time-consuming and requiring so much advance planning is, of course, done during pre-production.

Fig. 3-80 shows Smith making a clay model for the front of the face. The plaster head is covered with clay, the clay is sculpted as shown here, and then the clay model is used to shape its own negative mold. (Note all the photos in Smith's workshop; it is important for a makeup artist to study faces, and the best of these artists know more about bone structure and facial tissues than most doctors do.) When that mold has been cleaned and dried, it is filled with beaten-up foam latex (**Fig. 3-81**). This particular mold is of the sides of the face and neck. Next, Smith inserted the plaster cast of Hoffman's face; thus the outside of the hardened appliance would look the way the clay had been sculpted, and its inside would fit perfectly onto the actor's face.

When the latex had been baked and cured, the plaster cast removed, and the latex itself peeled from the mold, the resulting masks were painted with liver spots and implanted with hair. They were then ready to be put on Hoffman.

First, the foam latex prosthesis of the eyelid was glued on (**Fig. 3-82**); it was very thin, designed to fold and unfold naturally. The nose and lip piece was attached next, and then the chin and lower lip (**Fig. 3-83**). Then came the ears, and then the largest of all the pieces, the one covering the neck and the sides of the face (**Fig. 3-84**). **Fig. 3-85** shows the latex shoulder hump being attached to

Figure 3-80

Figure 3-81

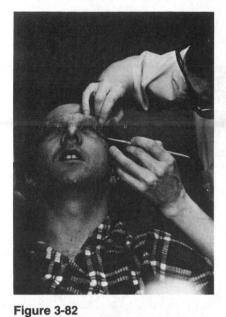

Figure 3-82

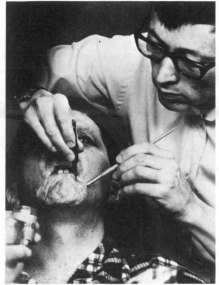

Figure 3-83

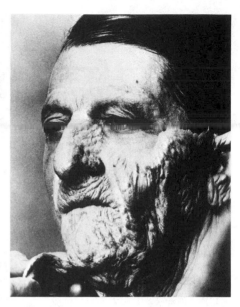

Figure 3-84

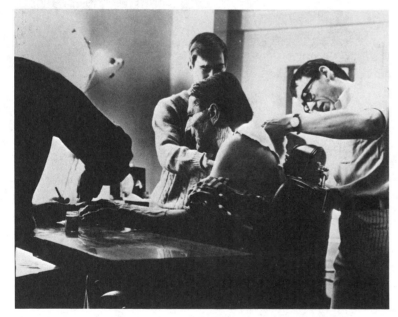

Figure 3-85

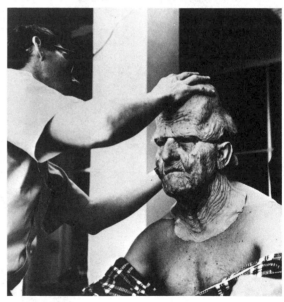

Figure 3-86

Hoffman's back while false fingernails are being glued onto his latex-covered hands. Then the headpiece (a "bald head appliance") was put on (**Fig. 3-86**). Although the prosthetics had been precolored and almost completely painted, it was still necessary to stipple on the last touches of pigmentation (**Fig. 3-87**). **Fig. 3-88** shows Hoffman in character, the final product of weeks of work.

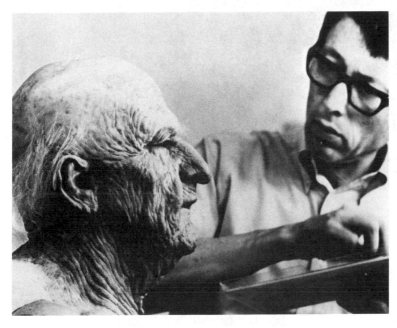

Figure 3-87

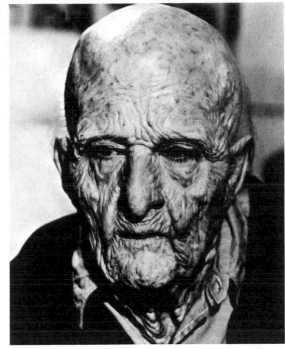

Figure 3-88

Special Effects Makeup. An arrow in the eye, the exit wound created by a .44 magnum, and countless other delights are created with **special effects makeup**. Whether optical or mechanical, and whether or not they involve makeup, the general function of special effects is to show something that would be difficult or impossible to just go out and shoot. Chaney's transformation into the Wolf Man, which required 21 separate makeups, depended on an optical effect (dissolves bridged each phase of the character makeup) and was not special effects makeup. But the on-camera transformation designed by Rick Baker for John Landis's *An American Werewolf in London* (1981) was, and it required a series of models with mechanically operated snouts that could be lengthened at will, hairs that would seem to erupt from their follicles, and fingernails that would stretch and deform.

The movies can be a violent place, and many of the things that an actor would not want to undergo in reality can be made to appear real through a good makeup job. In the color section **Fig. C-79** shows an exit wound created with a squib by Tom Savini for Romero's *Dawn of the Dead*. For Sean Cunningham's *Friday the 13th* (1980), Savini devised a way for an arrow to be shoved through actor Kevin Bacon's neck (**Fig. 3-89**) — but of course it was not *his* neck.

The neck and shoulders were an appliance (**Fig. 3-90**); it had a plaster backing and a foam latex skin and was attached to Bacon — who was sitting on the floor — along the underside of his jaw. The arrow was fitted just inside the appliance and extended down under the "bed." Flexible tubing ran from a "blood"-filled ice bag to

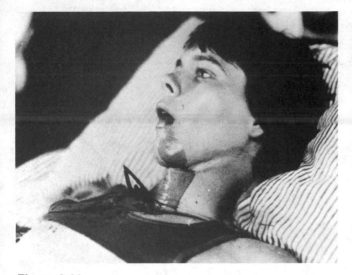

Figure 3-89

Figure 3-90

a pump (or **syringe**) operated by Savini's assistant. Savini pushed the arrow through a hole that had been prepared in the plaster and then through the latex "skin" of the throat; at the same time, his assistant pumped the syringe so that stage blood filled the ice bag and then flowed out over the appliance. While this effect was being shot, however, the air pressure popped the tubing off the syringe, and the assistant improvised. Blowing through the end of the tube, he caused the blood to bubble around the wound, much as if it were being mixed with air from the actor's throat. That "bungled" take was used in the film; it looked more realistic than what had been planned.

Special effects makeup can, of course, be used to create something beautiful and spectacular, not just something violent. If you wanted to make a film of James Thurber's *The Thirteen Clocks*, in which there is a woman whose tears turn to jewels, you would depend on special effects makeup.

Production and Mechanical Special Effects

Many special effects are staged during production. As distinct from optical special effects, which are typically geared toward producing composites and are created during post-production, **production special effects** are those that can actually be staged before the camera. Those that involve machines are called **mechanical special effects**, sometimes shortened to **mechanicals**. It would be a mechanical effect to suspend Christopher Reeve from wires so that he appears to be flying as naturally as Superman, a production effect to send a stunt double flying through a breakaway window. Detonating a squib is a mechanical special effect, and so is setting

Figure 3-91

off a series of explosions to give a peaceful Philippine beach the look of Vietnam at war.

Such effects are the responsibility of the **key special effects technician**. An **assistant special effects technician** helps out, perhaps by identifying hazardous areas on the set or by cleaning up after a blast. Whenever explosives are used, one assistant must be licensed as a **powder expert**. Such effects can be dangerous. Vic Morrow and two child actors were killed while shooting a battle scene for the portion of *Twilight Zone — The Movie* (1983) that was directed by John Landis, and some of the production personnel were held legally accountable. On the other hand, the 200 stunts in Irwin Allen and John Guillermin's *The Towering Inferno* (1974) were pulled off without any injuries. The key effects technician on that picture was A. D. Flowers, who also did *The Poseidon Adventure* (1972) for Allen. The fires, fed by propane tanks, were not allowed to burn more than 30 seconds at a time, and 30 real firefighters were present in case anything went out of control. In any event, a **first-aid technician** is always present on the set.

Wind, rain, snow, fog, and similar effects are part of the technician's basic repertoire. You can be sure that Gene Kelly did not have to wait for a major storm before launching into "Singin' in the Rain." **Fig. 3-91** shows an assistant scattering phony snow in front of a wind machine. To suggest the effect of a flood in *Fatty and Mabel Adrift* (1916), technicians designed a special set and filled it with water. In **Fig. 3-92** Fatty Arbuckle and Mabel Normand are shown in the bedroom as their cottage floats along. In addition to burning and flooding the set, special effects technicians can also do a lot of moving and shaking. It was they who made the sets

Figure 3-92

revolve in *Royal Wedding*, where Fred Astaire appears to dance on the walls, floor, and ceiling.

Wire work entails hanging an actor or a prop from a wire to produce the effect of suspension or flight. Although fishline can be used in many cases, and is both strong and transparent, piano wire is more dependable if the object in question is heavy.

Breakaways are props and set elements that are meant to break under light or moderate impact. When a cowboy is slugged on a

Figure 3-93

Figure 3-94

Figure 3-95

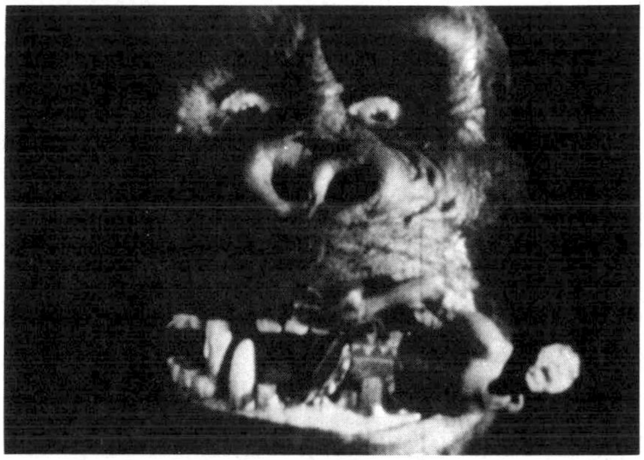

Figure 3-96

saloon balcony and goes crashing through the banister, the breakaway banister ensures that the effect will come off and that the actor will not be bruised. (The stunt coordinator and the effects technicians work together in the interest of performer and crew safety.) Breakaway "glass," designed to shatter on impact, is usually made from resins that will not yield sharp edges and, in fact, would hardly cut a doughnut. **Fig. 3-93** shows how a breakaway wall, made of light-weight bricks held in place by wallpaper, was used in a 1917 Keystone comedy.

Production effects can be done with **models** — for example, to make a boat in a bathtub look like an ocean liner in a typhoon — or they can be done **full scale**, with life-sized objects. Several full-scale **mechanical** ants were constructed for Gordon Douglas's 1954 bug epic, *Them!* One of "them," shown in **Fig. 3-94**, was complete to the midsection and was used when only the front of the insect would be visible on camera. Only expense and sophistication separate this ant from the mechanical sharks in *Jaws*, which were operated by a complex system of hydraulics.

In most cases, King Kong was a small-scale, stop-motion model. For some scenes, however, full-scale working models were built of his head, hand, and foot. **Fig. 3-95** shows the full-scale head and shoulders under construction, and **Fig. 3-96** shows its mouth in action, chewing on a screaming native. That shot, of course, required no stop-frame animation and was simply staged in front of the camera.

Figure 3-97

Choreography

The bearded gentleman in the ballet outfit (**Fig. 3-97**, from *Entr'-acte*) has an absurdity about him, a clash of expectations. There are times when dance and film refuse each other's aesthetics and working methods, and others when they interact to create something new, neither one art nor the other. To appreciate the vital difference between a "filmed dance" and a "film dance," it is necessary to think first about dance as an independent art.

The Stage and the Frame. Dance is the art of interrelating space and time via movement. Although it is usually done to music, what is definitive is the organization and execution of movement in relation to rhythm, even if that rhythm (or "count") is heard only in the dancer's consciousness. As distinct from performance, **choreography** is the art of *making* a dance: of planning, arranging, directing, and sometimes of notating the work.

A dance can be designed for and performed in any space: around a campfire, on a loading dock, in a parking lot, or on a stage. But to simplify the discussion, let us consider the stage as the normal site for theatrical dance and the *frame* as the site for cinematic dance.

Both for dance and for plays, what gives the stage its power is its unshifting presence. The stage is a dynamic and three-dimensional field, a place for the gathering and organizing of energy and space. Compositions shift in relation to each other and to the stage, within the field of the stage. The continuity of space and time develops its own momentum and presence — something that would be destroyed by the equivalent of a cut.

The frame, on the other hand, is a two-dimensional space with an impression of three-dimensionality. Gene Kelly once said, "On stage your dancing is like sculpture. It's three-dimensional. The camera has one eye; it changes the dancing to a painting — a flat thing." Furthermore, the filmed dancer is not physically present to the audience but has been abstracted into a moving picture. The frame is a temporary space — ephemeral in that it shifts with every cut — but it is also a record, something permanent. To set up a dance for the stage requires a great deal of preparation, and the dance itself is *gone* as soon as the performance has ended. The incontestable advantage of filming a dance is that it remains available, that one can have it "performed" simply by loading a projector.

The essential vocabulary of movement and gesture — the dancer's signifying system — remains intact on film, but those actions are modified by the camera and must be planned for it. Like composition, film choreography is designed in relation to the limits of the frame and takes into account the paradox of apparent depth. The crucial *continuity* difference when one is choreographing for film is that both the spatial and the temporal fields can be discontinuous, as they cannot be on the stage.

It is interesting to note that two of the greatest women directors,

Leni Riefenstahl and Maya Deren, were initially trained in dance rather than in cinema. Perhaps that training contributed to the enormous rhythmic sophistication and energy of their films. One of Deren's most perfect works is *A Study in Choreography for Camera* (1945). It lasts 3 minutes and is silent. Deren described it as a pas de deux, though only one dancer (Talley Beatty) is on the screen; his partner was the camera.

In this film, Deren choreographed a dance that could not have been performed in any but a cinematic space. Whereas a **filmed dance** is a nonfictional record of a stage performance, this is a **film dance**: a dance created for the spatial and temporal continuum of the cinema. It is a dance that uses film to achieve its purposes, not a preexisting work that is flattened and cropped into the terms of a foreign medium.

At first, the dancer is shown in a wooded landscape. He moves from a curved to a more expansive and open position (**Fig. 3-98**), and one of his legs extends toward screen right. Then he brings his leg down, but in another setting. Just after the cut, his leg enters the upper left frame of a shot of a living room (**Fig. 3-99**), and when it descends, he is standing in that room (**Fig. 3-100**). This movement, which could not possibly have been executed on-stage, in the woods, or anywhere but in the "made" space and time of the cinema, is presented as single and continuous; the shift of location does not even feel like a jump cut. (The French call this as-if-seamless jump cutting **faux raccord**, a false impression of continuity. The term could also describe the bone-to-spaceship cut in *2001*.) The dancer continues to execute this same developing dance over numerous space/time shifts until a leap that begins in another room is completed on a mountainside overlooking the ocean.

Although Deren's movie is a definitive example of how space and time are created for and with film, and of how a film dance can take advantage of these cinematic options, there is an equally good example of a film dance that works along opposite lines: the "Oceana Roll" from *The Gold Rush*. It is done in a single take with an unmoving camera. The tramp, who is having a dream about entertaining Georgia and her girlfriends, spears two rolls on forks and then bends his head near the table. In medium close shot we see Chaplin's face, the top of the dinner table, and between them the rolls — which look like feet — on the forks, which look like legs. These "legs" and "feet" dance beneath his face as if together they were the dancer. This dance was created for the camera just as surely as was Deren's. In thinking about how to shoot it, Chaplin evidently reasoned that the central point of interest would be the "Oceana Roll" itself, a continuous unit that would be enhanced by being presented as a unity. This dance would not have worked on the stage — it would have been too small to see. What film contributed was the ability to move in close; the fixed framing and absence of cutting added the proper sense of concentration. It must always be remembered that the cinema is a system of interrelated options, not of rules. Deren and Chaplin selected different

Figure 3-98

Figure 3-99

Figure 3-100

cinematic options in creating their dances, yet both made the right selections for their purposes.

The Choreographer. In film production, not every choreography is of a dance. An elaborate fight scene, whether in a Bruce Lee movie or in a musical, involves very intricate blocking, and the director may require the assistance of a choreographer. Choreography comes to the fore when the most important aspect of what is being filmed is the integrity, logic, coherence, and flow of planned movement. Thus you will sometimes find a choreographer listed in the credits of a film that includes no dancing. Some of the best choreography ever put on film was created for Kurosawa's *Seven Samurai* (1954). Nevertheless, most choreographers work at making dances and making them work on film.

When Jerome Robbins choreographed *West Side Story* for the stage, he worked out every detail; the production was fully realized, *tight*. When it was decided that Robbins and Robert Wise would co-direct *West Side Story* as a film (1961), Robbins took along the musical assistant who had been with him on Broadway, Betty Walberg. Robbins and Walberg figured out precisely how to revise the music and the choreography so that they would work in the new medium, and Wise took responsibility for the dialogue scenes — until Robbins was fired in the middle of production, that is.

"I counted the whole time we shot that thing," recalled Walberg. She and Robbins worked for three months before production began, storyboarding the dances. When Goldwyn secured the rights to use an area of Manhattan that was being torn up for the construction of Lincoln Center, they went on location and timed, with a stopwatch, exactly how long it would take the dancers to get from one position to another. Then they knew how much music they would need to accompany that action. No camera was present, so they put Walberg on a dolly with an umbrella and a piano and pulled her while the actors danced. It took about a month to work all that out, down to the exact tempo. Then they went to Los Angeles to sign up more dancers and rehearsed with them under similar conditions. The Hollywood studio streets were marked off so that if a given movement had gone on for 35 feet in New York, only 35 feet of studio street would be used. That kept the rehearsals coherent with the space that would eventually be used.

Then they went to New York and shot the prologue. Its music had by now been recorded, and they had the playback during shooting. At the command to "Play back!" Walberg would turn on the tape and begin counting at the top of her lungs: "One Two Three Four FIVE SIX SEVEN EIGHT!" On the count of five, for example, the camera might pan left while a dancer passed a basketball; on the count of six, another dancer would catch the ball and the camera would stop moving; on seven, the camera would move forward as the dancers regrouped and began to move back. *Every* action and camera movement happened on a count, and that care is immediately obvious in the film itself. While she was yelling out the counts for the dancers, Walberg was literally beating out those counts on the camera operator's back.

Next they went back to Hollywood to prepare the "America" and "Cool" numbers, planning additional music and counting it out again. The "Cool" ballet took a long time to rehearse, light, and shoot. Robbins asked that 14 days be allowed for shooting the dance-hall sequence. Wise had allowed 10, and the picture was beginning to go over budget. The upshot was that Wise — in his capacity as producer — fired Robbins. (In the end, it took Wise *18* days to shoot the sequence — partly because Natalie Wood kept spilling catsup on her costume.) Walberg stayed on at Wise's request — which is one reason the rest of the production kept up to the standards that Robbins had set — and the way she put it, "Everything went bananas when Jerry was gone. It got crazy."

The orchestrators, for example, considering Walberg a "spy" for Robbins, refused to let her into the recording sessions — but the conductor would often go out and ask her what the tempo was. As for Robbins, he eventually shared the Best Director Oscar with Wise and won his own special Oscar for his contributions to the art of choreography, but he never made another movie.

Although it is possible that the days of the perfectly realized and totally professional musical are over — partly because it costs "too much" to take the time to do the job right, and partly because, in Walberg's words, "there's no one to do them" — there have been some distinguished pieces of choreography in relatively recent films. Bob Fosse's *Cabaret* (1972) and *All That Jazz* (1979), which he both directed and choreographed, approach in quality the classical choreography of *West Side Story* and *Seven Brides for Seven Brothers* (1954, directed by Stanley Donen and choreographed by Michael Kidd). Carlos Saura's *Blood Wedding* and *Carmen* (1983), both of which were choreographed by Antonio Gades, make brilliant use of flamenco and open up radically new formal and expressive potentials for the dance film. All of these movies, and others not mentioned (like Luis Valdez's *Zoot Suit* [1981]), bring the arts of dance and film to a highly charged meeting ground and allow them to enrich one another. Although it is simple to note that both dance and film depend on movement, it is still magical to see how the right movements — professionally executed, appropriately shot, and edited with an eye to their integrity *as* movements — can become utterly different from those same movements on a stage, or even on a loading dock.

Sound Recording

A soundtrack goes through several distinct stages: recording, re-recording, editing, mixing, and printing. **Production sound** covers all sound operations and tracks recorded during the period of principal photography, whether on or off a sound stage.

The principal categories into which soundtracks are divided are dialogue, music, and effects. The **dialogue track**, which is the most important concern in production sound, consists of the words spoken by the actors or personages on- or offscreen. The **music track** includes music played within the world of the story — for instance, when a character turns on a car radio — and extra-diegetic music that is laid over the film to set a mood, to comment on the action, and so on. The **effects track** covers all the other sounds that may become part of a film: footsteps, helicopter blades, the creak of a saddle, and even the sound of an empty room (ambient air, or simply **air**).

Sound Design. One term that is coming into wide use and that is primarily associated with the major achievements of the San Francisco Bay Area sound artists (Walter Murch, Ben Burtt, and Alan Splet) is "sound design." **Sound design** is comparable to production design in that the job is to come up with a comprehensive aural concept for a movie. It is a matter of deciding how the film's world should sound and what sound can do to realize that world most fully. This might entail emphasizing certain natural sounds above others, establishing significant and interrelated clusters of sound, or inventing new ones. But unlike production design, sound design lasts through post-production; the mix is crucial.

In a fantasy or science fiction picture, where the world of the story does not properly exist, the sound designer needs to create its sound virtually from scratch. The sounds that Murch designed for Lucas's *THX-1138* (1971) were meant to generate, in Murch's words, the impression of "a film *from* the future, rather than a film about the future." But similar considerations can apply even in a realistic narrative film like *Apocalypse Now* or *The Conversation* — both designed by Murch — or in an avant-garde feature like *Eraserhead* (designed by Splet).

As a working example of sound design, Ben Burtt's story of creating the laser swords for *Star Wars* is instructive. As he told a National Public Radio audience:

The idea was that the weapon was very dangerous, that it would cut through you or burn you if it touched you, and so we wanted to have a sound that seemed ominous. At the same time, we didn't want to have a sound that was blasting away and would distract you from the dialogue; it had to be understated to some degree.

Eventually I was swinging a microphone around behind my television set. When you'd turn the TV on, sometimes you could hear a strange buzz. . . . I got a very nice, sputtery kind of hum sound, and I said "That's a pretty good element for the laser sword." But I needed something a little bit stronger to mix with that, and so I recorded a motor that was on an old projector at USC. I took that projector hum and the television hum, put them on two tracks, and blended them together so that there was now a composite of the two different kinds of hum.

The next step, of course, was to get the sensation that the sword was moving, or that the sword could swish back and forth. The characteristic of movement was not *in* the sound yet; it was just a steady hum. So to do that I played the sound on a tape recorder, over a speaker just sitting in a room. And then with another tape recorder and microphone I made a new recording of the sound as it was played over the speaker. Instead of holding the microphone stationary in front of the speaker just to duplicate the sound, I swished the microphone around the room and was able to come up with a variety of sounds which then were, at a later date, synchronized with the action in the picture. This was all done before the laser sword was even filmed.

Now there were two swords, of course, in the original film — Ben Kenobi's light saber and Vader's light saber — and they were both derived from the same sound. It was really the same sound just pitched about a quarter-tone apart from one another. Vader's sword was equalized — that is, the tone was controlled when we re-recorded the sound — to have a little more edge to it, a little more high frequency, so that it sounded like it was a little "sharper" in a sense, more vicious than Kenobi's sword, which was more pleasant.

This story reveals many important creative considerations: that sounds can be biased to encourage the audience to side with or against a particular character, that a created sound can augment and help to realize an invented image, and that various tracks are designed so that they will work well with other tracks. But the most interesting image here is that of Burtt swinging his mike around the room after having kept his ears open to the buzz from his TV. Whether he or she is a designer, a recordist, an editor, or a mixer, the sound artist must be alert to the sounds of the world. To gather and combine the sounds for a wheat field at dawn, it is essential to know how such a landscape actually sounds. If the necessary sounds do not exist in a tape library, the designer will find them in the world or find a way to make them. If the equipment for processing the sound as desired does not exist, the designer will often have to make that up, too.

Tracks and Terms. A track can be in sync or wild. A **sync track** is one recorded in synchronization with the camera; a **wild track** is not. **Live sound** is that recorded during shooting, whether in sync or wild.

Once the film has been edited, there is a critically useful distinction between sounds that appear to be motivated onscreen and those that appear to come out of nowhere. **Motivated sound** is analogous to motivated light: the sound has a source that is part of the world of the film. That source may be onscreen, in which case the sound is **direct** or **indigenous**, or offscreen, in which case the sound is **indirect** or **off**. If John Wayne fires a rifle onscreen, its report will be direct — whether the sound effect is live or is created during post-production; if he steps out of the camera's range before firing the rifle, its report will be indirect.

Whether motivated from on- or offscreen, indigenous sounds are varieties of actual, as opposed to commentative, sound. **Actual** or **diegetic** sound (which may be live or post-synchronized) comes from the world within the film; it is capable of being heard by the characters. **Commentative** or **extra-diegetic** sound comes from outside the immediate world of the story — from the level of the discourse, where the artist or the narrator hangs out — and it often expresses the storyteller's attitude toward the material being presented, like a commentary; it is off or over. When the Karloff character is gunned down in the bowling alley in *Scarface,* the onscreen pins and the offscreen guns are both actual. But if the gangster had simply been told to get out of town, and machine guns were then heard on the soundtrack, they would be commentative, a playful way to suggest that his career was finished. Of course, actual sounds can have commentative functions. In Robert Altman's *M*A*S*H* (1970), when Frank Burns (Robert Duvall) is carted away from the camp, the PA system plays "Sayonara," which is both the song for the day (actual) and authorial notice that this character will not be seen again in the film (commentative).

Within the industry, tracks are identified simply as **direct** (motivated onscreen source), **off** (motivated offscreen source), and **over** (laid over the other tracks, like an orchestral score or a voice-over narration, and usually unmotivated).

Crews and Procedures. A good soundtrack begins with a well-made recording. Just as a cinematographer tries to keep the elements of the image distinct and to indicate clearly what is the center of visual interest, a recordist works at getting each sound on tape in its fullest and cleanest form.

The minimal sound crew consists of a single person equipped with a tape recorder, a microphone, and a set of earphones that relay what the mike picks up. Assuming a reasonable budget, however, the most common small crew consists of two people, one of whom operates the mixing panel and the recorder while the other takes care of the microphone. On a union set, a cable handler may also be employed.

The head of the production sound category is the **production mixer**. His or her job includes making sure that the set or location has been modified to produce optimum sound quality, that the recordings are free of unwanted background noise and reverberation, and that both sync and wild tracks carry audible identifications (**voice slating**). In consultation with the cinematographer, he or she decides where the microphones should be placed, whether they are boom mikes or tiny wireless mikes that can be hidden in the knot of a necktie or pinned with "vampire clips" just inside a shirt or dress; ideally the mike should be as near the mouth as possible and with a clear shot at it, but invisible to the camera. The production mixer operates a mixing console into which the microphones' signals are fed and where they are balanced on their way into the tape recorder.

The **sound assistant** or **boom operator** holds the boom mike or fits the actors with smaller mikes, as already described. When working with a boom, he or she takes special care to "ride the line" (of the frame), keeping the mike as near the actor as possible but out of camera range. The job also includes voice-slating wild tracks. The **cable handler** sees that any wires are properly run from the mike to the console or recorder and also provides the cable that links the recorder to the camera for sync takes.

Some actions are filmed to the accompaniment of a pre-existing track called **playback material** or simply the **playback**, and this recording is the responsibility of the **playback operator**. The playback makes it possible for singers or dancers to remain in sync with the music, especially when the action will be covered in more than one shot. It would be nearly impossible for a singer to break off at a cut and then resume the song with full energy and the proper rhythm and vocal coloration in midstream for the next take; so the song is recorded first and is then played back during shooting, while the singer makes the appropriate lip and body movements. The playback ensures that each shot will be acceptably synchronized with the continuous sound, so that all of them can be cut together.

After each day of shooting, the acceptable or "printed" sound takes are re-recorded or **transferred** onto magnetic stock in a sound transfer bay — usually in up to three thin stripes running the length of the stock; for that reason, such mag stock is called **35mm magnetic stripe** (see page 461). During the transfer, sync is maintained by playing back the recording at the rate that the camera was operating.

The sync pulse on the tape may be generated by the camera and fed to the recorder by a cable, but today it is more common to have the pulse broadcast to the recorder by means of electronics similar to those in wireless microphones. **Crystal sync,** a state-of-the-art wireless system that has become the norm within the industry, uses a piezoelectric crystal to generate a perfectly regular pulse on the sync track and an identical crystal to govern the camera's motor. Quartz wristwatches operate on the same principle. Every quartz crystal of a certain type produces an identical pulse or frequency under identical conditions. There is no need to wire every quartz watch in the world to one big clock.

Because it is common practice to screen the result of each day's shooting as soon as possible, and to do it in double system with the picture and sound rolls run by interlocked machines, this immediate transfer to magnetic film (whether striped or fullcoat) ensures that the dailies can be projected in sync. The ¼-inch original tapes and the 35mm magnetic stripes are then filed away and stored as carefully as the camera negatives.

On the set, the following are the final steps that precede a recorded sound take. The rehearsals are completed, any mechanical effects are ready to go, the actors have had their hair brushed out and their makeup touched up at the last minute, and the cinematographer is satisfied with the intensity and arrangement of the lights. Things are "ready to roll." The A.D. checks that the production mixer and the camera operator are ready, and after making sure that the director is, too, says "Quiet on the set! Give me a bell." On that signal, the production mixer hits a buzzer, bell, or horn and turns on a red light mounted over the outside door(s) of the stage. That red light, or a similar sign on location, is an absolute command; roughly translated, it means *Shut up, keep out, and don't move!* Then the A.D. says, "Roll 'em!" The sound — actually the tape — then starts rolling, and the mixer will say "Speed" when the tape is up to the proper recording speed and locked into sync. Then the camera operator turns on the camera and will call "Mark it!" (in MOS shooting, "Speed") to the second camera assistant when the motor gets up to 24 fps.

The production mixer will already have voice-slated the tape ("Scene 28, Take 3"). Now the second assistant places the slate within view of the camera. When everything is up to speed, the second assistant says "Mark!" or "Marker!" and hits the sticks, then gets out of the way. The director says "Action!" and the take proceeds until the director says "Cut!"

Do that often enough and you've got the makings for a movie.

The Production Team

It's 3 A.M. and you're shooting on location in the rain. You're waiting for the stuntman to get his costume changed and his hair dried for the fourteenth time; otherwise, Take 15 is ready to go. The shot calls for him to dive out of a truck and take a roll in the mud while the truck careens toward a munitions plant. Finally he shows up, takes the dive, and executes a perfect roll — but the truck's engine dies, and the vehicle just stands there. You turn to the person next to you, or to no one in particular, and say a little litany that sustains you, because its ironies are legitimate: "I love Hollywood, and show business is my life." There is an Irishman now working in the industry who has "I love Hollywood" tattooed on the sole of one foot, "Show business is my life" on the other. Among some camera crews, the expression used when announcing that the set is ready for the actors is "Wheel in the meat!" There is a second unit T-shirt that reads, "To hell with dialogue — let's wreck something." It's little things like that that keep you going, along with bigger things like crew solidarity and creative accomplishment.

Teamwork. There are many ways to tie individuals together into crews and crews into an efficient team. It is common for many production teams to surround themselves with items that bear the name of the picture. The makers of *The Right Stuff* used nonslip *Right Stuff* coffee mugs, *Right Stuff* Cinzano ashtrays, and *Right Stuff* T-shirts. These collector's items, never sold to the public, help the filmmakers to feel like a unit, part of a special group charged with a single and often obsessive project.

Sometimes the crew that sticks together learns how to crack up together. There is a point in many high-stress projects at which things just become amusing — where they have to be made into fun, to take off the pressure. Howard Hawks was particularly good at keeping his set a fun place to be, without any loss of discipline and working efficiency. **Fig. 3-101** shows one of the lighter moments during the shooting of *Gone With the Wind*.

But the best way to get a group of professionals to work as a unit is to acknowledge each person *as* a professional and to take every contribution seriously.

Figure 3-101

There is little real fairness in the attribution of creative contributions in the film business (part of the job of a film historian is to establish just who did what), and this is often reinforced by poorly informed or prejudicial discussion. A production mixer might do the same excellent job on two pictures and find the sound in the successful picture praised, the sound in the other ignored or attacked. A cinematographer might save a movie, might make the director "look good" no matter how poorly the production has been managed and the scenes staged, and then read an article about that director's brilliant use of the camera. One reason that this book includes so much production and technical information, in addition to more conventional discussions of cinematic structures and aesthetics, is to make you as aware as possible of just what *does* go into a movie, how many experts are involved and how each of their contributions matters. To understand production realities is to be armed against critical oversimplifications.

Of all the people on the set, the director is the one who ought — who *needs* — to respect the contributions of every member of the production team. The director provides artistic and practical guidance — in a word, *direction* — for the project. The director's guiding vision can inspire the crew, can give them the sense that they are all working together on a good and worthwhile picture, not just putting in their time and building up their résumés. When a studio executive says "Trust me," there may be something in the voice that suggests piranha in the swimming pool. When a director says "It'll work" and it doesn't — when a stunt kills an actor, to take an extreme example — trust can be forfeited permanently. Most people know not to trust executives who say "Trust me," just as it is difficult to believe someone who keeps saying "To tell you the truth . . ." But on the set, where time is money, nerves may be frayed, and reputations are at stake, the director and the heads of the production categories must be able to be trusted. The context of production is both aesthetic and practical, and administrative decisions must prove appropriate, if not inspired, in both respects.

A set runs on a tight schedule, and much of its efficiency depends on careful planning during pre-production. But production is rarely a matter of simply carrying out previous decisions. Creative improvisation, working with what is actually on hand — a landscape, for instance — can yield superior results and can help to generate real artistic excitement, a mood that often survives in the finished picture. Improvisation flourishes in an atmosphere of respect and encouragement, particularly if the director is open to suggestions. As a practical business venture, activity on the set must be well planned, organized, and efficient. But as a crucial stage in the making of a work of art, production activity must be open to the intuitive and spontaneous insights that arise when one is in the midst of a developing project.

And, of course, the director is not the only person who gets good ideas or becomes immersed in the project with absolute dedication. Up to now, we have been examining the contributions of those production personnel whose work fits into familiar aesthetic categories (like acting or choreography) and is immediately evident onscreen. It is now time to look at those team members whose work is, at first, less evident and whose job titles, listed in the tail credits of a picture, are often less than descriptive: "best boy," for example. We shall also survey the chain of command on the set.

Other Team Members. The person ultimately in charge of the production team is the producer, and the following people answer to the producer directly: the supervising editor, the film publicist, the director, the art director or production designer, the production manager, and the production secretaries and assistants.

The **film publicist** helps to generate interest in a production by leaking stories to columnists, issuing formal press releases, arranging on-the-set interviews, putting together the press book, and helping to design a publicity campaign that will peak just before the movie's release. The still photographer works closely with the publicist but answers to the cinematographer.

The production manager is the producer's representative, the behind-the-scenes expediter. On location that job may be delegated to a **location manager**, who is assisted by a **location auditor** or accountant. In some cases the production manager will be an executive in charge of several projects and will delegate the day-to-day responsibilities to a **unit manager**, now usually referred to as a **unit production manager**. When second and third units are at work, each has its own unit manager. Whether the first unit is supervised by the production manager, a location manager, or a unit manager depends largely on how the picture has been financed and where it is being shot, but in all cases that person works closely with the first A.D.

As a single example of how the production manager represents the interests of the producer while arranging matters in the interest of team efficiency, consider the **call sheet**, which is distributed

CALL SHEET

weath.	SCATTERED THUNDERSHOWERS
sunrise/	558A - set/ 803P

1st UNIT
5TH DAY OF SHOOTING ''FOOL FOR LOVE''
400P LV HOTEL SHOOTING CALL 530P
PRODUCER GOLAN/GLOBUS
DATE FRI 5/17/85

PICT. ''FOOL FOR LOVE'' 984-2591 NO. _____ DIRECTOR Robert Altman

CAST

SET		SCS.		LOC.
SET	EXT. JUNKYARD (DUSK)	4, 7, 10	(1 DBL, 2)	EL ROYAL MOTEL
SET	EXT. MOTEL (DUSK)	14	(1 DBL, 2)	"
SET	CONT AND COMPLETE: INT MAY'S UNIT (DUSK)	26 PT	(1, 3)	"
SET	INT./EXT. MOTEL (N)	27	(1, 3)	"
SET	EXT. MOTEL (N)	28	(1, 2, 3)	"
SET				
SET				

CAST AND DAY PLAYERS	PART OF	LV. HOTEL	MAKE-UP	REMARKS
Sam Shepard	1. Eddie		600P	RPT TO LOCATION 600P
Harry Dean Stanton	2. Old Man	400P	430P	RPT TO LOCATION 430P
Kim Basinger	3. May	530P	600P	RPT TO LOCATION 600P

ATMOSPHERE AND STANDINS		THRU GATE
	16. EDDIE DBL	W/N

ADVANCE SCHEDULE OR CHANGES

SAT. 5/18	EXT. MOTEL (DUSK)	SC 3 EST SHOT MOTEL	
	INT. RESTAURANT (DUSK)	SC 5, 11, 13	CAST #3
	EXT. RESTAURANT (DUSK)	SC 8	" #1, 3
	IF NOT COMP. EXT. MOTEL (N)	SC 28 PT	" #1, 2, 3
MON. 5/20	INT./EXT. RESTAURANT (DUSK)	SC 16	CAST #3, 1 DBL
	INT./EXT. MAY'S UNIT (DUSK)	SC 18, 20, 23	" #1, 3
	EXT. MOTEL/JUNKYARD (DUSK)	SC 17, 21	" #7
	INT. MAY'S UNIT (N)	SC 29	" #1, 3

NO.	ITEM	LV.	NO.	ITEM	LV.	NO.	ITEM	LV.
1	CAMERAMAN	400P	1	MAKEUP/hair	400P	1	prod. van	ON LOC
	OPERATOR			EXTRA MAKEUP MEN		1	INSERT CAR	ON LOC
1	ASSISTANT	400P		HAIR STYLIST			STANDBY CAR	
1	ASSISTANT	400P		EXTRA HAIR STYLIST		1	set dressing trk	ON LOC
	EXTRA CAMERA			BODY MAKEUP WOMAN		1	prop trk	ON LOC
	EXTRA OPERATOR					1	VAN	ON LOC
1	EXTRA ASSISTANT	400P		COSTUMER (Men)		1	VAN lv hotel	400P
	PHOTO FXS. REP.		1	COSTUMER (Women)	400P			
1	KEY GRIP	400P		EXTRA COSTUMER (Men)			PICTURE CARS & TRUCK	
1	2nd GRIP	400P		EXTRA COSTUMER (Women)		1	EDDIE'S RIG	ON LOC
1	EXTRA GRIPS	400P						
	CRANE & CREW		1	GAFFER	400P		TRUCKS	
	CRAB DOLLY		1	BEST BOY	400P	1	pick up trk	400P
2	laborers on loc	400P	1	LAMP OPERATOR	400P			
	LANDSCAPE MAN			LOCAL #40 MAN			SCHOOLROOM TRAILERS	
1	PAINTER	O.C.	1	PROPERTY MAN	400P	5	DRESSING RM. TRAILERS	ON LOC
1	const. cord	O.C.	1	ASST. PROP. MAN	400P	2	prop. trlr	ON LOC
1	const. foreman	O.C.		EXTRA ASST. PROP. MEN				
	MECH. EFFECTS MEN		3	SET DRESSER	O.C.	1	SOUND MIXER	400P
1	SCRIPT SUPERVISOR	400P		DRAPERY MAN			SOUND RECORDER	
	EXTRA ASST. DIR.			FIXTURE MAN		1	BOOM OPERATOR	400P
	STILLMAN			WARDROBE RACKS		1	CABLE MAN	400P
1	REGISTERED NURSE ON LOC	430P		MAKEUP TABLES			EXTRA CABLE MAN	
	FIREMAN		55	HOT LUNCHES RDY BY	900P		P.A. SYSTEM	
	FIRE WARDEN			BOX LUNCHES			PLAYBACK MACH. & OPER.	
1	MOTORCYCLE POLICE ON LOC	430P		DINNERS		2	WRANGLERS ON LOC	430P
	POLICE PERMITS		XX	GAL COFFEE			LIVESTOCK:	
1	location manager	O.C.				3	HORSES ON LOC	430P

PROD. MANAGER: NICHOLLS ASSIST. DIRECTORS DOWD/DUNN

SPECIAL INSTRUCTIONS

VEHICLES: EDDIE'S RIG PROPS: BOTTLE OF TEQUILA
OWNER'S CAR SADDLE
VALLIANT

Figure 3-102

at the end of each shooting day and lets cast and crew members know what will be shot the next day and when and where to show up for work. It is prepared by the second A.D., revised if necessary by the first A.D., and approved by the production manager. **Fig. 3-102** is the call sheet for the fifth night of first unit shooting on Robert Altman's adaptation of Sam Shepard's *Fool for Love* (1985), and by now you have enough technical background and know enough terms and abbreviations to understand its every instruction and nuance. The complementary piece of paperwork, prepared by the same people, is the **production report**, a daily record of what was actually accomplished: the footage shot, the pages of script covered, the number of setups, and so on.

Working directly under the production manager are the unit manger; the **production accountant**, who keeps track of expenses; the **production secretary**, who coordinates the office paperwork; and one or more **production assistants**, who can be deeply involved in the creative enterprise or who might spend all their time running errands (that is, as "go-fers"), depending on their own skills and the extent to which those are considered valuable. Some production assistants are assigned to the director. The production manager also supervises the work of the first-aid technician; the **studio teacher**, who instructs child actors for at least three hours every school day in a quiet and "morally wholesome" environment; the **utility crew**, who guard the set, keep it clean, restock supplies, and run errands; the **craft service** person, who keeps the crew supplied with beverages and snacks; and the **transportation crew**.

The transportation category is headed by the **driver captain**, who is in charge of all vehicles that will be used by production personnel for official purposes and who assigns a **driver** to each of them. Tractor-trailers are manned by **rig drivers**. The mobile studio — a trailer-sized van stocked with production equipment — is driven and maintained by the **mobile studio operator**. **Stunt drivers** operate on-camera vehicles used in stunts; other on-camera vehicles are simply driven by actors.

The art director, who also answers directly to the producer, supervises the set, prop, wardrobe, and makeup categories. His or her immediate team consists of the set decorator, the key set builder, the costume designer, the wardrobe master, the scenic artist, and the artist/illustrator. The set decorator, in turn, supervises the prop master.

The set decorator selects and directs the placement of all set dressings. **Set dressing** consists of all furnishings, fixtures, appliances, and objects attached to the walls, floor, and ceiling of an interior set; for an exterior set, it includes items that appear to be integral parts of the set, including fences, brick paths, sheds, and even animals. **Set props** are those items that appear to be "fixed" — floor lamps, pictures hung on the walls, refrigerators, large potted plants, etc. They are distinct from **hand props**, which are carried or handled by the actors: money, food, glass paperweights, chain saws, baseball bats. The property master is in charge of all hand and set props and supervises the greens handler, the assistant prop handlers, the set dressers, and the home economist.

A number of specialists work under the prop master but also report to the director. These are the key and assistant special effects technicians, who handle mechanical special effects; the **animal specialist** or **trainer**, who feeds Toto and gets him to jump out of Miss Gulch's basket; and the **wrangler**, who takes care of livestock and animals that require no special training and are not inherently dangerous. Venomous snakes have to be handled by an animal specialist, regardless of whether they can do tricks.

The key set builder constructs or directs the construction of the sets, the scaffolding, the furniture, and the set dressing. He or she supervises the **carpenter** and the **assistant carpenters**, who do the planing, sawing, hammering, gluing, and framing that can turn an acre of desert into a town of false fronts or a sound stage into an undressed hotel lobby. The **key painter**, whose assistant is simply called a **painter**, paints the sets and also does special production artwork: filling a pond with red dye, for example, as was required for the bloody sea battle in *Kwaidan*. The **upholsterer** applies padding and material to the furniture, and the **draper** arranges, modifies, and hangs curtains, nets, and similar set dressings. The **paperhanger** puts up wallpaper, and the **tiler** puts up tiles. The **ornamental plasterer** constructs and installs decorative moldings and sculptures. Models and miniatures are constructed by the **model builder**, and special hand and set props by the **propmaker**. Other **construction specialists** are called in for such special jobs as cabinetmaking, bricklaying, wood carving, pipe fitting, plumbing, excavating, and concrete pouring. Special **equipment operators** are hired to run cranes, bulldozers, and fork-lifts.

The **scenic artist** executes — and often designs — painted backgrounds. Whereas the key painter does on a set what you might do when painting a bedroom, the scenic artist paints pictures that will stand behind the set (**backdrops**) or that might appear to *be* the set (**matte paintings**, usually done on masonite or glass). The view of ancient Rome near the start of Kubrick's *Spartacus* (1960) was a matte painting, as was the cliff through which a torrent of water poured in *Indiana Jones and the Temple of Doom*.

The director answers to the producer and supervises the director of photography, the production mixer, the chief re-recording mixer, and the supervising editor. The director of photography, in turn, supervises the technical crew. The director is in charge, then, of getting the picture and the sound tracks.

It is significant that the supervising editor, who oversees the cutting of both picture and sound tracks, communicates with the director but answers to the producer. The rigor of these chains of command and communication is one reason that some directors prefer to act as their own producers, so that less will be out of their hands, but it is also essential for optimum set operation.

Although the actors are employed by the producer, they answer to the director; some big stars, however, take their problems to the producer and can even demand that the director be replaced.

Much of *Gone With the Wind* had been shot by George Cukor before Clark Gable came on and insisted on working with Victor Fleming. Bette Davis often said that she would accept direction only when the director knew what he was doing; otherwise she would direct herself.

The director of photography, as the head of the technical crew, supervises the camera operator, the first and second camera assistants, the process projectionist, the aerial and underwater camera operators, the second unit cinematographer, and the still photographer. Electricians and grips are part of the camera crew. The director instructs or consults with the cinematographer, who then deals directly with the gaffer, the key grip, etc.

The **gaffer**, or **key electrician**, is the head of the electrical category. Most of the electrical work on a set involves setting and powering the lights, whose placement is determined by the cinematographer and is supervised by the gaffer. The gaffer also makes all hot or mainline electrical connections, checks lamps for their color-temperature output, keeps an eye on safety conditions, sometimes operates a dimmer board (a console of rheostats), and is rarely seen without a light meter. The gaffer is assisted by the **best boy**, who may be of any sex or age. Sometimes the best boy is the gaffer's right-hand person on the set — making electrical connections, operating wind machines, and pre-lighting the next set to save time — but often the best boy (and, analogously, the best boy grip) is on the truck where the equipment is stored, making sure that it is there and in working order, or off the set doing repairs and ordering new equipment.

Whether on a sound stage or on location, most electrical equipment is powered by a fixed or portable generator, which is run by the **generator operator**. A set is rarely wired the way a house is. Typically, when an actor hits a wall switch and the lights come on, the switch is just a prop and an electrical assistant has hit a live ("hot") switch off-camera — sometimes a bit too gradually, as you may occasionally have noticed. A crew of **electricians** report to the gaffer and sometimes to the best boy; they are the ones who, in most cases, do the physical work of setting up, operating, and taking down the lights, the cables, and the light-modifying equipment directly attached to the lights (like scrims). **Riggers** work before the shooting, laying cable and setting up big lights in their rough positions. **Operators** or **lamp operators** are on-the-set electricians who work during shooting.

Grips do most of the moving and hauling on the set. The bigger the production and the heavier the equipment, the more grips are employed. They move such camera equipment as dollies and cranes; pull cables when the camera is moving; set up and take down flags, gobos, backdrops, and reflectors; lay down tracks and boards for tracking shots; set up portable dressing rooms and toilets; hang flats to make walls or remove pieces of ceiling and floor for extremely high- and low-angle shots; and generally set up, support and anchor, and strike (take down) the set. All of these activities are supervised by the **key grip**, the head of the grip category, who works with the gaffer and reports to the director of photography. The key grip is assisted by the **best boy grip**, or **first assistant grip**, who may well be off in a trailer full of equipment or on the set as the key grip's right-hand person. The key and best boy grips supervise the other grips and **riggers**. The rigging crew in grip, like the electric riggers, come on the set before shooting and set up or build major constructions (such as dropping, from the permanent scaffolding, temporary scaffolding on which lights are set). The **dolly grip** (or if a crane is being operated, the **crane/boom grip**) operates or pushes the mobile camera platform after laying tracks, placing marks, or perhaps leveling the crane bed.

The production mixer and the sound recording crew have already been discussed in detail, and the jobs of the chief re-recording mixer and the supervising editor will be taken up in the next section. Working with the mixer and the supervising editor allows the director to oversee the treatment of what he or she has been responsible for getting on film and on tape.

The modification and assembly of those materials, the final gathering-together of the best takes and tracks and their organization into a finished, releasable motion picture, is the essence of post-production. For a director/theorist like Pudovkin, all of the work we have examined so far would be considered merely preparatory, the gathering of raw materials that will take on life and meaning only when they have been edited. (Hitchcock, on the other hand, felt the job was completed in pre-production.) Most filmmakers have some kind of editing and mixing plan in mind during shooting and often even during development. But whether the piles of cans filled with film and mag represent a disaster waiting to happen or a masterpiece on its way to a major award, those cans will have to be opened, the reels unrolled and broken down, and the parts joined into a whole. It is time to put the pieces together.

5. Post-production

A well-known 1977 film begins in the following manner. A brief fade-in presents the 20th Century-Fox logo; this fades out and a second title fades in and out: "A Lucasfilm Limited Production." Over both these shots the Fox fanfare is heard. Shot 3 presents another title: "A long time ago in a galaxy far, far away." The Lucasfilm logo has been green; this title is blue, and the soundtrack is silent. Then John Williams's fanfare starts, exactly as Shot 4 begins with the title, *Star Wars*; that title is in yellow, and it rapidly disappears into the background. As the fanfare continues, yellow rolling titles enter from the lower foreground and move toward their vanishing point in the upper background. These titles for "Episode IV: A New Hope" set the scene for the opening action and — because they are modeled on the opening titles of the *Buck Rogers* and *Flash Gordon* serials of the 1930s — anchor this film in the context of film history. Behind the titles is an expanse of stars.

Eventually the titles dissolve, leaving only the star field; the music changes mood, and the camera tilts down to show the horizon of a blue planet. A ship enters the frame from the top foreground and heads for the center background. This is Princess Leia's ship, and it is being pursued by a larger Imperial ship. Both these vehicles are miniatures, matted against the star field, and the blasts from their weapons are seen and heard: heard as sound effects and seen as individually rotoscoped streaks. By the end of this shot, the Imperial ship nearly fills the top of the frame. There is a reverse cut to Shot 5, showing the chase from the front. Shot 6 shows an explosion on the surface of Leia's ship, and the sound of the explosion carries over into Shot 7, where three robots are shown inside Leia's ship, reacting to the blast.

Out of all of these sounds and pictures, only the visual elements of Shot 7 were created during production. All the rest was planned during development and pre-production and was executed during post-production ("in post").

"That's a wrap!" is how the director announces to the crew that a shot has been satisfactorily completed. The ultimate **wrap** declares the end of production work on the set or on location. But after the wrap party, after all the sets have been struck and many of the filmmakers have gone on to other projects, there is still a great deal of work to do. Special photographic effects work, which may have been proceeding independently during the period of principal photography, goes into high gear during post-production. The picture has to be edited before the composer and the music editor can develop a coordinated music track. The sound, which has already been transferred to mag, must be edited and mixed. Then the laboratory makes a print of the first cut, which may be accepted, refined, or rejected. Only when a final cut has been approved and is ready for duplication does the entire production process — which began with development — finally end, and at that point the picture will either sit on a shelf or it will go into distribution.

Special Effects Cinematography _____

There are some things that just cannot be shot on a set, full scale and in real time, and others that could be shot that way but only with an unacceptable expense of time and money. **Special effects** is the domain of showing the impossible or the impractical, the art of making things appear to have happened. Production effects, including mechanicals, are those that can be staged during principal or second-unit photography and that can be photographed in a single pass by an unmodified production camera. **Special photographic effects**, often called **special effects cinematography**, employ photographic techniques to achieve their illusions. They may call for a modified production camera, a special process camera (used in the optical printing house or the laboratory rather than on a set), unconventional lighting, fixed and traveling mattes, bipack and optical printing, and an unusual degree of creative resourcefulness. Because of the extreme care and precision required, special effects cinematography is usually handled by a separate unit, working at its own pace without tying up production personnel and full-scale sets. But the most important reason that these effects are consigned to post-production, besides the obvious consideration that production footage must be on hand before it can be integrated into a composite, is that there is usually no way to achieve the desired effect with normal procedures.

Special photographic effects are divided into two major categories, depending on whether the effect is achieved on the original negative (**in-camera effects**) or on a fresh piece of stock (**laboratory effects**). In-camera effects avoid rephotography, which is their principal advantage. A picture of a picture will have more grain, higher contrast, and less resolution than the original, whether one is duplicating a release print or assembling a composite. With every succeeding **print generation** (not with every copy; all prints made from the same negative belong to the same generation and are nearly equivalent in quality), these problems become more noticeable, just as re-recording compounds the noise level on a soundtrack. The disadvantage of in-camera effects is that they can tie up production personnel for a long and expensive time, whereas laboratory effects can be done off the set. Lab effects generally take more time than in-camera effects, but the time is less expensive.

Improvements in the technology of optical and contact printing during the last 35 years have mitigated some of the problems associated with rephotography, rendering some in-camera effects nearly obsolete. The problem of resolution, for example, is less serious when an effects shot can begin its career on 65mm filmstock or in VistaVision; by the time it is ready for the final 35mm composite, it might have as much surviving detail as a 35mm camera original. Even the contrast and grain problems can be tackled on a good optical printer and with the help of low-contrast, fine-grain duplicating stocks.

If you have ever noticed an effects shot that is free of matte lines but still looks somehow "wrong," chances are that you are responding to the degraded quality of the overduplicated image. Even in *Star Wars* there are a few blue-screen shots of Solo and crew against the Falcon's viewing portal and the star field beyond, where Solo appears to have been bleached out and flattened. In general, however, laboratory effects are now capable of passing for camera originals, at least in image quality, and they account for most of the work being done today. In this section we shall take a look at those effects most commonly used in the 1980s as well as at older technologies that work on related principles.

Simple In-Camera Effects. In the context of special effects cinematography, what we have been calling a camera is known as a **production camera**. Its job is to expose a single length of filmstock to the imagery of the outside world. In contrast, a **process camera** may happily work one frame at a time and may be loaded with several lengths of filmstock. "In-camera effects" refers only to those achieved with a production camera.

The production camera has only a few ways of modifying what it photographs, notably a variable aperture, a variable-speed motor, a matte box, and a behind-the-lens filter (or aperture plate) slot. These are entirely adequate for day-for-night and slow- and fast-motion effects. Slow motion is one effect that *always* looks better when done in the camera. (An optical printer cannot supply images of the intermediate positions recorded by the camera at, say, 120 fps; instead, it must repeat the available frames.) Mattes and counter-mattes, mounted precisely in the matte box, allow for split-screen effects and in-camera matte shots, which will be discussed shortly.

Effects can also be created by stopping and starting the camera's motor. The first known special effects shot was of this type and was taken by Alfred Clark for the 1895 Edison film, *The Execution of Mary, Queen of Scots*. The actor knelt down before the chopping block, the camera was stopped, and everyone held their places while a dummy was exchanged for the actor. Then the camera started up again, and the dummy was beheaded. Fades, dissolves, and multiple exposures can also be done in a production camera, although it is wiser to make such decisions during the editing phase.

Prestylization and Process Shots. One alternative to special effects cinematography is to prestylize the material that is being photographed: to create an illusion full scale and in real time. Tod Browning's *Devil Doll* (1936) made its characters appear tiny by photographing them in oversized sets (**Fig. 3-103**).

In general, the effectiveness of an effects shot depends on the care with which it is executed and the context into which it is edited. Just as a film can be salted with lip-sync shots and appear to be completely lip-sync, a film like *Devil Doll* or *King Kong* can interweave normal production shots, production effects shots, and

Figure 3-103

laboratory matte shots, yielding the impression that the scale effects are continuous. Having seen the actress climb onto a gigantic prop, the viewer will carry over some of that impression of realism when watching the actress being held aloft by the mad doctor in a traveling matte shot; the matte shot will seem less "faked," and both will give the impression of having really happened, which is what "realism" means in this context.

Some **process shots**, notably front and rear projection, are done on the camera original during first exposure. In rear projection, as explained previously, footage of the background is projected onto a screen from behind, and the actors and other foreground objects are photographed along with the background footage onto the negative in the camera. In front projection the setup is more complex but less expensive. The background, which is often a slide but can also be movie footage, is projected from the side into a treated two-way mirror called a **beam-splitter**, or **beam-combiner** (see the glossary). The projected image is reflected by the mirror onto a screen in the background. The camera shoots directly through the beam-combiner and photographs both the actors or objects in the foreground and the image on the screen. Front projection was pioneered for *2001*, where it provided all of the backgrounds for the "Dawn of Man" sequence (see **Fig. 2-55**). A front projection screen can be much larger than a rear projection screen.

Process shots are also done during post-production. **Fig. 3-104** shows such a shot from *King Kong*. The dinosaur was stop-motion animated on a miniature set, and when that footage was ready, Fay Wray reported back for work. She took her position in a tree, and the animated footage was rear-projected. One of the ways the makers of *Kong* kept their audiences guessing was to reverse this prac-

Figure 3-104

tice at many points during the film. Often they used footage of the principals (or of other people and locations) as *background* while animating models in the foreground. The rear-projected footage could be shown one frame at a time, with the animators adjusting the models frame by frame as usual.

Models and Miniatures. Whereas some miniatures are used as three-dimensional plans for full-scale sets, there are others that are intended to pass for full-scale sets and figures. Although the terms are often used interchangeably, a **miniature** usually denotes a set, whereas a **model** is an individual component of that set — one of the buildings in the miniature downtown landscape of Ridley Scott's *Blade Runner* (1982), for instance, or a figure like King Kong. Shots of these small-scale objects may appear on their own, or they may be optically combined with other shots through in-camera or laboratory techniques. **Fig. 3-105** shows one model of the ship used in *Battleship Potemkin*. The full-scale ship remained at dockside throughout the shooting.

In the years since *Potemkin* was made, the construction and photographing of models have come to be done with much greater precision and expertise. Not only have the models themselves become more detailed, to the point where they can pass for full scale in close shots, but reliable **time/scale formulas** have been worked out. For a model to look convincing, its apparent mass and the velocities of its moving elements must be made to conform with those of the full-scale objects. A miniature car will fall off a miniature cliff at a rate determined by its own mass, not that of the full-sized car. The solution is to shoot the model in slow motion. If the model is one quarter of normal scale, the camera's operating speed

Figure 3-105

Figure 3-106

must be doubled; if the model is one hundredth of normal scale, the camera must be sped up by a factor of 10. In the color section **Fig. C-80** shows the crew at Industrial Light and Magic (ILM) shooting an explosion on the surface of the model of the Death Star for *Star Wars*. However detailed the model, this shot would not have worked if the camera had not been overcranking for slow motion.

Fig. 3-106 shows one of the miniature sets used in Cooper and Schoedsack's *Son of Kong* (December, 1933), complete with the table on which it was constructed. It was against such a background that the model of Kong, Jr., went through its stop-motion paces. Although they had access to more sophisticated equipment, Jon Berg and Phil Tippett used many of the techniques perfected by Willis O'Brien for the Kong films when they were creating the chessboard scene for *Star Wars* and the Tauntaun scenes for *The Empire Strikes Back*.

In the opening sequence of *Empire*, both Luke and Solo are shown riding Tauntauns through a snowy landscape. The snow was baking soda, the landscape was a miniature, and the Tauntauns and their riders were stop-motion-animated models. There were also full-scale medium shots of the real actors on Tauntaun mockups, and these were intercut with the miniature shots to produce the impression of action and scale continuity. Like Kong, the Tauntaun was a flexible puppet with a wire **armature** that functioned as a kind of skeleton and held the model in each of the discrete positions determined by the animator. Around the armature was a body of claylike material, and onto that was glued the animal's coat. In **Fig. 3-107** the Tauntaun's coat receives its final trimming. If you look at *Empire* very closely, you can see the Tauntaun's fur

Figure 3-107

Figure 3-108

rippling as it runs. This effect is much more noticeable in *King
Kong*, where Kong's coat is alive with the imprint of O'Brien's fingers. Rather than approaching that as a technical failure, it is exciting to find the evidence of Kong's making on his "person" and
to consider it the artist's signature: O'Brien's presence in the work.
In **Fig. 3-108** Phil Tippett is shown using height gauges for reference as he shifts the model Tauntaun and its rider from one exposure position to another.

The Tauntauns and the Walkers were animated on a miniature
set of the ice world of Hoth. In the color section **Figs. C-81** and
C-82 show how this was done with the Walkers. In **Fig. C-81** you
can see the height gauges alongside the models. The animators are

wearing surgical masks so that they will neither disturb nor inhale the baking soda snowscape. The background is a painting. **Fig. C-82** offers a more comprehensive view of the set and the backdrop. In the central foreground you can see the VistaVision camera; off to the right, the video monitor is part of an instant-replay video animation system developed by Lyon-Lamb. The Walkers were not animated through video techniques, but the system allowed the animators to check the results of the work they had prepared for the camera.

Miniatures can also help to generate weather effects. The tornado in *The Wizard of Oz* was a large-scale mechanical effect, though its 35-foot-long muslin sock was much smaller than a real twister. The top of the windsock was attached to a movable steel structure (a gantry) that tracked forward and backward along the ceiling of the soundstage. The bottom was attached to a small car that could make faster and more intricate movements. For the tornado in *Poltergeist* (**Fig. C-83**), the technicians at ILM worked on a smaller and relatively less expensive scale. Much like those in *Close Encounters*, the cloud effects in *Poltergeist* were created by the injection of paint into an aquarium filled with salt water. The tornado was made in a similar tank — a true tempest in a teapot — using a high-speed impeller to create the vortex and a bubble wand (courtesy of Marineland) to make the spinning water effervescent. Front and center, you can see the VistaVision camera, and off to the left, the video monitor. The coloring of the tornado and its matting into various composites were done later.

The making of models can be an extremely elaborate task. The longer a model is onscreen, the greater the danger that the audience will see that it *is* a model. One way around this problem is to keep the effects shot as short as possible; the better alternative is to make the model so detailed that it can pass for the real thing even in a leisurely shot.

The effects work for *Blade Runner* was done by Douglas Trumbull and Richard Yuricich's Entertainment Effects Group (EEG), which, with Lucas's ILM and John Dykstra's Apogee, is one of the three most accomplished and prestigious special effects houses now active in America. In *2001, Close Encounters*, and other films, Trumbull raised the slow-paced effects shot to a high order of art; for *Blade Runner*'s majestic opening sequence, Trumbull insisted on a highly detailed miniature set that could stand up to the scrutiny of the audience and convey a vivid impression of twenty-first-century Los Angeles. The model of the pyramid — the mile-high office building of the Tyrell Corporation, which the camera tracks up to in the opening shots and where the first interview scene is set — was designed by Tom Cranham. Once the rough designs had been sketched, a draftsman drew up a detailed pattern for the exterior of the pyramid (**Fig. 3-109**). Clear resin molds, cast in this pattern, were attached to the frame of the model and painted. Some of the paint was scraped away from inside so that a light source planted within the model would give the effect of lighted office windows. After precise touch-up work (**Fig.**

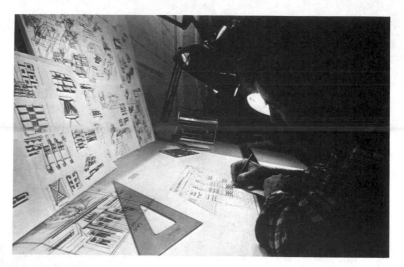

Figure 3-109

Figure 3-110

Figure 3-111

Figure 3-112

Figure 3-113

3-110), the model was photographed with a motion-control camera (**Fig. 3-111**). Because the light levels were low and Trumbull wanted maximum depth of field, the exposures were very long. The computerized motion-control camera executed many "passes" over the various miniatures (a **pass** is an effects take, a single passage of filmstock through the gate of a camera or printer, or a motion-controlled camera movement), each one capable of being repeated precisely.

Another use of the miniature, now more-or-less obsolete, is to suspend it between the camera and a partial but full-scale set: the **hanging miniature** technique. For MGM's 1925 version of *Ben-Hur,* Arnold Gillespie designed and rigged a hanging miniature that made the Circus Maximus appear to be a fully realized set. In **Fig. 3-112** you can see the full-scale portions of the set: the track and the bottom of the stands. Between that set and the camera, Gillespie hung a miniature of the upper stands, and the result can be seen in **Fig. 3-113**.

Glass Shots and Matte Paintings. Instead of a three-dimensional hanging miniature, the **glass shot** interposes a mirror or a matte painting between the camera and the rest of the set. In the color section **Fig. C-84** shows the camera, painted glass, and miniature set in position to create **Fig. C-85**, an exterior from Michael Benveniste's *Flesh Gordon* (1972).

A matte painting usually has several areas that are left transparent, through which the camera can see the set. How those areas are determined and cleared depends on how the shot is to be taken. In the simplest case, the completely detailed painting is mounted between the camera and the set, and then paint is scraped off the glass in specific areas; an assistant looks through the viewfinder to make sure that all the transparent areas are in

Figure 3-114

the right place. Another method is to do the matte painting on a stiff board and then to cut holes in it. The most common technique is to shoot the live action first, process that footage, and then load it into the camera (with the back of the camera left open) and project it onto a blank matte board or sheet of glass. The matte artist can then outline the areas on the matte board that will need to remain transparent so that the desired full-scale material will be visible when that footage and the completed matte painting are rephotographed (usually with a bi-pack camera).

Figure 3-115

Most matte paintings are done in a realistic, representational style because they are usually intended to strike the audience as genuine locations. **Fig. 3-114** is one of the matte paintings that Albert Whitlock did for Mark Robson's *Earthquake* (1974). The matte painting of Kane's Xanadu (**Fig. 3-115**) is more painterly and slightly less realistic.

Some glass-shot elements are photographed rather than painted. Cloud backgrounds are often shot onto oversized transparencies. In some cases a photograph can itself be blown up, be mounted onto composition board, and then have portions physically carved out. Whether painted or photographed, the "glass" has to be very carefully positioned so that both it and the set are in focus and so that the correct elements of the set are in view.

The **mirror shot** is a variation on the glass shot; it allows a three-dimensional model or miniature set (or a painting, photo, or projection — any image a mirror can reflect) to be combined with live action in the camera. The mirror is placed between the camera and the set, at a 45° angle relative to the optical axis of the lens. Off to the side, and reflected by the mirror back into the lens, is the miniature, artwork, or model. The set, where the actors perform, is straight ahead. If the mirror is partially silvered, the camera will see the set as well as a **phantom** or transparent image of what is reflected. (A two-way mirror or beam-combiner need not produce phantoms.) If the mirror is completely silvered, the set will be completely blocked. If the mirror is silvered, but only in certain discrete areas, then the camera will see the set through the glass where the silver has been scraped away, and will also see — but not as a phantom — what is reflected by the rest of the mirror. Among other things, mirror shots can be used to create split-screen effects, to fill out a partially constructed set, or to combine live action with miniatures. In the **Schüfftan process** (developed by Eugen Schüfftan and used throughout Fritz Lang's *Metropolis* [1926, released 1927]) the "immense" sets, which were usually hanging miniatures and painted backdrops, were reflected by a discretely front-silvered mirror; through the areas from which the silver had been removed, the camera saw the actors and the full-scale elements of the set. **Fig. 3-116** shows a Schüfftan shot from *Metropolis*; the actors, gong area, and lower level of the central buildings are full scale.

In-Camera Matte Shots. A matte may be made of metal, wood, masonite, or cardboard, may be painted on glass, or may be created through entirely photographic means; in some areas it is opaque, in others transparent. Its function is to block light from reaching the film in some areas and to admit light in other areas. A keyhole matte card, placed in the matte box (or, as a thin metal cutout, immediately behind the lens as an aperture plate), will admit light through the keyhole-shaped opening in its center and will block light everywhere else. Aside from the fact that a matte card affects the photograph and a matte painting *is* photographed, the essential difference between a matte card or plate and a matte painting is that although both of them allow the camera to photo-

Figure 3-116

Figure 3-117

graph certain information directly — that which is seen through the clear areas — the matte painting supplies information for the blocked areas, whereas the matte card or plate simply renders those areas opaque. Onto the opaque area, a second image can later be photographed, and neither the foreground nor the background information will be transparent. In-camera mattes are **fixed**: as opposed to traveling mattes, they do not change from frame to frame.

An early in-camera matte shot is shown in **Fig. 3-117**, from Edwin S. Porter's *The Dream of a Rarebit Fiend* (1906). First Porter mounted a matte card in the matte box, blocking off the top of the frame, and took a panning shot of New York City (note the Brooklyn Bridge). Then he covered the lens, cranked the film back to the beginning, took out the matte card, and inserted a **countermatte**: one that was opaque where the matte had been clear and clear where the matte had been opaque. The counter-matte blocked off that portion of the film where the cityscape had been recorded but left the top area open. Porter then re-exposed the same length of film, shooting the bed and the hapless dreamer (suspended by wires against a black background). For this second exposure, the camera did not move, and the effect when the two halves of the image were seen simultaneously was that the camera kept pace with the dreamer as his bed flew over the city.

A matte can be much more subtly contoured than the horizontal card used by Porter, and it can be used in combination with many other image-replacement techniques. **Fig. 3-118** shows the first stage of an in-camera matte shot that was used in the 1939 version of *The Hunchback of Notre Dame* (the one starring Charles Laughton and directed by William Dieterle). The effects supervisor was Linwood Dunn, who helped to develop the modern optical printer

Figure 3-118

Figure 3-119

and who did much of the photographic effects work on both *King Kong* and *Citizen Kane*. The Parisian set was partially constructed, and the upper background was matted out. The matte was not a piece of cardboard this time. Instead, a piece of glass was mounted between the camera and the set, and flat black paint was applied to the glass in the area that is opaque in **Fig. 3-118**. An assistant looked through the camera lens to make sure that the matte was painted in the proper areas, closely following the roof lines. The background was then painted on a separate pane of glass (a simple matte painting). A counter matte was prepared, blocking out the previously photographed areas of the frame. The matte painting was then photographed onto the original length of footage, and the result can be seen in **Fig. 3-119**. This can serve as a summary example of a sophisticated in-camera effect performed on the original negative.

Laboratory Effects. In order to appreciate some of the more complex effects that can be achieved with mattes, as well as to gain an overview of the whole range of "SPFX" cinematography, it is necessary to examine the various ways in which images are reproduced, whether when printing a film or when photographing a composite. A **composite** — any image made by combining two or more separately photographed images or elements, usually without phantom effects — is a representative laboratory effect.

An effects house or laboratory revolves around its printers. Most laboratory effects are created with the aid of an optical printer, which might be thought of as a camera facing a projector. The lensless rephotography done with a contact printer is far less selective, and so it has limited use in effects work. The bi-pack camera is used exclusively for effects, and it, too, is a printer.

Contact Printing. The simplest way to copy any length of film-stock is to use a contact printer. In a **contact printer** the original (previously exposed and processed) and the printing stock (unexposed) are loaded with their emulsions facing each other; when they pass the shutter, they are actually touching (in contact). The printer light shines through the shutter and the original, thereby exposing the print footage.

A contact printer is used for the simple duplication of a film — for example, when one is making release prints from a final negative — but it can also create fades, dissolves, and simple superimpositions, as well as modify exposure. The printer light can be made brighter or fainter, and the printer's variable shutter can be opened or closed or anywhere in between. If the original is too dark, for example, the printer light can be intensified, yielding a better-exposed copy; this process is called **timing** a print.

Film normally runs through a contact printer at a relatively high rate of speed. For especially precise tasks, it is necessary that the original and print stocks be kept absolutely unmoving and perfectly aligned during the instant of exposure, and for this purpose a step printer is used. A **step printer** is one in which registration pins descend to engage the sprocket holes of both filmstocks. These pins, which you might want to imagine as blunt needles on a sewing machine, keep the two frames in perfect **registration** (fixed alignment); then they get out of the way while the film advances. Many of the best production cameras and projectors use registration pins; they are not found only in printers.

Bi-Pack. A **bi-pack camera** is both a process camera and a step-contact printer. When film is loaded in bi-pack, what that means is that two loads of film are sandwiched together. Each load has its own feed and take-up reels, but both loads are threaded over the same sprocket wheels and both are simultaneously exposed when the shutter opens. Both contact printers and bi-pack cameras are loaded in this manner. The bi-pack camera can be fitted with a prism and an auxiliary lamphouse: the pressure plate — which keeps the filmstock flat against the aperture plate during the instant of exposure — can be removed, and a prism and lamp can be set behind the film. This temporary modification allows the camera to function as a projector, throwing the image onto a screen mounted a few feet in front of the camera. The prism-and-lamphouse assembly is called a **rotoscope**, and it is essential in the making of hand-drawn traveling mattes, which will be discussed later.

These are the stages involved in making a matte shot with a bi-pack camera. First, the live action is shot with a production camera, and then that processed footage is loaded into the camera on its own (that is, in **monopack**). The rotoscope assembly is installed, and a representative frame is projected onto an easel. The easel supports a piece of glass that has been painted entirely black and then repainted white. The matte artist traces the outlines of the live-action areas that will be retained in the final image. Of particular importance is the placement of the **matte line**, which will be the border between the live and painted areas. The artist then takes down the glass and paints the **replacement detail** (the image to be added to the live action) in the areas that will be or that have already been blocked out of the live-action shot. (The production footage could have been pre-matted in the camera, but more often it is shot full-frame.) The completed painting is returned to the easel. At this point the live frame is again projected onto the easel, and the artist makes the final decision about where to place the matte line. Where the live action will eventually appear on the composite, the artist scrapes all the paint away from the glass, including the black and white undercoats.

There are lights behind the easel as well as in front of it and to the sides. When a black cloth is hung behind the easel and the glass is lit from the front, all you can see is the painting and one or more opaque areas. When a white card is put behind the easel and the glass is lit from the back, the painted area becomes a silhouette, and the rest of the glass looks white. These setups create the matte and the counter-matte.

The bi-pack camera is now loaded with a fine-grain low contrast print of the live-action footage (or the camera original) *and* fine-grain negative raw stock, in bi-pack. When the shutter opens, light passes through the original and onto the raw stock. If the card or glass on the easel is completely white, it will provide an even illumination sufficient to expose the raw stock, and in that case the bi-pack camera will be functioning simply as a contact printer. But if some areas of the glass are opaque, light from those specific areas will not be reflected into the lens, through the original, and onto the raw stock. The first time the bi-pack load is run through the camera, the easel is lit from behind, and the painted area functions as a matte. Only those areas of the original that correspond to the white areas on the glass will be exposed and printed onto the raw stock, and the result will look something like **Fig. 3-118.** Then the original is removed, and the selectively exposed raw stock is wound back to its start. This time the easel is lit from the front, with a black cloth hung behind it. During this pass, the black area functions as a counter-matte (preventing the live-action area from being re-exposed), and the painting is exposed to the remainder of the frame. The resulting composite will look something like **Fig. 3-119.**

The advantage of using conventional glass shots rather than bi-pack printing is that in the former case, all of the image elements are captured on the original negative. As previously explained, every time a length of stock is duplicated (**duped**), the quality of the image is slightly degraded. The bi-pack composite is one generation removed from the original. Although optical printing is indispensable in contemporary post-production activity, its composites are often two or more generations removed. The advantage of bi-pack printing over production glass shots is that the production need not be held up while the matte artist prepares the painting. These trade-offs are typical of those the special effects supervisor must consider when deciding which process to use.

Optical Printing. An **optical printer** is a heavy and expensive piece of equipment; it is used to take a picture of a picture. The original and the raw stock are never in contact; instead, one or more optical systems intervene. As previously mentioned, the optical printer may be thought of as a projector and a camera that are facing each other. The "projector," called the **printer head**, is loaded with previously exposed footage, whether in monopack or bi-pack, and it projects the image directly into the lens of the process camera. The process camera can also be loaded monopack or bi-pack.

The printer head and the camera are mounted on rails and can move in relation to one another; the closer together they are, the more the original will be *reduced,* and the further apart they are, the more the original will be *magnified.* The camera lens, mounted on a bellows, may also be moved forward or backward for variable magnification. At an intermediate distance, the original can simply be copied (a magnification ratio of 1 : 1). Magnification is important when only part of the original is needed or desired; by blowing up the original and carefully positioning the camera, what is recorded on the raw stock (the **dupe negative**) will be a *cropped* version of the original. Reversing the process allows an entire original frame to occupy only a portion of the dupe frame; that is how the majority of split-screen and multiple-image effects are created today.

Fades, dissolves, and superimpositions can be made on an optical printer simply by controlling the opening of the variable shutter on the process camera, with the magnification set at 1 : 1. To ensure precise alignment within the bi-packs and exact frame-to-frame correspondence between the original and the dupe, most optical printers use registration pins (step-optical printing), and the entire assembly is massive to ensure against any vibration; the average optical printer weighs over a ton.

To appreciate the versatility of the optical printer and the ways in which it can create effects that would be impossible to shoot from nature, let us take a look at the final shot of Truffaut's *The 400 Blows* (1959). Antoine Doinel (played by Jean-Pierre Léaud) has run away from reform school, all the way to the beach. He has always wanted to see the ocean; now that he has arrived, he is at loose ends. Where will he go from here? What should his next goal be, and would achieving it accomplish any more than has his finally reaching the beach? Truffaut used to say that the conventional ending of a narrative film, in which the camera pulls away from the action (reversing the standard pattern of the establishing sequence), revealed a lack of understanding of or simply a withdrawal from the subject. Whether or not he was right about that, he was certainly committed to ending his own first feature with a forward movement, *toward* the subject. Using the optical printer, he and the effects supervisor achieved this movement in a radically original way.

As the shot begins (**Fig. 3-120**), Antoine slows to a walk. The camera moves toward him, and he appears to stop (**Fig. 3-121**).

Then the camera appears to rush forward so that Antoine's head nearly fills the frame (**Fig. 3-122**). Some people think that this last movement is a forward zoom executed by the production camera, but clearly it is not. The production camera did move forward during the shot, and it may well have gone all the way in for a closeup, but Truffaut used only the first half of the production footage, up to the frame shown in **Fig. 3-121**. That footage was then loaded into the printer head of an optical printer, with raw stock in the process camera. For the first half of the shot, the original was simply duplicated onto the negative. Then the printer head was stopped on the frame shown in **Fig. 3-121**, while the camera continued to run. The result was a **freeze frame**, a still image created by reprinting the same original frame many times. (You can identify a freeze frame not by the stillness of the action but by the way the film grain suddenly takes on a fixed pattern.) As the frame was being rephotographed, the printer head was moved farther from the camera. Both Antoine and the film grain were magnified, and the result was that the camera appeared to zoom in on an utterly arrested landscape and figure.

In addition to what this effect reveals about the workings of the optical printer, it also shows something about the origin of clichés. Ever since Truffaut conceived this use for the freeze frame — which in the context of *The 400 Blows* provided an appropriately open and closed ending — less original filmmakers have come to use freeze frames to end their pictures in midaction and to provide a background for the tail credits. **A cliché** is something that, more often than not, begins as an original metaphor but over the course of time becomes an automatic figure of speech (or cinema or whatever); by that time, what made it original and appropriate has been buried to the point of insignificance.

Other Optical Effects. The optical printer is most often used to effect such **optical transitions** as the fade, the dissolve, and the wipe, and it can do all of that when loaded in monopack. Bi-pack loads are used to make the majority of matte shots. Here is a brief catalog of the most common and representative optical effects, beyond those already mentioned:

Push-Offs. In a wipe, one image is gradually revealed while another is gradually obscured. In a push-off, the complete new image appears to displace the previous one — virtually to shove it off the screen.

Reduction Printing. A large-format original is copied onto raw stock of a narrower gauge. A 35mm feature might be copied onto 16mm for use in classrooms or similar nontheatrical situations, or a 65mm effects shot might be reduced to 35mm.

Blow-Ups. The reverse of reduction printing. A film shot in 16mm might be blown up to 35mm for theatrical exhibition.

Cropping. Part of the original frame is made to fill up the dupe frame. This is one way to fix a take that inadvertently included a boom mike, or to censor part of an image. This process leads to an increase in the size of the film grain.

Figure 3-120

Figure 3-121

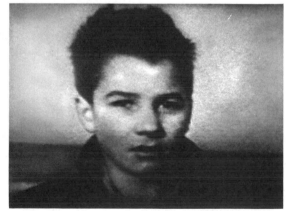

Figure 3-122

Pan and Scan. A wide image is selectively rephotographed so that its most essential action area will be copied onto a standard-sized frame. Sometimes the dupe area appears to pan across the space of the original; sometimes the original shot is cut into two or more shots; most often, the original is simply cropped.

Skip Framing. A way of achieving fast motion. The original, which was photographed at 24 fps, is run through the printer head, and the camera rephotographs only every second frame, doubling the apparent rate of motion. If faster motion is desired, the camera can be set to skip more frames between exposures.

Multiple Printing. The reverse of skip framing, producing a somewhat jerky variety of slow motion. The printer head holds each original frame while the camera rephotographs it as many times as desired. In *The Empire Strikes Back*, when Luke confronts his image of Darth Vader in a cavern, the slow-motion effects were achieved in this manner.

Flip Shots. The original is flipped left-to-right on the dupe. Sometimes this can remedy a director's having crossed the line, or reverse an image that had to be shot in a mirror.

Double Printing. More than one original is copied onto the dupe, and the images are superimposed. Relatively underexposed images will appear transparent (like "phantoms"); fully exposed images will appear solid. If one of the latter is perfectly white (clear), so that it can "burn" away whatever has been recorded in that area of the negative during a previous pass, it will be entirely opaque on the negative and clear on the print. That is how white titles and subtitles are superimposed over previously shot footage; if they are to be colored, it is necessary to use traveling mattes or bi-pack printing.

Reverse Printing. The original runs from tail to head while the dupe runs from head to tail. The result is that the action proceeds in reverse.

Back-and-Forth Printing. The original runs forward and backward while the camera runs forward. The action appears to advance and retreat. You could take a shot of a cat waving its paw once, back-and-forth print it, matte in a bag of cat food, and end up with a product endorsement ("Chow chow chow!").

Split Screen. Two or more originals are copied onto discrete areas of the dupe.

Rotary Movements. The printer head turns on its horizontal axis while the camera remains stationary. Newspaper headlines spin toward the audience!

Film Within a Film. One original is placed, without ghosting, within the area of another original on the dupe. Like split screen, of which this is a variety, this process inevitably involves the use of mattes. It is especially useful when an image is supposed to appear on a filmed television; when real TV is photographed by a movie camera, in most cases there is a wide black bar moving up through the image.

Day-for-Night. The original, shot day-for-day, is rephotographed through a neutral density filter or with the camera's aperture closed down two stops.

Scratch Removal. One of the many ways an optical printer can be useful in restoring an old film or salvaging wrecked new footage. The printer is fitted with a **liquid gate** so that the original is coated, just before the instant of exposure, with a transparent fluid that has the same refractive index as the filmstock. The liquid fills in the scratches and keeps them from showing; the dupe will appear scratch-free.

Mixing Black-and-White and Color. Both color and black-and-white originals are copied onto color stock. When a dissolve is made between a color version of a shot and a black-and-white version of that same shot, the image can appear to lose its color. The reverse of this was done at the start of Leonard Nimoy's *Star Trek III: The Search for Spock* (1984), in which black-and-white footage gradually takes on (that is, dissolves to) color.

In virtually all cases, once the final answer print has been approved, release prints are made on a contact printer. Optical printing is expensive and time-consuming, and there is little reason to use it for simple copying. But if you've ever tried to achieve a *Flash Gordon*–style wipe in a production camera, you will appreciate the versatility of this superior piece of equipment.

Traveling Mattes. Say that you wanted to make a film like Jack Arnold's *Tarantula* (1955), in which a giant spider lumbers across a desert landscape. The animal specialist is fresh out of 40-foot tarantulas. You get hold of a normal tarantula and photograph it in closeup and slow motion, then you shoot the desert in long shot, and then you double-print these originals. You end up with a giant transparent spider, which isn't what you wanted. Next you try making a matte in the shape of the spider, use that to block out a spider-shaped hole in the landscape, make a counter-matte so that the area around the original spider will not show, and print the results. This time the spider appears to be in the landscape rather than superimposed over it — but only for this one frame. As soon as the spider moves, the matte no longer works properly: it is in the wrong place. What you need is a matte that changes its shape every time the spider moves, and the only practical way to do that is to make the image of the spider *itself* generate a matte.

A **traveling matte** is one that changes from frame to frame. In this case, if there were a way for a strip of film to be completely transparent except for a completely opaque silhouette of the moving spider, that footage would be the traveling matte. The negative of that footage, opaque except for a clear area in the shape of the moving spider, would be the counter-matte. Once those mattes were available, bi-pack optical printing would allow you to get the effect you want. The question is: How would the initial matte be photographed?

The most time-consuming method would be **rotoscoping**, a technique for drawing a traveling matte by hand. It is reminiscent of the prehistory of photography, when the camera obscura was used as an aid to sketching. Using a bi-pack printer equipped with a rotoscope, you would project the closeup of the spider on the matte card. You would trace the outline of the spider on the card, then get a new card and project the next frame. At your leisure, you could fill in the outlines with black paint and have a series of mattes. Negatives of these would become the counter-mattes. Rotoscoping was used in the *Star Wars* trilogy to color in the light sabers and weapons blasts, providing a traveling matte for each white streak. It was also used in *Snow White and the Seven Dwarfs*, especially on the human figures. First live actors were photographed with a production camera, and then each frame was projected onto a card where its outline was traced. The animators filled in the details and colors, following the rotoscoped outlines of Snow White and the Prince, even to their lip movements. The special advantage there was that the animated figures were in lip sync with the dialogue tracks that had been recorded while the production footage was being shot. Rotoscoping has many uses, then, but the production of traveling mattes for live actors and big spiders is not among them, because a much simpler technology is available.

Jack Arnold and effects supervisor Clifford Stine achieved the traveling mattes for *Tarantula* by using a multi-film system called the **sodium-vapor process**, which is sometimes referred to as beam-splitting. There are actually many kinds of beam-splitting traveling-matte processes, only one of which uses sodium-vapor lamps, but it is convenient for our purposes here to treat them as one and to distinguish this process from the blue-screen process, which will be discussed shortly. The spider was photographed against a yellow screen that was illuminated by sodium-vapor lamps; these lamps put out monochromatic yellow light. The foreground — that is, the spider and its shadow — was lit with standard incandescent lamps that were filtered so that their light included *no* monochromatic yellow.

The camera used was a three-strip Technicolor production camera, and it was loaded with two separate rolls of film. The stock (Eastman Type 5251) was insensitive to monochromatic yellow. The camera was equipped with a **beam-splitter**, a filtered prism that transmitted the light gathered by the lens to both strips of film simultaneously. Because of the filter, however, one strip — which became the traveling matte — was exposed *only* to monochromatic yellow; the other was exposed to the full spectrum. Both stocks were negative.

The action negative, as a result, picked up only the foreground, and in full detail; the background area was clear. The matte negative, exposed only by the light reflected by the background, was clear in the area of the spider and opaque (completely exposed) everywhere else. Positive prints were then made of both of these; the matte was printed onto very-high-contrast stock. In the resulting action footage, the background was opaque and the foreground showed the spider. The positive of the matte footage was opaque in the area of the spider and clear in the background. This moving silhouette became the traveling matte; the original (matte) negative became the traveling counter-matte.

Through bi-pack printing, the matte was laid over the simple production footage of the desert landscape. The result was a shot of the desert with an opaque spider moving across it. The action footage of the spider was printed in bi-pack with the counter-matte, to make sure that there was no bleed-through of the background. That yielded a sharply outlined image of the spider against a black field. When both of these were printed onto a new strip of film, the image of the spider filled in the spider-shaped hole in the landscape, frame by frame. Most of this matte work was done with an optical printer, loaded first in bi-pack and then in monopack, with multiple passes.

The advantage of this and similar multi-film systems is that the matte is produced at the same time that the action is recorded. But there are also single-film systems capable of producing a superior color action negative, where the matte is generated later on.

The most widely used of these is the blue-backing or **blue-screen process**. The actor is photographed against a bright blue background and lit with conventional white light. The camera exposes a single length of ordinary color negative stock. From this negative, a black-and-white master positive is made: one that is allowed to record only the blue elements of the image. This master positive is opaque in the background. When it and the full-color negative are printed in bi-pack onto black-and-white stock, the result is a black-and-white positive with a clear background area. This process is then repeated with a master positive that contains only the *red* elements of the image, yielding a positive that is black in the background. A high-contrast dupe negative is made of this opaque-background positive; the result shows the actor in negative, the background clear. When the blue-filtered positive and the red-filtered high-contrast negative are rephotographed together — via bi-pack optical printing — onto high-contrast black-and-white stock, the result is the traveling matte. Its background is opaque, with a moving hole in it in the shape of the actor. The negative of this traveling matte becomes the traveling counter-matte.

Then the color original and the traveling matte are printed in bi-pack, producing a color image of the actor against a black background. (The resulting composite need not be in color, of course, if the film is to be released in black-and-white.) When the color original and the traveling counter-matte are printed in bi-pack, the result is a color image of the background with an opaque hole in the shape of the actor. When these two are double-printed, the foreground and background areas appear to have been photographed at the same time and in the same location; this composite is the end product, and it can then be cut into the rest of the film like any normal shot.

In the color section **Figs. C-86** through **C-92** show how the blue-screen process was used to create the speeder bike chase for *Return of the Jedi*. First, the forest background was shot. Garrett Brown, who invented the Steadicam, is shown in **Fig. C-86** in the act of shooting the background with a specially modified version of that system. What may look like a scratch on the print is actually a string that he followed on his trek through the woods. The camera took one frame per second, and the result was a rushing background (**Fig. C-87**) — in principle, not much different from Porter's pan of the New York skyline.

Luke and Leia were photographed on the full-scale speeder bike against a blue screen (**Fig. C-88**). In **Fig. C-89** you can see some of the supports for the bike; these were picked up along with the bike and the actors and later had to be rotoscoped out. **Fig. C-89** is a production still, but it is very similar to the color action negative photographed by the production camera; for purposes of discussion, we will treat it as if it were the actual **blue-screen element**. (**Elements** can be joined into composites). From this element, the traveling matte (**Fig. C-90**) was generated. It is called the **holdout matte** because it "holds out" the part of the background where the bike will go. The counter-matte (**Fig. C-91**) is called the **cover matte**; it allows everything but Luke, Leia, and the bike to be blocked out of the blue-screen element. **Fig. C-91** is an unusual cover matte; you can see that it is gray around the actors, but opaque around the gray area. It takes a lot of rephotographing, even onto high-contrast stock, to achieve a true clear/opaque matte; at the early stages, the background is gray rather than black. This cover matte was enhanced by a "garbage matte" made through rotoscoping, and it blocked out the crane and other bike supports. For purposes of discussion, imagine that the entire background is opaque. The composite is shown in **Fig. C-92**. **Figs. C-90** and **C-91** are the actual mattes used in the making of the film, and **Fig. C-92** is a frame enlargement.

New effects techniques are constantly being invented. For Clint Eastwood's *Firefox* (1982), Apogee made good use of Jonathan Erland's ultraviolet "reverse blue-screen process." The technique of **aerial-image printing** — where one of the elements is actually focused in the air — has made traveling mattes relatively affordable to the independent filmmaker and for the first time made it possible to get good effects in 16mm. The only way to keep up with such developments is to subscribe to a journal like Don Shay's *Cinefex*, which reports on them in detail even before the films are released.

Five Composites. To sum up, let us examine a number of composites from *Citizen Kane* and *King Kong*, all of which were produced on an optical printer. **Fig. 3-123** shows the explorers' landing on the beach of Skull Island. The live action, which takes up the bottom third of the frame, was shot on the California coastline. The island, complete with the wall and the mountains, was painted on glass. The birds were cel animations. These three elements were composited seamlessly, and the effect was clearly necessary

Figure 3-123

Figure 3-124

for the film, since the audience would expect to see Skull Island and the entire wall at some point and since these would have been entirely impractical to construct.

This composite would have been destroyed by phantom effects. But in **Fig. 3-124**, from the opera montage in *Citizen Kane*, the use of mattes would have been highly inappropriate. The point here is that all of these forces are pressuring Susan at once; both visually and as an aspect of the story, they overlap.

Figure 3-125

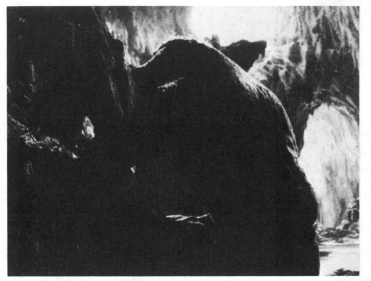

Figure 3-126

434

Figure 3-127

Finally, let us look at three frames from *Kong* that show how realism can be advanced while the audience is encouraged to fantasize. When we speak of realism in *Kong*, what is at issue is not the documentary quality of the imagery, nor the verisimilitude of the story, but the willing suspension of disbelief. An audience that is paying attention to how the effects were created is firmly entrenched in disbelief; it has withdrawn from the fantasy. If the same technique is used repeatedly, sooner or later the audience will pick up on it. In the following frames, which occur within minutes of each other, the effects techniques are brilliantly varied, and the audience is encouraged to accept both Kong and the two humans, Ann and Jack, as sharing the same space and time.

In the first shot (**Fig. 3-125**) Kong prepares to set Ann down on a ledge inside his cave. Both Kong and Ann are models. In the foreground, a little volcano puts out smoke that could not have been stop-motion animated. In the next shot (**Fig. 3-126**) Kong completes the action begun before the match cut, leaving Ann on the ledge. This time, however, Ann is live, whereas Kong is still a model. The audience cannot help reading the live and model Ann as the same figure and may even imagine that they saw the real Fay Wray in the previous shot. A few minutes later, Jack arrives in the cave just in time to watch Kong bash a snaky reptile (**Fig. 3-127**). Even assuming that the audience has figured out by this point that it is possible to have a live Ann in the background and a model Kong in the foreground, they would hardly be prepared for the addition of a live figure in *front* of Kong. Yet here they all are: the live Ann on her ledge, Kong and the snake in the middle, and the live Jack in the foreground. This effect could not have been achieved through rear projection and is a real surprise in the visual context of the scene. But in the dramatic context it makes perfect sense. The drama, then, wins out over the technical wizardry, and the audience is free to enjoy the spectacle. So well considered are these effects, so perfectly planned and crafted, that they do *not* call attention to themselves. Instead, they let the story and the characters carry the action, allowing Kong, however he was animated and however he was made to dwarf the humans, to become a fully accepted and genuine character.

Film Editing

"Always the same joy, the same astonishment," wrote Robert Bresson, "at the fresh significance of an image whose place I have just changed." Virtually any shot has significant content, but its meaning and effectiveness are finally determined by how it is trimmed and ordered, how it is made to work with other shots.

A shot is not a literal fragment of pre-filmic reality but an independent cinematic structure. As shots are arranged, a particular cinematic reality is defined. The world of *Marienbad* consists of 94 minutes of shots. Although some of those shots appear more "real" or more "imaginary" than others, the fact is that all of them are equally hypothetical. There is no two-year story, scrambled into a confusing discourse; instead, there is the clearest possible presentation of a paradoxically objective and subjective world whose "temporal" and "causal" relationships have been created through editing and whose "actions" are shots. *Marienbad* is, in other words, *a movie*. And any movie erects narrative coherence on foundations shared with *Marienbad*.

Although most filmmakers would have us forget this and read "through" the filmed to the pre-filmic, the fact is that what we see is what we get: a series of shots, not of events. Even in the most realistic film, the pre-filmic is transformed by the camera and then again by the editing, the two most significant encoding systems in the cinema. The event-on-film becomes, in Pudovkin's term, "plastic material" with which the editor can work. The shot is a paradoxical presence, a sign, a building block.

Editorial Freedom. As Bresson pointed out, an image changes its meaning when its position is changed. The Soviet theorists provided a simple test case for exploring this. You have three available shots: (1) a man pulls out a gun; (2) a second man frowns; and (3) the second man smiles. If you cut these in the order 3-1-2, you assert a dramatic context in which the second man becomes disturbed when he sees the gun. If you cut them in the order 2-1-3, you imply that the second man laughs at danger and is a very different sort of character. If you cut them so that Shot 1 does not intervene between Shots 2 and 3 but comes before or after them, you avoid setting up a readable cause-and-effect situation and begin to traffic in the territory of the avant-garde.

In the sound film the editor typically has less freedom to rearrange events in this manner, especially if he or she is answerable to a script. But to understand the resources of editing, you have to appreciate that such drastic reinterpretations of the plastic material are perfectly possible. And the sound film does allow the editor a considerable degree of freedom in any case. Let us say that you have one long take of a man giving a political speech, a continuous soundtrack of the speech, and 20 usable closeups of members of the audience. Some of these closeups show people smiling and nodding; some show them nodding off; some show them scowling. Cut in as reaction shots at particular moments in the speech, these can determine what the speech means in context. If the politician endorses equal rights for women, and you follow that with a shot of a smiling man, that would be very different from following it with a shot of a frowning man or a woman who has fallen asleep or the politician's daughter with a briefcase on her lap.

Editing is the art of making decisions about shot length, selection, and sequence. **Cutting** is the act of splicing lengths of film together. To decide how much of a shot to include in a film, and to suggest or manipulate its interpretive matrix by cutting it between other shots, is the job of the film editor; the sound editors will generally follow his or her lead. It is the editor who determines the overall pace and specific internal rhythms of the finished picture, who gives it jaggedness or an easy flow, who makes the parts come to life.

The editor will have to consult several different visions while assembling the text: not only his or her own sense of rhythm and timing, and the producer's demands for a finished product of a certain marketability and running time, but also what — on the basis of the contents of the shots and the director's instructions — the production team has intended each shot to mean. Shooting is not a random process, as by now should be quite obvious. Although most of the shots will have been filmed out of sequence, the script remains as a guide to their reassembly, and in most cases continuity will have been built into each take. The editor (who cuts both picture and dialogue) cannot reverse the order of Shot 1, in which the actor delivers the first half of a sentence, and Shot 2, in which that sentence is completed. Of course they could be reversed if the other filmmakers were agreeable, but it is very unusual for an editor to take on that drastic a level of decision-making independently. One could imagine a situation in which the rushes of *Marienbad* were turned over to an editor who insisted on bashing them into narrative coherence, just as one could imagine setting *Marienbad*'s editors loose on five hours of situation-comedy footage. But in practice the editor usually tries to realize fully what is latent in the printed takes — to help them to blossom like those Japanese paper flowers that uncurl when dropped into water.

The Birds. We can appreciate the continuity restrictions under which the editor works, and the creative freedom he or she nevertheless enjoys, by looking at part of a memorable scene from Hitchcock's *The Birds* (1963). Hitchcock was notorious for shooting in such a way that the editor had only minimal freedom: out of the order Hitchcock had intended, the shots would not make sense. Hitchcock controlled this, among other ways, by building continuity into the shots, as we shall see in the case of the cigarette smoked by Melanie Daniels (Tippi Hedren) and the number of birds on the schoolyard equipment behind her. Even so, it is plain that this scene has been edited for maximum suspense and that the timing of its cuts is crucial. The editor (George Tomasini, who also edited *Vertigo* and *Psycho*) could not have changed the order of the shots, but he did decide which parts of each to use and when to cut from one to another.

Melanie has gone to the Bodega Bay schoolhouse with a warning about the murderous behavior of the local birds. She decides to wait for the students to finish singing a song before going in to contact the teacher, and so she walks over to a bench and sits down. Behind this bench is a wooden fence, and beyond it the schoolyard filled with swings and other equipment, notably a jungle gym. We pick up this scene at the moment when Melanie has just begun to sit down.

Shot 1 begins on a match cut as Melanie finishes sitting on the bench. As she reaches into her purse to extract a cigarette case, a solitary crow lands on the gym behind her. She doesn't see it; we do. This medium shot last 10 seconds.

Shot 2 also begins on a match cut as Melanie extracts a cigarette from the case. She is still in medium shot, but the camera angle has changed so that the gym is no longer seen in the background; what is now behind her, from the audience's perspective, is the school building. She lights her cigarette — and the brief delay she experiences as it fails, at first, to catch fire initiates the rhythm of suspense.

Suspense is most often created by introducing a *delay* in the action, by suspending or deferring what the audience either wants to happen or dreadfully expects. "Expects" is appropriate because there is usually some other activity or process going on at the same time as what the audience is confined to watching, and the audience knows about it — knows, for example, that the killer is on the way to the onscreen bungalow where the tender lovers are wasting time, or that the time bomb in the clock factory is ticking away unheard. Appealing to the same emotional hook, suspense may also be created by *extending* an action, making it take longer than normal to disarm the bomb. In either case, the filmmaker need not cross-cut between the suspended action and the threat; what matters is that the audience retain an awareness of the threat — in other words, *supply* it to the action onscreen.

Charles Dickens is said to have remarked, "Make them laugh, make them cry, and make them wait!" If the audience has no emotional involvement in the action, delay or extension simply creates boredom. In this scene the audience is manipulated to want Melanie to look behind her (offscreen left) to *see the birds* gathering in the yard; the more she looks to screen right or fiddles with her cigarette, the more impatient and tense the audience should become. Appropriately, it is the lengthiest shots of Melanie, in which nothing can be seen going on behind her, that the tension is greatest. In any case, once the cigarette is burning, Melanie leans back on the bench and tries to relax. The song is heard in the background, and as its refrain ends (on the dramatically ironic words "now now *now*"), there is a straight cut. This shot lasts just over 16 seconds.

Shot 3 is a view of the fence with the gym behind it. There are four crows on the gym. After a brief pause the song goes into another verse, and this increases the suspense: *another* verse?! Let's get on with the warning! Just at that moment, a fifth crow lands on the gym. This shot lasts 12½ seconds.

Shot 4 is a tighter medium shot of Melanie; the bottom edge of the frame is just below her breasts. By now a pattern of cross-cutting, rather than of match cutting, has been established: alternating views of Melanie and the jungle gym. She exhales heavily, then looks over her shoulder at the school building; finally she looks more or less in the direction of her half-smoked cigarette and appears to be thinking. She is waiting for the song to end as much as for the cigarette to be finished; both become criteria of time, and this sense of waiting is directly communicated to the audience, which must wait 11 seconds for the end of this apparently uninteresting shot.

Shot 5 is a return to the setup of Shot 3. The shorthand for this is simply **as 3**; it indicates that the same setup was used in both shots and that they could have come from the same take. Now there are eight birds on the gym. A ninth bird lands, and the others shift position. This shot lasts 3½ seconds.

Shot 6 is an even tighter shot of Melanie; this time the lower edge of the frame is at her collarbones. This gradual moving in on the subject, which Hitchcock obviously engineered in continuity (the cigarette is now even shorter), further increases the tension. Again she glances impatiently at the school building and at the cigarette. This shot goes on for a very long time: all of 28 seconds. At its end, Melanie looks up and offscreen (toward the upper left foreground) as if something has caught her eye.

Now there is an eye-line match cut, creating the impression that what we see in Shot 7 is what Melanie is looking at from the vantage point of Shot 6. It is a long shot of the sky, and in it a single crow. The camera pans to the right to follow the flying bird. This is the first bird she has noticed in this scene. The shot lasts 3¾ seconds.

Shot 8 is as Shot 6. In this case there was one continuous take of Melanie on the bench, which the editor interrupted long enough to cut in Shot 7. She continues to look up, as if at the bird; the "as if" is important here because the actress is obviously not seeing any bird but is only looking off-camera.

Less than a second into Shot 8, Melanie's face begins to express concern: maybe more birds are coming! This is an ironic moment for the audience because we are well aware that this is not the first bird to have shown up. She turns her torso and head to watch the bird more intently. By the end of the shot, she is looking toward screen left — but where we want her to look is offscreen left and to the *rear*. The next shots accomplish this, pulling her gaze fully around. Shot 8 lasts just over 4 seconds.

Again there is an eye-line match. Shot 9 is a long shot of the flying crow, and the camera pans with it to the right. At the end of the pan, the schoolyard comes into view; the crow lands on the jungle gym. For exactly 1 second, the audience has a view of the schoolyard, filled with *thousands* of birds. This view shocks us almost as much as it does Melanie, because although we knew that more birds were arriving — one by one — we have had no way to expect that so many could have arrived during the 40 seconds that have elapsed since we last saw the schoolyard. The fact that there are so many is almost supernaturally startling, and it suggests a kind of time warp, a nightmarish discontinuity. It is not the time of the cigarette's burning down (2 or 3 minutes — but the song is continuous; hence another warp), nor of the 40 seconds of screen time; the time in which the thousands of birds have arrived one by one is the time of Melanie's *not having looked* — the awful period of having relaxed one's vigilance. Shot 9 lasts for 5½ seconds; the crow lands 4½ seconds into the shot.

Shot 10 shows Melanie's reaction. She stands up into the frame — the camera does not tilt, but she enters its field of view — and looks offscreen. This close shot lasts just over 2 seconds.

Just as reverse-angle shots had clarified that Melanie was looking at the flying crow, another reverse-angle cut now establishes that Shot 11 is Melanie's view of the birds in the yard. The setup here is naturally the same as that at the end of Shot 9, which had pulled her POV to this sight, and the shot lasts for 2½ seconds. Then there is a cut to a profile of Melanie as she begins to edge toward the schoolhouse, the song and the cigarette at last concluded.

These 11 shots last a total of 1 minute and 40 seconds. Short of watching the actual sequence, one way to get a sense of the cutting rhythm here is to compile a shot breakdown:

Shot 1:   Melanie, yard behind her, no crows. 10 sec.
Shot 2:   Melanie, schoolhouse behind her. 16⅛ sec.
Shot 3:   Jungle gym, 4 crows, 5th arrives. 12½ sec.
Shot 4:   Melanie. 11⅓ sec.
Shot 5:   Jungle gym, 8 crows, 9th arrives. 3½ sec.
Shot 6:   Melanie. 28 sec.
Shot 7:   Flying crow. 3¾ sec.
Shot 8:   Melanie, turning. 4⅛ sec.
Shot 9:   Crow lands on crowded gym. 5½ sec.
Shot 10: Melanie, standing. 2⅛ sec.
Shot 11: Bird city. 2½ sec.

Doing a little math here, we realize that four crows land during the 16 seconds of Shot 2. Three more crows show up during the 11 seconds of Shot 4. That's about one crow every 4 seconds: a fairly regular rate. Seeing all the crows at the end of Shot 9, the audience — expecting, in the terms of this progression, that about ten more birds will have arrived in the intervening 40 seconds — suddenly has to compute the acceleration of their landings. In context, this acceleration is almost astronomical.

The effectiveness of this mathematical shock depends on exactly how long, each time, we look away from the birds. (We don't count the seconds, but our experience through time is manipulated.) Although Hitchcock clearly determined the internal rhythm of Shot 6 — the crucially long one — it was Tomasini who decided *exactly* how long that shot would last: where exactly to cut in Shot 7, interrupting the take and establishing the end of Shot 6, and how early in the take to start Shot 6. Hitchcock could not have directed the scene this precisely if he did not know a great deal about editing, but Tomasini was hardly his slave, and it was he who made these 9 takes into *this* 11-shot sequence. In the hands of another editor these shots might have conveyed the same story information but would have had a different rhythm, a greater or lesser degree of suspense, and a correspondingly deeper or shallower level of

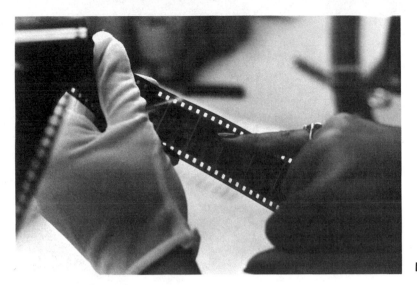

Figure 3-128

irony. For examples of considerably greater editorial freedom, review the sequences at the end of Part II of this book.

Editorial Procedures. For the moment, put yourself in the position of an independent filmmaker who has just wrapped production and is wondering what to do next. Your sound takes have been transferred onto mag film, and you have reserved space in an editing room, where you have laid out scissors, cement, splicing tape, a multi-channel synchronizer, a sound reader, a viewer, a table, a trim rack and bin, and a set of rewinds. Here is what you would do:

The camera original, let us assume, was a negative, and from it a positive copy has been made. This copy, called the **workprint**, is the one you will edit, the one it is all right to scratch, tape, untape, retape, accidentally roll your chair over, scream at, work on. The negative remains pristine in a cool vault until all of the editorial decisions have been made.

When the workprint arrives from the lab and the mag arrives from the sound transfer house, you cut them into separate shot takes, roll them up together (picture with sound), and number and save those you intend to use. (The alternative printed takes are saved, too, but not where they will get in your way.) When you need them, you can unroll them and hang them from pins over a large cloth-covered container called a **trim bin**. When matching picture and sound takes, you find their sync marks and line them up with each other. This is usually a matter of finding the frame of picture where the clapstick closed (**Fig. 3-128**) and placing it alongside the frame of sound where the sticks are heard. Each reel of picture and track is then sent out for edge coding, which will be explained shortly. The same number appears on each matching foot of picture and sound, so that they can still be synchronized after the slating frames have been trimmed out.

Figure 3-129

When you want to look at and trim the shot, you thread the picture into a viewer and run the mag film past a sound head in sync. The viewer may be an **upright**, like a Moviola — called an "upright" because the film moves through it vertically — or a **flatbed**, like the Steenbeck or Kem editing table (**Fig. 3-129**), which runs the film horizontally. Both uprights and flatbeds keep picture and sound in sync from head to tail — assuming, of course, that they have been threaded in sync.

When editing, it is best to have both picture and mag stock wound not on reels, which are bulky and apt to introduce scratches, but on **cores**: plastic cylinders that function as the hubs of sideless reels. If you do not have access to an editing table, you can still view the picture on a Moviescope or similar apparatus. The Moviescope is a small boxlike instrument equipped with a ground-glass screen; the image is reflected onto this screen from behind, thanks to a lamp and prism in the threading path. A sound head, wired to a speaker, can be mounted separately so that you can hear the sound take. To keep picture and sound in editorial sync (lined up in parallel, rather than displaced for projection), you will thread them both through a synchronizer (**Fig. 3-130**), a system of sprocketed wheels that turn on a common shaft. The editor in this picture is wearing cotton gloves because she is using the synchronizer while cutting negative, which is extremely susceptible to permanent damage from dust and fingerprints.

Then you can begin the fun part: trimming the unusable heads and tails and stringing the shots into a tentative order. Most editors leave some extra footage at head and tail so that there will be room to polish the rhythm later on. Right now you will be concerned with establishing the basic sequence of the picture and with providing sync dialogue tracks to accompany it. Music and sound effects are usually dealt with after the picture and the dialogue have been locked into their final pattern. As you approve

Figure 3-130   **Figure 3-131**

each picture and sound couple, you splice them onto the takes that have come before them, and eventually you will have two synchronized reels (or sets of reels), one with the picture and one with the spine of the soundtrack. This is your **rough cut**, the cinematic equivalent of a first draft.

You will encounter several possible methods for making splices. Workprints are normally held together with tape splices, negatives with cement splices. You make a **tape splice** by cutting the shots to be juxtaposed down the center of the frame line — so that the frames butt up together — and then laying a piece of transparent, sprocketed tape over both adjoining frames. The tape is applied to the base side of the film, not the emulsion, so that it can be torn off without wrecking the image. If you want a tape splice to go through a projector, however, you have to tape both sides, rendering the splice more-or-less secure but damaging to change.

Cement splices are (ideally) permanent. A heavy-duty cement splicer is shown in **Fig. 3-131**. You make a glue or **cement splice** by scraping the emulsion off the head of one shot, thus exposing the base, and gluing that to the base of the tail of the other shot. In 16mm one frame will show slight overlap from the frame welded onto it, but in 35mm the splice occurs on the relatively wide frame line and will not show up during projection. High-stress projection stocks (like Kodak's Estar, used for Imax) are spliced ultrasonically, also on the frame line.

Sound takes are spliced together with translucent white tape applied to the base side, the same kind used to splice ¼-inch magnetic tape. And like recording tape, mag film is cut on the diagonal so that there will not be an audible pop when the cut passes over the sound head.

After living with the rough cut for awhile, you trim the shots for content, rhythm, and running time, trimming the edge-coded mag tracks as well to maintain sync. A feature might be four hours in rough cut, less than two hours when released. All this trimming and rethinking is the crucial creative phase of editing, and it results in a **fine cut**.

As explained in the section on the producer, the fine cut may be subject to approval by executives or backers, not just by the editor and the director (and, in most cases, the cinematographer). In the film industry, the normal approval procedure begins when the fine cut, the tightened and polished version, is approved by the director and shown to the producer(s) as a first cut. Recutting often follows. The last fine cut approved by the director — the director's cut — will not necessarily be the version released, unless the director has the right of final cut. *The* **final cut** is the version to which the negative will be cut; it would be more than foolhardy to make irrevocable editorial decisions before the release version has been agreed upon or, in any case, determined. All of the cuts from rough to final are in double system and editorial sync.

Let us say that the second or third cut meets with your approval as well as that of the director, the producer, and perhaps a preview audience: What next?

You get the negative out of the vault, take it into a perfectly dust-free environment, put on cotton gloves, say your prayers, and start to cut it. Any mistake at this stage will be catastrophic; the negative cannot be replaced. If you were on the ball during production, you will have been cutting up the negative all along: isolating the takes and winding them onto cores, labeling them, logging edge numbers, and storing them in useful groupings. An MGM breakdown operator is shown doing this in **Fig. 3-132**, using a specially designed rewind to wind the negative onto the core. This stage is called **negative breakdown**, and it is often performed on the dailies as soon as they have been approved by the lab, the cameraman, and the director. Some of these takes will be forwarded to those who might need them to make optical composites (such as traveling mattes, dissolves, or titles with images in their backgrounds); this is called **pulling scenes**. If you have not done all that breakdown work before, you will have to do it now.

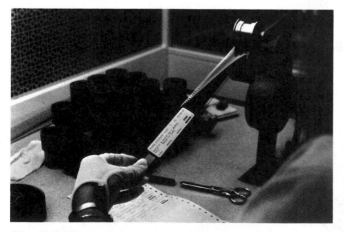

Figure 3-132

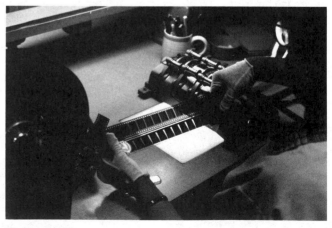

Figure 3-133

Your workprint has been completed, and copies of it have been forwarded (usually one reel at a time) to the sound effects editor and the music editor. Along the outside edge of the workprint is a series of sequential, unique (never repeated) numbers; these are called **key numbers** or **edge numbers**, and they were put on the negative when it was manufactured. They are the same on the print as they were on the negative — having been copied along with the picture onto unnumbered printing stock — and they allow you to identify any frame by its distance from a particular edge number. **Logging** or **keying** is the process of listing the key numbers for reference. **Edge coding**, which also is called **keying**, is the process of mechanically inking the key numbers from the camera rolls onto the transferred sound rolls that are, foot by foot, their mates (or inking a fresh set of code numbers onto both). While you are editing, these matching numbers allow you to maintain level sync between picture and sound; once the workprint has been edited, they allow you to match workprint and negative.

There are, however, edge numbers that are not specifically key numbers. If you examine the edge of a 35mm release print, you will find a set of sequential numbers, one for each 35mm foot (that is, every 16 frames), that more-or-less begin at zero at the start of each reel.

It is worth explaining that "more-or-less," and to do so requires a brief review of the reel. From the point of view of the camera operator, the Foley artist, the film editor, the sound editor, and anyone in silent film, a reel is just under 1,000 feet of 35mm film. From the point of view of the laboratory and the projectionist, a reel is a "double reel," just under 2,000 feet of 35mm film. What was a 12-reel picture would now be wound on 6 double reels. It is in the laboratory that the editor's reels are translated into the projectionist's reels. Given an 8,100 foot (90 minute) movie, consisting of 9 reels of approximately 900 feet each, Reel 1 and Reel 2 will become Reel 1A and Reel 1B, respectively, Reel 3 will become Reel 2A, and Reel 8 will become Reel 4B. The edge numbers on release prints (which are copied from the soundtrack negative, onto which they have been inked, or sometimes the picture negative) identify each foot by its distance from the start of its reel. Thus the foot whose first frame is marked 2A0100 is 100 feet from the beginning of Reel 2A. The number 1A0000 is found at the first frame of the head leader, which in the British system is the number 12 and in the American system is "PICTURE START." By the head leader's number 3 is the edge number 1A0009, and the first frame of picture in the first reel is 1A00012, as the first frame of the first foot of picture in what the editor considered the ninth reel (and which is now Reel 5A) is 5A00012.

Let us assume that you are now ready to match the workprint with the negative. You **pull the takes** from the previously broken-down rolls of negative, using the edge numbers on the log sheet or the workprint and matching them with the negative takes that have the same numbers. Then you **match and cut**: the negative is cut as it is matched to the edge numbers of the workprint running parallel to it in the synchronizer (**Fig. 3-133**). The shots are attached together with a scratch-proof clip and are wound onto a core, with white leader in the place of any missing shots.

If you are working in a studio or through a film laboratory, you then send the negative to the negative-assembly department; if you're on your own, you do the job they would do. The negative assembler removes the clips and splices the shots together with cement. Then the negative is returned to the negative-cutting department, where it is checked for synchronization with the optical soundtrack negative. Obviously this little scenario has left out all the work that has been done in creating, mixing, and transferring the soundtrack, but all that will be discussed in a later section. The spliced negative and the workprint are compared frame by frame, in order to verify that everything has been done as the editor desired. Late-arriving shots (titles, opticals, and inserts) are cut into the negative at this point, and everything is checked again.

Then the picture and sound negatives are sent to the laboratory, where they are printed together, in projection sync, onto fresh stock; the result is a **trial composite print**. The final trial composite is called the **answer print**. Some people say that this print "answers" the question of whether you in fact have a releasable movie. When an answer print is approved, **release prints** are struck.

Editorial Personnel. In a professional operation, the only major difference from the gauntlet you have just run is that there are more people to share the work. The head of the editorial category is the **supervising editor**, and he or she coordinates the schedules of the other editors; checks cue sheets for dialogue, effects, and music; supervises the final mixing process; encourages an air of "creative craftsmanship"; and sometimes serves as picture editor. The **picture editor**, also called the **film editor**, is the one who edits the workprint and the voice tracks. The picture editor, who has usually been on the set and has been present at the screenings of the rushes, marks the workprint with instructions for the negative cutter, checks the synchronization of *all* the soundtracks, prepares loops for dubbing sessions, orders opticals, and approves the quality of the answer print and the internegative. The picture editor is assisted by the **negative cutter** — whose job can be as maddeningly intricate as sewing cobwebs, as Brakhage once put it — and the negative cutter is assisted by the **breakdown operator**, part of whose job was shown in **Fig. 3-132**.

The **sound editor** (sometimes called the **supervising sound editor**) reports to the supervising editor and assumes responsibility for coordinating the editing of the effects and music tracks, or personally does that editing. These jobs may also be divided between a **sound effects editor**, who edits the effects tracks, and a **music editor**, who edits the music tracks and provides vital information about picture content and editing rhythm to the composer. The **sound effects specialist** prepares the Foley tracks, which will be taken up in a later section. All these edited tracks are later mixed by the **key re-recording mixer**, who is assisted by the **re-recording mixer** and the **music** and **sound effects mixers.** Sometimes the sound designer serves as key re-recording mixer.

All these editors have their assistants. The **assistant editor** and the **second assistant editor** work with the picture editor, the sound effects editor, and the music editor. An assistant might sync dailies, load the guillotine splicer with a fresh roll of tape, and generally make sure that the editing room functions smoothly. The creative side of the job might entail building a reel of picture or sound in tentative form.

In the last few years more of the editor's tasks have been made easier through the advent of computerized video technology. With a good program, the computer can keep track of edge and code numbers, call up a digital video copy of the shot and display it on a computer monitor, and keep a running record of all the cuts while making it possible to view those shots in sequence. The script supervisor's notes can be displayed along with the relevant breakdown data. Instructions for post-synchronization can be logged along with similar notes and keyed to, or even called up with, the shots, which usually are stored on an array of hard drives.

But even in the computerized editing room, some meticulous artisan is still going to have to splice the negative, and some editor is still going to have to know how to edit. When I was running around the MGM lab taking pictures for this discussion, an assistant cutter grabbed a mess of film from a trim bin (**Fig. 3-134**). Wonderfully summing up the intermittent chaos of the editing room and the physical realities of this business of making what appear to be perfectly incorporeal and instantaneous transitions on the screen, he said, "And *this* is the finished product!"

Figure 3-134

Music

About halfway through Roland Joffe's *The Killing Fields* (1984), an American reporter (Sam Waterston) sits in his comfortable living room and plays a videotape and a record. The tape contains news footage of Nixon and the war in Cambodia, a war the reporter has covered and from which he is now in a kind of insulated retreat. The record is Puccini's final opera, *Turandot,* and in this scene we hear the tenor's extremely moving aria from Act III, "Nessun dorma" ("No One Will Sleep"), which concerns secrecy, vigilance, and the triumph of love. The reporter has erected barriers against the emotional reality of his Cambodian experiences, but in this scene they sneak around those barriers and, empowered by the music, head straight for his heart.

The intensity of the aria increases as the reporter uses the remote control to scan the tape; it is as if he wants to make the footage get over faster. His pain is perfectly conveyed by the juxtaposition of the music and this action.

The political irony of his situation is conveyed visually by the contrast between his tasteful apartment and the horrors on the television. The fact that he is listening to an opera might be part of the critique of his disengagement, if the only point were that he has elitist tastes. But the music itself — the self-declaring fact that this is a magnificent piece — makes its own communication. It acts directly on us, much as it does on him, and allows us to understand how he is moved. And if we are moved with him, that makes sense for many reasons: for we, too, are a comfortable audience, jaded by the ways horrors are neatly wrapped up in the media, unable to take in their reality without making a judgment about our own distance from them, equally susceptible to the direct appeal of great music, and equally in need of having our barriers evaded. The scanned footage becomes more powerful than it would have been at normal speed; accompanied by the aria, it creates an emotional and political climax whose pathos is overwhelming.

The Role of the Music Track. Since they were first introduced, movies have been accompanied by music. To the extent that the silent film was a kind of visual music, an organized flow of pure form, it was intended to be complemented by real music. There were not always specific scores written for specific movies; more often a live accompanist or a small orchestra provided mood music that matched the tempo of the images and brought out their emotional content, or familiar songs whose tone and remembered lyrics commented on the individual scenes. When a character came home after a long absence, for instance, the song "Home Sweet Home" might drift in for a moment. Some sound effects could be created with music, particularly on an organ: a loud, sharp chord at the slamming of a door. Music was part of the "universal language" of silent film (whose original titles could easily be replaced with native-language titles).

The only reason that a synchronized soundtrack was *needed* was to allow the audience to hear dialogue rather than read it on intertitles that disrupted the visual rhythms. But the soundtrack had further advantages: it let nonmusical sound effects be recorded and presented, with increased opportunities for realism; it provided equally interesting but less widely practiced options for playing sound *against* image; it let the performer act with both voice and body; and it made it possible for a film to be accompanied by a carefully determined and repeatable musical score.

It is interesting to note that throughout the sound period, the music track has behaved in much the same way and has used many of the same strategies as in the silent period. It brings out rhythms, it enhances emotional moods, it manipulates the audience both subtly and directly, and it brings in songs that comment on the action. It interprets the film for the audience while enhancing its sense of flow. It is a text within the text of the film.

The transition can be studied most effectively in the score Chaplin wrote for *Modern Times* (1936), which is a changeling in the nursery of the sound film. While it has some recorded dialogue, *Modern Times* employs the narrative and emotional strategies of the silent film, many intertitles, and a score with pronounced affinities to the tones and devices of the silent film's loosely synchronized accompaniment. The music from popular songs often interprets or augments the action. When the tramp is out of luck, the strains of "Hallelujah, I'm a Bum" are heard in a melancholy tone; when he is marched off to jail, we hear a martial version of "If I Had the Wings of an Angel." The audience knew the lyrics to these songs and appreciated their references. Chaplin used "pure" music (not associated with lyrics) to enhance the tone of certain scenes and actions — for example, fast music for frenzied action — and musical sound effects. He also used what Wagner called **leitmotifs**: original musical themes that are consistently juxtaposed with particular actions and symbols, and that when repeated in other contexts bring their original associations along. Throughout *Modern Times* specific characters, ideas, and running themes are accompanied by specific leitmotifs, of which the most memorable is a tune that Chaplin later released as the song "Smile"; it brings along and intertwines all that the picture has to say about the problem of optimism in the world of the Depression, and this is especially noticeable when "Smile" is played as the picture's closing theme, where both it and the final scene, each in its own way, effects an emotional and thematic synthesis.

The use of this complex of familiar and original music is typical of the film music track. Popular songs continue to underscore scene content, ironically or directly — "Blue Moon" in *An American Werewolf in London*, for example, or "I Heard It Through the Grapevine" at the start of Lawrence Kasdan's *The Big Chill* (1983). Original songs, like "Over the Rainbow" or "When You Wish Upon a Star," have been composed for films and have become part of world culture, and some original scores have become popular hits (like Anton Karas's "*Third Man* Theme") or have entered the light classical repertory, like Miklos Rozsa's "*Spellbound* Concerto" or Sergei Prokofiev's "*Lieutenant Kije* Suite." Musical themes string together related scenes and characters — as when, in *The Wizard of Oz*, Miss Gulch rides her bicycle to the same music as the Wicked Witch of the West rides her broom.

The setting and varying of emotional tones continues to be a primary task of the score. A scene of a woman alone in an apartment at night could be rendered suspenseful and creepy with the addition of suspenseful and creepy music, whereas a more light-hearted and smooth track could change the tone entirely, suggesting perhaps that this woman is at peace with herself in her solitude. Such tracks let the audience know how to feel about a scene. Emotional underscoring can work in more complex ways, of course. In *From Here to Eternity*, a brutal knife fight in an alley is accompanied not by tense "fight music" but by subdued "Hawaiian music," which contrasts powerfully with the urgency and violence of the visuals and, in fact, makes the scene.

As the example from *The Killing Fields* demonstrates, music is also an independent text with its own history and power, and its use can constitute a leap into another language. That is how Godard used one of Beethoven's late string quartets at several crucial moments in *2 or 3 Things I Know About Her* (1966, rel. 1967). When Juliette (Marina Vlady) crosses a downtown street and thinks about how she and her world are, for that moment, one, the few seconds of Beethoven lend their own self-sufficiency and integration to hers. When a man sits in a café and stares into his espresso cup while Godard whispers voice-over about the limits of language and the problem of Being, finally expressing the hope that consciousness and conscience might simultaneously be reborn, it is again Beethoven whose music suggests the range and value of that hope.

The Composer. The score for *Citizen Kane* was composed by Bernard Herrmann, who also wrote the music for *Vertigo* and *Psycho*. His work on *Kane* can serve as a classic example of the art of the film composer and the function and structure of a complex score.

This score is organized around two recurring and systematically varied themes, which Herrmann referred to as "Power" and "Rosebud." The "Power" theme is announced in the first four notes of the score; the "Rosebud" theme is first heard fully and clearly over the first shots of the snowy globe. The meanings of these themes are established gradually and depend on their being juxtaposed with particularly resonant shots. "Rosebud," for example, is played with the globe, with the first shot of Kane on his sled, with the snow-covered sled after Kane has left with Thatcher, when Kane first walks into the boarding house where Susan is staying, when Kane tells Susan about his mother's death and the "sentimental journey" he had planned to the warehouse where her goods are being stored, and when the sled burns in the furnace. It is a leitmotif, and it strings together the various scenes in which Kane's innocence is displayed and his longing for love is foregrounded. In addition to preparing the audience for the identity of Rosebud — a realization that depends as much on the juxtaposition of the burning sled and the ongoing musical theme as it does on our ability to read the name of the sled — this theme interrelates the various expressions of this aspect of Kane's character. Only on second viewing is the audience likely to realize that the music has been identifying and explaining Rosebud all along.

The "Power" theme begins by accompanying the "No Trespassing" sign and occurs intermittently (alternated with preliminary snatches of "Rosebud") as the camera sneaks up on Xanadu. As "Rosebud" links up with Susan and with Kane's mother, "Power" links up with Thatcher, big capitalism, personal isolation, interpersonal domination, and Xanadu. It is played at its most subdued over the date "1929" in Thatcher's memoirs, most imposingly in the first exterior view of Xanadu after the sled has burned. The end of the picture expresses the interrelation of these two themes in Kane's character, as the "Power" and "Rosebud" themes first alternate and then merge — a musical surprise that Herrmann saved for the finish — before "Rosebud" wins out. The final shot, with its iron *K* (power) and dissipating smoke (Rosebud), has the same complexity and accepts the same conflict that the score does, and the final chords express the same heightened sense of resolution as the title that is superimposed at this point: "The End."

There are several minor themes tied to particular characters and story elements. A graceful waltz, played as Kane rides off with his fiancée Emily, becomes the "Emily" theme (though I have no idea what Herrmann called it). It expresses the ease and charm of Emily's social background and perhaps the way that marriage was supposed to have whirled off into a ballroom dance. (Susan, by contrast, is associated with jazz.) But in the breakfast sequence, where the "Emily" theme is presented differently in each of the breakfast scenes, it becomes more jagged and skittery until it at last subsides into a subdued and wistful minor key. It has traced the history of the marriage with the same precise trajectory as the breakfast scenes, but in its own self-sufficient terms. *Salaambo*, the opera Herrmann wrote for Susan to sing, undergoes a metamorphosis from an imposing but innocuous piece (sounding as if Richard Strauss had done his own version of *Aida*) to a syncopated percussive nightmare in the montage that immediately precedes Susan's suicide attempt. Her electronically modulated voice, as it dies out along with the filament in the stage light, is one of the most creative musical achievements in the entire film.

Herrmann also made use of "found" music, characteristically turning it to his own purposes. Susan has told some reporters that Kane will build her an opera house (that is, if no existing house will book her), and Kane has said that he expects that not to be necessary. Then comes the headline "Kane Builds Opera House," followed by an insert of that building. On the music track Herrmann provided the opening ·chords of the overture to Wagner's *Tannhäuser*. This could be simply explained as a recognizable snatch from a well-known opera, a way of accompanying the picture in an operatic mood. And it does do that. But *Tannhäuser* is an opera about the dream of love and its relations with power, control, and death. The musical quotation, by distant implication, thus links the Chicago Opera House with another Kane project, Xanadu, the "pleasure dome" (like the Venusberg of *Tannhäuser*) that is organized around Romantic idealism but leads its inhabitants into a trap of magic and sin. Susan becomes trapped in the opera house and in Xanadu by Kane's exercise of power, just as Tannhäuser is trapped by Venus; music becomes her nightmare just as passion becomes Tannhäuser's cross — but his story has a happier ending. And the quotation also tells us something about Kane; it is another example of how he uses power in his search for love, creating his own Venusberg and playing the roles of both Venus, the captor, and Tannhäuser, the idealistic victim who would prefer to return to the simple pleasures of the unspoiled natural world.

An original song was also composed for *Kane*. Its music is structured by the "Power" theme. Its lyrics describe a man who "doesn't like that 'Mister,' / He likes 'good old Charlie Kane!'" This is what Kane might say about himself (he has clearly endorsed the song and might even have written it); it is the "citizen" part of his nature. The song is played at the party held to celebrate the *Inquirer*'s having hired the staff of the *Chronicle,* and it is played without lyrics just after Kane has given a major political speech about what he intends to do to Jim Gettys after he wins the governorship. When Leland trudges through the confetti on his way to confront Kane about his confused vision of power and love, this music is played again, but in a sadder and quieter tone. This shift in the rendering of the song parallels and expresses the change in Leland's feelings about Kane's version of populism as well as the downbeat ending of the campaign. When the song is played again, over the final credits, it takes on another level of meaning: another interpretation of Kane, one that complements and rivals the Xanadu and Rosebud interpretations. In that context, it almost has the authority of the newsreel as an independent attempt to sum up Kane, throwing the emphasis onto his desire to be accepted and to lead a relatively normal life — and, of course, to be a celebrity, because such songs are not commissioned for just anyone, so perhaps the song is itself a Rosebud/Power synthesis as well.

The Music Editor. The composer does not simply sit down in front of an edited film and begin to write music that happily coordinates with every nuance of the picture. And there are many films that do not require a composer because they do not have original scores. A movie score calls on the services of many besides the composer: a music adaptor or **arranger**, a conductor, musicians, engineers who are particularly skilled at recording music, sometimes singers, and always a music editor.

The music editor edits the music track, works closely with the composer and arranger, and is usually the one responsible for selecting pre-existing pieces of music (though the writer and the director may contribute their own suggestions). He or she edits the music to the picture and in some cases — with the permission and cooperation of the picture editor — edits the picture to the music or refines the ways they work together.

The actual process of scoring begins with a **spotting session** in which the music editor, the composer, and the director look over the rough cut and consult about which sequences ought to have music. In the words of Elmer Bernstein, "Usually the director wants all the weak scenes scored, and the composer wants to score all the good scenes, because they're the most stimulating ones." The director often supplies the composer with adjectives describing the moods that he or she wants. The music editor plots the rhythms and the significant actions in the picture track.

The composer, who is typically given four or five weeks to write the score, relies on these notes when establishing and varying the tempo of the composition. Recall the moment in *Kane* when the globe falls to the floor and the crash is heard as a musical chord. In order to write this segment, Herrmann had to depend on the music editor's indication of exactly when the globe would hit the floor (identified in the spotting session as an **accent point**). Such notes are keyed to the length, in thirds of a second, of the sequence to be accompanied; these can readily be translated into metronomic beats. The music editor, then, translates movements and cutting rhythms into terms with which the composer can work.

Among the more technical of the music editor's responsibilities are the preparation of timing sheets and click tracks. The **timing sheets** begin at the **cue point** (where the music is supposed to start), which is taken as time zero. From there on, every potential accent point is identified, together with how many seconds after the cue point it occurs. Dialogue is included so that the composer will not inadvertently obscure significant lines.

Film tempo is measured in clicks rather than metronome settings. A **click** indicates the number of frames for each musical beat; for precision, each frame is divided into eighths. A 14/5 click would mean that there are 14 5/8 frames per beat — or for that particular beat. A regular 12/0 click would denote 12 frames/beat, 2 beats/second, 120 beats/minute, and 120 on a metronome. The music editor builds a **click track** for every scene or sequence that is to have musical accompaniment; it is a soundtrack consisting only of beats, and it is particularly useful when a new performance, recorded in post-production, must match the tempo of a live or playback track.

To prepare for the **scoring session**, where the music is recorded after it has been composed and arranged, the music editor marks the workprint with **streamers**: vertical grease-pencil lines that travel from screen left to right in two seconds. When they hit screen right, that is the cue point.

The music is then played by studio musicians in real time. The picture is shown on a screen that faces the conductor, who is cued by the streamers and who may listen to the click track on earphones. Quoting Bernstein again: "You come back with an orchestra and the music is recorded while the film is running on a screen. Usually everybody on the scoring stage is enthralled . . . because it's the only thing in films which happens fast."

Then the music editor neatens up the synchronization between the picture and the music track, or the picture editor polishes up the final cut to the music.

Cutting to Music. The most dazzling music/picture integrations are usually the result of intense collaboration between the music and picture editors. One scene in *Cabaret* offers a particularly fine example of the coordinated editing of picture and music — clearly directed with these effects in mind — and it is worth studying in detail.

Cabaret was choreographed and directed by Bob Fosse. It was based on a Broadway musical with songs by John Kander and Fred Ebb, which was itself based on a book by Christopher Isherwood. The music was supervised, arranged, and conducted by Ralph Burns, and the picture was edited by David Bretherton. The music editors were Robert N. Tracy, Illo Endrulat, and Karola Storr.

In the year of *The Godfather* it was *Cabaret* that won the Oscars for Best Scoring (Burns), Editing (Bretherton), Director, Art Director, Cinematography, Sound, Actress, and Supporting Actor. (*The Godfather*, however, won Best Picture, Screenplay, and Actor; its great original score, by Nino Rota, was ruled ineligible on a technicality.)

The story of *Cabaret* is set in Berlin in 1931, when the Nazis were on the verge of coming into power. Brian (Michael York), a Cambridge grad student, has been taken under the wing of a gabby narcissist, Sally (Liza Minnelli), who wants to become a film star and who sings in a cabaret where the Master of Ceremonies (Joel Grey) resembles a decadent vampire. Just as Brian and Sally make a sexual connection, Max (Helmut Griem) comes into their lives; both of them are attracted to this aristocrat, and an equilateral love triangle begins to take shape. Max suggests that the three of them go on a weekend outing in his chauffeur-driven car. As they pass the site of some Nazi butchery, Max observes to Brian that "The Nazis are just a bunch of stupid hooligans. But they do serve a purpose. Let them get rid of the Communists; later we'll be able to control *them.*" "We," he explains, means "Germany — of course."

Most of the musical numbers in *Cabaret* are presented as keys to this political environment. The decadence of the cabaret is shown as a flight from political engagement, a moral vacuum ready to be occupied by Nazism; the performers are partying on the edge of hell, and they realize this but don't really care. At one point the Master of Ceremonies performs with dancers in local-color hiking outfits while an old man is beaten up by Nazis outside the cabaret; these two actions are cross-cut, making the point that these two cultural expressions must be considered in relation to each other. In the scene we shall now examine, where "Tomorrow Belongs to Me" is sung in an outdoor country tavern, the political situation is foregrounded with extreme force.

After the discussion of controlling the Nazis, there are several dramatic scenes that include little or no music; one is a pastoral interlude during which Max suggests that they take a pleasure trip to Africa. Then they are seen partying in the back seat of the car as the chauffeur drives them to the tavern. Sally takes a "nap" in the car (too much champagne) while Brian and Max take a table in the courtyard.

As the tavern scene begins, sprightly accordion music dispels the tension of the previous scenes: things get off to a bright and rapid start. In the first shot, beer is drawn into a mug just as the accordion starts to play. Then a horn joins in, and we see a man with a dog, two horses frisking in a field, and several other shots of the customers engaged in such innocent pursuits as eating, chuckling, and playing chess. Max and Brian enact a subtle seduction scene until their attention is captured by a singing youth. The accordion had stopped playing a few seconds ago, and in the silence Max and Brian had drunk a toast "To Africa." But their dream of self-indulgence is about to be interrupted.

From the beginning to the end of the song there are 42 shots; these last for exactly 3 minutes and end this 4-minute scene. To make the music/picture cutting pattern clear — and there is really no way to appreciate these rhythms without screening the film — we shall take the song verse by verse and key the cuts to its lines. Each vertical line indicates the beginning of a new, numbered shot. This is the first verse:

|1
|The sun on the meadow is summery warm.

|2
|The stag in the forest runs free;

But gather |3 together |4 to greet |5 the storm;

|6
|Tomorrow belongs to me.

Shot 1 is a two-shot of Max and Brian after the toast; it ends as they look offscreen. Shot 2 is a close shot of the singer, with the thick leafy branch of a tree just beside him. Smiling and tilting his head, with his blue eyes, white teeth, and straight blond hair, he looks like your basic Flower of German Youth. His face is gentle, the song soothing and pastoral (recall the frisky horses). It appears to be the start of an idyllic moment, just what Max and Brian have been hoping for. Shot 1 lasts for a complete line, establishing the three-quarter time of the music and the regular pace of the poetic line. When Shot 2 starts at the start of the second line, the cutting pattern seems particularly regular, as if it will go on to match the rhythm of the line breaks. But in the third line, on the significant word "together," we begin to see reaction shots from the audience; the cut to the first of these (Shot 3: a woman with a white bow in her hair) implies that the singer is linked to these people, that they may be part of the same community. "To greet" is heard over Shot 4 — an older woman — and "the storm" over Shot 5, two youths in profile. Shot 6 returns to the singer, as if it were he to whom the future belongs. For the first time, we can see that he is wearing some kind of uniform.

Here is the second verse:

. . . 6
The branch of the linden is sleepy and green,

The Rhine gives its gold to the sea,

|7
|But somewhere a |8 glory awaits |9 unseen:

|10
|Tomorrow be|11longs to me.

As the youth continues to sing in Shot 6, and the horn joins the accordion, the camera tilts down his left arm. At "branch," it lingers on his swastika armband. That swastika immediately changes the tone of the scene and clarifies the meaning of the song (the future belongs to the Nazis); significantly, it comes into frame on, and is emphasized with, the beat: not just the downbeat of the three-quarter time, but also the stress on the syllable. Then the camera pans to the left, surveying the audience. We won't see the tree again, although the singer does not move.

The words of the song are given special meaning by the cutting and by the choice of reaction shots. On "glory" we see a young woman in a black dress with white dots on it, a woman who later in the scene will take on a formidable presence. At "unseen" there is a close shot of a middle-aged man with a goatee and an expression that is neutral at this point but that has squintingly nasty overtones; he has the eyes of a rattlesnake. Shot 10 is centered on a boy who watches the singer; if the man with the goatee is "unseen," the boy is part of the future. It is significant that Shot 11 begins on the beat and stress of "longs." To cut on the beat is to give a word or an image special importance; both beat and cut establish metrical units, and when they come together, the movie's audience cannot help but pay extra attention.

Stresses and Beats. Rhythm is a crucial aspect of any art that occurs in time. The alternation of stressed and unstressed syllables provides one of the essential elements of rhythm in poetry (in a "stressed" language like English, not in an "unstressed" one like Japanese). "Belongs," for example, cannot be pronounced "*be-longs*": the stress is on "*longs*." Each metrical unit, called a "foot," includes one stressed and one or more unstressed syllables. It is called a foot in an analogy with walking or with the dance, as if the foot hit the ground and bore one's weight on the stress, and both step and stress are analogous to the downbeat in music. In the theater a "beat" usually comes at a significant pause; although there have been beats throughout the action, one of them is emphasized by occurring in — or as — an instant of silence. The control of these beats, and of larger units of emphasis and release, creates the rhythm of the scenes and of the whole. Cinema can make use of all of these rhythmic devices and some of its own.

In a film, cuts often create beats; there are also movements and sounds within the shot that establish beats. The variation of shot duration creates a rhythm, and this rhythm works with the inner rhythms of each shot, which may depend on blocking, theatrical beats, or camera movement. In this song the rhythm of the cutting is precisely engaged with the rhythms of language, music, and action; to appreciate how, let us notate the next two verses.

A poetic stress is conventionally notated with a slash, or /, an unstressed syllable with a check, or u. The basic meter here has the stress pattern /uu. The waltz time has the same pattern: /uu. When the singer pauses, the music continues — so that these lines, as notated, may appear to contain extra stresses. To keep things as clear as possible, the stressed syllables are underlined, and the / and u marks are used to indicate *musical* rhythms:

```
...11            |12
u  /  u  u  /  |u u  /  u  u  /  u
The babe in his cradle is closing his eyes,

|13
|u  /   u   u  /   u   u  /uu/u
|The blossom embraces the bee,

|14                    |15
|u  /  u   u  /  u  |u/ u u / u
|But soon says a whisper, |"Arise, arise—

|16          |17
|u  /  u  u|/  u  u  /uu/u
|Tomorrow belongs to me."


    |18                        |19
u  |/  u  u  /  u  u  |/  uu  u  /
O |Fatherland, Fatherland, |show us a sign

|20
|u   /   u  u  /  u  u  /uu/u
|Your children have waited to see!

|21                    |22
|u  /  u   u  /   |u  u  u  /  u  u  /  u
|The morning will come |when the world is mine:

|23
|u  /  u  u  /  u
|Tomorrow belongs,

|24          |25
|u  /  u  |u  /  u
|Tomorrow |belongs,

|26              |27
|u  /  u  u  /  u  u  /uu/u
|Tomorrow belongs to me.
```

   Shot 12 begins on an offbeat; it is a medium long shot of the audience, with a horse-drawn coach in the background on the country road, and with the lyrics, it implies that the pastoral vision is "closing its eyes" to something. The waltz accompaniment picks up in energy and tempo. Shot 13 returns us to a close view of the singer. The tree has not been seen in his shots for some time; now he begins to squint. Shots 13 and 14 both begin after line breaks; by now the interdependence of the cutting and the metric patterns has been firmly established. In Shot 14, which comes from the same take as Shot 5, the two youths begin to sing along. From now on, whenever there is a close shot of a singing member of the audience, we hear the individual voice distinctly over the other voices in the sound background.

Shot 15, the turning point of the scene, is a close shot of the lead singer, now squinting markedly. The cut gives special emphasis to his implicit command to the audience: "Arise, arise." Dramatically, the audience's rising to their feet indicates their solidarity with the aspirations of the Nazis. The rest of the scene becomes an inventory of who rises and who doesn't, and the camera's sympathy is clearly with those who remain seated. Sympathy is manipulated here by the choice of camera angle and by the juxtaposition of certain facial expressions with discrete parts of the song; a true Nazi, in other words, would be more likely to be offended than inspired by this scene. In Shot 16, a young woman in a blue top stands into the frame (on "To-") and begins to sing, right on the beat ("-mor-"). She is the first to get up. Her standing into the frame happens on the offbeat and the unstressed syllable; on the beat and the stress, she is powerfully present. On the beat of "longs," Shot 17 takes us back to the lead singer and stays there through a significant change in the music: between verses it picks up in pace; it pumps itself up and then changes key. The downbeats become heavier, and a drum and cymbals become prominent in the accompaniment. The musicians join in much as the rising audience does, and the scene begins to feel like a political rally.

The martial tone takes over in the fourth verse, and the carefully established cutting pattern becomes even more forceful while increasing in metrical sophistication. Shot 17 ends as the singer gets out his "O." The cut to Shot 18 comes on the downbeat, not at the start of the line; that makes the word "Fatherland" all the more powerful, and it is reinforced by the appropriate image of two uniformed Nazi adults standing to attention and singing. In this shot all the elements cohere perfectly: Nazism, "Fatherland," cut, stress, and drumbeat. "Show us a sign" returns us to the world of Max and Brian, who are now faced with a "sign" of Nazi power; cutting to them on these words makes that point, and from their perspective. (On those same words, a Nazi filmmaker might have cut to a shot of a soaring eagle.)

Just after "sign" an offbeat is skipped. In that instant of silence comes the cut to Shot 20, and this is a clear example of how a cut can function as a beat on its own. In Shot 20 the camera is centered on a perturbed-looking old man and is at his eye level; the four people around him stand up and begin to sing, and the shot ends as he scratches his head. The shot lasts for a complete line, with an extra measure at the end. We have time to ask ourselves how this man feels about the younger generation ("children"). Shot 21 is a relatively tight closeup of the lead singer, now firmly predicting the coming of the new morning.

In Shot 22 the woman in the black dress stands up and sings; she was last seen in Shot 8, and by now she looks truly scary. In Shot 23 the bearded man from Shot 9 stands up. As 9 followed 8, 23 follows 22; this helps to knit the montage together in a neat pattern whose logic is beginning to emerge: the close reaction shots have been waiting to be joined into a coherent and regular system. That in itself has shades of fascism, and one begins to hope that the metrical editing pattern will be disrupted. Shot 23 begins as an eye-level closeup; the camera follows the bearded man as he stands, creating a low-angle shot of this overtly threatening figure. As the verse continues, other characters rise and sing.

The fourth verse ("O Fatherland") is repeated two more times. We see that the singer is on a podium, flanked by the two columns of the standing audience. The singer is conclusively intertwined with his audience in a highly ordered pattern of regular cross-cutting — for a while, one shot per word, sometimes one shot per stress. The climax of the scene comes when the singer repeats "Tomorrow belongs" three times (Shot 38); as he does so, he puts on his military cap (A), straightens its brim (B), and raises his right arm in the Nazi salute (C), like this:

A   B   C

Tomorrow belongs, tomorrow belongs, tomorrow belongs

The business of straightening the brim would be unnecessary unless the point were that it *is* on the beat; Fosse directed the visual rhythm to support the musical and poetic ones. In Shot 39 Max and Brian are at the door of the car. "Still think you can control them?" asks Brian, and Max shrugs. The singing continues in a hearty chorus as they drive away (Shot 40). Shot 41, a commentative intrusion, shows the Master of Ceremonies, apparently in a dressing room. Looking like Dracula after a day without sleep, he smiles and nods. The song and the picture then fade out as the car continues to drive away (Shot 42).

This scene was clearly directed for this song and was cut to a completed music track. Although the cuts and the camera movements have their own logic — interrelating the singer, the crowd, and Max and Brian as observers, then cutting in the Master of Ceremonies for overt commentary — they take on even more significance and considerably greater emotional power from having been so precisely coordinated with this rousing and perversely beautiful song.

Sound Editing and the Stereo Mix

The final soundtrack is a **sound composite** whose **elements** are individual sound *tracks*. Hundreds of tracks are recorded during production, hundreds more are created during post-production, and all of these tracks must be transferred to mag film, synchronized with the picture, edited, and finally integrated into one monaural or several stereophonic tracks. Once the picture, music, and dialogue had been cut to one another, for example, "Tomorrow Belongs to Me" was far from completed. The dialogue and music tracks still had to be adjusted so that they would play well together — so that important lines of dialogue would not be covered up by music, so that the volume would change as the camera drew nearer to or away from the singer(s), etc. Effects tracks had to be created, cut, and balanced with the dialogue and music, often with a different balance for each shot. This interplay of sounds, this balancing and combining of tracks, this final realization of the sound environment is all done in an arduous series of mixing sessions.

To **mix** tracks is to combine them into a sound composite; to **dub** a track is to re-record it. A mixing session, however, is sometimes called a "dubbing session." To keep the terms straight, think of the differences between a **dubber** (a transport and playback machine for mag film, capable of being interlocked with a projector and with other dubbers) and a **mixer** (an electronic console with more input channels than output channels, capable of modifying the sound characteristics of each channel as the tracks are combined and fed to a recorder). In the typical mix, whether preliminary (the **pre-mix**, in which tracks are combined or **mixed down** into manageable bundles) or final, the tracks to be combined are played back on dubbers (as many as twenty-four 3-track machines) that are synchronized with each other and with the picture, so that they all may be advanced and backed up in lockstep. At the mixer (the console), the mixer (a person) adjusts the volume, equalization, and echo of each input channel, creating the desired balances and interplay within the tracks as well as among them as they are combined (mixed) and re-recorded (dubbed).

Like "dubbing," which is used to refer to everything from sound transfer to foreign-language dialogue replacement, "mix" is a term that has many uses and applications. A picture dissolve is sometimes called a "visual mix" or simply a "mix," whereas a sound dissolve or **cross-fade** is called a **segue** (pronounced "seg-way"). The key re-recording mixer, who supervises the making of the intermediate and final sound composites, is usually called the **mixer**. The person who has creative control over the mix might, however, be the sound designer, the key re-recording mixer, or the supervising editor. Ben Burtt had creative control over the sound design of all three *Star Wars* pictures, but *Jedi* was the first on which he was also the key re-recording mixer. To keep things simple, we shall use "mixer" to identify the person in creative control — or, of course, the mixing console.

Before a reel of sound can be mixed, its component elements must be cut together, modified, and pre-mixed. They must be made as ready as possible for the mixer to work with; their internal relationships must be sorted out, synchronized, and settled. The reel of sound must be cut and built as precisely as the reel of picture, and *to* the picture. Reels of music, dialogue, and effects are built separately, often by different editors. And ever since stereo reared its two or more heads, all this work became rather more complicated. Before treating the mix in greater detail, then, let us take a look at some of the most common preparations for the mix, most of which involve some form of re-recording.

Music. We have already covered the work of the music editor, so this discussion will be brief. In a high-quality operation, the music is recorded onto 16 or 24 tracks on wide magnetic tape, sometimes digitally. By the time they reach the final mixing stage, these tracks will have been mixed down in the recording studio and transferred onto 3-track 35mm stripe. During the preliminary mix, individual instruments can be brought out or subdued, and the desired orchestral or ensemble coloration can be established and manipulated. The three tracks are divided so that they carry synchronized left-, center-, and right-field information.

It may be useful at this point to reprise and introduce a few terms. "Quarter-inch" is magnetic tape, run through a conventional tape recorder. "Mag film" is sprocketed stock that has been magnetically coated; the soundtrack for a 35mm film is edited and mixed on 35mm mag, and 16mm mag is used in 16mm filmmaking. **Fullcoat** is mag stock that has been coated across its entire width; in other words, it looks completely brown, and from one to six tracks may be recorded on it, depending on the configuration of the heads. When the entire width of the fullcoat is occupied by a single track, that is a "full-track recording." When it has only a single track, but that track runs in a narrow band rather than full-width, it is called "single stripe" or "1-stripe." Three parallel tracks, or "3-stripe," is a common configuration. "Stripe" in the above definitions refers to a narrow path, one of several parallel bands, on fully coated stock; it may also refer to an actual stripe of mag oxide painted onto clear polyester stock; some 3-stripe, then, has three brown stripes on a clear support. As a separate term, however, **stripe** is clear stock painted with a single stripe of mag oxide onto which *one track* is recorded. There is also a second, narrower band of mag oxide, called a "balance stripe," whose function is to make sure that both edges of the stock are equal in thickness; if there were only one stripe, the stock would not ride on a level plane or lie flat against the recording and playback heads. Stripe is the most convenient medium in which to edit any single track (virtually all Hollywood dialogue is edited on 35mm stripe); fullcoat is the best for the recording and trial playback of mutually synchronized tracks. Most 16mm work, however, is done full-track and on fullcoat.

Dialogue. Dialogue is sometimes modified and is often replaced during post-production. In a poem called "Fresh Air" Kenneth Koch once wrote about a man whose voice "had the sound of water leaving a vaseline bathtub," and if someone wanted that effect in a movie, the production dialogue track would have to be re-recorded through a **filter**. Most of the dialogue of the Oz Munchkins was played back at double speed for a high-pitched effect after having been recorded with the actors speaking slowly. Ingmar Bergman had some of his dialogue tracks re-recorded in reverse to characterize some of the more baffling and threatening environments in his films of the late 1960s. But what is most commonly done to dialogue tracks is simple *repair*, not transfiguration. These procedures may be as subtle as dialogue splitting or as drastic as dialogue replacement.

Dialogue splitting is a matter of isolating the dialogue of various characters, heard in the same scene, onto different tracks so that they may be individually modified; it is usually done by an assistant sound editor. Perhaps two characters are having a shot/reverse-shot conversation (also called, from the sound editor's perspective, an **A and B dialogue**). It turns out that a breeze is blowing in the sound background of one actor's track, perhaps because of the directions in which the microphones were pointed. The sound editor cannot simply cut the two actors' lines together without creating a noticeable "bump" in the sound. Each actor's dialogue, then, is put on a separate track (in other words, the dialogue track is split) so that its volume, equalization, filtration, and echo can be adjusted and also to create a sound background that *can* support a cut.

The mixer segues, rather than cuts, from one dialogue track to another, eliminating the bump. For this segue to be possible, the tracks have to be **extended** so that there are instants of relative silence at their heads and tails. In the pre-mix, then, the mixer can cross-fade from tail to head, from one sound background to the other, without affecting the level of the actual dialogue. The tracks are extended not with silence but with ambient air or room tone. If wild recordings of air have not been made during shooting, the dialogue editor will have to **pull air**, searching through the production tape to find an instant during which no one was speaking. This fragment of background tone is pulled (taken) from the tape, spliced in a loop, re-recorded, and cut in where needed.

It very often happens that even perfectly synchronized production dialogue tracks either are not or cannot be used. Instead, new dialogue tracks are recorded during post-production and synchronized, as much as possible, with the picture. **Post-synchronization** is the process of adding sounds to shots during post-production, whether they were shot silent or had only partly usable production tracks. Most of the effects tracks and virtually all of the music tracks are post-synchronized as a matter of course, but when dialogue is post-synchronized, that may be a reflection not of a normal procedure but of a production problem. "We'll fix it in post" is a very common remark.

A post-synchronized track that replaces an original or production track is called a **replacement** track. The general term for the process of **dialogue replacement** is **looping**. As we shall see in a moment, looping is often done with dubbers, and the post-synchronizing of dialogue is sometimes loosely referred to as "dubbing." In this context, however, what **dubbing** properly refers to is the replacement of an *entire* dialogue track, as when one is changing the language in which the dialogue is spoken, and it may also refer to "voice replacement," where a new actor (that is, a new voice) records the dialogue track originally spoken by the production performer.

Anyone who has seen *Singin' in the Rain* knows that there are some voices that need to be replaced. With proper attention to lip sync, both Jean Hagen and Donald O'Connor can appear to sing with the voice of Debbie Reynolds. The most common use of voice replacement techniques, however, is to create subtitle-free versions of foreign-language sound films. But dubbing is not restricted to the translation of entire movies from one language to another. It also proves useful in many international productions. In a Sergio Leone Western, for instance, the actors on the set may be addressing one another in Italian, Spanish, and English, and the original *domestic* release version will have to be dubbed into a single language.

Foreign-language dubbing drives film purists up the wall, though many audiences prefer it to the distracting job of reading approximately accurate subtitles. The problem with dubbing is that it violates the integrity of the filmed-and-recorded world; it sacrifices the impression that *that* person said *those* words *then*. It defeats the willing suspension of disbelief and also shears away a considerable portion of the original actor's performance.

But some of the same problems may arise even when the language is not being changed and even when the original actor records the replacement track. The new performance may not mesh dramatically with the original, even if the sync is perfect, or the new performance may play right but be out of sync. When lip sync is lost in domestic (same-language) dialogue replacement, the results can be both amusing and disastrous; for a few really flagrant examples, check out *The Cotton Club*, which was almost entirely post-synced. The apparently seamless correspondence of person, action, and speech is an essential tool of the realistic cinema, and in comparison with indigenous production sound (live sound), even the most carefully post-synchronized track may strike the audience as artificial. That is why so much effort is expended in the direct recording of dialogue during production. In some industries it is common practice to post-sync the entire soundtrack, using the original actors to record their lines. Shooting is much easier when one does not have to plant and dodge microphones, and the sound recordist's dream of having the actor close to the mike in a windless environment is easy to achieve in a studio. On *The Empire Strikes Back*, 83 percent of the dialogue was post-synced; that is an unusually high figure, but it is also the sign of a trend.

Production dialogue tracks are replaced for a variety of reasons. A line might need to be censored for a TV print, for example, and replaced with a less offensive line of the same length. A line might even be *rewritten* at the last moment, something that generally happens only when a picture is being "saved in the editing," though it may also happen when a relatively well-planned picture is being polished or recut. The most common reason to replace dialogue tracks is that simple, unwanted background noise has rendered them unusable. Perhaps a plane drones overhead while *Spartacus* is being shot, or the camera has not been well-blimped, or one actor gets her lines right while the other flubs his. In such cases, it becomes necessary to record a replacement track for the whole scene. The new, post-synchronized dialogue track may be created through conventional looping or through a process known as ADR or EPS; either way, the general process is referred to as "looping." Looped dialogue may be direct (onscreen source) or off (offscreen indigenous source); what it is *not* is live.

In conventional (and now nearly obsolete) **looping**, the original lip-synced production dialogue, now on mag, is attached to a piece of blank stock (fill) of exactly the same length, and the tail of the fill is then attached to the head of the dialogue in a continuous loop, which is played back through a dubber in sync with a projector. The machine plays back the production line and then a precisely-timed silence. The actor (or the looping artist, if there has been a substitution) faces a screen on which the picture, also spliced into a loop, is repeatedly projected, and listens to the loop on headphones. After hearing the line over and over, the actor eventually achieves sync with the original performance; the replacement line is spoken during the silent half of the loop, and as each new try is recorded (on another, "virgin" loop), the previous one is erased. The end result is a studio-delivered line that is in sync with the picture, to the extent that it exactly matches the timing of the line on the production track. Background noises and/ or location air are laid over the replacement dialogue later on, so that the lines will not sound as if they have been recorded in a studio (a typical example of the use of artifice in the construction of an impression of the natural).

Most "looping" today is accomplished through **ADR**, which used to stand for "Additional Dialogue Recording" and now stands for "Automatic Dialogue Replacement." The process is also known as **EPS**, which stands simply for "Electronic Post Sync." The essential difference between looping and ADR is that in ADR, the projector and dubber are interlocked and run forward or backward, whereas in looping they run forward in endless loops. One can loop only a few seconds at a time, but with ADR one can run through an entire scene and then crank back for another try. (Since ADR, like conventional looping, erases each previous replacement performance, a quarter-inch permanent copy of all attempts may be recorded for the editor's use.) The clear advantage of ADR is that the performer has the opportunity to watch and to act through the entire scene, rather than the same fragment, more-or-less out of context, over and over again. The advantage of looping, however, is that it invariably yields better lip-sync results.

In ADR, as in looping, the actor faces the screen and listens to a production track through headphones (which keep the playback from being picked up by the microphone). Imagine, however, how difficult it would be to say a line while hearing yourself say it. What usually comes over the headphones, then, is the dialogue *leading up to* the lines to be replaced. When the actor speaks, the only background might be atmosphere or silence. The sounds played back are channeled from one of several separate tracks on 3- or 4-stripe mag, and the performer may ask the engineer to switch from channel A (which might be the other actor) to B (sync production dialogue) to C (effects), and so on.

The performer also hears something else over the headphones, however, which is where the "automatic" aspect of ADR comes into play: three electronic beeps. On the fourth (imaginary) beep, the performer begins — as if hearing and acting on the pulse BEEP BEEP BEEP SPEAK. A computer produces these beeps at the right time, following the assistant or ADR editor's coded instructions. The picture is marked with streamers, and the streamer hits the side of the frame at the third beep. The picture becomes the guide to lip sync.

The newest development in EPS technology is a computerized system called "Wordfit." Using the sync production track as a reference, the system stretches and compresses the replacement track until it *is* in perfect sync. As of this writing, the results of this truly electronic post-synchronization are mixed: the sync is great, but the readings tend to sound unnatural if not a little weird.

Effects. The effects ("FX") tracks are the most numerous and diverse.

The sound effects editor re-records and assembles the various elements recorded during production, along with wild recordings from sound effects libraries and those specially created under the supervision of the sound designer. The effects editor also orders, and then cuts in, synchronized replacement live sound effects, a process called **Foley editing**.

"Effects" describes all of the sounds heard in a film other than dialogue and music — but not every effect one might want to include in a soundtrack can be found in a tape library, and some authentic effects may not sound "right," that is, may not sound the way the audience *expects* those things to sound. The crash of a real wooden structure, for example, sounds "wooden," but the sound of crashing *glass* may produce just the right impression and, furthermore, be accepted as natural because it fulfills the audience's expectations. Even if one can find 20 tapes of gigantic pine trees falling through timber to the ground, consider how long are the odds against finding one whose duration and peaks exactly match those of the action: the sync points when the tree first hits the tops, then the branches, of the other trees and when it bounces, thumps, and at last hits the ground. All this is a great deal more than a long crash. Even the simplest effects have their starts, peaks, and stops, and they all have to match those in the picture; the starts and stops are, in fact, the crucial instants, the ones that must be in sync. (That is true in those cases where sync is desired. Where audience reaction time must be allowed for, and in the case of many big effects such as car crashes, the sound is advanced 2 frames.) Considering all of this, and the amount of work it would be to splice together tapes of footsteps and lengths of clear sound leader in order to match the footsteps of an actor who was recorded MOS or whose mike did not pick up the footsteps, it is now common practice to create or synthesize sound effects, in real time, to match the picture. This customized effects track is produced by the **Foley artist**.

A **Foley**, then, is a replacement sound effect, created live while the picture is shown on a screen and the Foley artist's sounds are recorded. The effects-replacement process, invented by Universal's Ed Foley, was used at first for *body movement* effects — footsteps on the sidewalk, in particular, which is why you will not hear Jean Harlow's footsteps but you will, since the advent of Foley work, hear Kathleen Turner's. Other body movement effects include the sounds made by a raincoat as you take it off, a slug to the jaw (or a roast), a body fall, slogging through the mud, and so on. To create those last muddy sucking gooshy sounds, say for a shot in which a soldier is marching through the stuff, the Foley artist (also called the **sound effects specialist**) watches the film while duplicating the actor's motions — in this case, wears boots and trudges up and down in a box filled with mud. Like the looping artist, the Foley artist is cued by streamers.

At this point a great many of the sound effects in films, and not only those made by moving bodies, are Foley work, and most of them are created much less literally than the "footstepping" described above. This is where the Foley artist may work with how an action is "supposed" to sound, or how, in context, it has to sound. If Robin Hood bumps into a castle wall that happens to be made of plywood, that sound effect will have to be replaced (in exactly the same sense as "dialogue replacement") with the sound of the Foley artist's bumping into the equivalent of thick stone, perhaps the concrete wall of the Foley stage. The whooshing kicks in *The Karate Kid* were made with a badminton racquet. Toss three BIC pen tops into a glass, and you'll know where movie ice cubes come from. Foley artists now create all of the sound effects one might have heard on a radio show — doors, drawers, opening and breaking windows, horns, snapping wires, silverware, creaking branches — as well as many that have, in the past, traditionally been "cut effects" (effects that are cut by a sound editor), such as explosions, falling debris, squeaky banisters, and monsters.

A **looping group** may work with the Foley artists or independently, but the thrust of their work is similar: to synthesize a post-sync soundtrack. The typical looping group comprises three men and three women, and they divide up the "voices" in the scene among them. They may be crowds, kids leaving a bus, "other" diners in a restaurant, a politician's audience, passing pedestrians — whatever. They deliver lines, take body falls, crinkle cellophane for fire, scamper around making a racket with anything useful, keep looking at the picture and the streamers, and all together say "walla walla walla" in order to create that old standby crowd sound, "crowd walla." (Try it.) They may also dub domestic versions of foreign-language films.

Nevertheless, there is still a great deal of effects cutting going on in contemporary practice, and Foley artists are not the only people who invent sounds. We turn, then, to the work of the sound designer and the sound effects editor.

Sound effects tracks are **built** more often than they are found: put together out of many individual sound elements, recorded and re-recorded, pre-mixed and cut and pre-mixed again. The elements themselves must be built before the reel of sound can be built. To make a helicopter approach and then recede, for example, Walter Murch had to assemble and modify at least four tracks for each pass of every copter in *Apocalypse Now*:

There's something about the sound of the helicopter as it flies that tells you it's moving quite fast. It's a very complicated sound, and there's a shift of frequency, a Doppler shift, as it goes by. There are very complicated phase differences that are going on, so that the equalization of the sound is very complex. When it's first coming toward you, it goes phut-phut-phut, and then there's a turbine sound that comes in and then the slight whirring of the blades. It's a very colorful sound, and it changes as it moves.

Some effects might have to be put through a process Murch calls **worldizing**: making the sound appear to have been recorded in its purported environment. This could be a matter of playing a studio-recorded song through a real car radio and then recording that, to give the impression that the song is being heard over a radio by a character. Many of the tracks that sound as if they were coming over loudspeakers and megaphones in *Apocalypse Now* and *The Right Stuff* were worldized over the PA system at a California racetrack.

The sound editor cuts tracks for the mix. One typical procedure is called **splitting for perspective**. Say that views from inside and outside a car are to be cross-cut; outside it is raining, and inside two characters are talking. As the camera appears to be inside and outside the car, so must the sound. At a minimum, these are the sound elements that would be used: the characters' dialogue, the car's ambient air, the windshield wipers, the rain, and such traffic sounds as horns, tires on pavement, and rain hitting the car bodies. For the sound environment inside the car, the air and the dialogue would be at normal volume, whereas the exterior ambient sounds would be subdued. For the outside views, the air would be dispensed with, the dialogue would be muted, and the wipers, rain, and traffic noises would be louder. Each cluster of sounds would require separate volume, echo, and equalization settings. The sound editor prepares one set of tracks for the interiors and another for the exteriors; the sounds are split, then, to facilitate the mixing of perspective sound.

In Murch's words, most effects tracks have to be "added to or augmented or surgically fiddled with." And in the words of Alan Splet:

You process these sounds through the different devices, combine them, overlap them. It's like making a stew. You have a few potatoes, a few peas, some carrots, a little beef. I put it in the pot and taste it every so often to see how it's coming along. Then maybe you need a little more of this or that, and you blend it all together until you get your sound. You know when it's finally right by instinct. It just begins to feel right.

The Mix. It is desirable, by the end of all the pre-mixing sessions, to have as few as three music tracks, six dialogue tracks, and six effects tracks. All of these are sound composites, of course, but care has been taken not to introduce too many dubbing generations, since any sound degrades slightly with duplication, although not as drastically as an image does. Effects, typically, are pre-mixed in batches of six, onto 6-stripe fullcoat, with separate pre-mixes for atmosphere (like the background rumble of a *Star Wars* ship, or the "caw" of the jungle), for such complex sounds as helicopters and giant spice-worms, and so on. Eventually the pre-mixed reels are loaded on dubbers that are interlocked with each other and with a projector, as previously explained, and the final mix proceeds, one reel of sound at a time.

The simplest mixing console consists of two inputs and one output. Discrete signals enter the mixer, where they may or may not be modified as they are combined into one signal. The average professional mixer, of course, has many more inputs and outputs than that, and its diverse controls allow the signals to be modified in a great many ways. Level (volume) is adjusted via a big knob called a **pot** (potentiometer), one in line with each channel. Equalization is adjusted via sliding levers. Echo may be created with a spring-reverberation unit or, more recently, with digital delay. ("Spring reverb," which creates an artificial echo electronically, replaced the echo chamber; "digital echo" or "digital delay" allows one to program a computer with the dimensions and surfaces of the room in which the scene is set, and the computer will then calculate and create the right amount of echo — will, in fact, develop an electronic representation of that acoustical space.)

Volume, equalization, and echo are the principal concerns and adjustments, but there are many other modifications that can be made by external units (such as digital-delay or spring-reverb units). "Outboard signal processing," as it is called, has very few limits; typical modifications include the *compression* of the signal in order to narrow its dynamic range, the interposition of a *sound filter*, the use of a *limiter* to cut off the peaks in order not to blow away the average optical-sound projector with a track to which only mag is adequate, echo/reverb, and others.

In the very simplest monaural mix, the dialogue, music, and effects tracks are combined into a single channel while the mixer watches the picture on a screen (**Fig. 3-135**), below which there is an oversized footage counter. In some cases the immediate product of the mix will be a 3-stripe fullcoat, with one track each for dialogue, music, and effects. That is called a **D-M-E** mix, and it saves a good deal of work in case a line or effect needs to be redone, because one can redo the dialogue track, for example, without having to "tear down" the entire mix. To facilitate the dubbing of foreign release versions, a separate mix is done without the dialogue track (and without the effects that happen to have been in the background of the dialogue track); this is called an **M-E** or a **minus-dialogue mix**. At some point in the development of a stereo soundtrack, there might be one D-M-E or M-E per channel.

Sooner or later, however, the product of the final mix appears: a fullcoat with one fully mixed track per channel: one for mono, or two, four, or six channels for stereo.

In the contemporary, state-of-the-art mixing room, instruments adequate to the vision of the creative mixer may have to be invented. In *Apocalypse Now,* as noted before, the beach attack alone had more than 140 separate sound elements. A special mixing console — capable of handling 34 tracks at once, with computerized fader settings — was built for the purpose, at a cost of $200,000, and Walter Murch is shown at it in **Fig. 3-136**.

Stereo. A **channel** is a discrete reel- or film-long unit of sound information that is to be played through a particular theater speaker. A film **track** (in the sense of "soundtrack," not an individual element of the mix) is a reel- or film-long unit of *stored* sound information, and it may include more than one channel. A four-track mix will yield four channels, each on its own composite mag track. In the Dolby Stereo optical format, used for 35mm release prints, these four channels are electronically processed into two variable-area optical tracks; during projection they are electronically decoded into four separate channels (this is called the **4-2-4 process**). In the Dolby Stereo magnetic format, which is used on 70mm release prints, the six channels are carried on six mag tracks.

As a noise reduction process, Dolby encodes sound information and then decodes it, allowing sounds of particular frequencies to be moved around in the sound spectrum in relation to the noise floor. (The first film to use Dolby NR throughout production was *Star Wars.*) But encoding and decoding can also be used to isolate entire sound channels from each other, and it is this other use of Dolby technology that proves crucial in Dolby Stereo. In a 70mm six-track Dolby print, Dolby is used simply for noise reduction. But in a 35mm four-track Dolby Stereo optical print, the channels are encoded in different *phase* relationships. Noise reduction circuitry is also employed here, and it is particularly valuable because optical soundtracks have an unusually high degree of inherent background noise. The **Dolby sound consultant**, who is as important to the contemporary sound team as the Technicolor consultant was to the filmmakers of the 1940s and 1950s, helps the sound editors and mixers to bring all the tracks up to a precise standard, whether or not the recordings were originally encoded for noise reduction, and advises them on how to mix the tracks so that they will perform at an optimum level when played back in a correctly balanced theater.

Most 35mm theaters have three speakers behind the screen, identified as left, center, and right. In mono they all play the same information, though special circuitry may concentrate low-frequency music and sound effects in the larger central speaker. In the stereo theater (or "house"), there are usually at least four channels: left, center, right, and surround. The **surround channel**, which may be fed to speakers all around the side and back walls, or simply to one in the rear, allows the audience to be surrounded by the sound field. *Apocalypse Now* used a **split-surround** matrix (also called **stereo surround**) that produced a true quadrophonic effect, as the sounds from screen right were made to wrap around to the rear like a wing of right-field information, and the same on the left; the result was that left-front, left-rear, right-front, and right-rear all became discrete sites from which sounds could originate, or coordinates for orienting the sound field. Both the on-camera and off-camera sound fields were fully dimensionalized.

One of the re-recording mixers on *Apocalypse,* Dale Strumpell, described one use of the quadrophonic sound field as follows:

Martin Sheen is staring up at the fan. You're in his mind, and the sound is coming from both the front and back of the house. As he gets off the bed and goes to the window, the sound fades from the back speakers to the front — left, center, and right — and then, as the hand comes in and moves the venetian blinds, it moves from the left and right speakers to only the center channel. So you have this whole thing where the sound is narrowing, narrowing, narrowing, as the dolly shot is moving in closer.

Many contemporary films are released in multiple sound formats. A film like *Star Wars* is now available in 70mm six-track, 35mm four-channel/two-track, 35mm mono, 16mm mono, mono and stereo videocassettes, and a two-track laserdisc that is capable of being decoded for surround. The mixing crew may well have to mix the sound in four- and six-channel stereo *and* mono versions as well as those same versions without dialogue.

Dolby channels are encoded and decoded through a **stereo matrix**. Left-channel information is sent to the left track at normal volume and in phase; right-channel information is sent to the right track at normal volume and in phase. The center channel appears in both the left and right tracks, in phase, and at a lower level (3 dB below the "unity gain" at which the left and right channels are re-recorded). The surround channel is also on the left and right tracks, 3 dB down and *out* of phase. The point about -3 dB — which in oversimplified but plain English means "half volume" — is that the two half-volume tracks add up to a single channel that will be heard at normal volume.

In six-track Dolby the additional two channels are reserved for low-frequency information: explosions, earthquake rumbles, bass music, and so on. These are called **boom channels**, and they are fed through Speakers 2 and 4 behind the screen; they are free of noise reduction. The normal setup in a contemporary 70mm house is to have five speakers behind the screen (numbered sequentially from screen left) and between one and ten surround speakers. Speaker 1 plays the left track, Speaker 2 plays the left-center boom track, 3 is the center, 4 is the right-center boom, and 5 is the right track. Speaker 6 is surround. The boom channels are used to extend the bass response in the theater; the Dolby people refer to this *bass-extension* process as the **baby boom** system. It was used to spectacular effect in *Days of Heaven* and was quite imposing in *Close Encounters, Alien,* and *Dune.* The 70mm mixer determines the exact content of the boom channels because he or she is mixing six discrete mag tracks. But it is also possible to get boom-channel information out of the Dolby Stereo optical matrix.

There are a number of ways to create a stereo sound field, of which the simplest is to divert a particular sound to a particular channel. One can make a sound travel from screen left to screen right by turning down the level for the left channel while increasing that for the center, then reducing the center-channel level while increasing that for the right. All of these cross-fades can be controlled by a single knob called, appropriately, a **panpot**. For more complex effects it is usually necessary to divert an input to one or more outputs at different levels, sometimes with **delays**. Rear information is almost always presented later than front information, like a kind of echo; this delay keeps dialogue audible and increases the sense that the sound comes primarily from what Mike Todd called a "hole" in the screen rather than from everywhere at once. To make sense of the sound field, the mixer must establish a hypothetical center for that field, one that roughly corresponds to the center of the theater, not the middle of the screen.

Creative Mixing. What virtually any mix has to do is to render the important sounds audible at the proper times. In the tavern scene in *Cabaret*, for instance, when the camera was on Max and Brian at their table, the tavern effects and the music both had to be turned down and the actors' dialogue turned up. A mix is judged by how well it juggles its elements, leaving each with the desired sound coloration and quality. If a mix works brilliantly in six-track but sounds wrong in mono, the mixer would be faulted for not having designed a mono-compatible mix or for not having prepared a separate mono mix. Some final soundtracks are clean and sharp, with every element precisely audible — like those for *Citizen Kane* or *The Right Stuff* — whereas others might be praised for the richness of their overlapping textures, like those for *Eraserhead* or *Marienbad*. As we examine two particularly well-mixed sequences, try to visualize the mixer sitting in the dark and fiddling with the knobs and levers.

The first of these sequences comes about 20 minutes into *The Right Stuff*. Yeager (Sam Shepard) has just broken the sound barrier and is laughing and cuddling with his wife (Barbara Hershey) outside a bar and grill. Inside the bar the juke box is playing an old standby: "Those faraway places with strange-sounding names, / Calling, calling me." After an interior shot in which two men talk about the flight, there is a straight cut to an exterior shot of the Yeagers; the song is heard, less loud than it was inside. Mrs. Yeager is laughing, and Yeager is howling like a happy wolf. The sounds of their feet on the dirt road are heard, along with some crickets. Then there is a straight cut to the moon overhead. In this shot the song becomes slightly louder, and the howl and the crickets become slightly softer. Ordinarily we might interpret all this as simply showing Yeager, in an exuberant moment, howling at the moon. But together with the words of the song (over this shot, "calling, calling me"), the howl and the moon add up to a statement that the moon will be the next target for Yeager and those like him.

The second sequence comes from early in the uncut — that is, the unabridged — version of Sergio Leone's *Once Upon a Time in America* (1984). Most of the story concerns four street kids who form a gang in childhood and stick together as bootlegging adults. The main character is Noodles (Robert De Niro), and his major friendship is with Max (James Woods). Late in the movie — and "before" the sequence we will look at (the story is presented out of chronological order) — Max figures out a way to fake his own death and join up with "the Syndicate"; Prohibition has just ended, and it's time for Max to strike out in new directions. He tells Noodles and the other two friends, Philip and Patrick, about his plan to rob a Federal Reserve Bank, then indirectly encourages Noodles to call the police. The idea is that if the gang is put in jail for a few months on a minor bootlegging charge, Max will have time to get this fatally impractical plan out of his head. Noodles does call the police, expecting all four of them to be arrested together while picking up some of the liquor that other bootleggers are selling at cut rates. Then Max talks him out of going along on the job. The police, however, kill the three men as soon as they find them, and for a long time Noodles and the audience both believe that one of the corpses was Max's. Noodles is overwhelmed by guilt and spends the next 35 years in moral pain.

Shortly after the massacre, Noodles goes to an opium den and tries to forget his troubles. In the meantime, the Syndicate — which is in league with the police — has sent thugs out to look for Noodles and kill him, too; Max's sparing him had not been in their plans.

Hours before we understand what is really going on here, then, we see Noodles reclining in an opium den and being roused by some attendants. At what we will call time zero, right after Noodles has looked at Max, Philip, and Patrick's adult faces in the newspaper report of their deaths, the extremely loud ringing of a telephone is heard on the soundtrack. There is no phone in the den. Noodles reacts to the sound, however — suggesting to us that the sound is in his mind — and lights another pipe, looking upset. The phone rings at 10-second intervals. Soon the sounds of the opium den segue into those of a rainy street at night; the camera has pulled up to a lamp in the den, and now it pulls back from a streetlight in the new scene. We see three bodies lying side by side. A photographer pops a flashbulb onto the pavement. Noodles is in the crowd, watching the firefighters and the police cover the corpses. If we had any doubt what we were watching here, we would understand as the bodies are covered that this is a mind-screen — Noodles's personalized and drug-affected memory of the massacre — because the first two corpses have the faces of Patrick and Philip *as boys*. (The third, apparently Max, is an adult burned beyond recognition.) The ringing continues over this scene, at the same high level at which it began, but the intervals between rings gradually become longer.

Then there is a straight cut to a party in a speakeasy — a wake for the death of Prohibition, complete with a coffin cake. The ringing continues, and after a while Noodles leaves the main party and goes into another room; we assume that he is going to answer the phone. After all this ringing, we certainly want someone to answer it! Three minutes and 20 seconds after the ringing has begun, Noodles picks up a desk telephone and dials — and the ringing doesn't stop. Eighteen seconds later, there is a cut to the desk of a police sergeant, notably equipped with a phone. After 5 seconds, a hand reaches into the frame and picks up the receiver — and the ringing stops. We understand that what has been bothering Noodles all along, coloring all these memories, is the ringing of the *policeman*'s phone, the one Noodles called when turning in his friends. The ringing has been extended back over these memories as a metaphoric expression of Noodles's feelings of guilt.

As soon as the receiver is lifted, after 3 minutes and 43 seconds of ringing, there is a straight sound cut to a terribly loud electronic shriek, and then a straight picture cut to Noodles as he wakes up in alarm. This shriek accomplishes two things: it indicates, in sound terms, that the guilt has become unbearable, and it puts Noodles on alert. For he is in danger from the Syndicate, even if he knows next to nothing about them, and at just this moment they are seen entering the den and beginning to search for him. Noodles ducks out the back door and starts to take care of business. At the very end of the film, we again see Noodles living through this scene, but without the telephone. His guilt has vanished (he has confronted the elderly Max in the interim and has treated him, quite brilliantly, as if this man had nothing to do with the long-dead Max he continues to mourn), and when the drug takes effect, he smiles broadly, as if he can see his old friends once again. It is significant that this final scene is done with Noodles as a young adult, not as the old Noodles at the end of the story; it is, in other words, the "same event" as that at the beginning of the film, but this time it both proceeds and feels like a different scene. Having transcended the betrayal, Noodles has healed his younger self and has recovered the good past.

After the Mix. The final product of the mix is called the **composite master**, and it has one mag track per channel. For Dolby optical, the four mag tracks are transferred in sync to a four-track composite master, which is matrixed and transferred to a two-track **printing master**, an optical negative from which the final soundtrack is printed. A simple, monaural, magnetic composite master is transferred to an optical negative from which the normal optical soundtrack is printed.

Should the final soundtrack be magnetic, the composite master is copied onto a **magnetic dubbing master**, and the sound from that is re-recorded onto the magnetic oxide stripe(s) on the release print — in real time and therefore at greater cost.

A copy of the composite is forwarded to the negative cutter for a final synchronization check. Then titles and other opticals are cut into the negative, and the negative and the sound composite are sent to the lab for processing.

The Laboratory

The motion picture laboratory does not simply process film. It is responsible for correcting exposure levels and light values, which are often inconsistent in even the most professionally produced footage. The laboratory creates and stores several generations of pre-print and printing material. It monitors everything from the choice of printing stock to the storage conditions of the camera original and the fine-grain dupe negative master. It provides the production team with rushes overnight, makes meticulous corrections as the picture is refined and recut, and is responsible for quality control and for the shipping of release prints. The lab's job is to help the filmmakers produce the best possible movie — all along, not just after the wrap — and to ensure that the fruits of their labors will be preserved.

Without getting too deeply into the chemistry and optics on which all this work depends, let us take a brief look at how a full-scale film lab helps to bring a releasable movie out of an edited picture and a mixed sound composite. The model here is MGM Laboratories, which is located on the late MGM lot and whose work can be identified by the Metrocolor credit. What this lab does is very similar to what is done in the other major domestic labs, Technicolor and Deluxe General, and also in such high-quality but smaller operations as DuArt in New York.

Lab Procedures. The day's shooting comes into the lab in camera rolls, and these **daily rolls** are developed and printed overnight, then put into projection sync with the transferred sound (which is also on daily rolls; thus there are **picture dailies** and **sound dailies**). Rushes are usually **one-light prints**, which means that the negative is contact-printed onto raw stock with the printer's lamphouse at a more-or-less medium setting for each of the primary light colors: red, green, and blue. (Throughout this discussion, we shall assume that the film is in color.) One-light printing saves time and allows the filmmakers to evaluate what they have actually shot. After sync coding, the daily rolls are broken down into scenes and takes, which can be accessed by their key or edge numbers. The key numbers for each take are entered into a computer, which spits out a label to be taped onto the core-wound negative; these numbers will be consulted at every subsequent stage of the negative cutting and the color and density correction.

As the cutting of the workprint proceeds, it becomes clearer how much of each usable take can be discarded and which takes are really the best. **Trims** (parts cut out of a take) and **outtakes** (complete takes not approved for printing) are cut out of the daily rolls, are labeled, and are stored near at hand in case the editor decides to use them anyway. But let us skip ahead a bit and assume that the workprint and the mix have been completed, and that the original negative has been cut and spliced into 1,000-foot units (reels). We will also assume that the sound composite master has been transferred to a mono or stereo optical negative, also in reel-long units.

Color Timing and Print Generations. Considering that a film is shot out of sequence over a period of months, it is not surprising to find that inconsistencies in exposure will show up when the shots are lined up in sequence, especially in exteriors. Joe's face might be slightly pink when he is seen downtown, slightly green at the beach. Night Shot A might not be quite as dark as Night Shot B, and Night Shot C might have been taken in broad daylight with day-for-night instructions to the lab. Where exposures do not have to be corrected — which is the case for virtually all interiors — one-light printing is used.

To regularize all other exposures, the negative is duped onto new stock under varying intensities of color-balanced light. To correct exposure values is called "timing a print," and it is the responsibility of the **color timer**. The most drastic timing corrections are performed on the intermediate printing generations; the majority of release prints are one-light.

There is a hierarchy of printing materials. At one extreme, occupied firmly by the camera original, the material is handled only when absolutely necessary. At the other extreme, the release print, the material is handled fairly roughly. Camera negative is *never* projected, is step-contact-printed at low speeds, and is stored as quickly as possible in the dark and at about 60°F — for instance, at the bottom of a converted salt mine. Release prints, no matter how carefully handled, are yanked around by the moving parts of a projector and are exposed to the dangers of scratching and debris. Although their color dyes will not fade noticeably for many years under proper storage conditions (below 70°F, 30 percent relative humidity, air conditioned, and dust-free), and although they may be made on stock that can stand real abuse, the fact that they are projected means that they will suffer mechanical injury long before any dye-fading would be likely to become a problem. Some release prints are specially manufactured to hold their dyes and shape for at least 50 years under scrupulous care; these are called **archival release prints**, and they are just up the hierarchy from standard release prints.

The cut original negative is copied as soon as possible and is then put in permanent storage. It is copied two ways. First, it is printed onto a fresh length of fine-grain negative printing stock. The result is a positive, and it is called the **intermediate positive**, shortened to **interpositive** and abbreviated **IP**. The IP is kept in the lab, and it is from this IP that further intermediate or printing negatives are made. Second, the negative is copied onto **RGB records** or **YCM separations**. On separate passes through a specially designed step-contact printer, the cyan, magenta, and yellow information on the negative is selectively filtered and exposed onto three separate strips of black-and-white film, which are called the **red, green,** and **blue records** or **positive masters**. (RGBs are made from negatives; YCMs are made from IPs or prints.) All color dyes fade eventually, but the black-and-white "silver image" will last virtually forever under proper storage conditions. If you wanted to re-release an old color film and had only the inevitably faded negative to work from, the new prints would have the wrong colors. But if you put a red filter between the red record (made when the movie was new) and a fresh piece of color negative, the original and unfaded cyan/red information would be transferred to the new stock with its layers of fresh dye-couplers, and after three passes you would end up with a full-color dupe negative whose values would match those of the original negative.

Although printers work with red, green, and blue lights, the negative stock reads these as cyan, magenta, and yellow, respectively. Some color timers actually think in YCM but give instructions in RGB; as long as you remember that these are complementary color systems and that most lab work is done with negative stock, it shouldn't prove confusing that the terms are used interchangeably. The RGB records are stored as carefully as the camera original, and they can be taken out of storage if a dupe negative needs to be made.

The IP is copied onto a fresh piece of fine-grain negative, yielding a negative from which positive release prints can be struck. This negative is called the **intermediate negative**, shortened to **internegative**, abbreviated **IN**. The IP becomes the laboratory's "protection" in case a new IN needs to made. The hierarchy, then, descends from the camera original to the RGB records to the IP(s) to the IN(s) to the release print. That is also the order in which all these are made. If the filmmakers are in a hurry — and for the majority of 16mm and TV prints — it is possible to skip one of these stages by copying the original negative onto *reversal* stock, which immediately yields a printing negative. This is called the **color reversal intermediate** process, abbreviated **CRI**. 16mm CRI prints of older films are often made from the best available INs. A reversal print struck from a release print will inevitably be of lower quality; that is not CRI, but **duping**.

The frames from *The Godfather* in the color section of this book were made directly from 35mm IP. (They are full-frame, with a green stripe in the area where the soundtrack will go.) The source of those frames, then, is two generations better than the best possible release print. The frames from *Citizen Kane* and *King Kong* were made directly from 35mm IN, and the prints in this book should look as good as the images in a brand new release print. The frame enlargements from *Hiroshima, mon amour* and *Napoleon* were rephotographed from 35mm release prints, and their quality is accordingly a bit poorer. The least detailed, like those from *Queen Christina* and *Vertigo*, were rephotographed from 16mm release prints.

Most of the timing corrections are done on the IP and the IN. For black-and-white films, these corrections are made by adjusting the overall light level of the lamphouse in the printer. For color films, the RGB lights are individually controlled, and the printer is equipped with an **additive lamphouse**. ("Additive" means that it works with an additive rather than with a subtractive color system; the lights add to white.) In the color section **Fig. C-93** shows a Bell and Howell additive lamphouse; the door is open so that you can see how it works.

The additive lamphouse is found on both contact and optical printers. White light is broken into red, green, and blue light as it is selectively reflected by dichroic mirrors. The surface of a

dichroic mirror reflects certain wavelengths, like red, while allowing others to pass through, like blue-green; its exact effect is governed by its angle in relation to the light source. In each of the RGB light paths there is a slit governed by an attenuator; the wider the slit, the more light passes through. This governing mechanism is called a **light valve**, and it can be adjusted through 50 positions, with each step or **point** corresponding to a light increment of .025 log E, or logarithm of exposure. (One stop is .3 log E.) At a setting of 50, approximately six times more light is passing through than at a setting of 1. Timer settings are expressed in numbers like 30/28/27, where each number is a light valve setting for a particular color, expressed in points, in the order RGB (as read by the negative, CMY).

In order to correct the color, the timer must first discover precisely what the densities of RGB are on the negative as shot. The negative is run through an electronic **color analyzer** (the most widely used model is made by Hazeltine) that determines its RGB values (for example, 20/18/23). The Hazeltine displays the image on a monitor in color-positive form. Next to the monitor, the timer hangs a photo whose color values are perfect — usually a close shot of a young Caucasian woman. You may have seen her flash by during a reel change in a theater, because that photo (a new one comes out every decade or so) is sometimes found on projection leader as a color reference for that print. The photo keeps the timer's eye from "drifting" — that is, from becoming used to poor color. The implications of that photo's being of a young Caucasian woman, I leave to you.

The timer can experiment with the color-positive image by entering new light values and seeing how the correction will look. The process is a bit like fiddling with the color controls on a TV set. When the correction looks right, the timer transfers those settings into the computer memory. The final settings are those at which the RGB light valves should be set during the split second when that particular shot is being copied. Let's say that these settings are 22/22/24 and that an IN is to be made from an IP.

When the IP and the raw stock for the IN are in the printer, the computerized light-valve information is carried on a length of punched tape. A counter keeps track of how many frames have been exposed, and when that number indicates that the shot we are concerned with has finally arrived, the lamphouse valves are almost instantly adjusted from wherever they were to 22/22/24. After developing, the IN is looked over by the timer, the cinematographer, the editor, and sometimes the director, and if any further corrections need to be made, the process will be repeated.

Printing and Processing. To take a walk through a lab is a jam-packed sound experience. From the Model C step-contact printers, copying negative and IP at 180 feet/minute in a leisurely chugging sound, you may pass a silent, auditorium-sized daily vault and then find yourself in a huge dark area filled with the overwhelming noise of the high-speed contact printers, which run at about 1,000 feet/minute. A handler may go by with a hand truck piled high with filmstock, calling out, "Truck . . . truck . . . truck" for the benefit of those whose eyes have not yet adjusted to pitch dark. In the developing area, the sound is like that of a dam, all engines and churning fluids. Then comes the relative silence of the inspection and shipping areas.

Electronic light valves adjust at great speed — something like 5 milliseconds. In a step-contact printer, the change can be made on a frame line, but it might take half a frame to adjust in a high-speed printer. The high-speed printer is loaded with 4,000-foot rolls of stock, on cores, and the printing is done in two passes, back and forth. On each pass, every other shot is printed; that gives the light valves the extra time they need to get to the proper setting for Shot B while the previously (or not yet) printed Shot A runs by.

Once printed, the stock is developed. Assuming that what is being developed here is a composite release print (that is, one with an optical soundtrack), the developing takes place in two stages. The first one takes care of the picture, chemically affecting the silver crystals and the color dyes. Because the whole strip of film is developed at once, the soundtrack area is pre-processed just as the color image is. But color dyes are inadequate for soundtrack information, which might drop off 20 dB (in signal-to-noise ratio, not in volume) if the next step were not taken. Before the silver halides have been removed in a fixing bath, more developer is applied to the soundtrack area alone. The soundtrack area is then re-developed; as a silver image, it provides excellent modulation. The entire film is then fixed, washed, dried, and inspected.

Approval and Release. While it is being cut, the workprint is continually evaluated and revised. Eventually a release version is approved, and the negative is cut.

When the go-ahead is given, a **first trial composite print**, or answer print, is made from the picture and sound negatives in projection sync. The version that receives final approval is called the **final trial composite**; it is the model for the prints that are to be released — not just one of many answer prints but, for legal purposes, *the* answer print.

A **release negative** is used for making **release prints**, which are intended to be projected. The lab makes release prints in several different gauges and sometimes of both standard and superior quality. The highest quality prints, used for special showings — perhaps in the director's living room or at the White House — are called **show prints**. The show print is normally the final corrected print that will be struck from the original negative prior to release. Archival prints cost about 10 percent extra and unfortunately are not ordered as often as you might think.

The date on which prints are ready to be shipped to distributors and/or exhibitors is, as far as the laboratory is concerned, the film's

release date, although the term also refers to the date on which a film begins its first run for a paying audience, in one theater or a thousand.

Once the answer print has been approved, the movie can be considered to have been *made*. In accounting, the production budget is closed, and further expenditures are charged to the distribution budget. A picture will be in distribution as long as people are willing to pay to see it. When it goes out of distribution, it becomes harder for the would-be audience to encounter a freshly struck print; one might find only spliced and scratched release prints or, at worst, reversal **dupes** — duplicated, often illegally, directly from a used release print. In the larger sense, however, distribution is a permanent gesture, sharing the film with generations of audiences and allowing it to become part of the culture, perhaps even to be recognized as a classic.

The **distributor** is the person or the company that provides **exhibitors** (theaters and their managers) with release prints. Distribution begins with the approval of the answer print and has three phases:

A. Principal or primary distribution: for theatrical release and exhibition, domestic and foreign.
B. Secondary or ancillary distribution: for 16mm lease, TV exhibition, and videocassette rentals and sales, domestic and foreign.
C. Re-release or rerun distribution.

6. Distribution

Theatrical and Nontheatrical Distribution

There are several distinct markets for films, and in some cases different companies or branches of companies serve each of these markets. Their responsibilities and priorities vary considerably. The theatrical distributor of a film in first release typically spends more on publicity and advertising (and earns more) than the nontheatrical distributor who is making an established film available for classroom showings in 16mm.

Theatrical distribution is the business of making prints available to movie theaters and ancillary commercial outlets. **Nontheatrical distribution** addresses limited and usually nonprofit markets: educational institutions, military bases, hospitals, airlines, hotels, nursing homes, summer camps, galleries, museums, film societies, and private homes. The nontheatrical exhibitor is not allowed to compete with a local theater that has booked the same movie.

Some distributors specialize in particular types of films. The Filmmaker's Co-op, Millenium, Picture Start, and the Collective for Living Cinema concentrate on distributing avant-garde films. The Museum of Modern Art (MOMA) and the Images Video & Film Archive are famous for scrupulous research and resourceful treasure-hunting, and they regularly make restored prints of classic films available, primarily for classroom use.

The film scholar must be particularly grateful to the nontheatrical distributor, much as the enthusiast of oddball features is thankful for the late movie on a local TV station, for these are often the only sources for pictures that have long been unavailable in standard theaters or that might never have played theatrically at all. Although an art house might show *Seven Samurai* or *The Magnificent Ambersons* every year or so, and a mainstream blockbuster like *Gone With the Wind* might be re-released to theaters as long as people will flock to it, you will have a long wait if you expect your local cineplex to mount a double bill of, say, *M* and *Fury*, or *Metropolis* and *Dr. Strangelove*, or a Michael Powell festival, or, for that matter, a Strother Martin festival. Without the nontheatrical distributor, the daring exhibitor, the late late show, the laserdisc, and — despite its degraded image quality — the videocassette, access to the classics and also-rans of film history would be absurdly limited, as if the world's bookstores and libraries were to stock only those books published in the previous six months and in extremely large editions. From the theatrical distributor's point of view, however, this situation makes obvious business sense. It costs the distributor a great deal of money to promote *any* picture; the audience has to be there to justify the expense; and the audience does appear, on the whole, to be interested in seeing new releases rather than old ones and narrative films rather than documentaries or film poems. For better or worse, then, the major source of exhibition revenue is the brand-new feature.

Ratings, Previews, and Marketing

The essence of marketing a picture lies in getting a movie and an audience together. Audience interest will have been consulted when the project was in development, but several years may have passed since then. The distributor and the advertising and marketing specialists usually have two related options: to find the audience that, if they only knew, would love to see this picture, and to convince the more general audience that they want to see this picture even if, in fact, they don't.

To the distributor, the audience is often a statistical abstraction, not a deeply understood community. (The exhibitor, on the other hand, typically knows a great deal about the locals and their viewing habits.) Surveys are taken, box-office receipts are scrutinized, and demographics become crucial. Once there is a working notion of what people currently want to see, those factors have to be matched with the characteristics of the movie in question. Sometimes there will be no easy fit, with the result that the most marketable aspect of a picture may be touted as its central characteristic even if it is, in fact, utterly marginal.

A **primary** or **target audience** — the people most likely to want to see a certain picture — is identified, and the marketing campaign attempts to hook its interest. A more general campaign is addressed to the **secondary audience**, the people who might find the picture of interest but would not be expected to line up the week it opens.

Many aspects of a picture can be emphasized in marketing. Perhaps the most important of these are the genre and the names of the stars. The distributor can be expected to make a big deal out of the fact that the executive producer of the new picture happens to be Spielberg, that it is the greatest romantic comedy since sliced bread, and that it stars Barbra Streisand, Cary Grant, and Michael J. Fox.

Sex and Violence! What many people first want to know, however, and what the Motion Picture Association of America (MPAA) makes a point of telling them, is how much sex and violence the picture contains. That information is contained in the **MPAA rating** of the film, and it is intended to help the audience pick a movie that will suit its taste. In most cases the producer and the distributor are stuck with this rating, but some films (like *A Clockwork Orange*) are recut in order to get a different rating. R films typically earn more than X films, and PG films earn more than G films.

The MPAA rating system began in 1968 and replaced the **Production Code**, a set of moralistic prohibitions by which the industry had policed itself since the mid-1930s. Rather than simply not *make* a picture about, say, interracial marriage between successful criminals, the industry became free to produce such a film and to release it with an R. The original ratings were G, M, R, and X. Later M (*mature audiences*) was changed to PG, and in 1984 John Milius's *Red Dawn* became the first feature to be released with a rating of PG-13. As they stand in 1986, the ratings are:

G: For general audiences; all ages admitted.

PG: Parental guidance suggested; anyone can buy a ticket, but some parents may not want their children to see this picture.

PG-13: Parental guidance suggested for children under the age of 13, who probably ought not to see this picture; those between 13 and 17 can see it without undue parental concern.

R: Restricted; children under 17 not admitted without an adult.

X: No one under 17 admitted.

The exact film content that may trigger a particular rating has changed over the years. In 1956 Mervyn LeRoy's *The Bad Seed* (about a sweet little girl who kills people) was "Adults Only"; now it is shown uncut on TV. In 1969 John Schlesinger's *Midnight Cowboy* (seedy promiscuity), Dennis Hopper's *Easy Rider* (counterculture), and Haskell Wexler's *Medium Cool* (radicalization) all received X ratings, though today each would be sure to receive an R. The violence in *Temple of Doom* (PG) was so extreme that parents demanded that the new PG-13 rating be created.

What the ratings do reflect with some consistency is the picture's sexual content. As MPAA President Jack Valenti put it in 1984, "If a woman is stepping out of a shower and you see her breasts, it will probably be a PG-13. But if sexual orientation is seen with nudity, it still would be an R." Language is a significant consideration, and the use of some words mandates an automatic R. It is possible for a film with "full frontal female nudity" to obtain an R, even if it also shows simulated intercourse. A shot of a penis, however, earns an automatic X — reflecting an obvious cultural double standard — and really extreme violence (*Dawn of the Dead*) or unsimulated intercourse (the stag film) also get the X. The X rating is the only one that can be self-imposed, which was in fact the option chosen by the makers of *Dawn of the Dead*.

The producer submits the film for a rating when it is in final cut, usually in the form of a show print. Every member of the ratings board has to be a parent; their job is to represent the community, not the industry. They never censor films, and they do not rate quality. The rating seal becomes part of the final release print.

Previews. As a way of checking out audience reactions before cutting the negative and mounting an advertising campaign, a final workprint — with opticals cut in — or a trial composite may be previewed for a nonpartisan audience.

In a **production preview** the movie is shown while it is still in post-production, tested on an audience that is not personally concerned with whether it will be a success or a flop. After one such preview, Frank Capra deleted the first two reels (forever) from *Lost Horizon* (1937). It is hard for any artist to know for sure how his or her work will be received by an audience, and it makes sense to open oneself to feedback before releasing a picture. Sometimes the filmmaker will decide that the previewed film is perfect as it stands or needs only minor revision, but the producer will pay more attention to audience reactions.

Marketing sneaks, or **sneak previews**, take place after the film has been rated, presumably when it will no longer be recut. These are usually arranged by the releasing company rather than by the producer. The sneak audience may be given special tickets by a promotional or recruiting organization, or they may just walk in off the street. Audience reactions are carefully studied, and a film that bombs in previews might not even be released, whereas good preview reactions are counted on to start a "word-of-mouth" campaign, the most reliable promotion of all.

Although some artists appreciate the advance feedback, many others react less happily. As Brian De Palma put it, "It's appalling that 325 people recruited from shopping malls can shake the confidence of professionals who've been working in the industry for decades." Paul Brickman's *Risky Business* (1983) provides an instructive example. As Rebecca De Mornay, who played the female lead, told *American Film* (April 1985):

There was a much more downbeat, ambiguous ending, with Joel not getting into Princeton. And the final scene of the movie was the breakfast scene, which is now cut to shreds. That was an extended scene where there were pauses and silences with them just looking across the table at each other. Then all of a sudden an overwhelming tenderness, a mature tenderness comes up out of him, even though he's lost because of her. . . .

They screened that film to audiences and the majority said: "I don't get it. Are they going to get together or aren't they? Gee, it's really a bummer." I guess those people were raised on sit-coms where everything ends up happily, so they could not relate to an ambiguous and somewhat depressing ending.

And then the critics got on Paul Brickman's case and said: How dare you try to make a satire of American capitalism and then in the end sew it all up — not knowing, of course, that Paul, Tom, and I were just flabbergasted by what the studio made us do.

There is nothing new in that story. Lillian Gish was upset by the exhibitors who insisted that Victor Sjöström's *The Wind* (1927), which she produced and starred in, be given a happy ending. She called them "ex-abiders: we used to say they were a race apart."

Marketing analysts study the preview cards filled out by some audiences, form subjective impressions of audience satisfaction, and conduct interviews and surveys. They are especially concerned with two statistics: "want-to-see" and "satisfaction." These indicate, respectively, how much people want to see a film they have not yet seen, and how much they actually liked it when they saw it. A film with high want-to-see and low satisfaction will probably open in **wide release** — that is, in a great number of theaters — so that by the time people realize how bad it is, the picture will already have earned some money. A film with low want-to-see but high satisfaction will usually open in **limited release** — perhaps one theater per major potential market — so that good reviews and word-of-mouth will support a later, wider release pattern. A film that is low in both may well be shelved. A film that is high in both may open widely in the hope of setting a box-office record.

To show how this is actually done, and the language in which it is worded, here are some excerpts from the marketing analysis of *Poltergeist*. In December 1981 a "promotional strategy survey" determined the following:

A. Selected Findings
  1. Highly favorable market potential; outstanding interest among teenagers; older moviegoers are at best only moderately interested.
  2. Spielberg name, once linked to prior films, adds significant dimension to movie's appeal.
  3. The word "poltergeist" is largely unfamiliar to moviegoers.
B. Recommendations
  1. Prevent "settling" on any specific genre — rather present full range of suspense thriller/special effects/event movie with colorations of science fiction and supernatural.
  2. Ad image should be intentionally vague to heighten curiosity and add to aura of mystery and surprise.

In April 1982 there was a "recruited audience survey":

Well above-average playability reported. Exceptionally strong reaction among younger moviegoers, but also among older males. Violence (particularly the technician nightmare sequence) produces some hesitancy about the movie from older females.

After an "ad test," surveying the effect of various advertisements on want-to-see:

Recommended a combination of "TV/child" visual with copy that specifically mentions Spielberg *and* his other work. Artwork creates a feeling of quiet menace, scariness, and mystery.

When *Poltergeist* opened in the fall of 1982, both the producing/releasing company (MGM/UA) and an independent agency conducted "opening weekend studies":

A. CinemaScore reports a high A rating, Spielberg the primary draw.

B. MGM/UA study shows outstanding reaction, male and female alike. Audience young: 71% under 30. Patrons' characterization of film indicates that campaign has successfully avoided slotting the film into narrow horror genre.

If we keep all that in mind, it is easy to see why the film was not marketed as "from the director of *The Texas Chain Saw Massacre!*"

Marketing. Once a way has been devised to match the inherent characteristics of the movie with the anticipated demands of the contemporary audience, marketing goes into high gear. Throughout production the unit publicist will have been leaking information to gossip columnists and reporters in an attempt to build up long-term want-to-see, but the publicity mill really begins to grind once the film is in post-production. It is then that the stars plug the picture on talk shows and give interviews to film magazines — interviews in which the forthcoming picture is strongly emphasized. The gossip columnist is an effective collaborator in the weeks just before a picture opens, when the stars allow themselves to become highly visible. Liz Smith, for example, could find the stars of Lawrence Kasdan's *Silverado* (1985) dining in "the glamorous River Cafe," make some guesses about their romantic entanglements, and then give a brief review of the film ("Beautifully photographed and stunningly played, I'd say offhand it's the most entertaining movie-movie of the year — something of an American frontier fairy tale, but surely the most remarkable Western since *Red River*"). That last phrase is a good example of hype.

When the picture is screened for reviewers and prospective exhibitors, the unit publicist provides them with a **press kit** containing the complete credits of the film, production and publicity stills that can be reproduced in newspapers and magazines, "one-sheets" (small posters), and press releases. All this helps the distributor and the exhibitor to increase local market awareness of the picture (reviews are largely considered fodder for ads), and these efforts are often supplemented by the coordinated marketing of products related to the picture. Sometimes these tie-ins sell better than the picture itself (notably true of soundtrack albums), and in most cases they provide significant royalties to the producer, but their main function is to help the picture, as a cultural event, pop up in several markets like a leisure imperative.

Marketing gags have their pleasures. Producer William Castle gave out playthings to preview and first-release audiences, like those shown in **Fig. 3-137.** When you saw *13 Ghosts* (1960) in "Illusion-O," you were given a "ghost viewer" equipped with red and blue filters. Looking through the red filter (the ghost viewer), you could see the ghost; if you were too scared, you could look through the blue filter (the ghost remover). The audiences of *Mr. Sardonicus* (1961) were given glow-in-the-dark "punishment poll" cards that allowed them to vote on the fate of the villain while Castle, on screen, pretended to count them.

But the ultimate core of a marketing campaign is advertising. Advertising is always open to charges of misrepresentation and

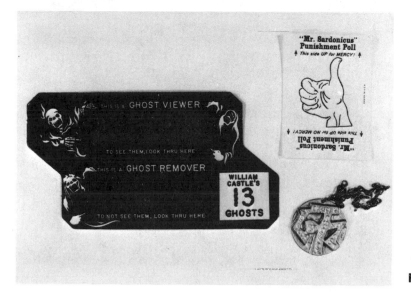

Figure 3-137

coerciveness — often with good reason — but its proper function is to alert the prospective customer to a product in which he or she might truly be interested. And in the context of film advertising, the movie is definitely a product.

Movie ads — whether printed or broadcast — emphasize what the ad agency and the distributor consider the most salable elements of the film. In the color section you will find an original one-sheet for *Forbidden Planet* (**Fig. C-94**). Besides telling us that the film is "AMAZING!" and providing a science fiction background similar to the cover art of 1950s SF magazines (to attract the target audience), this poster puts together two of the film's characters (Robby and Altaira) in a way they never interact in the actual movie.

All the way back to *Caligari,* the image of "the monster and the girl" has been a standard horror icon. What usually happens is that the heroine faints and is carried somewhere by the threatening and usually male monster. But Robby the Robot, who is carrying the scantily clad maiden in this poster, is actually one of the good guys in *Forbidden Planet.* The only person he ever actually carries is a dying male doctor. In the ads Robby was encoded as a figure of the future and therefore of science fiction (as a robot), but also as a conventional "monster with girl" in order to draw in the horror audience and to expand on the sexual and thriller overtones of "forbidden." And if you read the robot as carrying out, in the poster, the unacknowledged sexual and controlling impulses of Altaira's father (who built Robby) and recognize how much of the movie is organized around the danger of advanced technology in the absence of self-knowledge — the danger of being able to take desire too far, into compulsive acts of murder and destruction — this implicit interpretation of "forbidden" does cohere with the narrative project of the movie.

Jean-Luc Godard's TWO OR THREE THINGS I KNOW ABOUT HER
A New Yorker Films Release

Figure 3-138

It has always been a useful marketing strategy to give out free samples, to let the customer taste the product. Posters, printed ads, and lobby cards often show the prospective moviegoer a frame or two from the picture or an "artistic rendering" of a major scene. **Lobby cards**, which are sometimes just production stills with labels and are sometimes miniature posters, are generally placed where the customer can see them after having been attracted by the poster and the marquee, or in the lobby after having bought a ticket. Above is a 1968 American lobby card for *2 or 3 Things I Know About Her* (**Fig. 3-138**), and the color section ends with original lobby cards for *Snow White and the Seven Dwarfs* (**Fig. C-95**) and Leo McCarey's *Duck Soup* (**Fig. C-96**, rel. 1933). If you know the films, you can readily see which aspects of them were considered likely to have the greatest audience appeal.

The most time-honored of free samples is the **trailer**, the brief "coming attractions" film shown just before a feature.

Exhibition, Revenues, and Archiving

Whereas the copyright date indicates the year in which a movie was completed, the release date indicates when the film was "published" (in the sense of "made public") and officially entered the mainstream of the culture. From the perspective of the laboratory, as previously mentioned, the release date is that on which release prints are ready to be shipped to distributors; otherwise the release date is the exact *date* when the picture first opens on a regular basis for a paying audience in one or more theaters, and beyond that it is generalized as the *year* in which a picture opens in its country of origin. Only upon release does a film begin to earn money.

Exhibition. The conditions of exhibition can have great impact on the audience's appreciation of a movie. If the floor is sticky with old cola, the popcorn stale, the image out of focus, the sound inaudible, and the ticket overpriced, the movie will have to be *wonderful* in order to captivate an audience. Even so, if you had to clamber down into a smelly garret to see a great painting, you'd probably still appreciate the painting.

A clean, well-maintained, first-run theater (sometimes called an "A house") lends some of its own polish and poshness to the film in order to make seeing the film an enjoyable and special event. In many second-run theaters and drive-ins the emphasis may be on the social experience. To paraphrase a song from the 1950s, "Saturday Night at the Movies," you're not likely to care what picture you see when you're hugging with your baby in the last row of the balcony.

Whatever the social context, it is the exhibitor's absolute responsibility (even if this responsibility is delegated to the projectionist) to make sure that the picture is in focus and that the sound is clearly audible. The scrupulous **projectionist** will make sure to have the proper aperture plate in the gate and to keep the projector clean and in perfect working order. A dirty projector and an inattentive projectionist can ruin the best release print in a single showing. Compared with the absolutely dust-free environment of the lab, the conditions in many projection booths are incredible.

The audience around you affects your experience. This is not just a matter of whether they are polite or whether they are continuously and loudly explaining to each other what just happened on the screen. Watching a film by yourself, you can have as private an experience as when you are reading a book; however, you may miss the community experience that can catalyze the movie into its complete power. A comedy may seem funnier when more people are laughing at it, which is one reason that TV comedies have laugh tracks or studio audiences. You may never fully appreciate a slasher picture until you have seen it in a major urban center in a cheap theater in the middle of the night. The same is true of a teen sex comedy (or *Dawn of the Dead!*) in a shopping mall cineplex, the new Godard at a film festival, or *Apocalypse Now* with an audience of Vietnam veterans.

Revenues. Although significant amounts of money can come from tie-ins, network and cable TV sales, and home video markets, the principal source of revenue is the domestic and foreign ticket dollar. Many people have claims on that dollar: the exhibitor, the distributor, the producer, the loaning agency, and a host of **profit participants** who have contracted for a share of the revenue, often instead of a larger or guaranteed salary.

The total amount of money taken in at the box office (to date) is known as the picture's **box office receipts** or its **gross**. The exhibitor keeps a portion of the gross — how much depends on the contract with the distributor — but often makes most of its money from the concession stand. What remains — the portion of box office revenue forwarded to the distributor — is called the **gross rentals** or **gross proceeds**.

From this figure the distributor deducts sales tax, refunds, benefit showings, etc., and the remainder is the **gross receipts**, all the money gathered by the distributor. The gross receipts may be divided into the **distributor's gross** and the **producer's gross**, from which each must pay back all expenses before seeing a profit. Otherwise, the distributor pays back virtually *all* of the expenses until the remainder, the **net profits** or **net** of the picture, is divided between the producer and the distributor.

One way or the other, the distributor collects a fee (often 30 percent of the gross receipts); deducts the cost of prints, advertising, and licensing; pays off **gross profit participants**; and forwards a share to the producer. It is common for the distributor's share of the gross receipts to be much larger than the producer's until the costs of distribution have been recouped; then the pattern is reversed.

For the producer to reach net profits, the **negative cost** — everything charged to a picture's budget from the hiring of the writer through the approval of the answer print, in other words, the total cost of producing the release negative — must be paid back, with interest. From the remainder, **net profit participants** are paid, and the rest is the producer's share of the net profits.

As a rule of thumb, a picture must earn at least three times its negative cost in order to reach the net profit level. When you hear that a film has made $150 million, that figure is probably the gross, not the net.

The box office fate of a picture will be carefully monitored during the first few weeks of release. The trades (notably *Variety*) carry weekly listings of the biggest-grossing films: how much they made that week, how many screens they were playing on, and how much they have grossed since release. If one picture on 600 screens and a different picture on 1,700 screens each made $2 million in their second week of release, the former would be considered the better moneymaker and would probably be scheduled for wider release. (The widest release pattern is called **saturation booking**.) The picture on 1,700 screens that made $6 million that same week and $4 million the previous week, however, would be considered the hit. When it is discovered that audiences are paying to see a film over again, the scent of a blockbuster is in the air. When a picture stops making enough money to justify current marketing expenses, it may continue to play (accompanied by smaller ads), may be shifted to a "B house" or put on a double feature, or may be **pulled** (withdrawn) from distribution.

Availability and the Question of Video. Once a picture has gone out of first release, it may become very difficult to find. A reader can usually count on being able to find an out-of-print book in a store or library; the filmgoer is in the position of having to see every interesting film as soon as it comes out, as if the fiction audience had been recruited into some Book-of-the-Day Club.

The home video market is significant in this context. Even if a film on TV is inevitably a TV experience, complete with scan lines and presenting only part of the image, it is better than nothing. Almost the same can be said of a 16mm print of a 35mm original, as there is such a drastic fall-off in resolution and sharpness. When watching TV, you forget how *big* a closeup is; when watching 16mm, you can become used to a degraded image. Commercials and the abridgments and censorship that plague broadcast TV showings are an abomination, but they may be the price you have to pay if you want to watch a movie you cannot find anywhere else.

Out of all these alternatives, the videocassette, laserdisc, and 16mm formats offer the most acceptable compromises. In these formats the movie is usually uncut. The best thing about the 16mm image is that it is a *film* image. The major advantage of the laserdisc is that it can reproduce the full theatrical soundtrack, something that 16mm presently does not offer (unless the film was made in mono). With an **interactive** or **CAV laserdisc**, individual frames can be accessed by number and studied for hours. The conventional CLV laserdisc, however, plays straight through. The Voyager Company's Criterion Collection includes superb CAV laserdiscs of *Citizen Kane* and *King Kong*, which ought to be considered basic supplements to this text (see bibliography). The laserdisc produces a TV image, but an unusually sharp and steady one. A ¾-inch videotape yields an acceptable image but is not a home format. The image quality of ½-inch videotape is, at best, half as good as that of the laserdisc, but the convenience and wide availability of ½-inch videocassettes make them a real boon. The now-legalized home video library allows you to pull a "film" off the shelf as easily as a book. You can study editing decisions frame by frame on a CAV laserdisc, with theatrical sound. Should you be writing about the film, a video copy can allow you to check the text against your memory. But you still will not be looking at *the* film, and the ideal remains to see a movie in its original release format.

Festivals. The major role of a film festival is to put filmmakers and distributors together. Sometimes it is easier to convince a panel of judges and festival bookers that your film is worth screening once, in a prestigious environment, than to entice a distributor into committing millions of dollars to marketing it untried. Many independent filmmakers bring their completed works to festivals, present them to an educated audience, and with luck make on-the-spot deals with distributors who may be attending the festival in the hope of discovering marketable pictures.

To place a movie in the New York Film Festival is to have a one-day engagement in New York, testing the responses of the urban audience and of major reviewers. The special importance of the annual Cannes Film Festival in southern France is that it is an international marketplace. International distribution is a vital source of revenues, and at Cannes distributors from many countries can check out the new Eastwood or the new Resnais or the new Oshima just by going from one screening room to another, deciding in the process which ones to bid on. The prizes awarded at Cannes and Venice are significant honors, and like the Oscars they feed directly into the machinery of advertising and promotion.

The Telluride Film Festival, held annually in the mountains of Colorado, is part of the international film-marketing system, but it also is something more, and it may serve as an example of what a comprehensive film festival might be. In addition to showing the highlights from that year's Cannes and selected domestic independent features, Telluride screens important new avant-garde, animated, and nonfiction films, so that the presentation of world film activity in all categories is relatively comprehensive. Silent and early sound treasures, available nowhere else, are screened regularly, so that at Telluride the ongoing celebration of new work is complemented by the continuing discovery of film's past. The field of cinema is much more than a matter of recent features. At Telluride's tribute to Abel Gance, *Napoleon* was shown in the longest available version at the proper projection speed, and in related showings, Gance saw many of his own films in restored versions for the first time since their release, including his two greatest sound films, *J'accuse* (1937) and *Un Grand amour de Beethoven* (1936). And although there is the usual amount of deal making, there are also opportunities for filmmakers to get together and discuss substantive political and aesthetic issues — then to break for softball or get in line for the sixth movie of the day.

Libraries and Archives. The materials of film scholarship are vast and diverse, but they are often very difficult to get hold of. The studios will have most of their old payroll records, contracts, scripts, and production stills on file, but these are company files, and access to them is difficult to obtain. Many of the important early film journals were not collected by public and university libraries because while they were coming out, cinema was not widely considered a significant art form. And some studios have sold or simply destroyed their archives because it was perceived as too expensive to warehouse materials that were not likely to be used in the making of new pictures. Even if they have been saved, uncopyrighted scripts are rarely shown to outsiders, and reproduction rights on virtually all studio material — all the way down to production stills — are tightly controlled. The studio is in the business of film's present, and the scholar or simple enthusiast who is interested in film's past needs the resources of an excellent library.

A great film library, like that in the Academy of Motion Picture Arts and Sciences, should open its doors to scholars and industry personnel, and its staff should speak both their languages; that is, have a sense of their respective interests and needs. It should have complete runs of periodicals, from scholarly journals to fan magazines and trade papers, extensive clipping files, and first and revised editions of books on film in their original languages and in translation. It should have files of original production materials, from contracts to cutting continuities. And it should have, or have access to, a good film archive.

An archive is a permanent library of films, although many archives also have special collections of production materials, books, and journals. Some loan or rent their prints out on a nontheatrical basis or run their own programs of screenings (like MOMA), but their main purpose is to secure the best original prints, to restore them if necessary, and to store them properly so that they will be available and in the best possible condition for years to come.

Treasure Hunting and Restoration. Once a film goes out of copyright, it enters the **public domain**. A film in the public domain may be copied and distributed without any reimbursement to the producer. The nontheatrical distribution of works that are out of theatrical release corresponds, more or less, to the circulation of classic books throughout a culture. If, however, the ball is dropped when a film goes out of release and no one is interested in distributing it on any basis, it is to be hoped that a good print will still find its way into an archive or a private collection. Otherwise there is considerable danger that the film will be lost.

A truly lost film is one that was produced but of which no print remains extant anywhere in the world — like the complete *Greed*. A "lost" film is one that was considered lost but was then found — like *Napoleon*, which was restored over a period of more than 20 years by British film historian Kevin Brownlow and is now circulated by the Images Video & Film Archive (nontheatrical) and Universal (theatrical).

Because producers and exhibitors often treat films as marketable commodities with a limited time frame in which they are liable to earn significant money, it is the enthusiasts, creative filmmakers, scholars, and archivists who have the greatest interest in seeing that films are preserved. Ask yourself where English literature would be if someone had not made sure that Shakespeare's plays were printed — a matter in which Shakespeare apparently had no interest. Imagine if Hammett's *The Maltese Falcon* or Cain's *The Postman Always Rings Twice* had been considered forgettable entertainments and had gone 100 percent out of print after a few years of sales, and if there were no surviving copies from which new editions could be reset. The words from a surviving book can always be printed in new type — they remain the same words — but if you want to make a new print of *The Birth of a Nation*, you will have to copy an old print, with all its flaws, or seek out (good luck) the original printing negative; you could not go out and reshoot what you found in the print, because that process would result in a completely new text. The original materials have to be available.

And the original materials are physical, deteriorating over time. The nitrate base on which most films were shot before the 1950s yielded a wonderfully rich image but buckled and shrank alarmingly. Because the base was explosive, some distributors got rid of old prints by dumping them into lakes. Such prints could never be restored, thanks mainly to the water damage, but even well-stored nitrate prints cannot simply be run through a step-contact printer and copied onto safety-base stock. The copying has to be done on an optical printer, with each frame lined up individually to compensate for buckling and shrinkage. Even with safety base there is the problem of fading color dyes, and if no YCM separations are available, there is no way short of computer enhancement to restore the original colors — assuming that one remembers what they were and that the computer does not produce a "color TV" image. And there is the question of cost: film restoration is extremely expensive, and there is rarely an audience lining up outside the archive to subsidize the new print. Available funds must be allocated to restoring those films that are considered the most historically and aesthetically significant and that are in the most desperate physical condition. Other films just have to wait, and in the interim they may become impossible to restore or even to find.

As Brownlow once put it, "Areas of copyright in the film business are minefields in a maze." Tracking down the rights to films long out of release can be a legal nightmare. The past of film is not just waiting out there to be put into distribution, even assuming that it can be restored. In that context it seems appropriate to end with a success story.

When Brownlow and David Gill were looking for Chaplin materials to include in their documentary series *Hollywood*, they discovered that Chaplin had saved a tremendous amount of unreleased original material. These were short films, "made for fun," like *How to Make Movies* (from which several of the stills in this book were taken). There was a whole reel of *Shoulder Arms* (1918) that had never been released. There was an opening for *City Lights* that Chaplin had deleted because it was *too* funny. All of these were original camera negatives and prints, lovingly preserved by Chaplin's business manager.

Shortly afterward, collector Raymond Rohauer told Gill and Brownlow that he could provide them with another set of treasures: the complete rushes, on original camera negative, of Chaplin's Mutual comedies (1916–1917). Brownlow described that as "roughly the equivalent of an art collector offering the long-lost sketchbooks of Rembrandt." Gill managed to secure exclusive rights to the footage for Thames Television in Britain, so that all these unreleased materials could be presented in three superb documentaries (*Unknown Chaplin* [1983], perhaps the best films ever made about a filmmaker at work, and models of film scholarship). Then Rohauer gathered up the Mutual rushes, in what Brownlow described as "a cloak-and-dagger operation," from a number of secret vaults in France. When the rushes arrived at British customs, Brownlow took a snapshot of his co-workers and the open truck filled with 300,000 feet of nitrate (**Fig. 3-139**). From

Figure 3-139

left to right, the men are Rohauer, Gill, and editor Trevor Waite, but the real star is in the background: the cans with their priceless images of the living past.

Film and Society

The release of a film is the end of one process (production) and the beginning of another that is far more problematic: reception. When the film trickles or gushes into the mainstream of world culture, the mechanics of evaluation and interpretation come into play, and these are both social and aesthetic. A society may rate a film on the basis of its respect for or violation of cultural taboos; in America this begins with the MPAA rating and might extend to the point where a government official or the defender of a particular cause might endorse or denounce the picture. The aesthetics, themes, appeal, and power of the movie are evaluated by reviewers, critics, scholars, the givers of awards, and, of course, audiences. For the reviewer, the issue may be whether a film is "good" or "bad" or "compelling" or "boring"; for the social critic, however, the important considerations may be whether the film is "right" or "wrong," "welcome" or "pernicious." All of these value judgments are, of course, relative to the values endorsed by the critic, the film community, and the culture.

On another level, the ways in which films are interpreted by their audiences are much harder to define or evaluate. What happens when we watch a film? Do we "identify" with some of the characters, and if so, exactly how does that happen? If the film sets out to manipulate our emotions, ideas, and sense of structure, are we unconscious of that project or do we agree to go along? How innocent is the passive viewer, how willing a collaborator, how determined an antagonist? Do films really influence the behavior of people when they are not in the theater? How many of us assume that we are looking at *the* world rather than at a selective presentation of it? These questions are both endless and important.

Ideology and Nature. An **ideology** is a set of interlocking assumptions and expectations held by a person, a group, or a culture — a set of ideas about how the world works, a system of values. As distinct from a philosophy, an ideology can readily become a program for action. On the broadest level, it so entirely infuses a culture that its members may not even be aware of sharing certain assumptions about the nature of people and the best ways they can live together. An ideology can be so taken for granted that it comes to seem "natural," *the* way the world works or ought to work. If you have absorbed the ideology at the same time that you learned how to think and express yourself, your very thoughts may be little more than a reflection of that ideology, or your perceptions may be continuously filtered through it. One of the better definitions of ideology — though it was not intended as such — is offered as a joke in *Flashdance*: "This place is so small that you have to go outside to change your mind!"

The key to ideology is its apparent naturalness, and the way to free oneself from it — to the extent that that is possible — is to become aware of its arbitrary and limited nature. One way to do that is to look at the ideology of a different culture and to respect what it offers that culture. Another is to look at the ideology of your own culture and to ask whose interests it primarily serves. An ideology that asserts the "natural" link between democracy and free enterprise may actually work in the interest of major corporations rather than private individuals, and one that denounces the link between free enterprise and heartless capitalism may work to keep its people in a cleverly disguised social factory.

Ideologies normally give their subscribers the satisfying sense that they live under conditions of freedom and justice, that their world, or their program, is the right one. In most wars, for example, each side is convinced that it is fighting for the right, that its side is good and that its enemies are bad. This also describes the majority of Westerns, political melodramas, and horror films. Emotional associations are manipulated so that one set of characters becomes more appealing than another, and the audience is encouraged to root for the good guys and to anticipate the punishment or destruction of the bad guys. When the good guys triumph, so does the ideology that they have been encoded to represent. It is in this sense that the narrative film can be as potent a form of social control and propaganda as the most biased documentary.

Flashdance. Take an "innocent" picture like *Flashdance*, directed by Adrian Lyne and released by Paramount in 1983. The story was by Tom Hedley, the screenplay was by Hedley and Joe Esterhas, and the music was supervised by Phil Ramone. Jennifer Beals played Alex, an 18-year-old welder who can take care of herself, who talks dirty, whose sexuality has elements of innocence and experience, and who is also a self-trained dancer. In the evenings she is a highly polished and expressive jazz dancer at Mawbry's Bar (the story is set in Pittsburgh), but what she really wants is to join the local prestigious ballet and repertory company. She falls in love with her factory boss, Nick (Michael Nouri), who happens to have a friend on the arts council that helps to fund the ballet.

Alex is torn between the upper and lower classes. As a welder, a casual dresser, and a militant bicycle rider, she is one of the proletariat. When she dresses up with an apparently effortless elegance, rides with her lover in his black Porsche, or attends the ballet with her mentor Hanna (Lilia Skala), she is a temporary member of the aristocracy. Between those poles, she is encoded as natural ("just like me," Paramount doubtless wanted the audience to feel) and good (a devout Catholic, a strong person, a hard worker). She aspires to move upward in class, but this desire is presented ("naturally") as a simple aspiration to work in the art she most loves, ballet. She loves ballet because it is ballet, not because it is upper class — or at least, that is what she thinks about what she is doing.

But for the audience, things are a little different. In the final scene, when she tells Nick that she has passed her company audition and has realized her dreams, she is wearing a slick red coat. Nick stands by the Porsche with her dog (showing that he feels he has reconciled their two worlds) and gives her a bunch of long-stemmed red roses (elegant, upper class, and *matching* her proletarian coat). And they hug and kiss and twirl around. Visually, what is going on here is "as-if innocent." There are genuine class-identified elements in that scene, notably the Porsche and the roses. The romantic resolution of Alex and Nick's relationship and her career aspirations implies that she *has* joined his class — it is a kind of marriage — but the throwing together of all these elements (worker and boss, bike and Porsche, raincoat and roses) implies that these class distinctions do not really matter, that love and determination can reconcile all polarities. In other words, the class content of the scene is both *asserted and denied* at once. The audience may notice this contradiction — Alex does not — or it may buy the message and enjoy how everything works out for the best in contemporary America.

The problem is that *Flashdance* has highlighted such contradictions all along, whether or not it called attention to the fact that they are contradictions. Alex's problem and her character are identical: she wants "so much," as she confesses to her priest. She wants to be an independent worker, an expressive artist, a good Catholic, a hot and unmarried lover, her own woman, a woman's woman, and a man's woman. She wants to function in the world of males as an equal (welder) and as an object of the male gaze (barroom dancer). She is committed to a network of sisterhood: her mentor is an older woman who encourages her to join the ballet, and her friend Jeanie (Sunny Johnson) is a figure skater who becomes a stripper. What happens to Jeanie is presented as the career/aspiration trap that Alex must avoid. Jeanie flubs in a skating competition and then gives up; she becomes the girlfriend of a violent, obnoxious, and very lower-class pitchman for a strip joint; and she becomes a degraded sex object as a stripper. Although Alex finds Jeanie's strip act morally repellent (and the audience is given no reason to disagree) and saves her from continuing in that job as an act of sisterly solidarity, no one in the film ever points out that Alex's barroom dancing just as clearly puts her on a stage to be ogled by male customers while she performs her sometimes sexually enticing dances.

The test of Alex's "feminism" is whether she will apply to the repertory company. She has already proved that she can function in a man's world, and she has no problem expressing her femininity when it suits her. But she can dance in the bar only because she cannot see her audience; she likes to "disappear" into her dances, lose her sense of being Alex for a while. For the company, she will have to audition before a panel of judges whom she can see; in other words, she will have to dance as herself. To be able to do that would be to have become more mature as an artist and as a person. But the audition is not automatic: it is by invitation, once the application has been approved. After a great deal of soul-searching and after seeing what has happened to Jeanie (the wages of giving up), Alex applies, and she is invited to audition. But she finds out that the invitation was actually arranged by Nick, a favor in the old-boy network.

Funding has a great deal of power in the arts, and though the matter is not overtly discussed in the film, it is not hard to figure out that Nick can ask this favor — and get it — because he is part of the power structure. Alex feels she has to earn the audition on her own merits, and so she breaks up with Nick and decides not to perform. Then Nick gives her a lecture about the importance of cleaving to her dream, and Hanna dies. Alex decides that the dream is more important than her vision of perfect independence; she auditions and passes. The dance she performs, however, *is* quite personal, an integration of all the forms of dancing she enjoys. The most notable of these is breakdancing, which she has picked up from a street group and which clearly represents the crossing of a class barrier: the stuffy judges respond positively to this breath of fresh air (actually, they behave like idiots; the scene becomes silly), as if Alex's dance has reconciled the class distinctions among certain kinds of dance. Thus she gets to be her own person/dancer *and* the beneficiary of Nick's male connections.

The title song, "Flashdance . . . What a Feeling," is associated throughout the movie with Alex's moments of career determination and self-knowledge. It preaches that "you can have it all . . . you can dance right through your life." The "flash" comes when the "dream . . . takes hold" and the dancer is totally integrated, at one with her movement and expression. If Alex's problem is that she wants so much, the solution is that she can have it all. And that is where *Flashdance* and the ideology of Reagan's America come together, but it does not reconcile any of the contradictions we have been noting.

The choice Alex really is given is between becoming Jeanie and becoming Mrs. Nick Hurley. She chooses the latter. She has autonomy only up to a point and does not push it any farther. For example, she at first puts Nick off by saying that she doesn't approve of dating the boss. Eventually he says — when she has turned him down for a dinner date — "You're fired. I'll pick you up at eight." That's a cute line, and it catches her off guard, but it is also a direct exertion of the power of his position, which she has been acknowledging all along. At that point she could have agreed, or she could have refused the date and looked for another job, or she could have worked out a way to keep her job and not date him. Instead she just smiles. She has not really been fired, and she does go on the date. So Nick wins that round, and unconditionally. It is presented, however, not as a fight but as if Nick's exercise of power were purely benevolent — he never "really" intended to fire her — and as if the power structure between them has suddenly vanished in the moment it is most clearly being asserted; in other words, they immediately become social equals, on *his* social level and on his terms. She has already made a version of her ultimate decision, to become Mrs. Nick and to make the best of the compromising terms of the audition.

An important element in American ideology is that ours is a society without true class distinctions. Out of the melting pot of immigrant and native groups, anyone can rise to the top on the basis of talent, ambition, determination, and a host of other virtues preached by Benjamin Franklin, Horatio Alger, and, when *Flashdance* was made, Ronald Reagan. Although we never hear much about their backgrounds, Nick — or the actor — appears to have come from Italian stock, Jeanie has an Eastern European name (Stabo), and Alex — or Beals — is mulatto. The social landscape of *Flashdance*'s Pittsburgh is that of the American melting pot, where bosses and workers can socialize in a bar or in a factory and where the cream naturally rises to the top. It is acknowledged that class distinctions exist — the staff and members of the repertory clearly look down on Alex when she first shows up for her application form — but by the end, those distinctions do not function as impermeable social barriers, and Alex can crash through them because she has genuine talent. "Pluck and luck," Alger called it. If she has to surrender some of her more-or-less feminist priorities in order to make it, the filmmakers apparently saw that as no serious problem. The story, in other words, is a forthright presentation and reflection of the dominant ideology of contemporary America, and it asserts by implication that there is no contradiction between capitalism (often tied to the interests of big business and social control) and populism (which sees the people as the primary source of power and values). *Flashdance* simply accepts the conflicts that *Citizen Kane* deeply investigates. The story shows all of this flowing quite "naturally" together — it is, after all, what just happens to happen to Alex, right? — and disguises the fact that it is actually presenting a specific and political argument: America works.

Now imagine what the starving, diseased peasants in Buñuel's

Land Without Bread (1932) would think of this picture. Imagine its reception at a convention of feminists. Ask yourself whether the Soviets would go out of their way to import it. How "natural" would its assumptions appear to audiences with other ideologies? How "natural" would we find a pro-Nazi spy melodrama, and would we resist the mechanisms that encode a Nazi as a good guy, "one of us"? In fact there is nothing at all natural about the social assumptions in *Flashdance*: they are highly structured and intensely ideological. And there clearly are some people who will look at *Flashdance* and feel that the road to the top is also open to them, even if it may not be. If they go on to accept the social and economic conditions of contemporary America, and their role in it, rather than resisting and examining those conditions and assumptions, the picture will have served, ultimately, as propaganda in the interests of the current power structure — in effect, a sweetened pill.

So was Paramount part of a national conspiracy? Not likely. The point is that an ideology tends to replicate and express itself at every level of a culture, and the people who facilitate that expression are often simply doing what they consider natural and factual. (It is to guard against this kind of thinking that "truth" and "realism" are put in quotes in analyses of ideological processes. It's like the difference between being in a pleasantly cool room on a hot day and going outside to discover the exhaust blast of an air conditioner.) *Flashdance*, one of the original "high concept" pictures, was conceived to appeal to a target audience of young adolescent women. It set out to display and endorse the fantasies of contemporary American 13-year-olds (its R rating was notoriously unenforced) who are aware of the women's movement yet who would like to imagine themselves leading the full "feminine" life as well as the fully "human" one: who want to compete in the world of males, be recognized as autonomous and significant individuals, and still find Mr. Right. They want to take risks yet be watched over, to be sexy and innocent, to succeed in the terms that the culture has defined for them and to do that without compromising their personal integrity. Paramount read those fantasies correctly, as can be measured by the picture's extreme box office success with that age group. It told them what they wanted to hear. It provided exhibitors with a lucrative product. And whether or not Paramount was pushing a social program, the effect of that fantasy on that audience cannot be ignored. It is not hard to find in *Flashdance* a double-edged treatment of feminism: praising Alex within the network of women *and* showing her succeeding when she compromises with the male/aristocratic power structure. By implication, what it says is that feminism is all right in its place. And the same used to be said about women.

Now you might not want to leap onto the barricades to prevent *Flashdance* from being shown, but you might well become upset if you find those around you reading that film as an innocent endorsement of American aspirations that, after all, only reflects the "inherent" contradictions of feminism and couldn't do anyone any real harm. If you consider the film pernicious, the fact that it is so professionally shot and edited, so efficiently scripted, and so musically engaging might come to bother you very much. If you find yourself screaming about how well the pill has been sugar-coated ("Don't they realize what this picture's *saying?!*"), then you will understand how the structure of an illusion can become an ideological problem.

"Realism" As a Self-Effacing Code. For many leftist filmmakers and critics, the codes of "realism" are themselves pernicious because they encourage the audience to absorb a highly contrived and manipulative fantasy as if it corresponded to the real conditions of the world. Some of them are upset by such "innocent" practices as continuity editing because it attempts to deny the schisms between shots in the instant that they are most obvious. It obscures the "madeness" of the structure, pretending that it was "found" or natural. In that respect, many of Griffith's narrative practices could be examined not as the "natural laws of cinema" but as a particular narrative and ideological system. Even the industry preference for the "normal" lens becomes suspect because it imposes a conventional order on the visible world. You can appreciate that point by comparing Egyptian, Cubist, and Italian Renaissance paintings, all of which have very different concepts of perspective, all of them interesting and artistically satisfying. There could easily be a film industry that considered the telephoto lens "normal" and worked to defeat any impression of depth — why not? Or there could be a cinema that rejected continuity editing entirely, and another in which the narrative film had never been conceived. There is nothing "natural" about the cinematic apparatus. Even photography, which depends on a simple chemical reaction that is itself an element of the natural world, produces an object very different from the subject that was photographed. A cut is impossible in the physical world as we know it. And nothing "just happens to happen" in a story. As we observed in relation to the problem of the "eye-level" camera, eye level for the tall Hawks was very different from eye level for the short Akerman, and each imposed a perceptual norm on the system. You can run through this book and find evidence of ideology at every level of the filmmaking system, from the Caucasian photo used by the color timer as a norm of proper skin tones to the careful trimming of a match cut.

To read the ideology of a picture, one must be able to read a picture in the first place. To do that requires familiarity with a vast number of structuring codes, not all of which are visual or visible. The following story, told in the words of William Costanzo in his introductory textbook *Double Exposure: Composing Through Writing and Film*, makes the point neatly:

One day artist Pablo Picasso was showing a young visitor some paintings in his studio. The visitor, an American soldier, admitted that the artwork was beyond him; these strange, abstract canvases did not show life as it really looked. Later on, when the conversation turned back to the United States, the soldier showed Picasso a wallet-sized photograph of his girl back home. With a twinkle in his eye, the artist said, "She's an attractive girl, but isn't she awfully small?"

What Picasso did with the soldier's photograph, among other things, was to demonstrate the naïveté of reading any picture as absolutely realistic. He made the soldier realize the difference between a sign and a referent. Photos and paintings are equally artificial and encoded, and the filter of ideology is itself a system of codes.

The way that an ideology maintains its appearance of naturalness is to efface itself, to disappear into the givens and norms of the structure. Its assertions are erased and denied even as they are presented. But the contradictions are there to be noticed if you look hard enough. As a dancer, Alex was constructed out of two dancers: Beals for the head and shoulders, or for relatively undemanding full-body movements, and a more energetic and accomplished dancer for the torso and lower body. Occasionally you can see that this is going on, especially in one scene where "she" does a fast solo workout. The match cutting presents two dancers — their being in different shots asserts their difference — but it also denies that difference and insists that the two are one dancer. Alex is a construct, then, and perhaps a model for the construction of the split female subject, but we are encouraged to regard her as a simple signified, not as the product of two unrelated signifiers. In *Flashdance*, if we notice this doubleness, we are yanked out of the illusion. It becomes a condition of enjoying the story that we ignore the evidence of our eyes and accept these two women as Alex, or Alex as an integrated subject. In other words, we have to buy into the structure, not just pay for a ticket. If we resist doing that, or if we get upset at Nick's as-if-it-weren't-happening power play over the dinner date, we don't get the payoff that the picture has prepared for us, and it isn't any fun. We run the risk of being called a killjoy — and sometimes that will be just what we intend.

If you run through a picture like *Flashdance* looking for contradictions, you will find them in two intriguingly different categories. On the one hand, there are those that appear to have been unnoticed or glossed over by the filmmakers, like the "happiness" of its happy ending. These contradictions simply hang out together within the boundaries of the film. They cannot be reconciled, but some of them can be ignored in the interest of enjoying the illusion. If you insisted on neatness, you might say the picture was incoherent or poorly thought out. Or you might enjoy the plurality of meanings in the text and realize, like a follower of Derrida — whom we'll get to in a moment — that absolute coherence may well be an elusive abstraction. Rather than attacking the text for its incoherence, you could simply appreciate how one set of tentative meanings both leads to and conflicts with another in an endless and intriguing process.

On the other hand, there are some statements that appear to have been deliberately chosen in order to conflict with or perform a twist on the rest of the picture. As an example of a *subversive* statement, recall the joke — delivered by the cook at Mawbry's who "just happens" to be Jeanie's boyfriend — about how the bar is so small that you have to go outside to change your mind. That *might* have been a comment about the ideological claustrophobia of *Flashdance*. Even if that were not its programmatic intention, the line raises its own interpretation and critique of the dominant ideological program of the film.

In other words, some of the contradictions in *Flashdance* are those of contemporary America, like its celebration of upward mobility and its denial/assertion of class barriers, whereas others might function as internal critiques of that contradictory structure. To say that the film has a single, simple meaning is to miss out on its complexity. To assume that Paramount did not perceive all these *as* contradictions, that they felt the story was simple, is not only reasonable but also a good way to understand how self-effacing ideological statements are produced. These matters would not appear contradictory to those who subscribe to the ideology and do not see *it* as contradictory. To do that, they would have to leave the room.

Deconstruction. One practical method for analyzing and critiquing the plurality of meanings in a text, whether or not they were deliberately subversive, was pioneered by Jacques Derrida and is called **deconstructive criticism**. An elegant definition of this (appropriately) elusive term was written especially for this text by James Kincaid:

Deconstruction is most easily understood as a process of exposing or dismantling the logical or fictional structures that support any text, literary or otherwise. It seeks to expose the *un*naturalness of the assumptions that we take to be natural in writing — to show, for instance, that any positive assertion not only depends on but calls into being its contrary. Working from a philosophic position rooted in Neitzsche and with the most radical implications of Saussure's linguistics, the major figure in the field, Jacques Derrida, has argued that meaning is not only based on endless difference but is also endlessly deferred. We are constantly searching for a voice behind a text, a presence, a solidity that we can never quite catch up with. For instance, as Terry Eagleton points out, should we want to know what a single word means, we can look in a dictionary. But there we find not essences but other words, other pointers or signals that lead us to yet more words, never the thing itself.

In practice, deconstruction can work in several directions: exposing the arbitrary nature of received opinions or interpretations; exposing the ideological basis of presumably natural critical stances — objectivity, for instance; focusing on figurative language to show how the text "deconstructs itself"; engaging in a playful demonstration of its own "logocentrism," circling back on itself to reveal the fact that it could never have begun its demolition work without assuming some center, a center every bit as arbitrary as the one being attacked. A kind of happy pessimism is suggested by Derrida's assertion that no centers are valid but that we must assume one anyhow. We can do our best to understand and reveal our own false securities, the centers of our arguments — but we can never make that understanding or revelation complete, precisely because we cannot free ourselves from the notion of "being," the most delusive, if compulsory, center of all.

As you may remember from Part I of this book, Saussure conceived of the sign as a relationship between signifier and signified. The signifier is a sound-image, the signified a mental construct. Together they make up the sign, of which the referent is no part. Derrida posited that the signified is itself an elusive if not an ineffable construct, not something that can simply be evoked by the signifier. Between signifier and signified is a relationship called **différance**, a French pun on "difference" and "deferment." The signifier and the signified are categorically different from each other, and that difference makes signification as possible as it ever gets. As one attempts to close in on the definition of a term, however, meaning recedes; it is put off or deferred, just around the bend of the next signified, and the next. Instead of a straightforward "this goes with that" relationship, the parts of the sign are "joined" by what you may want to think of as an endlessly stretchable piece of chewing gum, whose texture is that of signification and which is, in fact, a process rather than a correspondence. In this context, referents become both self-evident and inconceivable. In place of the sign/referent model, in which the sign is made up of signifier and signified, the Derridean more often proposes the model of signifier/signified, with the signifier being what used to be called the sign and the signified being what used to be called the referent. The implication is that it is naive to talk about referents because they are outside the system of signification. Where was the soldier's actual girlfriend in the snapshot he showed Picasso? Toledo, maybe, but not in the "small woman."

Rather than allowing a field day for ambivalence and incoherence, deconstructive criticism acknowledges the problematic nature of signification. It provides a critical tool for seeing past the "official" interpretation imposed on a text by its makers, and so it has obvious uses in an ideological critique. Deconstruction shows that the world is not so simple a place as we sometimes imagine it and argues that any signifying practice — including thought itself — is a constant circling around a noncenter. Deconstruction goes beyond the standard ideological critical project because it does not simply say, "Here's reality, here's the filter through which it is represented, and here's the filter through which you perceive it." It implies instead that you, your perceptions, any intermediate filters, the critic, and reality are all in quotes and are equally not-quite-present. Reality, perception, and the perceiver are all finally ungraspable, receding like the end of a rainbow.

A deconstructive reading would be quite appropriate for a picture like *Flashdance* because it could easily acknowledge the artificiality of its statements, their incoherence, their mutual contradictions, and the "self-deconstructing" elements that refuse to cohere with the others or undermine their authority — and it could do all this without misdescribing the text or imposing an inadequate or one-sided interpretation on it. It will be perfectly all right — in fact, terrific — for the split Alex to be played by two women, or for the class system to be presented as there and not there at the same time. In the case of *The Last Laugh* the fact that the ending makes no sense in relation to the main body of the picture — and that an intertitle was so bold as to acknowledge that fact — could be read as an instance of différance between the two segments of the picture, somewhere between or beyond which is the as-if-single "meaning" of *The Last Laugh*. It becomes a relatively simple matter to accept *Caligari* as being about resistance to insane authority *and* the desire to submit to all-knowing authority, even if both authority figures are the "same" doctor.

Beyond prompting you to distrust the simple meanings of apparently simple pictures, deconstruction is remarkably well suited to the analysis of collaborative projects. The complex of meanings introduced by the writer, the producer, the director, and others do not always cohere, as the production history of *Caligari* demonstrates. Whereas the auteurist might gloss over these intricate complications in search of ultimate authorial coherence, the deconstructionist can acknowledge and appreciate them. It is ironic that this extremely sophisticated critical methodology provides an appropriate way to analyze and appreciate the nuts-and-bolts filmmaking process as it really works and the deeply complicated statements that movies actually make.

For example, what does it mean to be "citizen"/"Cain"? And what exactly is the attitude of *King Kong* toward civilization? Is Kong's story simply, as Denham prefers to read it, a variation on Beauty and the Beast? If so, when does Kong turn into a handsome prince or "stay his hand from killing"? Who was "right" about whether the lovers in *Marienbad* had met the year before, Resnais or Robbe-Grillet? How are we supposed to feel about Michael at the end of *The Godfather*? And how do the *Godfather* films, as big business ventures, remain exempt from their own critique? (They don't.) Is it a tragedy that Michael destroys his family by trying to protect it; or is that a gesture of social criticism by the filmmakers; or does it appeal back to a structure of différance within the Mafia construct of "the family," which depends on an absolute separation between "it's personal" and "it's business," but which also collapses that distinction? To attempt to answer such questions is to confront a movie in a radically comprehensive way — but with the understanding that no answer will ever be final.

Genre and Social Critique. *High Noon, Alien,* and *Heaven's Gate* all had social programs. *High Noon* (1952, dir. Fred Zinnemann) targeted Hollywood's unwillingness to resist the House Un-American Activities Committee's anti-Communist witch hunts of the late 1940s and early 1950s. *Alien* attacked the military-industrial complex. *Heaven's Gate* offered a revisionist history of the American West in which big business was evil and the melting pot a pipe dream. All three of these pictures worked within the confines of established genres, and in some ways they *also* worked against generic expectations. They used the generic code as one dominant line within their narrative structures, and that line approached, paralleled, and diverged from the line of the story — that is, the story as it might have been told outside the structuring constraints of the genre.

In *Heaven's Gate*, for example, there is what appears to be a formulaic Cavalry-riding-to-the-rescue, but when they show up, they rescue the *bad guys*. In that case Cimino was using a generic expectation to frustrate the audience and to remind us that even in the movies, things do not always work out the way they do in the movies. The implication is that the heroic fantasies of the Western are at least partly a lie: not only was the West *not* a simple landscape out of the Medieval romance, but it also could become a highly adequate metaphor for the vicious exercise of power and the defeat of idealism in the contemporary corporate and social landscape. So *Heaven's Gate* cast itself as a Western in which the Western was critiqued and displayed its own contradictions. The fact that many critics and audiences rejected *Heaven's Gate* just as the preview audiences rejected the original ending of *Risky Business* could be considered an ideological reaction.

Alien is relatively simple in comparison, and one of the reasons it was so much more successful at the box office than *Heaven's Gate* may have been that it stuck more closely to generic expectations. The good guys are workers in a spaceship. The bad guys are their employers, who want the Alien brought back to Earth so that it can be developed into some kind of weapon by the military branch of the mining company. The worst of the bad guys, who metaphorically incarnates the evils of a system that considers people "expendable" and yummy, is the Alien; next in line is the scientist/robot who bleeds milk (the ship's controlling computer is nicknamed "Mother") and represents the company's interests. So the bad guys are monsters, and this is a horror film, and everything is in order. We root for the workers against the bosses and celebrate the triumph of the lone female survivor. In this case the generic expectations and the narrative project work together, and what is interesting is to notice how the genre makes these politically radical perspectives seem perfectly appropriate.

High Noon is like many other Westerns in that it is set in a landscape that is in transition from wilderness to law-abiding city — but this time the town is as corrupt as the forces that threaten it. The movie builds to a showdown between the marshal and the major villain, but the showdown leaves a bad taste in the mouth. Considering its covert subject — and 1952 was not a safe time to launch a forthright attack on the House Un-American Activities Committee (HUAC), nor to denounce the Hollywood community as a bunch of moral and physical cowards — all this guarded ambivalence is not surprising. The movie looks like a simple attempt to discuss the modern world in generic terms, to use the Western much as *Alien* uses "the monster and the girl" but does not have the woman faint. But if we examine the treatment of the heroine in *High Noon*, we will discover some far more unsettling contradictions, ones that the filmmakers may have deliberately ignored, never become aware of, or consciously emphasized. While praising the hero's integrity, *High Noon* also praises the heroine's surrender of hers.

The story of *High Noon* covers about two hours; the discourse lasts 85 minutes. As the movie opens, at about 10:20 A.M., three bad guys are on their way into town to wait for the noon train; on that train is Frank Miller, the just-released leader of their gang. They intend to help Miller avenge himself on Marshal Will Kane (Gary Cooper) and the do-gooders in the town of Hadleyville, which used to be a rowdy place until Kane cleaned it up and threw Miller in jail. That same morning, Kane turns in his "tin star" and marries Amy Fowler (Grace Kelly), who is a convert to the Society of Friends — in other words, a Quaker by moral conviction. Kane plans to open a store in another town and to live a peaceful life, but he does not see himself as a Quaker. He does, however, wear a black hat — rather like a Quaker of the period and deliberately unlike the white hat of the ritual sheriff or cowboy hero. His hat color is a twist on a generic norm, and it alerts the audience that this will not be a simple Western. *High Noon* belonged, in fact, to a slightly different and relatively short-lived genre, the "adult Western"; that genre emphasized the psychological and moral conflicts of its characters rather than opting for a simple dichotomy between good and evil.

When Kane and the townspeople find out that Miller is on the way, Kane has to decide between leaving the town and staying to defend it. He decides to stay, and that drives a wedge between him and Amy. He has promised her to live a life of nonviolence, and when he decides to stay and fight, she tells him that she will leave on, of all things, the noon train. While the blond Amy waits in the hotel, she meets her husband's — and Frank Miller's — former lover, a dark-haired Mexican woman (Katy Jurado) who gives her a lecture about fighting for her man and being a real woman, rather than abandoning him in his time of need. (The distinction between fair/pure and dark/effective women is older than American literature.) Their conversation takes place at 11:43 A.M., and from then until noon, story and discourse time are in sync; 17 projection minutes later, the clocks in the film are at noon. That gives this particular phase of the story a special claim to being "realistic" — though it is also a simple and effective way to build up suspense, to keep the audience waiting in real time along with the characters. Once the train arrives, the careful monitoring of story time stops entirely, as if the characters had entered the mythical "time" of the Western as they stepped into their archetypal roles.

While Amy is confronting the implications of her decision to leave, Kane discovers what it means to have decided to stay. He tries to round up a posse and finds that no able-bodied adult male is willing to risk his life in order to preserve law and order. Some of the townspeople even blame Kane for having cleaned up the town in the first place, and others blame him for being the target that has lured Miller back for revenge. If the price of liberty is "eternal vigilance," these people are prepared to become slaves and toadies.

Even the judge leaves town — permanently — and before he goes, he says this to Kane: "This is just a dirty little town in the middle of nowhere. Nothing that happens here is really important. Now get out!" It is not hard to interpret this as a comment on the village of Hollywood. Carl Foreman, who wrote the script after uncredited input from Howard Hawks, was a Hollywood insider/outsider in the early 1950s, and later he was not allowed to receive screen credit for his script for David Lean's *The Bridge on the River Kwai* (1957); both Foreman and *Kwai*'s other uncredited writer, Michael Wilson, had been blacklisted by then. In this context, Frank Miller and his gang are comparable to the HUAC. Although the HUAC paid lip service to American values, it consistently violated the letter and the intent of the Bill of Rights, and it denounced those filmmakers who pointed that out — one of whom, Abraham Polonsky, had taught at Columbia Law School and certainly knew what he was talking about. Those who provided the committee with the names of "Reds" and "fellow travelers" were lionized — unless, like Larry Parks, they had had to be badgered and worn down and threatened into violating their sense of honor and "naming names." It wasn't enough to go along with the HUAC: one had to do it with a full heart and a sense of conviction. Hollywood tried to protect itself by blacklisting "unfriendly witnesses," denying the right to work to any known "or suspected" Communist, and churning out we-love-America pictures like Leo McCarey's infamous *My Son John* (also 1952).

In that context, and in the generic context of the Western, there is no question about the rooting interest in this picture. We are encouraged to want Kane to stand up to the bad guys; we wait for the showdown. The fact that nothing in Hadleyville "is really important" makes Kane's decision to stay an existential one, done for its own sake in a moral vacuum. He becomes the "one man alone" who is both the traditional Westerner — a man who often rides or strides off into the sunset even though he has the opportunity to settle down — and the brave knight of the Medieval romance. Foreman apparently felt that quivering Hollywood could benefit from having such a hero in its midst, and Zinnemann may well have agreed.

Where all this becomes truly complicated and revelatory — the most serious question about the film's social program — is in producer Stanley Kramer's attitude toward Foreman. Although Kramer is usually given credit for having conceived the project, having asked Foreman to write it, and having hired Zinnemann to direct the finished script, it is crucial that late in 1951, when the script had been completed, Foreman came under HUAC displeasure and Kramer fired him. Foreman had given Kramer the most socially conscious of his previous scripts — notably Mark Robson's *Home of the Brave* (1949) and Zinnemann's *The Men* (1950) — and he was bitter at the turn of events. When one knows that story, the vaunted integrity of *High Noon* becomes evasive, problematic, and even hypocritical. Frank Miller's gang could, after all, be read as the commies who threaten to invade the village. *High Noon* appears by turns to be making a radical statement and to be effacing its radicalism as a simple following-out of the conventional logic of the Western (a confused retreat to simple values). By the time of the gun battle, Kane has become both the hero and the underdog — when the shooting starts, he is outnumbered four to one — and the audience has been manipulated to root for him without question. We are glad that someone has the guts and the integrity to stand up to Miller, even if it does upset his personal plans.

But what about Amy? When she hears the first shots, she runs from the hotel into the street, expecting to find her husband dead; what she discovers is a dead villain. She goes into the marshal's office and waits. A holstered gun is prominent in several of the shots of her in the office, and like the empty space that the camera in *Top Hat* includes, almost begging for Astaire to dance in it, that pistol is waiting for Amy to decide to use it. When she sees that Kane is caught between the crossfire of the two surviving villains, she takes the pistol and shoots one of them to death — in the back, while his guns are empty. She had become a Quaker after seeing her brother murdered, and she has an absolute moral conviction against doing what she has just done. But the audience is encouraged to be *glad* that she has shot the man. That is part of her duty as a wife. As the ballad "High Noon" keeps insisting, in Tex Ritter's marvelous rendition (lyrics by Ned Washington):

> Do not forsake me, O my darling,
> You made that promise when we wed.
> Do not forsake me, O my darling —
> Although you're grievin',
> I can't be leavin'
> Until I shoot Frank Miller dead.
> Wait along, wait along.

From the song to the dark-haired woman, everyone is giving Amy the same instruction: put off the new moral order for just an hour, and then everything will be fine. Support your husband, who is doing the right thing even if you can't appreciate it and who ought to be able to count on his wife, of all people, especially when everyone else is deserting him. Stand by your man. And the audience, to the extent that its response is manipulated by generic expectations, roots for her to have the *courage* to go against her deepest ethical convictions rather than to have the courage to stick to them. What Kane does is within generic expectations; what Amy eventually does is, too. But if you back away from the neatness of all this for a moment, you can see that Kane and Amy are in exactly the same ethical quandary. Both of them are "torn 'twixt love and duty," as the song says, but the song is about Kane's problem only ("supposin' I lose my fair-haired beauty"). Kane feels as responsible to his sense of duty and honor as a marshal as Amy does to her sense of "a better way for people to live" and the moral imperatives of nonviolence. Both of them are inflexible, each waiting for the other to come around. In short, they are perfectly matched, and it was appropriate for them to marry; surely there is no one else in town who is even sensitive to these moral problems, much less who has the courage to live morally. The situation brings Will and Amy into conflict with each other, and that makes for good drama.

But how the drama is resolved makes more than a dramatic statement: it also advances a moral argument, a sense of what is right and proper. And that message is that Amy is right to shoot a man in the back in defense of her husband, and later to throw Miller off balance so that her husband can shoot him. The other side of the message is that Kane is a true Western hero, an idealist in a world of moral cowards. And although the ending is brilliantly subdued, it is clear that the couple has been brought closer together by the experience and will live together happily in some other town. As Grace Kelly enacted her, Amy is truly shaken by what she has done and will clearly have to revise her self-concept as she attempts to come to terms with her reasons for becoming a killer. But her wedding ring is prominent in the shot where she embraces her husband, and they clearly have an understanding as they get into their buggy and ride away.

In other words, while *High Noon* was going about its social critique, it also presented a program for the roles of the sexes. Kane should be a "real man" and follow his sense of duty, which is more important than the demands of marriage. Amy should be a "real woman" and abandon her sense of duty, which is less important than the demands of marriage — for a woman. The momentum of the genre wraps all this up into a neat package: the problem at the end is with the town, not with Amy.

It could be that the filmmakers were too concerned with Kane's (and their own) problem to think seriously about Amy's. It could also be that there is no place for nonviolence in the Western. (*The Big Country,* by the way, features a strong woman and a strong, nonviolent man.) But it is just as possible that *High Noon* reflects what Foreman, Washington, Zinnemann, and Kramer considered proper behavior for a woman, and that they were actually pushing that sex-role philosophy as hard as they could. In that sense, *High Noon* could be considered part of the postwar propaganda campaign to get women out of the factories and back into the home, to become again the princesses of drudgery and nurturance. Women's strength could not be denied, but it could be redirected and reinterpreted: put in its place. And whether or not those were its makers' intentions, *High Noon* is a solid example of how a film can imply a social program and can encourage the audience to endorse a certain kind of behavior. The generic code, in this case, makes everyone's behavior seem morally and socially appropriate — the way things work in a Western — even if, in the real world, people may behave very differently. In the real world, for instance, Amy would have been more likely to bury her husband and leave town. Or she might have saved his life but then refused to consummate the marriage. But neither of those actions would have felt "right" to the audience, even in an adult Western of the period.

"Life's Parade at Your Fingertips." To pull together these observations on genre and deconstruction, let us take a look at two scenes from Douglas Sirk's *All That Heaven Allows* (1955, rel. 1956). Carrie Scott (Jane Wyman) is an attractive middle-aged widow with two grown children: Kay, a know-it-all psychology major, and Ned, a prig. Theirs is an upper-middle-class family in a bourgeois town in the full flower of the Eisenhower era. Carrie falls in love with Ron Kirby (Rock Hudson), the neighborhood tree surgeon, whose favorite author is Thoreau. Ron lives in the woods outside town, as if he would create his own Walden; the buildings on his property are large, solid, and old, and they display their natural materials even after he has lovingly remodeled them. In contrast, the world of the town appears superficial and overdecorated, claustrophobically materialistic.

Ron asks Carrie to marry him and move to his place. She agrees, but her resolution falters when she realizes that she has become the object of town gossip. She is swayed most by her children's selfish and intolerant rejection of her plans, and eventually she makes the "noble sacrifice" of breaking off the engagement. Later on, it turns out that her children do not really need her to devote her life to them, nor do they understand the dimensions of her sacrifice. She decides to return to Ron, but he is not at home. He is just returning from a hunting trip, and he sees her as she gets into her car to leave. While trying to attract her attention, he loses his footing and falls off a cliff. A mutual friend tells Carrie that Ron is seriously hurt, and Carrie goes to the mill he has remodeled for their new life together. When he regains consciousness, they are reconciled, and the picture ends.

The genre here is romantic melodrama, but it has some connections with the radio/TV genre of soap opera. Soap operas very often introduce "complications" in order to defer resolution, so that their plots can continue for years; Ron's accident is just that sort of complication. Its value in the story is that it allows Carrie to realize what is truly important in life: in the fear of losing him forever, she realizes that social disapproval and the demands of her children are ultimately irrelevant and that love is what matters — something Ron has been telling her all along. (Men in soap operas are unusually sensitive to the thoughts and needs of women.) Beyond that, *All That Heaven Allows* is not particularly a soap opera, but many critics have called it one. In *Sirk on Sirk,* for instance, interviewer Jon Halliday calls this film "a standard women's magazine weepie — mawkish, mindless, and reactionary. Yet just beneath the surface it is a tough attack on the moralism of petit bourgeois America." To be fair to the picture, however, one must note that it is a *wonderful* melodrama and not at all "mindless," especially on its surface. Its intelligence comes not just in its critique of its own genre but also in the care and understanding with which it *realizes* the genre. And if you dismiss soap operas as mawkish entertainments whose only serious project is to sell soap to housewives, what you are probably dismissing is the audience. There is nothing inherently dumb about an infinite structure or an open-ended narrative, and there is something extremely interesting about a form that allows you to follow a set of characters from day to day. Furthermore, there is no clear ideological distinction between using a story to sell soap between scenes, as is done in the soap opera, and using a story to promote cultural norms *within* scenes, as is done in a great many narrative films. What distinguishes *All That Heaven Allows* from the soap opera is that it has a tight structure and a clear sense of closure. It is attacked as a soap because it addresses many of the concerns of middle-class women and sees them, rather than the males in their lives, as having to make the important decisions about how families are run and how moral and societal values are to be reconciled. The "weepie" adds to this worldview the formulaic element of the noble sacrifice. None of this is trivial.

As it happens, *All That Heaven Allows* was directed by a male who had real contempt for the story and for the genre. Even as Sirk made this film as beautiful and richly composed as possible, he parodied the limits of the structure. His intent was subversive — of the genre and of the accepted social norms of the period — but at the same time, he turned out a definitive example *of* the genre. As Sirk told Halliday, "with a picture like that your only saving point is to take a tree out of the garden and put it down in a salon." The Thoreau in Sirk — and Ron — would have preferred the tree to remain in the woods, but as Universal's in-house director, assigned to the project, Sirk had to make a film that would please its target audience of Eisenhower-era women. By encouraging that audience to want Carrie and Ron to get together, Sirk could prompt them to share in Carrie's education in values; by letting the highest of those values be romantic love, however, he made fun of the audience he was courting. To the extent that *All That Heaven Allows* is a great romantic melodrama, the joke may have been on Sirk. His distaste for the form he had mastered was, however, expressed with a resonant ambiguity in the lushness of the mise-en-scène — beautiful and claustrophobic, too "arranged" even in the woods — and in two intriguingly ironic scenes.

A salesman has been selling televisions in the town, promoting them as prestige items (remember that the story is set in 1955) and as a means for lonely women to have "company." Carrie doesn't want one; she wants to live in the world and have living companions. The most depressing phase of the film coincides with the Christmas season — a fairly obvious irony. The season of family reunions becomes the site of separation. Ned and Kay make it plain to their mother, with unconscious cruelty, that they are ready to marry (Kay) and to travel (Ned), and that they no longer care whether she marries Ron or sells the house. As a Christmas present, they give her a television. Carrie has just told Kay that "the whole thing's been so pointless," by which she means her sacrifice and, in a way, her life. The children, especially Ned, appear content to release her into a lonely life, and rather than give up their own personal plans — as Carrie has — they expect the TV to provide all the company she will need.

In the final shot of this scene the camera tracks toward the TV screen as the salesman tells Carrie, "All you have to do is turn that dial, and you have all the company you want, right there on the screen: drama, comedy, life's parade at your fingertips." When he says "screen," he points to it, and the TV screen comes to fill the movie frame. The set is turned off, and the screen is a dull green-brown, with a bright ribbon and bow crossing its upper left corner. The screen reflects an image of Carrie in her living room. She is shown, then, both to herself and to the audience, as a member of "life's parade" as it is presented and interpreted by the media: she becomes a TV program. She also sees herself as a prisoner of the screen, as if it were a mirror in which she could see the coming emptiness of her life, alone with the tube.

Her reflection is, of course, in color, and this was the era of black-and-white TV. The reflection is matted in, for visual clarity, *and* muddied as if by the underlying color of the picture tube. As a color image, it is encoded not only as "Carrie's life" but also as "like the images in this color film." (The TV frame encodes it as "like a TV program.") What that expresses is the danger of slipping from vividness into murkiness, from life into artificial imagery — and by implication, it reflects back on the "life" in the film and judges *that* as artificial imagery. It is a reflexive use of the inner frame, and the attack on film's competitor, TV, just as surely critiques the movies, whose illusions are only slightly closer to reality and can be just as empty.

The TV reflection is one of those "figures" or resonant metaphors by which a text can appear to deconstruct itself. It is a statement that evokes the counter-statement on which it depends. It dismantles the illusion of *All That Heaven Allows* from within its own boundaries — but it also asserts and carries forward the illusion. It is both emotionally moving *and* calculated to heighten the audience's awareness of responding to an illusion with easy emotions. It is not just a parody of the romantic melodrama and a critique of its falsity; it is also the single most emotionally moving image in the entire film. It is a devastating revelation for the character, whose children have effectively sold her down the river. It is a reflexive gesture by Sirk, who here judged the "reality" of this world as itself an artificial production: not the real world, but a movie that is like a TV program. What Carrie discovers about her life, Sirk has known all along. The audience realizes that if Carrie does not run back to Ron fast, her life will become a total loss, "pointless" no matter how "noble." Her getting together with Ron in a world far from TV ought to be rooted for as an act of personal salvation, a happy ending that would flout the artifices of her culture and of the film in which she has been cast.

But the romantic resolution itself contains an unsettling element. There is really no way for Carrie to get out of this film. The woods and the old mill are as beautiful as everything else and, by implication, as artificial. She has not really "left the room." By doing the socially incorrect thing and the romantically correct thing, she helps to bring a generic formula to its formulaic resolution — so she is still part of the "program." Deconstruction is one of the few critical methodologies adequate to this level of paradox. In this film the romantic formula is a "noncenter."

In several scenes Ron and Carrie's love is encoded as "natural" in contrast to the "artifice" of life in the gossipy town. The most symbolic of these instances is a scene in which Ron is shown petting a deer that has come up to his house; the landscape is covered with a thin, even blanket of snow. When Ron and Carrie begin to have romantic trouble, the deer goes away. At the very end of the movie, when Carrie has come back to Ron, the deer comes "home" too. On the face of it, this is a sweet way to suggest that their love is in harmony with nature, that even the creatures of the woods approve of their being together.

In the final shot, Carrie kneels by the couch on which Ron is convalescing; a large window with neat rectangular panes is right behind them, looking out on the winter landscape. As she says, "Yes, darling, I've come home," the camera tilts up and tracks forward so that there is only a view of — and through — the window. We see the deer nosing around in the snow and approaching the house. Although this may sound as uncomplicatedly celebratory as the ending of Disney's *Bambi* (1942), it isn't at all. The view is from the civilized side of the window, and the landscape seen through it is chopped up into neat little rectangles, like the bread in *Sunrise*. The implication is that this is as unstructured as nature can get in "this sort of film" or "this world." The deer has come home, but it is also excluded from the artifice (if we read the window as a network of wooden bars, a cage) *and* made artificial as a condition of entering the system at all (if we read it as a graph). Another way to put this is to say that a natural/artificial deer has come home to bless this natural/artificial resolution. The tree is in the salon. The generic program has been fulfilled, but it has strongly been suggested that what is wrong with the genre is what is wrong with the Eisenhower era. In this sense, *All That Heaven Allows* is subversive rather than radical, "burrowing from within" the genre and the social codes it reinforces rather than rejecting them outright.

Movies As an Influence on Behavior. Athol Fugard once told a Telluride audience that poetry, plays, and films "are civilizing influences in any community." Percy Shelley called poets "the unacknowledged legislators of the world." In the United States movies are protected as acts of "free speech," which is a way of acknowledging their status as art as well as their makers' rights to express their convictions. But it is also worth remembering W. H. Auden's remark ("In Memory of W. B. Yeats") that "poetry makes nothing happen." Yeats had been deeply involved in Irish politics, both as a poet and as a senator, but for all his labors, Ireland retained "her madness and her weather." The politics of art may not depend at all on its motivating a change in the way the world is run, however desirable that might be. Instead, it bears witness to a vision, a way of seeing things, a commitment to expression. It discovers and advances insights; it delves into the logic of integrity itself — and if its radical self-sufficiency can serve as an inspiration to others, well and good. But its proper job, as Ezra Pound argued, is to be "news that *stays* news."

The question whether an artistic statement can prompt an audience to change their minds about important matters in the world outside the theater has yet to be resolved. More than 20 years after *Dr. Strangelove* and *The War Game*, we still are threatened by the arms race. There have, however, been many cases in which movies have brought matters to wide public attention and have stimulated debate.

There is a good deal of evidence to suggest that movies do prompt audience identification with characters and story situations. Like Woody Allen in Herbert Ross's *Play It Again, Sam* (1972), we may have a Bogart in the back of our minds, giving advice and setting a fantasy example, a role model. Like Don Quixote or Emma Bovary, some of us live in a world whose most real figures are those out of the compelling imaginations of favorite artists. Like the hero of *Sullivan's Travels*, we sometimes need to escape into a more simply organized world in the interest of sheer mental health. In some cases, to wonder how Jimmy Stewart or Katharine Hepburn would have handled a situation is to discover the solution to a personal quandary; in others, that can be the wrong turn in a labyrinth of personal and social options, at the center of which is the bull of the status quo. But whether it works by fantasy or by example, forthrightly or manipulatively, if art can influence real-world behavior at all, there is reason to suspect that a film *could* become the focus for a social movement, a political change, or a renewal of the human spirit.

Cimino's *The Deer Hunter* (1978) was primarily about the psychological stresses of having fought in Vietnam and the effect of the war on a once-integrated and stable Pennsylvania community. To make his point, Cimino offered Russian roulette as a metaphor for stress and waste. Whereas the ideal of the film is encapsulated in De Niro's efficiency as a hunter — "one shot" to kill a deer — Vietnam is presented as a nightmarish landscape in which the player can never know whether or not there is a bullet in the chamber. At the climax of the film Nick (Christopher Walken) takes charge of his own death as if he has willed the roulette game into a "one shot" system, blowing out his brains and finding peace. Many audiences were confused by all this, pointing out that Russian roulette was not practiced in the prison camps nor in the gambling halls of Saigon. They wanted the story to have been more "real" and less sophomorically symbolic. But many members of the audience were entranced by the Russian roulette scenes and, in fact, went home to experiment for themselves. There was a rash of accidental and planned suicides, particularly among teenagers who had recently seen the film.

It is hard to establish how many "copycat crimes" (like jewel heists) have been inspired by scenarios played out in the movies, or whether movies have made it easier for people to think about using guns, but the following story has been well documented.

Late in 1984 Farrah Fawcett played a battered wife in a TV movie called *The Burning Bed*. Joseph Brandt, aged 39, watched the film and was particularly taken with a scene in which Fawcett kills her husband by setting his bed on fire. Deciding to "scare" his wife, as he later told police, he went into the bedroom, doused his 37-year-old wife Sharon with gasoline while she lay in bed, and burned her to death. After a TV showing of *The Exorcist* in 1975, a nun became convinced that her mother was possessed by Satan and murdered her that night.

It has been speculated that there is an increase in aggressive behavior in children and adults exposed repeatedly to violence in the media. In April 1985 a gang of toughs who had just seen the fifth episode of *Friday the 13th* assaulted the passengers on a Boston subway.

Even when there is not a question of direct influence, some real-world events are reported and interpreted in the context of analogous films. Bernhard Goetz, who shot four muggers on a New York City subway late in 1984, was called "the *Death Wish* killer"—even if Goetz didn't kill anyone—because his actions were perceived as comparable to those of the Charles Bronson character in Michael Winner's *Death Wish* films, and a Goetz/Bronson composite became the focus of a nationwide reexamination of the problems of vigilante violence and police inertia.

It has long been clear that movies can influence trends in music and fashion. And it is clear that they can reflect shifts in the prevailing ideology. Where the Eisenhower era had Mervyn LeRoy's *The FBI Story* (1959), the Johnson era had Arthur Penn's *Bonnie and Clyde* (1967). William Goldman once observed that which films are *made* is a reflection of executive mentality, but which films are *successful* is a reflection of audience mentality. *The FBI Story* could have been released in 1967, but the audiences would still have gone to *Bonnie and Clyde* because it spoke to their current concerns in a contemporary style. The fact that a movie is embraced by a particular culture in a specific period can be taken as a useful guide to the current ideology; it is almost as simple a matter as consumer preference for a point of view.

But movies can also have a subtle and profound psychological impact. In 1985 there was a news story about a young girl who had had bad dreams for *two years* after watching *Alien* on TV. There was a boy who was asked what he felt when watching a figure get stabbed in a movie, and he answered, "like I was getting stabbed but it wasn't really killing me — and like I was doing it." When Ross Carlson (who later died in a mental hospital) shot his parents to death in 1983, this is how he said it felt: "I pulled out a gun. Things were speeding up like I had been shot out of a cannon. My mind was doing 200 miles an hour. I seemed to be watching it. I'm big on movies. It seemed like a movie. I was watching it from another place. I saw my shoulder. The camera concentrated on my shoulder." A court psychiatrist interpreted this as an instance of "depersonalization," and Carlson is certainly not your average moviegoer, but his story is relevant as a partial key to the way a movie can present an action and make it be not quite real, can show violence that does not hurt, can prompt identification with assailant and victim at once and yet not bring home the consequences of such an encounter in the real world. It is even possible that audiences become used to the idea of watching life as if it were a movie and seeing themselves as figures who can flit from one set of conditions to another, one position to another, without ever becoming grounded in a coherent self-construct. If the experience of watching a movie can be remotely compared to a psychotic episode of radical depersonalization, it would be wrong to assume that filmgoing created Carlson's problem, but it would be whistling in the dark to assume that the filmgoing experience cannot encourage an involved/detached relationship with the world. Identification with a character is temporary; few of us are likely to hold up a bank because we enjoyed watching Bonnie and Clyde do it in a movie. But identification with the *camera* may be a common and continuously reinforced habit with far-reaching psychological effects.

Bringing the News. A movie is one way for a point of view to find expression within a culture and even for an entire culture to declare its existence. In the late 1960s the "counter-culture" made its presence felt in films like *Easy Rider, Medium Cool,* and *Alice's Restaurant* (1969, directed by Arthur Penn from a script by Venable Herndon). *Sugar Cane Alley* (1983), the first feature film made in *and* about Martinique, was written and directed by Euzhan Palcy, who supervised a racially mixed production team. When the film was released, she said, "Now we feel that we really exist; at last people are talking about us." By "us," she meant not her filmmaking team but the indigenous culture of Martinique. The movie did extraordinary business in Martinique, and one elderly man said as he left the theater, "Now I can die happy." To be on film is to become an acknowledged part of the world community, to come to public notice; in this case it was also an opportunity for cultural self-definition. A film like Mark Lester and Stephen King's *Firestarter* (1984), which takes for granted the inadvisability of trusting the U.S. government, could be read as expressing the attitudes of the generation that protested the arms race and the war in Vietnam now that it is, as King said in a different context, "our turn to tell the stories."

Movies can bring the public "the news," can let us know more about what is significant in the world. They can also systematically exclude important aspects of life from the screen or consistently present a false vision. Throughout film history, wildly inaccurate versions of the lives and preoccupations of women, blacks, Indians, and other groups have become formulaically entrenched. But in response to the "Charlie Chan" image of the Asian detective in a Western environment, Wayne Wang made *Chan is Missing* (1982), a Chinatown mystery in which detection proceeds according to Eastern rather than Western logic. "Chan" is "missing" from this film, and its "mystery" is never solved in a conventional manner. Wang asserted a different reading of his culture and broke through the stereotypes of character and the conventions of the mystery genre as a way of bringing the "news."

During the Depression in America there was a minor industry devoted exclusively to making films in Yiddish, pictures that expressed the major cultural and ethical convictions of that immigrant audience and gave them the sense that those values applied — or ought to apply — in America just as they had in "the old country." The most fascinating of these were the Yiddish Westerns. There is nothing about a Yiddish-speaking cowboy that is any less "realistic" than an English-speaking ancient Roman in an American movie, but to encounter one is still a startling cultural experience. In the Yiddish cinema — fragments of which can be examined in an excellent compilation documentary called *Almonds and Raisins* (1983) — an immigrant culture found a place to be "at home," to have its values acknowledged and its language spoken.

Documentaries can bring the news, too. Marcel Ophuls's *The Sorrow and the Pity* represented the first public acknowledgment of the anti-Semitism that informed France's collaboration with the Nazis. Despite their postwar pronouncements, not everyone in Vichy France was a covert member of the Resistance, and Ophuls documented the Occupation as it had never been seen before. Although a documentary can be as manipulatively arranged as any fiction, it has special claim to presenting the factual (whether it does or not) because it is assembled from factual materials. The nonfiction movies of the victims of the Nazi concentration camps are virtually irrefutable, and they have done more to bring the news and evoke profound reactions than all the fictions about the Holocaust put together.

Yet fictions do have their own kind of power — something that has been obvious ever since *The Birth of a Nation* led to the rebirth of the Ku Klux Klan. Even the most transparent emotional manipulation of the audience can be effective and can appear to address the real conditions of the world. As a genre, the "problem picture" has consistently brought to wide notice such social problems as racism, teenage pregnancy, political corruption, and religious intolerance. *Broken Blossoms* was not only a lyrical melodrama but also a problem picture about child abuse; beyond that, it argued for mutual understanding between East and West (with considerable irony: whereas the Buddhist wants to bring the doctrines of peace and love to the West, a Christian missionary wants to warn Asians about Hell). After impressing on the audience how horrible violence could be in the domestic microcosm, Griffith encouraged a comparison with the macrocosm. While the audience is grieving about Lucy, we are reminded — in a scene set in a police station — about the thousands of casualties in that week of the First World War. Robert Rossen's *All the King's Men* (1949) provided an intense indictment of political corruption, and its Willie Stark (Broderick Crawford) was intended to be recognized as a version of Huey Long. The fact that the movie was based on Robert Penn Warren's Pulitzer-winning novel gave its radicalism the mantle of social respectability, so that the picture was less dangerous to make; *Citizen Kane* had no such luck, and its distribution was nearly suppressed.

2 or 3 Things I Know About Her is a problem picture, too, though a far less conventional one. It investigates the economic conditions in a Parisian suburb and the related problem of prostitution, which Godard extrapolated into a critique of capitalism. The solution he proposed was a reevaluation of language, a rethinking — in fact, a deconstruction — of the systems by which we organize our understanding of the world and our behavior within it. The problems he saw were not the type that could be handled by a social worker. What Godard and many radical filmmakers have attempted is a *structural* analysis of the interlocking conditions of art and the lived-in-world, which reflect and influence each other. By grappling with the form of a truly problematic film, we may gain a new perspective on the other structures that surround and inform us. We might even learn a new way of thinking. The majority of problem pictures have used conventional structures to address immediate and pressing social concerns, with an emphasis on content; they have taken the world and its presentation for granted. But it can certainly be argued that radical content demands radical forms and that a new conceptual model may demand a new type of frame.

A movie may dramatize a viable solution to a social or political problem, offering a light at the end of the tunnel. But as a self-sufficient work of art, it may also be thought of as a light shining *down* the tunnel, a projected beam of insight.

Conclusion

Throughout this book we have been examining the cinema as a system. In "Parts and Wholes" the point was made that in a movie, selected fragments taken from the visible and audible world are linked into a functioning whole. Those parts act as a system, and the audience — encouraged by the filmmakers and by the implicit logic of the interrelatable fragments — creates an imaginary field, which is the whole. It is built from the fragments as a mosaic is from tiles. Where a "tile" is missing, we tend to imagine it. While watching a cowboy tear over the landscape, we generate our own image of the rustlers he wants to intercept; even if we do not see them at that moment, we assume that they are still going about their business.

But it is one thing to generate a personal imaginary field from a series of images and quite another to ask how that psychological process works and which signifying practices make it possible. To appreciate any given movie and our response to it, we must seek to discover how movies work in general, what their basic elements are and how they interrelate. Throughout Part II, then, we looked at film as a structure. That was partly an attempt to establish an illustrated glossary of basic cinematic terms — a common working vocabulary — but it was also a way to demonstrate how the most complex cinematic statements are built up gradually out of such essential components as the shot and the frame.

Behind even the simplest shot is the whole apparatus of the filmmaking enterprise. In Part III we have seen how a movie is built, not from frame to sequence (cinema as a signifying system) but from an idea to a completed movie (filmmaking as a creative system). Although that structure is less abstract than the one advanced in Part II, it is just as systemic, and it has allowed us to look closely at each of the sub-arts of film and to give credit to those artists whose work is sometimes overlooked or taken for granted. We have also seen how the various contributing arts themselves — from writing, acting, choreography, and set design to special effects and sound design — cluster with and catalyze each other into something more: the art of film.

All this has drawn on our knowledge of the other arts, personal experience with the movies, and intellectual care. It has led us through a matrix of interdependent concerns. There is no way to appreciate the aesthetics of shot and sequence construction (Part II) without knowing a good deal about how (Part III) and why (Part I) such decisions are made. Each part of this book has the other two for legs. The coherent center of this book is not in any of the parts but outside the text, in the conception you have been invited to share and develop, a vision of the nature of cinema.

A film should be approached in its wholeness, and from yours. A movie is an artistic structure, but it is also a concrete text. It is a communicated vision, but it is also a manufactured product. It is a fossil and a mirror, a record and a hallucination. It has its own internal logic, but it hooks your creative consciousness. To explore a film and appreciate its artistry fully, you will want to know everything you can about it. You will want to know its production history. You will want to become familiar with other works by its makers. You will check out its critical reception, what audiences and commentators have made of it. You will set it in historical perspective, to see how it relates to earlier and later pictures and to developments in the world outside the theater. You will ponder how it relates to the cinema in general, whether it opens up any theoretical insights that could be applied to many other films, or even to all films. You will examine how it affects you emotionally and how it stimulates or deadens your thinking. And you will apply what you have learned from that film, or from all films, to the other arts and to the whole range of human activity.

A movie can change your life. It can test you, make you work hard. It can open you to realms of experience and expression. It can enlarge the way you think and train you to look carefully and with loving understanding at any object worth the care, whether that be a text or the world itself. If you have a grasp of how movies work, then — like the fellow in *Entr'acte* (**Fig. 3-140**), on whom we close — you are at the end of one process and the beginning of another. All this is where you start.

Figure 3-140

521

FOR FURTHER READING

Film Studies is a growing field; every year brings new journals, brilliant articles, and books one cannot imagine having done without. There is no space here to list even a respectable proportion of the best books on production and critical studies. What follows, then, is a very selective bibliography of those books that one might want to read *first*. Each of them enlarges on a critical issue or a production technique addressed in this text, and each proved to be a useful and reliable source while this book was being researched. The few magazines and journals that are listed are, again, among the first one might consider subscribing to.

There are, however, several sources that ought to be considered desk companions to *How Movies Work*: two reference works (Spottiswoode et al., *The Focal Encyclopedia*; Katz, *The Film Encyclopedia*); an industry manual (Hines, *Job Descriptions*); a critical anthology (Mast and Cohen, *Film Theory and Criticism*); a comprehensive history (Mast, *A Short History of the Movies* or Cook, *A History of Narrative Film*); and two interactive laserdiscs (The Criterion Collection's editions of *Citizen Kane* and *King Kong*). Many of the films discussed in this book may be rented from Biograph Entertainment (phone 1-800-346-3144). For other distributors, notes on laserdiscs, and screening suggestions by chapter, see page 531.

Film Studies is conventionally divided into "production" and "critical studies," and the latter is often separated into "aesthetics," "history," "special topics" (genres, major figures, social issues, and so on), and "theory." Because most of these areas and concerns necessarily overlap (film history, for example, is inseparable from aesthetics, production, social context, and theory), the following list has not been arranged by topic.

In most cases, reprints are given with their current publishers. Levels of difficulty are indicated as "intro-ductory," "intermediate," or "advanced." Publications addressed explicitly to professional filmmakers are noted as "technical."

ABEL, RICHARD. *French Cinema: The First Wave, 1915–1929*. Princeton and Surrey: Princeton University Press, 1984. A critical history of the relations between the avant-garde and commercial cinemas in France, with chapters on *La Roue*, ciné-clubs, etc. Intermediate.

AGEE, JAMES. *Agee on Film*. 2 vols. New York: McDowell, Obolensky, 1958. The first volume contains Agee's collected writings on film, including all of his reviews (some of the best prose ever devoted to the art); the second contains his screenplays (reset) for *Noa Noa, The African Queen, The Night of the Hunter*, etc. Introductory.

——— AND WALKER EVANS. *Let Us Now Praise Famous Men*. Boston: Houghton Mifflin, 1960. Words and photos in the service of an intense respect for life. Introductory.

ALMENDROS, NESTOR. *Man with a Camera*. New York: Farrar, Straus & Giroux, 1984. A great cinematographer discusses the art. Introductory.

American Cinematographer. See Turner.

American Cinematographer Manual. See Clarke.

American Film. See Biskind.

ANDREW, J. DUDLEY. *Concepts in Film Theory*. New York and Oxford: Oxford University Press, 1984. An introduction to the terms of poststructuralist film theory and a guide to several academic debates of current interest. Intermediate.

———. *The Major Film Theories: An Introduction*. New York and Oxford: Oxford University Press, 1976. A textbook in classical theory, from Münsterberg to Metz. Intermediate.

ARNHEIM, RUDOLF. *Film as Art*. Berkeley, Los Angeles, and London: University of California Press, 1971. A theoretical discussion emphasizing the useful differences between cinema and ordinary reality. Intermediate.

BACH, STEVEN. *Final Cut: Dreams and Disaster in the Making of Heaven's Gate*. New York: William Morrow, 1985. A front-office production history, engagingly written by the frank and perceptive executive who worked on *Heaven's Gate* from start to finish; a credible portrait of Cimino, a short history of United Artists, and a compelling look at the world of the producer. Introductory.

BARNOUW, ERIK. *Documentary: A History of the Non-Fiction Film.* New York and Oxford: Oxford University Press, 1974. An excellent history as well as a careful critical consideration of the form. Introductory.

BARSACQ, LÉON. *Caligari's Cabinet and Other Grand Illusions: A History of Film Design.* New York: New American Library, 1978. The history, materials, techniques, and concerns of set design; superbly illustrated and written by a professional. Introductory.

BAZIN, ANDRÉ. *What Is Cinema?* 2 vols. Berkeley, Los Angeles, and London: University of California Press, 1967 (Vol. 1), 1971 (Vol. 2). Brilliant critical and theoretical articles, emphasizing the nature of the photographic image, the problem of montage, and the challenge of realism; intriguing and beautifully written. Intermediate.

BISKIND, PETER (ED.). *American Film.* A popular monthly, owned by the American Film Institute; noted for its informative critical articles, excerpts from forthcoming books, and snippets of industry news. Introductory.

BLACKWELL, MARILYN JOHNS. *Persona: The Transcendent Image.* Urbana and Chicago: University of Illinois Press, 1986. A sustained close reading of Bergman's masterpiece. Intermediate.

BLAKE, LARRY. *Film Sound Today: An Anthology of Articles from Recording Engineer/Producer.* Hollywood: Reveille Press, 1984. A short, invaluable collection of Blake's authoritative articles on Dolby, sound design, mixing, the history of film stereo, etc. Technical, introductory to intermediate.

BORDWELL, DAVID. *The Films of Carl-Theodor Dreyer.* Berkeley, Los Angeles, and London: University of California Press, 1981. A precise, well illustrated, intriguing analysis. Intermediate.

BORDWELL, DAVID, ET AL. *The Classical Hollywood Cinema: Film Style and Mode of Production to 1960.* New York: Columbia University Press, 1985. A sophisticated analysis of Hollywood narrative conventions. Intermediate.

BRAKHAGE, STAN. *Film Biographies.* Berkeley: Turtle Island, 1977. Extraordinary personal essays on Méliès, Griffith, Chaplin, Vigo, Dr. Caligari, etc. Intermediate.

BRAUDY, LEO. *The World in a Frame: What We See in Films.* Chicago and London: University of Chicago Press, 1984. An important discussion of open and closed structures in representational art. Intermediate.

BRESSON, ROBERT. *Notes on Cinematography.* New York: Urizen Books, 1977. A masterful collection of brief, intense meditations. Intermediate.

BROWNLOW, KEVIN. *Napoleon: Abel Gance's Classic Film.* New York: Alfred A. Knopf, 1983. The making and reconstruction of *Napoleon.* Introductory.

———. *The Parade's Gone By.* . . . Berkeley and Los Angeles: University of California Press, 1976. A passionate and authoritatively researched history and defense of the silent film, including interviews with filmmakers. Introductory.

CALLENBACH, ERNEST (ED.). *Film Quarterly.* A critical academic journal, published by the University of California Press; noted for its rigorous articles, in-depth reviews, and annual survey of film books. Intermediate.

CARRINGER, ROBERT L. *The Making of Citizen Kane.* Berkeley, Los Angeles, and London: University of California Press, 1985. A fascinating and comprehensive production history. Intermediate.

——— (ED.). *Citizen Kane.* Los Angeles: The Criterion Collection, 1984. An interactive laserdisc of the complete movie, including a visual analysis of major sequences, single-framed key production materials, and the original trailer; an essential reference and a landmark in the development of Film Studies. Order from The Voyager Company, 2139 Manning Avenue, Los Angeles, CA 90025; phone 1-800-446-2001 (in CA: 1-800-443-2001). Introductory.

CASE, DOMINIC. *Motion Picture Film Processing.* Stoneham and London: Focal Press, 1985. A compact, clear, and detailed introduction to the film lab, lens properties, color systems, and so on; the chemistry and physics of film. Technical, intermediate.

CAVELL, STANLEY. *Pursuits of Happiness: The Hollywood Comedy of Remarriage.* Cambridge and London: Harvard University Press, 1981. An extraordinary meditation on the cinema, comedy, and remarriage, via close readings of seven films. Intermediate.

———. *The World Viewed: Reflections on the Ontology of Film.* Enlarged ed. Cambridge and London: Harvard University Press, 1979. A personal and philosophically rigorous exploration of the phenomenology of film. Advanced.

CEPLAIR, LARRY, AND STEVEN ENGLUND. *The Inquisition in Hollywood: Politics in the Film Community, 1930–1960.* Berkeley, Los Angeles, and London: University of California Press, 1983. A scholarly and very well-written history of political activity in Hollywood, emphasizing the Screen Writers Guild, the congressional hearings, and the fate of the Hollywood Ten. Introductory.

CERAM, C. W. *Archaeology of the Cinema.* New York: Harcourt, Brace & World, 1965. A superbly illustrated history of the invention of the cinema; long out of print, but the best of its kind. Introductory.

CHAMNESS, DANFORD. *The Hollywood Guide to Film Budgeting and Script Breakdown.* Revised ed. Los Angeles: Stanley J. Brooks, 1984. A practical and detailed guide; covers script breakdown, logging, the production board, the budget, location shooting. Technical, advanced.

CHASE, DONALD (ED.). *Filmmaking: The Collaborative Art.* Boston and Toronto: Little, Brown/American Film Institute, 1975. Interviews, panel sessions, and fine editorial glue; professional discussions of the producer, writer, actor, cinematographer, production designer, costume designer, script supervisor, editor, composer, and special effects artist. Introductory.

CHATMAN, SEYMOUR. *Story and Discourse: Narrative Structure in Fiction and Film.* Ithaca and London: Cornell University Press, 1978. Observations on the trail of a comprehensive theory of narration. Intermediate.

Cinefex. See Shay.

Citizen Kane. See Carringer.

CLARKE, CHARLES G. (ED.). *American Cinematographer Manual.* 5th ed. Hollywood: American Society of Cinematographers, 1980. Practical and detailed information about cameras, lenses, filmstocks, etc.; the standard, indispensable reference manual in the industry. Technical, advanced.

COLE, HILLIS R., AND JUDITH H. HAAG. *The Complete Guide to Standard Script Formats: Part I—Screenplays.* Los Angeles: CMC Publishing (1003 N. Alfred St., Los Angeles, CA 90069), 1980. The definitive manual; read this before typing an author's final or a shooting script. Technical, introductory.

COOK, DAVID A. *A History of Narrative Film.* 2nd ed. New York: W. W. Norton, 1990. A comprehensive and detailed survey. Introductory.

CORSON, RICHARD. *Stage Makeup.* 6th ed. Englewood Cliffs: Prentice-Hall, 1981. Comprehensive, definitive, and practical; see Kehoe. Technical, intermediate to advanced.

COSTANZO, WILLIAM V. *Double Exposure: Composing Through Writing and Film.* Upper Montclair: Boynton/Cook, 1984. An introductory composition textbook, addressed to students and teachers, that shows how the careful study of films can help to make one a better writer. Introductory.

CRAFTON, DONALD. *Before Mickey: The Animated Film 1898–1928.* Cambridge and London: MIT Press, 1982. A fine history, culminating with Felix the Cat. Introductory.

DOANE, MARY ANN, ET AL. (EDS.). *Re-Vision: Essays in Feminist Film Criticism.* Frederick: University Publications of America/American Film Institute, 1984. The title says it all. Intermediate to advanced.

DOWDY, ANDREW. *The Films of the Fifties: The American State of Mind.* New York: William Morrow, 1975. A vividly entertaining history of the American narrative film in the 1950s, emphasizing social context and audience response. Introductory.

DUNN, LINWOOD, AND GEORGE E. TURNER (EDS.). *The ASC Treasury of Visual Effects.* Hollywood: American Society of Cinematographers, 1983. An invaluable anthology of articles on the history of optical special effects, beautifully illustrated and written by practicing experts. Introductory to intermediate.

EISENSTEIN, SERGEI M. *Film Form: Essays in Film Theory.* New York: Harcourt Brace Jovanovich, 1969. Essential discussions of the nature and development of film language, especially montage; one of the most important works in film theory. Intermediate.

———. *The Film Sense.* Rev. ed. New York: Harcourt Brace Jovanovich, 1969. Articles on color, sound, and the senses, together with representative production materials. Intermediate.

EISNER, LOTTE H. *The Haunted Screen: Expressionism in the German Cinema and the Influence of Max Reinhardt.* Berkeley and Los Angeles: University of California Press, 1969. An insightful analysis of German Expressionist cinema, its roots in theater and folklore, and the major masterpieces. Intermediate.

———. *Murnau.* Berkeley and Los Angeles: University of California Press, 1972. An excellent critical biography of the director, with adequate attention to his major collaborators; includes the script of *Nosferatu* (translated and reset). Intermediate.

FELL, JOHN. *Film and the Narrative Tradition.* Berkeley, Los Angeles, and London: University of California Press, 1986. A pioneering study of the roots of narrative techniques previously considered exclusively "cinematic," and of the range of the narrative tradition itself (including 19th century melodrama, comics, sheet music, etc.). Intermediate.

——— (ED.). *Film Before Griffith.* Berkeley, Los Angeles, and London: University of California Press, 1983. A very fine collection of scholarly articles on the first years of the cinema and of the film industry. Intermediate.

FIELD, SYD. *Screenplay: The Foundations of Screenwriting.* Expanded ed. New York: Dell, 1982. Although its vision of narrative structure is formulaic and simplistic, this book has been accepted as a practical guide to the "basics": how to write for contemporary Hollywood. Technical, introductory.

FIELDING, RAYMOND. *The Technique of Special Effects Cinematography.* 4th ed. Stoneham and London: Focal Press, 1985. A comprehensive, definitive, and practical survey of optical special effects, including specific instructions. Technical, intermediate to advanced.

——— (ED.). *A Technological History of Motion Pictures and Television.* Berkeley, Los Angeles, and London: University of California Press, 1967. Authoritative scholarly articles, memoirs, and other historical papers. Intermediate.

Film Quarterly. See Callenbach.

The Focal Encyclopedia. See Spottiswoode.

GOLDMAN, WILLIAM. *Adventures in the Screen Trade: A Personal View of Hollywood and Screenwriting.* New York: Warner Books, 1983. Witty and accurate; the best single introduction to the way Hollywood works today. Introductory.

GOLDNER, ORVILLE, AND GEORGE E. TURNER. *The Making of King Kong: The Story Behind a Film Classic.* New York: Ballantine Books, 1976. An excellent, authoritative production history; Goldner worked on the film. Introductory.

GOMBRICH, E. H. *Art and Illusion: A Study in the Psychology of Pictorial Representation.* Princeton and Surrey: Princeton University Press, 1960. A crucial study of the history and psychology of "realism" in art. Intermediate.

GORDON, PAUL L., ET AL. *The Book of Film Care.* Rochester: Eastman Kodak, 1983. A well-illustrated discussion of the nature, handling, and preservation of filmstock. Technical, introductory.

GUZZETTI, ALFRED. *Two or Three Things I Know about Her: Analysis of a Film by Godard.* Cambridge and London: Harvard University Press, 1981. A shot-by-shot analysis, containing all the dialogue (in French and English) and music as well as anamorphic frame enlargements from every shot (the film was in color; these are black-and-white). Intermediate.

HALLIDAY, JON. *Sirk on Sirk*. New York: Viking Press, 1972. A book-length interview with Douglas Sirk, conducted in 1970. Introductory.

HAPPÉ, L. BERNARD. *Your Film and the Lab*. 2nd ed. Stoneham and London: Focal Press, 1983. Detailed information on lab procedures, especially as they affect the editor. Technical, intermediate.

HARMETZ, ALJEAN. *The Making of the Wizard of Oz: Movie Magic and Studio Power in the Prime of MGM — and the Miracle of Production #1060*. New York: Limelight Editions, 1984. A superior production history, both above- and below-the-line. Introductory.

HASKELL, MOLLY. *From Reverence to Rape: The Treatment of Women in the Movies*. Harmondsworth and Baltimore: Penguin Books, 1974. An influential study of recurring images of women in the narrative film, with special attention to the compelling power of the star who rises above the limits of her scripted role. Introductory.

HAVER, RONALD (ED.). *King Kong*. Los Angeles: The Criterion Collection, 1984. An interactive laserdisc of the complete movie, perfect for frame-by-frame study, together with a "video documentary" and an optional voice-over commentary; see the reference to Carringer's disc of *Citizen Kane* for ordering information. Introductory.

HEATH, STEPHEN. *Questions of Cinema*. Bloomington: Indiana University Press, 1981. Densely and even poorly written, these essays on film narrative, the cinematic apparatus, and the application of Lacanian psychoanalysis, Marxism, and semiotics to an understanding of cinema are both important and influential. Advanced.

HENDERSON, BRIAN (ED.). *Five Screenplays by Preston Sturges*. Berkeley, Los Angeles, and London: University of California Press, 1985. Complete facsimiles of Sturges's brilliant final draft screenplays for *The Lady Eve, Sullivan's Travels*, etc.; further volumes are planned. Intermediate.

HINES, WILLIAM E. *Job Descriptions: Responsibilities and Duties for the Film and Video Craft Categories and Classifications*. Los Angeles: Ed-Venture Films/Books, 1985. A detailed, comprehensive, and authoritative listing of exactly what each below-the-line job entails; an indispensable reference and the only one of its kind, available by mail order (P.O. Box 23214, Los Angeles CA 90023). Technical, intermediate.

HOLLYN, NORMAN. *The Film Editing Room Handbook: How to Manage the Near Chaos of the Cutting Room*. New York: ARCO, 1984. An authoritative and pleasantly informal introduction to the world of the assistant editor and to post-production in general. Technical, introductory to intermediate.

JOWETT, GARTH. *Film: The Democratic Art: A Social History of American Film*. Stoneham and London: Focal Press, 1985. An important study of how American film and society have influenced each other. Introductory.

KAEL, PAULINE, ET AL. *The Citizen Kane Book*. Boston and Toronto: Little, Brown/Atlantic Monthly Press, 1971. Contains the final shooting script (reset), the RKO cutting continuity, and Kael's interpretation of the Welles-Mankiewicz collaboration. Introductory.

KATZ, EPHRAIM. *The Film Encyclopedia*. New York: Putnam, 1979. Although not entirely error-free, this is the most comprehensive one-volume reference to the biographies and the major achievements of a host of significant filmmakers now available; it also has entries on major terms, movements, and techniques. Introductory.

KAWIN, BRUCE F. *Mindscreen: Bergman, Godard, and First-Person Film*. Princeton and Surrey: Princeton University Press, 1978. More on film narration and reflexivity. Intermediate.

———— (ED.). *Faulkner's MGM Screenplays*. Knoxville: University of Tennessee Press, 1982. Complete facsimiles of four treatments and three screenplays, in various formats, all written by Faulkner during his first year in Hollywood; an introduction to the materials of textual editing and historical scholarship, with much information on MGM Story Department procedures. Intermediate.

KEHOE, VINCENT J-R. *The Technique of the Professional Make-up Artist for Film, Television, and Stage*. Stoneham and London: Focal Press, 1985. An excellent technical introduction, not as comprehensive and mature as Corson's classic text (*Stage Makeup*) but more film-oriented. Technical, intermediate.

KINDER, MARSHA, AND BEVERLE HOUSTON. *Close-Up: A Critical Perspective on Film*. New York: Harcourt Brace Jovanovich, 1972. Out of print, but worth looking for; a superb introduction to the close reading of films. Introductory.

King Kong. See Haver.

KRACAUER, SIEGFRIED. *From Caligari to Hitler: A Psychological History of the German Film*. Princeton and Surrey: Princeton University Press, 1947. A complex study of the ways in which films may express latent social and psychological conflicts; includes the production history of *Caligari*. Intermediate.

LASZLO, ERVIN. *The Systems View of the World*. New York: George Braziller, 1972. A clearly written introduction to systems theory; the best of its kind. Introductory.

LEES, DAVID, AND STAN BERKOWITZ. *The Movie Business*. New York: Vintage Books, 1981. A realistic introduction to the business practices and environment of contemporary Hollywood. Introductory.

LE GRICE, MALCOLM. *Abstract Film and Beyond*. Cambridge and London: MIT Press, 1977. A critical history of the abstract film, with discussions of art and cinematography, Structuralist film, etc. Intermediate.

LEYDA, JAY. *Kino: A History of the Russian and Soviet Film*. Rev. ed. Princeton and Surrey: Princeton University Press, 1982. Definitive; written by Eisenstein's principal translator. Intermediate.

———— AND ZINA VOYNOW. *Eisenstein at Work*. New York: Pantheon Books/Museum of Modern Art, 1982. A first-class collection of sketches and other pre-production materials. Introductory.

LIEHM, MIRA. *Passion and Defiance: Film in Italy from 1942 to the Present*. Berkeley, Los Angeles, and London: University of California Press, 1984. A powerful and well-informed critical history, emphasizing political context. Intermediate.

MacCANN, RICHARD DYER (ED.). *Film: A Montage of Theories*. New York: E. P. Dutton, 1966. A stimulating collection of articles and excerpts from classic texts, arranged to highlight major theoretical controversies and oppositions. Introductory.

MAST, GERALD. *A Short History of the Movies*. 4th ed. New York: Macmillan, 1986. An engagingly written history of the art, with emphasis on masterpieces of the narrative film. Introductory.

———— (ED.). *The Movies in Our Midst: Documents in the Cultural History of Film in America*. Chicago and London: University of Chicago Press, 1982. An exceptionally revealing anthology of original documents (1882–1977) bearing on social responses to the American cinema. Introductory to intermediate.

———— AND MARSHALL COHEN (EDS.). *Film Theory and Criticism: Introductory Readings*. 3rd ed. New York and Oxford: Oxford University Press, 1985. A comprehensive selection of classic and recent articles and book excerpts; an excellent guide to further reading. Introductory to advanced.

MAYER, DAVID. *Eisenstein's Potemkin: A Shot-by-Shot Presentation*. New York: Grossman, 1972. A thorough listing of every shot in the film. Introductory.

McBRIDE, JOSEPH. *Hawks on Hawks*. Berkeley, Los Angeles, and London: University of California Press, 1982. An extremely useful and well-edited series of interviews (1970–1977). Introductory.

McCLINTICK, DAVID. *Indecent Exposure: A True Story of Hollywood and Wall Street*. New York: Dell, 1983. A devastating history of the Begelman scandal; a fly-on-the-wall view of how Hollywood, as a transcontinental business, is actually run; and a cool account of human failure. Introductory.

McCONNELL, FRANK D. *The Spoken Seen: Film and the Romantic Imagination*. Baltimore: Johns Hopkins University Press, 1975. Frankenstein meets Bazin. Intermediate.

METZ, CHRISTIAN. *The Imaginary Signifier: Psychoanalysis and the Cinema*. Bloomington: Indiana University Press, 1982. The leading contemporary French theorist formulates an approach to the viewer–film relationship. Advanced.

MICHELSON, ANNETTE (ED.). *Kino-Eye: The Writings of Dziga Vertov*. Berkeley, Los Angeles, and London: University of California Press, 1984. Articles, notebooks, diaries, and proposals. Intermediate.

MILLERSON, GERALD. *The Technique of Lighting for Television and Motion Pictures*. 2nd ed. Stoneham and London: Focal Press, 1982. The nature and uses of light. Technical, advanced.

MONACO, JAMES. *American Film Now: The People, The Power, The Money, The Movies*. 2nd ed. New York: New American Library, 1984. A perceptive and well-informed discussion of contemporary Hollywood by a leading critic. Introductory.

MÜNSTERBERG, HUGO. *The Film: A Psychological Study: The Silent Photoplay in 1916*. New York: Dover, 1970. A brief and extremely insightful analysis of the relations between cinema and consciousness; a relatively overlooked classic of film theory. Introductory.

NEWHALL, BEAUMONT. *The History of Photography: From 1839 to the Present Day*. Rev. (4th) ed. Boston and New York: New York Graphic Society/Museum of Modern Art, 1964. Definitive and superbly illustrated. Introductory.

————. *Latent Image: The Discovery of Photography*. Garden City: Doubleday, 1967. A short, clear, and technically detailed history of the first years of the art. Introductory.

NICHOLS, BILL (ED.). *Movies and Methods: An Anthology*. 2 vols. Berkeley, Los Angeles, and London: University of California Press, 1976 (Vol. 1), 1985 (Vol. 2). Major critical and theoretical articles, arranged by methodology. Both volumes are extremely useful and stimulating. Intermediate to advanced.

NILSEN, VLADIMIR. *The Cinema as a Graphic Art: On a Theory of Representation in the Cinema*. New York: Hill & Wang, 1959. A practical as well as theoretical discussion of composition and camerawork, by one of Eisenstein's assistants. Intermediate.

NISBETT, ALEC. *The Technique of the Sound Studio*. 4th ed. Stoneham and London: Focal Press, 1979. The nature, recording, editing, and reproduction of sound. Technical, advanced.

PANOFSKY, ERWIN. *Meaning in the Visual Arts: Papers in and on Art History*. Garden City: Doubleday, 1955. Panofsky's subject is Renaissance art, but his definitive discussions of iconography and iconology and his sustained close interpretations of great visual structures are extremely instructive. Advanced.

PEARY, GERALD AND DANNY (EDS.). *The American Animated Cartoon: A Critical Anthology*. New York: E. P. Dutton, 1980. Historical and critical articles on everyone from Winsor McCay to Chuck Jones. Introductory.

PERKINS, V. F. *Film as Film: Understanding and Judging Movies*. Harmondsworth and Baltimore: Penguin Books, 1972. A provocative yet commonsense approach to film theory and criticism. Introductory.

PINCUS, EDWARD, AND STEVEN ASCHER. *The Filmmaker's Handbook*. New York: New American Library, 1984. A practical, clearly written introduction to independent filmmaking (and video) techniques. Technical, introductory.

PUDOVKIN, VSEVOLOD I. *Film Technique and Film Acting*. New York: Grove Press, 1970. Two classic works, both practical and theoretical. Introductory.

PUIG, MANUEL. *Kiss of the Spider Woman*. New York: Alfred A. Knopf, 1979. A great novel about movies, politics, sexuality, imprisonment, and language. Introductory. Of all the novels written about or with an eye on the cinema, this and Pynchon's *Gravity's Rainbow* may well be the two most insightful, well-informed, structurally sophisticated, brilliantly written, and ethically complex. Ironically, the 1985 screen adaptation of Puig's novel, although critically well-received, failed markedly to convey the cinematic energy of the original.

PYNCHON, THOMAS. *Gravity's Rainbow*. New York: Viking Press, 1973. See Puig. Advanced.

REISZ, KAREL, AND GAVIN MILLAR. *The Technique of Film Editing*. 2nd ed. Stoneham and London: Focal Press, 1968. The history and aesthetics of film editing; practical, sophisticated, and authoritative. Intermediate.

RICHIE, DONALD. *Ozu*. Berkeley, Los Angeles, and London: University of California Press, 1974. A superb discussion of Ozu's philosophy, working methods, and major films. Intermediate.

———. *The Films of Akira Kurosawa*. Rev. ed. Berkeley, Los Angeles, and London: University of California Press, 1984. A comprehensive career overview, now updated through *Kagemusha*. Introductory.

ROSENTHAL, ALAN. *The New Documentary in Action: A Casebook in Film Making*. Berkeley, Los Angeles, and London: University of California Press, 1971. The contemporary documentary in general and direct cinema in particular. Introductory.

ROTHMAN, WILLIAM. *Hitchcock — The Murderous Gaze*. Cambridge and London: Harvard University Press, 1982. Intensive shot-by-shot readings of *The Lodger, Murder!, The 39 Steps, Shadow of a Doubt*, and *Psycho*. Intermediate.

SALT, BARRY. *Film Style and Technology: History and Analysis*. London: Starword, 1983. An extremely well-researched and technically oriented history of film practice, together with a controversial program for the statistical analysis of visual style; *the* place to find out when and how a specific technical development (e.g., the zoom lens) entered industry practice. Advanced.

SARRIS, ANDREW. *The American Cinema: Directors and Directions, 1929–1968*. Chicago and London: University of Chicago Press, 1986. The "Bible" of auteur criticism; capsule evaluations of directors, both opinionated and perceptive. Introductory.

SATO, TADAO. *Currents in Japanese Cinema*. Japan: Kodansha International, 1982; distributed by Harper & Row. Selected historical and critical essays by Japan's leading film critic. Introductory.

SAVINI, TOM. *Grande Illusions: A Learn-by-Example Guide to the Art and Technique of Special Make-Up Effects*. Pittsburgh: Imagine, 1983. Detailed, entertaining, and gruesome. Technical, introductory.

SCHAEFER, DENNIS, AND LARRY SALVATO. *Masters of Light: Conversations with Contemporary Cinematographers*. Berkeley, Los Angeles, and London: University of California Press, 1984. Fifteen interviews, from Almendros to Zsigmond. Introductory.

SCHECHTER, HAROLD, AND DAVID EVERITT. *Film Tricks: Special Effects in the Movies*. New York: Dial/Harlan Quist, 1980. An enthusiastic, comprehensive, and technically precise survey of mechanical and optical special effects, from Méliès to schlock. Introductory.

SHAY, DON (ED.). *Cinefex*. A quarterly "journal of cinematic illusions"; long, authoritative, and detailed articles on special effects, especially in recent or forthcoming films. Technical, intermediate.

SINGLETON, RALPH S. *Film Scheduling: Or, How Long Will It Take You To Shoot Your Movie?* Beverly Hills: Lone Eagle, 1984. An excellent introduction to script breakdown and all that goes with it, including the complete 41-day shooting schedule for Coppola's *The Conversation* and a color-foldout production board as well. A companion volume, *Film Budgeting*, promises to be equally useful. Technical, introductory.

———. *Film Scheduling/Film Budgeting Workbook*. Beverly Hills: Lone Eagle, 1984. This workbook for *Film Budgeting* and *Film Scheduling* contains the complete shooting script for *The Conversation* (retyped, but in the original format). Technical, introductory.

SITNEY, P. ADAMS. *Visionary Film: The American Avant-Garde*. 2nd ed. New York and Oxford: Oxford University Press, 1979. A comprehensive and intensive critical history of American avant-garde film since 1943, with discussions of Deren, Brakhage, etc. Intermediate.

——— (ED.). *Film Culture Reader*. New York: Praeger, 1970. An essential — and out of print — anthology of articles on the American avant-garde film, reprinted from *Film Culture*. Intermediate.

SPOTTISWOODE, RAYMOND, ET AL. *The Focal Encyclopedia of Film and Television Techniques*. Stoneham and London: Focal Press, 1969. Expensive and worth it; by far the single most reliable and precisely written technical reference book in the field. Technical, advanced.

SQUIRE, JASON E. (ED.). *The Movie Business Book*. Englewood Cliffs: Prentice-Hall, 1983. Informative articles on the business aspects of filmmaking, written by professionals (agents, independent producers, financiers, etc.). Introductory.

TELOTTE, J. P. *Dreams of Darkness: Fantasy and the Films of Val Lewton*. Urbana and Chicago: University of Illinois Press, 1985. A fine critical study of the creative producer, with resonant readings of all of Lewton's films. Intermediate.

TURNER, GEORGE (ED.). *American Cinematographer*. The monthly journal of the American Society of Cinematographers, reporting on film and video production techniques, both classic and recent, together with superior in-depth articles and regular columns. Technical, intermediate.

WALLER, GREGORY A. *The Living and the Undead: From Stoker's Dracula to Romero's Dawn of the Dead*. Urbana and Chicago: University of Illinois Press, 1986. The vampire in literature and film; a close study of adaptation and an exemplary tracing of a single figure through a genre. Introductory.

WEIS, ELIZABETH, AND JOHN BELTON (EDS.). *Film Sound: Theory and Practice*. New York: Columbia University Press, 1985. A comprehensive critical anthology with a particularly useful glossary by Stephen Handzo. Intermediate.

WHITNEY, JOHN. *Digital Harmony: On the Complementarity of Music and Visual Art*. Peterborough: Byte Books/McGraw-Hill, 1980. A brilliant theoretical study of harmony, color, time, and scales in music and images; a manifesto for "visual harmony" together with a guide to computer/film applications. Intermediate.

WILSON, ANTON. *Anton Wilson's Cinema Workshop*. Rev. ed. Hollywood: American Society of Cinematographers, 1983. A collection of Wilson's columns in *American Cinematographer*; explanatory and problem-solving chapters on film, cameras, formats, lenses, filters, sound, etc. Technical, intermediate to advanced.

WOLLEN, PETER. *Signs and Meaning in the Cinema*. 3rd ed. Bloomington and London: Indiana University Press, 1972. Essays on Eisenstein, Godard, and the auteur theory buttress an influential essay on the semiotics of film. Intermediate.

WRIGHT, WILL. *Sixguns and Society: A Structural Study of the Western*. Berkeley, Los Angeles, and London: University of California Press, 1975. A significant application of Structuralism to genre study. Intermediate.

YELLIN, DAVID G., AND MARIE CONNORS (EDS.). *Tomorrow and Tomorrow and Tomorrow*. Jackson: University Press of Mississippi, 1985. William Faulkner's story "Tomorrow," together with Horton Foote's adaptations of it for TV and film. Introductory.

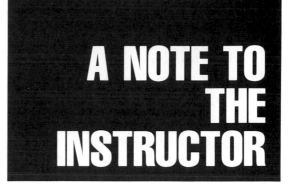

A NOTE TO THE INSTRUCTOR

What follows is a list of films one might want to screen in coordination with the specific chapters and discussions in this book. Virtually all of them may be rented in 16mm at classroom rates.

James L. Limbacher's *Feature Films: A Directory of Feature Films on 16mm and Videotape Available for Rental, Sale, and Lease* (New York and London: R. R. Bowker Company, 1985) is now in its eighth edition, and its information on 16mm rental sources is regularly updated. A less expensive alternative to Limbacher, and a good way to locate non-feature films as well, is to write to the following distributors and request their current catalogs. Space does not permit the listing of more than a few of the most comprehensive and reliable sources:

Biograph Entertainment Ltd.
(formerly Images Film Archive)
2 Depot Plaza, Suite 202B, Bedford Hills, NY 10507
(914) 242-9838, (800) 346-3144

Corinth Films
410 E. 62nd St., New York, NY 10021
(212) 463-0305, (800) 221-4720

EmGee Film Library
6924 Canby Ave., Suite 103, Reseda, CA 91335
(818) 881-8110; FAX (818) 981-5506

Films Inc.
5547 No. Ravenswood Ave., Chicago, IL 60640
(800) 323-4222

The Museum of Modern Art (MOMA), Circulating
   Film Library
11 W. 53rd St., New York, NY 10019
(212) 708-9530

New Yorker Films
16 W. 61st St., New York, NY 10023
(212) 247-6110

Kit Parker Films
1245 Tenth St., Monterey, CA 93940
(408) 649-5573, (800) 538-5838

Swank Motion Pictures
201 S. Jefferson Ave., St. Louis, MO 63166
(314) 534-6300, (800) 876-5577

Some of the films discussed in this book are prohibitively expensive in 16mm but cost between $25 and $40 in laserdisc, which, given the right playback equipment, allows the full theatrical soundtrack to be presented. The interactive or CAV laserdisc is an ideal student format for frame-by-frame study, second only to hands-on analysis at an editing table. Many of the films listed below are available on laserdisc, and almost all of them can be found on videocassette. The letterbox format, which preserves the theatrical aspect ratio, is the format of choice.

For each chapter or major subchapter in this book — that is, for each aspect of film study to which you might want to devote a class or a week of class or a screening assignment — one or two particular films have been suggested. Their titles are in boldface, and they provide at least a year's worth of showings that coordinate closely with the text. The list is, of course, suggestive rather than exhaustive.

Part I

1. FILM APPRECIATION

Olympia diving sequence + Workers Leaving the Lumière Factory + The Conjuror
and/or one of the following: *Casablanca, City Lights, His Girl*

Friday, It's A Wonderful Life, Modern Times, Only Angels Have Wings, Red River, Sullivan's Travels, The Treasure of the Sierra Madre, The Wizard of Oz.

1A. Critical Approaches to Film Appreciation
The Critic + A Clockwork Orange
All That Heaven Allows, The Cabinet of Dr. Caligari, Blow-Up, Carmen (Saura), Céline and Julie Go Boating, Chinatown, Citizen Kane, Dr. Strangelove, Earth, Edvard Munch, 8½, Flashdance, Fury, The Godfather I & II, Heaven's Gate (uncut), High Noon, Hiroshima, mon amour, Metropolis, Paths of Glory, Psycho, The Shining, Vampyr, Tout va bien, Vertigo, Vivre sa vie, We All Loved Each Other So Much, Young Mr. Lincoln.

IMAGES OF WOMEN IN FILM: *Act of the Heart, Adam's Rib, Alien, Aliens, All About Eve, An American in Paris, The Big Country, Blonde Venus, The Blue Angel, Le Bonheur, Broken Blossoms, Carnal Knowledge, Carrie, Cat People (1942 & 1982), Caught, La Chienne, Claire's Knee, Dawn of the Dead (uncut), The Decline of the American Empire, Detour, Double Indemnity, A Dream of Passion, 8½, Entre nous, Flashdance, Frances, Frenzy, Friday the 13th, Gaslight, The General, Gertrud, The Godfather, Goldfinger, Gone With the Wind, Gun Crazy, High Noon, His Girl Friday, I Married a Witch, Intolerance, Iphigenia, It Came from Beneath the Sea, Jeanne Dielman, Johnny Guitar, Jules and Jim, Kwaidan, The Lady from Shanghai, Last Tango in Paris, Leave Her to Heaven, The Leech Woman, The Life and Times of Rosie the Riveter, Lola Montès, The Lonedale Operator, Love and Anarchy, Mad Love, Meetings with Anna, Metropolis, Mildred Pierce, The Mothering Heart, Mourir à tue-tête, Muriel, My Son John, Niagara, Not a Love Story, Now, Voyager, Of Human Bondage, The Outlaw, Pandora's Box, A Passage to India, Peeping Tom, Portrait of Jennie, Psycho, The Quiet Man, Public Enemy, Queen Christina, Rabid, Rain, Red Desert, Red River, Repulsion, Romancing the Stone, Salt of the Earth, Sansho the Bailiff, Scarlet Street, The Searchers, Sheer Madness, Shoot the Piano Player, Snow White and the Seven Dwarfs, Some Like It Hot, The Stars Look Down, Stella Dallas, The Stepford Wives, The Story of Adèle H., La Strada, Straw Dogs, Sunrise, Swept Away . . ., Sybil, Thriller (Potter), Tokyo Story, Tout va bien, Ugetsu, Vertigo, A Very Curious Girl, Vivre sa vie, Way Down East, White Heat, The Wind, The Women Men Long For.*

1B. Electric Shadows
Sherlock Jr.
Abel Gance: The Charm of Dynamite, Beauty and the Beast, La Jetée, Mothlight, Orpheus, Vampyr.

2. PARTS AND WHOLES

Man With a Movie Camera
Betrayal, Dead Men Don't Wear Plaid, Don't Look Now, Intolerance, Je t'aime, je t'aime, La Jetée, Last Year at Marienbad, Lumière Premier Program (Images), Lumière Program I & *II (MOMA), Georges Méliès Program (MOMA), Mother, Rules of the Game, That Obscure Object of Desire, 2 or 3 Things I Know About Her, Walkabout.*

3. PRIMARY CATEGORIES

3A. The Narrative Film
Citizen Kane
THE NARRATOR: *Diary of a Country Priest, La Jetée, The Lady from Shanghai, Red River ("book version" available on laserdisc, "voice version" in 16mm), Zoot Suit.*

STORY AND DISCOURSE: *Betrayal, Henry V, Rashomon, Tout va bien.*

ESCAPISM: *Sullivan's Travels.*

TALE-SPINNING: *The Company of Wolves, Dead of Night, The Fatal Glass of Beer, Targets.*

HOLLYWOOD FORMULAS: *The Adventures of Robin Hood, 42nd Street, Gunga Din, I Married a Witch, Mr. Blandings Builds His Dream House, Mr. Smith Goes to Washington, Raiders of the Lost Ark, Rocky.*

GENRE: *The Day the Earth Stood Still + The Thing From Another World; 42nd Street + The Red Shoes + Flashdance; Shane + The Searchers + Paris, Texas.*

NARRATIVE STRUCTURE: *A Corner in Wheat, Une Dame vraiment bien!, The Great Train Robbery, Intolerance, The New York Hat.*

ACTS: *Battleship Potemkin, The Godfather, Return of the Jedi.*

NARRATIVE COMPLEXITY: *Dead of Night, Harakiri, Last Year at Marienbad, La Jetée, Mishima, Muriel, That Obscure Object of Desire, Persona, Rashomon.*

SUBJECTIVITY AND VOICE: *Apocalypse Now, Badlands, Dead of Night, DreamChild, Un Grand amour de Beethoven, Lady in the Lake, Last Year at Marienbad, Life Upside Down, Meshes of the Afternoon, Rashomon, State of Siege, Strangers on a Train, Taxi Driver, Vampyr, Wild Strawberries.*

REFLEXIVITY: *Les Carabiniers, Peeping Tom, Persona, Sherlock Jr., Sullivan's Travels, Targets, Those Awful Hats, 2 or 3 Things I Know About Her, Tout va bien, Uncle Josh at the Picture Show, We All Loved Each Other So Much.*

CREATING UNDER PRESSURE: *Abel Gance: Yesterday and Tomorrow, Andrei Rublev, La Roue, Unknown Chaplin #2.*

OTHERS: *Alphaville, L'Atalante, The Bicycle Thief, The Birth of a Nation, Black Narcissus, Cabaret, Caught, The Children of Paradise, Chushingura (1962), The Crime of M. Lange, Diabolique, Faces, From Here to Eternity, The General, The Gold Rush, Grand Illusion, Greed, J'accuse, Johnny Guitar, KAOS, The King of Comedy, Kiss Me Deadly, Kiss of Death, The Last Wave, Letter from an Unknown Woman, The Love of Jeanne Ney, The Maltese Falcon, The Man in the White Suit, Mean Streets, Modern Times, Mother, North by Northwest, Los Olvidados, Once Upon a Time in the West, Orpheus, Rules of the Game, The Sacrifice, Seven Samurai (uncut), The Seventh Seal, Shadows, The Sin of Harold Diddlebock, Stagecoach, The Third Man, To Be or Not To Be*

(1942), *Tokyo Story, Top Hat, Twentieth Century, Ugetsu, Vivre sa vie, Voyage to Italy, The Wages of Fear, Way Out West, The Wind, Zero for Conduct.*

3B. The Nonfiction Film
Hiroshima-Nagasaki, August 1945 + The War Game
Abel Gance: The Charm of Dynamite, Abel Gance: Yesterday and Tomorrow, The Battle of Chile, The Battle of San Pietro, Berlin: Symphony of a Great City, Blood Wedding, Burden of Dreams, The City, Don't Look Back, Edvard Munch, Enthusiasm, Glass, Grass, Granton Trawler, The Great Ecstasy of the Sculptor Steiner, High School, Hospital, Le Joli mai, Kino Pravda, Land Without Bread, Let There Be Light, The Life and Times of Rosie the Riveter, Louisiana Story, Lumière films, Man With a Movie Camera, A Married Couple, The Memory of Justice, Monterey Pop, Nanook of the North, The Negro Soldier, Night and Fog, Night Mail, North Sea, Olympia I & II, The Picasso Mystery, Point of Order, Primary, The Quiet One, Salesman, Song of Ceylon, The Sorrow and the Pity, La Soufrière, Streetwise, Taris, Titicut Follies, To Die in Madrid, The Trials of Alger Hiss, Triumph of the Will, 28 Up, Unknown Chaplin, Warrendale, Why We Fight.

3C. The Animated Film
The Cameraman's Revenge + Popeye Meets Sinbad
Bambi Meets Godzilla, Betty Boop cartoons (e.g., Bimbo's Initiation & Crazy Town), The Bugs Bunny/Road Runner Movie, Bugs Bunny, Superstar, Emile Cohl Compilation (Images), Closed Mondays, A Colour Box, Composition in Blue, Drame chez les Fantoches, Duck Amuck, Experiments in Motion Graphics, Gertie the Dinosaur, The Hole, Horse Over Teakettle, Les Joyeux microbes, Lapis, Moonbird, Mothlight, Motion-Painting I, NY, NY, Permutations, Pinocchio, The Pumpkin Race, A Short History of Animation (MOMA), A Short Vision, Snow White and the Seven Dwarfs, Superman cartoons (e.g., The Mummy Strikes & Volcano), Symphonie Diagonale, Through the Mirror.

3D. The Avant-Garde Film
Meshes of the Afternoon
L'Age d'or, Allures, Anemic Cinema, At Land, Ballet mécanique, Bardo Follies, Breathdeath, The Cabinet of Dr. Caligari, Castro Street, Un Chien andalou, A Colour Box, Entr'acte, Eraserhead, Étoile de mer, The Fall of the House of Usher (Webber and Watson), Film in Which There Appear Sprocket Holes, Edge Lettering, Dirt Particles, Etc., La Folie du Dr. Tube, Ghosts Before Breakfast, Heart of Glass, Lapis, Mothlight, Motion-Painting I, A Movie, My Name is Oona, N:O:T:H:I:N:G, Now That the Buffalo's Gone, Offon, Oh Dem Watermelons, Pacific 231, Palindrome, Pas de Deux, Re-entry, Return to Reason, Rhythmus 21, Ritual in Transfigured Time, Samadhi, Scorpio Rising, Standard Gauge, The Stars are Beautiful, A Study in Choreography for Camera, Surface Tension, Symphonie Diagonale, Text of Light, T,O,U,C,H,I,N,G, Überfall, The Very Eye of Night, Wavelength, Window Water Baby Moving, Zorns Lemma.

4. MONTAGE AND MISE-EN-SCENE

Ménilmontant
Battleship Potemkin, Citizen Kane, City Lights, Close Encounters of the Third Kind: The Special Edition, The Color of Money, Days of Heaven, Don't Look Now, Open City, The Last Laugh, Lola Montès, Psycho, Rules of the Game, The Wild Bunch.

Part II

1. RAW MATERIALS

Unknown Chaplin #1
Abel Gance: The Charm of Dynamite, Abel Gance: Yesterday and Tomorrow, Entr'acte, La Folie du Dr. Tube, Man With a Movie Camera, Offon, Standard Gauge, Tom, Tom, The Piper's Son.

1A. Lighting
Mad Love
Alien, Black Narcissus, Citizen Kane, Greed, Kwaidan, The Last Laugh, The Love of Jeanne Ney, The Magnificent Ambersons, Psycho, Queen Christina, Vampyr.

2. THE FRAME

Napoleon
THE INNER FRAME: *Citizen Kane, Duck Amuck, Rear Window, Sherlock Jr.*
ASPECT RATIO: *Andrei Rublev, Ben-Hur, The Big Country, Brainstorm, The Devils, East of Eden, Exodus, Forbidden Planet, Jules and Jim, A King in New York, Land of the Pharaohs, Lawrence of Arabia, Once Upon a Time in the West, Red and White, Silk Stockings, 2 or 3 Things I Know About Her, 2001, West Side Story.*
3-D: *Creature from the Black Lagoon, Dial M for Murder, Friday the 13th III, House of Wax, It Came from Outer Space.*
COMPOSITION: *Battleship Potemkin, Black Narcissus, From Here to Eternity, Ivan the Terrible, Queen Christina.*

3. BLACK-AND-WHITE AND COLOR

Black Narcissus
BLACK-AND-WHITE: *Ashes and Diamonds, The Big Heat, The Big Sleep, Citizen Kane, Day of Wrath, Double Indemnity, The General, Gertrud, Greed, Harakiri, King Kong, Kiss Me Deadly, The Last Laugh, The Long Voyage Home, Mad Love, The Magnificent Ambersons, Morocco, Night of the Living Dead, La Notte, Open City, Persona, Psycho, La Roue, Sawdust and Tinsel, Sunset Boulevard, Sweet Smell of Success, This Gun for Hire, To Have and Have Not, Touch of Evil.*

BLACK-AND-WHITE AND COLOR: *Andrei Rublev, Ivan the Terrible II, Night and Fog, Night of the Living Dead + Dawn of the Dead* (uncut), *Rumble Fish, The Wizard of Oz.*

TINTING AND TONING: *Broken Blossoms, Napoleon.*

COLOR: *Aguirre: The Wrath of God, Alien, An American in Paris, The Boy Friend, La Chinoise, Chushingura* (1962), *Composition in Blue, Cries and Whispers, Dawn of the Dead, Days of Heaven, Dial M for Murder, Dodeskaden, Edvard Munch, Fanny and Alexander, The Godfather I & II, Gone With the Wind, Heart of Glass, Henry V, The Horse's Mouth, Kwaidan, Liquid Sky, The Mirror, Muriel, Peeping Tom, Pierrot le fou, The Quiet Man, Ran, The Red Shoes, The River, The Sacrifice, Singin' in the Rain, Snow White and the Seven Dwarfs,* any original IB Technicolor print, *Tout va bien, The Trouble with Harry, 2 or 3 Things I Know About Her, Vertigo, Weekend.*

4. THE SOUNDTRACK

Singin' in the Rain
L'Age d'or, Apocalypse Now, Blow Out, Citizen Kane, The Coming of Sound (MOMA), *The Conversation, Days of Heaven, Duck Amuck, Dune, The Empire Strikes Back, Enthusiasm, Eraserhead, Un Grand amour de Beethoven, I Married a Witch, India Song, The Jazz Singer, Land Without Bread, Lights of New York, The Man Who Knew Too Much* (1956), *Modern Times, Once Upon a Time in America* (uncut), *Once Upon a Time in the West, Raging Bull, Star Wars, The Right Stuff, Way Out West, What's Up, Tiger Lily?*

5. THE SHOT

The 39 Steps
TAKES: *Unknown Chaplin #1* and/or *#2.*

SHOTS AND SHOT RELATIONS: *Battleship Potemkin, The Birth of a Nation, Breathless, Intolerance, Last Year at Marienbad, The Love of Jeanne Ney, Man With a Movie Camera, Ménilmontant, Mother, Napoleon, October.*

NEW AND OLD FOOTAGE: *The White Gorilla.*

FAST MOTION: *Onésime horloger.*

SLOW MOTION: *Olympia, Ritual in Transfigured Time.*

MOVING CAMERA: *After Hours, Citizen Kane, Hiroshima, mon amour, I Married a Witch, The Last Laugh, Lola Montès, The Magnificent Ambersons, Ordet, The Passenger, Red and White, Rope, Sunrise, Tout va bien, 2 or 3 Things I Know About Her, Vertigo, Young and Innocent, Weekend.*

6. THE SCENE

It's A Wonderful Life
All About Eve, Betrayal, The Gold Rush, Gone With the Wind, Hiroshima, mon amour, King Kong, Lawrence of Arabia, The Quiet Man, Rules of the Game, The Servant.

7. THE SEQUENCE

"Raising of the Bridges" sequence from October + The Godfather
Battleship Potemkin, Don't Look Now, The Godfather II, Mother, Napoleon, October, Our Daily Bread, Seven Samurai, Strike.

Part III

1. WHO MAKES A MOVIE?

The Cabinet of Dr. Caligari + Unknown Chaplin #2
Abel Gance: Yesterday and Tomorrow, Day for Night, Singin' in the Rain, Sullivan's Travels, Tout va bien, Unknown Chaplin #1.

AUTHORSHIP, COLLABORATION, AND INFLUENCE CLUSTERS: *The Bicycle Thief + Shoeshine + A Brief Vacation; The Bicycle Thief + Battleship Potemkin + We All Loved Each Other So Much; The Cabinet of Dr. Caligari + The Phantom of the Opera + The Last Laugh + The Mummy + Mad Love; Mad Love + The Long Voyage Home + Citizen Kane + The Fugitive + The Pearl + Under the Volcano; Un Chien andalou + L'Age d'or + Spellbound + Los Olvidados + The Phantom of Liberty; Intolerance + Way Down East + Mother; La Chienne + Scarlet Street; Metropolis + Dr. Strangelove; Piranha + The Howling + The Brother from Another Planet + Gremlins; Sunrise + City Girl + Badlands + Days of Heaven; Tender Mercies + Breaker Morant + Tomorrow + 1918; The Funhouse + E.T. + Poltergeist; Yojimbo + Fistful of Dollars.*

1A. Production Studies
[Pick a single movie and refer to it throughout Part III.]

Vertigo
Apocalypse Now, Casablanca, Citizen Kane, The Conversation, Dr. Strangelove, From Here to Eternity, The Godfather, The Gold Rush, Gone With the Wind, Hiroshima, mon amour, It's A Wonderful Life, King Kong, The Maltese Falcon, Muriel, Olympia, Once Upon a Time in America, Once Upon a Time in the West, Pennies from Heaven (1981), *Persona, Psycho, Queen Christina, Red River, Strangers on a Train, Top Hat, 2001, The Wizard of Oz, Zelig.*

2. DEVELOPMENT

Sullivan's Travels
EXECUTIVE DECISIONS: *Abel Gance: Yesterday and Tomorrow, The Cabinet of Dr. Caligari, Superman III, Suspicion.*

THE WRITER: *Chinatown, From Here to Eternity, Hiroshima mon amour, The Lady Eve, Lawrence of Arabia, Manhattan, Rules of the Game, The Servant, Sunset Boulevard.*

THE PRODUCER: Lewton: *Cat People, The Curse of the Cat People, Isle of the Dead, The Leopard Man, The Seventh Victim, I Walked With a Zombie.* Selznick: *Duel in the Sun, Gone With the Wind, Portrait of Jennie, Rebecca.*

BUDGETS: *Ben-Hur, The Conversation, The Creeping Terror, Foolish Wives, Greed, Hollywood Boulevard, King of the Z's, Macbeth (1948 & 1971), Monty Python and the Holy Grail. Night of the Living Dead, Plan 9 from Outer Space, 2001.*

3. PRE-PRODUCTION

Gone With the Wind

LOCATION VS. STUDIO SHOOTING: *All That Heaven Allows, The Bicycle Thief, Don't Look Now, The 400 Blows, The Godfather II, Greed, Hiroshima, mon amour, Kwaidan, Lawrence of Arabia, Medium Cool, Muriel, One from the Heart, Open City, Outback, Perceval, Pixote, The Quiet Man, Ran, The River (1951), The Searchers, Stagecoach, Tabu, La terra trema, Two for the Road, 2 or 3 Things I Know About Her, Uncle Tom's Cabin (Porter), Under the Volcano, The Valley Obscured by Clouds, The Wild Bunch, The Wind.*

PRODUCTION DESIGN: *Alien, Alphaville, Beauty and the Beast, The Boy Friend, Bride of Frankenstein, The Cabinet of Dr. Caligari, Casablanca, Dr. Strangelove, The Earrings of Madame De, Frankenstein, French Can-Can, The Godfather I & II, Grand Illusion, Henry V, Intolerance, Kwaidan, Life Upside Down, Macbeth (1948 & 1971), Mishima, Muriel, Napoleon, Pennies from Heaven, The Phantom of the Opera (1925), The Poseidon Adventure, Ran, La Ronde, The Servant, The Texas Chain Saw Massacre, This Island Earth, Thunderball, Ugetsu, The Wizard of Oz.*

COSTUMES: *American Gigolo, Beauty and the Beast, Days of Heaven, Diane, Fanny and Alexander, The Godfather 1 & II, Ivanhoe, Kwaidan, Persona, Ran, The Treasure of the Sierra Madre, Two Rode Together, Vertigo, The Wizard of Oz, Zoot Suit.*

4. PRODUCTION

Queen Christina

THE DIRECTOR: *Ali: Fear Eats the Soul, Arsenic and Old Lace, L'Atalante, Badlands, The Birth of a Nation, Bride of Frankenstein, Bringing Up Baby, La Chienne + Scarlet Street, Citizen Kane, The Color of Money, Days of Heaven, Dr. Strangelove, 8½, The 400 Blows, Fury, The General, Un Grand amour de Beethoven, Grand Illusion, His Girl Friday, J'accuse, The Lady Eve, M, Macbeth (1948 & 1971), A Man Escaped, Mother, Mouchette, Muriel, Napoleon, Nosferatu (1922 & 1979), Notorious, The Passion of Joan of Arc, Persona, The Phantom of Liberty, Pickpocket, Plan 9 from Outer Space, Raging Bull, Ran, La Roue, Rules of the Game, The Sacrifice, The Searchers, The Servant, Shoot the Piano Player, To Have and Have Not, 2 or 3 Things I Know About Her, Ugetsu, Unknown Chaplin, Vertigo, The Wages of Fear.*

THE DIRECTOR AS ACTOR: *Citizen Kane, The Gold Rush, The Green Room, Love and Death, Manhattan, Mon Oncle, Rules of the Game, Touch of Evil, The Wild Child.*

THE ACTOR: *The Adventures of Robin Hood, Aguirre: The Wrath of God, Ashes and Diamonds, The Bicycle Thief, Brewster McCloud, Bride of Frankenstein, Bringing Up Baby, Broken Blossoms, Casablanca, The Children of Paradise, Citizen Kane, City Lights, Dr. Strangelove, Duck Soup, The 400 Blows, The Godfather I & II, Greed, Henry V, Holiday, The Horse's Mouth, Ikiru, The Lady Eve, The Last Laugh, Lawrence of Arabia, The Love of Jeanne Ney, Marathon Man, The Marriage of Maria Braun, Ménilmontant, Metropolis, Mouchette, The Mystery of Kaspar Hauser, Napoleon, On the Waterfront, The Passion of Joan of Arc, The Philadelphia Story, The Quiet Man, Raging Bull, The Red Balloon, Red River, The Treasure of the Sierra Madre, Tout va bien, 2 or 3 Things I Know About Her, Unknown Chaplin #2, The Verdict, Vertigo.*

THE CINEMATOGRAPHER: *Aguirre: The Wrath of God, Alien, The American Friend, Barry Lyndon, The Birth of a Nation, Black Narcissus, Citizen Kane, The Conformist, Day for Night, Day of Wrath, Days of Heaven, Dr. Jekyll and Mr. Hyde (1932), Dr. Strangelove, 8½, Fanny and Alexander, La Folie du Dr. Tube, The 400 Blows, The Fugitive, Gertrud, The Godfather I & II, Gone With the Wind, Greed, The Green Room, Heart of Glass, Heaven's Gate, Hiroshima, mon amour, It's A Wonderful Life, Jules and Jim, Kwaidan, The Last Laugh, Last Year at Marienbad, Lawrence of Arabia, The Love of Jeanne Ney, Mad Love, The Magnificent Ambersons, The Maltese Falcon, Mishima, Morocco, The Mummy (1932), Muriel, Napoleon, Nosferatu (1922 & 1979), La Notte, Olympia, Only Angels Have Wings, Open City, Ordet, Paris, Texas, A Passage to India, The Passion of Joan of Arc, The Pearl, Peeping Tom, Persona, Psycho, The Quiet Man, Ran, Red River, The Red Shoes, The River, Rosemary's Baby, The Sacrifice, Salvatore Giuliano, Sawdust and Tinsel, The Searchers, Seconds, Seven Samurai, Shoot the Piano Player, The Story of Adèle H., Sunday in the Country, Sunrise, Sunset Boulevard, This Gun for Hire, To Have and Have Not, The Tree of Wooden Clogs, 2 or 3 Things I Know About Her, Ugetsu, Under the Volcano, The Valley Obscured by Clouds, Vampyr, The Verdict, Vertigo, The War Game, Zelig.*

REAR AND FRONT PROJECTION: *Foreign Correspondent, North by Northwest, Suspicion, 2001, Vertigo.*

MAKEUP: *Beauty and the Beast, Bride of Frankenstein, Citizen Kane, Dawn of the Dead, Dr. Jekyll and Mr. Hyde (1932), The Elephant Man, The Exorcist, Frankenstein, The Funhouse, The Godfather, The Hunchback of Notre Dame (1923 & 1939), Liquid Sky, Little Big Man, The Mummy (1932), The Phantom of the Opera (1925), The Wolf Man.*

PRODUCTION SPECIAL EFFECTS: *Alien, Apocalypse Now, Dawn of the Dead, A Nightmare on Elm Street, Superman I & II, Them!, The Towering Inferno.*

CHOREOGRAPHY: *All That Jazz, An American in Paris, Blood Wedding, Carmen (Saura), The Gold Rush, Moses Pendleton Presents Moses Pendleton, Olympia diving sequence,*

The Red Shoes, Seven Brides for Seven Brothers, Seven Samurai, Singin' in the Rain, A Study in Choreography for Camera, Swing Time, Top Hat, West Side Story (scope), Zoot Suit.

SOUND RECORDING: Apocalypse Now, Applause, Blood Feast (example of poor), Blow Out, California Split, Citizen Kane, The Coming of Sound (MOMA), The Conversation, Lights of New York, Singin' in the Rain.

SOUND DESIGN: Apocalypse Now, The Black Stallion, Days of Heaven, The Empire Strikes Back, Eraserhead, Star Wars, THX-1138.

5. POST-PRODUCTION

King Kong

SPECIAL EFFECTS CINEMATOGRAPHY: Blade Runner, Close Encounters, The Empire Strikes Back, Metropolis, Poltergeist, Tarantula, 2001, 2010, Young Sherlock Holmes.

OPTICAL PRINTING: Apocalypse Now, Citizen Kane, any Flash Gordon serial, The 400 Blows, Pas de Deux, A Place to Stand.

IN-CAMERA EFFECTS: The Dream of a Rarebit Fiend, Napoleon.

FILM EDITING: All That Jazz, Battleship Potemkin, The Birds, The Birth of a Nation, Cabaret, Citizen Kane, Dr. Strangelove, Don't Look Now, The Godfather II, Harakiri, Intolerance, Jaws, Last Year at Marienbad, Napoleon, October, Olympia II, The Passion of Joan of Arc, Psycho, Raging Bull, La Roue, Seven Samurai, Strike, To Die in Madrid, Zoot Suit.

MUSIC: Cabaret, Citizen Kane, Days of Heaven, La dolce vita, Frenzy, The Godfather, Gone With the Wind, Un Grand amour de Beethoven, The Horse's Mouth, The Killing Fields, Kwaidan, Manhattan, Modern Times, Muriel, Psycho, Red River, The Right Stuff, Spellbound, Strangers on a Train, The Thing (1982), The Third Man, 2 or 3 Things I Know About Her, The Treasure of the Sierra Madre, Vertigo, The Wizard of Oz.

SOUND EDITING AND MIXING: Apocalypse Now, The Black Stallion, Citizen Kane, Days of Heaven, Dune, The Empire Strikes Back, Un Grand amour de Beethoven, Once Upon a Time in America (uncut), The Right Stuff.

POST-SYNCHRONIZATION: Abel Gance: Yesterday and Tomorrow, Blow Out, The Cotton Club, 8½ (compare dubbed and subtitled versions), Fright Night (Foley work), I Married a Witch, What's Up, Tiger Lily?

6. DISTRIBUTION

Unknown Chaplin #3
MARKETING: Forbidden Planet, Poltergeist, Risky Business, The Wind.

RESTORATION: Napoleon, Unknown Chaplin #1

6A. Film and Society
J'accuse (1937)

OVERT POLITICAL CONTENT: All the King's Men, Antonio das Mortes, The Battle of Chile, The Birth of a Nation, La Chinoise, Dr. Strangelove, Eternal Monument, Go Tell the Spartans, Grand Illusion, Medium Cool, Muriel, My Son John, Open City, Rambo: First Blood II, State of Siege, To Die in Madrid, Triumph of the Will, 2 or 3 Things I Know About Her, The War Game, Why We Fight, Wind from the East, Z.

IMPLICIT, BURIED, OR DISGUISED POLITICAL CONTENT: Alien, Bonnie and Clyde + The FBI Story, The Cabinet of Dr. Caligari, Dawn of the Dead (uncut), DeathDream, Flashdance, Heaven's Gate (uncut), High Noon, The Hill, Invasion of the Body Snatchers (1956), The Last Laugh, The Negro Soldier, Night of the Living Dead, Olympia I, The Thing From Another World, Young Mr. Lincoln.

GENRE AND SOCIAL CRITICISM: All That Heaven Allows, DeathDream, Heaven's Gate (uncut), High Noon, Zoot Suit.

SOCIAL CONTEXT: Almonds and Raisins, Chan is Missing, The Deer Hunter, Leadbelly, Nothing But a Man, Pixote, Pull My Daisy, Sugar Cane Alley, Zoot Suit.

Condensed Recommended Primary Syllabus

Note that these have been arranged so that the course may begin with Part I, II, or III:

PART I

Film appreciation: Lumière, Méliès, Olympia diving sequence, and The Wizard of Oz
Film criticism: The Critic and A Clockwork Orange
Electric shadows: Sherlock Jr.
Parts and wholes: Man With a Movie Camera
Narrative film: Citizen Kane
Nonfiction film: Hiroshima-Nagasaki, August 1945 and The War Game
Animated film: The Cameraman's Revenge and Popeye Meets Sinbad
Avant-garde film: Meshes of the Afternoon
Montage and mise-en-scène: Ménilmontant

PART II

Raw materials: Unknown Chaplin #1
Lighting: Mad Love
Frame: Napoleon
Black-and-white and color: Black Narcissus
Soundtrack: Singin' in the Rain
Shot: The 39 Steps
Scene: It's A Wonderful Life
Sequence: "Raising of the Bridges" from October and The Godfather

PART III

Authorship: *The Cabinet of Dr. Caligari* and *Unknown Chaplin #2*
Comprehensive production study: *Vertigo*
Development: *Sullivan's Travels*

Pre-production: *Gone With the Wind*
Production: *Queen Christina*
Post-production: *King Kong*
Distribution: *Unknown Chaplin #3*
Film and society: *J'accuse*

GLOSSARY OF KEY TERMS

Above-the-line costs. The contracturally fixed expenses, incurred or agreed to before shooting begins, related to the hiring of the key creative personnel (notably the writer, the director, the producer, and the cast) and their staffs, the acquisition of story rights, and certain administrative responsibilities (such as employee fringe benefits); see "below-the-line costs" and "line."

Abstract film. A film whose imagery is nonrepresentational.

Academy. The Academy of Motion Picture Arts and Sciences.

Academy aperture. The standard size (0.864 in. × 0.63 in.) of a 35mm aperture plate, found in printers and projectors; it yields an aspect ratio of 1.33:1 while leaving room for a soundtrack.

Academy ratio. A standard aspect ratio of 1.33:1.

Act. (1) A major structural division within a script or narrative (the majority of narrative films today have three to five acts; many silent films had one act per reel); a long sequence of scenes with a consistent dramatic project; (2) to perform a dramatic role.

Actualité. A nonfiction film that consists of unbiased, objective recordings of actual people, objects, and events.

Actual sound. Also **diegetic sound** and **indigenous sound**. (1) Any sound that is presented as originating from an on- or offscreen action area and that is therefore capable of being heard by the real or fictive inhabitants of the filmed world, whether or not it was recorded during production; (2) loosely, live sound; see "commentative sound," "direct sound," "live sound," "off," and "over."

Adaptation. A film based on a pre-existing work.

Additive color system. Also **additive process**. A system in which colors are produced by the combination of various amounts of red, green, and blue light; if complementary spotlights overlap, their hues will add to white; see "subtractive color system."

ADR. Automatic dialogue replacement; also **EPS**, electronic post-synchronization. A dialogue replacement technique that has largely replaced conventional looping and in which the performer is cued by streamers and electronic beeps; picture and sound move forward/backward in interlock rather than endlessly forward in repeating loops, and the picture serves as the guide to lip sync.

Aerial image. A real image that is focused in the air rather than on a card, a screen, or a piece of glass.

Aerial shot. One in which the camera support (e.g., a helicopter) is off the ground.

Ambient air. Also **air**. Atmospheric sound, especially that of a particular set or location at normal quiet; see "room tone."

Ambient noise. Atmospheric sound, especially background noise.

Anamorphic. Colloquially, **scope**. Adjective for any wide-screen process or format in which a broad field of view is squeezed (horizontally compressed) during shooting and unsqueezed (restoring normal height/width relationships) during projection.

Anamorphic lens. A lens that compresses or expands the horizontal dimension of the subject or the frame without affecting the vertical dimension; see "flat" and "spherical lens."

Angle. See "camera angle."

Animation. (1) The process of creating in an unmoving object the impression of autonomous movement, usually through frame-by-frame shooting; (2) cartooning; frame-by-frame shooting of sequential paintings or drawings; see "cel animation."

Answer print. (1) Any in a series of trial composite

prints, with picture, sound, and all optical effects; (2) the first copy of a movie in its final, approved form; the final trial composite print.

Aperture. An opening.

Aperture plate. (1) A metal plate with a rectangular opening that determines the proportions of the frame; found in cameras, printers, and projectors; (2) a full-frame camera aperture plate, whose standard size in 35mm cinematography is 0.98 in. × 0.735 in., yielding an aspect ratio of 1.33:1; see "Academy aperture."

Appliance. A three-dimensional makeup item worn by or attached to the actor (e.g., a latex prosthetic).

Arc light. Also **arc lamp**. (1) A luminant that produces a hard, intense white light by causing an electric current to jump or arc, usually between two carbon rods; found in many projectors and large lighting instruments; (2) a light with such a lamp.

Armature. The flexible skeleton of a puppet or a stop-motion model.

Art director. The person who designs or selects the sets and decor of a picture.

ASC. The American Society of Cinematographers.

Aspect ratio. The ratio of the width of the image (written first) to its height (a constant); for example, Panavision is 2.35:1, and American widescreen is 1.85:1.

Auteur. (1) French for "author"; the guiding creative intelligence behind a picture; the person presumed to have made the most significant creative decisions during the collaborative production of a film and therefore to be responsible for its coherence and dominant style; (2) a filmmaker who writes, directs, and edits "his" or "her" movie.

Auteur theory. Also **auteurism**. The critical methodology that attributes the thematic and stylistic coherence of a movie to the artistic vision, the recurring personal concerns, and the specific instructions of a single artist, usually the director, and that adopts as a primary criterion of value the "personal signature" or the felt presence of the "author" in the work.

Author. The sole creator and original owner of a work.

Authorized narration. A narrative whose presenter is aware of the act of telling a story to or sharing a vision with an audience.

Avant-garde. (1) Any artist, critic, group, or movement in the vanguard of artistic innovation, usually informed by a particular theoretical perspective on the nature and evolution of the arts in general; (2) the work of an independent film poet.

Axis. See "line."

Balance. The tonal range and lighting design of a shot.

Base. The flexible component or vehicle of filmstock, currently made of cellulose triacetate or polyester and coated with an emulsion; see "nitrate film" and "safety-base film."

Beam-combiner. A device, usually a two-way mirror, that both transmits and reflects light, allowing the reflected and direct views to be photographed simultaneously; sometimes called a "beam-splitter."

Beam-splitter. (1) A device, usually a prism or a partially silvered mirror, that directs the light gathered by a lens in two or more directions, for example, onto different loads of filmstock; (2) loosely, a beam-combiner.

Beat. (1) A stress or pulse in a metrical, musical, theatrical, or editing rhythm; (2) a short, effective pause occurring on or held for a beat.

Below-the-line costs. Those expenses incurred in the actual, physical making of a movie (filmstock, sketches, sets, props, extras, technical personnel, processing, etc.) up to and including the cost of the final answer print; see "above-the-line costs" and "line."

Best boy. Also **first assistant electrician**. The gaffer's principal assistant. The key grip's principal assistant is the **best boy grip**.

Bi-pack. A double load of film; two lengths of film are run simultaneously through the gate of a camera or a printer, where they are in contact.

Bird's-eye view. A shot taken from directly above the subject; the most extreme high-angle shot.

Black body. A perfectly efficient radiator; an abstraction used in the determination of color temperature.

Blimp. A rigid cover placed over the camera for soundproofing.

Blimped camera. A camera with internal soundproofing.

Blockbuster. (1) A movie with high production values that costs and expects to earn a great deal of money; (2) any movie that grosses over $100 million.

Blocking. (1) The deployment of actors on a set and the planning of their movements; (2) the planning and rehearsal of a camera movement.

Blue-screen process. The technique of shooting action against a bright blue backdrop, yielding footage from which a traveling matte may be generated.

Booking. A contract for a specific theatrical engagement.

Boom. (1) The arm or jib of a crane; see "crane" and "crane shot"; (2) a lightweight pole; see "boom microphone"; (3) a channel reserved for low-frequency information.

Boom microphone. A microphone suspended from a

boom or pole, capable of following an actor while remaining out of camera range.

Boom shot. See "crane shot."

Break down. To separate into parts. **Breakdown** is the noun and the adjective.

Build. To assemble, especially a reel of picture or sound.

Camera angle. The tilt or inclination from which the camera views the subject; the angle between the camera's line of sight and the forward and/or lateral horizontal axes.

Cameraman. (1) The Director of Photography, also called the "first cameraman"; see "cinematographer"; (2) a camera operator or camera assistant of either sex. The **camera operator**, who runs the camera, is the "second cameraman"; the **focus puller** is the "first assistant cameraman" or the "first camera assistant"; the **clapper/loader** is the "second assistant cameraman" or the "second camera assistant."

Camera original. The actual footage, usually negative, exposed in a production camera.

Cast. (1) All of the performers in a movie; (2) to select an actor for a role.

Category. A union-represented job classification or cluster of related jobs; the primary Association of Film Craftsmen (NABET) craft categories are camera, sound, electrical, grip, art, set construction, property, wardrobe, makeup, directorial, transportation, editing, special services, and video.

Cel. A transparent sheet of celluloid on which an image (or one element of a layered composite image) may be painted.

Cel animation. Cartooning; frame-by-frame shooting of images that have been painted on cels.

Changeover. The switch from one projector to another at a reel break.

Channel. A discrete or decoded reel- or film-long unit of sound information that is to be played through a particular speaker; see "track."

Choreography. (1) The art of creating, directing, and notating a dance; (2) the art of planning and directing the movements of a group of performers.

Cinema. (1) The "language" that all movies "speak"; (2) the medium-specific process of intermittent photography, movement and projection; (3) a collective term for the art of motion pictures; (4) a movie theater.

CinemaScope®. Colloquially, **scope**. An anamorphic process and format; its original aspect ratio of 2.55:1 was reduced to 2.35:1 in order to make room for the soundtrack.

Cinematographer. Also **Director of Photography**, abbreviated **D.P.**, and **lighting cameraman**. The head of the camera crew, responsible for supervising the lighting of the set and all details relating to the camera; a motion picture photographer; see "cameraman."

Cinematography. (1) The process of recording motion with a movie camera; (2) the art of lighting and shooting a movie.

Cinéma vérité. French for "film truth," from Vertov's **kinó-pravda**; also **direct cinema**. A nonfiction film genre that acknowledges the presence of the camera and the interaction between filmmaker and subject; an unscripted documentary in which the camera serves as a catalytic agent.

Circle of confusion. The largest blur that can be accepted as the image of a point.

Circle of least confusion. The small circle that is the image of a perfectly focused point.

Clapper/loader. See "cameraman."

Clapstick. Colloquially, **the sticks**. A device for making a short, sharp noise that will allow picture and sound takes to be synchronized during editing; usually a thin board mounted to the top of a slate with a hinge.

Close shot. Abbreviated **CS**. A shot whose field of view is slightly broader than that of the closeup; in terms of the human figure, the head and upper chest might fill the frame.

Closeup. Abbreviated **CU**. A shot whose field of view is very narrow; the camera appears to be near the subject. In terms of the human figure, a face might fill the frame.

Code. (1) A consistent method for translating information from one signifying system to another; (2) a private language for storing information in a condensed or altered form so that it may ultimately be retrieved and translated back into its original form or language; (3) a means of organizing and selectively emphasizing information, or the shorthand that indicates how that information is to be interpreted; (4) a set of rules.

Color temperature. The specific energy distribution of a black body that has been heated to a particular temperature.

Color timing. See "timing."

Commentative sound. Also **extra-diegetic sound**. (1) A sound or track whose source is not within the recounted or presented world of a film; see "actual sound" and "over"; (2) a sound or track that comments on the action.

Complementary colors. A pair of hues with opposite properties, for example, red and cyan, green and magenta, or blue and yellow.

Composite. (1) Any image created by combining elements from two or more separately photographed images, usually on an optical printer; (2) any recording created by mixing other recordings; also **sound composite**; (3) a composite print.

Composite print. Also **married print**. A single-system print; one with picture and sound on the same piece of film.

Composition. (1) The arrangement of the elements of an image in relation to the boundaries of the frame and to each other; (2) an original piece of music.

Composition in depth. The composition of a visual field in relation to the axis that runs from camera to subject, often including the placement of significant information in widely separated image planes.

Compound lens. See "lens."

Consistency. The continuity of lighting balance from shot to shot.

Constructive editing. See "linkage editing."

Contact printer. A printer in which the emulsions of the processed original and the raw printing stock are touching one another during the instant of exposure; see "bi-pack" and "optical printer."

Continuity. (1) The created impression that events flow seamlessly from one shot to another; (2) the created impression that the conditions established in one shot apply in sequential or related shots, thanks to the careful matching of details from one shot — and shooting day — to another.

Continuity editing. Also **continuity cutting**. The art of editing shots together so that the action appears to develop "naturally" (i.e., in continuity) and the cuts are not called to the audience's attention.

Continuity flaw. The impression, accidental or otherwise, that events and conditions that ought to be consistent from shot to shot are, in fact, not consistent.

Contrast ratio. The ratio of key plus fill light to fill light; the higher (brighter) the fill light, the less difference there is between key and fill, the softer and lighter the shadows are in relation to the more brightly lit areas, and the lower the contrast ratio.

Core. A plastic hub onto which film is wound.

Counter-matte. The negative image of a particular matte, opaque where the matte is transparent.

Coverage. (1) The process of shooting relatively tight views of a scene, from a number of setups, after the master shot has been taken; (2) the process of making sure that every significant aspect of the scene has been **covered**, or rendered in a usable shot, so that the editor has a relatively high number of options (i.e., a variety of shots to work with); by shooting in this manner, the director "covers" himself or herself against the need to reshoot.

Crane. A vehicle equipped with a mechanically or hydraulically operated boom or arm at whose end is a camera platform that can be lifted and moved through the air.

Crane shot. Also **boom shot**. (1) A shot taken from a crane; (2) any nonaerial shot in which the camera platform moves through the air.

Credit. A title card that identifies one or more of the people or organizations who worked on the film, and in what capacity.

CRI. A color reversal intermediate negative; a printing negative optically printed, on reversal stock, from the original negative; a reversal duplicate negative.

Crop. To trim out part of an image area, especially by tightening its original borders.

Cross-cutting. Also **parallel montage**. The art of cutting back and forth between recurring setups or independent scenes; the intercutting of ongoing actions.

Crossing the line. Also **crossing the axis**. A violation of screen direction caused by failing to keep the camera on one side of the axis of action; see "line."

Cut. (1) An instantaneous transition from one shot (a **visual cut**) or track (a **sound cut**) to another; (2) the point at which one shot ends and another begins; (3) to splice a picture or a soundtrack.

Cutaway. Also **cutaway shot**. A cut away from a setup, figure, or action to which the camera will soon return.

Cutback. Also **cutback shot**. A cut to a previously established setup, figure, or action.

Cutting continuity. The shot-by-shot transcript of the release version of a film, including all dialogue, action, camera setups, and shot lengths measured to the frame.

Dailies. Also **rushes** and **daily rolls**. (1) One-light prints of each day's shooting, processed on a rush basis; it is usually the daily picture rolls that are cut up for the workprint; (2) the rolls of live production sound that accompany the picture rolls; while the rushes are being printed, the sound dailies (also called "track dailies") are transferred to stripe, and then both picture and sound daily rolls are screened in double system so that the filmmakers can evaluate the results of the previous day's shooting.

Day-for-night. A shot taken in the daylight but exposed, filtered, or printed so that it appears to have been shot at night.

Deconstruction. Also **deconstructive analysis**. The critical process of dismantling the logical, ideological, or fictional structures that support any text; an activity that uncovers the multiplicity of meanings and assumptions in a work while exploring the ways they threaten and refuse to cohere; see "différance."

Découpage. French for ordinary continuity editing, as distinct from the more dynamic "montage."

Deep focus. A visual field that is sharp from foreground to background (extreme depth of field) and whose foreground and background planes appear to be widely separated; often used to accentuate composition in depth.

Density. A measure of opacity.

Depth of field. The range before and behind the plane of focus within which objects remain acceptably sharp; a function of lens aperture, focal length, and camera-to-subject distance. Depth of field may be expressed as above, which is professionally preferable (e.g., 12 feet in front of and 12 feet behind the plane of focus), or as the total distance in question (e.g., in this case, 24 feet). Depth of field is often associated with, but is not the same as, the impression of depth within an image.

Development. The earliest phase of filmmaking, in which an idea is conceived and converted into a produceable property; officially it begins with the hiring of a writer and ends when the property is approved for production.

DGA. The Directors Guild of America.

Dialectical montage. Also **intellectual montage**. A variety of editing in which shots "collide" or significantly conflict with each other, ideally generating a metaphoric synthesis in the mind of the viewer; formulated by Eisenstein.

Dialectics. The study of generative oppositions in history, philosophy, economics, politics, and art; the **thesis**, or first term, gives rise to its opposite or opponent, the **antithesis**, and out of their conflict emerges a **synthesis** that becomes the first term in a new dialectical cycle.

Dialogue. Words spoken in a film.

Dialogue replacement. (1) Looping; see "replacement dialogue"; (2) voice or language replacement; see "dubbing."

Diegetic. Adjective for the conditions and events within a fiction; any part of a recounted world (the **diegesis**) that is accessible to the characters, capable of being part of their experience; see "extra-diegetic."

Diegetic sound. See "actual sound."

Différance. A French pun on "difference" and "deferment"; in deconstructive criticism, an elusive relationship whereby the difference between signifier and sig-

nified, on which the act of reference depends, itself suspends or defers the achievement of definite reference; the paradoxical, ironic, playful manner in which one sign leads only to another; the infinite putting-off of perfect reference and absolute meaning.

Diffusion. The dispersion, unfocusing, or scattering of light, creating **soft** effects; undiffused or parallel light beams create crisp, **hard** effects.

Direct. Setting aside such production distinctions as "live" or "wild" and such critical distinctions as "actual" or "extra-diegetic," the sounds in a movie may simply be identified as **direct** (the source is onscreen when the sound is heard), **off** (the source is offscreen when the sound is heard), or **over** (the source is not present in the scene at all or, like the source of a voice-over inner monologue, cannot *be* onscreen). These three terms cover all the possibilities.

Direct animation. Animation achieved without the aid of a camera.

Direct cinema. See "cinéma vérité."

Director. The captain and creative coordinator of the production team, responsible for the most effective use of production materials and personnel and often for the creative integration of camerawork, performance, and editing.

Director's cut. Also **director's fine cut**. The last edited version of a film that is approved by the director, which may or may not become the release version.

Direct sound. A motivated, actual sound, whether live or post-synced, whose source is onscreen; see "actual sound," "direct," "live sound," "off," and "over."

Discourse. The narrative line; the vehicle and manner (including plotting, word or image choice, tone, etc.) in which a story is told or presented to the audience; see "plot" and "story."

Dissolve. A superimposed fade-out and fade-in, whereby one image gradually vanishes while another gradually appears.

Distribution. The release and circulation of a completed movie.

Distributor. The person or company responsible for marketing, circulating, and licensing the exhibition of a completed movie.

Documentary. (1) A nonfiction film that has a particular point to make or perspective to advance about the factual material that it presents; (2) loosely, any nonfiction film.

Dolby NR®. Also **Dolby noise reduction®**; abbreviated **NR**. A process for reducing system noise, especially tape hiss.

Dolby Stereo®. (1) An NR-encoded optical soundtrack

carrying four channels on two variable-area tracks in encoded phase relationships; (2) a magnetic soundtrack with one track for each channel; all but the boom channels are Dolby NR-encoded.

Dolly. (1) A wheeled camera platform, capable of moving without tracks; (2) to move the dolly while the camera is running; see "track."

Dolly shot. (1) A shot within which the camera platform is wheeled across the floor or the ground without the aid of rails or tracks; (2) loosely, a track shot.

Double printing. Superimposition that is achieved not in a camera but in a printer; the duping of two or more shots onto the same series of frames, with or without phantom effects; see "multiple exposure" and "multiple printing."

Double reel. Two reels (approximately 1,900 feet) of 35mm film that have been spliced together and wound on a core or on a 2,000 foot reel for projection; 35mm films normally are shipped from the laboratory in double-reel lengths, whereas 16mm films normally are shipped in 1,200 foot (3-reel) or 1,600 foot (4-reel) lengths; see "reel," which is what a projectionist would call any of these as long as it fit *on* a reel.

Double system. The use of separate, interlocked machines to shoot/record, edit, or project picture and sound; see "single system."

Dub. (1) A copy of a recording; (2) to copy or to transfer a recording.

Dubber. A transport and playback machine for mag film; synchronized with a projector and/or other dubbers when looping or mixing.

Dubbing. (1) Re-recording; see "dub"; (2) loosely, the recording and post-synchronization of a replacement dialogue track; see "looping"; (3) specifically, the recording and post-synchronization of a dialogue track in a language different from that spoken in the original release version; foreign-language dubbing; (4) adjective for a recording session in which dubbers are used; looping sessions and mixing sessions are often called "dubbing sessions."

Dupe. (1) Short for a printed duplicate or copy; see "print"; (2) a print copied from a release print.

Dutch tilt shot. Also **Dutch angle** and **off-angle shot.** A shot in which the camera is tilted to the side, so that the top and bottom of the frame are not parallel to the lateral horizontal axis of the set; called an **oblique** rather than a Dutch or an off angle when in combination with other camera angles.

Dye transfer process. See "imbibition printing."

Eastmancolor®. See "monopack."

Edge coding. (1) Also **keying.** The act of inking the workprint's key numbers (which were latently imprinted by the manufacturer on the camera rolls and copied automatically onto the workprint) onto the matching mag footage or sound rolls; (2) the act of inking a fresh set of matching edge numbers onto synchronized rolls of picture and sound; (3) the act of inking the edge numbers that will appear on release prints onto either the soundtrack negative or the picture negative.

Edge numbers. (1) Also **key numbers.** The unique, sequential numbers imprinted by the manufacturer along one edge of camera filmstock, one number per 35mm foot; absent from printing stock, so that original and workprint footage will bear the same key numbers; (2) the sequential numbers, one per 35mm foot, found along the edge of release prints.

Editing. The art of selecting, trimming, coordinating, integrating, and cutting into projection sequence the shots and/or recordings that will become the film; organizing and assembling a workprint.

Editorial sync. Also **level sync.** The parallel alignment of sound and picture tracks so that synchronized frames are directly across from, or level with, one another; see "projection sync."

Effects. Abbreviated **FX.** See "sound effects" and "special effects."

Element. A part of a composite; thus, (1) one lens within a compound lens; (2) an individual recording that becomes part of a composite soundtrack; (3) an image area or shot that becomes part of an optical composite; (4) within a package deal, a creative person of notable skill and achievement.

Emulsion. The light-sensitive coating of filmstock.

Establishing shot. A shot that introduces or defines the location where an action takes place; usually a long shot.

Executive producer. One who is in charge of the larger financial and business aspects of a production; see "line producer."

Exhibitor. A person, group, or business that shows movies to patrons.

Expressionism. (1) The art of rendering inner states as aspects of the outer world; emotionally intense creative distortion; (2) capitalized, a specific reference to a movement in the literary, dramatic, and visual arts, beginning in the 1880s in northern Europe and peaking in Germany (1905–1920), and loosely to works in the tradition and spirit of that movement.

Extra. A background or "atmosphere" performer, hired on a daily or weekly basis, who usually has no lines but who must be paid at a higher rate if he or she speaks more than five lines in a picture.

Extra-diegetic. Adjective for that which comes from outside the world of the story and is not accessible to the characters but is still part of the discourse, for example, a "guided tour" voice-over narration or a commentative music track.

Extra-diegetic sound. See "commentative sound."

Extreme closeup. Also **tight closeup**; abbreviated **ECU**. A shot with a very narrow field of view; the camera appears to be extremely close to the subject. In terms of the human figure, a mouth or an eye might fill the frame.

Extreme long shot. Abbreviated **ELS**. A shot with a very broad field of view; the camera appears to be extremely far from the subject. A human figure might take up less than one tenth of the height of the frame.

Eye-level shot. (1) A shot in which the camera appears to be as high off the ground as the eyes of the principal subject, and in which the angle of view is neither high nor low; (2) loosely, a shot that shows the field of view as it would be seen by a standing adult looking more-or-less straight ahead.

Fade. (1) A transitional device in which the image evenly appears out of a black field (a **fade-in**) or evenly disappears into a black field (a **fade-out**); (2) a dissolve to a white or monochromatic field (e.g., a **fade to red**).

Fast motion. Also **undercranking**. The effect of faster-than-normal movement, achieved by shooting at less than projection rate; see "slow motion."

Faux raccord. French for "false accord"; a jump cut with a false impression of continuity; often a match of action over a change of scene.

Fill light. The supplementary light(s) illuminating the subject, used to balance the overall lighting effect and often to soften shadows created by the key light or to reveal detail in otherwise shadowed areas; see "contrast ratio" and "key light."

Film. (1) The celluloid strip on which images are photographically imprinted; (2) a collective term for the art of motion pictures; (3) a motion picture; (4) exposed stock.

Film editor. Also **picture editor**. The person who edits the workprint and the dialogue tracks of a movie; see "sound editor."

Film noir. An American genre (named by French critics who noticed its resemblance to the series of violent mystery novels published as "Série noire") that flourished in the 1940s and 1950s, characterized by sudden violence, romantic intensity, low-key lighting, themes of entrapment and spiritual corruption, and an idealistic defeatism.

Filmstock. Also **raw stock** and **stock**. Unexposed motion picture film, consisting of a cellulose (acetate, triacetate, or nitrate) or polyester base coated with a photosensitive emulsion; see "magnetic stock."

Final cut. (1) The completely edited workprint to which the negative is cut; (2) the contractually guaranteed right to approve a particular edited version of a film for release without further revision.

Fine cut. A completely edited workprint.

First cut. The first fine cut of a movie that is approved by the director and that is shown to the producer(s); see "director's cut."

Flashback. (1) A cut or leap from the narrative present to a direct view or an objective presentation of a past event; a **flash forward** cuts to the future; (2) loosely, the direct presentation of a memory; see "mindscreen."

Flat. Adjective for (1) any process or format that is not anamorphic; see "spherical lens"; (2) the nonanamorphic version of an anamorphic film; (3) the two-dimensional version of a 3-D picture; (4) a dull or nonreflective surface.

Floodlight. Also **flood**. Any lighting instrument whose light beam spreads out rather than narrows; see "spotlight."

Focal length. The distance from the film plane to the optical center of the lens when it is focused at infinity.

Focal point. The point from which light rays appear to diverge (**virtual focus**) or to which they converge (**real focus**).

Focus. The sharpness and definition of an image.

Focus puller. See "cameraman."

Foley. A replacement sound effect, performed by a Foley artist who watches the picture and, cued by streamers, duplicates the actor's movements and creates a sound that is recorded in post-sync with the picture; originally the process was used simply to provide "body movement effects," such as footsteps, that had not been picked up by production microphones, but now it is used for a much wider variety of sound effects.

Footage. A specific length of exposed film.

Format. The gauge and other characteristics (e.g., 3-D, flat, or scope) of a print and/or the aspect ratio of the image.

Fps. Abbreviation for **frames per second**, the rate of exposure and/or projection; usually 24 fps for sound film and 16 (or more) fps for silent film. "Silent speed" on most 16mm projectors today is 18 fps.

Frame. (1) An individual photograph on a strip of film; (2) the perimeter or boundary line of the picture area; (3) a story or narrative situation within which another story is bracketed or presented.

Frame enlargement. An uncropped, printed enlargement of an individual frame from a movie; see "production still."

Frame line. The unexposed boundary between adjacent frames on a strip of film.

Framing. The act of determining the boundaries of the image.

Freeze frame. A still image created by the continual reprinting of the same frame.

Front projection. The projection of a slide or footage (reflected by a beam-combiner) onto a background screen from the same direction as the camera.

F-stop. A standard lens-aperture setting, derived by dividing the diameter of the diaphragm opening into the focal length of the lens; each f-stop lets in twice (or half) as much light as the adjacent one; used when one is calculating depth of field; see "T-stop."

Full shot. Abbreviated **FS**. A medium long shot offering a relatively complete view of the set and showing the human figure from head to foot.

Fullcoat. Magnetic stock, one face of which has been entirely coated with magnetic oxide; from one to six tracks may be recorded on the fullcoat; see "stripe."

Gaffer. Also **key electrician**. The chief electrician on the set.

Gate. Also **film gate**. The apparatus through which film passes as it is exposed to light; the aperture unit of a camera, a printer, or a projector.

Gauge. The width of a strip of film, expressed in millimeters.

Genre. (1) A particular genus or type of film; a subcategory defined by the choice and treatment of subject; within the nonfiction film, for example, cinéma vérité and the newsreel are distinct genres; (2) especially within the narrative film, a group of films that deal with a particular subject (or a specific avenue of human experience, concern, relationship, action, or consciousness) in a characteristic and often ritual manner, transforming the discourse and structuring the story in relation to a shared set of terms, themes, values, figures, and codes; for example, *Mad Love* (horror) and *My Fair Lady* (musical) transform *Pygmalion* according to the terms of their respective genres.

Gobo. A large black panel that can hide a light from the camera or restrict a light beam to a certain area.

Grain. Also **film grain**. (1) An individual crystal of metallic silver within a photograph or frame; the smaller the crystals, the finer the grain; (2) the degree to which these crystals are perceived, as a pattern of visual "noise," within a photographic image.

Grip. A stagehand attached to the camera crew.

Hand props. Props that are handled by the performers; see set props.

Hard lighting. See "diffusion."

Hazeltine. A brand of electronic color film analyzer.

Head. (1) The beginning of a continuous strip or reel of film or tape; see "tail"; (2) in a tape recorder, the transducer that converts electrical into magnetic energy for recording or magnetic into electrical energy for playback.

High-angle shot. A shot in which the camera looks downward toward the subject.

High-key lighting. A lighting plan in which the set is brightly lit and there is a relatively low contrast ratio.

Hollywood montage. A variety of montage in which the images overlap as they succeed each other, often with rapid dissolves and complex optical-printing effects; what in Hollywood, especially in the 1930s and 1940s, was called simply a "montage."

Hook. (1) That which immediately captures the audience's interest in a story; (2) the central, intriguing action or premise that motivates and structures the story and dictates its primary elements.

House. A theater.

Housing. Also **fitting**. The part of a lighting instrument in which the lamp is mounted; see "luminaire."

Hue. Spectral color.

Icon. Also **iconic sign**. A sign that functions by the resemblance or likeness between its elements (e.g., a representational painting).

Ideology. A set of interlocking assumptions, values, and expectations held by a person, a group, or a culture.

Imbibition printing. Abbreviated **IB**. Also **dye transfer process**. The process of applying dyes directly onto the print by means of a matrix; see "Technicolor."

IN. See "internegative."

Independent producer. (1) One who produces a film and arranges for its distribution without studio support; (2) one who produces a film autonomously but has a financing or distribution deal with a studio; see "negative pick-up."

Index. Also **indexical sign**. A sign that points to or indicates its referent and that depends on some essential or causal link between its elements (e.g., a weather-vane).

Indigenous sound. See "actual sound."

Indirect sound. See "off."

Insert. A shot of an object, usually unmoving, that is cut into a scene or sequence; not considered principal photography.

Integral tripack. See "monopack."

Intercut. A screenplay direction indicating that two scenes are taking place simultaneously.

Intercutting. (1) The process of inserting one or more shots into another series of shots or into a master shot; (2) the interweaving of shots from separate scenes, not necessarily in a cross-cutting pattern but usually to imply relatedness or simultaneity.

Interlock. A mechanical link between two or more motors, ensuring that they will operate in exact sync.

Internegative. Also **intermediate negative**; abbreviated **IN**. A negative copy of an interpositive, from which prints may be struck.

Interpositive. Also **intermediate positive**; abbreviated **IP**. A positive copy of the edited negative, from which an internegative is struck. The first IP is called the **master positive**.

Intertitle. Any title card or subtitle, whether or not it is superimposed on another image, that appears after the head credits and before the tail credits.

IP. See "interpositive."

Iris. (1) A circular mask; (2) a transitional device in which the image appears as an expanding circle (an **iris-in**) or disappears as a contracting circle (an **iris-out**).

Iris diaphragm. A system of thin metal plates whose arrangement creates a hole whose size may be varied, allowing more or less light to pass through the lens and reach the film.

Jump cut. A disjunctive and often disorienting straight cut, especially within a scene; a sudden, illogical, or mismatched transition.

Key. (1) Principal; (2) supervisory.

Key grip. The head of the grip category.

Keying. (1) See "edge coding"; (2) see "logging."

Key light. The principal light(s) illuminating the subject and establishing its basic look, form, and texture; see "contrast ratio" and "fill light."

Key numbers. See "edge numbers."

Lamp. Also **luminant**. The light source within a lighting instrument; see "luminaire."

Leader. (1) A length of transparent, black, or colored film base; (2) the "countdown" **head leader** found at the start of a reel; (3) the color-coded protective leader found at the extreme head and tail of a reel.

Leitmotif. A recurring musical theme associated with a particular character, object, idea, or other narrative element.

Lens. (1) A piece of transparent glass whose outside edge(s) may be curved in order to cause light rays to converge or diverge; a **refracting lens** bends the light passing through it so that the rays diverging from the subject will converge on the film; (2) a system of lenses permanently mounted in a tube, also known as a **compound lens**.

Lens aperture. (1) The opening or light passage created by the iris diaphragm; (2) the diameter of that opening at any particular setting; see "f-stop"; (3) the maximum diameter to which the iris of a specific lens can be opened, which is *the* aperture or speed of that lens (e.g., an $f2$ 50mm lens).

Level. Volume; amount of power.

Level sync. See "editorial sync."

Light. See "luminaire."

Line. Also **the line**. (1) The axis of action; an imaginary line dividing the set or location in half; also **the axis**; see "crossing the line"; (2) on a budget form, the division between "creative" and "technical" personnel and expenditures; see "above-the-line costs" and "below-the-line costs."

Line producer. One who is directly responsible for supervising a production; see "executive producer."

Linkage editing. Also **constructive editing**. A variety of montage in which short shots, conceived as complementary and related parts, accumulate into a whole, like a wall made out of bricks; formulated by Pudovkin.

Lip sync. The perfect synchronization of picture and dialogue tracks, notably flawless when lip movements are on-camera.

Live sound. Tracks recorded during shooting, whether in sync or wild; indigenous production sound; see "actual sound."

Location. An off-studio shooting site.

Logging. (1) Also **keying**. The act of listing the inclusive edge or key numbers of individual shots; (2) the act of keeping a **log**, or detailed record, of any filmmaking activity.

Logo. A graphic trademark, for example, Paramount's

mountain and stars (and the place and way the name is printed).

Long lens. In 35mm cinematography, one with a focal length greater than 50mm; see "telephoto lens."

Long shot. Abbreviated **LS**. A shot that gives a wide view of the visual field; the camera appears to be far from the subject. Typically a human figure will be less than half the height of the frame.

Long take. A shot that lasts longer than a minute.

Loop. (1) Anything whose head is joined to its tail; (2) to post-synchronize dialogue; (3) in a threading path, a short length of film that is left slack.

Looping. (1) The recording and post-synchronization of a replacement dialogue track, whether through ADR or conventional looping; (2) the process of recording post-synchronized replacement dialogue, specifically by running loops of film and mag through a projector and dubber, repeatedly recording the replacement dialogue until the performer (the original or a replacement) achieves or approximates lip sync.

Low-angle shot. A shot in which the camera looks upward toward the subject.

Low-key lighting. A lighting plan with a relatively high contrast ratio and in which the set is dimly lit, with rich shadows and occasional highlights.

Luminant. See "lamp."

Luminaire. Also **light**. A complete lighting instrument, including the lamp, the lens, the fitting or housing, the support, and the cable.

Mag. Short for "magnetic" or for "magnetic filmstock."

Magnetic soundtrack. Also **mag track**. One or more stripes of magnetized iron-oxide particles bearing the final soundtrack and either bonded onto the release print (single system) or played back in sync with it (double system).

Magnetic stock. Also **fullcoat**, **magnetic film**, **magnetic filmstock**, **mag film**, and **mag stock**. Perforated film base coated with magnetic oxide.

Magnetic stripe. See "stripe."

Magnetic tape. See "tape."

Marks. The lines or pieces of tape on the floor of a set that indicate where the actors are to stand or arrive.

Married print. See "composite print" and "single system."

Mask. A sheet of metal or cardboard (a matte card or plate) or a strip of exposed film (a fixed matte) that admits light only to specific areas of the frame, used to reshape the frame or in connection with the making of optical composites; see "matte."

Master shot. A long take, usually a full or long shot, that covers all the major action of a scene and into which closer or more specific views are often intercut; see "coverage."

Match cut. A cut over which an action appears to continue seamlessly.

Matrix. (1) In imbibition printing, the celluloid strip bearing various thicknesses of hardened gelatin, capable of absorbing and shedding dyes; (2) in Dolby Stereo, a channel encoder/decoder.

Matte. (1) Any surface or coating that is flat black rather than shiny; (2) a mask that admits light freely to certain areas of the frame and completely blocks it from reaching other areas; as a rule of thumb, a mask is a rigid physical object or camera accessory, and a matte is a selectively opaque shot or shot element; see "traveling matte."

Matte box. A device mounted in front of a camera lens, sometimes fitted with a sunshade and capable of holding matte cards and filters.

Matte card. See "mask."

Matte line. (1) In a matte shot or painting, the border between original and replacement detail; (2) in a flawed composite, the noticeable outline of a matted-in figure or area.

Matte painting. In most cases, a sheet of glass or masonite on which replacement detail has been painted.

Matte shot. A composite image created through the use of mattes and counter-mattes, so that image areas from separate shots or exposures are incorporated into one shot without phantom effects.

Mechanical special effects. Also **mechanicals**. Production special effects created by or entailing the use of machines; the machines, critters, or gadgets themselves are also called "mechanicals."

Medium long shot. Abbreviated **MLS**. A shot whose field of view is narrower than that of a long shot but much broader than that of a medium shot.

Medium shot. Also **midshot**; abbreviated **MS**. A shot whose field of view is between those of the long shot and the closeup; in terms of the human figure, a view from head to waist or knees might fill the frame.

Melodrama. A popular narrative form characterized by extreme emotion and often drawing broad distinctions between good and evil.

Methodology. A systematic critical method for approaching and analyzing a subject.

Mindscreen. (1) Any first-person cinematic narration, whether authorized or unauthorized; (2) a visual and sometimes aural field that is encoded to appear to be generated, remembered, perceived, or related by a mind (usually that of a character).

Miniature. (1) A small-scale three-dimensional replica of a set; (2) a small-scale model.

Mise-en-scène. (1) French for "made into a scene" or "put in place"; the decor, layout, and theatrical and cinematic staging of a scene; (2) the general term for what has been arranged within a shot, also known as **mise-en-shot**.

Mix. To balance, combine, and re-record separate tracks, creating an intermediate or final composite soundtrack.

Mix down. Also **sub-dub**. To reduce the number of tracks by mixing them; see "pre-mix."

Model. (1) An individual component of a miniature set; (2) a three-dimensional replica, usually on a small scale.

Monopack. (1) Also **integral tripack**. A compound emulsion used in color photography, introduced as **Eastmancolor®**; (2) a single load of film; see "bi-pack."

Montage. (1) French for "mounting" or "raising"; the intensive, significant, and often abrupt juxtaposition of shots; (2) the dynamic editing of picture or sound; see "découpage"; (3) a series of brief shots or overlapping images; (4) loosely, film editing in general.

MOS. Minus Optical Sound; shot silent.

Motion-control photography. The use of a tape or, more often, a computer to control, record, and precisely repeat the movements of a camera.

Motion picture. (1) Any image that has been given the illusory quality of movement; (2) an individual movie.

Motivated. Adjective for (1) a lighting effect or sound whose literal or diegetic source can be identified and is usually on the set; (2) a shot, cut, or action that proceeds from, is causally related to, or can be accounted for by a previously established source, character, event, or intention.

Movie. (1) A moving picture; (2) in the plural, a collective term for the art of motion pictures.

MPAA. The Motion Picture Association of America.

MPAA rating. The audience-age restrictions placed on a film that is about to be released; the MPAA rating board's evaluation of the maturity level or the viewer suitability of a movie.

MPPA. The Motion Picture Producers Association.

Multiplane camera. A device for mounting and lighting cels in order to create an impression of depth.

Multiple exposure. Also **double exposure**. A shot created by exposing the film more than once, usually in a production camera, so that two or more images are superimposed; see "double printing."

Multiple printing. An optical effect whereby each successive individual frame is duped several times, re-sulting in a variety of slow motion or, in the extreme, a freeze frame; see "double printing."

Narration. (1) The act of telling or relating, whether or not the account is fictive, the presenter is personalized, the act is deliberate, or words are employed; (2) a voice-over commentary; in a silent film, the intertitles attributed to a narrator.

Narrative. (1) The adjective for "narration"; (2) as a noun, that which is told or related, comprising story and discourse.

Narrative film. A movie that presents an account or tells a story, usually but not always a fiction.

Narrative present. The time frame in which the primary action is taking place.

Negative. (1) Filmstock that turns black where it has been exposed to light; an image whose color values are complementary to those of the subject or whose black and white values are the opposite of those in the subject; see "positive" and "reversal"; (2) the camera original; the negative filmstock run through the camera; (3) the edited and spliced original negative, from which intermediate or final prints may be struck; (4) in some cases, the final, timed, intermediate negative; (5) the completed movie; see "negative cost."

Negative cost. The total expenses incurred in the production of a movie, up to and including the final answer print struck from *the* negative."

Negative pick-up. Also **pickup**. A deal whereby a studio buys an independently produced film and distributes it under the studio logo.

Nitrate film. Camera or printing stock with a base made of cellulose nitrate; explosive an obsolete, but often visually superior; see "safety-base film."

Noise. Random information.

Nonfiction film. A movie that presents factual material, usually in a relatively objective manner; see "documentary."

Normal lens. (1) A lens that reproduces perspective much as it is seen by the human eye and that has a field of view midway between wide-angle and telephoto; (2) in 35mm cinematography, a lens with a focal length between 25mm and 50mm.

Oblique-angle shot. See "Dutch tilt shot."

Off. Also **indirect sound**, **off-camera**, and **offscreen** (abbreviated **OS**). A motivated indigenous sound or action whose source or location is now outside of camera range; see "direct" and "over."

Off-angle shot. See "Dutch tilt shot."

One-light print. A print struck in a contact printer

whose lamphouse or printing light is at a medium or normal setting; a print whose timing has not been or does not need to be corrected.

Optical effects. Also **opticals.** Photographic effects achieved through optical printing, especially fades, dissolves, wipes, and superimpositions; see "special effects."

Optical printer. A printer in which the original and the printing stock are not in physical contact during the instant of exposure; instead, one or more optical systems intervene.

Optical soundtrack. A continuous black-and-white image area containing the final soundtrack and designed to allow varying amounts of light to pass through it to a photocell.

Outtake. A take that is either not approved for printing or not included in the final cut.

Over. A commentative sound or track, not motivated by an onscreen (direct) or diegetic offscreen (off or indirect) source, but laid over the other tracks in the mix; some voice-over tracks, however (e.g., interior monologue), can be considered motivated and diegetic; see "direct" and "off."

Over-the-shoulder shot. A shot or setup in which the camera has a view from behind and over the shoulder of one person to the face of another.

Pan. Also **panning shot** and **panoramic shot.** (1) To pivot or swivel the camera from side to side; (2) a shot within which the camera pivots on a vertical axis, turning in a horizontal plane.

Pan and scan. The process of selecting a 1.33:1 image from a wide-format image by cropping or panning across the original.

Panavision®. (1) A particular line of cameras and lenses, and the company that markets them; (2) the 35mm anamorphic process and format that replaced CinemaScope; the frame has an aspect ratio of 2.35:1.

Panchromatic film. Filmstock whose emulsion is sensitive to the entire visual spectrum, from blue to red.

Paradigm. The totality of signs that are capable of making sense at a given point in any discourse; a group from which a selection may be made.

Parallel montage. See "cross-cutting."

Pass. (1) A single effects take; (2) a single motion-controlled exposure; (3) a single passage of filmstock through a camera or a printer; (4) to decline an opportunity.

Persistence of vision. As applied to cinema, the phenomenon by which the retina retains a brief after-image of an individual, projected frame.

Persona. Latin for "mask" and the root of "personality"; a voice or identity adopted by a narrator as a mask or filter.

Perspective sound. The art of making a sound appear to originate at a certain distance from (and in stereo, at a certain angle and orientation to) the camera.

Phantom. Also **ghost.** A transparent image superimposed over an apparently solid background or shot.

Phi phenomenon. As applied to cinema, the preconscious process of deducing and hallucinating movement from a series of still frames.

Photocell. Also **photoelectric cell.** A transducer that converts light into electrical impulses, for example when reading an optical soundtrack.

Photo double. A stand-in performer who physically resembles a principal.

Pickup. See "negative pick-up."

Picture. (1) A motion picture, usually one currently in production or distribution; (2) the image track of a movie, as distinct from the soundtrack.

Picture editor. See "film editor."

Pixel. (1) A picture element; (2) the smallest bit of information on a TV or computer screen, a dot with a particular color and brightness; see "raster."

Pixillation. The art of animating a person or an object that is capable of moving under its own power.

Plot. The strategic order in which selected story events are arranged and revealed; a key element of discourse; see "story" and "discourse."

Polyvision. Multiple imagery (see "split screen"), multiple superimposition, and/or the use of multiple screens; formulated by Gance.

Point of view. (1) The conceptual or experiential vantage point of a character; (2) the narrative technique of limiting the presentation of a story to what a given character experiences or understands.

Point-of-view shot. Abbreviated **POV**; also **subjective camera.** A shot or setup in which the camera adopts the vantage point of a character's physical eye or literal gaze; see "mindscreen."

Positive. An image whose color or black-and-white values correspond to those in the subject; in most cases, a negative of a negative.

Post-production. The phase of filmmaking during which picture and sound are augmented and edited into final form; officially it begins with the conclusion of principal photography and ends with the delivery of the answer print.

Post-synchronization. The process of recording, during post-production, a track that is to accompany a particular MOS shot or to be substituted for a track recorded during production (especially replacement dialogue) and of synchronizing this and other wild tracks with the picture.

POV. See "point-of-view shot."

Pre-filmic continuum. That in the real world which is available to be photographed and recorded.

Pre-mix. Also **predub** and **preliminary mix.** A dubbing session in which individual tracks are combined into preliminary composites.

Pre-production. The planning phase of filmmaking in which a developed and approved property is systematically prepared for production; officially it begins with the setting of a start date for the picture and includes all the work that must be done before shooting can get underway.

Preview. The screening of an unreleased movie to a trial audience.

Primary colors. Colors that cannot be mixed from any other colors and can be combined to generate all other colors; the **additive primaries** are red, green, and blue; the **subtractive primaries** are their complements: cyan, magenta, and yellow.

Prime lens. Also **primary lens.** A lens with a fixed focal length.

Principal photography. Also **principal cinematography.** (1) The process of shooting (with or without sound) the principal performers and every dialogued scene in the script; (2) the production phase of filmmaking, as distinct from pre- and post-production.

Principals. Actors who play the most significant speaking roles in a film.

Print. (1) A positive, projectable copy of a shot or a film; (2) any dupe or printed copy, whether positive or negative; (3) to duplicate a frame, a shot, a reel, or a complete film.

Print generation. Also **printing generations.** The number of copying stages separating a particular print or set of prints from the original release negative.

Printed take. (1) The workprint of an approved, unedited shot; (2) an approved sound take that has been transferred from tape to stripe.

Printer. An image-duplicating machine that directs light through processed film onto raw stock.

Process camera. Unlike a production camera, any movie camera designed primarily for laboratory or effects use.

Process cinematography. Shooting against a rear- or front-projected background, or against a blue screen, using a production camera.

Producer. The head and supervisor of a filmmaking enterprise; the person who hires and provides funds for the filmmaking team and who often owns and licenses the finished product; see "executive producer," "independent producer," and "line producer."

Production. (1) The phase of filmmaking in which the bulk of a movie is staged and shot; the period of principal photography; (2) the process of making a film; the entire period from development through post-production, as distinct from distribution; officially it begins with the hiring of a writer and ends with the delivery of the answer print; (3) collective term for a filmmaking enterprise.

Production board. Also **breakdown board.** The board or box that holds color-coded scene (shot breakdown) strips in their shooting order; the rearrangeable shooting plan of a picture.

Production budget. A form on which the complete anticipated and actual costs of making a movie are listed.

Production camera. Any ordinary movie camera, designed to expose continuously a single load of filmstock; see "process camera."

Production designer. An art director who designs the overall look of a movie, coordinating and integrating its sets, costumes, props, and color schemes.

Production manager. The below-the-line producer, who approves production costs, handles the payroll, and reports to the line producer; sometimes an executive who delegates these responsibilities to one or more unit production managers.

Production sketch. A preliminary or fine drawing, usually of a shot, a set, a costume, or a model.

Production sound. All sound operations and tracks recorded during the period of principal photography.

Production special effects. Special effects that can be staged for the camera during production, as distinct from post-production optical special effects.

Production still. A photograph taken on the set or relating to the making of a film; see "frame enlargement."

Production values. (1) Expensive or high-quality on-screen items, especially sets, props, and costumes; (2) a measure of the apparent quality and expense of a production.

Project. (1) To throw an image onto a screen; (2) an undertaking, such as a film in development; (3) the artfully hidden goal of a narrative process or strategy.

Projection sync. Also **printing sync.** The displacement of synchronized sound and picture tracks by the distance that will separate them on a married print; see "editorial sync."

Prop. Also **property.** A physical object handled by an actor or displayed as part of a set; the term excludes costumes and set dressings; see "hand props" and "set props."

Property. (1) An owned work; (2) a concept, script, or pre-existing work that is being considered for production; (3) a script or film currently in production; (4) see "prop."

Rapid cutting. A variety of montage in which a great many shots follow one another in a short period of time; pioneered by Gance.

Raster. A single image field made up of pixels.

Ratings. See "MPAA rating."

Raw stock. See "filmstock."

Real focus. See "focal point."

Realism. (1) A representational style that attempts to present a state of affairs without distortion; (2) a style, quite apt to date, that attempts to present the world to an audience as they already see and normally conceptualize it.

Rear projection. Also **back projection**. The projection onto a translucent screen, from behind it, of stills or footage, usually to provide a background for live action.

Reduction. The opposite of enlargement.

Reel. (1) Up to 1,000 feet of 35mm film (usually 950 feet) or 400 feet of 16mm film (usually 380 feet); at sound speed, approximately 10 minutes long; at silent speed, approximately 14–16 minutes long; see "double reel." (2) a metal or plastic spool on which film or tape is wound; as distinct from a core, a reel has outside rims or flanges.

Referent. That to which a sign refers, usually a real object or an idea.

Reflexivity. (1) A posture or condition of self-referentiality; (2) the implication that a work of art is "aware of itself" as a work of art, either as an entry in a particular creative tradition or as an autonomous and self-directing structure.

Refraction. See "lens."

Registration. Repeatable, steady alignment; the process of placing and holding one frame after another in exactly the same exposure, printing, or projection position, or of perfectly aligning two or more frames simultaneously.

Release date. (1) The date (loosely, the year) when a film is first shown publicly to a paying audience; (2) the date on which release prints are ready to be shipped from the laboratory to the distributor.

Release negative. The final internegative, from which release prints are struck (usually without correction).

Release print. An original positive print (not a duplicate of such a print) officially put into distribution and designed to be projected.

Release version. The approved, final cut; the text or version of a movie that is first released.

Replacement detail. An image or area that is substituted for or fills in an area masked or matted out of another frame or shot.

Replacement dialogue. A line or track of dialogue recorded after shooting and post-synchronized to substitute for dialogue recorded during shooting; see "looping."

Resolution. The degree of fine detail within an image; see "sharpness."

Reversal. Filmstock that can be processed to yield directly a positive rather than a negative image; used as a camera stock only when one feels comfortable projecting the camera original, as in the home movie, or when one needs a projectable image in a hurry, as in newswork; used as a printing stock when directly duping a positive print or when making a negative directly from another negative (see "CRI").

Reverse shot. Also **reverse-angle shot**. (1) A shot that reverses the field of view over a cut, as if the camera had turned nearly or completely to the rear; (2) one in an alternating series of complementary views whose angles are usually separated by 120°–160°; see "shot/reverse-shot."

Review. A critical description and evaluation of a film, usually addressed to an audience that has not yet seen the film.

RGB. Abbreviation for "red/green/blue," the additive primaries; see "YCM."

RGB records. Also **master positive separations**. Separate black-and-white (silver) records of the red, green, and blue values (taken from the cyan, magenta, and yellow values on the original negative) in a color image, from which a new color negative may be generated if the original deteriorates or is lost; see "YCM separations."

Room tone. Still, ambient air; the sound made by an empty room.

Rooting interest. A character, conflict, or situation in which the audience is led to believe that it has an enthusiastic or urgent personal stake; the favorite.

Rotoscope. A prism and lamphouse assembly, usually set behind the lens of a bi-pack camera in order to throw an image onto a card or a screen, especially for the purpose of tracing a matte line, preparing a drawing from a photograph, or hand-drawing a traveling matte.

Rough cut. The preliminary edited version of a work-print; see "fine cut."

Rushes. See "dailies."

Safety-base film. Camera or printing stock that has a slow-burning base made of cellulose acetate (since 1951, cellulose tri-acetate); see "nitrate film."

Scene. (1) A complete unit of action, capable of being covered in a single shot; (2) a significant dramatic action or interaction taking place in a single location; (3) the shot(s) in which a scene is presented.

Scope. Short for "CinemaScope"; by extension, any anamorphic lens, process, or format.

Screen direction. The trajectory of movement (or of a gaze, a chase, etc.) within, across, and in relation to the frame; its orientation to real or hypothetical three-dimensional space; and the continuity of that space as it is created by the continuity of trajectory from shot to shot.

Screen left. The left side of the movie screen or image as seen by the audience.

Screenplay. Also **script**. The text from which a motion picture is produced, containing all of the dialogue and indicating most of the significant action planned to appear in the film; literally, a play written for the screen; see "shooting script."

Screen right. The right side of the movie screen or image as seen by the audience.

Script. Any full-length screenplay, from the author's final to the shooting script.

Segue. Also **cross-fade**. A sound dissolve.

Semiotics. Also **semiology**. The study of signs and signifying systems.

Sequence. A succession of coordinated elements; thus, (1) any group of consecutive shots and/or scenes; (2) a series of interrelated shots that is not restricted to covering an action in a single location and that has its own beginning, middle, and end (subtly limited structure) and distinct project (function, style, or concern) within the whole of the film; (3) a series of tightly or necessarily interrelated scenes; loosely, an act; (4) the chronological order of story events or the projection order of shots, to violate which, in the interest of production efficiency, is to shoot **out of sequence**.

Sequence shot. Also **plan-séquence**. A single, often intricately blocked shot that presents a complete scene.

Set. (1) An indoor shooting location; (2) a decorated sound stage; (3) colloquially, any shooting location.

Set dressing. (1) Furnishings, fixtures, and objects attached to the walls or the floor of an interior set; (2) integral parts of an exterior set.

Set props. Fixed (rather than hand) props.

Setup. The position of the camera, fitted with a particular lens, at the start of a take; any number of shots may be taken from the same setup.

Sexist. Prejudiced against the members and interests of a sex, as racist prejudices are targeted against a race; the term also describes a work, a culture, or a system of representation within which oppressive and artificial sexual or sex-linked codes are presented as natural.

Sharpness. The degree to which an image has clear, well-defined edges; see "resolution."

Shooting script. (1) The final version of a screenplay, used on the set, from which the film is actually shot; (2) a standard final screenplay format.

Short lens. In 35mm cinematography, a lens with a focal length less than 25mm; see "wide-angle lens."

Shot. (1) A continuously exposed piece of film; (2) a printed and edited take; (3) the view provided by a continuously exposed series of frames; (4) in animation and special effects, a series of individual or composite frames that gives the impression of having been continuously exposed.

Shot/reverse-shot. An editing pattern in which complementary reverse-angle shots are cross-cut; used especially for conversations and showdowns.

Shutter. A device that does, when open, and does not, when closed, allow light to reach the film in a camera, a printer, or a projector.

Sign. (1) A unit of reference; a word, picture, gesture, etc. that evokes, stands for, or indicates something; (2) a construct composed of a signifier and a signified.

Signified. Within the structure of the sign, a mental image or concept evoked by a signifier; a construct of a referent, not the actual referent of the sign, as the mental image of a tree (attendant upon the recognition of the signifier's attempt to refer to a tree) is not an actual tree.

Signifier. Within the structure of the sign, a sound, graphic, or image that evokes a particular signified, as the sound "tree" or a picture of a tree or the letters t-r-e-e each may evoke (or at least invoke) the notion of a tree.

Single system. (1) A **composite print** or **married print**, with picture and soundtrack on the same strip of film; (2) any camera, editor, or projector with both picture and sound capabilities; see "double system."

Slate. A portable chalkboard, usually fitted with a clapstick, bearing key information identifying the production and each take.

Slow motion. Also **overcranking**. The effect of slower-than-normal movement, achieved by shooting at a rate greater than projection rate.

Sodium-vapor process. A technique for shooting the action negative and the traveling matte at once, using a beam-splitter and yellow/yellow-free lighting.

Soft lighting. See "diffusion."

Sound composite. See "composite."

Sound cut. See "cut."

Sound design. The comprehensive aural concept of a movie; the art of deciding how a film or its presented world should sound.

Sound editor. One who edits the tracks for music or effects; see "film editor."

Sound effects. Any sounds in a movie, excluding dialogue and music.

Sound montage. (1) The rich multilayering of a great many tracks; (2) the complex and dynamic editing of tracks.

Sound stage. Also **soundstage.** A windowless, sound-proofed, professional shooting environment, approximately the size of a large barn.

Soundtrack. (1) The final sound composite; all the sounds heard in a film; (2) the optical or magnetic track in which that composite is stored.

Special effects. Abbreviated **SPFX.** Also **optical special effects**, **special optical effects**, **special photographic effects**, and **special effects cinematography.** Photographic illusions created through nonroutine shooting or printing techniques; see "mechanical special effects," "production special effects," and "optical effects."

Speed. (1) The widest possible *f*-stop on a lens; the rapidity with which it is capable of gathering and transmitting light; see "lens aperture"; (2) the degree to which filmstock is photosensitive; the rapidity with which its emulsion reacts to light; (3) the rate at which the motor of a camera, tape recorder, dubber, printer, or projector operates; see "fps"; (4) the announcement that a camera or a tape recorder has reached the correct operating speed.

Spherical lens. Also **flat lens.** A lens that preserves the normal horizontal and vertical relationships found in the subject; a lens designed for a nonanamorphic format; see "anamorphic lens" and "flat."

Splice. (1) The physical bond joining two pieces of film, tape, or magnetic stock; (2) to cut shots together.

Split-screen. Any frame containing two or more distinct frames or images.

Spotlight. Also **spot.** Any lighting instrument whose light beam narrows rather than spreads out; see "floodlight."

Sprocket. The toothed wheel that engages and advances film.

Sprocket holes. The regularly spaced perforations along the outside edge(s) of the film, engaged by the teeth of sprocket wheels.

Squib. A gelatin capsule with a gunpowder charge; when detonated inside a blood bag, it simulates a bullet wound.

Steadicam®. A camera support, worn by the operator, that ensures extremely smooth hand-held camera movements.

Step printer. Any printer in which registration pins engage the original and printing stocks during the instant of exposure.

Stock. See "filmstock."

Stop-motion animation. Frame-by-frame shooting of a model, a puppet, or a cutout; see "pixillation."

Story. The series of hypothetical events as they "happen" in the time of the fiction, or of factual events in history, regardless of the order in which they may be presented in a narrative; see "discourse" and "plot."

Storyboard. A panel on which drawings or paintings of major phases of action, key scenes, and significant settings are mounted, much like the comic-strip version of a cartoon or a live feature.

Straight cut. Also **cut.** A transitional device, free of any optical effects, in which the last frame of one shot is immediately followed by the first frame of the next shot.

Stripe. (1) Clear stock on which there are two mag oxide stripes; the wider stripe is used for the recording of a single track, and the narrower stripe, thanks to which both edges of the stock are of the same height or thickness, allows the stock to "ride" the heads on a flat or level plane; the majority of individual tracks are edited while on stripe, and reels of production dialogue are transferred to stripe as a matter of course; (2) loosely, one-track fullcoat; (3) clear stock on which there are three or more mag oxide stripes; (4) a narrow band of magnetic oxide that has been painted on or bonded to a length of filmstock, and onto which a magnetic track may be recorded.

Stunt. A hazardous action staged for the camera and executed by a **stunt player** (also **stunt actor**, **stunt man**, **stunt performer**, or **stunt woman**), who may also be a photo double for a principal player.

Subjective camera. See "point-of-view shot."

Subjective sound. A track that presents what a character hears, or remembers or imagines hearing.

Subtitle. A line of words double-printed (without phantom effects) over the bottom of a shot.

Subtractive color system. Also **subtractive process**. A system in which colors are produced by the mixing or layering of various dyes or filters, each of which absorbs certain wavelengths from the spectrum (subtracting them from white light); if complementary colors are combined, the result will be black; film color is subtractive, whereas color TV is additive; see "additive color system."

Superimposition. The shooting or printing of two or more images on top of one another, usually with phantom effects; see "double printing" and "multiple exposure."

Surrealism. An avant-garde movement, founded by André Breton in 1924, that sought to pursue within artistic structures the juxtapositions, transitions, and bizarre logic characteristic of dreams and the unconscious.

Surround. A channel played from the rear and/or sides of a theater.

Swish pan. A panning movement so rapid that the image is reduced to streaks.

Symbol. (1) Also **symbolic sign**. A sign in which the relationship between signifier and signified is arbitrary or agreed-upon (e.g., a word or a flag); (2) a figure that stands for more than itself.

Sync. Short for "synchronization," especially between picture and sound.

Sync track. A track recorded in sync with a camera; see "wild track."

Syntagm. Also **syntagma**. A sign or a cluster of signs in a particular syntactic position.

System. A composite whole, greater than the sum of its parts; a functioning group of interrelated elements.

Tail. The end of a continuous strip or reel of film or tape; see "head."

Take. (1) An attempt to photograph and/or record a usable shot; (2) an unedited shot.

Tape. Also **magnetic tape**; colloquially, **quarter-inch**. A length of plastic, friction-fed and unperforated, that is coated with magnetic oxide onto which sounds may be recorded.

Technicolor®. (1) The company that perfected imbibition printing; (2) an imbibition print, usually produced from three dye-transfer matrixes.

Telephoto lens. (1) A very long lens that takes in a much narrower field of view than that of the normal lens (i.e., has a higher factor of magnification) and that flattens depth relationships; (2) in 35mm cinematography, a lens with a focal length greater than 200mm.

Text. Literally, something woven; thus, (1) a book, or any shorter written or printed verbal entity, and the words and wording that constitute it; (2) a movie, as something edited, printed, significative, and — via its own semiotics — readable; (3) a composition, such as written or performed music; (4) any particular work, speech, paragraph, film clip, epic, scene, shot, graffiti, series or pattern of interrelated signs, etc., that has been excerpted or offered whole for discussion; (5) a particular wording, arrangement, cut, or version of a work; a complete, original, historically verified version of a book, a play, a poem, or a movie would be called a "good text," as the *Fractured Flickers* version of *Intolerance* would be called a "bad," "unreliable," or "corrupt text"; (6) an imprinted code, which can range from an "unwritten law" to the DNA in our genes; a script that one follows or manifests; logically extended, this sense of the term may imply that any culture is a system constituted by texts and within which texts are exchanged.

Tightness. The relative narrowness of a field of view.

Tilt. Also **tilt shot**, **tilting shot**. (1) To pivot the camera upward and downward; a tilting movement; (2) a shot within which the camera pivots on a horixontal axis, moving in a vertical plane; (3) see "Dutch tilt shot."

Timing. Also **grading**. (1) The process of determining the printing exposures and color corrections to be used when one is making a print; (2) corrective printing exposure.

Tinting. The process of evenly and monochromatically coloring an originally black-and-white image; see "toning."

Title. (1) The name of a work; (2) the legal ownership or control of a property; (3) also **title card**; a shot consisting only of words; see "intertitle" and "subtitle."

Toning. The process of chemically converting a black-and-white image to a color image; the darker the image — that is, the greater the concentration of exposed silver crystals — the deeper the color; see "tinting."

Track. (1) Also **truck**. To move — rather than pivot — the camera during a shot; see "track shot"; (2) a steel rail (or the equivalent) along which the wheels of a camera platform roll; (3) a continuous unit of stored sound information; a single recording; see "element"; (4) a reel- or film-long unit of stored sound information, sometimes containing more than one channel; see "soundtrack."

Track in. Also **track forward**. To move the camera closer to the subject; the reverse is to **track out** or **track back**.

Track shot. Also **tracking shot**, **trucking shot**. (1) Generally, a shot in which the camera moves forward, backward, to the side, or along a curve; in most cases the movements are smooth, whether the operator holds the camera or is on a rolling platform; aerial and crane shots and simple pivoting movements are excluded; (2) specifically, a shot in which the camera platform moves along tracks; see "dolly shot."

Trades. Newspapers addressed to industry professionals (those in the trade).

Transducer. A device that converts one form of energy to another.

Transfer. To re-record onto another vehicle, for example, to dub from ¼-inch tape to 35mm stripe.

Transitional device. A cut, fade, wipe, dissolve, segue, or similar means of ending one shot or track and beginning another.

Traveling matte. A matte that can vary the contours of its opaque area(s) from frame to frame; a filmed, moving silhouette.

Trial composite. See "answer print."

Trim. (1) To delete the superflous portions of a take, usually by cutting off its head and tail; (2) the deleted portion of a shot.

Trope. (1) A figure of speech; by extension, the figurative use of signs and structures within any discourse; (2) a sophisticated artistic flourish that depends on and often stretches the basic signifying practices of the medium.

T-stop. A standard aperture setting, like an *f*-stop, but calibrated for an individual lens to compensate for its own light-transmitting characteristics; used when one is setting exposure; see "*f*-stop."

TV safe area. Also **safe action area**. That portion of a 1.33:1 image that will be visible on a picture tube; inscribed on some reflex viewfinders to guide composition. Further inside this area is the **safe title area**.

Two-shot. A shot of two people.

Unauthorized narration. A narrative whose presenter is not aware that his or her story or vision is being shared with an audience.

Uncredited. A significant contribution for which the responsible party did not receive screen credit.

Uncut. Unabridged.

Unit. A production group with its own director and crew.

Unit production manager. Also **unit manager**. An on-the-set production manager in charge of the day-to-day functioning of a first, second, or insert unit and sometimes of an entire production.

Variable area track. An optical soundtrack whose amplitude or contour varies but whose density remains constant.

Variable density track. An optical soundtrack whose dimensions remain constant but whose uniform degree of opacity varies.

Variable shutter. A shutter whose degree of openness can be adjusted, allowing additional control of exposure.

Virtual focus. See "focal point."

VistaVision®. A large-negative format that runs 35mm film horizontally through the camera, often with an aspect ratio of 1.66:1 in double system and 1.85:1 in single system.

Voice-over narration. Abbreviated **V-O**. A commentative dialogue (sometimes interior monologue) track; see "narration" and "over."

Wide-angle lens. (1) A short lens that takes in a broader field of view than that of the normal lens and that deepens or exaggerates depth relationships; (2) in 35mm cinematography, a lens with a focal length shorter than 20mm.

Wide format. Also **wide screen**. Any film, in any gauge, whether flat or anamorphic, with an aspect ratio greater than 1.33:1; see "widescreen."

Widescreen. (1) In America, a flat format with an aspect ratio of 1.85:1; (2) in Europe, a flat format with an aspect ratio of 1.66:1; (3) loosely, wide screen; any wide-screen format, whether flat or anamorphic; see "wide format."

Wild track. Also **wild recording**. A recording made without camera synchronization, or in the absence of any camera; see "post-synchronization" and "sync track."

Wipe. A transitional device in which parts of one shot are removed while parts of the next shot appear in their place.

Workprint. (1) A positive print generated directly from the camera original; a working copy; (2) an edited version of the picture, created from workprint footage; the edited dailies; see "fine cut" and "rough cut."

Worm's-eye view. A shot taken from directly below the subject; the most extreme low-angle shot.

Wrap. A wrap-up, the successful conclusion of an effort.

YCM. Abbreviation for "yellow/cyan/magenta," the subtractive primaries; see "RGB."

YCM separations. Separate black-and-white records of the yellow, cyan, and magenta values in a negative, usually taken from an IP or best surviving print; see "RGB records."

Zoom in. Also **forward zoom**. To increase the focal length of a zoom lens while the camera is running, narrowing the field of view; also, a shot created in that manner. The reverse is a **zoom out** (or *to* zoom out), also called a **backward** or **back zoom**.

Zoom lens. A lens with a variable focal length.

INDEX